END OF

END OF DAYS

*Essays on the
Apocalypse from
Antiquity to Modernity*

Edited by
Karolyn Kinane *and*
Michael A. Ryan

McFarland & Company, Inc., Publishers
Jefferson, North Carolina, and London

LIBRARY OF CONGRESS CATALOGUING-IN-PUBLICATION DATA

End of days : essays on the apocalypse from antiquity to modernity /
    edited by Karolyn Kinane and Michael A. Ryan.
        p.   cm.
    Includes bibliographical references and index.

    ISBN 978-0-7864-4204-1
    softcover : 50# alkaline paper ∞

    1. End of the world.   I. Kinane, Karolyn.   II. Ryan, Michael A.
BL503.E53 2009
001.9 — dc22
                                                    2009004328

British Library cataloguing data are available

On the cover: Cristoforo De Predis (1440–1486), *The End of
the World and the Last Judgement: "The Great Babylon,"* c.153r.,
Biblioteca Reale, Turin, Italy (photograph by Alinari/Art Resource,
New York); background ©2009 Shutterstock

Manufactured in the United States of America

McFarland & Company, Inc., Publishers
  Box 611, Jefferson, North Carolina 28640
    www.mcfarlandpub.com

Editors' Acknowledgments

We are honored to have worked with the many talented and diligent contributors to this volume. Very special thanks go to Richard Emmerson for talking with us about this project in its early stages and offering most welcome advice. We also would like to thank Darren Dochuk, Lisa Riley, and Naomi Fosher for their enthusiastic assistance, discussion, and thoughts regarding this edited volume. The deepest levels of appreciation, as always, go to our respective partners, James Kinane and Gary Massey, for their unflagging love, support, and patience as they had to hear endlessly about all things apocalyptic.

Karolyn Kinane and Michael A. Ryan

Table of Contents

Introduction

Karolyn Kinane and Michael A. Ryan

In the summer of 1310, a Franciscan friar caused significant uproar on the island of Majorca. This unnamed preacher had gone around the city, appropriating the apocalyptic utterances of the physician and mystic, Arnau de Vilanova, and putting a particularly frightening twist on it. The preacher told the people that the Antichrist's arrival was nigh and that physical tribulations of all stripes would plague the world and hearken his advent. The people were apparently so badly frightened by this itinerant preachers' sermons that there were not "enough preachers, nor friars minor, nor clergy to hear [the people's] confession.... [T]he king of Majorca, knowing the fear of the people ... requests that the bishop of Majorca, who was in Perpignan, come back to comfort the people and that ... the preaching friar be imprisoned."[1]

In the autumn of 1983, the American Broadcasting Corporation aired the television movie "The Day After." In this movie, which portrayed the effects of a nuclear war waged between the United States and the Soviet Union, one of the most arresting scenes comes right before the detonation of a nuclear bomb over Kansas City, Missouri. As a siren blares, panicked people run in every direction in the streets of the doomed city. The camera pulls tightly away from the street scene, providing a panoramic view of the city, which is then washed out by a bright, white light. The then state-of-the-art special effects show the city's inhabitants being incinerated, evaporating by the resulting force of the blast and firestorms.

These two accounts, separated by time and geography, point to a powerful theme that runs throughout the course of this present volume of essays: the idea of the apocalypse and its reception within culture and society. In both of these vignettes, we see people reacting with fear to the idea that the end of their individual, social, and cultural existence was looming. The notion of the utter and complete end of all temporal and physical existence is a powerful and culturally universal concept. As human societies around the globe have produced creation myths, so too have they created narratives concerning the destruction of their worlds.[2] The idea of a universal annihilation,

1

whether it were to occur in either a spectacular or a subtle manner, has held an enduring grip on the popular imagination across time as well as cultures. Though the modern era is distinct in many ways from the premodern, its apocalyptic reckonings nonetheless carry echoes of and connections to those of the classical and medieval worlds. The essays collected here explore both the influence and innovation of apocalyptic ideas from classical Greek and Roman writings to the foreign policies of the contemporary United States. Within the cultural and intellectual framework of the Western world, which is the focus of this study, the narrative of the end of the world is tied intimately with the notion of the Judeo-Christian Apocalypse.[3]

The term apocalypse comes from the Greek word *apocalypsis,* meaning a lifting of the veil or, simply put, a revelation. It is a term of significant importance for biblical exegesis and religious studies. Apocalypses, such as those from the Old Testament Book of Daniel or the New Testament Apocalypse of St John, were prophetic texts that hinted at future times of great trauma, although the Greek term for that genre of text would not have been applied to pre–Christian sources.[4] This trauma, described as a series of trials and tribulations in apocalyptic sources, presaged a time when the mighty, powerful, and wicked would be brought low, while those who suffered at the hands of the powerful would be redeemed and justly rewarded for their suffering. Within the early Christian frameworks, the might and force of the Roman Empire provided the perfect background for many of these apocalyptic ideas to take root and flourish.

As the ultimate book of the Christian Bible, the Apocalypse of St John contributed momentously to European intellect and culture. The authorship of the Apocalypse, also known as the Book of Revelation, is attributed to the youngest of Jesus' disciples, John, who was purportedly living on the remote island of Patmos. This heavily symbolic, and at times disturbingly graphic, book outlines a course of the future that would hearken the Second Coming of Jesus Christ. The Evangelist depicts a world that would suffer powerful physical trials and tribulations, yet the arrival of Christ and the fulfillment of history would be a joyous event, one in which Christian adherents would be justly rewarded for their lifetimes of devotion, patience, and suffering. During the initial years of the Christian faith, in which Christians suffered from periods of intense religious persecution at the hands of some Roman emperors, this message was appealing. Thus, John's text functioned to encourage the community of the Christian faithful, to give them aid and succor during bleak times. The Second Coming of Christ would be a traumatic time, yet also a redemptive time, a time when old scores would be settled.[5]

When the presaged Second Coming did not immediately happen, however, subsequent Christian adherents reread the message of St John's Apocalypse and contextualized it in relation to later contemporary crises they endured. Medieval prophetic insight, which drew heavily on the textual and visual sources contained in the Apocalypse of St John, reached its height in the apocalyptic and exegetical writings of the twelfth century Calabrian abbot, Joachim di Fiore.[6] The message and imagery of the Book of Revelation spread from the domain of religious studies and became a powerful hermeneutical source in the Middle Ages, affecting significantly the arenas of medieval society and culture.[7]

Although the majority of modern Western society and popular culture today is purported to be avowedly secular, the Apocalypse nonetheless still resonates. Apocalyptic rhetoric and tropes appear continually throughout the history of the West and the advent of modernity did not sweep away these apocalyptic fascinations, as they appear in art, cinema, and literature and take on "an archetypal function."[8] Within the realm of modern popular culture, the apocalypse acquires another level of meaning and functions as a revealed vision of the end of the world that can be horrifying, frightful, and impending, as well as one that can be hopeful, humorous, and in the distant future.

On the brink of the year 2000, PBS launched a popular two-hour edition of *Frontline* about the Apocalypse, complete with scholarly and popular perspectives. At the close of 1999, the apocalypse was so pervasive as to be called by at least one U.S. reporter "the most fundamental and timely question of the hour."[9] The proliferation of blogs both secular and religious chronicling signs of the end of times, in addition to the many apocalyptic scenarios, themes and names (such as *rapture, revelation, tribulation, Antichrist, Armageddon)* in comic books, games, music and movies, attest to this enduring fascination with how the world ends. And scholars have noticed. The literature of apocalyptic studies is, in a word, immense.[10] Within the domain of modern popular culture, scholars have investigated apocalyptic rhetoric and themes within topics that range from reading the magazine *Soldier of Fortune* as a modern apocalyptic text, to Soviet peasants' visions of an impending apocalypse, to apocalyptic representations in the art of Picasso during the Spanish Civil War.[11] There are, of course, many more examples, but these studies illustrate an important point: it is within the realm of popular culture where apocalyptic ideas continue to endure and, in some cases, flourish.

Although there are starker boundaries between the domains of popular and elite culture in modernity, there is nonetheless a transference of cultural norms and *topoi* between the two spheres, just as in premodernity.[12] This transfer and endurance of apocalyptic ideas within the cultures of premodern and modern societies guide and connect the essays in this present collection.

Division of the Book

This collection begins with Brett Edward Whalen's essay on teaching the
End of Days, a piece that serves as a microcosm for this project. In his essay,
Whalen discusses the points of convergence and divergence among medieval
Christian and contemporary secular apocalyptic ideas. As a scholar, Whalen
had been immersed in biblical exegesis and medieval historiography, yet his
students brought what he calls "secular images of catastrophic destruction" to
the table. His experiences in the classroom thus illustrate the themes in this
collection, such as the ongoing interaction between high theology and popular religion, high art and popular culture. Whalen's essay further articulates
"the sense of relevancy between past and present" that this volume encourages readers to discover.

In the first half proper of our book, "Development and Dissemination,"
we invite readers to explore ancient, medieval, early modern, and modern popular conceptions of the apocalypse with such a "sense of relevancy" in mind.
Casey Starnes' essay explores classical visions of the apocalypse, examining
particularly how eschatological elements of Judaism are indebted to Greek,
Roman, Egyptian, Babylonian and Persian influence. The essay also briefly
considers how these elements survived into early Christian, late antique, and
medieval religious views. Kevin R. Poole's essay on Beatus of Liébana traces
notions of the "last world emperor" and the Antichrist as well as methods for
calculating the End Times in early medieval Spain. Poole proposes that what
started as Christian propaganda against Muslims in Spain expanded to
influence boarder apocalyptic rhetoric across Europe. Tessa Morrison considers how medieval illustrators and writers attempted to render the New
Jerusalem as described by John in the New Testament and illustrates how
such renderings often require the spectator to be simultaneously within,
beyond, and above the city. Lisa LeBlanc shows the centrality of the apocalypse in medieval morality plays and to what extent those dramatists used
apocalyptic *topoi* in leveling their criticisms of contemporary society. Carmen
Gómez-Galisteo's essay brings us squarely into the early modern period when
she demonstrates that one impetus for the Puritan's migration to America was
the fear of the impending apocalypse looming over an ever-degenerating
England. Gómez-Galisteo suggests, however, that Puritan anxiety about grace
ensured that apocalyptic threats would nonetheless be ever-present, and the
apocalypse thus migrated along with the Puritans in spite of their attempted
flight.

Apocalypticism shapes not only how medieval and premodern western
cultures imagined the past, present and future, but it also shapes modern literature, politics, and religion, the subject of the three essays that round out

the first half of our book. Richard Smith's essay explores how the early twentieth century Jamaican author J. Edmestone Barnes used medieval and later apocalyptic ideas to critique modern imperialism. The study by Eric Michael Reisenauer which follows considers how apocalyptic concerns, which bore the mark of the scientific method rather than religious fanaticism, were used by British authors in the late nineteenth and early twentieth centuries as they articulated relations among Britain, Israel, and the Ottoman Empire. Finally, David Redles demonstrates the incontrovertible connection between particularly medieval millenarian ideas and their appropriation by ideologues of Nazi Germany.

The second half of the book, "Political and Popular," focuses on the continuance of apocalyptic fears and expectations and how they are understood within the realms of contemporary politics and popular culture. Husam Mohamad's essay, for instance, illustrates how Christian fundamentalist coalitions' views about Armageddon influence U.S. foreign policy, particularly with regards to Israel. Lorenzo DiTommaso then works with the novels of Cormac McCarthy, Walter Miller and Philip K. Dick, as well as the *The Matrix* film franchise, in an attempt to define "apocalyptic fiction," and urges readers to consider not only images but worldviews such as cosmological dualism as key to linking ancient and medieval eschatology to contemporary iterations. Therese-Marie Meyer explores how Puritan eschatology is parodied in the 1990 novel *Good Omens: The Nice and Accurate Prophecies of Agnes Nutter, Witch* by Neil Gaiman and Terry Pratchett. Although the novel begins with parodic downsizing of the religious, Meyer claims that the metaphysical ultimately reigns supreme. And Johann Pautz explores how the philosophies of the John Birch Society, the Militia Movement, and contemporary Christian apocalyptic fiction all inform U.S. social and economic policies.

The convergence and divergences of the political and popular continue further in Nancy A. Shaefer's article, where she explores the "thriving evangelical subculture" in the United States via the *Left Behind* books and movies. Shaefer attempts to account for the persistence of beliefs in prophecy and preoccupation with end-time speculation in one of the most technologically advanced, industrialized nations in the world. Evelyn Stiller looks at rapture fiction from the 1970s and illustrates how modern evangelical notions of race and gender are "updated" in the real-time strategy videogame *Left Behind: Eternal Forces.* Benjamin E. Zeller demonstrates the relationships among apocalyptic reckonings and contemporary UFO-based religions and, finally, Rikk Mulligan notes how medieval notions of plague fuse with modern conceptions of technology, vampires, and zombies within contemporary speculative fiction.

Regarding apocalyptic expectations and their place in modern society,

Caroline Walker Bynum and Paul Freedman have commented that, unlike premodern people, we moderns "are neither very apocalyptic, nor very eschatological, nor even very scared. Not, perhaps, as much as we ought to be."[13] However, as the authors of the essays in this volume have shown, both premodern and modern Western cultures share many apocalyptic similarities. In their respective societies' worldviews, prior apocalyptic ideas were constantly transmitted and refashioned over the centuries. And as seen in modern popular culture, just as in premodern culture people are still apprehensive, if not outright frightened, by their revelations of a potentially apocalyptic future.

NOTES

1. "E di es que prehicadors ne frares menores ne clergues qui i sien no basten a les confessions oir, si que l rey de Mayorca sabe l espaordiment de les gens e prega lo bisbe de Mallorca que era ab el a Perpinya que se n passas e que confortas les gens e encara que l prior que preses lo frare prehicador." Martí de Barcelona, *La cultura catalana durant el regnat de Jaime II* (Barcelona: Estudios Franciscanos, 1991) 179–180.

2. David Adams Leeming, *The World of Myth* (New York: Oxford University Press, 1990).

3. We have focused on the Judeo-Christian notions of the apocalypse, but this is not the sole cultural tradition to focus on the end of cycles. Many indigenous American societies, such as the Hopi, have crafted significant apocalyptic rhetoric and many people have read the Mayan calendar within an apocalyptic framework, as it hints at the end of a cycle to come in 2012.

4. John J. Collins, *The Apocalyptic Imagination: An Introduction to Jewish Apocalyptic Literature*, 2nd ed. (Grand Rapids, MI: Eerdmans, 1998) 3.

5. The scholar who has most espoused this intriguing, yet controversial, idea has been Norman Cohn, *The Pursuit of the Millennium: Revolutionary Millenarians and Mystical Anarchists of the Middle Ages* (New York: Oxford University Press, 1970). Robert Lerner, *The Powers of Prophecy: The Cedar of Lebanon Vision from the Mongol Onslaught to the Dawn of the Enlightenment* (Berkeley: University of California Press, 1983) has vociferously disagreed with Cohn's assertions.

6. Marjorie Reeves, *The Influence of Prophecy in the Middle Ages: A Study in Joachimism* (Oxford: Clarendon, 1969); Bernard McGinn, *The Calabrian Abbot: Joachim of Fiore in the History of Western Thought* (New York: Macmillan, 1985); Delno C. West and Sandra Zimdars-Swartz, *Joachim of Fiore: A Study in Spiritual Perception and History* (Bloomington, IN: Indiana University Press, 1983); Harold Lee, Marjorie Reeves, and Giulio Silano, *Western Mediterranean Prophecy: The School of Joachim of Fiore and the Fourteenth-Century Breviloquium* (Toronto: Pontifical Institute of Medieval Studies, 1989).

7. In addition to the other essays contained in this book, see Bernard McGinn, "Introduction: John's Apocalypse and the Apocalyptic Mentality," in *The Apocalypse in the Middle Ages,* Richard K. Emmerson and Bernard McGinn, eds. (Ithaca, NY: Cornell University Press, 1992) 3–19.

8. Frances Carey, "The Apocalyptic Imagination: between Tradition and Modernity," in *The Apocalypse and the Shape of Things to Come,* Frances Carey, ed. (Toronto: University of Toronto Press, 1999) 270–319.

9. Eric Mink, *New York Daily News Frontline Apocalypse! Press Page* November 1999 <http://www.pbs.org/wgbh/pages/frontline/shows/apocalypse/etc/press.html> (October 20, 2008).

10. For just some examples, see the following bibliographies: D. Brent Sandy and Daniel M. O'Hare, *Prophecy and Apocalyptic: An Annotated Bibliography* (Grand Rapids, MI: Baker Academic, 2007); Robert L. Muse, *The Book of Revelation: An Annotated Bibliography* (New York: Garland, 1996); and Harold R. Willoughby, *A Bibliography for the Study of Apocalypse Iconography* (Chicago: University of Chicago Press, 1940).

11. Philip Lamy, "Millennialism in the Mass Media: The Case of 'Soldier of Fortune' Magazine," *Journal for the Scientific Study of Religion* 31 no. 4 (December 1992): 408–424; Lynne Viola, "The Peasant Nightmare: Visions of Apocalypse in the Soviet Countryside," *The Journal of Modern History* 62 no. 4 (December 1990): 747–770; Timothy Anglin Burgard, "Picasso's Night Fishing at Antibes: Autobiography, Apocalypse, and the Spanish Civil War," *The Art Bulletin* 68 no. 4 (December 1986): 657–672.

12. See Aron Gurevich, *Categories of Medieval Culture* (London and Boston: Routledge & Kegan Paul, 1985) and idem, *Medieval Popular Culture: Problems of Belief and Perception* (Cambridge: Cambridge University Press, 1988). See especially Peter Burke, *Popular Culture in Early Modern Europe* (New York: Harper and Row, 1978).

13. See page Caroline Walker Bynum and Paul Freedman, "Introduction," in *Last Things: Death and the Apocalypse in the Middle Ages,* Caroline Walker Bynum and Paul Freedman, eds. (Philadelphia: University of Pennsylvania Press, 2000) 1–17 at 17.

WORKS CITED

Barcelona, Martí de. *La cultura catalana durant el regnat de Jaime II.* Barcelona: Estudios Franciscanos, 1991.

Burgard, Timothy Anglin. "Picasso's Night Fishing at Antibes: Autobiography, Apocalypse, and the Spanish Civil War." *The Art Bulletin* 68, no. 4 (December 1986): 657–672.

Burke, Peter. *Popular Culture in Early Modern Europe.* New York: Harper and Row, 1978.

Bynum, Caroline Walker and Paul Freedman, eds. *Last Things: Death and the Apocalypse in the Middle Ages.* Philadelphia: University of Pennsylvania Press, 2000.

Carey, Frances. "The Apocalyptic Imagination: Between Tradition and Modernity" in *The Apocalypse and the Shape of Things to Come.* Frances Carey, ed. Toronto: University of Toronto Press, 1999: 270–319.

Cohn, Norman. *The Pursuit of the Millennium: Revolutionary Millenarians and Mystical Anarchists of the Middle Ages.* New York: Oxford University Press, 1970.

Collins, John J. *The Apocalyptic Imagination: An Introduction to Jewish Apocalyptic Literature,* 2nd ed. Grand Rapids, MI: Eerdmans, 1998.

Gurevich, Aron. *Categories of Medieval Culture.* London and Boston: Routledge and Kegan Paul, 1985.

_____. *Medieval Popular Culture: Problems of Belief and Perception.* Cambridge, UK: Cambridge University Press, 1988.

Lamy, Philip. "Millennialism in the Mass Media: The Case of 'Soldier of Fortune' Magazine." *Journal for the Scientific Study of Religion* 3, no. 4 (December 1992): 408–424.

Lee, Harold, Marjorie Reeves and Giulio Silano. *Western Mediterranean Prophecy: The School of Joachim of Fiore and the Fourteenth-Century Breviloquium.* Toronto: Pontifical Institute of Medieval Studies, 1989.

Leeming, David Adams. *The World of Myth.* New York: Oxford University Press, 1990.

Lerner, Robert. *The Powers of Prophecy: The Cedar of Lebanon Vision from the Mongol Onslaught to the Dawn of the Enlightenment.* Berkeley: University of California Press, 1983.

McGinn, Bernard. *The Calabrian Abbot: Joachim of Fiore in the History of Western Thought.* New York: Macmillan, 1985.

_____. "Introduction: John's Apocalypse and the Apocalyptic Mentality" in *The Apoca-*

lypse in the Middle Ages. Richard K. Emmerson and Bernard McGinn, eds. Ithaca, NY: Cornell University Press, 1992: 3–19.

Mink, Eric. *New York Daily News Frontline Apocalypse! Press Page* November, 1999 <http://www.pbs.org/wgbh/pages/frontline/shows/apocalypse/etc/press.html> (October 20, 2008).

Muse, Robert L. *The Book of Revelation: An Annotated Bibliography.* New York: Garland, 1996.

Reeves, Marjorie. *The Influence of Prophecy in the Middle Ages: A Study in Joachimism.* Oxford, UK: Clarendon Press, 1969.

Sandy, D. Brent and Daniel M. O'Hare. *Prophecy and Apocalyptic: An Annotated Bibliography.* Grand Rapids, MI: Baker Academic, 2007.

Viola, Lynne. "The Peasant Nightmare: Visions of Apocalypse in the Soviet Countryside." *The Journal of Modern History* 62, no. 4 (December 1990): 747–770

West, Delno C., and Sandra Zimdars-Swartz. *Joachim of Fiore: A Study in Spiritual Perception and History.* Bloomington, IN: Indiana University Press, 1983.

Willoughby, Harold R. *A Bibliography for the Study of Apocalypse Iconography.* Chicago: University of Chicago Press, 1940.

Teaching the End of Days:
Medieval Meets Modern
Apocalypse in the Classroom

Brett Edward Whalen

In the fall of 2006, I had the fortunate opportunity to teach a small seminar titled "The Apocalypse in the Christian Middle Ages" at the University of North Carolina, Chapel Hill.[1] It was my second year at UNC and my first time teaching about medieval apocalypticism, although the subject has been of central importance to my own research for some time.[2] This being the case, I was particularly eager to approach the end of days from a pedagogical perspective. After some initial shuffling, the class settled down with fifteen students. It became apparent over the first few meetings that they comprised a motivated, enthusiastic, and intellectually curious group. As a general rule, however, they had little previous experience studying premodern Christianity or medieval European history. During our initial class meeting, when I asked them to share whatever popped into their heads when they thought about the end of the world, their responses for the most part involved secular images of catastrophic destruction, including such things as avian flu, a comet striking the Earth, nuclear war and alien invasions.

My principal goal for the semester was to draw the students back into a remoter world of apocalyptic thinking, one dominated by biblical exegesis rather than aliens, culminating with the Second Coming of Christ rather than a mushroom cloud. For our shared readings, I assigned two volumes by Bernard McGinn, whose name is justifiably well known among historians of apocalyptic thought: first, his work *Antichrist: Two Thousand Years of the Human Fascination with Evil*, which offers a sweeping survey of the Christian apocalyptic tradition from the Bible until the present; and second, McGinn's *Visions of the End: Apocalyptic Traditions in the Middle Ages*, a collection of primary source documents translated principally from medieval Latin.[3] I also assigned several chapters from Majorie Reeves' work *Joachim of Fiore and the Prophetic Future*, which examines the life and writings of medieval

9

Europe's most innovative apocalyptic thinker, along with portions of Norman Cohn's ground-breaking work *The Pursuit of the Millennium*.[4] In this influential and controversial book, Cohn argued that popular medieval and early modern apocalyptic movements manifested a radical agitation for social transformation among the poor and displaced elements of an increasingly industrialized European society.[5]

Broadly speaking, my aspirations for the course remained similar to those for all of my classes in medieval history. The students, I hoped, would become familiar with the major historical contours of our subject matter, learning about key trends, events, and actors in the development of apocalyptic thought during the Middle Ages. More importantly, through their own analysis of primary source documents, they would gain some sense of how historians ply their trade, in this case using evidence from the past to formulate conclusions about the meaningfulness of Christian apocalypticism for medieval society, politics, and religious life. As always, I wanted my students to immerse themselves in the *difference* of the Middle Ages, to experience the intellectual challenge of entering a less than familiar world. Almost all of my students, for example, had heard about the Rapture, the belief that the faithful followers of God will be lifted up into Heaven before the unleashing of apocalyptic tribulations (this idea was one of the few overtly religious concepts mentioned during our "brainstorming" session on the first day of class). Due in large part to the popular *Left Behind* series of novels about the trials of those who do not make the cut, but remain here on earth to confront the horrors of the end times, the Rapture constitutes one of the better known scenarios in the present-day American apocalyptic imagination. To general astonishment, I informed my class that this doctrine had emerged relatively recently from within modern, fundamentalist Protestantism. No one in the Middle Ages was waiting for the Rapture.[6]

At this point, however, my students had a surprise for me. One of them volunteered that a congregation of religious believers in her small home-town had spent New Year's Eve in 1999 on top of a hill waiting for the Rapture. Let me be clear. As a general rule of thumb, in the classroom I try to suggest connections between my medieval subject matter and present-day issues, particularly when religious values and beliefs are concerned. Teaching on the crusades, for example, provides ample opportunities to explore links between the Middle Ages and events "ripped from the headlines." Drawing such connections, in my opinion, does not mean crudely asserting or assuming direct continuities between the past and present, nor should it include the anachronistic projection of contemporary values into the past. Rather, when we explore how medieval Christian believers grappled with their own world, we can better understand how religion fits, comfortably and uncomfortably, into the broader matrix of politics, culture, and society, not just in the Middle Ages but also in our own times. This student's revelation — no pun intended — about the lived experience of apocalyptic expectation in her own local community, however, suggested a far more immediate sense of relevancy between past and present than I generally anticipate. This moment provided my first glimpse of the fact that medieval would meet modern apocalypse right there in my own classroom.[7]

One of the first challenges confronting me and my students was to establish some basic terms and concepts for discussing the end of days. Scholars have long debated over the precise meaning of "apocalypticism," "eschatology," and "millennialism," all of which are related but distinct ideas.[8] While they often agree to disagree, many historians find it helpful to distinguish between general forms of *eschatology,* which include any set of beliefs about the end of existence, including the fate of the individual soul, and *apocalyptic eschatology* or *apocalypticism,* the belief that the imminent end of history will involve a series of crises, followed by the defeat of evil and the triumph of the elect. *Millennarianism* is a specific form of apocalyptic eschatology, based principally on Revelation 20:2, that anticipates a miraculous "thousand-year" reign of Christ, completely transforming terrestrial institutions and bringing collective salvation.[9]

It is one thing to rattle off these terms in an academic article, but something else for an entire class of undergraduate students to feel comfortable using them. As we hashed over these concepts and jumped into our primary sources, the students increasingly focused on the historical orientation of apocalyptic eschatology, that is to say, on the idea that apocalypticism is concerned with the revelation of God's intention for the totality of history. In order to grasp the divine plan for the future, one must also look at the present and the past, both of which give meaning to developments on the apocalyptic horizon. To understand the Second Coming of Christ in Final Judgment, one must look back to Christ's Incarnation, his "First Coming" in the flesh. The Incarnation, in turn, leads one inexorably back into the pages of the Old Testament, the Hebrew scriptures that (from a Christian perspective) prophesied the future coming of Christ the Messiah, who would open the doors to Redemption from sin. The problem of sin, in turn, brings one back to the Garden of Eden and the Fall that started history in motion. The apocalypse, so to speak, points us toward Adam; the end of history reaches back to its beginning, and its beginning toward its end.[10]

To become experts in medieval apocalypticism, my students first needed to become Christian "theologians of history," immersing themselves in a foreign perspective on the nature of time as part of a providential dispensation that stretches from Creation until Final Judgment. Among other consequences, this step meant rethinking an implicitly secular assumption that the end of the world is something to be avoided. Consider a common scenario from popular culture, including movies such as *Deep Impact* and *Armageddon*: a comet or asteroid is heading toward Earth and will wipe out life on our planet, unless a heroic band of astronauts can somehow use technology to avert the danger by destroying the menacing object (usually, nuclear weapons are employed to divert or deflect that space-born threat, thereby turning one potential source of apocalyptic destruction into a means of saving humankind). In a medieval apocalyptic mentality, there is no avoiding the end. In some ways, apocalyptic commentators were looking forward to it. After the horrible trials and tribulations that would accompany the apocalypse, Christ would return to judge the living and the dead, bringing about the culmination of God's plan for Redemption. If you believed that you were among the saved, then the end of the world was still something to be feared, but beyond that fear lay hope. Needless to say, nuclear annihilation or environmental disasters hold no such promise of salvation hidden behind the veil.[11]

For a number of classes, we discussed some basic Christian theories about the meaning and organization of history, focusing mostly on the influential works of Augustine of Hippo (354–430). These schemes included the division of time into three stages: the era "before the law" (*ante legem*) that was given to Moses, the era "under the law" (*sub lege*) from Moses until Christ, and the Christian era "under grace" (*sub gratia*) from Christ until the end of time. Another important scheme divided history into seven ages, based on the seven days of creation: the first age, from Adam to Noah; the second, from Noah to Abraham; the third, from Abraham to David; the fourth, from David to the Babylonian Captivity; and the fifth, from the Babylonian Captivity to the coming of Christ, and the sixth, starting with Christ. The sixth age would be followed by the Sabbath of eternal rest. Some Christian thinkers believed that each age of history consisted of a thousand years and that one could therefore calculate the coming of the end (the precise date would depend on exactly where one dated the Incarnation).[12] Augustine, however, vehemently argued that the length of the sixth age, the *final* age of history, was known only to God. In fact, he believed that it was impossible to fathom any divine plan for the sixth age. Simply put, from Christ until the end of time, there would be no more developments in sacred history, only the long pilgrimage of the Church, the "mixed body" of the good and the wicked that would endure until the Second Coming.[13]

Regardless of Augustine's considerable influence, many subsequent Christian thinkers persisted in their attempts to read the ever increasing stretch of time following Christ through the prism of salvation history. According to many medieval theologians and historians, the fourth-century conversion of the Roman Emperor Constantine (272–337 CE) to Christianity represented a divinely ordained moment of triumph for the Church, establishing the power of the Christian Roman Empire throughout the world. In another scheme, popularized by Saint Jerome (347–420 CE), passages from the Book of Daniel revealed the preordained progression of "world empires" from the Babylonians to the Persians, next to the Macedonians, and finally to the Romans. Even before Constantine, some Christians had argued that history would not end until the power of Rome had somehow failed or lapsed.[14] For others, the rise of Islam in the seventh century represented another critical juncture in history, when the Muslims overran much of the Eastern Roman Empire. From that point forward, Islam began to play a crucial role in Christian apocalyptic scenarios.[15] In class, we read sections of the so-called "Pseudo-Methodius," an influential Syrian apocalyptic tradition dating from the late seventh century. This text describes the rise of the "sons of Ishmael" (i.e. the Muslims) as a punishment by God against Christians for their sins. In the future, however, a "Last World Emperor" would arise, who would smash the power of the non-believers and restore Christianity to a golden age of peace before the arrival of Antichrist, the final trials of the faithful, and Christ's Second Coming.[16]

Speaking of Antichrist, all of my students had hazy notions about the false Messiah, the "Son of Perdition" (II Thess. 2:3), who would come to persecute the faithful at the end of time. We began to explore the Antichrist tradition more closely, starting with the notion that belief in Antichrist formed an integral and not peripheral part of Christian messianic theology.[17] By placing Christ at the center of salvation, Christians almost inevitably began to assign his evil counterpart a prominent place in the end-times. As Adso of Montier-en-Der related in his popular ninth-century tract on the subject:

> Since you want to know about Antichrist, the first thing to observe is why he is so named. It is because he will be contrary to Christ in all things and will work deeds against Christ. Christ came in humbled fashion; he will come as a proud man. Christ came to raise up the humble, to justify sinners; he, on the other hand, will cast out the humble, magnify sinners, exalt the wicked and always teach the vices contrary to virtues. He will destroy the Law of the Gospel, call the worship of demons back into the world, seek his own glory, and call himself almighty God.[18]

As the semester progressed, my students became particularly attuned to the "political uses" of the Antichrist tradition. What better way to attack a political opponent than to associate him or her with "Antichrist"? Throughout the High and Late Middle Ages, during the famous clash between popes and emperors for supremacy over medieval society, both sides did not hesitate to smear each other with the label of Antichrist.[19] In other scenarios, increasingly popular after the development of the crusading movement in the twelfth and thirteenth centuries, Christians associated Muslims with Antichrist or his minions. When a prophet's prediction about the imminent arrival of Antichrist turned out to be wrong, reasons were found for the miscalculation and the hunt began for a new Antichrist. Apocalyptic thinkers were nothing if not flexible.

In addition to Antichrist, we also engaged with the contested nature of apocalyptic thought within the Latin tradition, above all where millennialism was concerned.[20] Generally speaking, modern observers often view the Middle Ages as an "age of faith," when Christians shared a monolithic worldview, unable, unwilling, or too scared to question the authority of the Church. Nothing could be further from the truth. In terms of apocalyptic eschatology, debate rather than consensus characterized medieval thinking about the end of the world. As described above, patristic theologians such as Augustine of Hippo were adamant that humans were living in the sixth and final age of history, which would quickly end after the coming of Antichrist and Christ's return. Others, however, basing their belief on the Book of Revelation's assertion that Satan would be bound for "one thousand years," argued that the climatic battle between good and evil under Antichrist would be followed by a "millennial" kingdom on earth, a new kind of terrestrial society in an age of peace and plenitude. Taking sides in a debate that stretched back at least to the second century, Augustine viewed this idea as a dangerous fantasy. The "binding" of Satan, he asserted, had already begun with Christ's resurrection and triumph over death. The "thousand years" referred to in the Book of Revelation was a symbolic figure denoting all of history from Christ until the end of time. Certainly, there would be no historical "Sabbath age" after the end of sixth era.[21]

I was especially keen for my students to grapple with the issue of what was at stake in medieval debates over millenarianism. Although Augustine's denial of the millennium would shape mainstream Christian attitudes for centuries to come, it did not entirely prevent subsequent thinkers from speculating about the potential for a millennial transformation in ecclesiastical life, politics, and society. During the High Middle Ages, the teachings of Joachim of Fiore (1132–1202) best illustrate the subversive potential of apocalyptic eschatology.[22] Among numerous creative insights, Joachim argued that all of history was organized on the principle of the Trinity. First, there had been the era (*status*) of God the Father, running approximately from the beginning of time until Christ. Second, there was the era of the Son, lasting roughly from Christ until Joachim's present. Within two generations, Joachim believed, there would begin a Sabbath era of the Holy Spirit, "when, after the destruction and cancellation of the false gospel of the Son of Perdition and his prophets, those who will teach many about justice will be like the splendor of the firmament and like the stars forever."[23] This striking and influential vision of the future, when a new order of "spiritual men" would inaugurate a new age "more fully in grace," marked a clear departure from the authority of Saint Augustine and others like him. During his lifetime, Joachim remained an orthodox figure, but about fifty years after he died, some of his more radical admirers argued that the third era of the Holy Spirit would mean an end to the institutional authority of the Roman papacy and church, including the superseded priesthood and sacraments of the second age.[24]

Suddenly, the dangers posed by millennial schemes for mainstream Christian thinkers seemed quite evident! This being the case, we decided to put Joachim on trial for heresy. In one of my less reserved teaching-moments, we engaged in some role-playing: I acted as the pope, and my students formed two parties of educated theologians, one prosecuting and one defending Joachim of Fiore, based on his own writings as presented in McGinn's *Visions of the End*. The prosecution argued that Joachim's efforts to read the course of history after Christ as part of the providential plan constituted a clear violation of patristic prohibitions, above all, those of Augustine. They cast aspersion on his claim that a future epoch of the Holy Spirit would somehow transform the world before the end of time. Joachim, the prosecution claimed, was presumptuously claiming spiritual insights into the meaning of history. The defense pointed out that the Calabrian abbot had submitted his works for papal approval on several occasions and received papal sanction to continue writing. Joachim, they argued, hardly represented an anti-clerical iconoclast, whatever his later followers claimed. This exercise was not only enjoyable; it also demonstrated just how comfortable my students had become with the language and logic of medieval apocalypticism. Although I felt that the arguments against Joachim were more convincing, having read Joachim's works for myself, I decided that the abbot was not guilty of heresy, much to the disgruntlement of the prosecution. The final decision lay with me — after all, I was the pope

The semester was more or less proceeding according to plan. Around a month into our class, however, two things had happened that began to change the tone and direction of our investigations into medieval apocalypticism. First, while driving home from work, I heard an interview with Pastor John Hagee on the NPR radio program *Fresh Air* with Terry Gross.[25] Hagee is the founder of "Christians United for Israel," a self-described "grassroots Christian movement" that strongly supports the modern nation of Israel. Israel, according to Hagee and others like him, is the only state that was deliberately and directly created by God, who bestowed its territory upon Abraham and his descendants. From this perspective, the "rebirth" of Israel in the year 1948 formed an historical turning point of eschatological significance. The Jewish presence in the Holy Land is a necessary part of Hagee's apocalyptic theology — there must be Jews in Israel to bring about end of days and allow the Second Coming, when the Jews will convert to Christianity or suffer the consequences of their unbelief.[26]

About a week later, I played this interview for my students in class. Although the theological framing of Hagee's apocalypticism is relatively new, developing from nineteenth- and twentieth-century American evangelical Protestantism, the idea that the Jews will have a key role to play at the end of time formed an important part of medieval apocalyptic thought. From a Christian viewpoint, during the progression from the Old Testament to the New Testament, the Jews had effectively lost their position as God's Chosen People due to their rejection of Christ, yielding their place to the Gentile Church. It was commonly believed that the Jews would serve Antichrist when he arrived on the scene, greeting him as their true Messiah. At the same time, based principally on Romans 11:25, medieval Christians also anticipated that the Jews (or a portion of them anyway) would convert to Christianity after the defeat of Antichrist. Joachim of Fiore, in particular, devoted a great deal of attention to this idea that Gentiles and Jews would be united harmoniously before the conclusion of history.[27] According to some theologians, this logic provided one reason why the Jews should be grudgingly tolerated by Christians and not destroyed, since there needed to be some Jews left around to convert.[28]

Listening to John Hagee, we suddenly confronted a similar, if distinctly modern Christian apocalyptic theology about the Jews. Around this same time, one of my students emailed me an article from the website of the satirical newspaper *The Onion*. The piece, dating from the turn of the millennium (that is, the second millennium), declared to its readers: "No Seven-Headed Dragon Appears in the East."[29] With cutting levity, the article explained that religious "experts" were puzzled by the failure of the much-anticipated draconic figure of evil from the Book of Revelation (Rev. 12:3) to emerge on the scene during such an appropriate moment. Enjoying the wry piece, I asked this particular student to share the article with the rest of the class. His presentation was such a success that I decided every student (as part of their participation grade) should bring some sort of modern "apocalyptic show and tell," that is to say, any kind of contemporary materials that intersected with our medieval course themes.

The spirit of modern apocalypticism had begun to haunt our class on the apocalypse in the Middle Ages. One of the students shared excerpts from a commentary being written on the Book of Revelation by David Koresh, the spiritual leader of the Branch Davidians, when the FBI stormed their compound in Waco, Texas, with disastrous consequences.[30] Another student brought copies of the periodical *Midnight Call,* an evangelical Christian publication dedicated to informing its readers about the approaching end of days. This glossy, professional-looking publication included essays about the need to support Israel, the dangers posed by the United Nations (commonly associated with the future "world government" of Antichrist), and the establishment of the Euro-zone as one step toward a universal currency (again, pointing toward the global rule of Antichrist).[31] During one of our final meetings, in some sense as a "fun day" after the students had completed their final essays, we spent one class searching Google and Youtube for apocalyptic-related materials and videos. The results were astonishing. The Internet fully displayed the political valence of apocalypticism, hosting sites that associated Saddam Hussein, George W. Bush, Pope John Paul II and others with Antichrist. Another site linked the "new age" pseudo-religiosity of the *Star Wars* film series and Hillary Clinton (in a connection that I still do not completely understand, nor am I sure that I want to) with evil forces at the end of time. Film clips displayed secular images of apocalyptic destruction, such as asteroids crashing into the earth, while scenes from the animated series *South Park* featured the ultimate battle between good and evil, a light-weight, slender Jesus Christ battling in a boxing ring with a heavy-weight, muscle-bound Satan (there is a dissertation waiting to be written on apocalyptic themes and imagery in *South Park*). Besides the sheer entertainment value of this exercise, if I may dignify it with that label, our exploration of modern apocalyptic images demonstrated just how far we had come from the beginning of the semester. Sights and sounds that might have previously shocked or amused my students could now be understood as recent manifestations of an apocalyptic complex that stretched back roughly two thousand years, encompassing the Middle Ages and much more.

By the end of the semester, I had started to realize that this classroom synergy between medieval and modern apocalyptic mentalities tells us something important about the changing circumstances of our own world. I am firmly convinced that if I had taught this same seminar ten or fifteen years ago (perhaps even less than that), our way of relating to the topic of apocalypticism would have been considerably different. First of all, I am struck by the advent of the Internet as a demotic vehicle for disseminating ideas about the end of the world, both the sublime and the ridiculous, the politically dangerous and quixotically harmless. In a sense, the proliferation of apocalypticism on the Internet is unsurprising. The first century of the "print revolution" in late-fifteenth and early-sixteenth century Europe facilitated an unprecedented explosion of (usually polemical) religious texts and images, including those of an apocalyptic orientation. Two examples include Albrecht Dürer's illustrations of the Book of Revelation and the first printed editions of works by Joachim of Fiore. Print opened up new vistas for apocalyptic speculation. Not surprisingly, the "information revolution" around the turn of the second millennium seems to be doing likewise, with results that are still taking shape.

More profoundly, recent years have witnessed a shift in the political impact or at least the visibility of religious motivations and sensibilities. For many Americans, the suicide attacks of 9/11 signaled this change, although it was already on display in many parts of the world well beforehand, particularly since the end of the Cold War. The belief (perhaps it was always a delusion) that we were living in a constantly secularizing world is no longer tenable. Indeed, it can be argued with good reason that nineteenth- and twentieth-century secular ideologies, above all totalitarian systems including fascism and communism, possessed their own forms of "apocalyptic" inspiration: the thousand-year Nazi Reich seems to provide one notable example of modern millennialism.[32] Religious-based apocalypticism, however, whether Christian or Islamic, has resurfaced in some circles with a vengeance. Contrary to what we might expect, my own students must confront a much more immediate sense of apocalyptic expectation in their political world than I myself would have, if I had taken a similar class on the medieval apocalypse during my own undergraduate career roughly two decades earlier.

To be clear, the apocalypticism of the Middle Ages does not lead us directly or transparently into the eschatological speculations of modern times. Just as no one in the Middle Ages was expecting the Rapture, few if any would now anticipate the arrival of an "angelic pope," who will unite the peoples of the world into "one flock" under "one shepherd" (Jn. 10:16) before the end of history — a popular scenario in the later Middle Ages. It is hardly surprising that there are substantial differences between medieval and modern apocalyptic thought, given that so much else has changed in politics, society, culture, Christian spirituality and nearly every other aspect of life. What modern apocalyptic thinkers seem to share with their premodern predecessors is an investment in understanding the ebb and flow of history, which sometimes seems to be rushing in a torrent toward its conclusion, along with the claim that they possess privileged insights into the transcendent plan for earthly events. This being the case, perhaps the final lesson of medieval apocalyptic traditions should be a healthy sense of skepticism about those who claim such knowledge of history's purpose, regardless of whether they do so in the name of God, Nation, Freedom or some other principle. So far, needless to say, everyone predicting the end of history has been dead wrong.

NOTES

1. Without my students, this essay would not exist. Accordingly, my thanks to Sarah Archer, Noah Brisban, Michael Chomat, Nathan Dankner, Caroline Fisher, Meredith Gilliam, Emily Kiser, Jillian Nadell, David Pollock, Patricia Ryan, Ian Sanders, William Schultz, Ian Shields, Justin Singer and John Tabor. My thanks also to Matthew Gabriele for his editorial suggestions and insights.

2. My forthcoming book, *The Pursuit of Christendom: The Medieval Church and the Conversion of the World,* examines the importance of historical and apocalyptic schemes for the imaging of a unified world order under the authority of the Roman papacy during the High Middle Ages. See also my article "Joachim of Fiore and the Division of Christendom," *Viator* 98 (2003): 89–108.

3. Bernard McGinn, *Antichrist: Two Thousand Years of the Human Fascination with Evil* (New York: Columbia University Press, 2000), and Bernard McGinn, *Visions of the End: Apocalyptic Traditions in the Middle Ages* (1979; New York: Columbia University Press, 1998).

4. See Marjorie Reeves, *Joachim of Fiore and the Prophetic Future* (1976; Stroud, U.K.: Sutton, 1999), and Norman Cohn, *The Pursuit of the Millennium: Revolutionary Millenarians and Mystical Anarchists of the Middle Ages,* rev. ed. (1957; New York: Oxford University Press, 1970). See also Gian Luca Potestà, "Radical Apocalyptic Movements in the Late Middle Ages," in *The Encyclopedia of Apocalypticism: Apocalypticism in Western History and Culture,* Bernard McGinn, ed. 4 vols. (New York: Continuum, 1998) 2: 110–142, and Robert Lerner, "Millennialism," in *The Encyclopedia of Apocalypticism,* 2: 326–360.

5. Some have criticized Cohn for exaggerating the subversive nature of apocalyptic eschatology and ignoring its potential for reinforcing authority. Among others, see Bernard McGinn, "Apocalypticism and Church Reform: 1100–1500," in *The Encyclopedia of Apocalypticism,* 2: 74–109, and Robert Lerner, "Medieval Millenarianism and Violence," in *Pace e Guerra nel basso medioevo: atti del XL convegno storico internazionale, Todi, 12–14 Ottobre 2003* (Spoleto, 2004) 37–52.

6. See the essays in *Rapture, Revelation, and the End Times: Exploring the Left Behind Series,* Bruce Forbes and Jeanne Kilde, eds. (New York: Palgrave Macmillan, 2004). More generally on American Protestant apocalypticism, see McGinn, *Antichrist,* 252–257, and Stephen Stein, "American Millennial Visions: Towards Construction of a New Architectonic of American Apocalypticism," in *Imagining the End: Visions of Apocalypse from the Ancient Middle East to Modern America,* Abbas Amanat and Magnus Bernhardsson, eds. (London: I. B. Tauris, 2002) 187–211. See also the essay by Nancy Shaefer, "The *Left Behind* Series and its Place Within the American Evangelical Subculture" in this volume.

7. For some thoughts on the relevance of medieval topics to modern concerns, see Caroline Walker Bynum, "Why All the Fuss about the Body? A Medievalist's Perspective," *Critical Inquiry* 22 (1995): 1–33, especially pp. 27–33.

8. I attended an international conference in Budapest called "The Apocalyptic Complex," December 7–8, 2007, where we spent a great deal of our time debating without resolution what "apocalyptic" really meant. My thanks to Matthias Riedl and the other conference participants, who, as much as my former students, helped me to think in new directions about the issues involved in this essay.

9. See McGinn, *Visions of the End,* 1–36, and Richard Landes, "Lest the Millennium Be Fulfilled: Apocalyptic Expectations and the Pattern of Western Chronography 100–800," in *The Use and Abuse of Eschatology in the Middle Ages,* Werner Verbeke, Daniel Verhelst and Andries Welkenhuysen, eds. (Leuven: Leuven University Press, 1988) 137–211 (including the terms in his appendix, 205–208).

10. See Brett Whalen, "From Adam to the Apocalypse: Post-Classical Christianity and the Patterns of World History," *World History Association Bulletin* 23 (2007): 21–26.

11. As summed up by Bernard McGinn, "The Apocalyptic Imagination in the Middle Ages," in *Ende und Vollendung: Eschatologische Perspektiven im Mittelalter,* Jan Aertsen and Martin Pickavé, eds. (Berlin: W. de Gruyter, 2002) 79–94: "Apocalypticism has always been characterized by an intricate mixture of optimism and pessimism" (quotation from p. 84).

12. In addition to Landes, "Lest the Millennium Be Fulfilled," see Richard Landes, "The Fear of an Apocalyptic Year 1000: Augustinian Historiography, Medieval and Modern," *Speculum* 75 (2000): 97–145.

13. On the seven ages of history, see Auguste Luneau, *Histoire du salut chez les pères de l'église: la doctrine des âges du monde,* Théologie historique 9 (Paris: Beauchesne, 1964), and Roderich Schmidt, "*Aetates mundi:* Die Weltalter als Gliederungsprinzip der Geschichte," *Zeitschrift für Kirchengeschichte* 67 (1955–56): 287–317. Generally, on Augustine's "agnostic" attitude toward post-biblical history, see Robert Markus, *Saeculum: History and Society in the Theology of St Augustine* (Cambridge: Cambridge University Press, 1989).

14. See Martin Haeusler, *Das Ende der Geschichte in der mittelalterlichen Weltchronistik,* Beihefte zum Archiv für Kulturgeschichte 13 (Cologne: Böhlau, 1980) 6–32, and Michael Allen, "Universal History 300–1000: Origins and Western Developments," in *Historiography in the Middle Ages,* ed. Deborah Mauskopf Deliyannis, Orbis mediaevalis 1 (Leiden: Brill, 2003) 17–42.

15. See Jean Flori, *L'islam et la fin des temps: l'interprétation prophétique des invasions musulmanes dans la chrétienté médiévale* (Paris: Seuil, 2007).

16. McGinn, *Visions of the End,* 70–76. For the Greek and Latin versions of the text, see *Die Apokalypse des Pseudo-Methodius: die ältesten griechischen und lateinischen Übersetzungen,* J. A. Aerts and G. A. A. Kortekaas, eds. 2 vols., Corpus Scriptorum Christianorum Orientalium 569–570 (Subsidia 97–98) (Leuven: Peeters, 1998). See also the comments of Flori, *L'islam et la fin des temps,* 133–141, 182–187.

17. In addition to McGinn, *Antichrist,* see Richard K. Emmerson, *Antichrist in the Middle Ages: A Study of Medieval Apocalypticism, Art, and Literature* (Seattle: University of Washington Press, 1981), and Kevin Hughes, *Constructing Antichrist: Paul, Biblical Commentary, and the Development of Doctrine in the Early Middle Ages* (Washington, D.C.: Catholic University of America Press, 2005).

18. Translation modified slightly from McGinn, *Visions of the End,* 84. For the Latin text, see Adso of Montier-en-der, *De ortu et tempore antichristi,* Daniel Verhelst, ed. Corpus Christianorum Continuatio Mediaevalis 45 (Turnhout: Brepols, 1976) 26. See also Richard K. Emmerson, "Antichrist as Anti-Saint: The Significance of Abbot Adso's *Libellus de Antichristo,*" *American Benedictine Review* 30 (1979): 175–190.

19. See McGinn, *Antichrist,* 114–172.

20. See Robert Lerner, "Refreshment of the Saints: The Time after Antichrist as a Station for Earthly Progress in Medieval Thought," *Traditio* 32 (1976): 97–144, and Robert Lerner, "The Medieval Return to the Thousand-Year Sabbath," in *The Apocalypse in the Middle Ages,* Richard K. Emmerson and Bernard McGinn, eds. (Ithaca, NY: Cornell University Press, 1992) 51–71.

21. See Paula Fredriksen, "Tyconius and Augustine on the Apocalypse," in *The Apocalypse in the Middle Ages,* 20–37.

22. There are numerous books and articles on Joachim. For a starting point, in addition to Reeves, *Joachim of Fiore,* see Bernard McGinn, *The Calabrian Abbot: Joachim of Fiore in the History of Western Thought* (New York: Macmillan, 1985), and Gian Luca Potestà, *Il tempo dell'apocalisse: vita di Gioacchino da Fiore* (Rome: Editori Laterza, 2004).

23. McGinn, *Visions of the End,* 134.

24. On this so-called "Scandal of the Eternal Gospel," see Marjorie Reeves, *The Influence*

of Prophecy in the Later Middle Ages (1969; Notre Dame: University of Notre Dame Press, 1993) 59–69, and David Burr, *Olivi's Peaceable Kingdom: A Reading of the Apocalypse Commentary* (Philadelphia: University of Pennsylvania Press, 1993) 1–25.

25. This interview originally aired on September 18, 2006. It can be heard online at the NPR website, <www.npr.org/templates/story/story.php?storyId=6097362> (August 4, 2008). See also the Christians United for Israel website, <http://www.cufi. org/site/Page-Server> (August 4, 2008).

26. See Paul Boyer, "The Middle East in Modern American Popular Prophetic Belief," in *Imagining the End,* 312–335, along with McGinn, *Antichrist,* 252–257.

27. See Robert Lerner, *The Feast of St. Abraham: Medieval Millenarians and the Jews* (Philadelphia: University of Pennsylvania Press, 2002); Anna Abulafia, "The Conquest of Jerusalem: Joachim of Fiore and the Jews," in *The Experience of Crusading,* Marcus Bull and Norman Housely, eds. (Cambridge, U.K.: Cambridge University Press, 2003) 127–146; E. Randolph Daniel, "Abbot Joachim of Fiore and the Conversion of the Jews," in *Friars and Jews in the Middle Ages and Renaissance,* Steven McMichael and Susan Myers, eds. (Leiden: Brill, 2004) 1–22.

28. See Jeremy Cohen, *Living Letters of the Law: Ideas of the Jew in Medieval Christianity* (Berkeley: University of California Press, 1999) 23–65.

29. "No Seven-Headed Dragon Rising in the East," *The Onion,* <http://origin.the onion.com/content/node/30030> (August 12, 2008). See also Stein, "American Millennial Visions," 188–189.

30. "The David Koresh Manuscript: Exposition of the Seven Seals," <http://ccat. sas.upenn.edu/gopher/text/religion/koresh/Koresh%20Seals> (August 4, 2008).

31. See the Midnight Call website, <http://www.midnightcall.com/> (August 4, 2008). I recently learned that there is a similar monthly journal published in Iran, titled *Mau'ud* (meaning "promised" or "predicted"), which offers a fundamentalist Islamic perspective on the end of days, including the role of the United States and Israel as eschatological agents of evil. I cannot help but think it ironic that the readers of *Midnight Call* and *Mau'ud,* in some ways sitting on opposite sides of an apocalyptic fence, would probably have a great deal to say to each other.

32. See Emilio Gentile, *Religion as Politics,* George Staunton, trans. (Princeton: Princeton University Press, 2006), along with the essay by David Redles "Nazi End Times: The Third Reich as Millennial Reich" in this volume.

WORKS CITED

Abulafia, Anna S. "The Conquest of Jerusalem: Joachim of Fiore and the Jews" in *The Experience of Crusading.* Marcus Bull and Norman Housely, eds. Cambridge, UK: Cambridge University Press, 2003: 127–146.

Adso of Montier-en-der. *De ortu et tempore antichristi.* Daniel Verhelst, ed. Corpus Christianorum Continuatio Mediaevalis 45. Turnhout: Brepols, 1976.

Aerts, J. A., and G. A. A. Kortekaas, eds. *Die Apokalypse des Pseudo-Methodius: die ältesten griechischen und lateinischen Übersetzungen.* 2 vols. Corpus Scriptorum Christianorum Orientalium 569–570 (Subsidia 97–98). Leuven: Peeters, 1998.

Allen, Michael. "Universal History 300–1000: Origins and Western Developments" in *Historiography in the Middle Ages.* Deborah Mauskopf Deliyannis, ed. Orbis mediaevalis 1. Leiden: Brill, 2003: 17–42.

Boyer, Paul. "The Middle East in Modern American Popular Prophetic Belief" in *Imagining the End: Visions of Apocalypse from the Ancient Middle East to Modern America.* Abbas Amanat and Magnus Bernhardsson, eds. London: I. B. Tauris, 2002: 312–335.

Burr, David. *Olivi's Peaceable Kingdom: A Reading of the Apocalypse Commentary.* Philadelphia: University of Pennsylvania Press, 1993.

Bynum, Caroline Walker. "Why All the Fuss about the Body? A Medievalist's Perspective." *Critical Inquiry* 22 (1995): 1–33.

Cohen, Jeremy. *Living Letters of the Law: Ideas of the Jew in Medieval Christianity.* Berkeley: University of California Press, 1999.

Cohn, Norman. *The Pursuit of the Millennium: Revolutionary Millenarians and Mystical Anarchists of the Middle Ages.* 1957; rev. ed., New York: Oxford University Press, 1970.

Daniel, E. Randolph. "Abbot Joachim of Fiore and the Conversion of the Jews" in *Friars and Jews in the Middle Ages and Renaissance.* Steven McMichael and Susan Myers, eds. Leiden: Brill, 2004: 1–22.

Emmerson, Richard K. "Antichrist as Anti-Saint: The Significance of Abbot Adso's *Libellus de Antichristo.*" *American Benedictine Review* 30 (1979): 175–190.

_____. *Antichrist in the Middle Ages: A Study of Medieval Apocalypticism, Art, and Literature.* Seattle: University of Washington Press, 1981.

Flori, Jean. *L'islam et la fin des temps: l'interprétation prophétique des invasions musulmanes dans la chrétienté médiévale.* Paris: Seuil, 2007.

Forbes, Bruce and Jean Kilde, eds. *Rapture, Revelation, and the End Times: Exploring the Left Behind Series.* New York: Palgrave Macmillan, 2004.

Fredriksen, Paula. "Tyconius and Augustine on the Apocalypse" in *The Apocalypse in the Middle Ages.* Richard K. Emmerson and Bernard McGinn, eds. Ithaca, NY: Cornell University Press, 1992: 20–37.

Gentile, Emilio. *Religion as Politics.* George Staunton, trans. Princeton, NJ: Princeton University Press, 2006.

Haeusler, Martin. *Das Ende der Geschichte in der mittelalterlichen Weltchronistik.* Beihefte zum Archiv für Kulturgeschichte 13. Cologne: Böhlau, 1980.

Hughes, Kevin. *Constructing Antichrist: Paul, Biblical Commentary, and the Development of Doctrine in the Early Middle Ages.* Washington, D.C.: Catholic University of America Press, 2005.

Landes, Richard. "The Fear of an Apocalyptic Year 1000: Augustinian Historiography, Medieval and Modern." *Speculum* 75 (2000): 97–145.

_____. "Lest the Millennium Be Fulfilled: Apocalyptic Expectations and the Pattern of Western Chronography 100–800" in *The Use and Abuse of Eschatology in the Middle Ages.* Werner Verbeke, Daniel Verhelst, and Andries Welkenhuysen, eds. Leuven: Leuven University Press, 1988: 137–211.

Lerner, Robert. *The Feast of St. Abraham: Medieval Millenarians and the Jews.* Philadelphia: University of Pennsylvania Press, 2002.

_____. "Medieval Millenarianism and Violence," in *Pace e Guerra nel basso medioevo: atti del XL convegno storico internazionale, Todi, 12–14 Ottobre 2003.* Spoleto: Fondazione Centro italiano di studi sull'alto Medioevo, 2004: 37–52.

_____. "The Medieval Return to the Thousand-Year Sabbath" in *The Apocalypse in the Middle Ages.* Richard K. Emmerson and Bernard McGinn, eds. Ithaca, NY: Cornell University Press, 1992: 51–71.

_____. "Refreshment of the Saints: The Time after Antichrist as a Station for Earthly Progress in Medieval Thought." *Traditio* 32 (1976): 97–144.

Luneau, Auguste. *Histoire du salut chez les pères de l'église: la doctrine des âges du monde.* Théologie historique 9. Paris: Beauchesne, 1964.

Markus, Robert. *Saeculum: History and Society in the Theology of St. Augustine.* Cambridge, UK: Cambridge University Press, 1989.

McGinn, Bernard. *Antichrist: Two Thousand Years of the Human Fascination with Evil.* New York: Columbia University Press, 2000.

_____. "The Apocalyptic Imagination in the Middle Ages" in *Ende und Vollendung: Eschatologische Perspektiven im Mittelalter*. Jan Aertsen and Martin Pickavé, ed. Berlin: W. de Gruyter, 2002: 79–94.

_____. *The Calabrian Abbot: Joachim of Fiore in the History of Western Thought.* New York: Macmillan, 1985.

_____. *Visions of the End: Apocalyptic Traditions in the Middle Ages.* 1979; New York: Columbia University Press, 1998.

McGinn, Bernard, ed. *The Encyclopedia of Apocalypticism: Apocalypticism in Western History and Culture.* 4 vols. New York: Continuum, 1998.

Potestà, Gian Luca. *Il tempo dell'apocalisse: vita di Gioacchino da Fiore.* Rome: Editori Laterza, 2004.

Reeves, Marjorie. *The Influence of Prophecy in the Later Middle Ages.* 1969; Notre Dame, IN: University of Notre Dame Press, 1993.

_____. *Joachim of Fiore and the Prophetic Future.* 1976; Stroud, UK: Sutton, 1999.

Schmidt, Roderich. *"Aetates mundi:* Die Weltalter als Gliederungsprinzip der Geschichte." *Zeitschrift für Kirchengeschichte* 67 (1955–56): 287–317.

Stein, Stephen. "American Millennial Visions: Towards Construction of a New Architectonic of American Apocalypticism" in *Imagining the End: Visions of Apocalypse from the Ancient Middle East to Modern America.* Abbas Amanat and Magnus Bernhardsson, eds. London: I. B. Tauris, 2002: 187–211.

Whalen, Brett. "From Adam to the Apocalypse: Post-Classical Christianity and the Patterns of World History." *World History Association Bulletin* 23 (2007): 21–26.

_____. "Joachim of Fiore and the Division of Christendom," *Viator* 98 (2003): 89–108.

Part I. Development and Dissemination

Ancient Visions: The Roots of Judeo-Christian Apocalypse

Casey Starnes

Apocalyptic literature, or simply *apocalyptic*, has as its hallmark a view of the end of the world and an accompanying vindication of past wrongdoings usually via some Final Judgment. This End is a revelation (=apocalypse) given to a man in the form of a vision or journey with an angelic mediator. It is a common view in recent scholarship to view apocalyptic literature as a natural extension of prophecy.[1] Today the term "Apocalypse" evokes myriad images: the Holocaust; nuclear annihilation; the return of the Messiah; the Crusades; Armageddon.[2] How did the word come to denote so many things? It is the nature of apocalypse to be redefined by each generation. The most common modern definition may be the "end of the world," while a sense truer to the word's roots would be a "revealing of things hidden." The book of Revelation from the New Testament is but one Biblical example of a larger corpus of Apocalyptic literature. This literature purports to reveal hidden visions of the end of the world. Such visions have always captivated the human spirit. The big question "what happens when we die?" is expanded to the all-encompassing questions "what happens to the universe itself when it dies?" and its corollary "what is the fate of human souls when the universe perishes?" There are many ancient answers to these questions.

The mission of this essay is to show the evolution of thought that led to the visions of apocalypse as perceived by Jews and Christians. The principles they espoused of cosmic destruction and the ultimate fate of the soul are heavily indebted to the beliefs of other peoples in the Middle East and Mediterranean. The early Egyptians, Babylonians, Persians, Greeks, and Romans have left a wealth of religious, epic and philosophical literature. Methodologically, I examine certain mythological and theological elements contained in this ancient literature, using comparative analysis, and interpret eschatology as a historical evolution of belief. Examining these sources in this manner, we can draw a picture of the various modes of thought that were to provide a definitive model for the later Jewish and Christian apocalypses that permeate the religious views of late antiquity, the Middle Ages, and today.

From the second century BCE to the second century CE, Jewish theologians molded a new syncretic Jewish conception of apocalypse from older and current traditions that nevertheless retained its Old Testament roots. These antecedent and contemporary traditions prefigured the major themes of Jewish apocalyptic writings including dualism, resurrection, Millennialism and a final victory of good over evil. Many of these ideas were readily absorbed by Christian doctrine. In this way were created two of the most prominent visions of Apocalypse popular today. It is important, however, to realize that the ancient core of Jewish belief has, by a dogged conservatism, maintained its solidarity through millennia of outside influence. The foreign developments around the Jews often had the effect not of simple infiltration, but of stimulating parallel Jewish developments. Thus the Jewish faith has always kept its unique precepts intact. Let us therefore turn to its beginnings.

The Jews began as the Hebrews, one of many Semitic peoples in the large group of cultures that comprise the Middle East. Neighboring states included ancient Egypt, Sumer (whose heirs were Babylon and Assyria), Canaan, and Syria. Despite linguistic, religious, and ethnic diversity, these peoples shared many features of a common mythology that can be summarized thus: various gods battle one another under a rubric of order versus chaos, a staple of Middle Eastern thought that recurs in the roots of apocalyptic. An example is the battle between the younger Babylonian gods of cities and order against the older, watery gods of disorder (e.g. the well-known Babylonian "succession myth" wherein Marduk conquers the salt-water dragon Tiamat). There existed little eschatology of an end-time event.[3] Demons walked the earth as minions of the greater gods. Humans had a dreary future in the underworld, yet systems of punishment and reward were developing to ensure a suitable fate for the dead. In brief, the ancient Middle Eastern view of the cosmic struggle was highly developed, whereas an end-time event held little sway. This then was the world in which Judaism emerged.

Prophets, Exile, and the Persian Impact

Around the year 1000 BCE, King David unified Israel. What were the belief systems of this people? To answer this question we must look at how the Jews of this period shared in the Middle Eastern system of polytheism and the combat myth. The chief god of the later Jews, Yahweh, was originally a sky/storm god, and subordinate to El, the supreme creator (and chief god of the neighboring Canaanites). Like the Canaanite god Ba'al and the

Babylonian Marduk, Yahweh was a fighter against chaos, sometimes embodied in the form of a watery dragon such as the Leviathan.[4] Soon however they began to see Yahweh as not only the patron deity of Israel but also the supreme god and finally the only true god.[5] This change was prescribed by a sense of persecution by neighboring peoples. Let us examine the historical events that led to this change in theological outlook. In the 730s BCE the Assyrians conquered Israel. Around 600 the Babylonians conquered Assyria and Israel became a vassal state. In 597 the Babylonian king Nebuchadnezzar besieged Jerusalem and deported the aristocracy to Babylon, instigating the Exile period. In 586 he leveled the walls of Jerusalem, destroyed the temple, and murdered the royal family. The Persian king Cyrus conquered Babylon in 539, however, making Israel a Persian province. The following year he allowed some Jewish exiles to return. Under Persian authorization the returned Jewish leader Zerubbabel rebuilt the temple in 536 and a new Jewish monarchy took power.

These events colored the writings of the Jewish Prophets. The Prophets are important for our purposes for two reasons. First, they show how a changing political and social environment had major effects on Jewish eschatology. More importantly the Prophets foreshadow many features of the apocalyptic literature that was soon to rise meteorically. Passages from Ezekiel, Zechariah, Isaiah and Joel prefigure many apocalyptic themes: visions or dreams delivered or interpreted by an angel; signs that mark the coming of the End and return of God; final battles and destruction of God's enemies; and final Judgments. As such they are often seen as "proto-apocalyptic."[6] Let us see now how the Jewish Prophets reacted to these changes in their spiritual outlook.

The pre–Exile Prophets painted an angry God and a bleak picture for Israel in response to the series of setbacks. God was punishing them for misdeeds as if they were unruly children. After the Assyrian subjugation, Hosea began a movement to establish Yahweh as the one and only God and reported that God was punishing the Jews at the hands of the Assyrians because of their failure to worship Him exclusively. Hosea 9.1 states, "Do not rejoice, O Israel; do not be jubilant like the other nations. For you have been unfaithful to your God.... Threshing floors and winepresses will not feed the people; the new wine will fail them." It was believed that if they converted to monotheism they might preempt these problems. During the Exile the Jews vehemently preserved this belief under the Babylonian regime, as often occurs when a minority is persecuted. Isaiah and Joel likewise prophesied at this time. While they shared a sense of punishment for Jewish misdoings, all hope was not lost. Isaiah, for example, prophesied the return of the Exiles (a hundred years before the Exile took place!), the rebuilding of Jerusalem on a mountain, rejoicing of the land, and decimation of enemies.[7] Yet generally the worldview was pessimistic.

Exile in Babylon exasperated a dismal situation. When the Persians took control of Babylon, Jews came in contact with Zoroastrian theology. This confluence was to have a major impact on Judaic eschatology. Persian contact at Babylon and the subsequent four centuries of Persian rule helped shape Jewish thought. Important Zoroastrian themes such as the coming of a savior, an imminent "putting things to right," dualism, individualism, resurrection, determinism, and Millennialism affected the thoughts and writings of Exilic and post–Exilic Prophets such as Ezra, Nehemiah, and Zechariah. An overview of Persian eschatology is therefore necessary at this point.[8]

The supreme god of *asha* (order), Ahura Mazda, is countered by an active god of *druj* (disorder), Angra Mainyu. Their battle is ongoing in a finite time period that will end when Angra Mainyu is destroyed, *asha* prevails, and an eternity of bliss begins. All this is under the divine providence and governance of Ahura Mazda. At the end of limited time, the dead are universally resurrected. The world undergoes an ordeal and purging of evil which involves the living and the resurrected dead. The earth becomes a river of molten metals through which all people must pass. For the righteous the stream is felt as warm milk.[9] The wicked dead are annihilated in the metal, while the righteous dead as disembodied souls in heaven receive an even more blissful existence: they are given new bodies on earth to enjoy a spiritual and corporeal life. Finally Ahura Mazda comes to earth as a priest and all the righteous become immortal. Angra Mainyu returns to the darkness and the molten metal seals the gate.

The return of Ahura Mazda at the end of time was called the *frashokereti* or the "making wonderful." It was thought to be imminent, and there was much disappointment at its delay. Zoroaster came to be seen as a savior who was sent, died, and would return reincarnated. Before Zoroaster's second coming a Saoshyant (future benefactor) will come at a time when earth becomes evil. Harbingers will be atmospheric disturbances, stunted growth among all life forms, and *druj* will almost triumph over *asha*. The Saoshyant will then eradicate all evil. The *frashokereti* is thus complete.[10]

In the fourth century BCE a modified (heretical) form of Zoroastrianism called Zurvanism came into vogue. A scheme of successive ages became prominent, influenced by the "Great Year" of Babylonian astronomers.[11] A 12,000-year pattern was conceived in which great events occur every 3000 years. The last period is subdivided into three millennia. Each terminates with a savior (the Saoshyant triplicated); each is a decline from good into decay, restored at millennium's end to goodness; it is concluded by the *frashokereti*. Zoroastrianism and its offshoot Zurvanism used the ancient myth of order combating chaos to create a new combat myth, realized most powerfully in the apocalyptic coming of a savior. This is the advent of dualism between active forces of good and evil at work in the world (as opposed to the older "taming of chaos"). Here we also find individualism (conscious siding with the good or evil forces), resurrection, Messianism, and determinism (the doctrine that all events are the inevitable consequence of factors outside of human control). Zoroastrianism also presents the first account of Millennialism, a scheme of defined worldly time divided into successive thousand-year periods, each of which will end in destruction, until a final overpowering of evil at the hands of a force of good.

[margin note: Summary of Contribution of Zoroastrianism]

The effect of Zoroastrianism on Jewish eschatology was rapid. A new vision came into place: the coming of a king of David's line as the agent of Yahweh, ushering in an age when Yahweh himself would effect the imposition of righteousness directly. This is logically a parallel development to the evolution of the Persian savior-figure Zoroaster, whose active intervention and return to ensure the people's welfare was a compelling innovation. Zechariah, writing as a returned exile, paints a vision of the king's return accompanied by the destruction of Israel's enemies:

> Shout, Daughter of Jerusalem!
> See, your king comes to you,
> righteous and having salvation...
> Open your doors, O Lebanon,
> so that fire may devour your cedars!...
> Listen to the wail of the shepherds;
> their rich pastures are destroyed!
> Listen to the roar of the lions;
> the lush thicket of the Jordan is ruined![12]

The coming of a king as agent of God is followed by the arrival of God himself to set things right. There will be decimation of the enemies' lands. People are symbolized by animals. All these elements formed the bridge between the Prophets and the apocalyptists. Zoroastrianism inspired a messiah figure, a vindication of wrongs and reward for the faithful, and a view that God is in control.

Post-Exilic Jewish leaders began to reconceptualize the Jewish position under the more humane Persians. Jewish religion was alive and convalescent but needed to undergo certain changes to accommodate the new political environment. Ezra and Nehemiah drew up a reformed law code, the "Law of Ezra." Under this set of laws the Jews received certain legal status under Persian sanction. These changes are crystallized in the oldest part of the Old Testament, the Pentateuch or Torah, which was given its definitive form soon after the Law of Ezra. The Pentateuch outlines a set of laws that reflect the new thinking. People now had an important role in fulfilling laws to keep God happy. This religious individualism reflects the influence of the Zoroastrians on the returned exiles. Post-exilic thinkers saw God as active in the lives of the Jews, and they longed for a return to security. The old *Weltanschauung* of static order and disorder was broken.[13] God was seen to be intervening according to a plan to achieve a new and better state of existence for his people. The post-exilic Prophetic writings of the Jews reveal for the first time a hopeful vision of the future. The Prophets were to dominate Jewish thought for the next several centuries.

The Hellenistic Age and the Rise of Apocalyptic

The Hellenistic period witnessed radical changes. The period began benignly enough for the Jews. Israel came first under the rule of the Hellenized Ptolemaic Dynasty, but in 170 BCE, fell into the hands of the Seleucids (a Hellenized Persian dynasty). Under the persecutions of the Seleucids, Jewish attitudes towards the Greeks quickly soured. In 169–167 Antiochus IV desecrated the second temple of Jerusalem, outlawed Judaism, and destroyed the city. This offense was avenged soon after by Jewish rebels, the Maccabees. The Jews were restored and the temple retaken. Nevertheless such actions embittered the Jews towards their rulers. This led to important theological developments.

The failure of the prophecies to come to fruition and the continual degradation of vassalage was to have a lasting effect. The growth of a new kind of literature takes its root at this time. In the new Hellenistic environment, Apocalyptic literature, or simply *apocalyptic*, arose from and replaced prophecy. The social and political situation changed in the Hellenistic period: the prophecies were unfulfilled and God's power seemed diminished. Therefore the prophetic outcomes shifted from the present to a future fulfillment to explain and interpret new events against Hellenistic and later Roman persecution. Paul O'Callaghan aptly summarizes the changed situation: "the prophetic spirit remains, but its form of expression changes with the circumstances."[14] After the Prophets there was a return to the mythic visions of God. This generally manifests in one of two forms: the otherworldly journey that has an interest in personal eschatology — the nature of heaven and hell, Judgment, etc.; or the dream or vision that concerns cosmic eschatology — the End Time. It is the latter on which we will focus.

Although the reaction against the rulers proved to be the impetus for these changes, many features of Hellenistic culture had seeped into the lifestyles and writings of the Jews through education, literature, and philosophy. Apocalyptic features the theme of immortality and a new vision of the afterlife — ideas taken from Hellenistic culture, not the Prophets. The Prophets wished to resurrect Israel, but the apocalyptists saw the difficulty in this. Thus the coming golden age was pushed forward beyond human time. They had little faith in the Prophets' "rescuing of history" and instead looked to the mythic past and the idealized future more than to the present.[15] In short, the apocalyptists produced a new kind of prophecy tinted with an admixture of Hellenistic, Persian, and biblical wisdom literature.

The apocalyptic writers also employed the Hellenistic artifice of archaizing, placing their new prophets or "apocalyptists" in the past to create an air of authenticity, a technique sometimes termed "pseudonymity." Examples are those books reportedly written by Daniel (sixth century exile), Enoch (the beginning of history), and the book of Jubilees (starring Moses). It was felt by the apocalyptists that "behind the pronouncements of the prophets lay a hidden meaning, which was understood only imperfectly by the prophets themselves."[16] The revelations received by the apocalyptists differ in other ways from those of the prophets: the future is predetermined and is not influenced by man; God spoke directly to the prophets, but via angels to the apocalyptists. These new themes show the influence of Babylonian cosmological wisdom, Zoroastrianism, and most importantly and for the first time, Greek theology and philosophy as well as Hellenistic literary conventions. Let us turn to the books themselves to examine these influences.

Daniel is the single canonical apocalyptic text found in the Old Testament. It was composed c. 165 BCE on the heels of the Maccabean Revolt. Daniel taught that only the elite followers of the wise (namely Daniel himself) could learn to endure worldly suffering and interpret eschatological wisdom. The theory of successive ages appears here in its first instance for the Jews. In Daniel 2, Nebuchadnezzar dreams of a metal statue. The four metals — gold, silver, bronze, and iron — have antecedents in a Zoroastrian cosmic tree with seven branches of various metals, and more firmly in Hesiod's Five Ages.[17] The meaning in each case is a succession of worldly kingdoms or empires. Each age slips into iniquity and is finally destroyed, to be replaced by a new kingdom. Each renewed kingdom is inferior to the last in the Greek model. Thus while each age experiences ethical deterioration, the whole of time is also deteriorating, pointing to a final time of total annihilation by Zeus. Each age also features portents of decline — natural phenomena, strange births, unmitigated violence, etc. It is debated whether Hesiod's presentation is cyclic or terminal; it is unspecified in the poem itself. The cyclic model has parallels in Orphism, a Greek cultic religion, while the terminal model may be rooted in Zoroastrianism and traditional Judaism. The cyclic theme played a role in early Jewish apocalyptic, but later seems to have been phased out to adhere to the more traditional Jewish belief of a singular creation and destruction.

Such symbolism is continued in Book 7 with its animals as kingdoms and beasts rising from the sea (representing the ancient chaos and evil) to ravage God's empires on land. The renewal of the ancient combat myth owes much to the spread of Greek myth throughout the Hellenized East.[18] God judges the final kingdom from his supernal throne surrounded by legions of angels and casts it into fire. Meanwhile, he appoints an eternal earthly reign to a "son of man," an early sign of Messianism.

Enoch, though not canonical, was very influential in apocalyptic thought. The book contains a series of apocalyptic dreams. These include the following: the Apocalypse of Weeks (91, 93) which overviews history as a succession of periods in microcosm, recalling the myth of ages; the Astronomical Book (72–82) which shows cosmic and astral phenomena known to Greek physics and Babylonian cosmological wisdom[19]; and the Animal Apocalypse (85–90), a dream vision culminating in a fiery destruction of earth. The Animal Apocalypse sequence depicts nations and generations allegorically as animals, reflecting Hesiodic mythic symbolism and Greek fable tradition: after the New Jerusalem, God makes a single white bull, magnificent, and all beasts stare and become white bulls. Adam himself becomes a white bull — the new Adam.[20]

Often in Enoch God appears like the Stoic *logos* with the variously ranked angels as subservient executors of the natural order. Stoicism arose in the early third century BCE as a Greek philosophical system in which a single force is in control of the entire universe, keeping harmony between all realms of the cosmos and life on earth. An exemplary passage from Enoch proclaims: "Contemplate all the events in heaven, how the lights in heaven do not change their courses, how each rises and sets in order, each at its proper time, and they do not transgress their law. Consider the earth, and understand from the work which is done upon it, from the beginning to the end, that no work of God changes as it becomes manifest."[21] Stoic in flavor are the single ruling force, determinism, and a system of static laws governing the universe. This popular "pagan monotheism" meshes well with Judaism on several levels.

Other Hellenisms can be seen in the Book of Jubilees, which relates the story of Moses receiving the Laws on Mt. Sinai via the angel Uriel. Here appears Prince Mastema, the first supernatural enemy of God in biblical writings, with his host of demons. Satan was still a minor figure, God's "prosecuting angel," and had little relation to the later Satan.[22] Angels become lustful and mate with the women of earth, producing a spawn of demons and giants, who then teach man the hidden arts of weaponry and magic. God perceives this as a loss of spiritual purity and decides to wipe out the offenders (man, demon, and giant). He engineers the Flood, eliminating the giants; the fallen angels are imprisoned in the earth.[23] This scenario strikingly evokes the Greek Prometheus, a lesser divinity who aided humans in the secret arts of fire, metallurgy, farming, astronomy, and many other useful skills, and as a consequence suffered imprisonment and torture along with his brothers and Titan relatives.[24] The fallen angels and giants take as their model the fallen Titans and giants of Greek myth.

Next in Jubilees we find that the spirits of the giants (and the fallen angels too? The language is ambiguous) roam earth's surface, corrupting man. God soon imprisons them as well, but allows one tenth to remain on earth to harry mankind in accordance with Mastema's wish.[25] Likewise in the Ages of Hesiod, some higher beings of the early Ages are allowed to frequent the earth, interacting with humans.[26] Often these beings enforce justice and Zeus's judgment. The Final Judgment also wears a new face in apocalyptic. Jubilees 23.25 declares that near the day of Judgment, such conflict and oppression will ensue that children will be born gray-haired and look like old men.[27] There will be a religious revival and purification of earth. Heathen nations are awed and convert; wicked angels are thrown into a new fiery abyss outside of heaven and earth. Jerusalem and the temple are replaced by a bigger and better Jerusalem and temple. The tone of this literature captures the mood of a people looking through the horrors of everyday life to a glorious future and divinely administered justice.

These Greek influences evidence the shared Greco-Jewish environment and exchange of learning.[28] The Diaspora (which began as far back as the Babylonian exile) had placed Jews alongside the inhabitants of Alexandria, Pergamum, Antioch, etc., Hellenized cities that hosted Greeks, Jews, Syrians, Egyptians, Persians, etc. living side by side. Such cosmopolitanism amounted to several Hellenistic effects on the apocalyptic thinkers: a reshaping of the conception of the underworld and the Judgment waiting there; the idea of flood and fire as forms of apocalyptic destruction; early signs of Messianism; and the nature of the soul and resurrection. It is also worth remembering that the Hellenistic world initiated by Alexander the Great was comprised largely of Persian areas. Thus Zoroastrian ideas became incorporated into greater Hellenistic culture.

The Romans, Messiah, and Birth of Christianity

While apocalyptic was developing, major political events were unfolding further west. Rome had arisen as the new superpower. By the mid second century BCE it had taken Greece, Macedon and Carthage, and eventually the Romans called the Mediterranean *mare nostrum*, "our sea." Pompey invaded Palestine in 65 BCE and took Jerusalem two years later, annexing Israel. Ptolemaic and Seleucid rule had come to an end. The Jews were now in the hands of Roman governors. Despite hostility between Romans and Jews, Roman influence in Jewish culture nonetheless occurred, albeit less abundantly than that of the Greeks and Persians. In many cases it is difficult to discern which way the influence flows. In any case, Roman doxology is largely appropriated from the Greeks and the mystery cults of the East via the Greeks, a process that continued from the earliest of Roman times, but became irreversible after the sack of Corinth in 146. In the famous words of Horace, "Captive Greece captured her fierce conqueror [Rome]."[29]

Several pieces of Latin literature had an influence on Jewish doctrine. Virgil's *Aeneid*, written in the 20s BCE, furthers the idea of the Orphic cathartic fire. Some souls are forced to remain in the underworld until their souls are purged after a thousand years. These are souls awaiting birth, and after they drink of the river Lethe, they are resurrected.[30] These ideas reflect Millennialism and Stoic ideas of resurrection. Moreover the tale is thematically relevant to the Jews as it involves an exile (Aeneas) whose city (Troy) is destroyed, who goes on to found a dynasty (Rome) that eventually avenges this wrong. Virgil's famous "Messianic" fourth Eclogue tells of the coming of a savior figure who ushers in a new era of prosperity when the land itself blossoms without tillage.[31] This hearkens back to the notion of a return to Hesiod's golden age when Saturn ruled. Such utopian thinking depends on the Stoic conception of cyclic time. Christians later adopted the Messianic Eclogue as a prophecy of Christ's coming and Virgil was made an honorary Christian. Likewise Ovid's Metamorphoses depicts a series of deteriorating ages at the end of which Jupiter becomes angered at humanity and ponders between two forms of universal destruction, fire and flood, choosing the latter "lest he light the axis of the world afire."[32] Such themes of ages, destruction, and Messianism probably furthered the impact of Hellenistic cataclysmic theory and portended their popularity in the Sibylline and Messianic literature soon to come.[33]

Messianism is rare in the Old Testament.[34] In the first century BCE the concept flowered in response to the non–Davidic kingship of the Hasmoneans and then to the cruelties of Roman subjugation.[35] One apocalyptic scheme noted above contains a messianic theme: the dream of four beasts from Daniel 7 symbolizes, like the statue, four empires of earth.[36] The last empire (Greek or Roman) is to destroy the world, but then the "Son of Man" restores order and makes a glorious kingdom for all earth. Soon the Son of Man was conceived as a Davidic king of super-human strength, more powerful as time progressed. Cohn states that, "As ... the conflict with Rome became more and more bitter, messianic phantasies became with many Jews an obsessive pre-occupation."[37] Josephus records that it was a (misread) belief in the advent of the Messiah that launched the Jews on the suicidal war against the Romans in 68 CE.[38]

When Jesus entered the scene, the Jews had experienced much hardship at the hands of the Romans. His miracles were seen as effecting the prelude to the End as depicted by the Prophets, e.g. Isaiah 35.5–6: "blind men shall see and the deaf shall hear." He fit the messianic mold of the Prophets and the apocalyptists. Yet his death did not accord with expectations. It was debated early on whether Jesus was the Messiah. In the first century CE the Christians revised the notion of a human messiah to accommodate a divine figure and equated this figure with Jesus. This reasoning explained his wretched and paradoxical death.[39] As divine and human, Jesus formed a new model of Messiah. As such he underwent human suffering and death, but was resurrected and took on certain divine roles of the Messiah. That is, he was now expected to return at the Second Coming and act as Final Judge. The idea of a second coming accommodated the new model and allowed Jesus to be the executor of the Apocalypse.[40]

The Christians adopted apocalyptic literature as well. The Book of Revelation is considered the Christian counterpart to Daniel. Its famous apocalyptic scheme can be summarized as follows: Satan, a dragon beast, and a false prophet beast attack the earth and Jesus comes as a warrior with an angelic host and casts down the evil (namely, the Romans) and dooms them and the two beasts to hell. Satan is chained in the abyss for a Millennium while martyrs are resurrected and reign with Jesus. Satan and the demonic hosts then are released and besiege Jerusalem, yet God destroys them ultimately with fire. Finally, a Last Judgment occurs wherein all the dead are resurrected and judged; the wicked are sent to hell while the good inhabit a new heaven/earth combined where God himself reigns over men and angels. The apocalypse presented here is essentially the combat myth revised: chaos in the form of dragon-like beasts is deposed by a younger god. All the Persian and Hellenistic elements are in place: Messianism, Millennialism, resurrection, final judgment, fiery underworld for sinners, and eternal reward for the true. The contemporary apocryphal works the *Apocalypse of Peter* and the *Shepherd of Hermas* present similar views, one voiced by the arisen Christ, the other by the Church.[41] These works were intended to parade the imminent advent of the Messiah and crushing of the Romans to give hope to the oppressed Christians. When Rome was not overthrown as soon as expected, the prophecies were again reinterpreted to fit the new situation. Meanwhile, during the development of apocalyptic, another literary form based on a Greco-Roman model became popular in Jewish and then Christian circles: the Sibylline oracles.

The Sibyllina, Messianism, and Honing of Christian and Jewish Orthodoxy

In the second century BCE, the Jews co-opted a new mode of apocalyptic expression from the Greeks and Romans. The Sibylline oracles were collections of prophecies given to the sibyls, famous prophetesses located throughout the Mediterranean world. The Greeks began the custom of consulting sibyls at least as early as the eighth century. The Romans adopted the practice of collecting the sayings of the Sibyl at Cumae and other sibyls into a codified book of oracles, which they consulted at periods of national crisis.[42] Around 160 BCE a Jewish propagandist began constructing oracles based on the Greco-Roman format with the intent to convert the Greeks.[43] The application of the oracular form entailed hexameter verse, prophecies through the agency of a sibyl, a thorough acquaintance with Greek mythology and epic, and Hellenistic forms, language, and themes (not to mention the use of the Greek language as medium, a feature shared with the whole of the New Testament). The effect is not a rewriting of Judeo-Christian doctrine into something Greek. Instead the oracles provide a new frame of reference for Jewish ideas to be presented to the Hellenized Jews and Greeks, while Jewish tradition remains fundamental.[44] Here is an excerpt of an underworld scenario from the Sibyllina:

> Bodies of humans, made solid in heavenly manner,
> breathing and set in motion, will be raised on a single day.
> Then Uriel, the great angel, will break the gigantic bolts,
> of unyielding and unbreakable steel, of the gates
> of Hades, not forged of metal; he will throw them wide open
> and will lead all the mournful forms to judgment,
> especially those of ancient phantoms, Titans
> and the Giants and such as the Flood destroyed.[45]

The tone is apocalyptic, although it is told directly as a vision from God (like the Prophets). The themes of resurrection, angelic warfare at the End Time, judgment of sinners, and interest in the underworld are apparent. The mixing of Biblical and Greek persons and events is characteristic of its amalgamated nature. Such literature was very popular into the Middle Ages and gave impetus to such works as Dante's *Inferno*.

Meanwhile Messianism had had a long evolution. After the Jewish War, it fizzled out among the Jews (though it was revived later). Yet slowly the idea came to dominate Christian doxology.[46] After Christ did not return as soon as expected, the mood towards Messianism changed. Many canonical apocalypses fell out of favor until only Revelation remained. In the second century Irenaeus compiled an anthology, *Against Heresies*, containing messianic and millennial prophecies from the Old and New Testaments. His *modus* was a scouring of what he considered non-orthodox beliefs. The recently translated Nag Hammadi library has revealed that although he and other early church fathers frequently misrepresented non-orthodox Christianities (sometimes lumped together with Gnosticism), nevertheless they saw messianic apocalypse as a just reward for the suffering of the people. Lactantius reiterates the idea in the fourth century, and Commodianus, the Christian Latin poet (perhaps third century) believed Christ would return at the head of a human, not angelic army, and urged that Christians should gather arms. He prophesied that the saints will gather to fight the armies of Gog from the land of Magog.[47] After defeating them they will reign in Jerusalem on an abundant earth.[48]

In the third century Origen discredited chiliasm (Millennialism) and substituted for it an eschatology of the individual soul, based on the Greek idea of spiritual progress from this life to the next.[49] In the following century when Christianity became the official Roman religion, the Church fathers disapproved of chiliasm and condemned it as a superstition, suppressing Irenaeus' book. Many early church fathers viewed apocalyptic literally and believed it fanciful and therefore insincere. St. Augustine, however, envisioned the Book of Revelation as a spiritual allegory, and that is probably the only reason for its preservation.[50]

Nevertheless the idea of millennial apocalypse and its focus on messiahs and anti-messiahs persisted in the popular imagination. The Millennialism of Revelation could not be uprooted from popular religion, so appealing it was to the oppressed. The Sibylline Oracles were adopted by Christians to accompany Revelations. The books portray leaders as far ranging as Cyrus, Nero, and the Ptolemies as messianic warrior kings or Antichrist tyrants.[51] Constantine was one such messianic king, a warrior-Christ as emperor. When he failed to become the human savior, the job devolved to his son Constans. When his sons fell out over the Arian controversy, it was told that a new Constans, Emperor of the West, would reunite the empire and rule over a golden age terminating in a final triumph over the heathens and conversion of the Jews. An Antichrist would next come for a period of tribulation, to be defeated eventually by the angel Michael. Finally, at the Second Coming, the Emperor of the Last Days would arrive to destroy earth and invoke Judgment.[52] This model thus features two saviors, one human and one divine (contrast the one-savior model of Revelation). The theme of Emperor of the Last Days points forward to the chiliastic militancy that pervaded the minds of medieval God-fearers. Charlemagne was thought to be "sleeping" until he should rise again and conquer the armies of Magog, equated in the Crusades to the soldiers of Islam. The clergy and other "prophets" fomented apocalyptic fervor through wide dissemination of the Sibyllina, touting various rulers such as Godfrey de Bouillon and Louis VII of France as Last Emperor or *Constans redivivus.* Later, Frederick II underwent a similar messianization according to prophecies interpreted from the Sibyllina. Like Charlemagne, he was to awake and conquer the enemies of Christ in the prelude to the End Times.

The Antichrist shows influence of the Persian figure Ahriman and the ancient combat myth with its dragon imagery. Already in Daniel, Antiochus appears as a horned creature that casts down a portion of heaven's angels and stars to the earth. Revelation separates the tyrant into two beasts: a red sea-dragon and a horned dragon-like monster from the depths of the earth. The concept of the second beast is merged with Satan himself. Like "Emperor of the Last Days," the moniker "Antichrist" was branded onto individual rulers and tyrants for political ends. The failure of these individuals to precipitate an apocalypse inevitably resulted in them being degraded to the rank of "precursor" to the true Emperor or Antichrist.[53] In some of the early Sibyllina, for example, Cleopatra VII appears as the embodiment of the Antichrist, but is later replaced by Nero.[54] Constantine and his sons represent this pattern as well in the 4th century CE. In the 1240's CE Frederick II was held to be the Last Emperor by many Germans, while the Papacy and Italians saw him as Antichrist. After he died prematurely, for generations "resurrected" Fredericks crawled out of the German woodwork, who experienced initial credibility and popular support but were inevitably deemed heretics and executed.[55] Thus the historicity of apocalypse is not denied, but endlessly postponed to the future.

Jews have developed an assortment of eschatological schemes since the Christian schism. Much of the shaping of these ideas is tied to Messianism and appeared during the Middle Ages. There is however much disagreement on the nature of the Messiah. Some insert the Messiah into the original, Prophet-era tradition of a future king of the Davidic line come to rule over the Jewish people in a Messianic age, while others see the Messiah as simply a symbol of the Messianic Age. Orthodox Judaism follows the former interpretation, positing a Jewish king who will gather the Jews to their homeland and instigate an age of peace. Reform Judaism foresees an age of peace but denies the coming of an actual Messiah figure. Judaism rejects the idea that God or his son will assume human form.[56]

Traditional Judaism retains the duality between this world, *Olam Hazeh,* and the world to come or the world of the afterlife, *Olam Haba.* The Talmud avers resurrection as a central tenant of its doxology, but not for the Messiah.[57] This revival of the dead will be ushered in by the Messiah, and followed by God's presence on earth and a Messianic Age of bliss. Medieval Jewish views of the afterlife in the Messianic Age differ from the classical. Some denominations envision a purely spiritual existence, while others describe a combined existence on earth, where physical and spiritual meld. This metaphysical state recalls the outcome for mankind after the *frashokereti* of Zoroastrianism. Destinations include Gan Eden (heaven) and Gehinom (purgatory/hell). Although Gehinom is an unpleasant place, it is in no way equivalent to the Christian Hell. Instead it has affinities with Platonic and Stoic notions of the underworld as a place of purification, as well as the cathartic molten river of late Zoroastrianism. No soul resides in Gehinom for longer than twelve months. It is seen as a preliminary stage for some souls to the passage to Gan Eden. Hassidic Judaism relies on the Kabbalah as primary text. This "mystical" version of Judaism offers the notion of *gilgul* or reincarnation, a doctrine nowhere mentioned in the Talmud.

Judaism says much about the coming of the Messiah and the End of Days. It is believed that the power of the Prophets was repealed after the destruction of the first temple in Jerusalem for misbehavior and failure to heed the prophecies. Thus no prophecy is available or interpretable for the prediction of the End, beyond the original pre–Exile Prophets. The Jews had long abandoned the Sibyllina when the Christians adopted them to great effect. Thus the Talmud features a scheme of the world's end based on the Prophets and slightly adapted, based on the fixed Hebrew calendar, outlined here.[58] The world will exist for 6000 years starting from the creation of Adam. Thus the beginning of time is the year 5760 BCE and the end will occur in the year 2240 CE.[59] The end is ushered in by a return of the Jewish people to Israel, defeat of all enemies, the rebuilding of the third temple in Jerusalem and resumption of sacrifice, and the resurrection of the dead. Next the mortal Davidic Messiah arrives to wage war with Gog and the people of Magog. This is the famed Armageddon, in which many perish until God intervenes and gives the Jews victory.[60] God then banishes all evil from the earth, and in the year 6000 of the Jewish calendar, the era of peace and prosperity begins, the *olam haba* where all people will know God directly. All Israel has a portion of the peace of the *olam haba*, even the sinners who must undergo purification.[61] This is the principal apocalyptic scheme of the Jews.

[handwritten margin note: Summary of Jewish apocalypse]

The End: Past and Future

Apocalyptic is a reactionary literature in times of crisis. It continually refashions itself to fit the changing time. When the Prophets failed, the vision of the future was rewritten. Vindication coincided with a loss of tangency with the present and a remythification of the past, fully realized in the Apocalyptic and the Sibylline oracles. Although the Church Fathers suppressed apocalyptic writings, nevertheless the idea flourished in the popular mind and was cemented in the Book of Revelation. The apocalyptic schemes were in place for the medieval era.

The Christian vision of the apocalypse has proliferated over the years to include diverse offshoots: Jehovah's Witnesses foresee the coming of Satan himself in place of the Antichrist, to lead a coalition of worldly kings against the chosen. The buildup to battle includes massive persecutions and the United Nations stamping out all religions. The Seventh Day Adventists believe that Armageddon will take place after the Millennium. These are but a few of the many variations. The prophets of ancient times repeatedly thought they were on the edge of the Apocalypse. History offers a series of such events for the Jewish people: the enslavement in Egypt and the exodus; the Babylonian captivity and Persian release; the maltreatment of Antiochus and the Seleucids; the persecutions of the Romans culminating in the destruction of Jerusalem in 70 CE and the Diaspora. Such events form a cycle of catastrophes and recoveries that continued to shape the perception of God's machinations among mankind and perpetuated a continual reconception of history. Likewise, many have perceived Armageddon in the medieval and modern world. The continued threat of nuclear annihilation and other forms of mass destruction based on everything from biological warfare and nanobots to aliens and global warming feed the frenzy for the apocalyptic mind, changing to fit the needs of a changing world, perpetuating that mild but mass hysteria that is always on the lookout for the End.

NOTES

1. Paul O'Callaghan, *The Christological Assimilation of the Apocalypse* (Dublin, Ireland: Four Courts, 2004) 111–12. O'Callaghan presents an excellent bibliography of such scholars.

2. For Holocaust as Apocalypse see Darrell Fasching, *The Ethical Challenge of Auschwitz and Hiroshima: Apocalypse or Utopia?* (New York: State University of New York, 1993); for nuclear annihilation and other modern apocalyptic scenarios see Richard Landes, *Encyclopedia of Millennialism and Millennial Movements* (New York: Routledge, 2000) 70–74ff. Bernard McGinn, *Visions of the End* (New York: Columbia University Press, 1998) adeptly treats popular views of the Apocalypse from the fifth to the fifteenth century. The connection of the Messiah and Armageddon to Apocalypse is inherent in Jewish and Christian doctrine. For the Crusades, see below.

3. Egypt had a limited eschatology wherein the earth ends by a return to chaotic ocean. See *The Book of the Dead*, chap. 175.

4. Psalm 74.13–14: "It was you who split open the sea by your power; you broke the heads of the monster in the waters. It was you who crushed the heads of Leviathan and gave him as food to the creatures of the desert."

5. Cf. the *concilium deorum* of Psalm 82 at which Yahweh resides.

6. See Mitchell G. Reddish, ed., *Apocalyptic Literature: A Reader* (Peabody, MA: Hendrickson, 1995) 29.

7. Isaiah 40–48, 52, 62–66.

8. Zoroaster reformed Persian religion, traditionally in the sixth century BCE. Studies in oral tradition have placed him much earlier. Our record of early Zoroastrianism comes largely from the Avesta, written in the fifth century CE, a quarter of which is extant. The lateness of its written form presents problems vis-à-vis its relation to Judaism. My analysis employs a standard theory that the precepts far antedate the writings. See also Norman Cohn, *Cosmos, Chaos and the World to Come: The Ancient Roots of Apocalyptic Faith* (New Haven, CT: Yale University Press, 1993) 77. This point is contended by T. Francis Glasson, *Greek Influence in Jewish Eschatology* (Saffron Walden, Essex, UK: Talbot, 1961) 1–7.

9. Yasna 44.15, 51.9. Cohn, in *Cosmos, Chaos and the World to Come*, 97, suggests that this detail is based on a trial ordeal in which molten metal was poured upon the accused.

10. The question of the position of apocalypse in Indo-European culture is problematic. I contend that the Iranian and the Germanic apocalyptic scenarios are modified relics of a common Indo-European end-time belief. See also Jaan Puhvel, *Comparative Mythology* (Baltimore: The Johns Hopkins University Press, 1987) 285: "Fraškart (*frashokereti*) and Ragnarök are remnants of an apocalyptic myth that survives elsewhere only in transmuted battle saga." Cf. Steven O'Brien, "Indo-European Eschatology: A Model," *Journal of Indo-European Studies*, Vol. 4, No.4 (1976): 295–320.

11. The "Great Year" is a Babylonian notion in which planets periodically and regularly line up, creating catastrophic cosmic events.

12. Zechariah 9.9, 11.1, 11.3.

13. Cf. Cohn, *Cosmos, Chaos and the World to Come*, 147.

14. O'Callaghan, *The Christological Assimilation of the Apocalypse*, 113. John J. Collins, *Seers, Sibyls, and Sages in Hellenistic-Roman Judaism* (New York: Brill, 1997) 57, argues that apocalyptic is a new creation, not a child of the Prophets.

15. Cf. G. von Rad, *Old Testament Theology* volume 2 (Munich: Christian Kaiser, 1962) 303ff., quoted in O'Callaghan, *The Christological Assimilation of the Apocaypse*, 118.

16. Cohn *Cosmos, Chaos and the World to Come*, 164.

17. Zand of Vahman Yasht, 7.3.1. Hesiod, *Works and Days*, 129–234. The late recording (sixth century CE) of the Persian source makes the primacy of the metal theme difficult to determine. Cf. Glasson, *Greek Influence in Jewish Eschatology*, chap. 1 passim.

18. The Greeks themselves had much earlier borrowed the combat myth and succession myth from the Near East. See M.L. West, *The East Face of Helicon: West Asiatic Elements in Greek Poetry and Myth* (Oxford, UK: Clarendon Press, 1997).

19. The exchange was not simple and linear, but a complex system of cross-fertilization, a cultural ebb and flow of ideas. Comparative analysis has e.g. shown the massive influence of Sumerian/Babylonian culture on the Hittites, Phoenicians and Greeks. See West *The East Face of Helicon*; Walter Burkert, *Babylon, Memphis, Persepolis: Eastern Contexts of Greek Culture* (Cambridge, MA: Harvard University Press, 2004).

20. Enoch's catabasis and description of the underworld in chapters 1 to 36 owes much to *Odyssey* 11, Plato *Phaedo* 114, and Pythagorean and Orphic descriptions of nekyiai and the underworld. Cf. Glasson *Greek Influence in Jewish Eschatology*, chapters 2–4. Orphic influence is seen in the underworld descriptions (1–32). There is a blissful realm and long life among the groves for the righteous, and a purifying yet punishing fire for the wicked. Fire had been seen in the Old Testament as a means of punishment, but not in an eschatological sense. Examples are God's destruction of Sodom and Gomorrah and individuals in the Pentateuch and Psalms. Fire as an instrument of eternal torment is Orphic in origin. For Orphic sources, see M.L. West, *The Orphic Poems* (Oxford, UK: Clarendon, 1983).

21. Enoch 1.2.1–2.

22. Cohn *Cosmos, Chaos and the World to Come*, 182.

23. Jubilees 5.

24. Hesiod, *Theogony,* 514–570, 717–721; Aeschylus, *Prometheus Bound,* 437–508.

25. It is clear that Mastema here represents the fully evolved Satan familiar to later biblical works (also called Beliar). This evolution of Satan into God's counterpart belies Persian dualism. Such dualism is inherent in most subsequent apocalyptic scenarios: the two opposing forces draw up their hosts for a final confrontation at the end of time.

26. Hesiod, *Works and Days,* 123–26.

27. Cf. Hesiod, *Works and Days,* 180–81: "And Zeus will also destroy this race of mortal men when they come to be born with gray hair on the temples."

28. Gnostic literature of the early Common Era has much in common with apocalyptic, e.g. vivid poetic and symbolic visions of end-times. O'Callaghan sees no historic relation, *The Christological Assimilation of the Apocalypse,* 109–11.

29. Horace, *Epistles,* 2.1.156.

30. Virgil, *Aeneid,* 6.736, 743–51. Virgil's underworld also elaborates the division between the isles of the blessed (Elysium) and Tartarus where the vilest criminals such as Tantalus and Ixion dwell in torment.

31. Virgil, *Eclogue,* 4.

32. Ovid, *Metamorphoses,* 1.163–265. Such fiery destruction occurs in Hesiod's *Theogony* during the Titanomachy, 687–710, and Zeus' final battle with Typhoeus, 820–52.

33. The views of the Qumran sect (c. 150 BCE to 68 CE), recorded in the Dead Sea Scrolls, show similar apocalyptic developments in thought.

34. There are some exceptions, e.g. Isaiah 19.20; Zechariah 9.9 (see above).

35. Cf. John J. Collins, *Jewish Cult and Hellenistic Culture* (Boston: Brill, 2005) 80.

36. See Kenneth Barker, ed., *The NIV Study Bible* (Grand Rapids, MI: Zondervan, 1985) 1298, 1302, 1311 for an analysis.

37. Norman Cohn, *The Pursuit of the Millennium* (Fairlawn, NJ: Essential, 1957) 5.

38. Josephus, *Jewish War,* 6.5.2–4.

39. Cohn, *Cosmos, Chaos and the World to Come,* 206.

40. There are signs of Orphic influence in the parallels between Jesus and Dionysus. The tablets of the Bacchic Mysteries tell of the dismemberment and resurrection of Dionysus via *sparagmos,* the ritual tearing-up of animals and eating of their flesh that is associated with his worship. He is killed at the hands of Titans who eat his flesh, signifying the ritual of homophagy, and later resurrected by his father Zeus. The ritual enactment of these rites celebrates the rebirth of the god as well as the spiritual rebirth of the devotee. Hence Dionysus was called the twice born god, or "born again." These may be superficial similarities; yet they reveal a shared network of ideas perpetuated throughout the Greco-Roman world.

41. *Apocalypse of Peter,* 1–14; *Shepherd of Hermas,* 4.1–5.

42. Dionysius of Halicarnassus, *Roman Antiquities,* 4.62.5–6. The Sibylline oracles as we possess them today are Jewish and Christian works written from the second to fifth century CE. Unfortunately, the early Roman versions were destroyed by events such as the fire of 64 CE. The extant Judeo-Christian Sibyllina are sometimes titled the *Pseudo-Sibyllina* to distinguish them from the lost originals.

43. Collins, *Jewish Cult and Hellenistic Culture,* 98; Erich S. Gruen, *Heritage and Hellenism* (Berkeley: University of California Press, 1998) 287, cautions the idea of proselytization.

44. Cf. Gruen, *Heritage and Hellenism,* 290.

45. Sibylline Oracles 2.225–32, John J. Collins, trans., in *The Old Testament Pseudepigrapha,* volume 1, James H. Charlesworth, ed. (Garden City, NY: Doubleday, 1983).

46. For Jewish continuances of Messianism see Cohn, *The Pursuit of the Millennium,* 6.

47. Gog and Magog first occur in Ezekiel 38–9 and are mentioned in Revelation 20.8.
48. Commodianus, *Carmen Apologeticum,* 791–1060. This battle is based on Ezekiel 38.
49. E.g. Plato, *Phaedrus,* 248E-249D: souls are incarnated every thousand years, up to ten times before they can enter heaven. This is likely an Orphic doctrine.
50. Augustine, *City of God* 20.6–17.
51. It has been observed that Revelation's Number of the Beast, 666, is a code for Nero's full name based on the number value of Greek letters. The ancients relished such puzzles.
52. Cf. Cohn, *The Pursuit of the Millennium,* 12, 56–7, and bibliographical notes at 384 n.56–57.
53. *Ibid.,* 20.
54. Sibylline Oracles 3.75–92, 3.63–74.
55. See R.E. Lerner, "Frederick II, Alive, Aloft, and Allayed," *The Use and Abuse of Eschatology in the Middle Ages,* Werner Verbeke et al., eds. (Leuven: Leuven University Press, 1988) 359–84.
56. Talmud, Bamidbar 9a (= Numbers 23.19): "God is not a man, that he should lie, nor a son of man, that he should change his mind." The Talmud is the classical rabbinic text for Judaism. It contains the Old Testament, the Mishnah (c. 200 CE), and the Gemara (c. 500 CE).
57. Mishnah, Sanhedrin 10.1.
58. These well-defined conditions are recorded in Avoda Zarah, 9a.
59. Many liberal Jews consider these years symbolic.
60. The term Armageddon is based on the Hebrew *Har-Megiddon,* the "Hill of Megiddo" near Jerusalem, where many ancient battles were fought. For logistical details of Armageddon, see J. Dwight Pentecost, *Things to Come: A Study in Biblical Eschatology* (Grand Rapids, MI: Zondervan, 1964) chap. 20.
61. Talmud, Sanhedrin 10.1.

WORKS CITED

Albinus, Lars. *The House of Hades.* Aarhus, Denmark: Aarhus University Press, 2000.
Barker, Kenneth, ed. *The NIV Study Bible.* Grand Rapids, MI: Zondervan House, 1985.
Boyce, Mary, ed. and tr. *Textual Sources for the Study of Zoroastrianism.* Totowa, NJ: Barnes and Noble, 1984.
Burkert, Walter. *Babylon, Memphis, Persepolis: Eastern Contexts of Greek Culture.* Cambridge, MA: Harvard University Press, 2004.
Charles, R.H., ed. *The Apocrypha and Pseudepigrapha of the Old Testament in English.* Oxford, UK: Oxford University Press, 1969.
Cohn, Norman. *Cosmos, Chaos and the World to Come: The Ancient Roots of Apocalyptic Faith.* New Haven, CT: Yale University Press, 1993.
_____. *The Pursuit of the Millennium.* Fairlawn, NJ: Essential, 1957.
Collins, John J. *Jewish Cult and Hellenistic Culture.* Boston: Brill, 2005.
_____. *The Old Testament Pseudepigrapha,* volume 1. James H. Charlesworth, ed. Garden City, NY: Doubleday, 1983.
_____. *Seers, Sibyls, and Sages in Hellenistic-Roman Judaism.* New York: Brill, 1997.
_____. *The Sibylline Oracle of Egyptian Judaism.* Dissertation Series, Number 13. Society of Biblical Literature and Scholars' Press for The Pseudepigrapha Group, 1974.
Fasching, Darrell. *The Ethical Challenge of Auschwitz and Hiroshima: Apocalypse or Utopia?* New York: State University of New York, 1993.
Glasson, T.F. *Greek Influence in Jewish Eschatology.* Saffron Walden, Essex, UK: Talbot, 1961.
Gruen, Erich S. *Heritage and Hellenism.* Berkeley: University of California Press, 1998.

Hengel, Martin. *Judaism and Hellenism,* volume 1. John Bowden, trans. Philadelphia, PA: Fortress, 1974.

Landes, Richard. *Encyclopedia of Millennialism and Millennial Movements.* New York: Routledge, 2000.

Lerner, R.E. "Frederick II, Alive, Aloft, and Allayed" in *The Use and Abuse of Eschatology in the Middle Ages.* Werner Verbeke et al., eds. Leuven: Leuven University Press, 1988.

McGinn, Bernard. *Visions of the End.* New York: Columbia University Press, 1998.

O'Brien, Steven. "Indo-European Eschatology: A Model." *Journal of Indo-European Studies* 4, no. 4 (1976): 295–320.

O'Callaghan, Paul. *The Christological Assimilation of the Apocalypse.* Dublin, Ireland: Four Courts, 2004.

Pentecost, J. Dwight. *Things to Come: A Study in Biblical Eschatology.* Grand Rapids, MI: Zondervan, 1964.

Puhvel, Jaan. *Comparative Mythology.* Baltimore, MD: The Johns Hopkins University Press, 1987.

von Rad, G. *Old Testament Theology,* volume 2. Munich: Christian Kaiser, 1962.

Reddish, Mitchell G., ed. *Apocalyptic Literature: A Reader.* Peabody, MA: Hendrickson, 1995.

Terry, Milton S, trans. *The Sibylline Oracles.* New York: AMS, 1973.

West, M.L. *The East Face of Helicon: West Asiatic Elements in Greek Poetry and Myth.* Oxford, UK: Clarendon, 1997.

_____. *The Orphic Poems.* Oxford, UK: Clarendon, 1983.

Beatus of Liébana: Medieval Spain and the Othering of Islam[1]

Kevin R. Poole

Historically, the eighth century in Spain marked a time of massive social, political, and religious upheaval. The year 711 saw the Berber invasion from North Africa and the subsequent arrival of Arabian Muslims, which drove Visigothic Christians to the far northern regions of the Iberian Peninsula. The Muslims established themselves as the ruling political and religious classes of much of Spain until the mid-eleventh century, with a continued presence in the southern regions until the late fifteenth century.[2] With the arrival of the invading armies from North Africa, Visigothic rule in Iberia came to a swift end as the Muslims pushed father north, threatening to cross the Pyrenees into Gaul. This, in turn, led to Charlemagne's counteroffensive, beginning in 778, in which he took possession of parts of what would become Aragon and Catalonia in an attempt to subdue the Iberian Muslims while also extending Franco-Christian territories. Farther south, Archbishop Elipandus of Toledo began preaching a new Christological belief known as Adoptionism (to be explained further on), which set into motion a series of ecclesiastical and political arguments that would, for the last two decades of the century, divide the Spanish church into two rivalling groups, one headed by the archbishop himself and the other by the Asturian monk Beatus of Liébana. The latter, observing the changes taking place around him, wrote his *Commentaria in Apocalipsin* in 776, supposedly believing that the apocalyptic end as recounted in the biblical Book of Revelation was at hand.

For no apparent reason other than the fact that Beatus lived in a changing society, he wrote in 776 the first draft of what would later become polemic against Adoptionism and, even later, be used as argument for establishing a "Muslim Antichrist" in Spain. Within a decade of writing this first draft, Beatus had written two more, the third being the definitive copy upon which the "Beatus tradition" was built. Combining the teachings of the Church Fathers regarding the end-time events with his thoughts on political and religious events of his own days, Beatus created a document that, during the remainder of the Middle Ages, would be copied at least thirty-four times in various parts of the Iberian Peninsula, France, and Italy. Twenty-six of those extant manuscripts contain illustrations, and others have blank spaces where illustrations would have been added if they had been completed. Because of the extent of the Beatus manuscript tradition, the Apocalypse became as popular a text to illustrate in Spain during the Middle Ages as did Books of Hours and the Book of Psalms in other parts of Europe. More importantly for the study of the cultural importance of Iberian manuscripts is that the Beatus family comprises the largest extant manuscript family from the European Middle Ages.[3]

Beatus of Liébana

As is the case with most writers of the Early Middle Ages, we know very little about the life of the man called Beatus of Liébana. We know neither in which year he was born nor in which part of Spain his birth took place. Some have speculated that he may have been born in a southern territory of the Iberian Peninsula and carried north at a young age with those who fled the rule of the Muslims. Likewise, the year of his death remains a mystery: based on the scarce documentation of the time in which he is named, most historians agree that Beatus's death probably occurred in the middle years of the first decade of the ninth century (ca. 805), although Jaime Marqués Casanovas claims that Beatus both became abbot of his monastery and died in the year 798.[4] We have very little evidence to support this claim: in correspondence between himself and Beatus, Alcuin of York (Charlemagne's late eighth-century advisor in Aachen) refers to Beatus as an abbot, though they never met one another in person.[5] Likewise, in letters that reference the Adoptionist heresy of the late 700s, Alvarus of Córdoba (†861) refers to Beatus as a *libanensis presbyter*, which could be interpreted as a "priest" from Liébana or simply as a "resident" of that place.[6] Again, though, with Alvarus's lack of personal knowledge of Beatus, it is difficult to determine Beatus's true social or religious status.

As a writer, Beatus's fame stems from the *Commentaria in Apocalipsin* that he wrote in the later decades of the eighth century. As has been pointed out, he wrote three versions of this work — one in 776,[7] the second in 784,[8] and the third in 786.[9] We also know Beatus for two other texts: as co-author of the *Apologeticum* (also known as the *Letter from Etherius and Beatus to Elipandus*), a two-book document written in 785 against the Adoptionist teachings of Archbishop Elipandus of Toledo; and as the possible author of a sixty-line acrostic hymn known as "O Dei Verbum." Though some scholars doubt Beatus's authorship of the latter, Manuel Díaz y Díaz reminds us that there is no evidence to disprove this belief.[10] As a participant in the battle against Adoptionism, seen in the *Commentaria* and the *Apologeticum*, Beatus gained notoriety within Asturias as a regional saint whose feast day was (and still is) celebrated on February 19. Interestingly, however, the Cult of Saint Beatus is incorrect in its dedication to and veneration of the body it believes to be that of Beatus, housed in the monastery of Valcavado: it is actually that of Obeco, illuminator of the Valcavado manuscript produced nearly two centuries after Beatus's death.[11]

Beatus, Adoptionism, and the Apocalypse

Having studied the New Testament Apocalypse and written a compendium of early Christian teaching regarding its interpretation, Beatus saw in his own surroundings what he believed to be the "signs of the times" that pointed to the Second Coming of Christ. The Adoptionist movement, headed by Archbishop Elipandus of Toledo and Bishop Felix of Urgel, became for Beatus the embodiment of the Antichrist. Known as the *haeresis feliciana*, Adoptionism taught that Jesus was the legitimate Son of God in spirit, but only an adopted son in human form. That is, the body of Jesus lacked divinity, whereas the spirit within it did not. Not accepting the divinity of Christ in all forms, this doctrine met opposition from both the northern Iberian Christians and those of Frankish kingdoms under Charlemagne's rule. Beatus and Bishop Etherius of Osma served as the voice of orthodox Christianity in Iberia, the former referring to Elipandus as the Antichrist in correspondence to both the Toledan archbishop and to other bishops of Northern Spain and Gaul.

Regarding the theological origins of Adoptionism, one must simply look to the years preceding its development, for it was in Elipandus's repudiation of the former Migetian heresy that he developed his own Christological belief.[12] The Spanish historian Marcelino Menéndez y Pelayo, as well as the German historian Heinrich Denzinger, have attempted to trace Adoptionism to the Arians, the Donatists, and the Priscillianists (all fourth-century heresies), as well as to the Jews and Muslims.[13] In a very generalizing way, Cesar Dubler claims that "there can be no doubt that [Adoptionism's] intellectual roots lay in the heresies of the Near East."[14] Though there may exist certain parallels among these various heresies and the Adoptionist beliefs, I am of the belief that those movements have only coincidental rather than direct influence on Elipandus's arguments, developed four centuries later. We have no tangi-

ble evidence to prove that Elipandus founded his doctrine on any of the afore-
mentioned heresies, and I prefer to see his as yet another in a series of attempts
at Christological interpretation that were taking place during these still early
and formative years of Catholic dogma. The main difference between this
interpretation and those preceding it lay not in the belief itself but in the person promoting it: many of the former heresies had their roots in individual
preachers who had managed to gather a following, later to be put down by
ecclesiastic officials. Adoptionism, however, began as *ex cathedra* teaching by
the highest ranking member of church hierarchy in Spain — as Archbishop of
Toledo, Elipandus also held the title of Primate of Spain, the most prestigious
and most powerful ecclesiastic office in Iberia.

Partly in response to the Migetian heresy, and partly as an attempt to
establish official doctrine regarding the person of Christ, the Creed of Seville
was written and approved in October 784, containing a clause that reflected
Adoptionist belief. Elipandus had consulted with the Catalan bishop of Urgel,
Felix, who had actually served as formulator of the doctrine that Elipandus
put forward, thus the name *haeresis feliciana*. With Elipandus's promulgation
of the new Christological doctrine, churches across Iberia began to teach the
new belief to followers. Because of the political and religious influence held
by Felix of Urgel over the churches of Northeastern Iberia and the southern
Frankish realms, Adoptionism also spread across the Pyrenees into lands controlled by Charlemagne. At this point, Beatus of Liébana once again enters
the scene.

Upon hearing of the spread of Adoptionist beliefs, Beatus immediately
wrote a letter (now lost) explaining to Elipandus the error of his ways. As
Jaime Marqués Casanovas explains, Beatus may have perceived of Adoptionism as "a new Muslim invasion on the spiritual plane" for

> [i]f Christ were merely the adopted Son of God, He was barely distinguishable
> from a prophet such as Mohammad was for Islam; He was no longer the true
> God. Beatus felt that he had been elected by God to play the part of a new,
> spiritual Pelagius and oppose the invasion, although he knew full well that he
> was like David confronting Goliath.[15]

That is, Beatus, having already written two drafts of his *Commentaria in Apocalipsin* and convinced that the end was near, took Elipandus as the force of
evil, arising from within the Church, whose aim was to destroy the Church —
the Antichrist. Like Pelagius, the great Visigothic warrior who defeated the
Muslims at the Battle of Covadonga and thus initiated the Spanish reconquest of Muslim-held territories, Beatus considered himself a spiritual warrior destined to save Christendom from the wiles of the Antichrist.

Reacting to Beatus's insults, Elipandus wrote to the Asturian abbot Fidel,
accusing Beatus of the sin of arrogance. In this letter he goes so far as to call

Beatus a mangy little sheep (*ovis morbida*) and a disciple of the Antichrist (*servi sunt antichristi*).[16] It was, of course, unthinkable that a lowly monk from the mountains of Asturias could teach anything to those of Toledo, especially the Archbishop:

> They do not question me, but try to teach me, they who are servants of the Antichrist [...] Yet never has it been heard that someone from Liébana taught a Toledan [...] It is known to all people that Sacred Doctrine clearly has its beginnings in the See, and it never puts forth anything schismatic. And now a fetid sheep desires to be our teacher.[17]

In the same manner, in other letters to the bishops of Spain and Gaul, Elipandus continuously refers to Beatus as the "fetid" disciple of the Antichrist who takes pleasure in prostitutes and bestiality—an apparent invention on the part of Elipandus in order to win the support of fellow bishops. Even more, as far as can be discerned, Beatus and Elipandus never actually met one another, and there is no extant textual evidence to link Beatus to the accusations made by Elipandus. Elipandus's sarcasm and name-calling must have served as Beatus's impetus to write his *Apologeticum*, for in this two-volume letter he turns the Archbishop's words back on him, entwining passages from the Bible and from the Holy Fathers in order to prove through his own form of logic that, in fact, Elipandus was the Antichrist, not himself. This, of course, brought on a doctrinal war in which the power that Elipandus enjoyed as Metropolitan of Toledo came under the scrutiny of bishops from all reaches of Europe. Beatus proved to be not the mangy sheep who could be dominated by the powerful Spanish Primate, but an acutely learned man who was able to gain the backing of the Church in various kingdoms, indeed the pope himself, in defense of orthodoxy.

In his two-volume letter to Elipandus, officially supported by Bishop Etherius of Osma (Asturias), Beatus tried to use the power of logic to prove that the Toledan archbishop embodied the Antichrist, basing his arguments on the Biblical passage from I John 2:22: "all who believe that Jesus is not the Son of God are liars and, therefore, the Antichrist." Simply put, by characterizing Jesus as the *adopted* son of God, Elipandus had implicitly claimed that He was not the *true* son of God. Therefore, Elipandus must be the Antichrist. Expounding upon this argument at great length and taking advantage of the episcopal support of Etherius, Beatus was able to incite both Iberian and Frankish bishops to take action against Elipandus. Recognizing his home kingdom of Asturias as the symbol of Iberian independence from the Muslims and from Christian heterodoxy, and comparing himself to Pelagius, Beatus turned to both Pope Adrian I and to Charlemagne for help in the ensuing battle. Both were interested in expanding Christian influence and eliminating Muslim control, so Beatus's ideological connection of Adoptionism to Islam proved beneficial to his efforts in gaining support. Beatus's arguments impacted Frankish religious leaders strongly: Alcuin of York (the English religious advisor to Charlemagne), Paulinus of Aquilaea, Theodulph of Orléans, Benedict of Aniane, and Richbod of Trier all wrote against the Adoptionist doctrine, and it was partly as a result of their writings that Bishop Felix of Urgel was brought to trial at Charlemagne's residence in Regensburg (792) and sent to his imprisonment in Rome. Other church councils — Rome (789), Ratisbon (792), Frankfurt (794), and Aix-la-Chapelle (799) — dealt heavy blows to the Adoptionist teachings, putting an end to them completely at the beginning of the ninth century when both Felix and Elipandus had grown too old to continue preaching and eventually died.

Beatus's Apocalyptic Calculations

Based on the fact that Beatus had already written his commentary on the Apocalypse before the Adoptionist controversy came into being, we can assume a prior interest in the Second Coming on his part. As has been pointed out already, it is entirely possible that Beatus believed that the apocalyptic events of Revelations would take place during his lifetime and that he searched within his own environment for the signs that would confirm his belief. Though the New Testament clearly points out that the day and time of Christ's coming is unknown even to Christ himself, it was not uncommon in the Middle Ages (indeed, it is not uncommon today) for the religious to search the pages of the Bible for clues that could lead them to unravel the mysteries surrounding the Parousia.[18] Julian of Toledo (7th century) and Juan de Bíclaro (mid–8th century), both Iberian Christians, had carried out calculations in order to predict when the Sixth Age of Man would come to an end, thus ushering in the beginning of the Apocalypse. Even the Venerable Bede, in the first third of the eighth century, had been suspected of heresy because of his own millenarian calculations that came too close to reflecting those carried out by Jewish exegetes.

In a letter to the bishops of Gaul toward the end of 794, Elipandus of Toledo rather sarcastically tells of an incident that, if taken as true, shows Beatus's millenarian ideas put into practice. Reflecting general medieval belief regarding the Final Judgment, Beatus had written in his *Commentaria*, book IV, chapter 5, that the Judgment would take place on a Sunday: since Jesus had resurrected from the dead on a Sunday, then the same would happen with the dead who must be resurrected to face the Final Judgment.[19] Playing off this idea and obviously attempting to discredit Beatus, Elipandus tells of a certain Easter Vigil in which Beatus had proclaimed to the multitudes that they should prepare for the Final Judgment, for it would take place that very night. As an act of penitence, Beatus had asked those present to abstain from food during the remainder of the night and into the following morning. When, at noon on Easter Sunday, Jesus had still not appeared in the eastern skies, Ordoño, the priest chosen to preside over the Vigil Mass, declared, "Let us eat and drink, for if we are to die, then we should do so with our bellies full!"[20] Though we have no evidence to prove this anecdote either true or false, we must admit it as a possibility — in his *Commentaria* Beatus had concerned himself with numerology and the calculation of the date in which the Final Judgment *could* take place. He admits that there is no way to know the exact time (which goes against Elipandus's anecdote), but he also shows zeal in proclaiming that the end must be very near since, according to his calculations, the Antichrist — Elipandus — had already come into existence.

For theologians of the eighth century the year 800 CE held special importance, for it was in this year that many believed the Sixth Age, or the sixth thousand years of earthy creation, would come to an end. Each millennium of the six thousand years represented one of the original days of creation as outlined in Genesis: since God rested after the sixth day of work, it was believed that God's creation would last six Ages of one thousand years each, and that the universe would be admitted to everlasting peace only in the Seventh Age, or the Eternal Sabbath. Relying on Biblical genealogies and events, both Saints Jerome (†420) and Julián of Toledo (†690) had calculated Jesus' birth as having taken place in either the year 5199 or 5200 of creation, respectively. If this were true, then the end of the Sixth Age, and, thus, the beginnings of the apocalyptic events of Revelations, would take place in either 800 or 801 CE in order for the six thousand years to come to fruition. Beatus repeated the calculations in the following manner:

> The six days in which the Lord realised his work is a week and represent the figure of six thousand years, which are expressed in a week. The first age, from Adam to Noah, are 2,242 years. The second, from Noah to Abraham, are 942 years. The third, from Abraham to Moses, are 505 years. The fourth, from the exodus of Israel's children from Egypt to their arrival to the Promised Land, were forty years. And from the arrival to the Promised Land until Saul, the first king of Israel, there were judges for 355 years. Saul reigned for forty years. From David until the beginning of the construction of the temple forty-three years passed. The fifth age, from the first building of the temple until the exile in Babylon, there were kings for 446 years. The people were held captive after the destruction of the temple for seventy years. From the restoration of the temple to the Incarnation of Christ passed 540 years. The time from Adam to Christ adds up to 5,227 years. And from the birth of our Lord Jesus Christ to the present era, that is, the year 822, there have been 784 years. If you add from the first man, Adam, to the present time, year 822, you will have a total of

5,987. Therefore, the sixth millennium has fourteen years remaining. With that, the sixth age will end in the year 838.[21]

Taking into consideration that eighth-century Iberia submitted to the Mozarabic calendar, which followed a calculation thirty-eight years ahead of the Roman calendar, the final year given in Beatus's calculations (838) turns out to be the year 800 CE of the official ecclesiastic calendar.

Further on, Beatus tells us that, although the calculated year of the Parousia is fourteen years into the future, God could see fit to shorten that period. Due to God's unpredictability, Catholics are urged to live as if the end could come at any moment:

> In which season, which year, which hour, which day, which period will the resurrection take place? We do not know if these fourteen days will be shortened, for only God knows that [...] All Catholics should understand, wait and fear, and consider these fourteen years as if they were one hour: day and night, in ash and cilice, cry as much for your own destruction as for that of the world, and do not become too interested in the computations of time; and do not try to investigate excessively the day or the season of the end of the world, which no one knows except for God. Everyone should think about his own end, just as the Scripture says: "in all your actions keep present your end, and you will never commit a sin."[22]

Without a doubt, Beatus must have felt that his writings would have an impact on the society in which he lived. As biblical exegesis, preachers would reference his commentaries in their sermons; during the meditative *lectio divina* practiced by the ordered religious, the commentaries would be used as a tool for spiritual training and preparation.[23] Whichever the case, it is evident in his writing that Beatus truly felt the Second Coming to be imminent, and with his added perception of Elipandus as the Antichrist, Beatus probably saw his religious and moral duty as that of warning other Christians of what lay ahead. In so doing, he would aid them along the path of perfection in preparation for the Final Judgment that he perceived so near.

When in the year 800 the Apocalypse did not come to pass, religious thinkers began to reanalyze their thoughts on the Book of Revelation and to revise their millenarian calculations. Some looked to historical events for new clues that would lead them to revised calculations for the year of the pending End, whereas others looked to the stars and even to magic.[24] While some set new dates for either the year 900 or 1000 for when the Apocalypse would take place, others simply awaited certain events such as the victory of Christianity over Islam. Since we have no documentation either by him or about him from which to draw conclusions, we have no knowledge of what Beatus of Liébana thought about his own mistaken calculations. Likewise, we know not what Elipandus must have thought about Beatus's error in identifying him as the Antichrist: based on the tone of his writings, however, we can be quite sure that the archbishop may have had a few spiteful comments to make regarding the matter. What we do know is that the religious and cultural interest in the millennium and in eschatological matters in general did not come to an end with Beatus's death or that of the authors of Adoptionism, for the *Commentaria in Apocalipsin* enjoyed several hundred years of being copied and illustrated throughout Northern Spain and Southern France. The reason for such widespread diffusion lies in Christianity's perception of Islam at the time, a religion that was quickly gaining political power in the Mediterranean regions.

Islam as Antichrist in Christian Iberia

Though Yarza Luaces presents the arrival of Islam to the Iberian Peninsula as one of the possible reasons for which Beatus of Liébana may have written his apocalyptic commentaries, nowhere in the texts of either the *Commentaria in Apocalipsin* or the *Apologeticum* does Beatus mention the presence of Islam in Iberia (though he does compare Adoptionism to Islam in various letters to the Iberian and Frankish bishops).[25] Toward the end of the eighth century, when Beatus was writing his texts, Islam still had not reached the necessary level of power in the northern Iberian territories to be considered a true threat to Christianity — many simply saw the new religion as yet another heresy that would eventually be put down by the Church.[26] Likewise, as Kenneth Baxter Wolf points out, the first invaders of Iberia in 711 and subsequent years were of questionable socio-religious status: most were Berbers who had been brought under Arab domination just a very short time before and who probably did not completely understand the new religion, which was, itself, still in its initial stages of formation.[27] Islam, though familiar to the ears of Beatus and his Northern Iberian contemporaries, did not present a direct menace to them, especially at the level of considering it the embodiment of the Antichrist. Not until the ninth century did the Arab population begin to have a noticeable stronghold on the peninsula, having established towns in major river valleys and created trade routes between Iberia and the East.

By the tenth century, the Muslim presence in Spain had grown to such extent that, in 912 under the leadership of Abd-ar-Raman, the land controlled by the Arabs was proclaimed a caliphate, taking the name of Caliphate of Córdoba. This marked the beginning of the period of greatest Muslim influence in Spain, stretching from the Caliphate and the subsequent Taifa kingdoms, the declining years of the Almoravids, the Almohads, the Benemerins, and the territorial reduction to the Kingdom of Granada in 1231. At the same time the Beatus *Commentaria in Apocalipsin* experienced a sudden rise in both readership and copy — twenty-three of the twenty-six extant illustrated manuscripts come from the years between the second decade of the tenth century and the year 1220. John Williams confirms this in his discussion of the tenth-century Beatus manuscripts when he says that the

> extensive glosses and correlations that mark such commentaries as the Vitrina 14-1, the Morgan 644, and the Gerona Beatus testify to readership and to the seriousness accorded the texts. Erasures that mark the face of Satan in such commentaries as Tábara (125r) and Lisbon (e.g., 186v, 201r) speak eloquently of individual contact with, and reaction to, the Beatus commentary.[28]

During this time there developed in Europe, particularly in Spain, the belief that either Mohammad or the Islamic religion embodied the Antichrist (whose face could not be looked upon, thus the erasures mentioned by Williams), and that extinguishing this religion would bring about the thousand-year reign of Christ on earth mentioned in the twentieth chapter of the Book of Revelation. It was partly to this end that the Crusades to the Holy Lands were declared in the eleventh through the thirteenth centuries and that the Christian reconquest of Spain was accorded the privileges of Crusade by Pope Calixtus II in 1123.

Because of the circumstances in which Spain saw itself in the tenth centuries and those that followed, as the only Western European Mediterranean territory in which Islam and Arabian culture had made a lasting impression, the desire to defeat the new religion held special importance. On the one hand, Christendom saw Spain, alongside the Holy Lands, as a battleground between the forces of good and evil as described in the text of the Apocalypse. On the other, during the Central and Later Middle Ages, there developed in Spain a belief that there would exist at some point in the near future a "Last World Emperor" who would turn his earthly empire over to God in Jerusalem. Angus Mackay explains that

> [i]n Spain this tradition, suitably influenced by Joachimite ideas and prophecies attributed to St Isidore of Seville, produced a Spanish messianic king and world emperor known variously as the *Encubierto* (the Hidden One), the *Murciélago* (the Bat), and the New David. The beginning of each new reign, therefore, aroused eschatological expectations. Was the new king the *Encubierto* or the Bat who would defeat the Antichrist in Andalusia, retake Granada from the Muslims, cross the sea, defeat all Islam, conquer the Holy City of Jerusalem, and become the last world emperor? When would the Hidden King reveal himself?[29]

The idea of the "hidden king" became especially important in the years following the fall of the Caliphate of Córdoba (1031) in which Christians all over Europe celebrated what they perceived to be a spiritual victory for the Kingdom of God. Nearly five centuries later, in 1516, when the Catholic Monarch Ferdinand of Aragón died after having conquered the last remaining Muslim stronghold in Spain with his wife Isabella, without later having crossed the Mediterranean to take possession of Jerusalem in the name of Christianity, the idea of the *Encubierto* came to an end. Beatus of Liébana did not write his *Commentaria* with these ideas or beliefs in mind since they developed well after his death, but there is no doubt that they greatly affected the later copyists and illustrators of his text, especially those of the eleventh, twelfth, and thirteenth centuries. Not only do we see the perceived "Muslim Antichrist" in illustrations from the later Beatus manuscripts, but we also find this idea in other writings of the time.[30] Probably the two most famous works to appear in Spain, in which Mohammad is conceived of in derogatory and even satanic ways, are the ninth-century *Indiculus luminosus* by Alvarus de Córdoba and the *Liber apologeticus martyrum* by Eulogius of Córdoba, from the same century. As Cantarino explains, the *Indiculus* takes as it target readers the *christiani muti*, the Mozarabs, those Christians who accepted life under Muslim rule to the point of assimilating Arabian social norms (style of dress, eating habits, learning to speak Arabic). In this text, Alvarus connects Muslim domination to the beast in the prophecies of the Old Testament book of Daniel 7:23, which in Biblical exegesis represents, of course, the Antichrist.[31] Eulogius's text portrays Mohammad as a brutal animal and a sexual deviant, the opposite of what one would expect of a divine prophet. Wolf explains that Eulogius

> concentrated his efforts on casting the Muslims as persecutors of the church of the classical pagan Roman type and depicting Mohammad as a false prophet who, like Arius, had challenged the divinity of Christ. For his part Alvarus followed the parallel but distinct path of identifying Muhammad with the Antichrist, by reinterpreting key passages of scripture.[32]

Though Wolf does not seem to believe that these two writers' works had much of an influence on later writers or theologians, I do not wholly agree. Other writers may not have directly quoted Alvarus or Eulogius in their texts, but these latter did contribute to the beginnings of Christian polemical and propagandistic literature against Muslims in Spain. The very same ideas presented by Alvarus and Eulogius would be repeated numerous times in the centuries that followed, both in and out of Spain.

Two examples from outside of Spain come from the Cluniac abbot Peter the Venerable (†1156) and from the Cistercian Joachim de Fiore (†1202). As a result of Peter the Venerable's visit to the Cluniac monasteries of Spain in 1141 and the translation of the Koran that he mandated,[33] the abbot wrote a treatise known as the *Liber contra sectam sive haeresim sarracenorum*, which, in the prologue, directly links Mohammad to the Antichrist:

> If you want to know who the greatest forerunner of Antichrist and the devil's
> chosen disciple, Muhammad, was or what he taught, read this prologue atten-
> tively, in which are briefly contained all this book contains: his most foul and
> false genealogy, his most impure and unspeakable life and doctrine, and the
> utterly laughable and insane fables produced by him and his followers.[34]

The book consists of an eighteen-part outline of the reasons for which a
Christian must not give in to the temptations of Islamic teachings. According to the author, the basic tenet of Islam that all Christians must understand
is that Muslims deny that Christ is the Son of God, though they do revere
him as a sinless prophet. As Beatus of Liébana had already argued, those who
deny Jesus as Son of God are the Antichrist, and for Peter the Venerable this
continued to hold true with regards to Islam. A question that we must ask,
however, is the following: if Mohammad had accepted Jesus as a divine
prophet, how, then, could he be the precursor of the Antichrist or, even more,
the Antichrist himself? As Peter explains, the answer lies in the deceptive
nature of the Antichrist: in order to gain converts, the Antichrist must express
an appealing proposition to those he wishes to win over. By preaching in
favour of a more "carnal" lifestyle, yet not fully denying the sanctity of Christ,
Mohammad had been able to take control of a large part of the known world.
Using Beatus's arguments and a series of logic-based explanations, Peter the
Venerable concludes that Mohammad was a minor antichrist preceding THE
Antichrist of the Apocalypse — Islam itself. For Peter, The apocalyptic
Antichrist of the last days is prefigured by many smaller antichrists and that
followers of Islam have allowed themselves to be led into the hands of the
Devil.

   In an attempt to explain the seven seals that are broken during the events
of the Apocalypse, Joachim de Fiore had calculated that his generation was
living at the time of the breaking of the sixth seal.[35] The Antichrist had already
been set loose into the world to persecute the Christian faithful, and the
breaking of the seventh and last seal would bring the Heavenly Sabbath. In
calculations that echo those of the exegetes of Beatus's days, Joachim de Fiore
explains that the time of the sixth seal consists of only one human generation, whereas the preceding seals had totalled forty generations all together.
Thus, Joachim expected the seventh seal to be broken and the Celestial
Jerusalem to be established on earth within his own lifetime. Considering himself to be of great spiritual insight and prophetic abilities, Joachim de Fiore
met with King Richard I of England in 1191 to tell him, erroneously, that he
would defeat Muslim forces in the Holy Land:

> When King Richard I was on his way to the Holy Land in 1191 he met Joachim
> de Fiore at Messina, and Joachim outlined to him a view of history which
> brought the apocalyptic visions of the ninth-century Spanish martyrs up to

date. For him, as for them, the end of the world was at hand, and for him also the chief instruments of Antichrist were the Saracens. On the two flanks of Christendom, in Spain and the Holy Land, he saw the strength of Islam renewed under the Almohads in Spain and Saladin in Palestine. But with regard to the future, he had to feel his way with care. He seems to have assured King Richard that he would defeat Saladin, and in this he was certainly wrong. But the most interesting addition he made to the apocalyptic picture was his assurance that the final Antichrist was already alive and in Rome, and that he was destined to obtain the papal see.[36]

Here we see that Joachim de Fiore did not consider Muslims to be the Antichrist, but simply the helpers of the Antichrist to come. The true Antichrist would come from within the Church, just as Beatus had suspected of Elipandus, thus allowing him more power over Christendom. Interestingly, we see the same idea of the "Last World Emperor" in this anecdote as Mackay explains regarding Spain: the prophet Joachim de Fiore had seen in Richard the image of the monarch who would defeat the Muslim rulers and, thus, open the way for the Kingdom of God to be established on earth.

Apart from the religious writings of the time, certain events transpired that brought about a general feeling of apocalyptic doom. The arrival of Islam to the Iberian Peninsula in 711 and the establishment of the Caliphate of Córdoba in 912 had marked important turning points in the history of European Christianity, but three other events in particular led Christians to view the Muslims as the forces of the Antichrist in the Early and Central Middle Ages: the sacking of the first basilica of St. Peter's in Rome in 846, Al-Mansur's attack on Santiago de Compostela in 997, and the destruction of the Holy Sepulchre by Al-Hakim's forces in 1009. Each of these events had a tremendous impact on Christianity, for all were important centres of pilgrimage to which the faithful travelled in penitence or to pray for their particular needs.[37] All had been locations of significant activity in the first years of Christianity: Jerusalem, on whose outskirts Jesus had been crucified and from which the Apostles had been sent into the world; Rome, the ancient pagan city that had been converted to Christianity and in which the Apostle Peter had been crucified, which later became the Holy See for all of Christianity; and Santiago de Compostela as the final resting place for Saint James, whose remains had been discovered there in the ninth century. The destruction of these sacred places struck a blow to Christianity that would later contribute to Pope Urban II's proclamation of the First Crusade in 1095 and to the admission of Spain to the crusading efforts in 1123.

In the summer of 997 the illegitimate ruler of the Caliphate of Córdoba, Muhammad ibn 'Amir ("Al-Mansur") made his way north to the territories of Galicia where he oversaw numerous attacks on the Christian populations of that area. Having made forty-seven attacks already, Al-Mansur led his men on what has been called a "jihad for domestic consumption" in order to turn Santiago into a Muslim stronghold from which further attacks on the northern territories could be launched.[38] In the course of the campaign against Santiago, Al-Mansur ordered the bells of the cathedral taken down and dragged back to Córdoba by Christian prisoners-of-war. Once in the caliphate's capital, the bells were made into decorative lamps for the new mosque. Blanks points out that "by removing (and silencing) the bells, al-Mansur opened public aural space for the call to prayer; by displaying them in Córdoba, he proclaimed his status as Muslim hero."[39] Due to the cruelty attributed to Al-Mansur and the large number of violent attacks he made on Christian villages of the central and northern regions of Spain, he came to be known as one of the primary agents of the Antichrist, with Córdoba "portrayed as the evil symbol of both wealth and heathenism."[40] From this point on in some of the copies of the Beatus *Commentaries on the Apocalypse*, the Whore of Babylon is depicted reclined on stacked cushions, in the Arabian style, and the feast of Balshazzar from the commentaries on the Old Testament book of Daniel is depicted as taking place beneath a red and white horseshoe arch that many would naturally associate with the architectural design of the Great Mosque of Córdoba.

The other two events parallel the destruction of Al-Mansor in Spain. Chronicles of the ninth century tell us that the church of St. Peter in Rome had suffered a similar fate at the hands of the Aghlabid rulers of Sicily. In 846 the church and its surroundings were completely sacked by the armies of this ruling family, only to be attacked yet again in 875 after a short rebuilding project. With the second attack Arab armies were able to take control of the regions just north of Rome, which they held until their defeat in 915. One can only imagine what this meant to Christians everywhere: the ecclesiastic center of Christianity had been taken over by the perceived Antichrist, which meant that the battle of Armageddon would soon be approaching. Even more, the destruction of the Holy Sepulchre in Jerusalem in the year 1009 caused widespread panic. In Blanks' opinion, this was the one event above all others that was seen by contemporary commentators to link the Muslims to the Apocalypse:

> In 1009 the Fatimid Caliph al-Hakim ordered the total destruction of the Holy Sepulcher in Jerusalem. If there was one event in the early Middle Ages that linked the Saracens to Apocalypticism, this was it. In his youth, Abbo of Fleury had heard a preacher in Paris promise the end of the world in the year 1000 and nothing happened — ten years later, the Apocalypse spoke. The destruction of the Holy Sepulcher was the portentous event that seemed to liberate suppressed millennial fears.[41]

Rudolfus Glaber, a Cluniac monk of the time, reports in his *Historiarum libri quinque* that, though the destruction took place on the orders of the Fatimid Caliph Al-Hakim, the actual cause lay in the deceptive nature of the Jews who lived in the Frankish regions of Orléans. Out of jealousy at the large numbers of pilgrims travelling to Jerusalem, those Jews had concocted a lie and had it sent to Al-Hakim: according to them, the Christians were secretly planning an attack on the caliphate during which Al-Hakim would be deposed as ruler. The only way to subvert such an attack would be for the "Prince of Babylon" to destroy the Holy Sepulchre. This destruction led Ademar of Chabannes, another monastic writer of the time, to connect the *rex Babilonius* (Al-Hakim) to the Antichrist, and the destruction of the temple to the persecution of the Christians that would take place in the last days. For this writer and preacher, the Muslims were to be seen as the primary sources of evil, with the Jews as their helpers; only by eradicating them could the Seventh Age of peace on earth be established.

Conclusions

This was the religious and social environment in which Beatus of Liébana's *Commentaria in Apocalipsin* were copied and distributed — an environment in which the Muslim (and Jewish) "other" was seen as the force of evil working against Christianity in the same manner in which the Antichrist would perpetuate deceit and destruction in the last days before Christ's second coming. It should be of no surprise that Beatus's text was copied and illustrated in such large numbers in the tenth, eleventh, and twelfth centuries, for both religious and laity alike during this time saw in the "infidel" invasions and takeovers the spiritual war described in the biblical Revelation. Likewise, it should come as no surprise that the *Spanish* monasteries in particular would produce so many copies of a commentary on that book, for the prolonged presence of Islam in Spain placed the Iberian Christians at the forefront of the Crusades against the opposing religion. Their own reconquest of lands taken over by the invading Berbers and Arabs became for them a crucial part of Christianity's battle against the Antichrist. The protection of the shrine at Santiago de Compostela as a place of Christian pilgrimage, and the recovery of Iberia for Christianity with the purpose of regaining the favour of God that the Visigothic kings had lost, created in Spain an eschatological environment in which the end was perceived as near. It was, however, a welcomed end inasmuch as it would bring Christian victory over evil and the establishment of God's kingdom as pictorially depicted in the Beatus illustrations.

NOTES

1. I would like to thank Vicente Cantarino and Louise Goodman for their comments and suggestions regarding both the content and the structure of this essay. Their help has proven invaluable to me.

2. Although the Muslim Kingdom of Granada was conquered by the Catholic Monarchs Fernando of Aragon and Isabel of Castile in 1492, the Muslim presence lingered on for several more years, secretly in many places.

3. Joaquín González Echegaray believes that we can add at least another six documents to the list of those comprising the Beatus family: "The number of copies that today constitute the series of Beatos is thirty-four, and to those we can add at least another half dozen copies, now lost, but of whose existence in libraries, until relatively recent times, we have had faithful historical evidence." Joaquín González Echegaray, Alberto del Campo, and Leslie Freeman, eds. *Obras Completas de Beato de Liébana* (Madrid: Biblioteca de Autores Cristianos, 1995), XXV–XXXIII. Author's translation. Unless marked otherwise, all subsequent translations are the author's.

4. Jaime Marqués Casanovas. "Beatus of Liébana." Part II of the introductory comments to *Sancti Beati in Apocalipsin Codex Gerundensis* (Oltun in Helvetia: Urs Graf, 1962) 41.

5. For a discussion of Alcuin of York's correspondence with Beatus, as well as his role in the Adoptionist heresy, see Marcelino Menéndez y Pelayo, *Historia de los Heterodoxos*, vol. 1. (Madrid: Biblioteca de Autores Cristianos, 1956) 355–387. Luis Vázquez de Parga supposes the letter from Alcuin to Beatus had been written in either 799 or 800. "Beato y el ambiente cultural de su época" in *Actas del Simposio para el Estudio de los Códices del "Comentario al Apocalipsis" de Beato de Liébana* (Madrid: Joyas Gráficas, 1978) 39–40.

6. Enrique Flórez, *España Sagrada: Theatro geográphico-histórico de la iglesia de España XI* (Madrid: Rodríguez, 1908) 120, 127.

7. The two extant copies of this manuscript are housed in the Biblioteca Nacional (Madrid) and the Bibliothèque Nationale (Paris).

8. The codex of the Real Academia de la Historia was made from this manuscript.

9. This version contains the added commentary on the Old Testament book of Daniel by Saint Jerome, following the commentary on the Apocalypse.

10. "[...] no positive argument has been found that directs us to the author of the hymn: it is not very possible that Beatus of Liébana composed it, but if we try to substitute this name with another, we find none other to use." Manuel Díaz y Díaz, *De Isidoro al siglo XI: Ocho estudios sobre la vida literaria peninsular* (Barcelona, El Albir, 1976) 260–261.

11. Antoni Cagigós Soro, *The Beatus of La Seu d'Urgell and All Its Miniatures* (La Seu d'Urgell: Museu Diocesà, 2001) 11.

12. The Migetian heresy, named for the Spanish preacher Migetius, is known for its development of an unorthodox Trinitarian belief: the Old Testament David was to be considered the first person of the Trinity, the Eternal Father from whom the line of Jesus had sprung; since Jesus had descended from David in human form (*qui factus est de semine David secundum carnem*), only in human form did He constitute the second person of the Trinity; the third person, the Holy Spirit, found its being in the person of Saint Paul since Jesus had commissioned him to teach the truth (*Spiritus qui a Patre meo procedit, ille vos docebit omnem veritatem*). Migetius's notion of the Holy Trinity lacked the mystic nature with which the Church had imbued it, thus turning each of the three persons into mere human symbols of the concepts of eternity (David), sacrifice (Jesus), and word (Paul). See Menéndez y Pelayo, *Historia de los Heterodoxos*, 353–354.

13. Menéndez y Pelayo, *Historia de los Heterodoxos* and Heinrich Denzinger, *Enchirid-*

ion symbolorum, definitionum et declarationum de rebus fidei et morum (Freiburg: Herder, 1921).

14. Cesar Dubler, "Antecedents of the Age of Beatus of Liébana" in *Sancti Beati in Apocalipsin Codex Gerundensis* (Oltun in Helvetia: Urs Graf, 1962) 19.

15. Jaime Marqués Casanovas, "Beatus of Liébana," 41.

16. Elipandus of Toledo, "Apologeticum I," paragraph 43, in Beato de Liébana, *Obras completas,* 742.

17. *Ibid.*

18. Matthew 24:36 states that "of that day and hour no one knows, neither the angels of heaven, nor the Son, but the Father alone."

19. "Regarding the day we read that, just as our Lord rose from the dead on a Sunday, we also hope to rise in the last age on a Sunday." Beato de Liébana, 378–380.

20. See Juan Gil, "Los terrores del año 800," in *Actas del Simposio para el Estudio de los Códices del "Comentario al Apocalipsis" de Beato de Liébana.* vol. 1 (Madrid: Joyas Gráficas, 1978) 222–223, for a discussion of this anecdote and its possible exaggeration on the part of Elipandus.

21. Beato de Liébana, 376–378.

22. Beato de Liébana, 380.

23. Jean Leclercq gives a concise description of biblical exegesis in both medieval and modern monasticism in his *The Love of Learning and the Desire for God: a Study in Monastic Culture.* Catharine Misrahi, trans. (New York: Fordham University Press, 1982). In his "Narrative and Illumination in the Beatus Apocalypse," Kenneth Steinhauser explains how the Beatus texts were used as both *lectio divina* as well as material for sermons and polemical invective. See *Catholic Historical Review* 81 (1995): 185–210. Likewise, Mireille Mentré outlines the importance of the apocalypse and, in particular, the Beatus manuscripts to the spiritual life of both the religious and the laity during the Spanish Middle Ages in *El estilo mozárabe* (Madrid: Encuentro, 1994) 237–252.

24. Laura Smoller explains, for example, how medieval Parisian scholars used the astronomical tables of thirteenth-century Castilian King Alfonso X to predict the world's end somewhere between 1750 and 1801. See her "The Alfonsine Tables and the End of the World: Astrology and Apocalyptic Calculation in the Later Middle Ages" in *The Devil, Heresy, and Witchcraft in the Middle Ages: Essays in Honor of Jeffrey B. Russell.* Alberto Ferreiro, ed. (Leiden: Brill, 1998) 211–240. See also Adela Yarbro Collins, *Cosmology and Eschatology in Jewish and Christian Apocalypticism* (Leiden: Brill, 1996). For commentary on the many uses of magic in the Middle Ages, including the prediction of future and apocalyptic events, I refer the reader to Richard Kieckhefer's *Magic in the Middle Ages* (Cambridge, UK: Cambridge University Press, 1989).

25. Joaquín Yarza Luaces, *Beato de Liébana: Manuscritos iluminados* (Barcelona, Moleiro, 1998) 50.

26. Speaking of the northern kingdoms of Spain during the early Reconquest, Stanley Payne states that "[u]p until the eleventh century, the Muslim population of the Christian states was small, consisting exclusively of prisoners carried back to the north. They were reduced to semislave status but were also more apt than not to be converted to Christianity [...] In the more settled areas, particularly Galicia, captured Muslims were frequently absorbed by the local society within a generation or two. No major centers of Muslim population were captured during the first three centuries of the Reconquest; most Muslims in the path of Christian advance withdrew, and only a comparative few were seized. Thus in the early Middle Ages they formed no ethno-religious bloc in the north." See *A History of Spain and Portugal,* 2 vols. (Madison: University of Wisconsin, 1973) 47–48. Likewise, John Williams tells us that "[n]ot long before Beatus composed his commentary, John of Damascus (d. ca. 749), in a Christian territory occupied by Muslims at

the other end of the Mediterranean, included Islam in his catalog of Christian heresies [...] Islam, poorly known as it was, would have been seen in the peninsula in Beatus's era as a heresy, not an antagonistic religion. See "Purpose and Imagery in the Apocalypse Commentary of Beatus of Liébana" in Richard Emmerson and Bernard McGinn, eds. *The Apocalypse in the Middle Ages* (Ithaca, NY: Cornell University Press, 1992) 227. As Williams goes on to discuss, it is not until the following century that Islam gains the apocalyptic reputation given by the Christian polemic writers.

27. "But the fact that the Latin documentation of eighth-century Spain as a whole is practically bereft of references to Islam as a religious phenomenon suggests that Beatus may simply not have regarded Islam as the kind of challenge to the peninsular church that would merit apocalyptic speculation [...] there are real questions as to the religio-cultural status of the men who comprised the invading armies. How Muslim could they have been, given that the bulk of their members were ethnically Berbers who had been brought under Arab domination only a few short years before? What did it mean to be a Muslim anyway at a time when the jurists in the East were still engaged in the process of defining precisely what an Islamic society should or could be? [...] the conquered peoples of Spain did not immediately conceive of the invaders from Morocco in religious terms. The original set-tlement of Arabs and Berbers was simply too sparse and, as a result, too militarily inse-cure to have any major immediate impact on the daily lives of the vastly larger Christian population." "Muhammad as Antichrist in Ninth-Century Córdoba." Mark Meyerson and Edward English, eds. *Christians, Muslims, and Jews in Medieval and Early Modern Spain: Interaction and Cultural Exchange* (Notre Dame, IN: University of Notre Dame, 1999) 4.

28. Williams, "Purpose and Imagery," 225.

29. Angus Mackay, "The Late Middle Ages: 1250–1500" in Raymond Carr, ed. *Spain: A History* (Oxford, UK: Oxford University Press, 2000) 92.

30. For a concise survey of anti–Islamic Christian writings of the period, see Vicente Cantarino, "Notas para la polémica contra el Islam en España," *Spanien und der Orient in Frühen und Hohen Mitterlater* (Mainz: Verlag Philipp von Zabern, 1991) 126–141. See also Jacinto Lozano Escribano and Lucinio Anaya Acebes, *Literatura apocalíptica cristiana (hasta el año 1000)* (Madrid: Polifemo, 2002).

31. Cantarino, "Notas para la polémica contra el Islam en España," 127–128.

32. Wolf, "Muhammad as Antichrist in Ninth-Century Córdoba," 6.

33. Dominique Iogna-Pratt tells us that Peter the Venerable ordered the Koran trans-lated "to enable him to refute Muhammad's sectaries in his *Contra sectam Sarracenorum.*" *Order and Exclusion: Cluny and Christendom Face Heresy, Judaism, and Islam (1000–1150)* (Ithaca, NY: Cornell University Press, 1998) 138.

34. Quoted in Iogna-Pratt, *Order and Exclusion,* 340.

35. Joachim de Fiore, *Expositio in Apocalypsin* (Frankfurt: Minerva, 1964). Facsimile edition published in Venice in 1527 by F. Bindoni and M. Pasini.

36. Richard W. Southern, *Western Views of Islam in the Middle Ages* (Cambridge, MA: Harvard University Press, 1962) 40–41.

37. David Blanks makes a very interesting point when he says that "[a]t the turn of the first millennium, Latin Christendom's greatest pilgrimage centers were anything but cen-tral; on the contrary, Compostela, Rome, and Jerusalem were situated on the cultural and military periphery. This made for good penance. The distance and difficulty involved in these pilgrimages accounted, at least in part, for their popularity. From an alternative per-spective, however, the shrines of these cities were located the center of the Christian spir-itual compass. Hence, cartographers placed Jerusalem at the center of the earth, and pilgrimage narratives nearly always describe the 'going to' and hardly ever the 'coming back.'" David Blanks, "Islam and the West in the Age of the Pilgrim." *The Year 1000: Reli-*

gious and Social Response to the Turning of the First Millennium (New York: Palgrave Macmillan, 2002) 257.
  38. Blanks, "Islam and the West in the Age of the Pilgrim," 258.
  39. *Ibid.*
  40. James Reston, *The Last Apocalypse* (New York: Anchor, 1998) 137.
  41. Blanks, "Islam and the West in the Age of the Pilgrim," 260.

WORKS CITED

Blanks, David. "Islam and the West in the Age of the Pilgrim" in *The Year 1000: Religious and Social Response to the Turning of the First Millennium.* New York: Palgrave Macmillan, 2002: 257–271.

Cagigós Soro, Antoni. *The Beatus of La Seu d'Urgell and All Its Miniatures.* La Seu d'Urgell: Museu Diocesà, 2001.

Cantarino, Vicente. "Notas para la polémica contra el Islam en España," in *Spanien und der Orient in Frühen und Hohen Mitteralter.* Mainz: Verlag Philipp von Zabern, 1991: 126–141.

Denzinger, Heinrich. *Enchiridion symbolorum, definitionum et declarationum de rebus fidei et morum.* Freiburg: Herder, 1921.

Díaz y Díaz, Manuel. *De Isidoro al siglo XI: Ocho estudios sobre la vida literaria peninsular.* Barcelona: El Albir, 1976.

Dubler, Cesar. "Antecedents of the Age of Beatus of Liébana" in *Sancti Beati in Apocalipsin Codex Gerundensis.* Oltun in Helvetia: Urs Graf, 1962.

de Fiore, Joachime. *Expositio in Apocalypsin.* Frankfurt: Minerva, 1964. Facsimile edition. Published in Venice in 1527 by F. Bindoni and M. Pasini.

Flórez, Enrique. *España Sagrada: Theatro geográphico-histórico de la iglesia de España XI.* Madrid: Rodríguez, 1908.

Gil, Juan. "Los terrores del año 800," in *Actas del Simposio para el Estudio de los Códices del "Comentario al Apocalipsis" de Beato de Liébana,* vol. 1. Madrid: Joyas Gráficas, 1978: 215–247.

Iogna-Pratt, Dominique. *Order and Exclusion: Cluny and Christendom Face Heresy, Judaism, and Islam (1000–1150).* Ithaca, NY: Cornell University Press, 1998.

Kieckhefer, Richard. *Magic in the Middle Ages.* Cambridge, UK: Cambridge University Press, 1989.

Leclerq, Jean. *The Love of Learning and the Desire for God: A Study in Monastic Culture.* Catharine Misrahi, trans. New York: Fordham University Press, 1982.

Liébana, Beato de. *Obras completas de Beato de Liébana.* Joaquín González Echegaray, Albeto del Campo, and Leslie Freeman, eds. Madrid: Biblioteca de Autores Cristianos, 1995.

Lozano Escribano, Jacinto, and Lucinio Anaya Acebes. *Literatura apocalíptica cristiana (hasta el año 1000).* Madrid: Polifemo, 2002.

Mackay, Angus. "The Late Middle Ages: 1250–1500" in *Spain: A History.* Raymond Carr, ed. Oxford, UK: Oxford University Press, 2000: 90–115.

Marqués Casanovas, Jaime. "Beatus of Liébana" in *Sancti Beati in Apocalipsin Codex Gerundensis.* Oltun in Helvetia: Urs Graf, 1962.

Menéndez y Pelayo, Marcelino. *Historia de los Heterodoxos,* vol. 1. Madrid: Biblioteca de Autores Cristianos, 1956.

Mentré, Mireille. *El estilo mozárabe.* Madrid: Encuentro, 1994.

Payne, Stanley. *A History of Spain and Portugal,* 2 vols., Madison: University of Wisconsin, 1973.

Reston, James. *The Last Apocalypse.* New York: Anchor, 1998.

Smoller, Laura. "The Alfonsine Tables and the End of the World: Astrology and Apocalyptic Calculation in the Later Middle Ages" in *The Devil, Heresy, and Witchcraft in the Middle Ages: Essays in Honor of Jeffrey B. Russell*. Alberto Ferreiro, ed. Leiden: Brill, 1998: 211–240.

Southern, Richard W. *Western Views of Islam in the Middle Ages*. Cambridge, MA: Harvard University Press, 1962.

Steinhauser, Kenneth. "Narrative and Illumination in the Beatus Apocalypse." *Catholic Historical Review* 81 (1995): 185–210.

Vázquez de Parga, Luis. "Beato y el ambiente cultural de su época" in *Actas del Simposio para el Estudio de los Códices del "Comentario al Apocalipsis" de Beato de Liébana*. Madrid: Joyas Gráficas, 1978: 33–45.

Williams, John. "Purpose and Imagery in the Apocalypse Commentary of Beatus of Liébana" in *The Apocalypse in the Middle Ages*. Richard Emmerson and Bernard McGinn, eds. Ithaca, NY: Cornell University Press, 1992: 217–233.

Wolf, Kenneth Baxter. "Muhammad as Antichrist in Ninth-Century Córdoba" in *Christians, Muslims, and Jews in Medieval and Early Modern Spain: Interaction and Cultural Exchange*. Mark Meyerson and Edward English, eds. Notre Dame, IN: University of Notre Dame Press, 1999: 3–19.

Yarbro Collins, Adela. *Cosmology and Eschatology in Jewish and Christian Apocalypticism*. Leiden: Brill, 1996.

Yarza Luaces, Joaquín. *Beato de Liébana: Manuscritos iluminados*. Barcelona: Moleiro, 1998.

"Seeing" the Apocalyptic City in the Fourteenth Century

Tessa Morrison

Introduction

In the thirteenth and fourteenth century the cathedral was the height of European achievement; it embodied the whole of Christian knowledge and attempted to mimic the divine in its architecture.[1] It was the ritual, spiritual and economic, as well as the physical, center of the city.

The cathedral was intended to be an image of heaven both mystically and liturgically. The dedication ritual of the cathedral explicitly related to the vision of the New Jerusalem, as described by John the Divine in the Book of Revelation.[2] The liturgy at Saint Denis for the church dedication on the vigil of the feast began:

> The Lord has sanctified His tabernacle; for this is the house of God, in which His name will be invoked, as it is written: and my name will be there says the Lord.

Followed by,

> I saw the holy city, New Jerusalem, coming down from heaven from God made ready as bride adorned for her husband (Revelation 21.2).[3]

This image of the descending New Jerusalem included in the dedication introduced the symbolic relationship between the Divine New Jerusalem and the earthly cathedral. The New Jerusalem is described in Revelation as being clear as crystal; it was cubic in shape with its length, height and width all being equal — twelve thousand furlongs; it had walls of a hundred and forty-four cubits with twelve gates, three on each side, and each gate was carved from a pearl. The foundations of the city were garnished with gems, "The first foundation was jasper; the second, sapphire; the third, a chalcedony; the fourth, an emerald; the fifth, sardonyx; the sixth, sardius; the seventh, chrysolite; the eighth, beryl; ninth, a topaz; the tenth, a chrysoprasus; the eleventh, a jacinth; the twelfth, an amethyst." The streets were made of "pure gold."[4] Both John the Divine's economy of words and his measurements in his description gave no end of problems to later authors and illustrators. Twelve thousand furlongs equals fifteen hundred miles.[5] The walls of this massive city were a hundred and forty-four cubits, (approximately two hundred and sixteen feet).[6] However, it is not stated whether this is the height or the width. Both would appear to be unsatisfactory; the height would seem inadequate for a city of twelve thousand furlongs high, and if the walls were hundred and forty-four cubits wide, the foundation would be inadequate. The early modern scientist and exegete, Isaac Newton, considered the hundred and forty-four cubits to be the volume of the walls, but that would make the walls twelve cubits in height. This would be even more disproportionate for a city of twelve thousand furlongs.[7] It is perhaps likely that these measurements were picked for their numerical quality rather than their architectural features and aesthetic qualities. Despite the problems with the plan of this New Jerusalem, it is the ultimate utopian city; the old city had passed away and a new city descended from heaven.[8]

The cubic shape, the disproportions and the exposed foundations in the description left a visual challenge to artists throughout subsequent eras. Another problem in the description was that John saw no temple within the New Jerusalem.[9] This left artists with a dilemma; if the cathedral was to be an image of heaven but there was no temple in the New Jerusalem, then how would the New Jerusalem be depicted? Generally, most of the features described by John were totally ignored or loosely reinterpreted by the medieval artists. In some of the earlier depictions of the city, symmetry, although not a cube, dominated the design, with the twelve gates represented. There are images from the tenth and eleventh centuries of the New Jerusalem that are seen at a bird's eye view as a symmetrical design that had elaborate patterned gates with key-hole arches and turrets.[10] The same style of a bird's eye view of the New Jerusalem is depicted with heavily patterned round arches and turrets, which reveal an architectural change.[11] There are many images of the City that display a round symmetrical design, with some as early as the ninth and tenth century being a simple set of rings with twelve divisions marking the gates.[12] Others are circular designs from the twelfth to the fourteenth century that are ornate with towers, turrets and the twelve gates stemming from the center.[13] Many other images of the City portray it from one side; the buildings have towers, turrets and are surrounded by elaborate fortifications.[14] Other images do not portray the city at all and depict God and the Lamb with the twenty-four elders or the tree of life.[15] The numerous images of the New Jerusalem reveal architectural, sartorial, and stylistic changes, and there is little continuity of design, shape, or features. Generally, the most dominant feature of the city in these designs is the walls. However, in John's description the walls are at most 0.0000273 percent of the height of the city; the walls would be a nearly invisible border much like a thin pencil line at the bottom of the cube.[16] Moreover, the image of the City, despite its description, more often than not completely contradicts the text that it is representing. The medieval artists dealt with the problems of John's description, or lack of description, by ignoring the main features and reinterpreting the principle elements of the design.

However, there is one feature from John's description that captured the imagination of the medieval artists and poets — the gems. John described the gems as single stones. Each foundation was of a massive individual stone and each of the gates was a single gigantic pearl. However, medieval artists depicted these gems as patterns of sets of stones.[17] Abbot Suger had the altar of Saint Denis studded with the twelve gems of the foundations and the pearls of the gates of the New Jerusalem, which he believed had magical properties that would transport him to a higher world, from the material world to the immaterial world. He claimed

> To those who know the properties of precious stones it becomes evident, to their utter astonishment, that none is absent from the number of these, but that they abound most copiously. Thus, when — out of my delight in the beauty of the house of God — the loveliness of the many-colored gems has called me away from external cares, and worthy meditation has induced me to reflect, transferring that which is material to that which is immaterial, on the diversity of the sacred virtues: then it seems to me that I see myself dwelling, as it were, in some strange region of the universe which neither exists entirely in the slime of the earth nor entirely in the purity of Heaven; and that, by the grace God, I can be transported from this inferior to that higher world in an anagogical manner.[18]

Micro-architecture in the form of shires and caskets mimicking the New Jerusalem were covered in these same gems.[19] These shires and caskets could offer the pilgrim sacred objects that could induce a transcendental experience of the beyond.[20] The aesthetic and divine quality of these gems was also praised in poetry, particularly in the Middle English poem *The Pearl*.

Pearl and the New Jerusalem

Pearl, preserved at the British Library (MS. Cotton Nero A. x), is an anonymous work dated 1360–1400.[21] The poem is divided into three parts. In the introduction a Dreamer, the narrator, loses an oriental pearl in a garden. His loss is great because the pearl was "So rounde, so reken in vche araye (So round, so perfect in every array)."[22] The Dreamer falls asleep complaining and aggrieved at his loss. In the second part of the poem the Dreamer finds himself in a magical realm where he comes to a steam paved with precious stones. Across the bank of this stream is a pure maiden, lavishly dressed in white and decked with pearls. The Dreamer identifies her with the lost pearl that he grieved for and she in turn addresses him as her jeweler, but she rebukes him for his grief. She counsels him that if he wants to join her across the stream, which is a place of peace and serenity, to have patience and faith. She tells the Dreamer that she is one of the brides of Christ and dwells in the New Jerusalem, a pure and divine City. The Dreamer longs to see the New Jerusalem and the maiden allows him to briefly gaze upon the City; but, overwhelmed by the vision of the City, he attempts to cross the stream to enter the City and in his attempt he breaks the dream and he awakens in the garden.

The sumptuous imagery of the poem has been well documented, and the symbolism of the colors and the gems has also been recognized.[23] However, a neglected area of the poem is the description of the City, the New Jerusalem. It has often been passed over as being a paraphrase of the description in Revelation. Many books of critical essays only mention it in passing and do not single it out for any special attention.[24] Although the description is based upon Revelation, it goes beyond John's economy of words and brings the full richness of medieval artistry to the image of the City.

Umberto Eco claimed that an important aspect of medieval aesthetics was people's spontaneous reaction to and love of color and light. He noted that in medieval poetry,

> colors were always decisive, unequivocal: grass was green, blood red, milk snowy white. There were superlatives for every color ... and while a color might have many shades, it was never allowed to fade and blur into shadows. Medieval miniatures testify to this love of integral color, to the vivacity of chromatic combinations.[25]

The poet of *Pearl* rendered the City in color and light.

> Þe borȝ watȝ al of brende golde bryȝt,
> As glemande glas burnist broun,
> Wyth gentyl gemmeȝ an-vnder pyȝt
> (The city was all of pure, shining gold,
> Like gleaming crystal burnished bright,
> With precious jewels set beneath).[26]

The poet describes the foundations not just as a listing, but singles out the gems for more description: jasper "lowest hemme (glistened green)"; chalcedony "purly pale (translucently paled)"; emerald "so grene of scale (so green of scale)"; beryl "cler & quyt (clear and white)"; topaz "twi-hued" and amethyst "þe gentyleste in vch a plyt, / De amatyst purpre with ynde blente (the noblest of all the gems amethyst purple with blue blent)." The walls of jasper glistened like "glayre,"[27] which is a preparation made of eggs whites for tempering pigments. With the burnished gold and the binding of brightly colored pigments, the poet appears to be describing a painted image.

The poet emphasizes the pictorial image of the city. Barbara Nolan claims that "his descriptions resemble those of thirteenth and fourteenth century illuminators of the Apocalypse."[28] Muriel A. Whitaker takes this idea further and examines thirty-five individual Apocalypse manuscripts in order to assess their influence on the *Pearl*-poet.[29] She claims that the language of the illuminator and the fact that the poet introduced the motifs of Revelation in a different order to the Vulgate Scripture may indicate pictorial sources influenced the *Pearl*-poet, but it is not possible to say which manuscript was the main source.[30] However, hints in *Pearl* strongly suggest two architectural influences: the stained glass windows of the Gothic cathedrals and the geometry of the architectural depictions in the Apocalypse manuscripts.

The Luminous Quality of the New Jerusalem in *Pearl*

The poet built up the image of the City as a mosaic of luminous gems. The City "Þat schyrrer þen sunne schafte3 schon (that shone with rays brighter than the sun)," was burnished bright as gleaming glass with glorious gems "set" beneath it. The gems have a luminous and glass-like quality; jasper glistened green, chalcedony was translucently paled and beryl was clear and white. This mosaic was of sets of luminous gems; it is a description that is similar to a stained glass window. The art of *Pearl* is high Gothic. The Gothic cathedral was designed to be an image of heaven and was illuminated by large stained glass windows. "The Gothic wall seems to be porous: light filters through it, permeating it, merging with it, transfiguring it."[31] In the combination of brilliant color and brilliance of light, Gothic stained glass work developed into a high art form that was accessible to the public. Abbot Suger was in awe of this uninterrupted translucent wall at the Abbey cathedral at Saint Denis and he wrote:

> The church shines with its middle part brightened.
> For bright is that which is brightly coupled with the bright,
> And bright is the noble edifice which is pervaded by new light.[32]

In the thirteenth century Saint Hugh, Bishop of Lincoln, praising the "circular radiance" of the two rose windows in his new cathedral, claimed that,

> The double majesty of the windows displays shining riddles
> Before men's eyes; it is emblazoned with the citizens of the
>   Heavenly City,
> And the arms with which they overcome the tyrant of Hell.[33]

Light emanated throughout the upper chapel of the western bays of the cathedral at Saint Denis and Suger claimed that it was "most beautiful and worthy to be the dwelling of angels."[34] Saint Bernard may have famously disapproved of art because he felt that it was a distraction from the pure message, yet he was struck by the divine beauty and purity of the transparent walls.[35] He claimed that the light had a divine quality, "As pure ray enters a glass window and emerges unspoiled, but has acquired the color of the glass ... the Son of God who entered the most chaste womb of the Virgin, emerged pure, but took on the form, and he clothed himself in it."[36] Within the massive and overwhelming frame of the Gothic cathedral the stained glass windows assisted in creating a space that was attempting to mimic the divine, a place worthy of the angels. The architecture of the Romanesque cathedral had marked the power and authority of the church. It also had attempted to encapsulate the description of the New Jerusalem, particularly by using the symmetry in John's description, but it was in the development of Gothic architecture that two clearly distinct architectural spaces were developed: the earthy space of the city and the "divinely" lit and symmetrical cathedral space. This illuminated cathedral created a space that was unlike any other space outside of its walls. In the Gothic cathedral there was an emphasis on two architectural features, both light and symmetric relationships of the architecture, which "conveyed an insight into the perfection of the cosmos, and a divination of the Creator."[37]

Between the twelfth and fifteenth centuries an enormous number of stained glass windows were fitted into churches and cathedrals throughout England. The cathedral walls "that had been inanimate became frames for heavenly visions, and no art, throughout the Middle Ages, had such power and prestige with the Christian congregation."[38] The narrative quality of these windows related a biblical story to the congregation through a series of luminous images. The stained glass windows were accessible to all people and were referred to as "the Bible of the Poor" since they could be "read" by the entire congregation. As Biblical "texts," they were a continuous influence in everyday lives.[39] There would be little doubt that the poet would have been familiar with the stained glass window and had "read" the illuminated Biblical stories, since this illuminated space of the cathedral was the very heart of the city.

The New Jerusalem was a mosaic of gems united together by color and light, and the poet left no doubt about its illuminated qualities. The garden, the stream and the City each are studded with gems and burnished with precious metals to various degrees. Not only does the landscape get more sumptuous as the Dreamer moves from the garden to the City, but the Dreamer's perception and perspective of the celestial world across the stream differs greatly from his perspective and description of the earthly world of the garden. Although the celestial world in *Pearl* was clearly marked with more pattern and greater intensity of light, the poet also creates a clear distinction between the earthly and the celestial world by giving them different geometrical spaces. Similar to the two distinct architectural spaces of the earthly city and the Gothic cathedral that mimicked the divine in its architecture, the poet creates two distinct poetic spaces to mark the earthly and the celestial in his poetry.

The Dreamer's Vision of the New Jerusalem

The Dreamer moves through the garden, then along the bank, moving up stream. The Maiden tells him,

> 'If I þis mote þschal vnhyde,
> Bow vp towarde þys borneȝ heued,
> & I anendeȝ þe on þis side
> Schal sve tyl þou to a hil be veued.'
> (If I this city reveal to thee,
> Bend upward toward this river's head,
> And I on this side opposite thee
> Shall follow till thou be in sight of a hill.')

And the Dreamer states,

> Þen wolde [I] no lenger byde,
> Bot lurked by launceȝso lufly leued,
> Tyl on a hyl þat I asspyed,
> & blusched on þbughe as I forth dreued.
> Byȝonde þe brok fro me warde keued
> (Then no longer would I delay,
> But stole on through the branches so beautifully leaved
> Till on a hill I espied it,
> And gazed on the city as I forward pressed.
> Beyond the brook from me low placed)[40]

From that single point on the bank of the stream the Dreamer views the New Jerusalem. He sees the foundations, the external and internal sides of each of the four walls, the streets, the lamb, God, and the Tree of Life. This is an impossible perspective, to see inside and outside from all sides, through the top and underneath from a single point. But the Dreamer's vision goes "Þurȝ woȝe & won (through wall and dwelling)."[41] The poet moves away from the Scriptures in an attempt to explain, at least, the bird's eye view and places the Dreamer at the "borneȝ heued (river's head)" and the City "Byȝonde þe brok fro me warde keued (Beyond the brook from me low placed)." In Rev-

Figure One. The Divine Architect, Bible in Vienna National Library, 2554, fol. 1. Copied from John Block Friedman, "The Architect's Compass in Creation Miniatures of the Later Middle Ages," *Traditio* XXX (1974): Figure VII (drawn by Tessa Morrison).

elation, the City is on a mountain's highest point and John is carried there, in spirit, to see the City. The Angel shows John the City as he measures the entire City, its walls and its height, its breadth, and length.[42] But the Dreamer remains in one position. This position of the Dreamer could partially explain the New Jerusalem as being depicted in a bird's eye view. However, this would not explain how the numerous angles of this very static set of images could be viewed from a single point. In Revelation, John is guided by an angel, but the Dreamer is separated from the maiden by the stream. This concept of a static image is compounded when he attempts to enter the City, but just as he charges the bank of the stream, he awakens from his dream.[43]

He is unable to move from one bank to the other, from the earthly world to the celestial world. Both worlds are divided by a spatial ambiguity — a different geometry. The world of the Dreamer and the garden has one perspective, i.e. it is perceived from one place at a time rather than from many points simultaneously, but the vision of the New Jerusalem, as described in *Pearl,* was a multi-perspective world, a geometry which is difficult to comprehend and nearly impossible to draw. Nonetheless, medieval artists and writers attempted to comprehend and to depict the celestial world of the New Jerusalem.

The Image of the New Jerusalem and the Mixed Perspectives of *Pearl*

The image of the Divine Architect who created a perfectly symmetrical universe where all things in the universe depended upon him was deeply rooted in the medieval period. The harmony of the symmetrical universe that could be constructed with a compass and straightedge was originally promulgated by Plato (429–347 BCE) in the *Timaeus* and the *Republic,* and built on by Ptolemy (c.85–161 CE) in *Almagest.* In Revelation, John "saw a new heaven and a new earth; for the first heaven and the first earth were passed away" and the New Jerusalem that descended from God was perfectly geometric.[44] The image of Creation and God with his compass and rule became intertwined with his creation of the New Jerusalem of Revelation.

As stated earlier, in the medieval period there were many different methods of depicting the New Jerusalem, from a set of twelve simple rings to elaborate symmetrical designs. Although the features of John's description are ignored by most medieval artists, the symmetry that he describes was retained in most of the images. This defined the city in terms of its designer, the Divine Architect with his compass and ruler. There are over forty surviving images of the Divine Architect wielding compass and rule from the medieval

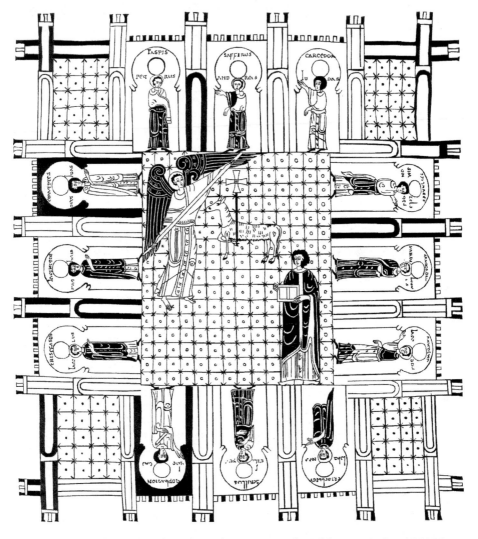

Figure Two. New Jerusalem, Facundus Beatus, 1047, Biblioteca National MS Vitrina 12-2, fol. 253v. Copied from Williams, *The Illustrated Beatus: A Corpus of the Illustrations of the Commentary on the Apocalypse, Volume One*, Plate 37 (drawn by Tessa Morrison).

period, highlighting the significance of symmetry.[45] This reverence for symmetry is echoed in the designs of the medieval cathedrals and in the images of the New Jerusalem.[46] Yet there is one style of symmetric images in particular that bears a strong resemblance to the Dreamer's vision of the City.

Examples of this style are found in the period from the eleventh to the thirteenth centuries. The style is a birds-eye view of the city as a square motif. There are three gates on each side. In the center square are depicted the lamb, the Angel and sometimes John. They are within the courtyard of the birds-eye city and are depicted at eye level with the viewer (Figure Two).[47] In a later version of this style John is placed in the corner of the image and overlaps the City motif.[48]

This style of image is complex and the city is symmetrical. It is an aerial view that is distorted with the four walls of the City lying 90° from their usual position and in the same plane as the aerial view. Each wall is lying 90° from the other, and the four walls border a square, central courtyard, which is at aerial view but at the same angle as the walls. The image of the lamb, the Angel, and occasionally John, are integrated into the one motif in the central courtyard and level view point to the viewer, which is 90° difference to the aerial view of the courtyard. This style presents an interesting dimension within the image plane. These images of the City are developed into an elaborate motif, but the City is viewed from different angles forming a complex perspective; it is possible to see the full 360° view of the exterior of the city and into the center of the interior of the city.

This square image endured and had been copied for over two hundred years. It was not just the image of the city but the entire manuscript that was copied. The architectural features of the city were styled to the audience's cultural and temporal taste of that time. The original image of this style can be found in the eleventh-century Facundus Beatus from Spain (Figure Two), which portrays key-hole arches typical of Mozarabic architecture. The twelfth century manuscript Saint-Sever from France has gates with round arches (Figure Three); these were the contemporary style of France. Yet in later copies, such as the English manuscript of the Trinity Apocalypse, the gates have pointed Gothic arches that were typical of thirteenth century England (Figure Four).[49] With the exception of the foundations, the view of the city in this image has the same angles of the city as seen by the Dreamer from the bank of the stream. The massive gems of the foundations are represented as patterns of gems in the walls of the city.

It would be wrong to expect medieval art not to have a tilted or "incorrect" perspective — mixed perspectives were often used as artistic devices. For example, at banqueting scenes with the figures seated, the table would be presented as tilted down so the contents of the table could be seen.[50] At other times, people sitting at a square table would all be presented from the front.[51] However, the complex mixed perspectives of Heavenly Jerusalem does appear to be a unique method of depicting the viewed (the city) and viewer (John and the Angel) in medieval art.

In the Apocalypse manuscripts the New Jerusalem was not the only city

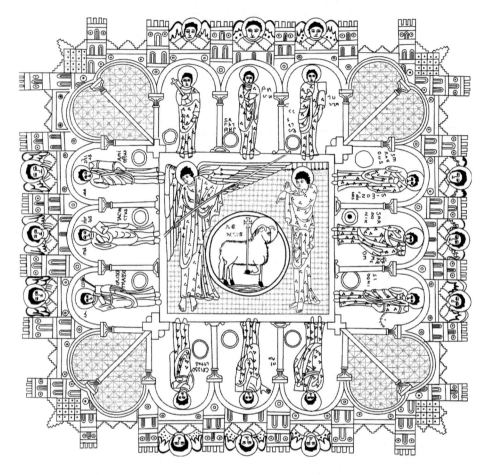

Figure Three. New Jerusalem, Beatus of Saint-Sever. Paris, Bibliothéque Nationale, MS lat 8878, ff. 207v-208. Copied from Mary Carruthers, *The Craft of Thought: Mediation, Rhetoric, and the Imaging of Images, 400–1200* (Cambridge, 2000) Plate 2 (drawn by Tessa Morrison).

to be depicted. In Revelation 18:1–20, the city of Babylon was seized and destroyed. Yet there is very little variation in the view of Babylon and the geometry of its depiction, and it is very different from the depiction of the New Jerusalem in the same manuscripts. For example, in the 1047 Apocalypse manuscript the Facundus Beatus, Babylon is depicted with one perspective which is viewed level with the viewer.[52] The city has almost bi-fold symmetry with the destroying angels above the city in the same plane (see Figure Five).[53] Compare Figure Five with the New Jerusalem from the same manuscript, Figure Four. The difference of the perspectives in the represen-

Figure Four. The New Jerusalem, Trinity College Cambridge, MS R.16.2 c.1260. Copied from Williams, *The Illustrated Beatus: A Corpus of the Illustrations of the Commentary on the Apocalypse, Volume Five* (drawn by Tessa Morrison).

tations is striking. The artist used minimal symmetry and one perspective of the earthly city while the New Jerusalem is a complex symmetrical and a multi-perspective world. The artist has used two different geometries or spaces to distinguish the earthly and the celestial. This concept of "the more the symmetry, the closer it gets to perfection" was well established by the Church Fathers.[54] The numerous medieval depictions of the Divine Architect with compass and rule along with the increase in symmetric architectural features in medieval cathedrals demonstrate that symmetry was a significant factor in depicting the divine in this period.

Conclusion

The description of the New Jerusalem in Chapter 21 of the Book of Revelation is brief and lacks any real detail. There is no one grand entrance or a single main feature for the artist to depict what would be emblematic of the New Jerusalem. In John the Divine's description, the main features were elements that cannot be seen from one angle, such as the four walls each with three gates, the twelve angels (three guarding each wall), the names of the twelve apostles at each gate and the twelve massive single gem foundations. To depict these main elements it is necessary to see from above, from below and all exterior sides of the City.

The *Pearl*-poet clearly described these features in the vision of the city; but this does not explain why the Dreamer remained in one position across the bank separated from both the city and the maiden. John's spirit was guided through the city by the Angel; however, the Dreamer could not enter the New Jerusalem. Instead, he stood at the threshold of the earthly and celestial world. When he attempted to enter this celestial world, the vision was broken. The use of geometry to define the divide between the earthly and celestial world in literature has a precedent in Dante's *Paradiso*. Dante introduced a geometric spatial ambiguity at the union of these two universes — he turned around *to* look up into the Empyrean.[55] Dante did not turn around *and* look up; if this was the case why would he have needed to turn around at all? The use of these different angles in Dante's *Paradiso* has intrigued mathematicians; for over eighty years it has been well recognized by them that the universe of the *Divina Commedia* is a four-dimensional structure.[56] This mathematics was well beyond Dante's comprehension, but his system was well-defined in the mathematics of his era; he would have been aware that to turn around *to* look up was impossible. Jeffrey Burton Russell explained this vision of Dante as a vision that, "reconfirms the view of the cosmos where up and out are better than down and in, because it is more open to the divine light."[57]

Similarly the *Pearl*-poet was not aware of the descriptive geometry of perspective that was perfected in the Renaissance. But creating these two different spaces of the earthly and the celestial with the use of visions of different angles makes the description of the celestial space more mystical and a little more mysterious. He created a multi-angled image that corresponded to the Trinity Apocalypse. Trinity Apocalypse was heavily laden with gold leaf and the image was painted with brightly colored pigments that was, among

Figure Five. The Burning of Babylon, from the Facundus Beatus 1047. Copied from Williams, *The Illustrated Beatus: A Corpus of the Illustrations of the Commentary on the Apocalypse, Volume Four*, Plate 415 (drawn by Tessa Morrison).

other manuscripts, like the poet's description of the city, as Whitaker has pointed out.[58] However, it is not in the gold and bright color where the true similarity lies — it is in the geometry.

The difference of the two architectural spaces that distinguished the Gothic cathedral from the city was defined by architectural features such as the illumination of the stained glass windows and symmetry of the architectural features. The difference of the two poetics spaces of the earthly and the celestial in *Pearl* is through radiance of the gems and an image of the city that can only be achieved with two-dimensional symmetry. The difference of the two artistic spaces of the earthly Babylon and the New Jerusalem is in their geometry. All three are an attempt to distinguish the earthly from the celestial. In the architectural, poetic and artistic spaces, the divine is distinguished by light from the architectural feature of the stained glass windows, the radiance of the gems, the pigment and gold leaf, and symmetry that is constructed with a compass and rule. All three use the tools of the Divine Architect in an attempt to illustrate the divine.

The description of the luminous mosaic-like city in the *Pearl* strongly resembles the theologian's description of the Gothic stained glass windows, and the alliance of the cathedral and the New Jerusalem would have enhanced this connection. However, the geometry in the description of the Dreamer's vision does closely match the geometry of the Trinity Apocalypse. This image was copied for over two hundred years and only three copies have survived: one from Spain, one from France and one from England. This was a widely traveled and valued image. The artists created a complicated multi-angled image in an attempt to replicate the vision of the New Jerusalem, a celestial world designed by God with his compass and ruler, and these images have become emblematic of the text. The poet of *Pearl* may have copied this spatial concept from the Trinity Apocalypse, or a similar manuscript that no longer survives, from the "divinely" lit cathedral or derived it himself from John the Divines' description. However, all constructed a geometric space that created a clear distinction between the earthly and celestial worlds, and it made the division between these worlds very mysterious.

NOTES

1. Otto von Simson, *The Gothic Cathedral: Origins of Gothic Architecture and the Medieval Concept of Order* (Princeton, NJ: Princeton University Press, 1988) 11
2. *Ibid.*, 10; Ann R. Meyer, *Medieval Allegory and the Building of the New Jerusalem* (Woodbridge, Suffolk, UK: D. S. Brewer, 2003) 80–91.
3. *Ibid.*, 81–82.
4. Revelation 21:11–21.
5. Paul S. Minear, *New Testament Apocalyptic* (Nashville, TN: Abingdon, 1981); Robert D. Russell, "A Similitude of Paradise: The City as Image of the City," in *The Iconography*

of Heaven, Clifford Davidson, ed. (Kalamazoo, MI: Medieval Institute Publications, 1994); W. Shaw Caldecott, *Solomon's Temple: Its History and Its Structure* (London: The Religious Tract Society, 1908).

   6. A cubit is approximately 18 inches (45.72 centimeters). See Caldecott, *Solomon's Temple: Its History and Its Structure,* 215.

   7. Isaac Newton, "The Day of Judgement and World to Come," in *The Religion of Isaac Newton* F.E. Manuel, ed. (Oxford, UK: Clarendon Press, 1974).

   8. Revelation 21:1.

   9. Revelation 21:22.

   10. "Heavenly Jerusalem," Biblioteca Nacional Madrid, MS Vitr 14–2, fol. 253v. Reproductions of this can be seen in Mary Carruthers, *The Craft of Thought: Meditation, Rhetoric, and the Making of Images, 400–1200* (Cambridge, UK: Cambridge University Press, 2000) Plate 3; Hana Sedinova, "The Precious Stones of Heavenly Jerusalem in the Medieval Book Illustration and their Comparison with the Wall Incrustation in St. Wenceslas Chapel," *Artibus et Historiae* 21, no. 41 (2000) 35 and "Heavenly Jerusalem," The Pierpont Morgan Library, New York, MS M. 644, fol. 222v. Reproductions of this can be seen in Sedinova, "The Precious Stones of Heavenly Jerusalem in the Medieval Book Illustration and their Comparison with the Wall Incrustation in St. Wenceslas Chapel," 32.

   11. The Heavenly City, Bibliothèque Nationale, MS lat. 8878, ff. 207v208. Reproductions of this can be seen in Carruthers, *The Craft of Thought: Mediation, Rhetoric, and the Making of Images, 400–1200,* plate 2.

   12. Bibliothèque Municipale Valenciennes, MS, 99 fol. 38r, and Bibliothèque Nationale Paris MS. Nouv. Acq lat 1132 fol. 33r; Sedinova, "The Precious Stones of Heavenly Jerusalem in the Medieval Book Illustration and their Comparison with the Wall Incrustation in St. Wenceslas Chapel," 38.

   13. Heavenly Jerusalem, Narodni knihovna, Praha, MS. XXIII C 124 (Velisias's) fol 168v. Reproduction of this can be seen in Sedinova, "The Precious Stones of Heavenly Jerusalem in the Medieval Book Illustration and their Comparison with the Wall Incrustation in St. Wenceslas Chapel," 40; Heavenly Jerusalem Bilbliothèque Paris, MS. Lat 8865 fol 42v. Reproduction of this can be seen in Sedinova, "The Precious Stones of Heavenly Jerusalem in the Medieval Book Illustration and their Comparison with the Wall Incrustation in St. Wenceslas Chapel," 41; Frontispiece, Berlin Staatsbibliothek, MS. Ham. 390. Reproduction of this can be seen in Helen J. Dow, "The Rose-Window," *Journal of Warburg and Courtauld Institutes* 20, no. 3/4 (1957): plate 15.

   14. Numerous examples of these can be seen in Muriel A. Whitaker, "'Pearl' and some Illustrated Apocalypse Manuscripts," *Viator: Medieval and Renaissance Studies* 12 (1981); Sedinova, "The Precious Stones of Heavenly Jerusalem in the Medieval Book Illustration and their Comparison with the Wall Incrustation in St. Wenceslas Chapel"; Francois Bucher, "Micro-Architecture as the 'Idea' of Gothic Theory and Style," *Gesta* 15, no. 1/2 (1976).

   15. Examples are Oxford, Bodleian Library MS Douce 180 fol 12; London, British Library MS Royal 19 B. xv fol 18. For reproductions of these and others of the same style see Whitaker, "'Pearl' and some Illustrated Apocalypse Manuscripts."

   16. Figure is determined by dividing the height of the walls by the height of the city.

   17. Some examples are "Jerusalem" and "Bethlehem" mosaic, Basilica di Santa Prassede, Rome, 9th century; "Heavenly Jerusalem" The British Library, London MS. Add 47672, fol. 473r, 13th–14th century.

   18. Suger, Abbot of Saint Denis, "De Administratione," in Erwin Panofsky, trans., *Abbot Suger* (Princeton, NJ: Princeton University Press, 1948) 61.

   19. Bucher, "Micro-Architecture as the 'Idea' of Gothic Theory and Style."

20. *Ibid.*, p.71

21. Anonymous, *The Pearl*, Edward Vasta, trans. (Notre Dame, IN: University of Notre Dame Press, 1961) xv.

22. Anonymous, *The Pearl,* 5.

23. See Wendell Stacy Johnson, "The Imagery and Diction of the Pearl: Toward an Interpretation," *A Journal of English Literary History* 20, (September 1953) 161–180; John Conley, ed. *The Middle English Pearl: Critical Essays* (Notre Dame, IN: University of Notre Dame Press, 1970). See also Robert J Blanch, "Precious Metal and Gem Symbolism in Pearl," in *Sir Gawain and Pearl: Critical Essay*, Robert J Blanch, ed. (Bloomington and London: Indiana University Press, 1966); Felicity Riddy, "Jewels in Pearl," in *A Companion to the Gawain-Poet*, Derek Brewer and Jonathan Gibson, eds. (London: D. S. Brewer, 1997)

24. Some examples are M. Madeleva, *Pearl: A Study in Spiritual Dryness* (Folcroft, PA: Folcroft, 1969); Conley ed., *The Middle English Pearl: Critical Essays*; Derek Brewer and Jonathan Gibson, eds., *A Companion to the Gawain-Poet* (London: D.S. Brewer, 1997). Two exceptions are Whitaker, "'Pearl' and some Illustrated Apocalypse Manuscripts" and Rosalind Field, "The Heavenly Jerusalem in the Pearl," *The Modern Language Review* 81 (1986).

25. Umberto Eco, *Art and Beauty in the Middle Ages* (New Haven, CT, and London: Yale University Press, 2002) 44.

26. Anonymous, *The Pearl,* 989–992.

27. *Ibid.*, 998–1018, 1026.

28. Barbara Nolan, *The Gothic Visionary Perspective* (Princeton, NJ: Princeton University Press, 1977) 199.

29. Whitaker, "'Pearl' and some Illustrated Apocalypse Manuscripts," 183.

30. *Ibid.*, p.191, 195.

31. Simson, *The Gothic Cathedral: Origins of Gothic Architecture and the Medieval Concept of Order,* 3

32. Panofsky, *Abbot Suger,* 22.

33. St. Hugh as quoted by Dow, "The Rose-Window," 280.

34. Sumner McKnight Crosby, *The Royal Abbey of Saint-Denis: From Its Beginnings to the Death of Suger, 475–1151* (New Haven, CT, and London: Yale University Press, 1987) 222.

35. M. B. Pranger, *Bernard of Clairvaux and the Shape of Monastic Thought* (Leiden and New York and London: Brill, E. J., 1994) 222.

36. St Bernard as quoted by Dow, "The Rose-Window," 289.

37. Simson, *The Gothic Cathedral,* 51.

38. John Baker, *English Stained Glass of the Medieval Period* (London: Thames and Hudson, 1978) unpaginated.

39. Lawrence Cunningham and John Reich, *Culture and Values: A Survey of the Humanities* (Belmont: Thomson/Wadsworth, 2006) 225

40. Anonymous, *The Pearl,* 972–982.

41. *Ibid., The Pearl,* 1049.

42. Revelation 21:10–17.

43. Whitaker, "'Pearl' and some Illustrated Apocalypse Manuscripts," 1169–1170.

44. Revelation 21.1.

45. Block Friedman, "The Architect's Compass in Creation Miniatures of the Later Middle Ages," 420.

46. Simson, *The Gothic Cathedral,* 9–20

47. Examples are in Beatus of Navarre, Bibliotheque Nationale Paris lat, 1366 ff 148v–149v. Reproduction in J Williams, *The Illustrated Beatus: A Corpus of the Illustrations of*

the *Commentary on the Apocalypse, Volume One* (London: Harvey Miller 1998) Plates 37–38; Silos Beatus, London, British Library Add MS 11695. Reproduction can be seen in J. Williams, *The Illustrated Beatus: A Corpus of the Illustrations of the Commentary on the Apocalypse, Volume Four* (London: Harvey Miller, 1998) Plate 326.

48. An example is Heavenly Jerusalem, Trinity Apocalypse, 1250, Cambridge, Trinity College MS R. 16.2, f. 25, Reproduction can be seen in Williams, *The Illustrated Beatus: A Corpus of the Illustrations of the Commentary on the Apocalypse, Volume One,* Plate 68.

49. Carruthers, *The Craft of Thought: Meditation, Rhetoric, and the Making of Images, 400–1200,* 120.

50. See "The Last Supper," Mosaic in the Nave of St. Apollinare Nuovo, Ravenna, early sixth century. Reproduction can be seen in John Beckwith, *Early Christian and Byzantine Art* (Harmondsworth: Penguin, 1986) 106.

51. For an example see "Heavenly Throng Praises God," Plate 74 in Williams, *The Illustrated Beatus: A Corpus of the Illustrations of the Commentary on the Apocalypse, Volume Four.*

52. The Facundus Beatus, Madrid, Biblioteca Nacional, MS Vitrina 14–2. See Williams, *The Illustrated Beatus: A Corpus of the Illustrations of the Commentary on the Apocalypse, Volume Four,* plates 225–350.

53. For example see "The Burning of Babylon," Las Huelgas Beatus Pierpont Library, New York, ff, 129–130. Reproduction in John Williams, *The Illustrated Beatus: A Corpus of the Illustrations of the Commentary on the Apocalypse, Volume Five* (London: Harvey Miller, 1998) Plate 415–416.

54. Tessa Morrison, "The Art of Early Medieval Number Symbolism," *Journal of the Australian Early Medieval Association* 2 (2006): 169–181

55. Dante, *La Divina Commedia — Paradiso* (Firenze: La Nuova Italia, 1966) XXVIII: 13–18.

56. Andreas Speiser, *Klassische Stücke Der Mathematik* (Zürich: Verlag Orell Füselli, 1925); J.J. Callahan, "The Curvature of Space in a Finite Universe," *Scientific American* no. 235 (August 1976); M. Peterson, "Dante and the 3-Sphere," *American Journal of Physics* 47 (1979) and R. Osserman, *Poetry of the Universe* (New York: Doubleday, 1995).

57. Jeffrey Burton Russell, *A History of Heaven: The Singing Silence* (Princeton, NJ: Princeton University Press, 1999) 175.

58. Whitaker, "'Pearl' and some Illustrated Apocalypse Manuscripts," 194.

Works Cited

Baker, John. *English Stained Glass of the Medieval Period.* London: Thames and Hudson, 1978.

Beckwith, John. *Early Christian and Byzantine Art.* Harmondsworth, UK: Penguin, 1986.

Blanch, Robert J. "Precious Metal and Gem Symbolism in Pearl" in *Sir Gawain and Pearl: Critical Essay.* Robert J Blanch, ed. Bloomington and London: Indiana University Press, 1966: 86–97.

Bucher, Francois. "Micro-Architecture as the 'Idea' of Gothic Theory and Style." *Gesta* 15, no. 1 (1976): pp.71–89.

Caldecott, W. Shaw. *Solomon's Temple: Its History and Its Structure.* London: Religious Tract Society, 1908.

Callahan, J.J. "The Curvature of Space in a Finite Universe." *Scientific American* 235 (1976): 90–100.

Carruthers, Mary. *The Craft of Thought: Meditation, Rhetoric, and the Making of Images, 400–1200.* Cambridge, UK: Cambridge University Press, 2000.

Conley, John, ed. *The Middle English Pearl: Critical Essays.* Notre Dame, IN: University of Notre Dame Press, 1970.

Crosby, Sumner McKnight. *The Royal Abbey of Saint-Denis: From Its Beginnings to the Death of Suger, 475–1151.* New Haven, CT, and London: Yale University Press, 1987.

Cunningham, Lawrence, and John Reich. *Culture and Values: A Survey of the Humanities.* Belmont: Thomson and Wadsworth, 2006.

Dante Alighieri. *La Divina Commedia — Paradiso.* Firenze: La Nuova Italia, 1966.

Dow, Helen J. "The Rose-Window." *Journal of Warburg and Courtauld Institutes* 20, no. 3 (1959): 284–97.

Eco, Umberto. *Art and Beauty in the Middle Ages.* New Haven, CT, and London: Yale University Press, 2002.

Field, Rosalind. "The Heavenly Jerusalem in the Pearl." *The Modern Language Review* 81 (1986): 7–17.

Friedman, John Block. "The Architect's Compass in Creation Miniatures of the Later Middle Ages." *Traditio* 30 (1974): 419–429.

Johnson, Wendell Stacy. "The Imagery and Diction of the Pearl: Toward an Interpretation." *A Journal of English Literary History* 20 September (1953): 161–180.

Madeleva, M. *Pearl: A Study in Spiritual Dryness.* Folcroft, PA: Folcroft, 1969.

Meyer, Ann R. *Medieval Allegory and the Building of the New Jerusalem.* London: D.S. Brewer, 2003.

Minear, Paul S. *New Testament Apocalyptic.* Nashville, TN: Abingdon, 1981.

Morrison, Tessa. "The Art of Early Medieval Number Symbolism." *Journal of the Australian Early Medieval Association* 2 (2006): 169–81.

Newton, Isaac. "Of the Day of Judgment and World to Come" in *The Religion of Isaac Newton*, Frank E. Manuel, ed. Oxford, UK: Clarendon, 1974: 126–36.

Nolan, Barbara. *The Gothic Visionary Perspective.* Princeton, NJ: Princeton University Press, 1977.

Osserman, R. *Poetry of the Universe.* New York: Doubleday, 1995.

Panofsky, Erwin *Abbot Suger.* Princeton, NJ: Princeton University Press, 1948.

The Pearl. Edward Vasta, trans. Notre Dame, IN: University of Notre Dame Press, 1961.

Peterson, M. "Dante and the 3-Sphere." *American Journal of Physics* 47 (1979): 1031–1035.

Pranger, M. B. *Bernard of Clairvaux and the Shape of Monastic Thought.* Leiden, New York and London: Brill, 1994.

Riddy, Felicity. "Jewels in Pearl" in *A Companion to the Gawain-Poet.* Derek Brewer and Jonathan Gibson, eds. London: D.S. Brewer, 1997: 143–155.

Russell, Jeffrey Burton. *A History of Heaven: The Singing Silence.* Princeton, NJ: Princeton University Press, 1999.

Russell, Robert D. "A Similitude of Paradise: The City as Image of the City" in *The Iconography of Heaven.* Clifford Davidson, ed. Kalamazoo, MI: Medieval Institute Publications, 1994: 146–161.

Sedinova, Hana. "The Precious Stones of Heavenly Jerusalem in the Medieval Book Illustration and Their Comparison with the Wall Incrustation in St. Wenceslas Chapel." *Artibus et Historiae* 21, no. 41 (2000): 31–47.

Speiser, Andreas. *Klassische Stücke Der Mathematik.* Zürich: Verlag Orell Füsell, 1925.

Simson, Otto von. *The Gothic Cathedral: Origins of the Gothic Architecture and the Medieval Concept of Order.* Princeton, NJ: Princeton University Press, 1984.

Whitaker, Muriel A. "'Pearl' and Some Illustrated Apocalypse Manuscripts." *Viator: Medieval and Renaissance Studies* 12 (1981): 183–96.

Williams, J. *The Illustrated Beatus: A Corpus of the Illustrations of the Commentary on the Apocalypse*, volumes one through five. London: Harvey Miller 1998.

Social Upheaval and the English Doomsday Plays

Lisa LeBlanc

Medieval English villages celebrated the Feast of Corpus Christi by staging and attending mystery cycle plays. These plays, of which the earliest record is 1376, were staged by the various guilds in the town and were performed over several days. These cycles provided both religious enlightenment for one of the high feasts of the Church and entertainment for the entire village. While records show that many villages performed these cycles, only four cycles of plays actually survive. The N-Town cycle, also known as the Coventry cycle, dates from 1425–1460 and consists of forty-two plays. The York cycle, which dates from the latter half of the fourteenth century, consists of fifty plays, three of which are lost. The Chester cycle, the earliest reference of which is 1422 (though the cycle may actually have been performed in the fourteenth century) consists of twenty-four plays which would have run over three days. The Wakefield cycle, also known as the Towneley cycle, dates from 1400–1450 and consists of thirty-two plays.

V. A. Kolve uses these cycles, along with the Beverly cycle, for which no plays survive but a list of plays that were performed is available, to develop a core of ten plays that were common to the cycles. These plays are Fall of Lucifer, Creation/Fall of Man, Cain and Abel, Noah and the Flood, Abraham and Isaac, Nativity (including Annunciation through Jesus and the Doctors), Raising of Lazarus, Passion (including Conspiracy through Harrowing of Hell), Resurrection (including the Watch through the Ascension), and Doomsday.[1] That the Doomsday play is one of the core plays should surprise no one. The plays are meant to trace the narrative of the world from the beginning, even before Creation, to the very end. Furthermore, the York cycle, one of the earliest cycles, started in the second half of the fourteenth century, after the city had become prosperous, but also after York had survived the Black Death in 1349. While the Black Death contributed to an increase in apocalyptic literature in late fourteenth century England in general, other events of this time period also caused great social upheavals, such as war with

France, rebellions in Scotland and Wales, the Great Western Schism, the Peasant's Revolt, an earthquake, the rise of Lollardy, and the ten-year-old Richard II taking the throne of England in 1377, all of which caused great interest in doomsday to appear.[2] Likewise, the rise of the commercial class, which quickly became wealthier than the aristocratic class, also brought about much social and economic change, as the middle class gained civic power in the cities and class structures became more fluid. This breakdown of the feudal structure contributed to the upheaval of the Middle Ages, thus causing a greater concern that the End Times may be immanent.[3] This trend of focusing on the afterlife continued into the fifteenth century, a period during which a larger number of lyric poems concerned with the inevitability of death were produced than in any other period.[4] The massive deaths, the social upheaval, and the consequent fears brought on by the Black Death turned the attention of many medieval writers to the idea of Doomsday.

The mystery cycle as a whole attempts to remind medieval audiences of the approaching End Times, running as it does from the Fall of Adam through the Redemption of the crucifixion and onto the Judgment of Doomsday.[5] The Doomsday play itself is, as one would expect, even more clearly a reminder of the End Times. As Pamela Sheingorn and David Bevington note, "The Judgment Day both completes the cosmic frame of the [mystery cycle] in ending all time and God's creation and makes an accounting of the individual life of each Christian."[6] To a medieval playwright, the Doomsday plays were a chance to make the audience, which consisted of all ranks of society, mindful of what was coming, as well as to provide spectacle.

Along with religious education and entertainment, the cycle plays also provided social criticism of the time. Anthony Gash argues that the playwrights could "woo the audience's approval for controversial social comments put into the mouths of comic or 'evil' characters."[7] To illustrate, he shows that the criticism of royal pardons, which Henry VI used to raise money, appears in the pardoning of Cain in the mystery cycles.[8] Kolve interprets anachronisms in the Wakefield cycle's shepherds' plays as the playwright's attempts to comment on the suffering of the poor in his own society.[9] Furthermore, Theodore Lerud discusses the criticism against those who proclaimed the king's decrees and against letters of patent of protection embedded within several Wakefield plays.[10] The Doomsday plays are the only plays in the cycles that are set in the future, not in the past. These plays suggest that this future could be near at hand; indeed, it could happen during the lifetime of the audience, and there were many social indicators that the apocalypse may be near. This setting allows the author to include social criticism in the plays easily; despite this fact, little research has been done on the use of social criticism in the Doomsday plays of the English mystery cycles. This paper will argue that the social upheavals of the high Middle Ages led the playwrights of the Doomsday plays to have, aside from entertainment, the salvation of the audience as their primary purpose. Additionally, two of the playwrights' secondary purpose seems to have been to critique situations caused by these apocalyptic upheavals.

The Doomsday play of the N-Town cycle, referred to in the manuscript as the *dies iudicii* or Day of Judgment, is probably the least developed of the four. It is incomplete and ends abruptly. Despite its brevity, just 130 lines, the play incorporates several apocalyptic images with spectacle to draw the audience into a warning about the coming of Doomsday. With the exception of St. Peter, who in this play is portrayed as a supernatural character like the angels, all humans are grouped into the saved or the damned, none having individual lines. Similarly, demons are largely grouped, but the supernatural characters remain distinct, including God and the archangels Michael and Gabryell.

Despite being more than twice the length of the N-Town Doomsday play, the York cycle Doomsday, with 380 lines, is no more developed. With the exception of God and Jesus, the characters in the play are not individualized at all. They are listed as three angels, two good souls, two bad souls, three demons, and two apostles, none of whom are named. Unlike the N-Town play, even the sins of the bad souls are not distinguished from each other; the souls are merely sinners. Even though these characters are generalized, there is still an urgency about Doomsday, although the play uses spectacle less than the other Doomsday plays do.

In the Wakefield cycle, the Doomsday play is much more developed, running to 830 lines. However, the characters, consisting of four evil (Malus) souls and four good (Bonus) souls, two demons and several angels, Jesus, and a third demon named Tutiuillus, still remain vague.[11] Most of the detail about sin comes from the discussions of the demons, not the bad souls.

The Chester cycle is also more developed, running to 708 lines. The sinners, as well as the saved souls, are distinguished from each other, but they are not developed characters; instead they are types identified by their roles in life: a saved and a damned pope (Papa Salvatus and Papa Damnatus), a saved and a damned emperor (Imperator Salvatus and Imperator Damnatus), a saved and a damned king (Rex Salvatus and Rex Damnatus), a saved and a damned queen (Regina Salvata and Regina Damnata), a damned justice (Justiciarius Damnatus) and a damned merchant (Mercator Damnatus). Their sins do differ from each other, but only the sins of the justice and the merchant are specific to the characters, rendering false judgments and filing false lawsuits for the Justiciarius and forcing the poor to sell land cheaply and buy and sell falsely for the Mercator; those of the other characters, lust, greed, vanity, could be easily interchangeable.

The Nearness of Doomsday

Since the plays go beyond simply enacting religious ritual to sounding a clear warning about the possibility of the coming of the apocalypse, the cycle plays use many strategies to draw the audience members in and remind them of the necessity to think of their own judgments. One strategy seen in all plays, in varying degrees, is the conflation of time. While the plays do set Judgment Day in the future, specific lines in the plays make the audience members present at the event, or at least remind them that this event could happen during their lifetimes.

In the York Doomsday play, God speaks of human inability to know when the end is coming:

> Ilke a day ther mirroure may thei se,
> Yoitt thynke thei noyot that thei schall dye.
> All that euere I saide schulde be
> Is nowe fulfillid thurgh prophicie,
> Therfore nowe is it tyme to me
> To make endyng of mannes folie.
> [On such a day they may see their reflection,
> Yet they do not think that they shall die.
> All that I ever said will be
> Is now fulfilled through prophecy,
> Therefore now, to me, it is time
> To make an ending of man's folly][12]

While God says that humans are not prepared for judgment, the clear implication to the audience is that the End Times may be soon and that they themselves might be the unprepared souls who do not realize that the end is upon them. To reinforce this idea, God says, "nowe is it tyme" [now it is time],[13] indicating that the judgment is about to take place within the time of the play as well as potentially tying it to the audience's "nowe."

The Wakefield cycle also moves Judgment Day into the audience's time. Once Jesus has initiated the Last Judgment, demons begin to argue for their rights to the evil souls using references recognizable to a medieval audience as terms of their own time period. During this discussion, they paraphrase "a pere in a parlamente" [a peer in parliament],[14] make reference to court practice, plan to go to Watling Street, and the first demon even says that he'd rather go on a pilgrimage to Rome than face the judge, Jesus. They continue their argument, using legal terminology, by discussing the books they must examine and the bag full of briefs one of them carries. Thus the demons become high medieval lawyers and court officials.

The Chester play seems least concerned with bringing the audience into the drama. The strongest attempt comes in the last lines of the play when John the Evangelist says:

> And all that ever my Lord sayth here,
> I wrote yt in my mannere.
> Therefore, excuse you, withowten were,
> I may not well, iwysse.
> [And all that my Lord ever said here,
> I wrote it in my manner.
> Therefore without doubt excuse you
> I may not well, I know][15]

According to the stage directions, the demons have already removed the damned souls from the staging area, so to whom is this warning addressed? Since there are no damned souls for John to be addressing, it is likely that the audience members are the intended recipients of the reminder that warnings about the Last Judgment can be found in the Gospels and Revelation.

The N-Town Doomsday play makes the most concerted attempt at drawing the audience into the action of the drama. The play opens with Michael summoning "All men [to] Aryse" [all men to arise] for judgment. [16] The manuscript indicates that only Jesus, Michael, and Gabryell are present at this time. Therefore, Michael's emphasis on "all," repeated again in the sixth line, could easily be a call to the entire audience. That this call is addressed to the audience is further emphasized by Michael's use of "3ow":

> And of 3our Answere 3ow now Avyse
> What 3e xal sey · whan þat 3e cum
> 3owre Ansuere ffor to telle
> for whan þat god xal 3ow appose
> ther is non helpe of no glose
> the trewth fful trewlye he wyl tose
> And send 3ow to hevyn or helle.
> [And of your answer, now you consider
> What you shall say, when you come
> Your answer to tell
> For when God shall sit opposite you
> There is no hope from glossing
> The truth full truly he will choose
> And send you to heaven or hell]. [17]

Since none of the human characters have yet appeared, the most obvious object of "3ow" is the audience. Thus the audience members are called to answer for their lives on the spot, much as the play's souls will shortly be.

Another strategy used by all four plays to make the apocalypse seem present to the audience is spectacle, that is, the use of dramatic sights and sounds to make the audience members feel as if they are experiencing Doomsday. Due to the scarcity of records, we cannot know the full extent of spec-tacle used in these plays, but David Leigh points out that "evidence from property lists for a Doomsday play at Coventry indicates that barrels were set on fire to symbolize the consummation of the world."[18] Three of the four plays indicate, either in dialogue or in stage directions, that horns, which are mentioned in the Book of Revelation as hearkening the apocalypse, are blown.

The same three plays show the wounds of Jesus quite visibly. The York cycle particularly emphasizes the wounds, as Jesus says:

> Here may yoe see my woundes wide,
> THe whilke I tholed for youre mysdede.
> Thurgh harte and heed, foote, hande and hide,
> Nought for my gilte, butt for youre need.
> Beholdis both body, bak and side,
> How dere I bought youre brotherhede.
> THes bittir peynes I wolde abide —
> To bye you blisse thus wolde I bleede.
> Mi body was scourged withouten skill,
> As theffe full thraly was I thrette;
> On crosse thei hanged me, on a hill,
> Blody and bloo, as I was bette,
> With croune of thorne throsten full ill.
> THis spere vnto my side was sette —
> Myne harte-bloode spared noght thei for to spill;
> Manne, for thy loue I wolde not lette.
> [Here you may see my large wounds,
> The which I suffered for your misdeeds.
> Through heart and head, foot, hand and skin,
> Not for my guilt, but for your need.
> Behold the body, both back and side,
> How dearly I bought your brotherhood.
> These bitter pains I would abide,
> To buy you bliss, thus would I bleed.
> My body was scourged without skill,
> As a thief full violently I was tormented;
> On a cross they hung me, on a hill,
> Bloody and bruised, as I was beaten,
> With a crown of thorns thrusted cruelly.
> This spear was stabbed into my side —
> They did not hesitate to spill my heart's blood;
> Mankind, for thy love I would not stop them.][19]

In Wakefield and Chester, Jesus draws attention to the fact that the souls, and the audience members, can see all the wounds he received for their sake. In the Chester Doomsday, Jesus is flanked by angels who carry the instruments used to torture and crucify Jesus.

The fourth play, the N-Town Doomsday, includes its own spectacle, with sounds and sights tied together. Once the archangels have finished summoning all to judgment, the stage directions say *Omnes resurgentes subtus terram clamavit* [All souls rising from beneath the earth cry aloud],[20] so even though this play has no horns mentioned, it brings dramatic noise to the audience as the souls of the dead break out of their graves.[21] While it is not clear how this escape from the graves was staged, having the souls suddenly appear, probably from under the stage carts, while claiming they were breaking out of their graves, likely caused a sensation in the audience. Along with the souls come a group of demons who are ready to take the damned souls to hell.

Finally, another characteristic found in all the plays is the use of Matthew 25: 31–46, a passage familiar to medieval audiences.[22] It is a fitting passage for judgment because it discusses the necessity for the people to live Christian lives, a reminder that becomes significant in times of social upheaval. In the N-Town play, the passage is used briefly as God condemns the sinners because they did not practice the corporal acts of mercy. This condemnation is followed by two demons identifying seven sinners as the seven deadly sins. They tie the sins directly to the neglect of the corporal acts of mercy. The proud sinner neglects to give bread; the covetous sinner refuses to give drink; the wrathful sinner neglects the sick; the envious sinner ignores the prisoner; the slothful prisoner will not bury the dead[23]; the gluttonous sinner ejects the homeless; and the lustful refuses even "A thred" [a thread][24] to the naked. Both the acts of corporal mercy and the seven deadly sins brought to mind the idea of particular, personal judgment, that each member of the audience would be judged by these standards. Wakefield and York use more of Matthew 25, measuring both the Good and Bad Souls by the works. The responses of the souls in York, that they never knew Jesus to be hungry, thirsty, and so forth, also comes from Matthew 25. Chester uses the passage in an interesting manner; Jesus explains that these works have merited the souls either heaven or hell, but he does this after they have been judged. While typical Doomsday images, like the apocalyptic horn, are often drawn from Revelation, the only passage that is truly Biblical in all the plays is Matthew 25, which describes the corporal works of mercy, the standard by which judgment occurs. The gospel passage would be familiar to medieval audiences due to the fact that it was the basis for medieval ideas of the apocalypse, so the playwrights attempted to tie the plays to ideas about judgment to which the audiences would already have had a strong relation: "The visual rendering of the scene [of the Last Judgment] as it developed in the Middle Ages is based largely on the description in Matthew 24:30–32 and, particularly, 25:31–46."[25] Because these images would have been present to audiences in church sculpture and sermons, they would readily have connected the audiences to their own roles in the End Times.

Social Criticism

Despite all of this effort by the playwrights to highlight the immediacy of Doomsday, the N-Town, Chester and Wakefield Doomsday plays are not focused on all audience members but rather target specific classes. York, due to its brevity and lack of development, does not distinguish between social classes, distinguishing only between good and bad souls. In contrast, N-Town, also brief and lacking development, does begin to distinguish between the classes by the emphasizing the judgment of the upper class. When Gabryell calls forth souls for judgment, he summons "Bothe pope prynce and prysste with crowne / Kynge and caysere and knyhtys kene" [Both pope, prince, and priest with crown / King and caesar and knights keen]. While he also refers to "pore ne ryche of grett renowne"[poor nor rich of great renown],[26] neither the peasant class nor the commercial class are singled out the way the upper class is. At the time the plays were written, the commercial class had become much more powerful. The merchant and artisan guilds were responsible for the mystery cycles. However, relations between the commercial class and the upper class were not always cordial. The aristocratic class often faced financial difficulties since they lived on land wealth which did not grow over the years. The commercial class, on the other hand, was growing more and more prosperous. As a result, the upper class often enacted laws to keep the classes separate and to keep the commercial class below them. Perhaps N-Town singles out the pope, prince, priest, king, caesar, and knight to launch a subtle attack on the strata that excluded the commercial class.

The social attacks, particularly on the upper classes, are stronger in the more developed Wakefield and Chester plays. The Wakefield play mentions all manner of sinners. The legal brief one of the demons carries concerns carpers, criers, cutpurses, thieves, lubbers, liars, rioters, receivers of stolen goods, shrewish wives, backbiters, and false indicters. Tutiuillus, who joins the other demons, continues the list with "rasers of the fals tax / And gederars of greyn wax" [raisers of the false tax / And gatherers of green wax],[27] those wearing "prankyd gownes and shulders vp-set" [pleated gowns and high shoulders], "kyrkchaterars" [church chatterers], "barganars and okerars / And lufars of symonee" [bargainers and usurers / And lovers of simony], and "runkers and rowners" [murmurers and whisperers].[28] He adds many more types of sinners to the list, so that it must have been difficult for any member of the audience not to see himself or herself somewhere in that list. However, certain sins are singled out. While Tutiuillus condemns many sins, the sin of fancy dress seems to be his favorite. Of one sin, he says:

> Thise laddys thai leven
> As lordys riall,
> At ee to be even,
> Pu[r]turd in pall
> As kyngys.
> [These lads that live
> Like royal lords,
> At once to be equal,
> Ornamented in rich cloth
> Like kings.][29]

He describes the various fashion offenses of several sinners of the time, and even claims this particular offense is greater than any of the seven deadly sins.

The amount of time spent on this sin, as opposed to others, is greatly disproportionate, with 87 lines discussing fashion's sins as opposed to other sins which are granted one line each, which links this speech to the sumptuary laws that came out of the social chaos caused by the Black Plague. Due to the Black Plague, there was a surplus of goods and a lack of buyers, as well as a surplus of work and lack of laborers, throughout England. Peasants were able to negotiate better working conditions, despite laws that attempted to keep them where they were before the plague, such as the 1349 Ordinance of Labourers:

> [E]very man or woman in our realm of England, whether free or unfree, who is physically fit and below the age of sixty, not living by trade or by exercising a particular craft ... shall, if offered employment consonant with their status, be obliged to accept the employment offered, and they shall be paid only the fees, liveries, payments or salaries which were usually paid in the part of the country where they are working in the twentieth year of our reign [1346].[30]

Furthermore, the bourgeois class became more powerful after the plague, as many commercial opportunities opened up. Because they were often wealthier than the aristocratic class, they began to dress as the upper class did. This chaos in social order led King Edward III to update England's Sumptuary Laws in 1363, restricting all clothing to reflect the social class of its owner:

> Item, for the outrageous and excessive apparel of many people, contrary to their estate and degree, to the great destruction and impoverishment of the whole land, it is ordained that lads (including the servants of lords as well as those employed in crafts and manufacturing) ... shall have cloth worth less than 2 marks a cloth and use no cloth of a higher value ... and shall use nothing of gold or silver, embroidered, decorated or of silk. And their wives, daughters and children shall do likewise and shall wear no veils worth more than 12*d*.[31]

The laws distinguished seven social classes and restricted what each class was allowed to wear.

Tutiuillus's comments, particularly his reference to the "laddys that leven / As lordys riall" [lads that live / Like royal lords][32] seem to support the sumptuary laws by condemning those who dress too elaborately. However, Tutiuillus is a comic and dishonest character, poking fun at his victims, satirizing his own role in judgment, and using guile throughout, which reduces the validity of his accusations. His emphasis on dress, over the adulterers, whores, knifers, extortionists, and others who get a brief mention, shows that his priorities are not on the more serious sins. His lack of credibility, therefore, turns his criticism of those who dress too elaborately into an implied mockery of the sumptuary laws. Those who feel that such dress laws are important have no more credibility than Tutiuillus does, at least according to the rising middle class who was responsible for the plays and to whom the sumptuary laws were largely aimed.

Another group targeted by the Wakefield play is made up of lawyers and court officials. The demons, as mentioned above, make reference to court practices and possess briefs. The first evil soul to speak laments that no amount of legal quibbling will get him out of trouble at this judgment:

> Ther may no man of lagh
> Help with no quantyce.
>
> Vokettys ten or twelfe
> May none help at this nede,
> Bot ilk man for hisself
> Shall answere for his dede.
>
> [There may no man of law
> Help with no cunning.
>
> Advocates ten or twelve
> May none help with this need,
> But each man for himself
> Shall answer for his deeds.][33]

Furthermore, Tutiuillus, in his role of collecting souls and keeping track of their sins, identifies himself as "chefe tollare / And sithen courte-rollar" [chief toll-collector / and also keeper of court rolls].[34] While Jesus does identify himself as the judge at the Last Judgment, he does not use any legal phrasing; law is portrayed as tied to the demons, only to be overthrown by divine law at the Last Judgment.[35] This harsh criticism of those involved in the medieval justice system is not unique to the mystery plays. G. R. Owst points out that condemnation of the vices of the justice system, both secular and ecclesiastical, was commonplace in the sermons of the mendicant preachers of the high Middle Ages, who attributed much of the turmoil of the period to a corrupt legal system.[36]

The Chester Doomsday play, too, focuses its social criticism on issues raised by the newly formed bourgeois class. The play opens with God the Father calling all souls to judgment. The first to arrive are a pope, emperor, king and queen. None of these figures were perfect in life; in fact they were all clearly sinners. The pope admits he ignored God's commandments and was interested only in worldly power. The emperor is vague about his sins, saying merely that he coveted riches and that "I to sinne were bayne and bowne" [I was willing and bound to sin]. The king is also vague, referring to the fact that he paid more attention to his body than his soul. The queen's sins are perhaps the clearest. She dressed in very fancy clothing and jewels so that "All ... might excyte lecherye" [All might excite lechery]. As a result of their having been cleansed in Purgatory, these three souls have shown contrition, and they will now be able to enter Paradise. They are followed by another pope, emperor, king and queen, who were also sinners during their lives, but who are not saved. The second pope admits he was covetous and craved "sylver and symonye" [silver and simony]. Furthermore, he says that "all the soules in Christianitie / that damned were while I had degree / now gyve accompt behoveth mee" [all the souls in Christendom / that were damned while I had the high seat / now give account against me].[37] The emperor is guilty of manslaughter, covetousness, wrong-doing, gluttony, and receiving ill-gotten gains. The king's sins include oppressing the poor and the church, lechery, and covetousness. The queen's sins are similar to her saved counterpart's; she admits she "never wrought" [never committed] lechery, but that it was not for lack of trying. However, there are two more damned souls, a merchant and a judge, who do not have saved counterparts. The justice argues that it is law itself that has condemned him to hell: "Alas, that ever I learned lawe, / for suffer I must manye a hard thrawe" [Alas, that I ever learned law, / for I must suffer many a hard death-throe]. As a justice of the courts, he "falsely causes tooke in hand / and mych woe dyd elles" [took false causes in hand / and also caused much woe].[38] He admits to corrupting justice for bribes as well as swindling the church. For all these sins, he feels he will fare poorly in his trial at the Last Judgment. The merchant is also damned because of his profession:

> Alas! Marchandize maketh mee,
> and purshasinge of land and fee,
> in hell-payne evermore to bee,
> and bale that never shall blynne.
> Alas! Merchandise made me,
> and purchasing of lands and fees,
> to be in hell-pain forevermore,
> and grief that never shall cease.[39]

This merchant forced the poor to sell him their lands, bore false witness in court, and ignored his obligations to the church. While these were clearly seen as wrong, he adds, as one of his sins, that "ofte I dealed with marchandyce" [often I dealt with merchandise].[40] There is no indication that the merchandise is anything illegal or immoral; the implication is that just being a merchant is sin enough to damn him.

Critics such as Phoebe Spinrad and David Leigh dismiss these two characters as later additions, but questions remain as to why they were added and why the person who added them did not add their saved counterparts.[41] The lack of balance, as well as the fact that, unlike the other damned souls, these sinners tie their damnation directly to their professions, seems like a more pointed attack. Martin Stevens presents the characters as simply representing the various levels of society in a *danse macabre*,[42] but this argument also does not explain why the lawyer and merchant are not represented as saved or why their sins are more particular to their professions. It also does not explain why the lower classes are excluded from the *danse macabre*.

The attack on the lawyer does seem to fit with the tying of law to the demons in the Wakefield Doomsday play. During this time in England, as Theodore Lerud points out, lawyers were seen as corrupt men, manipulating law to circumvent justice.[43] The merchant is a more difficult character to explain. In parsing out why a writer of the merchant class, or at least hired by the merchant class, would single out that class for an attack, it is important to keep in mind that the merchant guilds were separate from the craft guilds, and the Chester Doomsday play was put on by the webstars, or weavers, a craft guild. Due to laws passed that restricted textile guilds to selling only to local merchants, relationships between the textile guilds and merchant guilds were not always friendly. For instance, the law of the fullers and weavers of Winchester in 1209 states:

> Be it known that no weaver or fuller may dry or dye cloth nor go outside the city to sell it. They may sell their cloth to no foreigner, but only to merchants of the city. And if it happens that, in order to enrich himself, one of the weavers or fullers wishes to go outside the city to sell his merchandise, he may be very sure that the honest men of the city will take all his cloth and bring it back to the city, and that he will forfeit it in the presence of the aldermen and honest men of the city. And if any weaver or fuller sell his cloth to a foreigner, the foreigner shall lose his cloth, and the other shall remain at the mercy of the city for as much as he has. Neither the weaver nor the fuller may buy anything except for his trade but by making an agreement with the mayor. No free man can be accused by a weaver or a fuller, nor can a weaver or a fuller bear testimony against a free man. If any of them become rich, and wish to give up his trade, he may forswear it and turn his tools out of the house, and then do as much for the city as he is able in his freedom.[44]

These laws work clearly to the advantage of the merchants and greatly restrict the rights of textile guildmembers. Furthermore, a new merchant guild, which excluded craftsmen and many freemen from trade, was established by royal charter in Chester during the mid-sixteenth century.[45] For this reason, the textile guilds and the merchants often had hostile relationships, which may have made the merchants targets for social criticism from the writers employed by the weavers guild.

Conclusion

Despite the use of social commentary, or perhaps because of it, the Wakefield and Chester plays are entertaining but also serve their purpose of warning the audiences of the End Times as do York and N-Town. All four playwrights make use of several strategies to draw in their audiences and to make them aware of the possible nearness of the Last Judgment. The deaths, international and civic conflicts, religious unrest, and social upheaval would have made this world seem precarious and the next world seem nearer for the medieval audience. The same social dislocations that caused the focus on the next world to flourish also caused a reshuffling of society, and the social impact of that reshuffling prompted two of the playwrights to include a satire on these new social relationships in their plays. In these play cycles, the mirror with which audience members are expected to view themselves in order to prepare for their own judgment is suddenly turned outward towards society. This new view uses apocalypse to call for a reform of society, particularly those elements repressive to the guilds that sponsored the doomsday plays: powerful merchants, justices, and sumptuary laws. The playwrights use the metaphor of judgment to draw attention to those elements of society that they themselves condemn in order to raise awareness of the need for reform that would stabilize the new social order in which the power of the emerging commercial class would be strengthened.

NOTES

1. V. A. Kolve, *A Play Called Corpus Christi* (Stanford, CA: Stanford University Press, 1966) 50–51.
2. Penn Szittya, "Domesday Bokes: The Apocalypse in Medieval English Literary Culture," in *The Apocalypse in the Middle Ages*, Richard Emmerson and Bernard McGinn, eds. (Ithaca, NY: Cornell University Press, 1992) 374–397 at 383.
3. Glynne Wickham, *The Medieval Theater*, 3rd ed. (Cambridge, UK: Cambridge University Press, 1987) 66.
4. David Fowler, *The Bible in Middle English Literature* (Seattle: University of Washington Press, 1976) 79.
5. Wickham, *The Medieval Theater*, 63.

6. Pamela Sheingorn and David Bevington, "'Alle this Was Token Domysday to Drede': Visual Signs of Last Judgment in The Corpus Christi Cycles and in Late Gothic Art," in *Homo, Memento Finis: The Iconography of Just Judgment in Medieval Art and Drama*, Early Drama, Art and Music Monograph Series 6, David Bevington, ed. (Kalamazoo, MI: Medieval Institute Publications, 1985) 121–145 at 122.

7. Anthony Gash, "Carnival against Lent: The Ambivalence of Medieval Drama," in *Medieval Literature: Criticism, Ideology and History*, David Aers, ed. (New York: St. Martin's, 1986) 74–98 at 76.

8. Gash, "Carnival against Lent," 77.

9. Kolve's Chapter 5 focuses on anachronism and conflation of place. While some of these changes are only for convenience or humor, several are used to provide commentary on contemporary society.

10. Theodore K. Lerud, *Social and Political Dimensions of the English Corpus Christi Drama* (New York: Garland, 1988) 157–161.

11. Only one angel has a speaking part, but stage directions indicate other angels are on stage.

12. *The York Plays*, Electronic Text Center, University of Virginia Library, <http://etext. lib.virginia.edu/toc/modeng/public/AnoYork.html> (July 3, 2008). Lines 51–56. All quotations from the York play are taken from this text. All modernizations are my own except where noted.

13. *York*, line 55.

14. *The Towneley Plays*, 2 vols., Early English Text Society, Martin Stevens and A. C. Cawley, eds. (London: Oxford University Press, 1994) 406. All quotations from the Wakefield cycle are taken from this edition.

15. *The Chester Mystery Cycle*, Early English Text Society, R. M. Lumiansky and David Mills, eds. (London: Oxford University Press 1974) 463. All quotations from the Chester cycle are taken from this edition.

16. *Ludus Coventriae or The Plaie called Corpus Christi*, Early English Text Society, K. S. Block, ed. (London: Oxford University Press, 1960) 373. All quotations from the N-Town Doomsday play will be taken from this edition.

17. *Ludus*, 1.

18. David J. Leigh, "The Doomsday Morality Play: An Eschatological Morality," in *Medieval English Drama: Essays Critical and Contextual*. Jerome Taylor and Alan H. Nelson, eds. (Chicago: University of Chicago Press, 1972) 263.

19. *York*, 245–260.

20. *Ludus*, 374.

21. The stage direction has their voices come "subtus terram" and the voices call the "clowdys of clay" to "cleue a-sundyr" (27).

22. "And when the Son of Man shall come in his majesty, and all the angels with him, then shall he sit upon the seat of his majesty. And all nations shall be gathered together before him, and he shall separate them one from another, as the shepard separateth the sheep from the goats: And he shall set the sheep on his right hand; but the goats on his left. Then shall the king say to them that shall be on his right hand: Come, ye blessed of my Father, possess you the kingdom prepared for you from the foundation of the world. For I was hungry, and you gave me to eat; I was thirsty, and you gave me to drink; I was a stranger, and you took me in: Naked, and you covered me; sick, and you visited me: I was in prison, and you came to me. Then shall the just answer him, saying: Lord, when did we see thee hungry, and feed thee; thirsty, and give thee drink? And when did we see thee a stranger, and took thee in? or naked, and cover thee? Or when did we see thee sick or in prison, and came to thee? And the king answering, shall say to them: Amen, I say to you, as long as you did it to one of these my least brethren, you did it to me. Then he

shall say to them also that shall be on his left hand: Depart from me, you cursed, into everlasting fire which was prepared for the devil and his angels. For I was hungry, and you gave me not to eat: I was thirsty, and you gave me not to drink. I was a stranger, and you took me not in; naked, and you covered me not; sick and in prison, and you did not visit me. Then they also shall answer him, saying: Lord, when did we see thee hungry, or thirsty, or a stranger, or naked, or sick, or in prison, and did not minister to thee? Then he shall answer them, saying: Amen I say to you, as long as you did it not to one of these least, neither did you do it to me. And these shall go into everlasting punishment: but the just, into life everlasting" (Douay-Rheims translation).

23. Matthew 25 only lists six acts of corporal mercy. The N-Town playwright added burying the dead to the passage listing the acts of corporal mercy as well as to the seven deadly sins, very likely just so it would balance with the number of deadly sins.

24. *Ludus*, 377.

25. C. M. Kauffmann, *Biblical Imagery in Medieval England 700–1500* (London: Harvey Miller, 2003) 258.

26. *Ludus*, 373, 374.

27. Green wax referred to the seal put on official documents, especially those from the Exchequer to the sheriff.

28. *Wakefield*, 413.

29. *Wakefield*, 414

30. Rosemary Horrox, trans. and ed., *The Black Death* (Manchester, UK: Manchester University Press, 1994) 288. (Second brackets in original.)

31. Horrox, *The Black Death*, 340.

32. *Wakefield*, 414.

33. *Wakefield*, 401.

34. *Wakefield*, 410.

35. For a thorough examination of the use of legality in the mystery cycles, consult Lerud *Social and Political Dimensions of the English Corpus Christi Drama.*

36. G. R. Owst, *Literature and Pulpit in Medieval England* (New York: Barnes & Noble, 1961) 340–341.

37. *Chester*, 441, 443, 444, 445.

38. *Chester*, 447, 448.

39. *Chester*, 449.

40. *Chester*, 450.

41. Phoebe Spinrad, *The Summons of Death on the Medieval and Renaissance Stage* (Columbus: Ohio State University Press, 1987) 51. Leigh, "The Doomsday Morality Play: An Eschatological Morality," 266.

42. Martin Stevens, *Four Middle English Mystery Cycles: Textual, Contextual, and Critical Interpretations* (Princeton, NJ: Princeton University Press, 1987) 314.

43. Lerud, *Social and Political Dimensions of the English Corpus Christi Drama*, 60.

44. Paul Halsall, *Medieval Source Book,* <http://www.fordham.edu/halsall/source/1209 Weavers2.html> (July 5, 2008).

45. "Early Modern Chester 1550–1762: Economy and Society, 1550–1642," *A History of the County of Chester: Volume 5 part 1: The City of Chester: General History and Topography* (2003) 102–109. <http://www.british-history.ac.uk/report.aspx?compid=19195> (July 5, 2008).

WORKS CITED

The Chester Mystery Cycle. Robert M. Lumiansky and D. Mills, eds. Early English Text Society. London: Oxford University Press, 1974.

"Early Modern Chester 1550–1762: Economy and Society, 1550–1642." *A History of the County of Chester: Volume 5 part 1: The City of Chester: General History and Topography.* <http://www.british-history.ac.uk/report.aspx?compid=19195> (July 5, 2008).

Fowler, David. *The Bible in Middle English Literature.* Seattle: University of Washington Press, 1976.

Gash, Anthony. "Carnival against Lent: The Ambivalence of Medieval Drama" in *Medieval Literature: Criticism, Ideology and History.* D. Aers, ed. New York: St. Martin's Press, 1986: 74–98.

Horrox, Rosemary, trans. and ed. *The Black Death.* Manchester, UK: Manchester University Press, 1994.

Kauffmann, C. M. *Biblical Imagery in Medieval England 700–1500.* London: Harvey Miller, 2003.

Kolve, V. A. *A Play Called Corpus Christi.* Stanford, CA: Stanford University Press, 1966.

"The Law of the Fullers & Weavers of Winchester, 1209." *Medieval Source Book* (Paul Halsall). <http://www.fordham.edu/halsall/source/1209Weavers2.html> (July 5, 2008). From: A. F. Leach, ed. *Beverley Town Documents, Selden Society* Vol. XIV. London, 1900: Appendix II, 134–135. Reprinted in Roy C. Cave and Herbert H. Coulson, *A Source Book for Medieval Economic History.* Milwaukee: Bruce, 1936. Reprint New York: Biblo and Tannen, 1965: 242–243.

Leigh, David. "The Doomsday Morality Play: An Eschatological Morality" in *Medieval English Drama: Essays Critical and Contextual.* Jerome Taylor and Alan H. Nelson, eds. Chicago: University of Chicago Press, 1988: 260–278.

Lerud, Theodore K. *Social and Political Dimensions of the English Corpus Christi Drama.* New York: Garland, 1988.

Ludus Coventriae or The Plaie called Corpus Christi. K.S. Block, ed. Early English Text Society. London: Oxford University Press, 1960.

Owst, G. R. *Literature and Pulpit in Medieval England.* New York: Barnes and Noble, 1961.

Sheingorn, Pamela, and David Bevington. "'Alle this Was Token Domysday to Drede': Visual Signs of Last Judgment in The Corpus Christi Cycles and in Late Gothic Art" in *Homo, Memento Finis: The Iconography of Just Judgment in Medieval Art and Drama.* Early Drama, Art and Music Monograph Series 6th. David Bevington, ed. Kalamazoo, MI: Medieval Institute Publications, 1985: 121–145.

Spinrad, Phoebe. *The Summons of Death on the Medieval and Renaissance Stage.* Columbus: Ohio State University Press, 1987.

Stevens, Martin. *Four Middle English Mystery Cycles: Textual, Contextual, and Critical Interpretations.* Princeton, NJ: Princeton University Press, 1987.

Szittya, Penn. "Domesday Bokes: The Apocalypse in Medieval English Literary Culture" in *The Apocalypse in the Middle Ages.* Richard Emmerson and Bernard McGinn, eds. Ithaca, NY: Cornell University Press, 1992: 374–397.

The Towneley Plays, 2 vols. Martin Stevens and A. C. Cawley, eds. Early English Text Society. London: Oxford University Press, 1994.

Wickham, Glynne. *The Medieval Theater,* 3rd ed. Cambridge, UK: Cambridge University Press, 1987.

The York Plays. University of Virginia Library E-text Center. <http://etext.lib.virginia.edu/toc/modeng/public/AnoYork.html> (November 11, 2008). From Richard Beadle, ed. *The York plays.* York Medieval Texts. Second series. London: E. Arnold, 1982.

Flight from the Apocalypse: Protestants, Puritans and the Great Migration

Carmen Gómez-Galisteo

"And, behold, I come quickly; and my reward is with me, to give every man according as his work shall be. I am Alpha and Omega, the beginning and the end, the first and the last," God promises in the Book of Revelation (or Apocalypse), 22:12–13. Though the canonicity of this particular biblical book was being questioned by some thinkers, sixteenth- and seventeenth-century Europe was swept by a renewed interest in the apocalypse and God's "quickly" was assumed to make explicit reference to that era.[1] After all, this historical period saw a number of changes that would profoundly alter life as it had been understood up to then; this was an age that saw the fall of the Byzantine empire in 1453, the encounter with the Americas in 1492, the sack of Rome in 1527, and, of course, the Reformation. As Martin Luther's doctrines spread throughout Europe, not only were the authority and power of the Roman Catholic Church contested. The Reformation was also bringing about far-reaching changes in historical modes of thought that questioned the relationship between government and religion, helping to define and characterize a whole age. Traditionally, "apocalypticism was Western Christendom's response to historical crisis," and apocalyptic prophecies of all sorts were rife in the period, with every new Protestant group favoring its own interpretation of the apocalypse.[2]

Luther himself, believing that he was living in the last days, also contributed his share to the apocalyptic enthusiasm by declaring that "it is not to be expected that mankind will still see two or three thousand years after the birth of Christ. The end will come sooner than we think" and advancing that "I am sure that the Day of Judgment is just around the corner. It doesn't matter that we don't know the precise day ... perhaps someone else can figure it out. But it is certain that time is now at an end."[3] Thus, in the early modern world, the Book of Revelation became far more than a reservoir of vivid images. The Apocalypse buttressed theological doctrines of the providence and justice of God and historical outlines of world chronology. It provided rhetorical frameworks for political arguments both radical and conservative and for evangelical appeals for religious conversion. It supported plans for a return to primitive Christianity; it predicted the disso- lution of Church and world in the near future. ... It epitomised a passing stage of first-century religious imagination; it was an authoritative vision for all ages.[4]

In England, maybe more than in any other Catholic-turned-Protestant European nation, the Reformation played a decisive role in shaping the minds of the peoples of a whole country as well as their understanding of themselves and their country's role in world history. Closely intertwined with the Refor- mation, apocalyptic thought was especially influential in the English mental framework, having been totally absorbed into it by the end of the first decade of the seventeenth century.[5] The Protestant apocalyptic tradition, as used by English historians, was to help shape a distinctively English identity, which up to then had been considered inferior to other European nationalities.[6] Though it was not an exclusively British Protestant phenomenon, Revelation would decisively shape English Protestant thought more than that of any other nation, determining "English self-understanding, and religious thought well after the seventeenth century" as well as, later on, "apocalyptic thought in colonial and revolutionary America."[7]

Isolated from continental Protestantism, the English Reformation had developed in ways different from the German or Scandinavian examples. Many felt that Henry VIII's efforts in establishing a Protestant Church of England had not been thorough from the outset. To make matters worse, Mary I's bloody reign, with the restoration of Catholicism and the subsequent per- secution and martyrdom of Protestants, had delayed the course of the English Reformation. Therefore, the accession of Protestant Elizabeth to the throne filled Protestants' hearts with hope. Enthusiasm soared and many interpreted Elizabeth's reign as a sign of the impending millennium:

> With the rise of Elizabeth to the throne, the typological reading of English history received a boost, and the woman announced in Revelation 12:1–9 came to be read as a prefiguration of the queen: pregnant with Christ, persecuted by the popish Antichrist (personified in the Spanish Armada), and in pain, she is rescued by God, who removes her to the wilderness.[8] According to these escha- tological views, the reign of Elizabeth pointed to the imminent arrival of the apocalypse, as well as to England's providential election as the future location of the New Jerusalem.[9]

For sixteenth- and seventeenth-century Englishmen, England came to play a leading role in the world drama of salvation and redemption, with the Reformation being the culmination of English history.[10] So much was this the case that Elizabethans perceived themselves as God's chosen people, the dwellers of God's elect nation that would set the example for the rest of the world to follow.[11] It was inconceivable for Englishmen that this divine nation of the elect was any other than England, for all the other European countries failed to meet the requirements that God's chosen nation was to have. God's chosen nation would necessarily be a Protestant one, but the smallness of both the Swiss cantons and the German states, the extreme religious tolerance of Holland, and the remoteness of the Scandinavian nations made them all unable to fulfill this sacred role. There was no doubt in the minds of English Protestants, then, that England was the only nation that qualified as God's elect nation.[12] The Thirty Years' War (1618–1648) also helped support this theory: that England's sufferings had been lesser than those of other Protestant nations was evidence of God's special favor towards England, and pamphleteers called for English assistance to other Protestant nations.[13] For Puritan Thomas Hooker, the war proved that England played a leading role among the Protestant nations: "for whence comes it, whence is it, that the Lord hath had an eye unto me above all the rest, when the fire of God's fury hath flamed and consumed all the country round about us; Bohemia, and the Palatinate, and Denmark."[14]

However, Elizabeth, despite all the hopes put on her, soon disappointed many of her subjects with her determination to keep the Church as she had found it, to the point of telling the French ambassador, Malvesier, that "she would maintain the religion that she was crowned in, and that she was baptized in; and would suppress the Papistical religion that it should not grow; but that she would root out Puritanism, and the favourers thereof."[15] The failure of the Church of England to complete the Reformation led many a Protestant to think that England could not be regarded as God's chosen nation while Roman Catholic traces still remained. Elizabeth's successor, James I, was even less sympathetic to claims of reforming the Church of England. In the midst of such a hopeless state of incompleteness, William Perkins in his *Exposition of Christ's Sermon Upon the Mount* (1618) cautioned that

> religion hath been among us this thirty-five years, but the more it is published, the more it is contemned and reproached of many, etc. Thus not profaneness nor wickedness but religion itself is a byword, a mockingstock, and a matter of reproach; so that in England at this day the man and woman that begins to profess religion and to serve God, must resolve with himself to sustain mocks and injuries even as though he lived amongst the enemies of Religion.[16]

England began to be considered, instead, as a hindrance to the advancement of the true religion. Thus, England began losing its role as God's chosen nation and believers decided to look somewhere else for a more suitable place for their millennial ideas.[17]

Especially critical with the incomplete manner in which the Reformation was being carried out were the Puritans, who received this name for their intention of purifying the Church of England from Catholic vestiges. Given that England had failed to fulfill the role of God's chosen nation and that its sinfulness was rampant, the Puritans anticipated an imminent, divine punishment for having gone astray. God's wrath would fall on the English people because Protestantism was besieged abroad and changes were not carried out at home.[18] When the Puritans decided to flee from England, they did so out of the utmost conviction that, shortly after their departure, a punishment would fall on England because of its shortcomings.

Signs of England's imminent punishment that confirmed the Puritans' apocalyptic fears were not hard to find. Puritans, as well as other contemporary observers, found plenty of disturbing evidence to support their views of an England that was going dangerously astray. The lack of land for all Englishmen in England was a concern very much in the minds of contemporary writers, who proposed that the surplus of population be sent to America, thus alleviating the burden that this excess of population imposed on the land — not to mention the risk of population riots.[19] Several illnesses plagued England, with the black plague and smallpox combining their efforts to annihilate a large part of the population.[20] Financial failures also favored an interpretation of divine punishment falling on Britain, with agricultural losses from the 1580s to the 1660s (with the years between the 1590s and the 1620s being especially bad), a decaying cloth industry and the rapid disappearance of English forests, a raw material essential for several industries.[21] In short, with their flight, Puritans would be fleeing from an imminent judgment and subsequent punishment.

However, stressing that their flight from England did not involve cowardice was an important issue, too. By the very act of leaving the country, Puritans would be performing "a service to the Church of great consequence to carry the Gospel into those parts of the world, to help on the fullness of the coming of the Gentiles, and to raise a bulwark against the kingdom of AnteChrist [sic], which the Jesuits labor to rear up in those parts," as Puritan leader John Winthrop claimed around 1628.[22] More importantly, Puritans' flight would be a warning for those who stayed: "the departing of good people from a country does not cause a judgment, but warns of it, which may occasion such as remain to turn from their evil ways, that they may prevent it, or take some other course that they may escape it," Winthrop asserted.[23]

Many Puritan voices warned of the imminent disaster. Puritan minister Thomas Hooker became one of the most insistent ones in preaching about England's fate. His sermon "The Danger of Desertion" (1631) is representative of the context in England at the time.[24] Hooker himself would not leave for America till 1633, but in 1631, God was already giving his farewell to his formerly chosen people, who remained blind and deaf to His signs:

> When we observe what God hath done for us, all things are ripe to destruction, and yet we fear it not, but we promise to ourselves safety, and consider not that England is ready to be harrowed, and yet we cannot entertain a thought of England's desolation. When there are so many prophecies in it of its destruction, yet we cannot be persuaded of it. According to the conviction of our judgments, either it must not be, or not yet, as if it were unpossible that God should leave England, as if God were a cockering father over lewd (and stubborn) children. God may leave a nation, and his elect may suffer, and why may not England (that is but in an outward covenant with him)? England's sins are very great, and our warnings are and have been great; but yet our mercies are far greater. England hath been a mirror of mercies. Yet now God may leave it, and make it the mirror of his justice.[25]

Metaphysical poet and minister George Herbert similarly feared that: "Religion stands on tiptoe in our land, / Readie to pass to the American strand."[26] He was not unaware of the social and financial implications:

> Then shall Religion to America flee; ....
> My God, Thou dost prepare for them a way,
> By carrying first their gold from them away,
> For gold and grace did never yet agree
> Religion alwaies sides with povertie.[27]

These apocalyptic thoughts, rife in England during the 1620s and 1630s, would constitute the backdrop for the colonization of New England.[28] Thus, the planting of New England became tainted by this apocalyptic tone.[29] The Puritans' flight from incompletely reformed England was, also, a flight from Apocalypse itself. That they were persecuted by James I contributed its share to give rise to apocalyptic thoughts, too, for the oppressed have usually found solace in millenarian thoughts.[30] The Book of Revelation, a book specifically written for those suffering persecution, was particularly fitting for Puritans' circumstances.[31] Minister John Cotton, who only removed to America when persecution on him proved to be constant and not even his influential friends could help him, claimed that "we could offer a much clearer and fuller witness in another land than in the wretched and loathsome prisons of London."[32] Cotton justified the Puritans in their decision to flee to America in *Gods Promise to His Plantation* (1630) in the following way:

> how shall I know whether God hath appointed me such a place, if I be well where I am, what may warrant my removeall? ... there be evils to be avoided that may warrant removeall. First, when some grievous sinnes overspread a Country that threaten desolation.... This case might have beene of seasonable use unto them of the *Palatinate*, when they saw their Orthodoxe Ministers

banished, although themselves might for a while enjoy libertie of conscience. Secondly, if men be overburdened with debts and miseries, as *Davids* followers were; they may then retire out of the way (as they retired to *David* for safety).... Thirdly, in case of persecution, so did the Apostles in Acts 13. 46, 47.[33]

Anne Hutchinson, who went to America following her minister, John Cotton, before earning herself a reputation of religious unorthodoxy, declared when seeing Boston for the first time, that "if she had not a sure word that England should be destroyed her heart would shake."[34] While Puritans were certainly attracted to the New World for their conviction of an imminent apocalypse, the extent to which this conviction lured non–Puritans to New England remains a controversial matter.[35] For Alan Heimert and Andrew Delbanco, "ecclesiastical concerns were hardly the primary driving force, much less the exclusive one, behind the Great Migration of the 1630s. The literature of the 1620s discloses an increasing preoccupation among the Puritan clergy with the accelerating social and economic 'sins' of English culture."[36] Though references to the "desolation" of England are numerous in migration literature, the motives of non–Puritans more often than not went unrecorded (the most prolific writers by far being ministers and Puritans trying to attract more colonists).[37] Certainly, religious principles did not weight so heavily for all the migrants to America. Misled by praising reports speaking of the opportunities available in New England, many went to America with no clear goal in mind. Puritanism did help in providing a reason for migration, but not all migrants to the New World were Puritans and even some Puritans were not exclusively driven by religious purposes but by personal circumstances as well.[38]

In analyzing migrants' motivations, Nellis Crouse and Virginia DeJohn Anderson reached a similar conclusion: that though not all immigrants to New England were Puritans, many felt a certain sympathy for Puritan principles, concepts or motivations. Anderson's findings are that non–Puritan immigrants agreed to cooperation (and, up to certain extent, assimilation) with their Puritan neighbors for the sake of coexistence, though they might not share Puritan religious principles.[39] What is more, Crouse discards the importance of economic aspects in the Great Migration:

> we have few records suggesting financial difficulties; the colonists were, for the most part people of means, not likely to be affected by fluctuations in the cloth trade or even by a poor harvest; they chose the comparatively bleak shore of New England in preference to the fertile West Indies; their exodus caused Archbishop Laud serious misgivings for the future of the colony; ... and, lastly, their migration stopped suddenly with the election of the Puritan Long Parliament.[40]

To America the Puritans were to go, since England was beyond hope. In the same way and to the same extent that their very particular use of ecclesiastical history had enabled the English to see their country as a main actor in world history, now Puritans turned to ecclesiastical history "to explain the ultimate necessity of God's saints to depart from sinful England, to justify the meaning and significance of their migration to America, to construe the sacred, redemptive and revelatory meaning of the American wilderness, and last but not least, to interpret their life and experience in New England."[41] The sinfulness of England involved its de-sacralization, the loss of its importance within the framework of ecclesiastical or providential history. England, no longer leading the Reformation, had become an example of apostasy; the Church of England, no longer a role model among Protestants, had become the representation of the Antichrist. America, not England, now held Protestant millennial expectations and hopes.[42]

The interrelation between America and the Apocalypse dated back to the moment of discovery itself. In as early a date as 1500, Columbus claimed that "God made me the messenger of the new heaven and the new earth of which he spoke in the Apocalypse of St. John after having spoken of it through the mouth of Isaiah: and he showed me the spot where to find it."[43] Imbued by the apocalyptic zeal, Columbus encouraged priests to convert the Indians in the one hundred and fifty years remaining before the apocalypse, according to his calculations.[44] 1493, the year that saw the return of Columbus, also saw the publication of Sebastian Brandt's *Nuremberg Chronicles*, where, at the end of his book, he left just six blank pages to add what would happen before the imminent end of days.

New England, as its name indicated, was to become a new beginning for England, a second chance for those faithful English people who felt excluded in their mother country. Neither were the Puritans the only seventeenth-century individuals who believed that the apocalypse was coming nor chose America for their destination. Other settlements founded in seventeenth-century America were Woman in the Wilderness, Irenia, and Bohemia Manor, whose founders shared with the Puritans, for the most part, the idea that the decay of the Christian Church, going astray from the purity of Christianity of the first centuries, was irremediably lost and true Christians should wait in the New World for Christ's Second Coming.[45]

John Winthrop, the leader of the Massachusetts Bay Colony, took the matter of transplanting to America very seriously. For this fervent Puritan and respected member of his community, moving to the New World represented losing it all in favor of an uncertain future in an unknown location. In his 1629 "Reasons to be Considered, and Objections with Answers," Winthrop came to the conclusion that "God hath provided this place [New England] to be a refuge for many whom he meanes to save out of the general calamity."[46] In a letter to his wife on May 15, 1629, he expressed the same assurance that

England's "sinnes giues vs so great cause to looke for some heauvy Scquorge and Judgment to be cominge vpon us" so God "will provide a shelter and a hidinge place."[47] Puritan minister Francis Higginson, who readily moved to New England with his family, also stated that "New England might be designed by heaven, as a refuge and shelter for the non-conformists against the storms that were coming upon."[48] Should they decide to stay in England, people would not only face the danger of living in a God-forsaken country, they also ran the risk of losing their own status as God's chosen ones: "know it, we are in danger of most grievous judgement, namely, to be cut off from Christ, and to be made no people," as William Perkins preached in 1595.[49]

Once in America, news from England confirmed colonists' worst fears about a coming Apocalypse.[50] Bostonians held the unshakable "belief in the imminence of the millennium. Apocalyptic yearnings were common in the Puritan movement in the early seventeenth century, fed by the sense of crisis created by the building tensions between the Stuart monarchs and their non-conformist subjects."[51] Physical removal, then, did not imply that colonists had left their apocalyptic thoughts behind. In 1639 John Cotton, already living in Boston, dated the Apocalypse to 1655.[52] He writes: "I will not be two [sic] confident, because I am not a Prophet, nor the Son of a Prophet to foretell things to come, but so far as God helps by Scripture light, about the time 1655, there will be then such a blow given to this beast ... as that we shall see a further gradual accomplishment and fulfilling of this Prophecy here."[53] Although 1655 came and went and no Apocalypse took place, for the rest of his life Cotton kept seeing hints in everyday events that confirmed him that the Apocalypse was imminent. He claimed so in his 1651 Thanksgiving sermon and in a letter to Puritan English leader Oliver Cromwell.[54] By the end of the seventeenth century, his grandson, Cotton Mather, convinced that "God would not suffer Mr. Cotton to err," again warned of its imminence[55]: "I am verily perswaded, *The Judge is at the Door; I do without any hesitation venture to say, The Great Day of the Lord is Near, it is Near, and it hastens Greatly.* O That our Minds May be as deeply Engaged in Thinking on the Second coming of our Lord, as the Saints of old were in thinking on His First."[56]

Preparation for the imminent arrival of the Apocalypse was an ever-present thought in New England Puritans' minds. That they were separated by an ocean from sinful England did not decrease their apocalyptic-related concerns. If anything, the removal helped intensify their examination of New England society with the hope of finding signs of their role as New Jerusalem. God's second coming was especially significant because only then would it be disclosed who the true believers and who the sinners were. Questioning one's status as one of the Elect was at the core of Puritan existence, especially since reaching complete assurance was beyond their reach until death — "uncertainty of one's election was one of the signs of salvation, whereas complete assurance was a sure sign of damnation."[57] In declaring that "the greatest part of Christian grace lies in mourning the want of it," Thomas Shepard had defined the way to go for good Christians (that is, those receiving grace)— to constantly pine for their lack of grace.[58] Thus, the Puritans sheltered two contradictory feelings—optimistic hopes in their being the only true followers of God and pessimistic fears of not belonging to the select and restrictive group of the Elect. Permanently uncertain about whether they were one of the predestined ones, the Puritans lived in a state of constant fear and doubt about their salvation.

The fear that they might not be good enough to be saved gripped Puritans, sometimes paralyzing them with terror. The faithful believed that grace was not to be earned by Catholic ideas such as good works or lost on account of evil deeds. As the covenant of grace demanded, Puritans minutely examined their lives to try and discover signs of their possessing grace or being too sinful to receive it.[59] Life was considered a test, and failure to meet God's requirements meant eternal damnation in Hell. A permanent, internal psychological "struggle to preserve sanity and identity" ensued in a desperate attempt to discover one's true nature, to see if the wicked side prevailed or, if, on the contrary, one was to be saved.[60] Even the saints might backslide, so soul-searching, prayer, and introspection to prevent this were compulsory, lest New Englanders might follow Old England's pernicious example of once a chosen nation, now a decaying one.

In the most extreme cases, this permanent insecurity sometimes rendered Puritans indecisive and impotent, unable to do anything other than mull over their fears, forced to inactivity for fear they might be sinning.[61] Such a seemingly trivial issue as closing the door of a neighbors' barn, noisily being slammed by the wind during a storm, put minister Michael Wigglesworth in pains, uncertain whether this could be considered a breach of the command not to work during the Sabbath. Sometimes, if successful, Puritans could put this fear at the back of their conscious minds, but it was always ready to sneak into their lives. Madness was not too unusual an outcome. Winthrop records in his journal for the year 1637 a case illustrative of the tensions and stress that this uncertainty may cause on the individual psyche:

> A woman of Boston congregation, having been in much trouble of mind about her spiritual estate, at length grew into utter desperation, and could not endure to hear of any comfort, etc., so as one day she took her little infant and threw it into a well, and them came into the house and said, now she was sure she should be damned, for she had drowned her child.[62]

With these precedents, it is no wonder that the New England Puritan best-seller was one specifically dealing with the Apocalypse, Michael Wigglesworth's *The Day of Doom* (1662). Its popularity is testimony to the central role that the idea of Apocalypse occupied in the Puritan mind. Maybe more than any other text produced during this period, *The Day of Doom* illustrates the Puritan age of American history, capturing the spirit of the times in such an accurate way that Cotton Mather referred to it as the "Book of the Ages."[63] Heavily relying on the Bible (up to the point that some modern editions include the verses he made reference to within the poem itself), in *The Day of Doom* Wigglesworth attempted to make Christ's judgment vivid to a popular audience.[64] With the goal in mind of achieving as broad an audience as possible, Wigglesworth deliberately used a plain language (a distinctive feature of Puritan style) as well as common meter and folk ballad features.[65] Wigglesworth's text became extraordinarily well-known, used as a verse catechism and also as a primer for children to learn to read (though this goal was unintended by Wigglesworth). That such a dreary and scary poem became so commonplace and was considered to be a reading perfectly proper for young children, shows that, for the Puritans, the Apocalypse was a central part in their lives, and, accordingly, children should be acquainted with it from a very early age. Adults and children alike could quote the text by heart, which was referred to in daily conversation as well as in sermons.

Up to a certain extent, *The Day of Doom* can be considered a companion to Wigglesworth's *God's Controversy with New-England* (1662). In the latter, Wigglesworth warned his fellow colonists of God's displeasure with them and of its outcome:

> Our healthfull dayes are at an end,
> And sicknesses come on
> From yeer to yeer, becaus our hearts
> Away from God are gone.
> New-England, where for many yeers
> You scarcely heard a cough,
> And where Physicians had no work,
> Now finds them work enough.
>
> ...
>
> And one disease begins
> Before another cease, because
> We turn not from our sins.
> We stopp our ear against reproof,
> And hearken not to God:
> God stops his ear against our prayer,
> And takes not off his rod.
>
> ...
>
> We have been also threatened
> With worser things than these:
> And God can bring them on us still,

To morrow if he please.
For is his mercy be abus'd,
Which holpe us at our need
And mov'd his heart to pitty us,
We shall be plagu'd indeed.

...

Beware, O sinful Land, beware;
And do not think it strange
That sorer judgements are at hand,
Unless thou quickly change.
Or God, or thou, must quickly change;
Or else thou art undon:
Wrath cannot cease, if sin remain,
Where judgement is begun.[66]

In *God's Controversy with New-England* Wigglesworth mentions even "sorer judgements" though he dare not explicitly allude to the Apocalypse. That he would do later in *The Day of Doom*, where the situation described by Wigglesworth is a dreadful one, reminding his readers of images of decay and decline not too different from those that had been used a few decades earlier to describe England's fall from grace and to justify the coming to America. In *The Day of Doom* "vile wretches" feel safe despite the "all kind of sin" and even the good ones "through sloth and frailty slumber'ed," pay no attention to God's warnings of a future punishment were they to persist in their ways.[67] The opening scene, describing soundly sleeping people suddenly awakened by the force of God's punishment, suggests that the Apocalypse was not something to happen in remote England, but could befall upon familiar New England, not so righteous any more:

The Security of the World before
Christ's coming to Judgment.
Still was the night, Serene & Bright,
when all Men sleeping Lay;
Calm was the season, & carnal reason
though so 'twould last for ay.
Soul, take thine ease, let sorrow cease,
much good thou hast in store:
this was their Song, their Cups among,
the Evening before.[68]

The high sales of *The Day of Doom* (it is estimated that there was one copy of it for every twenty-five New Englanders and one for every forty-five colonists) show the pervasiveness of the Apocalypse in the New England Puritan mind.[69] That the book was only modestly successful in England shows that the poem contains a distinctive New England spirit, a sensibility differ-

ent from that of the English Puritans.[70] This was a New England-style Apocalypse and *The Day of Doom* is a distinctively New England Puritan poem.
Even removed from sinful England, physical distance did not provide Puritans with peace of mind. Because of the constraints of the doctrine of grace
and the impossibility of getting assurance of their status as "saved," Puritans
kept examining themselves and their fellow neighbors, always finding fault
in their own actions as well as those of others. It was as virtually impossible
to find a state of perfect grace in New England as it had been in England.
The New England Puritans had intended to flee from the divine punishment
that awaited England; fleeing from the Apocalypse proved impossible, though,
at least from a mental point of view. Despite attempts to flee the Apocalypse,
Puritans took it with them, and it would continue plaguing them. At the end
of the Puritan period, they still believed in Revelation 22:20: "He who
testifieth these things, saith, Yea: I come quickly. Amen: come, Lord Jesus.
The grace of the Lord Jesus be with the saints. Amen."

NOTES

1. "Erasmus [of Rotterdam] challenged the place of the Apocalypse in the New Testament canon in 1516 and in 1522. ... Finally, Erasmus accepted the book because of the *consensus ecclesiae* and because of its historical value." Irena Backus, "The Church Fathers and
the Canonicity of the Apocalypse in the Sixteenth Century: Erasmus, Frans Titelmans,
and Theodore Belza," *Sixteenth Century Journal* 29 (1998): 651. John Calvin neglected the
Book of Apocalypse, not certain about its standing in the Bible; Martin Luther eventually gave up the doubts he had once held about its canonicity, and Peter Martyr, William
Tyndale, William Perkins, and Martin Bucer (also spelled Butzer) chose not to make use
of the Book of Revelation at all, to keep matters simple. Richard Bauckham, *Tudor Apocalypse: Sixteenth Century Apocalypticism, Millennarianism, and the English Reformation:
From John Bale to John Foxe and Thomas Brightman* (n.p.: Sutton Courtenay, n.d.) 41–42
at 11.
2. Bauckham, *Tudor Apocalypse,* 232. Ira V. Brown, "Watchers for the Second Coming: The Millenarian Tradition in America," *The Mississippi Valley Historical Review* 39
(1952): 444.
3. Quoted in Bauckham, *Tudor Apocalypse,* 11. Quoted in Hillel Schwartz, *Century's End:
A Cultural History of the Fin de Siècle from the 990s through the 1990s* (New York and others: Doubleday, 1990) 90. Feeling that times were about to end, Luther accelerated the
publication of his translation of the book of Daniel in 1530, afraid that the apocalypse
may prevent its publication. Bauckham, *Tudor Apocalypse,* 147.
4. Christopher Burdon, *The Apocalypse in England. Revelation Unravelling, 1700–1834*
(Houndsmills and London: Macmillan / New York: St. Martin's, 1997) 209.
5. Katharine Firth, *The Apocalyptic Tradition in Reformation Britain, 1530–1645* (Oxford:
Oxford University Press, 1979) quoted in Burdon, *The Apocalypse in England,* 33.
6. The English colonial project was developed roughly at the same time as the Reformation as a means for the English to develop a distinctively national identity of their own
given that "many Elizabethan writers voice a nagging concern that — in military, commercial, and/or artistic terms — the English are a backward and peripheral nation." Louis Montrose, "The Work of Gender in the Discourse of Discovery," *Representations* no. 33 (1991):

17. The English relished the possibility of being able to compare themselves (most favorably, according to English propagandistic reports) to Spain in the colonial theater (not less than a world power, an empire with extensive territories throughout all of continental Europe and now also in the New World) to create a strong, national English identity. The English, who up to then had been "a reluctant, insecure, and insular people," now were thrown "from a marginal corner of Columbus's New World into the cockpit of an expanding world system." Carville Earle, "Pioneers of Providence: The Anglo-American Experience, 1492–1792," *Annals of the Association of American Geographers* 82, no. 3 (1992): 478.

7. Burdon, *The Apocalypse in England,* 209. Paul Boyer, *When Time Shall Be No More: Prophecy Belief in Modern American Culture* (Cambridge, MA, and London: Belknap, 1992) 57.

8. The defeat of the Armada in 1588 came to be universally regarded in England as a sign of God's being Protestant and on England's side against the Antichrist/popish Spaniards. This was a conviction Englishmen also brought to America with them.

9. Jorge Cañizares-Esguerra, *Puritan Conquistadors: Iberianizing the Atlantic, 1550–1700* (Stanford, CA: Stanford University Press, 2006) 77.

10. Avihu Zakai, *Exile and Kingdom: History and Apocalypse in the Puritan Migration to America* (Cambridge, UK, and others: Cambridge University Press, 1992) 7.

11. *Ibid.* 58.

12. Michael McGiffert, "God's Controversy with Jacobean England," *The American Historical Review* 88 (1983): 1153–1154.

13. Boyer, *When Time Shall Be No More,* 63. McGiffert, "God's Controversy with Jacobean England," 1154.

14. Quoted in Alan Heimert and Andrew Delbanco, eds., *The Puritans in America: A Narrative Anthology* (Cambridge, MA, and London: Harvard University Press, 1985) 62.

15. Quoted in W. H. Stowell and D. Wilson, *The Puritans in England,* in *History of the Puritans in England and the Pilgrim Fathers* (London, n.p.: 1849) 159.

16. Zakai, *Exile and Kingdom,* 207.

17. *Ibid.,* 7–8.

18. Francis J. Bremer, "In Defense of Regicide: John Cotton on the Execution of Charles I," *The William and Mary Quarterly* 37 (1980): 38.

19. Some authors doubt that there was a surplus of population in England at the end of the sixteenth century, but whether this perception was accurate or not overpopulation was a very real threat for contemporary English writers. Howard Mumford Jones, "The Colonial Impulse: An Analysis of the 'Promotion' Literature of Colonization," *Proceedings of the American Philosophical Society* 90 (1946): 146.

20. Gloria L. Main, *Peoples of a Spacious Land: Families and Cultures in Colonial New England* (Cambridge, MA, and London: Harvard University Press, 2001) 26.

21. Main, *Peoples of a Spacious Land,* 26. Bremer, "In Defense of Regicide," 38. Harvey Wish, *Society and Thought in Early America: A Social and Intellectual History of the American People Through 1865* (New York: David McKay, 1964) 15.

22. John Winthrop, "Reasons for the Plantation in New England," The Winthrop Society, <http://winthropsociety.org/doc_reasons.php> (March 31, 2008).

23. *Ibid.*

24. Heimert and DelBanco, *The Puritans in America,* 63.

25. Thomas Hooker, "The Danger of Desertion (1631)," in Heimert and Delbanco, *The Puritans in America,* 65–66.

26. Quoted in Mildred Campbell, "Social Origins of Some Early Americans," in *Seventeenth-Century America: Essays in Colonial History,* James Morton Smith, ed. (Chapel Hill: University of North Carolina Press, 1959) 87.

27. Quoted *ibid.*

28. Stephen J Stein, "Transatlantic Extensions: Apocalyptic in Early New England," in *The Apocalypse in English Renaissance Thought and Literature*, C. A. Patrides and Joseph Wittreic, eds. (Manchester, Dover, UK: Manchester University Press, 1984) 267.

29. Boyer, *When Time Shall Be No More*, 68.

30. Brown, "Watchers for the Second Coming," 443.

31. Bauckham, *Tudor Apocalypse*, 232.

32. Quoted in Bremer, "In Defense of Regicide," 38.

33. Reiner Smolinski, ed., *The Kingdom, the Power, and the Glory: The Millennial Impulse in Early American Literature* (Dubuque: Kendall/Hunt, 1998) 15–16.

34. J. F. Maclear, "New England and the Fifth Monarchy: The Quest for the Millennium in Early American Puritanism," *The William and Mary Quarterly* 32 (1975): 240.

35. Maclear, "New England and the Fifth Monarchy," 230. For a discussion of scholars' opinion in regards to the extent of the influence of millennial expectations in the Great Migration, see Smolinski, *The Kingdom, the Power, and the Glory*, 36–37.

36. Heimert and DelBanco, *The Puritans in America*, 62.

37. Maclear, "New England and the Fifth Monarchy," 230.

38. David Cressy, *Coming Over: Migration and Communication between England and New England in the Seventeenth Century* (Cambridge, UK: Cambridge University Press, 1987) 292.

39. Virginia DeJohn Anderson, "Migrants and Motives: Religion and the Settlement of New England, 1630–1640," *New England Quarterly* 58 (1985): 383. See Anderson for an in-depth analysis of the interconnectedness between religious motivation and immigration.

40. Nellis M. Crouse, "Causes of the Great Migration 1630–1640," *The New England Quarterly* 5 (1932): 35–36.

41. Zakai, *Exile and Kingdom,* 2.

42. *Ibid.*, 10, 63, 209.

43. Quoted in Schwartz, *Century's End,* 85. Smolinski further claims that the exploration of the New World was largely determined by religious convictions and millenarian cosmologies. Smolinski, *The Kingdom, the Power, and the Glory,* viii.

44. Bremer, "In Defense of Regicide," 85.

45. Woman in the Wilderness (founded by German Pietists in 1694), Irenia (founded by Moravians in 1695), and Bohemia Manor (founded by the Labadists in 1683). Steve Mizrach, "The Symbolic Invention of America-as-Utopia," Florida International University, <http://www.fiu.edu/~mizrachs/utopo-amer.html> (October 1, 2008).

46. Quoted in Zakai, *Exile and Kingdom,* 64.

47. Quoted *ibid.*, 59.

48. Quoted *ibid.*, 64.

49. William Perkins' *Lectures Upon the Three First Chapters of the Revelation* (1595), quoted *ibid.*, 208.

50. Cressy, *Coming Over,* 239. Even once the Great Migration had already began and was well under way, gloomy reports from New England helped confirm Puritans' worst fears. Letters informed them that England was in a state of progressive and alarming decay, the Scottish War being an indication of it. Cressy speaks of three phases in regards to the kind of information colonists received from England: "before 1640, through most of the period of the great migration, English affairs were seen as troubled but not desperate. ... From 1640 to 1660 the news from England was urgent, important and bewildering. The homeland was in crisis, with invasions, wars, revolution and revolutions within the revolution. ... After the Restoration, and for the remainder of the 17th century, ... the news itself ... was uninspiring." Cressy, *Coming Over,* 236.

51. Bremer, "In Defense of Regicide," 108.

52. Reiner Smolinski, "Apocalypticism in Colonial North America," in *The Encyclopedia of Apocalypticism*, Stephen J. Stein, ed. volume 3: Apocalypticism in the Modern Period and the Contemporary Age (New York: Continuum, 1998) 41–42.

53. Quoted in Maclear, "New England and the Fifth Monarchy," 233.

54. Bremer, "In Defense of Regicide," 108.

55. Wish, *Society and Thought in Early America,* 35. "Utopian Promise: Puritan and Quaker Utopian Visions, 1620–1750," American Passages: A Literary Survey, <http://www.learner.org/amerpass/unit03/pdf/unit03ig.pdf> (January 10, 2006), 35.

56. Quoted in Brown, "Watchers for the Second Coming," 446.

57. Elizabeth Reis, *Damned Women: Sinners and Witches in Puritan New England* (Ithaca, NY, and London: Cornell University Press, 1997) 14.

58. Jim Wohlpart, "The Dual Self in Bradstreet's 'The Flesh and the Spirit': The Never-Ending Conflict between Good and Evil," 1997, <http://itech.fgcu.edu/faculty/wohlpart/courses/bradstreet.htm> (October 1, 2008).

59. Reis, *Damned Women,* 13. Luther himself reminded his followers that "no one is sure of the integrity of his own contrition." Quoted in Schwartz, *Century's End,* 90.

60. Cynthia Griffin Wolff, "Literary Reflections on the Puritan Character," *Journal of the History of Ideas* 29 (1968): 21. Wohlpart, "The Dual Self in Bradstreet's 'The Flesh and the Spirit.'"

61. Still, men and women perceived their sinfulness and damnation differently. "Puritans never explicitly confronted their belief that women were more sinful than men. In fact, they maintained that women as well as men could share in the glory of conversion, oneness with Christ, and ultimately salvation. Nevertheless, the understanding women expressed about themselves betrays feelings about the souls and its relation to God and the devil which differed from those of men. ... Demonstrating freedom from all sin was, of course, an exceedingly difficult task for any Puritan; for a Puritan woman, so thoroughly permeated by her religion's ideology that she considered herself by nature a vile and evil creature hopelessly unworthy of Christ's love, the task was virtually impossible." Reis, *Damned Women,* 2–3. See Reis, *Damned Women,* "Introduction: Puritan Women and the Discourse of Depravity," 1–11, and chapter 1, "Women's Sinful Natures and Men's Natural Sins," for an analysis of Puritan perceptions of women's propensity to evil.

62. John Winthrop, *Winthrop's Journal: History of New England, 1630–1649,* James Kendall Hosmer, ed. vol. 1 (New York: Barnes and Noble, 1966) 230.

63. Wish, *Society and Thought in Early America,* 58–59.

64. Among these modern editions containing biblical verses, for instance, Michael Wigglesworth, *The Day of Doom,* World Library, 1996, <http://www.19.5degs.com/ebook/day-of-doom/341/read#list> (October 1, 2008).

65. A.M.E. Morris, "The Day of Doom: A poetical Description of the Great and Last Judgement," *The Literary Encyclopedia,* June 21, 2005, <http://www.litencyc.com/php/sworks.php?rec=true&UID=16350> (October 1, 2008).

66. Michael Wigglesworth, *God's Controversy with New-England,* in Smolinski, *The Kingdom, the Power, and the Glory,* 55, 58, 59, 60.

67. Wigglesworth, *The Day of Doom.*

68. *Ibid.*

69. "Wigglesworth, Michael." *The Chronology of American Literature,* 2004, <http://www.answers.com/topic/michael-wigglesworth> (October 1, 2008). *The Day of Doom* sold 1,800 copies in its first year of publication, a time when most people could hardly afford owning a book (they were shipped from England and were extremely expensive). No other book printed in seventeenth-century New England sold as much as *The Day of Doom.* Reis, *Damned Women,* 26. Morris, "The Day of Doom."

70. Morris, "The Day of Doom."

Works Cited

Anderson, Virginia DeJohn. "Migrants and Motives: Religion and the Settlement of New England, 1630–1640." *New England Quarterly* 58 (1985): 339–383.

Backus, Irena. "The Church Fathers and the Canonicity of the Apocalypse in the Sixteenth Century: Erasmus, Frans Titelmans, and Theodore Belza." *Sixteenth Century Journal* 29 (1998): 651–666.

Bauckham, Richard. *Tudor Apocalypse: Sixteenth Century Apocalypticism, Millennarianism, and the English Reformation: From John Bale to John Foxe and Thomas Brightman.* Oxford, UK: Sutton Courtenay, 1978.

Boyer, Paul. *When Time Shall Be No More: Prophecy Belief in Modern American Culture.* Cambridge, MA, and London: Belknap, 1992.

Bremer, Francis J. "In Defense of Regicide: John Cotton on the Execution of Charles I." *The William and Mary Quarterly* 37 (1980): 103–124.

Brown, Ira V. "Watchers for the Second Coming: The Millenarian Tradition in America." *The Mississippi Valley Historical Review* 39 (1952): 441–458.

Burdon, Christopher. *The Apocalypse in England. Revelation Unravelling, 1700–1834.* Houndsmills and London: Macmillan; New York: St. Martin's, 1997.

Campbell, Mildred. "Social Origins of Some Early Americans" in *Seventeenth-Century America: Essays in Colonial History.* James Morton Smith, ed. Chapel Hill: The University of North Carolina Press, 1959: 63–89.

Cañizares-Esguerra, Jorge. *Puritan Conquistadors: Iberianizing the Atlantic, 1550–1700.* Stanford, CA: Stanford University Press, 2006.

Cressy, David. *Coming Over: Migration and Communication between England and New England in the Seventeenth Century.* Cambridge, UK: Cambridge University Press, 1987.

Crouse, Nellis M. "Causes of the Great Migration 1630–1640." *The New England Quarterly* 5 (1932): 3–36.

Earle, Carville. "Pioneers of Providence: The Anglo-American Experience, 1492–1792." *Annals of the Association of American Geographers* 82, no. 3 (1992): 478–499.

Heimert, Alan and Andrew Delbanco, eds. *The Puritans in America: A Narrative Anthology.* Cambridge, MA, and London: Harvard University Press, 1985.

Hooker, Thomas. "The Danger of Desertion (1631)" in *The Puritans in America: A Narrative Anthology.* Alan Heimert and Andrew Delbanco, eds. Cambridge, MA, and London: Harvard University Press, 1985: 62–69.

Jones, Howard Mumford. "The Colonial Impulse: An Analysis of the 'Promotion' Literature of Colonization." *Proceedings of the American Philosophical Society* 90 (1946): 131–161.

Maclear, J. F. "New England and the Fifth Monarchy: The Quest for the Millennium in Early American Puritanism." *The William and Mary Quarterly* 32 (1975): 223–260.

Main, Gloria L. *Peoples of a Spacious Land: Families and Cultures in Colonial New England.* Cambridge, MA, and London: Harvard University Press, 2001.

McGiffert, Michael. "God's Controversy with Jacobean England." *The American Historical Review* 88 (1983): 1151–1174.

Mizrach, Steve. "The Symbolic Invention of America-as-Utopia." Florida International University. <http://www.fiu.edu/~mizrachs/utopo-amer.html> (October 1, 2008).

Montrose, Louis. "The Work of Gender in the Discourse of Discovery." *Representations* 33 (1991): 1–41.

Morris, A.M.E. "The Day of Doom: A Poetical Description of the Great and Last Judgement." *The Literary Encyclopedia.* June 21, 2005. <http://www.litencyc.com/php/sworks.php?rec=true&UID=16350> (October 1, 2008).

Reis, Elizabeth. *Damned Women: Sinners and Witches in Puritan New England.* Ithaca, NY, and London: Cornell University Press, 1997.

Schwartz, Hillel. *Century's End: A Cultural History of the Fin de Siècle from the 990s through the 1990s.* New York and others: Doubleday, 1990.

Smolinski, Reiner. "Apocalypticism in Colonial North America" in *The Encyclopedia of Apocalypticism. Volume 3: Apocalypticism in the Modern Period and the Contemporary Age.* Stephen J. Stein, ed. New York: Continuum, 1998: 36–71.

_____, ed. *The Kingdom, the Power, and the Glory: The Millennial Impulse in Early American Literature.* Dubuque, IA: Kendall and Hunt, 1998.

Stein, Stephen J. "Transatlantic Extensions: Apocalyptic in Early New England" in *The Apocalypse in English Renaissance Thought and Literature.* C. A. Patrides and Joseph Wittreich, eds. Manchester, Dover, UK: Manchester University Press, 1984.

Stowell, W. H. "The Puritans in England" in *History of the Puritans in England and the Pilgrim Fathers.* W. H. Stowell and D. Wilson. London, n.p.: 1849.

"Utopian Promise: Puritan and Quaker Utopian Visions, 1620–1750." American Passages: A Literary Survey. 36. <http://www.learner.org/amerpass/unit03/pdf/unit03ig.pdf> (November 6, 2008).

"Wigglesworth, Michael." *The Chronology of American Literature.* 2004. <http://www.answers.com/topic/michael-wigglesworth> (October 1, 2008).

Wigglesworth, Michael. *The Day of Doom,* World Library. 1996. <http://www.19.5degs.com/ebook/day-of-doom/341/read#list> (October 1, 2008).

_____. "God's Controversy with New-England" in *The Kingdom, the Power, and the Glory.* Reiner Smolinski, ed. Dubuque, IA: Kendall and Hunt, 1998. <http://digitalcommons.unl.edu/cgi/viewcontent.cgi?article=1036&context=etas> (November 9, 2008).

Winthrop, John. "Reasons for the Plantation in New England." The Winthrop Society. <http://winthropsociety.org/doc_reasons.php> (October 1, 2008).

_____. *Winthrop's Journal: History of New England, 1630–1649* vol. 1. James Kendall Hosmer, ed. New York: Barnes and Noble, 1966.

Wish, Harvey. *Society and Thought in Early America: A Social and Intellectual History of the American People Through 1865.* New York: David McKay, 1964.

Wohlpart, Jim. "The Dual Self in Bradstreet's 'The Flesh and the Spirit': The Never-Ending Conflict between Good and Evil." 1997. <http://itech.fgcu.edu/faculty/wohlpart/courses/bradstreet.htm> (October 1, 2008).

Wolff, Cynthia Griffin. "Literary Reflections on the Puritan Character." *Journal of the History of Ideas* 29 (1968): 13–32.

Zakai, Avihu. *Exile and Kingdom: History and Apocalypse in the Puritan Migration to America.* Cambridge, UK, and others: Cambridge University Press, 1992.

J. Edmestone Barnes, a Jamaican Apocalyptic Visionary in the Early Twentieth Century

Richard Smith

Introduction

Apocalyptic visions and beliefs in post-emancipation Jamaica are most often associated with the millenarian traditions of the black peasantry and urban dispossessed. The myalism of the 1860s Great Revival, the manifestations of Bedwardism from the 1890s and the emergence of Ras Tafari in the Kingston slums during the Great Depression have all been characterized by the fusion of preserved African religious beliefs with apocalyptic readings from the King James version of the Old Testament.[1] In contrast, aside from interpretations linked to the ideas of Marcus Garvey, the apocalyptic ideas of Jamaican intellectuals have not been examined in detail.[2] This essay aims to address this absence by discussing the reaction of a long-neglected black émigré Jamaican, J. Edmestone Barnes, to the imperial crises of the early twentieth century culminating in the First World War.

For a number of reasons, two of Barnes's essays, *Signs of the Times: Touching the final supremacy of nations* (1903)[3] and *The Economy of Life: Some Suggestions for World Betterment* (1921),[4] form the focus of this study. Perhaps most significant is the insight these texts provide into the role of religion in the evolution of an intellectual anti-colonial ideology, particularly how the "end of days" signaled the birth of a new optimistic, emancipatory era for colonial subjects. At first, Barnes's engrained loyalty to Imperial Britain led him to imagine a benevolent Empire extending the rights of citizenship to all its subjects. Angered by the failure of Britain to reward the loyalty of black subjects during the South African War (1899–1902) and, to a lesser extent, the First World War, Barnes started to imagine a new order of self-government for all subjects of African descent. However, he never argued for the complete severing of Imperial ties. In this process, non-conformist religion and Imperial education were fused in critiques not only of Imperial government, but also European civilization, focused on Catholicism, divine monarchy and the expansion of empire and military might.

Barnes was born into a peasant farming family, eight years before the Morant Bay Rebellion of 1865, a pivotal event which defined Jamaican society for generations to come. The unsuccessful revolt by the black Jamaican peasantry over disproportionate poll taxes marked the first organized attempt since emancipation from slavery in 1838 to assert black politics, rights and self-determination. For most white Jamaicans, Morant Bay signaled the end of the "Great Experiment" in free labor. Measures to force the black peasantry away from independent subsistence and towards plantation labor were intensified. The imposition of Crown Colony government imposed further limitations on black political representation.[5] Against this backdrop, Barnes received his education at the Kingston University School, established by James D. Ford in 1871. Ford claimed to provide a "sound practical and liberal education" and a curriculum including both ancient and modern languages.[6] Education was regarded as an important tool to inculcate European values of civilization among black Jamaicans, particularly after the Rebellion. However, it was not compulsory and remained under the control of non-conformist missionary organizations until well into the twentieth century. As a fee-charging institution aimed at the children of white planters, the University School was well beyond the reach of the majority of black Jamaicans. This suggests that the Barnes family were relatively wealthy farmers or had the support of a local benefactor. Barnes himself would certainly have been one of the few, if not the only, black pupils.

Barnes and the Black Atlantic World

In 1889, Barnes was the first Jamaican to be baptized into the Christadelphian faith and two years later arrived in Britain to conduct a speaking tour on behalf of the brethren.[7] As he traveled, he contributed a number of articles to *The Investigator*, a Christadelphian journal edited in Glasgow by Thomas Nisbet. In the autumn of 1893, following a bout of ill-health, Barnes sought a rest-cure in Germany, from where he continued to correspond with *The Investigator*. However, he was increasingly attacked for his forthright views on the resurrection of Christ and the possibility of eternal life, a theme he returned to in both *Signs of the Times* and *Economy of Life*. When it was suggested he had been given undue prominence on his tour of Britain, Barnes was moved to retort, "with few exceptions, the leaders of Christadelphianism have always acted with undue precipitance in the casting off and disfellowshipping [of] their brethren touching enquiry for understanding."[8] Possibly sponsored by a religious sympathizer, Barnes entered the University of Leipzig, Germany, where he studied geological and engineering sciences as well as philosophy and theology. Barnes subsequently pursued a career in mining and civil engineering which took him to Latin America, South Africa, Liberia and the United States and which included a number of business ventures. As well as his involvement with the Christadelphians, Barnes's life may be traced through his involvement with the Rationalist Press Association (RPA) between 1903 and 1921, his appointment by the government of Liberia as its representative in the boundary dispute with the British colony of Sierra Leone from 1910 to 1912, a later campaign to develop industrial schools in that country and his membership of the Royal Geographical Society, to which he was elected as a fellow in 1919. Barnes was also involved with several mining syndicates in Venezuela and South and West Africa.[9] By 1928, he had accrued sufficient funds to own a thirty per cent stake in the Lahun Syndicate Limited which had commissioned Barnes to establish the extent of diamond and mineral deposits in Sierra Leone.[10]

Between the turn of the twentieth century and 1928, his last year of documented activity, Barnes traveled widely on three continents, along the way becoming acquainted with non-conformists, rationalists, anti-colonialists, British Imperial officials, scientists, engineers, entrepreneurs, radicals, pan-Africans and intellectuals of the Harlem Renaissance. He may truly be regarded as both a product and an embodiment of the Black Atlantic.[11] Among this disparate, global audience Barnes circulated his pamphlets and short books, sustaining a number of key friendships of mutual influence and intellectual benefit.

Charles Garnett, minister of Arundel Square Church, Barnsbury, London wrote the introduction to Barnes's short pamphlet, *The Economic Value of the Native Races of Africa*.[12] Garnett had become a staunch advocate of racial equality after a tour of the United States in the 1890s, where he came into contact with the activist Mary Church Terrell and the universalistic Theosophical Society. Particularly interested in the rights of black South Africans after the Boer War, Garnett was a leading member of the League of Universal Brotherhood and Native Races Association, eventually retiring from his ministry in 1911 to campaign against racial injustice throughout the Empire. In 1907, Garnett defended Barnes against charges of impropriety in his diamond mining dealings laid against him by the South African authorities.[13] A shared knowledge of South African affairs may have influenced Barnes when he came to write *The Economy of Life*, a considerable portion of which is devoted to a critique of pre-apartheid institutionalized racism. Pivotal to the promotion of Marcus Garvey's activities in London, during the 1920s, Garnett also provides a possible connection between Barnes and the wider pan-

African movement. Barnes's interest in the promotion of industrial education and full citizenship for Africans suggests the influence of Edward Wilmot Blyden and Joseph Booth, the latter actively preaching in Cape Town while Barnes was present there.[14]

Signs of the Times was circulated in London and Barnes's Caribbean homeland where it was favorably reviewed in the *Daily Gleaner* of Jamaica.[15] When *The Economy of Life* appeared eighteen years later, Barnes's profile had risen considerably. Reviews were published in New York and London[16] and his influence within the Harlem Renaissance at this time was recognized by Richard B. Moore, the Barbadian Pan-Caribbeanist, who recalled Barnes's revolutionary public condemnation of the term "negro" in a public lecture at the Lafayette Hall, New York.[17] The *Economy of Life* was published by Sidney Campion, the socialist, journalist and critic, who at the time was a prominent member of the Independent Labour Party.[18] The forward was written by Joseph McCabe,[19] the leading freethinker and prominent member of the Rationalist Press Association. Both these connections testify to the continuing favorable reception to Barnes and his influences as a critical thinker in post-war Britain.

Barnes as Historicist and Eschatologist

Signs of the Times was published by a friend in South London, Henry Forsey Brion,[20] with whom Barnes had been staying as he prepared to leave for South Africa on business. At this time, Barnes, who had been christened Isaac, adopted the pen name, J. Edmestone Barnes, the *I* on his university certificates more closely resembling a *J*.[21] His critical reading of the Bible, informed by secular history, was intended to provide insight into the growing conflict among the European powers and the likely outcome of that struggle. Barnes emphasized his was a scientific analysis based on material circumstances as opposed to "supernatural revelation."[22] Barnes followed the historicism of Joseph Mede and Isaac Newton, although his most immediate influence appears to be John Thomas, founder of the Christadelphian movement. Historicism took the apocalyptic symbols and time spans of the Books of Daniel and Revelation to map the course of history, a method followed by Christadelphian theology, which also shared historicism's rejection of the Holy Trinity.[23] Within this eschatological tradition, the prophetic time spans of 1260, 1290, 1335 and 490 days in the Books of Daniel and Revelation are reckoned as years.[24] Barnes's Christadelphian background, with its interrogative, forensic approach to Biblical texts, was therefore not entirely incompatible with his membership in the RPA.[25] Indeed, that Barnes earned the respect of Joseph McCabe is perhaps in no small part due to his persistent anti–Catholic stance in both *Signs of the Times* and *Economy of Life*. In turn, Barnes praised McCabe's *The Evolution of Civilisation* which he regarded as "thoroughly disruptive of the pious stories of the orthodox religions."[26]

Anti-Catholicism and the Beginning of the End

For Barnes the beginning of a forty year "end of days" and the revealing of "a new order … the overturning of that long dark night of treachery and scarlet-coloured things" was marked by Italian unification in 1870.[27] Barnes held that the unification of Italy ended the rule of the Church of Rome — the scarlet Beast and scarlet-clad Whore of Babylon — which had established a false kingdom in place of God's reign on earth, in Barnes's terms, "politico-ecclesiastical despotism and lawlessness, by alliance of Church and State."[28] Here Barnes took the fourth great beast in Nebuchadnezzar's dream of the fate of nations (Daniel 7) as the Roman Empire, rather than Greek, which eventually gave way to the Church of Rome (the strongest of the beast's ten horns) from the time of Constantine.

According to Barnes, Constantine's opportunism in enlisting Christians to defeat Maxentius at the Battle of the Milvian Bridge (312 CE),[29] and the consequent granting of religious toleration under the Edict of Milan (313 CE), was responsible for placing the Catholic Church of Rome in a position to challenge God's authority and persecute the rightful followers of Christ. The status of the Catholic Church was further strengthened by the Justinian edict of 533 CE, which granted papal authority to Pope John, underpinned by the increasing unity of church and state during the Byzantine era, evident when Phocas conceded authority of all Christian churches to Boniface III (608 CE).[30] In 1868, 1335 years after the Justinian edict, Pope Pious IX issued the *non expedit* encyclical forbidding Catholics from participating in the new Italian state. *Non expedit* and the claim to infallibility of 1870 were almost immediately undermined as the remaining principalities joined the Italian state, swearing loyalty to King Victor Emmanuel, rather than the Papacy. Barnes suggests the name of the Italian monarch, Emmanuel — "God is with us" in Hebrew — was a sign of divine intervention. Furthermore, Barnes concluded that modernist critiques from within the Catholic Church, which asserted its teachings and institutions were human rather than divine, underlined "the end of the Dispensation which the Catholic Church represents."[31]

When Barnes began writing *The Economy of Life* around 1906, he could point to a further event which he believed marked the end of the Christian

Dispensation, "the ignominious defeat ... of the army and the navy of the Great White Christian 'Tsar of all the Russias' ... by the Mikado's army and navy."[32] Barnes's description of the defeat of Russia by Japan in the war of 1904–1905 was significant on another level, as it brought into question white European claims of racial superiority, "the Mikado and his people not being either white or Christian."[33] Principally, however, it was the failing power of the Papacy which marked the end of the Fourth Age for Barnes and the beginning of the "end," a forty year "period of political earthquakes, thunders, and lightnings foretold — the period when the hearts of nations are failing them for fear."[34]

The Condition of the British Empire During the End

Barnes asserted that the "British Empire and Nation ... will in no wise ... be exempted from the fiery scourge and trying vicissitude coming upon the nations of the world,"[35] and pointed to a panoply of threats in addition to the Papacy: Free Trade, the Great Powers of continental Europe, and the loss of Imperial dynamism. Barnes was deeply aware of the malaise believed to be taking hold of Britain that became increasingly evident in the recruitment crisis during the South African War (1899–1902). Barnes believed the "Wake up, England" speech by the Prince of Wales in December 1901 was "a direct appeal to the nation to rouse itself from the state of apathy and lethargy into which it has fallen by the exuberance of its delusion."[36] The Prince of Wales (later George V) had recently toured the British Empire, partly in order to promote the preeminence of British goods in the trade with the British colonies. But he also hinted at the condition of British manhood which was cause for much concern by suggesting that his "fellow countrymen ... prove the strength of the attachment of the motherland to her children by sending ... only of her best" to meet the demand for population in the white colonies of Australia, New Zealand and Canada. There "healthy living, liberal laws, free institutions," could be "exchange[d] for the over-crowded cities and the almost hopeless struggle for existence which, alas, too often is the lot of many in the old country."[37]

In 1899, around forty per cent of recruits for the British Army were found unfit within two years of service. Added to outright rejections, the rate of wastage among volunteers was closer to sixty per cent. As the Prince of Wales implied, the poor physique and health of military recruits was believed to be particularly evident among men from industrial areas,[38] a pessimistic attitude evident in earlier imperial crises. In 1871, six years after the Morant Bay Rebellion, Charles Kingsley visited the West Indies and suggested the black peasantry were more robust than the "short and stunted figures" of the white urban poor.[39] Barnes was also calling attention to another reason for this turn-of-century despondency — a belief the comforts of Empire and industry had produced complacency, lethargy, and moral enervation, further enfeebling the population and thereby undermining Imperial effectiveness. The journalist Arnold White fore-fronted the popularization of this dystopian vision, proposing that the rejection of family life had compounded the undermining of national stamina and had resulted in a loss of political resolve.[40]

To ensure the British Empire survived the tribulations that lay ahead, Barnes advocated support for Joseph Chamberlain's Tariff Reform campaign. With newspaper reports of Chamberlain's historic Birmingham speech of May 15, 1903,[41] presumably fresh in his mind, Barnes argued the end of Free Trade would not only benefit metropolitan manufacturing but British colonies also as they bought more goods from Europe and the U.S. than were sold in exchange.[42] Barnes's stance was in stark contrast to that of another émigré Jamaican, also published in 1903. Dr. Theophilus Scholes opposed tariff barriers on the grounds the Empire had benefited from Free Trade over many decades. Protectionism was likely to involve retaliation to which the Empire, particularly the metropole, would be highly vulnerable, being so dependent on imported food.[43]

More important for Barnes was his desire that the Empire substantiate its assertion to be the pre-eminent civilization and uphold the proclaimed mission to "deliver [its subjects] from error's chain,"[44] rather than embodying "sanguinary aggrandisement."[45] To ensure victory for the British Empire in the battle for "the final supremacy of nations," and to prepare the foundations for a new age of self-determination and global equality, Barnes argued:

> All thoughts must now be concentrated towards Britain's confederation and consolidation of the ... diverse subjects of the King to be schooled to unity and universality of action, irrespective of whatsoever colour, creed, or race ... the Empire occupies a highly exalted place.... Its peoples and rulers are a nation that possess high intelligence, and aim at the noblest ideal of life among the nations of the earth.[46]

Barnes's loyalty to the Empire and his belief it could be reformed, but remain intact, meant he delayed publication of *The Economy of Life* until the threat posed by the First World War had passed.[47] Then he declared that if the Empire were to survive, "Great Britain must wake up ... and weld her peoples of divers nationalities, and of varied complexional castes, into a strong, homogeneous band or body, by giving unto the peoples full opportunities to improve their conditions to the utmost capacity which they are capable."[48]

European Conflict and the End of Days

In 1899, Czar Nicholas II of Russia and Queen Wilhelmina of the Netherlands convened the Hague Conference, ostensibly to create the machinery for peaceful settlements of disputes and to limit the growth of armaments. Convinced the forty year "end of days" was drawing to a close, Barnes underlined the impossibility of achieving peace. He suggested any apparent rapprochement was the very opposite; "this is not the aeon ... for peace, but war"[49]—a war he believed would erupt between 1908 and 1910, 2400 years after Daniel's vision.[50] The rise of the Great Powers, subsuming the smaller nations in their wake, would inevitably lead to an escalation of the arms race, maintained Barnes, drawing his readers' attention to recent speeches by the Marquis of Salisbury and the Marquis of Dufferin and Ava, two leading British diplomats who had reached similar conclusions. Despite his Christadelphian background, Barnes did not present an alternative to war, declaring "There can be no permanent peace among nations until the final supremacy is decided between them by the arbitrament of the sword, and one of them ... is crowned Lord of all."[51]

Barnes placed the Russian Empire as the central threat to the British Imperialism. In Barnes's eyes, the claim of Czar Nicholas II to rule through divine right meant he placed himself above God's authority on earth. But, like Eve, the Czar was prevented from touching the "Tree of Life" and was ultimately doomed. In interpreting the kingdoms of Gog, Magog, Gomer and Tarshish of the Book of Ezekiel as Russia, Germany, France and Britain respectively, Barnes extensively paraphrases, but never cites, John Thomas's *Exposition of Daniel*.[52] Thomas in turn had followed the *Geographia Sacra* (1646) of French Protestant theologian, Bochart (1599–1667). Ezekiel named the Great Chief "Gog of the land of Magog" who will be met in battle by a formidable foe "to decide who shall subdue and vanquish the other, and become the chief of the European and Oriental cosmos."[53] "In modern phraseology that power is Great Britain of Europe and *Great Britain beyond the seas combined*," declared Barnes. "Every Briton, be he white or black, red or blue, at no distant date will be required to do duty to the Empire's cause."[54] Here Barnes stresses his support for a united Empire against a common enemy, anticipating the declarations of support for the war effort issued by Marcus Garvey's Universal Negro Improvement Association in 1914, in the expectation of post-war political and economic enfranchisement.[55]

Believing war was inevitable, Barnes was critical of proposals to cut the British naval budget and regarded those in favor guilty of "pusillanimous talk."[56] Barnes rejected retrenchment as defeatist and argued that Britain, with its vast Empire, was capable of defeating the combined forces of continental Europe if militarily prepared. Barnes was an admirer of Charles Dilke, a leading member of the "blue water" school, who feared a European war and believed the best deterrent was a strong navy. Dilke also advocated a command structure which linked the two services and Imperial and home defense.[57] Barnes's prediction of a mighty conflict was a mere four years adrift. In *The Economy of Life*, published three years after the end of the First World War (1914–1918), it is evident he was even more convinced the world was on the cusp of a new age. "'Armageddon' has come ... and it has scorched mankind with so terrific a heat as to cause millions of the human family to gnaw their tongues for their pain and torments."[58] But more importantly, the First World War had brought the downfall of worldly empires. Generals and world leaders were "prohibited from entering through the 'gateway' into the 'New City'" or "[t]o rule and reign in this New Dispensation upon which men have entered,"[59] underlining, for Barnes, that all humankind were ultimately accountable and subordinate to a higher authority.

The apparent dawn of a new era raised two key theological points for Barnes which had preoccupied him since he toured the British Isles in the early 1890s and which seem to have fractured his relationship with the Christadelphians. The concepts which Barnes wished to interrogate and were central to his understanding of the Apocalypse were the belief of everlasting life and the Resurrection.[60] In rather arcane terms, Barnes referred to the new age revealed after the "end of days" as *aionian zoe*, an expression he argued had been "incorrectly translated into the English tongue as 'Everlasting Life!'"[61] Barnes was convinced *aionian zoe* did not imply eternity, rather "the term *aion* is ... a fixed and settled order of things." Here Barnes sought the authority of Thomas Nisbet, the editor of *The Investigator* who had argued "*Aion* is not time, long or short, boundless or endless. It is stability and fixity as opposed to what is temporary."[62] Barnes went on to expound in a materialist, rationalist fashion that "every *aion* has its own peculiar characteristics, and it is these characteristics which constitute a given period, an *aion*, distinguishing it from preceding or succeeding *aions*."[63]

The second prong of Barnes's critique was his refutation of "the erroneous and superstitious belief" of resurrection.[64] According to Barnes this conviction had arisen through the incorrect translation of the Greek *anastasis* which he took to mean "to raise up" or "set up" rather than "rise again."[65] Barnes insisted the new age —*aionian zoe*—signified "the higher existence of man, on earth," as opposed to "Life ... everlasting or immortal," and therefore of this, rather than "another world."[66] His rejection of resurrection underlines the increasing influence of rationalism evident in *The Economy of Life* and differs significantly with the Christadelphian perspective outlined in John Thomas's *Anastasis*.[67] Barnes had drawn on Charles Turner Gorham's *The First*

Easter Dawn, which had been published by the rationalist publisher Watts and Company. Joseph McCabe wrote the preface for Gorham's study which was favorably reviewed in the RPA journal.[68]

The Plight of Africa and the New Age

Barnes's theological stance, particularly his fervent belief oppression could be transformed into justice in this world rather than the next, was pivotal to his growing preoccupation with the plight of Africans in Africa and the diaspora. As such, Barnes shared the present-world orientation of the millennial movements of his native Jamaica, premised on the belief God would intervene in worldly affairs, a source of encouragement to those suffering hardship under the colonial regime. In *Signs of the Times,* Barnes made only one direct reference to the plight of black Africans, doing so in order to make historical comparison with the tribulations of the Jews.[69] Barnes understood how the papacy had partly arisen due to the toleration of Emperor Constantine, who objected to the cruelty inflicted upon the Christians solely on the basis of their religion. Likewise he cited Thomas Macaulay's remarks on the treatment of the Jews in England, who "were persecuted only because they were Jews,"[70] who in turn, Barnes compared to black Africans who were ill-treated "in consequence of the colour Almighty God has given them."[71]

The immanent *Parosia*— presence — of Christ in the new age signaled the end of Gentile rule and, by association, the end of the iniquitous predicament of black Africa.[72] "Israelites, Jews and Africans" were the "true representatives and embodiment of the way of life, in contradistinction to the way of death among nations in general,"[73] and were destined to have their authority restored as written in the Book of Ezekiel (11:17 and 37:21). As Barnes completed *The Signs of the Times,* the First Aliyah (1882–1903) of Jewish migrants to the Holy Land was coming to a close and the Second, prompted by the Kishinev[74] pogrom of April 1903, was under way.[75] Barnes observed that "the Jews [of the Gentile nations] ... are ... becoming conscious of home ... and are putting forth efforts to back to the land of their ancestors."[76] The movement of Jews to their "father's land" was of deep significance for Barnes, "the *prima facie* bone of contention in the very last phase of the 'Great Eastern Question'"[77] with the potential for significant resonance among the African diaspora. Here Barnes followed the teachings of John Thomas, who had written at length of the return of Jews to the Holy Land in a coming new age. In the 1860s, Thomas declared that on Christ's return to earth he would send a proclamation to Britain to enlist British maritime power for the restoration of Israel. Ultimately, the British Empire would make "a peaceable surrender

... into his hand"[78] and Queen Victoria would be unthroned and pay homage to Jesus in Jerusalem. Thomas's perspective suggested that the British Empire, rather than the Roman Empire, was the fourth great beast of Daniel's vision, a position shared by James Cross whose eschatological study of the Great Powers's demise and the government of Jews in the new age may also have been consulted by Barnes.[79]

In *The Economy of Life*, Barnes was more forthright about the negative impact of the European empires on black Africans. During the book's preparation, Barnes had spent lengthy periods in South Africa, West Africa and the United States. Barnes argued "nothing could surpass that dastardly buccaneering and kidnapping which 'civilised' Christian European nations conducted on the West Coast of Africa ... from the 16th to the early 19th centuries" and "the continent of Africa has become devastated and bereft of its people. The African race, like the Jews, are scattered all over the world among other people."[80] However, Barnes believed the adversities Africans had suffered under slavery and colonialism prepared them, like the Jews, "for a great destiny in the next aion." The new age, promised Barnes, would be a time of upliftment, in which "men and nations" would follow the call of Jesus "to come up higher — to get away from animal life and take possession of the higher one."[81] But the end of days and the arrival of the new age, although a period of momentous events and passing of worldly powers, were not regarded as a time of judgment by Barnes. While unjust leaders might be swept aside, human beings in general would not be called upon to account for past behavior.

Barnes's views on resurrection and eternal life are crucial here. As Barnes argued in *The Investigator* during the 1890s, *anastasis* had been poorly translated to imply a physical raising from the dead, losing what he believed was the original, metaphorical sense implying improvement or rebirth through faith and upright living, paving the way for a just and equitable society.[82] Hence he chose the term "Economy of Life" to encompass "the whole or every part of life's purposes, and not merely the monetary aspect alone" and which should be based on "moral culture, responsibility, reciprocity [and] goodwill."[83] Any suggestion that in the new age the dead would be raised to be judged alongside the living and to be potentially damned in the process was, according to Barnes, "the scattering of papist blasphemy." He went on to ask: "Can rational beings conceive how a just and good God, whose attributes are founded on love, could have judged his creature man without righteousness, justice and equity?"[84] In other words, the mercy of a triumphant God would not be found wanting.

Between 1903 and 1909, Barnes lived at Kroonstad in the Orange Free State, South Africa, acting on behalf of two diamond mining syndicates.[85] South Africa was emerging from the bloody and bitter conflict of 1899–1902 and the administration of the former Boer republics — Transvaal and Orange Free State — and the British colonies of Natal and the Cape were under consideration by the Imperial government. Black South Africans had fought for both the Boer settlers and the British,[86] but Barnes felt the military service and greater support they had given the Imperial cause should be recognized in any decisions touching on their status within the future South African state. Barnes's major concern was that self-government, both of the four colonies after the war and in a united South Africa, meant the further erosion of black political and economic power, particularly in terms of the franchise and access to land. Barnes stressed his concerns by once again summoning the authority of the Radical Liberal Charles Dilke, who "feared the consequences [of South African self-government] would be fraught with danger for the ... coloured subjects of that part of the Empire."[87] Barnes complained the legislative arrangements for both the Orange Free State and Transvaal had been instituted with no regard to the rights of Indians and Blacks who had supported the British in the Boer War. "The self-government granted to the white subjects of these States, without any check for safe-guarding the rights and liberties of the coloured subjects, led the white men to use their power upon the unfortunate coloured people (loyal British subjects),"[88] concluded Barnes, culminating in the imprisonment of Gandhi as he led a campaign of civil disobedience against the 1907 Asiatic Registration Act in the Transvaal.[89]

Despite military victory in 1902, British imperialism was unable to halt the aspirations of Boer nationalists and British anti-imperialists, who dominated the legislatures of the four colonies. In October 1908, delegates from the four colonial governments organized a convention to prepare a constitution for a unified South Africa. By now, Barnes's business interests had foundered, largely due to obstacles he encountered on account of his race, culminating in malicious police investigations.[90] As a consequence he directed most of his energy towards political activity, including the production of a pamphlet entitled *White South Africa: Ethical Side Light on the South African Convention,* in which he argued Africa had descended from "an ancient land of light and learning" to a "Dark Continent" due to the mercenary acts of European buccaneers and the demoralization and seduction of Africans through "bribes and douceurs."[91]

In February and March 1909, Barnes attended two mass meetings in Cape Town and its suburb of Woodstock, called to discuss the draft constitution recently signed by the national convention. The most contentious proposal in the draft was the restriction of parliamentary membership to men of pure European descent. The franchise systems of the four participating states were to be preserved, but of these only the Cape granted voting rights to nonwhites. Even there, in 1909 the electorate included only ten per cent Coloreds (those of mixed heritage) and five per cent blacks. Effectively, non-whites were to have no say in the governing of the Union of South Africa.[92] Barnes later recalled his contribution to the Cape Town meeting of February 22, 1909, which was attended by around three thousand people, chaired by Mayor F. W. Smith and which included the prime minister of the Cape, John Xavier Merriman, on the platform. Despite his objection to the terms of the proposed constitution, Barnes's allegiance to Empire led him to mollify discontent among non-whites in the audience, "exhorted[ing] them to possess their souls in patience, to be loyal, and act only by constitutional means."[93] Barnes urged those barred from the franchise to forward constitutional amendments to the convention. If these were rejected, "then, like Roman citizens ... they were to appeal to Caesar — and England, the paramount authority, would vindicate them."[94] Barnes's level of faith in Imperial government highlights a longstanding aspect of colonial subjecthood. Parliament, and moreover the monarch, were regarded as dispensers of equity and justice, who could be called upon to overrule iniquitous colonial regimes.[95]

The consent of the Imperial government was required before the draft constitution could come into force and it was sent to London accompanied by delegates from the four South African colonies who were to scrutinize its progress through parliament. In effect, the draft constitution became the South Africa Bill which was debated in the British parliament during July and August 1909. Barnes had traveled to England in March, after the mass meetings in the Cape, probably to hear the parliamentary debate. He may have come into contact with a further Cape delegation, comprised of the former Prime Minister, W. P. Schreiner, and key black, Colored and Asian leaders, who hoped to address parliament in an attempt to extend electoral rights to non-whites throughout South Africa. The bar on non-white candidature for the Union parliament was regarded as "illiberal, unjust and offensive to King's subjects" which originated "for South Africa a disqualification based upon colour which has never yet been embodied in any Imperial Act of Parliament."[96] Despite enlisting the support of the Anti-Slavery and Aborigines Protection Society and Charles Dilke among others, the delegation made little impact on parliamentary proceedings.[97] As Barnes noted, the Bill was recommended to the House of Commons by the Liberal Prime Minister Asquith on the grounds it should trust the "generosity and the experience"[98] of the Union parliament and should certainly not risk further war. Other parliamentarians were less diplomatic in their language. As the House of Lords debated the Bill, the Archbishop of Canterbury stated the "The overwhelming majority of the people of South Africa must for some generations to come be regarded ... as quite unfit for ... functions of citizenship on a par with white men."[99] The Bill received Royal Assent in September 1909, was ratified by the Union parliament in May 1910 and served as the basis for the South African Constitution until 1961.

For Barnes, the South Africa Act was "a most scandalous and unfortunate *coup d'état...*" fraught with danger for the well-being of the state and the integrity of the Empire. The Imperial Parliament legislated a "colour line — a line of invidious racial distinction."[100] With the outbreak of European hostilities immanent, loyalist that he was, Barnes was reticent about broadcasting his strength of feeling to the Empire at large, but where once he had envisaged the British Empire would serve as the guardian of all races, forming the basis for a Godly kingdom in the new age, he was no longer so sure. The "Act ... sets up a kingdom which is divided against itself, 'a white South Africa' and 'a black' or 'coloured kingdom.' The black is intended for perpetual exploitation by the white."[101] Barnes was particularly incensed by the claims of the British government that it left the racialized franchise intact to avoid further military conflict with the Boers. He delivered a stinging critique that, given the subsequent violent history of Southern Africa, was perhaps the most prescient of his many discerning observations:

> the Empire is itself endangered by its dereliction of a sacred duty ... the safe-guarding of that large section of its "black or coloured" people whose interests it has sacrificed "for peace sake" ... a peace of the kind that passes all understanding ... as surely as righteousness exalts a nation, so surely unrighteousness, or injustice, lowers its standing and retards its evolution, and will ultimately destroy that nation as unfit to survive.[102]

Most tellingly, Barnes believed the passing of the South Africa Bill was a repudiation of the word of God and the teachings of Christ as it failed to apply justice to all, regardless of race. Barnes pointedly remarked that, as a non–European, Jesus himself would have fallen foul of the new South African constitution. If the British Empire did not redeem itself then it was potentially doomed to be eclipsed, like the defeated Central Powers in the First World War, and might not survive into the new age. Clearly alluding to the political triumph of the Boers in 1910, despite the costly and ultimately hollow victory of British arms in 1902, Barnes declared, "no nation can be strong enough in arms to indulge with impunity in such wrongs to one class of its subjects. If Britain attempts it, then in spite of all the good it has done to humanity, I am afraid all will be over with it sooner or later."[103]

Conclusion: The Prospects for a Pan-African New Age

Through the pages of *The Signs of the Times* and *The Economy of Life* it is possible to trace the transformation of J. Edmestone Barnes from a Christadelphian and Imperialist sympathizer to rationalist and pan-Africanist. But despite a pan-African outlook that came of bitter experience, he did not entirely lose his affection for Empire nor the hope that it could be redeemed to provide the basis of an enlightened new age, a heaven on earth. Barnes's belief in the possibility of Imperial reconstruction was evident in his continued admiration for the leading statesmen of Empire, such as Joseph Chamberlain and Charles Dilke. Although he felt the apocalypse of the First World War was inevitable, for which the Empire should have been more adequately prepared, Barnes desired that change should come through a combination of righteous, divine intervention and peaceful political agitation and therefore condemned the Bolshevik revolution.[104]

Hopeful the South African constitution could be overturned, Barnes was convinced the Imperial future could be assured if greater political equality and even a degree of self-determination could be conceded black subjects: "So long as the Constitutional laws of Great Britain do not give any preference to any class of citizens on the score of colour, the black or coloured subjects will recognise the king as their Sovereign Lord as loyally as any other subjects."[105] But what of the prospects for the African diaspora? Having observed Africans and those of African descent in a multitude of settings — the West Indies, West and South Africa, Great Britain and the United States — Barnes believed they would generate sufficient goodwill to "bring about contentment and happiness," a reiteration of his belief that Africans were indeed the "true representatives and embodiment of the way of life" in the new age.[106] Although he had frequently compared his fellow Africans to the children of Israel on the grounds they had dispersed so widely and with relative success, Barnes believed "the idea of their going back to Africa *en masse*, to live like the Hebrew children in their exodus out of Egypt and Palestine, could not possibly be realised."[107] More significantly, in the era of the Harlem Renaissance, the New Negro and the highpoint of Garveyism, he asked "where is the ideal Moses of the black race in the next aion who will perform this gigantic task?" Barnes responded to his own question firmly in the negative, "No sign of that individuality can be discerned in ... our day," highlighting an idiosyncratic political and theological independence maintained over many years.[108] For this critical legacy, J. Edmestone Barnes deserves greater attention within the realm of pan-African thought and the emergence of black independence movements after the first World War. As William H. Ferris, literary editor of Marcus Garvey's *Negro World* was moved to write in his review of *The Economy of Life*, "although we disagree with some of [Barnes's] conclusions, we must agree he is a thinker of the first rank."[109]

NOTES

1. See, for example, Barry Chevannes, *Rastafari: Roots and Ideology* (Syracuse, NY: Syracuse University Press, 1994); Barry Chevannes, *Rastafari and Other African-Caribbean Worldviews* (Basingstoke: Macmillan, 1995).
2. A notable exception is W. F. Elkins, *Street Preachers, Faith Healers, and Herb Doctors in Jamaica, 1890–1925* (New York: Revisionist, 1977).
3. London: H. F. Brion (hereafter *Signs*).
4. Chorley: Universal, 1921 (hereafter *Economy*).
5. See Gad Heuman, "*The Killing Time*": *The Morant Bay Rebellion in Jamaica* (Basingstoke: Macmillan, 1994); Thomas Holt, *The Problem of Freedom: Race, Labor, and Politics in Jamaica and Britain, 1832–1938* (Baltimorem MD: Johns Hopkins University Press, 1992); Brian L. Moore and Michelle A. Johnson, *Neither Led Nor Driven: Contesting British Cultural Imperialism in Jamaica, 1865–1920* (Mona: University of the West Indies Press, 2004).
6. *Daily Gleaner*, October 27, 1871, 3.
7. "First Caribbean Christadelphian," *Caribbean Pioneer* (online edition), January 2002, <http://www.tidings.org/pioneer/pioneer200201.htm> (July 17, 2008); L. Alan Eyre, "A 1909 Cape Town Publication and its Author: A Puzzling Mystery Solved," *Quarterly Bulletin of the National Library of South Africa* 59 no. 2 (2005): 62–71.
8. *The Investigator*, VII, no. 28 (October 1892): 88.
9. Joseph McCabe, *A Biographical Dictionary of Rationalists* (London: Watts, 1920) 921; Rationalist Press Association, *Annual Reports* for 1903, 1907–1913, 1919–1921; RPA Membership Registers, Vols. 1, 3, 6, Bishopsgate Institute, London; *West India Committee Circular*, June 8, 1922, 258; Royal Geographical Society, election certificate for J. Edmestone Barnes; *The Marcus Garvey and Universal Negro Improvement Association Papers*, Vol. VI (Berkeley: University of California Press, 1992) 521–2. George Washington Ellis, the African-American ethnologist and a Secretary of the American Legation in Liberia, noted Barnes's technological expertise. He was, like Barnes, a member of the Royal Geographical Society (RGS). See George W. Ellis, "Sociological Appraisement of Liberian Resources" *Journal of Race Development* 5, no. 4 (1915): 399–415.
10. The National Archives (UK) (hereafter TNA) BT31/24913/157827 Agreement September 15, 1919 and Summary of Share Capital to February 28, 1928.
11. The key introduction to this concept is Paul Gilroy, *The Black Atlantic: Modernity and Double-Consciousness* (London: Verso, 1993).
12. *The Economic Value of the Native Races of Africa in relation to the development of the resources of that continent* (London: Watts, 1908).
13. *The Marcus Garvey and Universal Negro Improvement Association Papers*, Vol. VII (Berkeley: University of California Press, 1992) 210–211; L. Alan Eyre, "Isaac Edmestone Barnes in Kroonstad, Orange River Colony: The Troubled Life of a Black Jamaican Mining Executive 1903 to 1909" *Quarterly Bulletin of the National Library of South Africa* 60, no. 4 (2006): 121.
14. Joseph Booth, *African for the African* (Blantyre, Malawi: Christian Literature Association in Malawi, 1996 [1897]) 32–34; Harry Langworthy, *Africa for the African: The Life of Joseph Booth* (Blantyre, Malawi: Christian Literature Association in Malawi, 1996); Donald Spivey, "The African Crusade for Black Industrial Schooling" *The Journal of Negro History*, 63, no. 1 (1978): 1–17.
15. "The Book of Barnes" *Daily Gleaner*, September 12, 1904, 8–9.
16. *The Literary Guide and Rationalist Review*, March 1921, 48; *Negro World*, September 3, 1921 cited in *The Marcus Garvey and Universal Negro Improvement Association Papers*, Vol. IV (Berkeley: University of California Press, 1992) 66.

17. Richard B. Moore "The Name "Negro"— Its Origin and Evil Use" in *Richard B. Moore, Caribbean Militant in Harlem*, W. Burghardt Turner and Joyce Moore Turner, eds. (Bloomington: Indiana University Press, 1988) 223.

18. Campion's autobiographical writings, *Sunlight on the Foothills* (London: Rich and Cowan, 1941); *Towards the Mountains* (London: Rich and Cowan, 1943); *Reaching High Heaven* (London: Rich and Cowan, 1944) and *Only the Stars Remain* (London: Rich and Cowan, 1946) capture his political and journalistic activities in depth for this period.

19. See Bill Cooke, *A Rebel to His Last Breath: Joseph McCabe and Rationalism* (London: Prometheus Books, 2001).

20. Brion was a map-maker and Fellow of the RGS.

21. Eyre, "1909 Cape Town Publication."

22. *Signs*, 11.

23. Robert Roberts, *A Declaration of the First Principles of the Oracles of the Deity* (Birmingham: The Author, 1867) 16–7.

24. 1260 days (Revelation 12:6), the most significant of these, is the product of "time, times and half a time" (Daniel 7:25, 12:7), "time" being taken as a year of 360 days, "times" as two years and "half a time" as 180 days. 1260 days also occurs as the "forty-two months" of thirty days (Revelation 13:5), 490 days as the "seventy weeks" (Daniel 9:24). The substitution of years for days originates in Ezekiel 4:6 and Numbers 14:34. See Stephen D. Snobelen, "'A Time and Times and the Dividing of Time': Isaac Newton, the Apocalypse and 2060" *The Canadian Journal of History* 38 (2003): 537–551.

25. Watts, which published *The Economic Value of the Native Races* for Barnes, was the publishing arm of the RPA.

26. *The Literary Guide and Rationalist Review*, December 1921, 192.

27. *Signs*, unnumbered preface. Scarlet is regarded as the color of government.

28. *Signs*, 14.

29. Barnes notes that Constantine is reputed to have ordered his soldiers to emblazon the first two Greek letters of Christ— Chi Rho — on their shields after a vision (*Signs*, 17).

30. *Signs*, 17–21. Like many other exegetes, Barnes relies on Gibbon's *Decline and Fall of the Roman Empire* to validate his apocalyptic vision, even though Gibbon himself had tended towards skepticism. See Stephen D. Snobelen, "A Further Irony: Apocalyptic Readings of Edward Gibbon's *Decline and Fall of the Roman Empire*" *The Canadian Journal of History* 33 (1998): 387–416.

31. *Economy*, 41. In September 1907, Pius X issued *Pascendi dominici gregis* condemning "modernism" as the "synthesis of all heresies" which strove to corrupt Catholic truth. *Pascendi* "virtually slammed the door on any historical study of the Bible, on theological creativity, and on church reform." Darrell Jodock, "The Modernist Crisis" in *Catholicism Contending with Modernity: Roman Catholic Modernism and Anti-Modernism in Historical Context*. Darrell Jodock, ed. (Cambridge, UK:Cambridge University Press, 2000) 1. In 1910 Pius X required all clerics and office holders to take oath against modernism. The leading figures of modernism, Maurice Blondel (1861–1949), Alfred Loisy (1857–1940), Friedrich von Hugel (1852–1925) and George Tyrrell (1861–1909), did not claim to be part of an organized, coherent group and were so-defined by the encyclical and declared enemies of the church (*ibid.*, 4–5, 20–3).

32. *Economy*, 39.

33. *Ibid.* The apocalyptic implications of the Russo-Japanese war were also discussed by another Jamaican, the writer and barrister, Frederick Charles Tomlinson, in his pamphlet *The End of the Age* (Kingston: Rainbow, 1915) 5.

34. *Signs*, 22.

35. *Signs*, preface.

36. *Signs*, preface

37. *The Times*, December 6, 1901, 10.

38. Richard A. Soloway, *Degeneracy and Degeneration: Eugenics and the Declining Birthrate in Twentieth Century Britain* (Chapel Hill: University of North Carolina Press, 1990) 41.

39. Douglas A. Lorimer, *Colour, Class and the Victorians: English Attitudes to the Negro in the Mid-Nineteenth Century* (Leicester, UK: Leicester University Press, 1978) 155.

40. Arnold White, *Efficiency and Empire* (London: Methuen, 1901) 55, 108. For a more detailed discussion of debates around national efficiency before and during the South African War see Geoffrey Searle, "'National Efficiency' and the 'Lessons of the War'" in *The Impact of the South African War*, David Omissi and Andrew S. Thompson, eds. (Basingstoke: Palgrave, 2002) 194–211.

41. *The Times*, May 16, 1903, 8; Richard Jay, *Joseph Chamberlain: A Political Study* (Oxford, UK: Clarendon Press, 1981) 248–303.

42. *Signs*, 47.

43. Bartholomew Smith (pseud. T. E. S. Scholes), *Chamberlain and Chamberlainism* (London: John Long, 1903) 55–67, 132. Scholes also highlighted the contradictory attitude of Chamberlain to West Indian peasant proprietorship (7–42).

44. *Signs*, preface. Here Barnes cites the missionary hymn "From Greenland's Icy Mountains" by Reginald Heber (1782–1826).

45. *Signs*, preface.

46. *Signs*, 47–8

47. *Economy*, 119.

48. *Economy*, 121.

49. *Signs*, 24–5

50. *Signs*, 27. In this calculation, Barnes follows John Thomas who had outlined the significance of 2400 days as years in *Chronikon Hebraikon* (1866) 26 and reiterated this in *Exposition of Daniel* (Birmingham: Walker, 1920 [1868]).

51. *Signs*, 9. The pacifism of the Christadelphians was established during the American Civil War, a pivotal moment in the organization of the sect which until that point was a more informal association of like-minded groups. Christadelphians refused military service on the grounds they did not recognize human government in any form. Federal law only permitted conscientious objection for known denominations so John Thomas was obliged to define the organization as "Brethren in Christ"— Christadelphians. See Frank Jannaway, *Without the Camp. Being the Story of Why and How the Christadelphians Were Exempted From Military Service* (London: The Author, 1917).

52. Thomas, *Exposition*, Chapter 24.

53. *Signs*, 44

54. *Signs*, 43 (my emphasis).

55. See Richard Smith, *Jamaican Volunteers in the First World War: Race, Masculinity and the Development of National Consciousness* (Manchester, UK: Manchester University Press, 2004) 43–44.

56. *Signs*, 47.

57. *Signs*, 46. Roy Jenkins, *Sir Charles Dilke: A Victorian Tragedy* (London: Fontana, 1968) 398–401.

58. *Economy*, 117.

59. *Economy* 121.

60. A primary Christadelphian interpretation of these concepts is Roberts, *Declaration*, 13–14, 22, 29, 34–7, 42–4.

61. *Economy*, 120.

62. *Economy*, 2.

63. *Economy*, 3.

64. *Economy*, x.

65. *Economy*, 25–6

66. *Economy*, 51.

67. John Thomas, *Anastasis: a treatise on the judgment of the dead at the appearing of Christ with reference to the nature of the body when it first emerges from the grave* (Birmingham: G. J. Stevenson, 1871).

68. Charles Turner Gorham, *The First Easter Dawn: An Inquiry into the Evidence for the Resurrection of Jesus* (London: Watts, 1908); *Economy*, x; *The Literary Guide and Rationalist Review*, October 1921, 147.

69. Eyre suggests Barnes may have had Jewish ancestry. Eyre, "1909 Cape Town Publication," 62, 67.

70. *Signs*, 16. Macaulay spoke in favor of Robert Grant's bill for the Removal of Jewish Disabilities. Edward Alexander, "Dr. Arnold, Matthew Arnold, and the Jews," *Judaism* (Spring 2002): 214–225.

71. *Signs*, 16.

72. *Signs*, 22. For Barnes's explanation of *parosia* and his preference that the translation be "presence," rather than "coming" see *The Investigator*, VIII, no. 32, (October 1893): 94.

73. *Signs*, 26

74. Formerly in the Czarist province of Bessarabia, but now usually known as now Chişinău, Moldova.

75. *Signs*, 32 and *Economy*, 8–9.

76. *Signs*, 32.

77. *Signs*, 33. See also the essay in this volume by Eric Reisenauer, "Tidings Out of the East": World War I, the Eastern Question, and British Millennialism."

78. John Thomas, *Destiny of the British Empire, as revealed in the Scriptures* (London, 1871) 19.

79. James Cross, *Coming Eschatological Events: or, the Future of the British Empire, Russia, the Papacy, the Jews, and Christendom as Revealed in the Pages of Holy Writ* (Bristol: John Wright & Co., 1893) particularly 164–218, 281–5.

80. *Economy*, 10, 111.

81. *Ibid.*, 10, 11.

82. *Investigator*, VIII: 30, (April 1893): 37.

83. *Economy*, 122, 1. See also the review of *Economy* in the *Literary Guide* (see note 53).

84. *Investigator*, VIII: 32, (October 1893): 93.

85. For full details of this period, including the malicious investigation of Barnes by the South African authorities, Eyre, "Isaac Edmestone Barnes in Kroonstad," 105–127.

86. See Pieter Labuschagne, *Ghostriders of the Anglo-Boer War (1899–1902): The Role and Contribution of Agterryers* (Johannesburg: University of South Africa, 1999); Peter Warwick, *Black People in the South African War* (Cambridge, UK: Cambridge University Press, 1983); Bill Nasson, "Black Communities in Natal and the Cape" in Omissi and Thompson, *Impact of the South African War*, 38–55.

87. *Economy*, 72–73. Although Dilke was a firm believer in white racial superiority, he nevertheless regarded the Empire as custodian of the rights of native peoples. As well as his concern for the position of black and Indian subjects in South Africa, he worked with the campaigning journalist E. D. Morel for the rights of black Africans throughout the continent. Jenkins, *Sir Charles Dilke*, 394–7.

88. *Economy*, 73.

89. Rodney Davenport and Christopher Saunders, *South Africa: A Modern History* (Basingstoke, UK: Palgrave Macmillan, 2000) 244–5.

90. See Eyre, "Isaac Edmestone Barnes in Kroonstad" for more details.

91. Cited in *Economy*, 90–91.

92. Leonard Thompson, *A History of South Africa* (New Haven, CT: Yale University Press, 1995) 146–153; Davenport and Saunders, *South Africa*, 255–264.

93. *Economy*, 81.

94. *Ibid.*, 82.

95. Significantly, although he had become a naturalized Liberian citizen, Barnes sought the aid of the British Foreign Office when he pressed claims against the Liberian government for dismissing him as its representative on the Sierra Leone boundary commission. The British representative, Major Cowie, testified to Barnes's diligence and devotion to duty. TNA FO367/279/14359 A. Nicholson, Foreign Office to P. Crommelin, April 23, 1912.

96. *The Times*, February 28, 1909, 6;

97. Thompson, *History of South Africa*, 149–153; *The Times* July 28, 1909, 6.

98. *The Times*, August 17, 1909, 5.

99. *Economy*, 77.

100. *Ibid.*, 79.

101. *Ibid.*

102. *Ibid.*, 79–80.

103. *Economy*, 85–86.

104. *Ibid.*, 120.

105. *Ibid.*, 85.

106. *Ibid.*, 111.

107. *Ibid.*

108. *Ibid.*

109. *Negro World*, September 3, 1921 cited in *The Marcus Garvey and Universal Negro Improvement Association Papers*, Vol. IV (Berkeley: University of California Press, 1992) 66.

WORKS CITED

Alexander, Edward "Dr. Arnold, Matthew Arnold, and the Jews." *Judaism* (Spring 2002): 214–225.

_____. *The Economy of Life: Some Suggestions for World Betterment.* Chorley: Universal, 1921.

Barnes, Isaac E. "Anastasis and Aeon Judgement." *Investigator*, VII, no. 28 (October 1892): 88.

_____. "Anastasis and Aeon Judgement." *Investigator*, VIII, no. 32 (October 1893): 93–94.

_____. "A Friendly Criticism." *Investigator*, VIII, no. 30 (April 1893): 37.

Barnes, J. Edmestone. *The Economic Value of the Native Races of Africa in Relation to the Development of the Resources of That Continent.* London: Watts, 1908.

_____. *Signs of the Times: Touching the Final Supremacy of Nations.* London: H. F. Brion, 1903.

"The Book of Barnes." *Daily Gleaner.* September 12, 1904: 8–9.

Booth, Joseph. *African for the African.* Blantyre, Malawi: Christian Literature Association in Malawi, 1996 [1897].

Campion, Sydney. *Only the Stars Remain.* London: Rich and Cowan, 1946.

_____. *Reaching High Heaven.* London: Rich and Cowan, 1944.

_____. *Sunlight on the Foothills.* London: Rich and Cowan, 1941.

_____. *Towards the Mountains.* London: Rich and Cowan, 1943.

Chevannes, Barry. *Rastafari and Other African-Caribbean Worldviews.* Basingstoke, UK: Macmillan, 1995.

_____. *Rastafari: Roots and Ideology.* Syracuse, NY: Syracuse University Press, 1994.

Cooke, Bill. A *Rebel to His Last Breath: Joseph McCabe and Rationalism.* London: Prometheus, 2001.

"Correspondence." *The Literary Guide and Rationalist Review.* December 1921: 192.

Cross, James. *Coming Eschatological Events: or, the Future of the British Empire, Russia, the Papacy, the Jews, and Christendom as Revealed in the Pages of Holy Writ.* Bristol: John Wright and Co., 1893.

Davenport, R., and C. Saunders. *South Africa: A Modern History.* Basingstoke, UK: Palgrave Macmillan, 2000.

Elkins, W. F. *Street Preachers, Faith Healers, and Herb Doctors in Jamaica, 1890–1925.* New York: Revisionist, 1977.

Ellis, George W. "Sociological Appraisement of Liberian Resources." *Journal of Race Development* 5, no. 4 (1915): 399–415.

Eyre, L. Alan. "Isaac Edmestone Barnes in Kroonstad, Orange River Colony: The Troubled Life of a Black Jamaican Mining Executive 1903 to 1909." *Quarterly Bulletin of the National Library of South Africa* 60, no. 4 (2006): 121.

_____. "A 1909 Cape Town Publication and its Author: A Puzzling Mystery Solved." *Quarterly Bulletin of the National Library of South Africa* 59, no. 2 (2005): 62–71.

"First Caribbean Christadelphian." *Caribbean Pioneer.* January 2002. <http://www.tidings.org/pioneer/pioneer200201.htm> (July 17, 2008).

Gilroy, Paul. *The Black Atlantic: Modernity and Double-Consciousness.* London: Verso, 1993.

Gorham, Charles Turner. *The First Easter Dawn: An Inquiry into the Evidence for the Resurrection of Jesus.* London: Watts and Co., 1908.

Heuman, Gad. *"The Killing Time": The Morant Bay Rebellion in Jamaica.* Basingstoke, UK: Macmillan, 1994.

Hill, Robert ed. *The Marcus Garvey and Universal Negro Improvement Association Papers,* Vol. IV, VI, VII. Berkeley: University of California Press, 1992.

Holt, Thomas. *The Problem of Freedom: Race, Labor, and Politics in Jamaica and Britain, 1832–1938.* Baltimore, MD: Johns Hopkins University Press, 1992.

Jannaway, Frank. *Without the Camp: Being the Story of Why and How the Christadelphians Were Exempted From Military Service.* London: The Author, 1917.

Jay, Richard. *Joseph Chamberlain: A Political Study.* Oxford, UK: Clarendon Press, 1981.

Jenkins, Roy. *Sir Charles Dilke: A Victorian Tragedy.* London: Fontana, 1968.

Jodock, Darrell. "The Modernist Crisis" in *Catholicism Contending with Modernity: Roman Catholic Modernism and Anti-Modernism in Historical Context.* Darrell Jodock, ed. Cambridge, UK: Cambridge University Press, 2000.

"Kingston University School." *Daily Gleaner.* October 27, 1871: 3.

Labuschagne, Pieter. *Ghostriders of the Anglo-Boer War (1899–1902): The Role and Contribution of Agterryers.* Johannesburg: University of South Africa, 1999.

Langworthy, Harry. *Africa for the African: The Life of Joseph Booth.* Blantyre, Malawi: Christian Literature Association in Malawi, 1996.

Lorimer, Douglas A. *Colour, Class and the Victorians: English Attitudes to the Negro in the Mid-Nineteenth Century.* Leicester, UK: Leicester University Press, 1978.

McCabe, Joseph. *A Biographical Dictionary of Rationalists.* London: Watts, 1920.

_____. "Rationalists and Religion." *The Literary Guide and Rationalist Review.* October 1921: 147.

"Mr. Chamberlain in Birmingham." *The Times.* May 16, 1903: 8.

Moore, B. L., and M. A. Johnson. *Neither Led Nor Driven: Contesting British Cultural Imperialism in Jamaica, 1865–1920.* Mona: University of the West Indies Press, 2004.

Moore, Richard B. "The Name 'Negro'— Its Origin and Evil Use" in *Richard B. Moore,*

Caribbean Militant in Harlem. W. Burghardt Turner and Joyce Moore Turner, eds. Bloomington: Indiana University Press, 1988.

Nasson, Bill. "Black Communities in Natal and the Cape" in *The Impact of the South African War.* David Omissi and Andrew S. Thompson, eds. Basingstoke, UK: Palgrave, 2002: 38–55.

The National Archives BT31/24913/157827 Agreement September 15, 1919, and Summary of Share Capital to February 28, 1928.

The National Archives FO367/279/14359 A. Nicholson, Foreign Office to P. Crommelin, April 23, 1912.

"New Books." *The Literary Guide and Rationalist Review.* March 1921: 48.

"The Prince and Princess of Wales in the City." *The Times.* December 6, 1901: 10.

Rationalist Press Association. *Annual Reports* for 1903, 1907–1913, 1919–1921.

_____. Membership Registers, Vols. 1 (1903–1904), 3 (1907–1914), 6 (1922), Bishopsgate Institute, London.

Roberts, Robert. *A Declaration of the First Principles of the Oracles of the Deity.* Birmingham: The Author, 1867.

Royal Geographical Society. Election certificate for J. Edmestone Barnes. 1919–1925.

Searle, Geoffrey. "'National Efficiency' and the 'Lessons of the War'" in *The Impact of the South African War.* David Omissi and Andrew S. Thompson, eds. Basingstoke, UK: Palgrave, 2002: 94–211.

Smith, Bartholomew [pseud. T. E. S. Scholes]. *Chamberlain and Chamberlainism.* London: John Long, 1903.

Smith, Richard. *Jamaican Volunteers in the First World War: Race, Masculinity and the Development of National Consciousness.* Manchester, UK: Manchester University Press, 2004.

Snobelen, Stephen D. "A Further Irony: Apocalyptic Readings of Edward Gibbon's *Decline and Fall of the Roman Empire.*" *The Canadian Journal of History* 33 (1998): 387–416.

_____. "'A Time and Times and the Dividing of Time': Isaac Newton, the Apocalypse and 2060." *The Canadian Journal of History* 38 (2003): 537–551.

Soloway, Richard A. *Degeneracy and Degeneration: Eugenics and the Declining Birthrate in Twentieth Century Britain.* Chapel Hill: University of North Carolina Press, 1990.

"South Africa Bill." *The Times.* August 17, 1909: 5.

"The South African Native Problem." *The Times.* July 28, 1909: 6.

"South African Natives and the Constitution." *The Times.* July 28, 1909: 6.

Spivey, Donald. "The African Crusade for Black Industrial Schooling." *The Journal of Negro History* 63, no. 1 (1978): 1–17.

Thomas, John. *Anastasis: A Treatise on the Judgment of the Dead at the Appearing of Christ with Reference to the Nature of the Body When It First Emerges from the Grave.* Birmingham: G. J. Stevenson, 1871.

_____. *Chronikon Hebraikon.* New York: Printed by E. O. Jenkins for the author, 1866.

_____. *Destiny of the British Empire, as revealed in the Scriptures.* London: G. J. Stevenson, 1871.

_____. *Exposition of Daniel.* Birmingham: Walker, 1920 [1868].

Thompson, Leonard. *A History of South Africa.* New Haven, CT: Yale University Press, 1995.

Tomlinson, Frederick Charles. *The End of the Age.* Kingston: Rainbow, 1915.

Warwick, Peter. *Black People in the South African War.* Cambridge, UK: Cambridge University Press, 1983.

West India Committee Circular. June 8, 1922: 258.

White, Arnold. *Efficiency and Empire.* London: Methuen, 1901.

"Tidings Out of the East": World War I, the Eastern Question and British Millennialism

Eric Michael Reisenauer

The surge in millennial expectation in Britain during the Great War (1914–1918) far surpassed all similar outbursts going back at least a century. Books and pamphlets streamed from the press announcing the imminent advent of Christ; religious newspapers increasingly noted the ominous signs of the times as the war progressed; public meetings sprouted up to try to untangle the cords of prophecy seemingly being fulfilled all around them. Not since the French Revolution and Napoleonic era had the end of days seemed so close at hand. An increase in eschatological anticipation is hardly remarkable in wartime, particularly when such upheavals involve the kind of horrors which accompanied the First World War.[1] Nightmares born from life and death on the Western Front would disturb the sleep of even St. John's Four Horsemen.[2] But horrific carnage alone was not enough to sustain, much less to increase, what Ernie Hilbert calls the "apocalyptic impulse" during the war years.[3] For many, the Great War's millennial *bone fides* were founded less in the war's scope and intensity than in its direction of focus — increasingly East.[4] While it was often the images and realities of the Western Front which attracted the most press and earned the war the common moniker "Armageddon," those who looked for a Biblical, rather than a merely figurative, apocalypse knew that their attention was warranted elsewhere.[5] The Eastern Question, which had vexed British foreign policy-makers since the early nineteenth century, was finally being answered — answered in ways which, while confounding the diplomats, seemingly vindicated the Biblical prophets. The question, in fact, lay at the center of a millennialist understanding of the First World War. Its centrality shows that Great War millennialism was less a panic-laden and fear-driven response to a crisis than a rather careful and thoughtful attempt to read God's plan into the history and future of nations. The

142

millennialist response to World War I was, in fact, the culmination of ideas found in eschatological exegeses on events in the Eastern Mediterranean going back several decades. Its intensity and prominence dwarfed those of previous outbreaks not simply because the cataclysm was so much more frightful but also because the long-expected events of prophecy were at last so clearly and unmistakably being fulfilled.

Eyes Fixed Upon the East

The Eastern Question was one of the greatest conundrums in British foreign policy of the nineteenth and early-twentieth centuries.[6] For decades the fates of Britain's central Asian possessions as well as of Russia, the Ottoman Empire and, more indirectly, the Jews seemingly depended on solving this riddle.[7] Indeed, answering the question to Britain's satisfaction was deemed important enough to bring the British into a mid-century war with Russia in the Crimea and to spark an intense bout of sabre-rattling in the 1870s. Britain's national and imperial interests required an agile diplomatic strategy which sought to soften any fallout and maximize any gain from a declining Ottoman Empire and an ascendant Russia. For much of the nineteenth century, fear of Russian control of the Eastern Mediterranean had induced successive British governments to adopt a solidly pro-Turkish stance by going to war against Russia in Turkey's defense in the 1850s and nearly doing so again in the Eastern Crisis of 1875–1878. But by the turn of the twentieth century almost everything was in a state of flux. Germany was actively challenging Britain as Turkey's European champion, and the attitude of the Porte had become, both before and after the Young Turk rebellion of 1908, increasingly pro-German and anti–British.[8] Lord Salisbury appeared to have been right when he declared in 1897 that Britain had backed "the wrong horse" in the Crimea as the Ottoman Empire, so long enjoying British protection, was by 1914 clearly under the sway of the German Kaiser.[9] So much had things changed that, during the war, the British completely abandoned their traditional policy of sustaining Ottoman territorial integrity and now sought to protect their interests in the region by directly controlling parts of a dismantled Turkish empire.[10] Britain's relationship with the Russian Empire was also changing. In 1907 the two nations had reached acceptable understandings regarding India and central Asia effecting something of a *rapprochement* between them. By the beginning of the Great War, British interests in the East had become dependent upon a powerful and stabilizing Russian presence in southeastern Europe and, in a dramatic reversal, in March 1915 the British Foreign Office hesitantly agreed to grant Russia guardianship of Istanbul pending Allied victory in the war and other conditions.[11] Benjamin Disraeli, who had written in 1876 of the dire consequences to the British Empire should Moscow ever control the Straits and had been instrumental in paring back Russian power in the Balkans at the Congress of Berlin in 1878, would have trembled had he lived to see it.[12]

Not even the most prescient of diplomats would have predicted such a turn about in international alliances just thirty years before. But what about the Biblical prophets? Had they foreseen that events would unfold in such a way in order to prepare for the Armageddon which would soon follow? Many in Britain believed they had.[13] Since at least the middle of the nineteenth century, three Scripture-based "signs of the times" had been the staple of Eastern Question prophetic interpretation. The details often differed in eschatological works not only from author to author but also from crisis to crisis; yet the general thrust of argument and core Biblical texts used (especially the books of Isaiah, Ezekiel, Daniel, and Revelation) remained remarkably constant over more than eight decades of commentary. Virtually all writers on prophecy agreed that in order for Armageddon to commence the following events must transpire in the East (though not necessarily in this order): First, the Ottoman Empire would decline in power and ultimately fall to pieces. Islamic control over the Holy Land would thereby be released, allowing for the second of the necessary events: the restoration of Jewish power in Palestine, most likely with the aid of Britain and under British protection. Third, Russia and its allied nations would become a threatening presence in Central Asia and the Eastern Mediterranean pushing constantly against Turkey and ultimately looking to control the Holy Land for itself. This would bring the crisis in the East to a climactic war between a hostile Russian confederation and a British-led alliance of nations offering protections to the Jews. Whether or not this conflict was Armageddon was a matter of some dispute, but that it would be at the very least a herald of the approaching end of days was beyond doubt.

Unlike the natural omens (i.e., comets, eclipses, earthquakes), social, political or technological transformations, or religious upheavals which often sparked millenarian responses, these signs had a specificity of agent, time, and place which required a more sober analysis. Their fulfillment, therefore, was not as dependent on an emotional urgency that often proved unstable and ephemeral. The Eastern Question held the potential to fulfill these way marks. British millennialists had long advised their countrymen to watch its unfolding closely and analyze its relation to Scripture with a kind of "scientific" scrutiny. They would not be disappointed by what such an analysis revealed.[14] "Our eyes are fixed upon the East at the present time," the Rev. Samuel Hinds Wilkinson assured his audience in 1916:

and we little know what the future of the Bible lands will be after the war. But
there is a great probability that they will pass from the hands of the Moslem
Power into the hands of other Powers. Some of us believe that our British
Empire will very likely obtain that protectorate over a good portion of Syria,
including Jerusalem; the French taking the northern part; and Russia taking
Constantinople and probably part of Asia Minor. But the present is certainly
a most interesting time as affecting the future of Israel, the re-peopling of
the land, and the working out of God's great purpose in connection with that
remarkable nation reserved for future blessing to the whole world.[15]

Never before, prophecy students loudly proclaimed by the end of the war,
had the events of history so nearly aligned themselves to the predictions of
the prophets.

However, such claims were, in fact, deeply rooted in a long tradition of
confident pronouncements regarding a prophetic solution to Eastern troubles.[16] Over the previous century, tumultuous affairs in the East had periodically inspired Biblical expositors to announce that the times were pregnant
with meaning. Napoleon's interactions with Turkey and his relationship to
the Jews had helped convince a number of authors of his identity with the
Antichrist (or, alternately, the Jewish redeemer).[17] Britain's growing influence
on the Indian subcontinent during the first half of the nineteenth century
apparently confirmed that it was being divinely prepared to assume its role
as the power who will prepare the way for the Jews, "the kings of the East,"
to be restored to Palestine.[18] In 1853, on the cusp of the Crimean conflict,
David Pae, a Scottish novelist who dallied in Biblical prophecy, produced his
first of a number of pamphlets on the subject entitled *The Coming Struggle
Among the Nations of the Earth*.[19] His work was extremely popular (selling
more than one hundred and fifty thousand copies in the United Kingdom
alone) and set off something of a pamphlet war as sides were taken to either
confirm or scoff at Pae's exegesis. Dr. John Thomas, the founder of the Christadelphians and a widely-respected writer on prophecy, angrily accused Pae
of having cribbed and reproduced (inaccurately) his ideas as outlined in his
much larger work *Elpis Israel* (1849) and he thus unintentionally gave it added
exposure among Bible students.[20] Other authors at the time added their own
take on Eastern events as fulfillment of prophecy.[21] Yet by 1856 the Crimean
conflict had come and gone and, while all parties were rather bruised by it,
Armageddon it certainly was not.

The issue emerged with a renewed vigor later in the century as a general European war over Turkey's fate loomed again on the horizon.[22] Pae
returned to the fray with another contribution and, while admitting that the
twenty four years which had elapsed since his first pamphlet had shown
unquestionably "that the system of chronology adopted by the author is not

more correct than other systems he rejected," he claimed that the same interval of time had proved to him that his "scheme of interpretation" held true. "The events which have transpired since the publication of *The Coming Struggle*," Pae asserts, "have been exactly in the line of the anticipations there announced. The Crimean War, the Austro-Italian War, and the Franco-German War, were all stages in the fulfillment of prophecy, according to the interpretations which had been offered. Every one of the events prognosticated have now assumed the form of impending occurrences; and the time is evidently fast ripening for their full accomplishment."[23] Walter Scott, another writer on prophecy, summed up the feelings of many in the opening words of his 1877 contribution to the literature: "The great political problem of the day is the solution to the Eastern difficulty, one which for many years has puzzled the wisest and most sagacious politicians and statesmen of Europe. That knotty question has fairly baffled the combined wisdom of the world.... All eyes are anxiously directed East. A very general feeling of disquiet is abroad. That we are on the eve of great political and other changes of importance, is clear to all reflecting persons."[24] Though no European-wide war occurred, the multi-national Congress of Berlin's controversial reworking of the terms of Treaty of San Stefano kept viable a prophetic interpretation of the events as being steps towards the final crisis.

In 1882, Scott revisited the Eastern Crisis and Congress of Berlin and found that, despite the failure of Armageddon to occur, what had transpired over the past five years only buttressed his claims of an imminent crisis. "The recent Jewish persecutions in Russia," he writes, "and also the present Egyptian difficulties, are matters of sorrow but not of surprise, being quite in keeping with statements penned five years ago.... The cession of the interesting and historical Island of Cyprus to Great Britain, and this country's direct interference in the internal government of Egypt, are indications that the commercial and political interests of England are circling round the east.... The crisis is rapidly approaching. The end is near."[25] Britain's acquisition of Cyprus from Turkey to serve as "a base and centre of military operations in the east" was especially noteworthy since this placement now brought the British "face to face with that great northern power, Russia — the Gog of Ezekiel."[26] In the end, of course, all of these developments failed to bring about the millennium and the solution to the Eastern Question eluded both diplomats and exegetes throughout the nineteenth century. The East retained its hold over the imaginations of the prophetically inclined, nonetheless. At the end of the century, the Rev. Joseph Tanner explained to his readers that "the final conflict of Armageddon in Palestine will be closely connected with what is called in political circles the Eastern Question. In fact, it will be the Eastern Question in its last phase."[27] Yet pronouncements concerning an imminent crisis went largely into abeyance until the eve of the First World War when the signs of the times once again showed themselves.

Drying Up of the Euphrates

Since the early seventeenth century, writers on the Biblical prophecies had interpreted Revelation 16:12 — "And the sixth angel poured out his vial upon the great river Euphrates; and the water thereof was dried up, that the way of the kings of the east might be prepared" — as well as passages in Daniel 8 and 11 as referring to the decline and ultimate destruction of the Ottoman Empire.[28] Over the course of the nineteenth century, as Turkey's power waned in Europe and Africa, these prophecies seemed to be in the process of fulfillment. Even Britain's pro-Turkish policies which had helped to stave off the death of the "Sick Man of Europe" for several decades were deemed necessary despite apparent contradiction of prophecy. Why should Britain, which was destined to play a prominent role in the restoration and protection of the Jews, work to preserve the Gentile oppressor of the land of Israel? "All things in good time," was the answer given most often. Dr. Grattan Guinness explained to his readers in 1886 that even though Disraeli had, by the terms of the Cyprus Convention of 1878, pledged England to uphold Turkish control over Syria and Palestine, "God has decreed, on the other hand, that Palestine and Jerusalem shall be freed, and freed speedily, from Moslem domination." Therefore, he determined, "this treaty cannot stand; it is in opposition to the revealed counsels of God." Once the time comes, "no effort to maintain Turkish power in Europe or Syria will be of any use."[29] Until then, however, God empowered Britain to maintain the Ottoman Empire for the following reasons: to safeguard Britain's eastern possessions, to arrange its interests in direct opposition of those of Russia thus preparing the way for the final battle, and to force the Ottoman Empire to engage in the types of economic and social reforms which would allow for the deserts of Palestine to truly blossom under future Jewish control.[30] God would ultimately arrange things otherwise, but "until such a time, He moves strong England to uphold the weakness of the Turk. It is the Russian's function again to endeavor to destroy Turkish rule, which he will eventually be permitted to accomplish, but only that he may be able to work out his own destruction."[31]

By the eve of the World War, the wait appeared nearly over as Turkey suffered losses at the hands of the Balkan states with the encouragement of Russia and, in 1912, surrendered almost all its European holdings. "Are we at the last days?" T. A. Gregg wondered in a column for the Toronto *Mail and Empire* early in 1913. "The Turk thrust out of Europe at the point of a bayonet, his prestige in Asia must be weakened and his hold enfeebled and made insecure.... The teaching is that the holy places will be trampled under foot by the gentiles until the Times of the Gentiles be fulfilled. Has that time come? Shall 1913 see the unclean foot of the Ottoman no longer profaning the sacred places, where so long it has left it unseemly mark?"[32] In his work of the same year, Reginald Moore detailed Turkey's "progress of decay" over the previous decades despite human attempts to stop it and suggests that its long death throes might soon be at an end:

> So rapid had the decay of Turkey in Europe for the last century been, that the Christian Powers of Europe have several times intervened to arrest it, lest the problems arising as to the disposal of the fragments should provoke European complications. This has constituted the "Eastern Question" which has taxed the resources of a generation of modern diplomatists, but for which, as these words are being written, a solution is apparently in the process of being found by the Balkan States.[33]

At the start of the Great War in August 1914, Turkey's professed armed neutrality seemed to afford it another reprieve from annihilation as the European powers now turned their military energies onto each other.[34] But the end of the year witnessed Turkish attacks, using German provided gunboats, on Russian shipping and ports leading to declarations of war on the Porte by the Entente Powers. Millennialists took note of this remarkable turn of events. The Rev. A. B. Simpson, who had been dismissive of the eschatological claims for the war in 1914, was by March 1915 more willing to entertain them. His change of heart was brought about by a number of developments, most notably, "the entrance of Turkey into this present war — her own headlong plunge into her final overthrow. And how solemnly this fulfils the sixth plague in Revelation xvi., the drying up of the Euphrates flood that the way of the kings of the East, the true leaders of the Orient, may be prepared."[35] The February 1, 1915 edition of the *Morning Star* had already come to the same conclusion. "The entrance of Turkey into the war is of the greatest significance," it noted. "It is the power of Darkness which has done for centuries the blackest of deeds.... There can be no doubt that the end of Turkey is now in sight."[36]

Turkey's formal entrance into the war on the side of the Central Powers made possible a number of prophetic events. Perhaps the most important of these was that the war was now gradually shifting eastward to Palestine where the final Battle of Armageddon would be fought.[37] As the war progressed, the Rev. Elijah Bendor Samuel noted that, "prophetic students have watched with great interest the breaking up of Turkey. Its disintegration has gone on steadily but surely.... It looks now as if she will lose Palestine soon."[38] The importance of this development was clear to the Rev. Charles Henry Titterton who, as the late Vans Dunlap Scholar in Hebrew and Oriental Languages at the University of Edinburgh, knew something of the area and its significance. "The moving of the nations towards Palestine is suggestive of most crucial coming events," he wrote in 1916, "and brings into near view the possible early fulfillment of Bible promises and prophecies, of which the world at large takes little or no cognizance."[39] Others sounded even more confident:

> When Turkey decided to fling herself into this fray, it brought even more clearly to view the possibility that this terrible grapple of the nations of the world is leading straight on toward Armageddon. While Turkey kept out and the war was confined to Europe, Armageddon did not seem so near. The old battleground of the ancient nations is located in Palestine, at the foot of Mt. Megiddo, in the plain of Esdraelon, north of Jerusalem, accessible from the north and south and from the sea. This region of the Near East is to be the storm centre round which the hosts of the nations will gather in the last mighty battles of this world.[40]

Turkey's destiny, so long the central mystery of the Eastern Question, now seemed clear.[41]

Throughout the war, millennialist authors kept close watch over Turkey's fortunes, charting its setbacks and anticipating its impending demise. The vast majority of prophecy investigators believed that clues as to the timeline of its death could be found in the book of Daniel by deciphering the terms "times," "days," and "weeks" as used therein.[42] From calculations derived from this so-called "prophetic chronology" most writers placed Turkey's times of troubles in the Holy Land as culminating during the years 1914–1918, with the regime's final overthrow within very few years after that.[43] Augusta Cook, in a course of lectures given in Westminster Hall during the winter of 1915–1916, remarked that Turkey's days were indeed numbered: "Do we not now see how remarkable is the approach to the fulfillment [of Turkey's doom] as seen in the present war, in which Turkey is engaged and getting the worst of it?" Yet she urged her listeners patience since according to the prophetic timeline, "until the years 1917 and 1918 are arrived we cannot expect any great events for the deliverance of Jerusalem."[44] Another noted that 1916 had seen critical and likely fatal defeats for the Islamic power:

> The loss to Turkey in 1916 of the holy cities of Mecca and Medina is widely recognized as being of high significance. We will only remark that as it occurs in the Closing Era [as determined by prophetic chronology], it is likely to be final or irreversible. It also stands on a higher plane of importance than merely a further shrinking of Turkish territory, which has been going on for many years as the drying up of the Euphrates.[45]

It was in December of 1917 that the event which all millennialists had anticipated finally happened. Jerusalem fell to British forces under the command

of General Allenby and the rule of the Turk over the Holy City had now
ended. No other event of the war was greeted with more enthusiasm in British
millennial publications than this one.[46] Jerusalem's liberation, though tremendous, could only have value were it to be followed by the demise of Turkish
control over the entire Holy Land and the return of Israel. Allenby's victory,
according to the *Monthly Bulletin of the Advent Preparation Prayer Union*, was
a strong indication that such a series of events was proceeding. "This was further confirmed," it noted in June 1919, "when the complete routing of the
Turks some ten months later brought about the collapse of Bulgaria and Aus-
tria, and the surrender of Germany. A third indication will be the handing
over of Palestine and Mesopotamia, i.e., the land promised to Abraham and
his seed, to Great Britain, as the mandatory power under the League of
Nations, and the bestowal of full citizen rights throughout this Promised Land
upon the Jews."[47] Indeed, it seemed, the Euphrates was now dried up and the
Jews had, at last, a way prepared for them.

The Exiles' Return

If any other development aroused as much enthusiasm among millennialists as the deliverance of Jerusalem from the Turks it was its correlative: the
restoration of the Jews to Palestine. The fates of these two peoples were
absolutely intertwined with the decline of the one to be accompanied by the
ascent of the other.[48] Long a staple of millenarian theory, the idea of a restored
Jewish nation (based largely on the prophecies found in Isaiah 11:11–12 and
Ezekiel 37) had come into its own in the nineteenth century as Britain's presence in and influence over the Near East increased.[49] In its most-fully developed form, nineteenth-century Jewish restoration theory had two parts. The
first was the establishment of a permanent settlement of Jews in the region of
Palestine in either an autonomous or semi-autonomous state. The second part
involved a prominent role for Great Britain in this project, as either negotia-
tor, financier, transporter, protector or perhaps some combination of these.
Britain was commonly identified as the great maritime merchant nation,
Tarshish, which according to Isaiah 60:9 would by its vessels bring the children of Israel home and, per Ezekiel 38:13, defend the Jews in their land
against the aggressor. Already in the 1830s and 1840s movement towards such
a restoration was evident.[50] Prominent figures such as Sir Moses Montefiore,
"the most famous practicing Jew in England during the nineteenth century,"
the evangelical Anthony Ashley Cooper, later the Seventh Earl of Shaftesbury,
and the former governor of South Australia, George Gawler, among others,
strongly promoted the idea, even offering detailed plans, of a future Jewish

state in Palestine.[51] Most of those behind such ideas (other than Montefiore) were part of the Christian Zionist movement which sought to bring about a restoration and conversion for Jews in line with millennial predictions.[52] Moreover, these decades witnessed events in the East that were interpreted at the time as providential steps along the way. The Egyptian Khedive Muhammad Ali's defeat of the Sultan in 1832, taking for himself (temporarily) almost all Palestine, not only further weakened the Ottoman Empire but put the Holy Land under a control of a government heavily indebted to Britain. Moreover, in 1841 the British government authorized the establishment of an Anglican Bishopric in Jerusalem naming a converted Jew, Michael S. Alexander, as its first bishop. Despite such encouraging signs, Montefiore's and the Christian Zionists' schemes ultimately came to little.

Events of the 1870s reignited interest in Jewish restoration with Britain gaining effective control over the Suez Canal in 1875 as well as its acquisition of Cyprus and the further weakening of Turkey as a result of the Russo-Turkish War. "At Cyprus the ships of Tarshish are now at anchor, waiting to do their errand for Israel," the Scottish evangelist Horatius Bonar announced in 1878.[53] Even Abraham Benisch, editor of the *Jewish Chronicle* during this period and long interested in Jewish restoration, noted that something Providential seemed to be afoot.[54] Some confident predictions were made that the end of days would come no later than 1882, but millennial expectations were dashed again when it failed to appear on schedule.[55] The one missing element, some suggested, was that few Jews were in fact all that interested in returning to Palestine. Jewish interest in resettlement only began to take on momentum near the turn of the century with the founding of the World Zionist Organization at the first Zionist Congress in 1897 by Theodor Herzl and the establishment of a number of Jewish colonies in the region of Palestine beginning in the 1880s.[56] This birth of political Zionism as well as the increased presence of Jews in Palestine (estimated to be between 50,000 and 100,000 on the eve of the World War) seemed to be the necessary and final steps in preparation for the prophesied Jewish exiles' return.[57]

As momentous as the prospect for return might be for the Jews themselves, there also was a strong conviction that their restoration would finally bring peace to Europe as a whole. Indeed, many believed that a Jewish Palestine, in the words of William J. B. Moore, "may be the only solution to the Eastern question."[58] As the threat of war loomed, the resettlement of the Jews in Palestine was being promoted as a prophetic and political solution to the rising problems in the East. In 1911, three years before the storm clouds broke, Sir Andrew Wingate, the uncle of the great future Zionist, Orde Wingate, suggested that it was in the interests of the peace of the world that the European nations cooperate in this venture. Wingate surmised that, by his read

of the prophecies, the "time may be drawing near" when those nations who
had persecuted the Jews for so long "may be moved to restore them to their
own land."[59] Promises of European money should be used to convince Turkey
to agree to such a scheme and Jewish "sobriety, industry, and intelligence"
would cause the desert to bloom and open a "practically inexhaustible field
to colonisation."[60] The political impact of this, Wingate suggests, would be
tremendous:

> Nothing would knit the Great Powers closer together than cooperating in
> settling the Jewish question, which, as the Jewish population increases, tends
> to become more and more troublesome. A Jewish colonization would also settle
> the Mesopotamian question. For this reason it would be worth while for the
> Powers to arrange with Turkey suitable guarantees for the Jewish loans, because
> the introduction of Jewish capital and population has the elements in it of peace
> to the nations.[61]

Solving the so-called "Jewish problem," therefore, was central to finding a sat-
isfactory conclusion to the Eastern Question; "for after all," the Rev. Francis L.
Denman informed his readers, "the Eastern Question is a Jewish Question."[62]

Very soon into the war, especially as Turkey joined the conflict, speculation began as to the effect of the war on the Jews and the likelihood of their
resettlement *en masse* into Palestine once the war ended with some type of
British involvement.[63] Millennialists were almost beside themselves in noting
how even those who thought nothing of prophecy were now seeing the importance of this development: "One of the most remarkable features arising out
of the present European conflict, is that way in which the secular and the religious press in various parts of the world are busy discussing the future of the
Holy Land."[64] As the war progressed, students of prophecy took special interest in any developments regarding the British Palestinian campaign.[65] Outside prophecy circles, the *Jewish Chronicle* echoed sentiments found in its
pages during the tenure of Abraham Benisch some forty years prior by noting that the idea of a British victory in the war being ultimately a victory for
the Jewish movement in Palestine was an opinion, "which is shared by every-
body who knows the position."[66]

Events of late 1917 brought the issue of Jewish restoration to the forefront. At the beginning of the year, the *Christian Herald and Signs of Our
Times*, in making reference to Grattan Guinness' prediction of some thirty
years before that the year 1917 would bring about a crisis in the Holy Land,
commented that while caution should be used in fixing dates, "the times are
momentous, and great events may transpire this year."[67] During the year a
number of millennial authors commented at how the pace of events in the
East seemed to indicate that the Jewish exiles' return to their lost inheritance
could not be far off. "Surely the 'Times of the Gentiles' are fast running out,"

the Rev. Samuel Schor announced: "Exit the Gentile from Jerusalem; enter once again the Jew."[68] A close interest in the fate of the Jews and Palestine was essential to those looking for the end of days since, "the affairs of the Jews, then, and matters concerning the land of Palestine, are the key to the Eastern problem and the destinies of nations can alone be learnt in connection with that land and people."[69] Given this level of anticipation, it is easy to imagine the response in millennialist circles to the Balfour Declaration of November 2, 1917, promising the British government's "best endeavours" to create in Palestine a national homeland for the Jewish people. Just six weeks later Jerusalem fell into British hands. "The age-long and cruel dominion of the Turk is now being relaxed from Palestine, and the Holy City itself is actually delivered by the conquest of our brave troops," William Bathurst triumphantly explained. "The ancient chosen race will come back to their land. A whole volume of prediction will thus be fulfilled. Scriptural prophecy teems with vivid literal promises to this effect. Even now the British Government has given its word that the Jewish re-peopling has our full sanction."[70]

It was largely in direct response to the Balfour Declaration that, just a few days later, the Advent Testimony Movement (later the Advent Preparation Prayer Union), the closest thing to an organized millennialist effort at the time, issued its founding Statement and Syllabus signed by ten prominent ministers representing both the established and dissenting churches.[71] Meetings were held under the auspices of the Movement in December, 1917 and the early months of 1918, where expectant crowds numbering into the thousands marveled at the fulfillment of the prophecies concerning the restoration of the Jews and other aspects of the Eastern Question.[72] Evoking the theme of the importance of 1917, in early 1918 the *Christian Herald*, which by this time boasted a weekly sales of a quarter million, reprinted a sermon from the Rev. Simpson wherein he announced that, "the best news in a thousand years reached this country a short time ago, and thrilled millions of hearts in the Christian world, and we rejoice with Jerusalem in her great and wondrous joy." Many serious persons, he continued:

> had been wondering if some extraordinary event in connection with the
> fulfillment of prophecy, the deliverance of Jerusalem and the judgment of
> the Turk would not come to pass in the year 1917, and as the last month came,
> and the year was almost over were you surprised that our hearts thrilled with
> strange, profound delight as we learned that the greatest event in Turkish and
> Jewish history had begun to develop, and that henceforth 1917 in our western
> calendar, and 1335 in the Turkish chronology, would be the year of wonder and
> of record in the works of God?[73]

To read a fulfillment of the prophecies into these events took very little imagination or casuistry. Almost no millennialist book, pamphlet, or conference over the next few years failed to mention the events of 1917. Indeed, as late as 1924 prophecy students continued to bolster their convictions of the approaching end times by referencing the Jewish return and its various consequences.[74] Moreover, as important as the liberation of Jerusalem and promise of the restoration of Israel were in and of themselves, what made them all the more remarkable was the fact that Great Britain was responsible for both, thereby completely fulfilling the anticipated conditions of the prophecies.[75]

King of the North and King of the South

The prophesied event which was the most difficult to initially square with the configuration and course of the Great War was that of a coming epic struggle between Russia and Great Britain. This was the one prophecy which seemed more likely to be fulfilled sixty years earlier than it did in 1914. The Crimean War had actually pit Russia against Britain and the Russo-Turkish War in the 1870s had threatened to do the same. Even in the late nineteenth century, as tensions increased between Russia and Britain over control of central Asia, war between the two at times seemed inevitable. Yet none of these incidents or developments brought about the predicted clash of empires. Since 1907 the two nations had seen their relationship improve dramatically and they were now allies in the war. Despite this difficulty, most First World War–era millennialist remained convinced that this battle must happen and that God would arrange the circumstances to allow it.

The Biblical texts which lay at the base of this interpretation were Ezekiel 38 and 39 and Daniel 11. These texts spoke of a great confederacy of nations led by Gog and the prince of Rosh, Meshech, and Tubal, collectively known as the king of the North, who would come up against Israel in their own land in the last days. Israel would seek the aid of the king of the South, a term denoting an alliance of nations consisting of Tarshish and all "the young lions" thereof as well as Egypt, Sheba, and Dedan. Their conflict would be the battle which would prepare the way for the Second Coming of Christ. Little disagreement existed as to the identity of the king of the North. Almost every expositor on the prophecies in recent times identified this power as Russia.[76] The identification was based primarily on the geographical position of Russia as well as on eponymy: Rosh being the source for Ross or Russia, Meshech or Mosoch signifying Moscow, and Tubal laying at the root of Tobolsk, a regional capital in western Siberia. If such an identification seemed fanciful, millennialists of the nineteenth and twentieth centuries were quick to point out that no less a scholar than the Rev. Arthur P. Stanley, Regius Professor of Ecclesiastical History and Canon of Christ Church Oxford, supported the identification of Rosh with Russia. "This early Biblical notice of so great an empire is doubly interesting from its being a solitary instance," he wrote in Dr. William Smith's renowned *Dictionary of the Bible*. "No other name of any modern nation occurs in the Scriptures."[77] Beyond this, however, Russia's advances in central Asia in the second half of the nineteenth century, its antagonism to Turkey and desire to control Constantinople and the Straits, its historical antipathy towards the Jews, and its 1907 agreement with Persia (one of the prophesied allies of Gog) cemented the image of an advancing, menacing presence ready to descend on the Holy Land from the north.

Identifying the king of the South, however, was not quite as easy. During the early nineteenth century, Egypt was held out to be the most probable candidate, and Muhammad Ali's actions against the Sultan in the 1830s seemed to support this view. In his 1839 pamphlet, *The Time of the End*, the Rev. Frederich Fysh suggested that Muhammad Ali's actions in Syria were absolute fulfillment of prediction that the king of the South would push against the "Wilful King," whom he identifies as the Sultan. Russia, the king of the North, and Egypt would fight together to destroy the Ottoman Empire but then Russia would surely turn on Egypt and, in the great battle of the end in Palestine, decimate it.[78] Yet Ali's loss of control over Syria in 1840, as well as Russia's support for its return to the Sultan, flew in the face of Fysh's interpretation. Since Egypt was mentioned in the prophecy by name it must in some way be involved, but clearly another more formidable power must be indicated. It was in the 1840s the idea that Britain may be this power began to take hold amongst prophecy students. In *The Two Later Visions of Daniel*, published in 1846, the Rev. T. R. Birks suggested that while Egypt had lately been rising in prominence as an independent power it was yet, "too feeble to undertake any serious resistance to a confederacy so vast and mighty." He suggests that Egypt may in fact simply be the "salient point of attack" and that the true prophetic king of the South would be that power which occupies Egypt, is one of wider influence, and holds other possessions. "The same power which holds the vast southern empire of India," he muses, "may then also have possession of Egypt." The course of current events seemed to be drawing the interests of Britain, India, and Egypt together. "Whenever, therefore," he concludes,

> all the continent shall be gathered under one head, as the king of the north, it seems not improbable that the maritime empire of Britain may be the rival power, and thus its acquisition of Egypt, as the emporium of its Indian commerce, will give to it the prophetic character of the king of the south.[79]

As the British interests in and control over the areas of India, Egypt, Arabia, and the Eastern Mediterranean grew in the second half of the nineteenth century, this identification only became stronger. Britain's acquisition of Aden in 1839, the transformation of India into a crown colony in 1858, its control of Cyprus in 1878, its occupation of Egypt in 1882, as well as events in the Sudan during the 1880s and 1890s firmly established by the turn of the century that Britain was indeed the king of the South. During the second half of the nineteenth century, this identification was asserted with increasing confidence.[80] As a further confirmation, the prophet's mention of the "young lions" of Tarshish clearly indicated Britain's settlement colonies as the lion had long been the emblem for Britain and thus her daughter nations, i.e. Canada, Australia, New Zealand, South Africa and even the United States, were undoubtedly these young lions.[81]

What was more, even those not prone to studying the prophecies seemed aware that world peace was now increasingly dependent upon how the British and Russian empires handled their Asian interests. General Lord Roberts declared in the House of Lords in 1898 that he believed that the "force of civilization will compel Great Britain and Russia to eventually meet in Asia," and even *The Contemporary Review* asserted in its issue of May 1895, that "Europe in Asia, for practical purposes consists of two Powers, England and Russia. The Empires of Britain and Muscovy have the overlordship, the one of the South the other of the North." Though it is doubtful that the use of these terms was deliberately eschatological, the author nevertheless contends that upon their relationship rested the peace of Asia and the whole world.[82]

The arrangement of alliances at the beginning of World War I, then, threw something of a wrench into this scheme. A few authors abandoned the traditional scheme and suggested that Germany, not Russia, was the leading nation of Gog.[83] But most others held firmly to the traditional prediction of a coming final war between a Russian-led northern confederation and a southern British one, despite their present entente. Their confidence in the traditional interpretation was built upon several supports. First, very few Great War-era millennialists believed that the present conflict was Armageddon itself. Rather it represented the "time of tribulation" that would set up the necessary configuration of nations to bring about the Final Battle. Disagreement existed as to whether the current war would morph seamlessly into Armageddon or if there might be an interlude of peace, but the fact that Britain and Russia were presently fighting on the same side caused little concern. If one accepted prophetic chronology which placed Armageddon some few decades on, there remained ample time and opportunity for a re-arrangement of alliances.[84] Moreover, the British alliance with Russia and France was an "unnatural one" and so it was easily accepted that Russia and Britain would resume their old rivalry (either at some point within the present conflict or shortly after its end), and, with new issues at stake, begin to build new arms and cultivate new allies for the coming battle.[85] "Is it not likely," the Rev. Earle

Legh Langston asked in August 1918, "that the forthcoming peace that must soon be declared will be most unsatisfactory to Russia, Germany and Turkey, especially with regard to the near Eastern question? These powers, therefore after some respite, will unite to set things right from their point of view."[86] This triple alliance would indeed be in a position to sweep down into Israel, as Ezekiel 38:9 described, "coming on like a storm; you shall be like a cloud covering the land, you and all your troops, and many peoples with you."[87]

Secondly, Russian and British cooperation was necessary in order to set up the conditions for Armageddon. An interpretation closely echoing Fysh's wherein the king of the North and the king of the South would work in concert to destroy Turkey was commonly offered. "It is of interest to notice," *The Christian Herald* told its readers in the spring of 1916 in an analysis of recent events in the East, "that the regions in which the fighting is taking place, both under British and Russian direction, are regions which, according to unfulfilled prophecy, are to have a glorious future, and one cannot but wonder if present events are a preparation for that time."[88] This joint activity in the region would have the two-fold benefit of shifting the focus of the war to Palestine where the final battle must be fought and of ultimately pitting British and Russian interests against each other.[89] Millennialists repeatedly reminded their readers that the place called Armageddon (Megiddo) was not in Europe but in Asia. "Before the battle of Armageddon can be fought," Salt explained to his readers, "there must, obviously, be some great incentive to incite the gathering of nations into Palestine."[90] The purpose of the Great War was to help develop that situation. Russia and Britain must engage in this development together so that each could claim interests in the Holy Land and thus serve as the pretext for war. The emigration of Russia's large Jewish population to Palestine as well as its claims over Istanbul would give the Russians a viable stake in the region very likely to be antagonized by Britain's military and commercial activities, not to mention its protection over a restored Jewish state there.[91]

And thirdly, too many other specific predictions were in the process of fulfillment to now believe that a rather uncomfortable and untraditional alliance between Moscow and London could thwart the ultimate purposes of God. As the course of the war unfolded, in fact, millennialists found themselves heartened by events. In late 1914, Britain took full possession of Cyprus, removed Egypt officially from the Ottoman Empire, and shored up its routes to India solidifying its southern position. After 1915 it was commonly conceded that Russia would gain effective control over the Straits as a consequence of an Allied victory, thus giving it control over the great northern approach to Palestine.[92] In addition, already in the early days of the war, millennialists noted the news reports that spoke of a planned federation of Europe or league of nations to be set up once the conflict had ended.[93] This proposed league, which would most likely fall under the control of Russia and its northern European allies, was identified as, "not only *the natural outcome of the present world-conflict*, and consequent international exhaustion, but also ... *the inevitable prelude of the Kingdom of the Antichrist.* In fact, it is the divinely-permitted preparation for that satanic consummation."[94] Britain and its empire, they argued, would be either be excluded, refuse to join, or eventually remove itself from this company.[95] In the plans for, and ultimately the founding of the League of Nations, millennialists believed that they could now discern the face and formation of the nations of Gog.[96]

But the two most important of confirmatory events were the Russian Revolutions of 1917 and the British Mandate over Palestine of 1920. The revolutions which first toppled the Czar and then introduced Bolshevik control during the course of 1917 were accepted by millennialists as acts of God — as truly miraculous as the unexpected entry of Turkey into the war. The upheavals were compared to the French Revolution of 1789 which had ultimately brought about an atheistic government and then a world-conquering dictator in the person of Napoleon.[97] By early 1918, Russia had pulled out of the alliance with France and Britain (as predicted), was openly negotiating with Germany, and the Bolshevik government had renounced all claims to Constantinople. Events of the near future, based upon all available information, were not difficult to predict. Russia would emerge from its political difficulties stronger than ever, either with a restored Czar who would use the revolutions as pretences to further consolidate his power or under another autocrat equally interested in power.[98] An alliance with an exhausted Germany would give Russia control over Northern Europe.[99] Even Russia's withdrawal of claims to the Near East was a necessary, but only a temporary, development — only lasting long enough to allow (under God's guiding hand) the firm establishment of a restored Jewish nation in Palestine under British protection.[100] It was in regards to this last point that the British Mandate over Palestine, anticipated during the waning days of the war and received at the San Remo conference in April 1920, seemed to be the final confirmation of the coming battle. Britain, which had proclaimed in the Balfour Declaration its support for a Jewish national home in Palestine almost three years before, now seemed to be given the authority to truly restore and protect the children of Israel as had been long anticipated. The Rev. Langston summed it up thus: "Great Britain has had conferred on her one of the greatest, if not *the* greatest honor she has ever had in all her glorious history — and that is to supervise all the affairs with regard to restoring the Jews to their ancient home, and to enable them to settle down in that land, and thus prepare the way for the coming of the King of kings."[101] By the beginning of the 1920s, then, everything in the East, the principal events, peoples, and circumstances, looked to be now in place for Armageddon.

Conclusion

It was to the East, then, that believers were exhorted to look in anticipation of the millennial dawn. As much as the Western Front might command the attention of the press and the politicians, prophecy students knew that this was but a sideline affair. "I would earnestly ask my readers to divert their attention away from Western Europe — which is of small account, 'a very little thing' in the Eyes of Him with Whom 'All the inhabitants of the earth are reputed as nothing,'" John J. Pearson wrote in late 1917, repeating a plea he had made very early in the war, "and look towards Palestine, Egypt, and Mesopotamia: for it is in these regions of the earth that the great closing scenes of the tremendous world-drama, now opening, will be enacted! ... Watch the East; for here God will pour out His Almighty Power!"[102] The centrality of the Eastern campaign to the course of the war seemed evident to millennialists and further buttressed their claims. Was it not remarkable, they asked, that the war dragged on for year after year until the complete liberation of Palestine and Syria only then to be ended within a matter of weeks?[103] For decades millennial enthusiasts had predicted specific events which one day must ultimately transpire in the East to signify the near approach of the Lord. These were now occurring with a startling and unprecedented precision. Those who expected the imminent coming of Christ during this period, then, can be fairly labeled wrong, but they should not be counted as crazy. Too many prominent, respectable, and even skeptical men and women had come to believe that developments in the Eastern theatre of the war were presaging the end of days. At the end of the war, the Rt. Rev. Handley C. G. Moule, Anglican Bishop of Durham, agreed that the "age of the Gentiles" did seem to be passing. "Many a noteworthy event in what we may call the Scriptural East," had taken place, he noted; above all, "we have seen Jerusalem set free by a Christian, Messianic power." In that achievement, wrought at that specific time, he confessed, "I think we feel the finger of God." He further recalled that he had been approached three years earlier about Moore's book *The Nearness of Our Lord's Return* by an old Cambridge friend, now a Fellow of the college and for thirty years a distinguished public school master, whose personality "would not suggest precisely the student of prophecy." Yet, the conditions of the time, "taken along with a sober statement of the case for the expectation on predictive lines," had led this man to the conclusion that, "the consummation of the age was coming." That a man of such character and temperament would be led to this belief, the Bishop concluded, was significant.[104]

In sum, in their testing of long-held hypotheses against the unfolding developments of the Great War, there was something more of scientific method than religious fanaticism in most British millennialist works. "In the study of prophecy," Samuel Hurnard reminded his readers, "there is a need to check results and conclusions by the sober test of time."[105] The Rev. Walter Wynn was so confident in the scientific methodology behind these interpretations that he went so far as to apply the test of falsifiability to them. After long and careful reading and analysis, he told his congregation in 1915, he had determined that, "if Christ does not return to this world previous to the year 1935, no interpretation of the prophecies need call for serious considerations. We can close the subject once and for all as unprofitable."[106] One should not overstate this case, however. Of course the apocalyptic impulse at this time was not entirely immune to the emotional urgency of the moment, and the human reactions to the catastrophe which was the First World War affected millennialists as much as anyone else. It cannot be denied, furthermore, that at the base of much eschatological expectation was a deep desire to make sense of all the carnage — to give it all some deeper meaning. The point here is that, as Richard Landes reminds us, millennial ideas and those who have held them should not be shunted to the margins of the historical record on the assumption that they constituted some kind of lunatic fringe of the cultural and intellectual landscape.[107] The Eastern Question had been long without a viable or permanent solution despite the efforts of the best and brightest politicians and diplomats from many nations and several generations. A good many educated and thoughtful men and women came to believe that the final answer to this perpetual problem was to be found not in dispatches out of the Foreign Office but in the pages of their Bibles. Who at the time was in a position to say with any certainty, especially as the events of the Great War seemingly gave confirmation after confirmation, that it might not be so?

NOTES

1. Very little analysis on World War I-era British millennialism has been done. Ernie Hilbert broaches the issue to some extent in his article "Prelude to Armageddon: Apocalyptic Clamour and Complaint in Britain, 1850–1914," *Journal of Millennial Studies* 1 (Winter 1999): 1–22, though his focus is on the period preceding the war. To a large degree this lacunae is understandable since the study of popular religious feeling in Great War-era Britain, something quite apart from official Church responses, is only now gaining the attention of historians. See Michael Snape, *God and the British Soldier: Religion and the British Army in the First World War* (Abingdon: Routledge, 2005) 4.

2. Jay Winter, in *Sites of Memory, Sites of Mourning: The Great War in European Cultural History* (Cambridge, UK: Cambridge University Press, 1995), examines the presence

of apocalyptic imagery in the cultural landscape of the time. This, however, was usually more a figurative application of traditional concepts and images onto modern realities than an attempt to identify and predict the biblical apocalypse.

3. Hilbert, "Prelude to Armageddon," 6.

4. "Leading Article," *The Record: The Church's Oldest Newspaper* (London), November 30, 1916. That same year, M. Harding Kelly remarked in her *Glory; or, Things to Come* (London: Marshall Brothers, 1916) that, "as we watch the great death struggle between the Allies and their enemies to-day, we note how the whole issue circles more and more around the great Eastern question" (30).

5. "Armageddon: Sacred History Recalled by Familiar Names in To-Day's Dispatches," *Daily News* (London), September 23, 1918.

6. The Eastern Question, or Eastern problem as it was sometimes called, concerned the diplomatic and strategic consequences of an Ottoman Empire in decline. Uncertainty regarding the balance of power in southeastern Europe and the Mediterranean, Russian access through the Dardanelles, and British trade to and through the Near East should the Turkish Empire collapse made this question an important and perennial problem for the Great Powers of Europe in the nineteenth century.

7. Richard Millman's work remains the best account of British interests involved in the Eastern Question in the mid to late nineteenth century: *Britain and the Eastern Question 1875–1878* (Oxford, UK: Clarendon, 1979). Though the question involved the fates of Christian, Jewish, and Muslim populations, analysis of the religious response to the Eastern Question has been nonetheless limited to accounts of specific Christian churches' responses to the issues, or in the case of the 1875–78 crisis, the role of Benjamin Disraeli's Jewish heritage in the debate of British policy decisions. See John P. Rossi, "Catholic Opinion on the Eastern Question," *Church History* 51 (1982): 54–70; Ann Pottinger Saab, "Disraeli, Judaism, and the Eastern Question," *International History Review* 10 (1988): 559–578; Anthony S. Wohl, "'Dizzi-Ben-Dizzi': Disraeli as Alien," *Journal of British Studies* 34 (July 1995): 375–411.

8. Marian Kent, "Great Britain and the End of the Ottoman Empire, 1900–1923," in *The Great Powers and the End of the Ottoman Empire*, Marian Kent, ed. (London: Frank Cass, 1996) 178–179.

9. For the context and controversy regarding this statement see Lillian M. Penson, "The New Course in British Foreign Policy, 1892–1902," *Transactions of the Royal Historical Society*, 4th ser., 25 (1943): 121–138.

10. Kent, "Great Britain and the End of the Ottoman Empire, 1900–1923," 186.

11. Robert Kerner, "Russia, the Straits, and Constantinople, 1914–1915," *The Journal of Modern History* 1 (September 1929): 414. For a contemporary view of the importance of Constantinople in the British and Russian alliance see, H. Hamilton Fyfe, "What Russia Will Want," *Daily Mail* (London), November 30, 1914.

12. G. E. Buckle and W. F. Monypenny, *The Life and Letters of Benjamin Disraeli, Earl of Beaconsfield* (London: J. Murray, 1910–1920) VI, 84.

13. The amount of millennialist literature produced during the war years in Britain, including books, pamphlets, and religious periodical articles, numbers into the several hundreds.

14. See Robert Roberts, *England and Egypt. Prophecy Fulfilled and Fulfilling* (Birmingham: R. Roberts, 1882) 3; and Robert Baker Girdlestone, *The Divine Programme: Suggestions for its Study* (London: Prophecy Investigation Society, 1915) 7–8.

15. Wilkinson, *The Future of Jerusalem in Its Successive Phases with Regards to Present Events* (London: Prophecy Investigation Society, 1917) 5; see also W. F. T. Salt, *The Great War in the Light of Divine Prophecy. Is it Armageddon?* (Bristol: F. Walker, 1915) 140.

16. Continuity of these claims throughout the period can be seen in a few ways. First,

a good many World War I-era millennial authors acknowledged their profound debt to writers from previous decades. For example, Harold Norris cites his indebtedness to Dr. Henry Grattan Guinness (1835–1910) in *When Will Our Lord Return? Prophetic Times and Warning Events*, 2nd ed. (London: C. J. Thynne, 1915). Secondly, prophetic works from the nineteenth century, long out of print, were re-edited and re-issued during the war as current events seemed to confirm the interpretations found in them. Two of Canon Edward Hoare's works from the 1870s were reprinted at least three times each during the war: *Rome, Turkey and Jerusalem*, edited by J. H. Townsend (London: C. J. Thynne, 1914, 1915, 1918 [original edition: London: Hatchards, 1876]), and his *Palestine and Russia* (London: Hatchards, 1877) was brought up to date by E. L. Langston under the alternate titles *Palestine, Russia, and the Present War* (London: C. J. Thynne, 1915) and *Great Britain, Palestine, Russia, and the Jews* (London: C. J. Thynne, 1918 [two editions]). Thirdly, some authors who had written prophetic tracts in the late-nineteenth century put out new editions of them during the war, often without any significant changes. For example, in 1915 Sir Robert Anderson put out a tenth edition of his *The Coming Prince* (London: Hodder & Stoughton), which he had originally published in 1881 remarking in the preface that, "the War has apparently created an increase interest in the prophecies of Daniel, and as this book is therefore in demand, it has been decided to publish a new edition without delay."

17. Stuart Semmel, *Napoleon and the British* (New Haven, CT: Yale University Press, 2004) 83–106.

18. John Thomas, M. D., *Elpis Israel: Being an Exposition of the Kingdom of God, with Reference to the Time of the End, and the Age to Come*, 4th ed. (West Hoboken, N.J.: The Author, 1867) 390–398; *"The Kings of the East;" An Exposition of the Prophecies* (London: Seeley and Burnside, 1842).

19. Pae, *The Coming Struggle Among the Nations of the Earth or, The Political Events of the Next Fifteen Years: Described in Accordance with the Prophecies in Ezekiel, Daniel, and the Apocalypse, Showing the Important Position Britain will Occupy During and At the End of the Awful Conflict* (London: Houlston & Stoneman, 1853).

20. Thomas quickly published a "corrected" version of the pamphlet and, while replicating Pae's title on his work, he makes it clear that his ideas are the more viable ones. Thomas, *The Coming Struggle Among the Nations of the Earth* (Toronto: Thomas McLear, 1853) 3. See also, "The Editor's Shanty," *The Anglo-American Magazine* 4 (April 1854): 427.

21. Along with Pae, John Cumming of the Scottish National Church was a prolific Crimean War millennial author. His many works on the subject include, *Signs of the Times; The Moslem and His End; the Christian and His Hope* (London: Arthur Hall, Virtue & Co., 1854), *The War and Its Issues: Two Sermons* (London: Arthur Hall, Virtue & Co., 1854), and *The End: or, The Proximate Signs of the Close of this Dispensation* (London: John Farquhar Shaw, 1855).

22. See, for example, George William Dalton, *Who Is to Have Constantinople? A Prophetical Answer to that Political Question* (Dublin: Hodges, Foster & Figgish, 1876); James Moir Porteous, *The Eastern Question. Turkey, Its Mission and Doom; A Prophetical Instruction* (London: n.p., 1876); and John Wilson, *The True Solution of the Eastern Question: England's Duty in Relation to the Christians of Turkey* (London: W. H. Guest, 1877).

23. David Pae, *The Russo-Turkish War and Its Issues: As Revealed in Scripture Prophecy* (London: William P. Nimmo, 1877) 2. *The Stirling Journal* devoted its lead article of August 17, 1878, to examining Pae's pamphlet in the light of Eastern events.

24. W. S., *The Eastern Question: and What the Bible Says About Coming Events*, 3rd ed. (London: Alfred Holness, 1877) 4.

25. Scott, "Introductory Statement," *The Eastern or Jewish Question Considered: and What the Bible Says about Coming Events* (London: Alfred Holness, 1882).

26. *Ibid.*, 4–6.

27. Tanner, *Daniel and the Revelation: The Chart of Prophecy and Our Place in It*. With a Preface by the Rev. Hubert Brooke, M.A. (London: Hodder & Stoughton, 1898) 213.

28. This interpretation is found in Thomas Brightman, *A Reuelation of the Reuelation, that is the Reuelation of St John Opened Clearely, with a Logicall Resolution and Exposition* (Amsterdam: n.p., 1615) and Joseph Mede, *The Key of the Revelation Searched and Demonstrated out of the Naturall and Proper Charecters of the Visions. With a Coment Thereupon, According to the Rule of the Same Key*, Richard More, trans. With a Preface by Dr. Twisse (London: n.p., 1643). By the nineteenth century it was standard in prophetic literature.

29. Guinness, *Light for the Last Days: A Study Historic and Prophetic* (London: Hodder & Stoughton, 1886) 152, n.1.

30. M. A. of Cambridge, *The Coming Collision Between England and Russia, Predicted by Ezekiel, Chapters XXXVIII and XXXIX* (London: W. H. Guest, 1879) 19.

31. *Ibid.*, 47–48.

32. Gregg, "The Drying Up of the Ottoman Power: The Doom of the Gentiles," *The Mail and Empire* (Toronto), January 13, 1913.

33. Moore, *The Nearness of Our Lord's Return, as Inferred from Studies in the Comparison of Prophecy with History* (London: Robert Scott, 1913) 107–109.

34. Lawrence Roberts had predicted in August 1914 that, based on his reading of the prophecies, Turkey must soon join the coalition of nations against Britain. Roberts, *Britain's Unveiling: Or Israel in the Book of Revelation* (London: R. Banks & Son, 1914) 4.

35. Simpson, "The Midnight Cry," *The Christian Herald and Signs of Our Times* (London), March 11, 1915.

36. "Turkey," *The Morning Star: A Herald of the Second Coming of Christ* (London), February 1, 1915.

37. "In the News," *The Jewish Chronicle* (London), December 31, 1915.

38. Samuel, *Palestine—Turkey—and Egypt* (London: C. J. Thynne, 1915) 19. Cf. Lancaster, *Prophecy, the War and the Near East* (London: Marshall Brothers, 1916) 168.

39. Titterton, *Armageddon, or The Last War, with a Foreword by the Rev. E. W. Moore, M.A., Incumbent of Emmanuel Church, Wimbledon* (London: C. J. Thynne, 1916) 2.

40. S. A. Wellman, *The World's Crisis in the Light of Prophecy* (Lucknow: International Tract Society, 1915) 44–45.

41. Diocesan Reader, *The War: Messiah's Advent: Is It Imminent? Israel's Restoration, 1916–1917* (London: Marshall Brothers, 1915) 8, 43.

42. Prophetic chronology involved identifying some historic event as a commencement point, an event usually involving ancient Israel, Islam, or the Church, and then applying the length of these periods, using the day-year theory (one biblical day being equal to one calendar year), to find where the terminus lay. Grattan Guinness, while not the originator of this practice, became its champion in the late nineteenth century and it informed much of the content of his work. He provides a rousing defense of the method in an appendix to *Light for the Last Days* (1886), "Appendix A: The Scientific Basis for Prophetic Chronology," 635–671.

43. In *Light for the Last Days*, Guinness had calculated the range of years for the final crisis of the Turk as being from 1915–1934, though he singled out 1917 as a particularly crucial year regarding the end of Turkish control of Palestine: "There can be no question," he writes, "that those who live to see this year 1917 will have reached one of the most important, perhaps *the* most momentous, of these terminal years of crisis" (326, 346).

44. Cook, *Light from the Book of Daniel On History Past, Present, and Future* (London: Robert Banks and Son, 1916) 233.

45. W. Bell Dawson, *The Close of the Present Age in the Light of the Periods Predicted by Prophecy* (London: Marshall Brothers, 1917) 48.

46. See, for example, "The Future of Jerusalem," *The Christian Herald and Signs of Our Times* (London), December 6, 1917; Francis L. Denman, "The Capture of Jerusalem," *The Record* (London), December 20, 1917; and Wilkinson, "Jerusalem!" *Trusting and Toiling on Israel's Behalf: Organ of the Mildmay Mission to the Jews* 24 (January 15, 1918): 1–2.

47. F. S. Webster, "The A.B.C. of Our Manifesto," *The Monthly Bulletin of the Advent Preparation Prayer Union* 1 (June 12, 1919): 2.

48. George John Emmerson, *The End in View* (London: Marshall Brothers, 1920) 109.

49. See Richard W. Cogley, "The Fall of the Ottoman Empire and the Restoration of Israel in the 'Judeo-centric' Strand of Puritan Millenarianism," *Church History* 72 no. 2 (June 2003): 304–332, and Mayir Vereté, "The Restoration of the Jews in English Protestant Thought 1790–1840," *Middle Eastern Studies* 8 (January 1972): 3–50.

50. Edward Bickersteth made note of some of these signs in his *The Restoration of the Jews to Their Own Land* (London: R. B. Seeley and W. Burnside, 1841) lxxvi–xciv.

51. W. D. Rubinstein, *A History of the Jews in the English Speaking World: Great Britain* (New York: St. Martin's, 1996) 79.

52. Eitan Bar-Yosef, *The Holy Land in English Culture 1799–1917: Palestine and the Question of Orientalism* (Oxford, UK: Clarendon, 2005) chapter 4.

53. "Prophetic Signs in the East," *The Christian Herald and Signs of Our Times* (London), October 16, 1878. A secular paper, *The Carlisle Patriot*, also remarked on the strange convergence of events in the East with the Biblical prophecies in its lead article, "Politics and Prophecy," July 19, 1878.

54. See, "Turkish Bonds and Palestine," *Jewish Chronicle*, April 28, 1876. These same sentiments of Providential design and preference for British protection appear in articles the previous year and in the years that followed. For Benisch's personal interest in the issue see, Jonathan Frankel, *The Damascus Affair: "Ritual Murder," Politics, and the Jews in 1840* (Cambridge, UK: Cambridge University Press, 1997) 316–328, *passim*.

55. C. W. E., *The Identity of the British Nation with The Lost Ten Tribes of the House of Israel: The Clue to the Eastern Question* (London: W. H. Guest, 1880) 8. The popular preacher, Joseph Wild, produced two works in which he made this prediction: *The Future of Israel and Judah: Being The Discourses on the Lost Tribes, From "How and When the World Will End"* (London: Robert Banks, 1880) and, *The Lost Ten Tribes and 1882* (London: Robert Banks, 1880).

56. For the rise of political Zionism in Britain see Stuart A. Cohen, *English Zionists and British Jews: The Communal Politics of Anglo-Jewry, 1895–1920* (Princeton, NJ: Princeton University Press, 1982).

57. Frank George Jannaway, *Palestine and the Jews: Or, the Zionist Movement and the Evidence that the Messiah Will Soon Appear in Jerusalem to Rule the World Therefrom* (Birmingham: C. C. Walker, 1914) 70.

58. Moore, *Ancient Tyre and Modern England; or, The Historical Type of Ancient Tyre in Its Prophetic Application to Modern England* (London: Elliot Stock, 1906) 350–351.

59. Wingate, *Mesopotamia, the Gateway to Palestine* (London: n.p., 1911) 23. Wingate repeats essentially the same argument on the very eve of the war in his *Modern Unrest and the Bible* (London: World's Evangelical Alliance, 1914) 20–22.

60. Wingate, *Mesopotamia*, 42.

61. *Ibid.*, 46.

62. Denman, *Turkey — Palestine — and Israel* (London: C. J. Thynne, 1915) 36.

63. W. S. Collis, *The War and Prophecy* (Dublin: E. Ponsonby, 1914) 10.

64. Frederick John Horsefield, *The Return of the King: Its Certainty; Its Meaning; Its Nearness* (London: Marshall Brothers, 1915) 118.

65. E. N. Dixon, *The Divine Plan in the Government of the World* (London: W. Hard-

wick, 1915) 13–14; Euston John Nurse, *Palestine and the War. With Sixteen Illustrations and Maps* (London: Skeffington & Son, 1918).

66. "Conditions in Palestine: An Interview with Mr. W. Gluskin," *The Jewish Chronicle* (London), December 31, 1915.

67. "1917 as a Fateful Year," *The Christian Herald and Signs of Our Times* (London), January 18, 1917, also "1917: A Fateful Year," *The Christian Herald and Signs of Our Times* (London), March 22, 1917. The article, "Striking Prophetic Dates," *The Record* (London), March 15, 1917 makes much the same point.

68. Schor, *The Future of Jerusalem* (London: C. J. Thynne, 1917). Also, John J. Pearson, *The Exiles' Return to Their Lost Inheritance* (London: Arthur H. Stockwell, 1917) 13–14; Augusta Cook, *Is It Armageddon? The Present War in the Light of Divine Prophecy*, 7th ed. (London: Robert Banks & Son, 1917) ii-iii.

69. Alfred Henry Burton, *Russia's Destiny in the Light of Prophecy* (London: Pickering & Inglis, 1917) 3–4. Such a sentiment was common and constant in millennial thought. Both Robert Middleton in *The Great War and its Place in Prophetic History* (London: Jarrold & Sons, 1916) 20, and George John Emmerson in *The End in View*, 93, use nearly identical imagery of the restoration of Israel as God's timepiece of prophecy as Bickersteth (*Restoration of the Jews*, 148) had some seventy-five years before.

70. Bathurst, *Significant Signs of the Present Times, 1918, in View of the Approaching Advent of Christ* (London: Robert Scott, 1918) 7–8.

71. "Advent Testimony," *The Record* (London), November 8, 1917. An Irish version of the same movement was founded by prominent churchmen at the end of the year: "An Irish Advent Testimony," *The Christian Herald and Signs of Our Times* (London), January 10, 1918. Meetings to discuss the issue were also held in other parts of the country. See, "Notes of the Week," *The Record* (London), February 14, 1918.

72. *Advent Testimony Handbooks, No. 1–6* (London: C. J. Thynne, 1918). For an account of the December 13, 1917, meeting see, "Advent Testimony," *The Record* (London), January 3, 1918.

73. Simpson, "Britain Fulfilling Prophecy: A Timely and Remarkable Sermon," *The Christian Herald and Signs of Our Times* (London), April 11, 1918.

74. Samuel Fennell Hurnard, *After Ten Years: A Sequel to "The European War and Prophecy"* (London: Morgan & Scott, 1924) 8–10.

75. See C. Askwith, "The Lord's Coming: As it Will Affect the Jews" in *The Lord's Coming: Its Near Approach* (London: Prophecy Investigation Society, 1918) 30–33; J. R. Kaighin, *The Bible: The Jew: And the War* (London: Samuel E. Roberts, 1918) 160–161.

76. For a particularly thorough case for this identity see John Hawker, M.A., *Russia's Limits* (London: Elliot Stock, 1878).

77. "Rosh," in *A Dictionary of the Bible Comprising its Antiquities, Biography, Geography and Natural History*, William Smith, ed., vol. III (London: John Murray, 1863) 1061–1062.

78. Fysh, *The Time of the End, or, The Sultan of Turkey the Wilful King, and Mehemet Ali the King of the South Pushing at Him, as Foretold by Daniel* (London: Simpkin & Marshall, 1839).

79. Birks, *The Two Later Visions of Daniel: Historically Explained* (London: Seeley, Burnside, and Seeley, 1846) 333–334.

80. See, for example, *The Destiny of the British Empire as Revealed in the Scriptures* (London: William Macintosh, 1865) 8–10; British Clergyman, *Who Are the British, What is Their Destiny?* (London: W. H. Guest [1880]) 53–61 and John Ellam, *Prophetic Studies: or, Some Present Day Facts as Seen in the Light of Prophecy* (London: C. J. Thynne, 1903) chapters 4 and 5.

81. John Thomas, *Destiny of the British Empire as Revealed in the Scriptures. Compiled*

Chiefly from the Writings of Dr. Thomas (London: G. J. Stevenson, 1871) 8–9; Herbert Aldersmith, M.B., F.R.C.S., *Coming Events in the East and the Return of the Jews to Palestine*, 3rd ed. (London: James Nisbet & Co., 1896) 14.

82. "The Coming Great Battle," *The Lyttleton Times*, June 6, 1898; "The European Partners in Asia," *The Contemporary Review* 67 (May 1895): 610.

83. James Bernard Nicklin, *"The Great Shaking"* (Halesowen & Blackheath: Parkes, 1918) 4; F. D. *The War and the Prophets* (London: Morgan and Scott, 1915).

84. R. K. Arnaud, *The New Prophecy* (London: Hodder and Stoughton, 1917) 159–181.

85. Henry Sulley, *Is it Armageddon?* (London: Simpkin, 1915) 82.

86. Langston, *Great Britain, Palestine, Russia, and the Jews: A Third Reprint* (London: C. J. Thynne, 1918) 36–38.

87. Alfred Taylor Schofield, *The Lord's Coming: Its Near Approach* (London: Prophecy Investigation Society, 1918) 21. See also George H. Lancaster, *Prophecy, The War and the Near East*, 5th ed. (London: Marshall Brothers, 1919) 244.

88. "Current Events: News from Constantinople," *The Christian Herald and Signs of Our Times* (London), March 16, 1916. Also George E. Watts, *The Prophecies of Daniel and Their Allusion to the Present War and Defeat of the Kaiser—The Beast, False Prophet and Infidel King—With Copious Notes* (Derby: Mee & Wilson, 1916) "Appendix."

89. This prediction seemingly received confirmation near the end of the war in an article in *The Daily News* which predicted that Palestine, which had for all of history served as the center of international rivalries, would do so again in the near future: "With the Turk gone, and the League of Nations in its place, there may be more fighting somewhere to make good its decrees, and that fighting, wherever it starts, will be sure to drift to the Cockpit of the World." Richard Whiteing, "The Cockpit of the World," *The Daily News* (London), October 9, 1918.

90. Salt, *The Great War*, 136; see also, Euston J. Nurse, *Prophecy and the War*, 8th ed., New and Revised (London: Skeffington & Son, 1918) 79; Cook, *Light from the Book of Daniel*, 218; and Sulley, *Is it Armageddon?* 82.

91. D. M. Patton, "Russia and Palestine," *Trusting and Toiling* 21 (February 15, 1915): 9–11.

92. William Baillie, *History in Prophecy: Studies for Pilgrims in the Present Crisis* (London: C. J. Thynne, 1915) 53–58.

93. "Europe to be Confederated," *The Christian Herald and Signs of Our Times* (London), September 24, 1914; Earnest Goode, "Prophetic Illustrations from Current Events: The Ten-Kingdomed Confederacy," *The Prophetic News and Israel's Watchman* (May 1915): 115.

94. Hope Charles Tiarks, *The King's Call for Advent Testimony* (London: C. J. Thynne, 1919) 38, original emphasis; also, Alfred Henry Burton, *The Future of Europe, Politically and Religiously, in Light of the Holy Scripture*, 4th ed. (London: Pickering & Inglis, 1917) 2.

95. Ernest Peter Cachemaille, *The Warfare of the End* (London: Prophecy Investigation Society, 1920) 14–15; also Percy F. White, *Armageddon: The Near Future Great War and the Golden Age of Peace Which Shall Follow* (London: J. F. Belmont and Co., 1918) 12–13.

96. W. M. W., "The Sequel to the Present War," *The Morning Star* (London), May 18, 1916; also Algernon James Pollock, *Things Which Must Shortly Come to Pass* (London: Central Bible Truth Depot, 1918) 107, 236.

97. Burton, *Russia's Destiny*, 62–63.

98. Charles Duncan Horatio McMillan, *The Harvest and the Vintage: An Interpretation of the Times* (London: Robert Scott, 1918) 89.

99. Cook, *Is It Armageddon?* ii–iii. Several decades earlier, Thomas had predicted that the autocrat of Russia would ultimately control both the Russian Empire and Germany:

Elpis Israel, 4th ed., 388. This seemed to receive confirmation in the Treaty of Rapallo of April 1922 which normalized relations between the Soviet Union and Germany. See Frank George Jannaway, *Palestine and the World* (London: Sampson Low, Marston & Co., 1922) 187–191.

100. Wingate, *Palestine, Mesopotamia, and the Jews: The Spiritual Side of History* (Glasgow: Pickering and Inglis, 1919) 76–82.

101. Langston, *The British Mandate for Palestine and its Significance* (London: Morgan & Scott, 1920) 31–32.

102. Pearson, *The Exiles' Return*, 335.

103. Hurnard, *After Ten Years*, 9; Dixon, *The Divine Plan in the Government of the World*, 2nd ed. (London: Imperial British-Israel Association, 1919) 17–18.

104. Moule, *The Hope and the Near Approach of the Lord's Return, and Its Influence on Life* (London: C. J. Thynne, 1919) 13.

105. Hurnard, *After Ten Years*, 2.

106. Wynn, *The Bible and the War: Thrilling Addresses* (Letchworth: Garden City Press, 1915) 13. Wynn repeated this assertion a year later (although he granted Christ an extension of one year) in his *Revelation in the Light of the War and Modern Events* (London: C. J. Thynne, 1916) 183.

107. Landes, "The Fruitful Error: Reconsidering Millennial Enthusiasm," *Journal of Interdisciplinary History* 32 (Summer 2001): 89–98.

Works Cited

"Advent Testimony." *The Record*. November 8, 1917: 750.

"Advent Testimony." *The Record*. January 3, 1918: 13.

Advent Testimony Handbooks. Nos. 1–6. London: C. J. Thynne, 1918.

Aldersmith, Herbert. *Coming Events in the East and the Return of the Jews to Palestine*, 3rd ed. London: James Nesbit and Co., 1896.

Anderson, Robert. *The Coming Prince*, 10th ed. London: Hodder and Stoughton, 1915.

"Armageddon: Sacred History Recalled by Familiar Names in To-Day's Dispatches." *Daily News*. September 23, 1918: 1.

Arnaud, R. K. *The New Prophecy*. London: Hodder and Stoughton, 1917.

Askwith, C. "The Lord's Coming: As it Will Affect the Jews," in *The Lord's Coming: Its Near Approach*. London: Prophecy Investigation Society, 1918.

Baillie, William. *History in Prophecy: Studies for Pilgrims in the Present Crisis*. London: C. J. Thynne, 1915.

Bar-Yosef, Eitan. *The Holy Land in English Culture, 1799–1917: Palestine and the Question of Orientalism*. Oxford, UK: Clarendon, 2005.

Bathurst, William. *Significant Signs of the Present Times, 1918, in View of the Approaching Advent of Christ*. London: Robert Scott, 1918.

Bickersteth, Edward. *The Restoration of the Jews to Their Own Land*. London: R. B. Seeley and W. Burnside, 1841.

Birks, T. R. *The Two Later Visions of Daniel: Historically Explained*. London: Seeley, Burnside, and Seeley, 1846.

Bonar, Horatius. "Prophetic Signs in the East." *The Christian Herald and Signs of Our Times*. October 16, 1878: 584.

Brightman, Thomas. *A Reuelation of the Reuelation, that is the Reuelation of St. John Opened Clearely, with a Logicall Resolution and Exposition*. Amsterdam: n.p., 1615.

British Clergyman. *Who Are the British, What Is Their Destiny?* London: W. H. Guest, 1880.

Buckle, G. E., and W. F. Monypenny. *The Life and Letters of Benjamin Disraeli, Earl of Beaconsfield*, vol. VI. London: J. Murray, 1920.

Burton, Alfred Henry. *The Future of Europe, Politically and Religiously, in Light of the Holy Scripture*, 4th ed. London: Pickering & Inglis, 1917.

_____. *Russia's Destiny in the Light of Prophecy*. London: Pickering and Inglis, 1917.

Cachemaille, Ernest Peter. *The Warfare of the End*. London: Prophecy Investigation Society, 1920.

Cogley, Richard W. "The Fall of the Ottoman Empire and the Restoration of Israel in the 'Judeo-centric' Strand of Puritan Millenarianism," *Church History* 72, no. 2 (June 2003): 304–332.

Cohen, Stuart A. *English Zionists and British Jews: The Communal Politics of Anglo-Jewry, 1895–1920*. Princeton: Princeton University Press, 1982.

Collis, W. S. *The War and Prophecy*. Dublin: E. Ponsonby, 1914.

"The Coming Great Battle." *The Lyttleton Times*. June 6, 1898.

"Conditions in Palestine: An Interview with Mr. W. Gluskin." *The Jewish Chronicle* . December 31, 1915: 12.

Cook, Augusta. *Is It Armageddon? The Present War in Light of Divine Prophecy*, 7th ed. London: Robert Banks & Son, 1917.

_____. *Light from the Book of Daniel on History, Past, Present, and Future*. London: Robert Banks and Son, 1916.

Cumming, John. *The End, or, The Proximate Signs of the Close of This Dispensation*. London: John Farquhar Shaw, 1855.

_____. *Signs of the Times: The Moslem, and His End: The Christian, and His Hope*. London: Arthur Hall, Virtue & Co., 1854.

_____. *The War and Its Issues: Two Sermons*. London: Arthur Hall, Virtue and Co., 1854.

"Current Events: News from Constantinople." *The Christian Herald and Signs of Our Times*. March 16, 1916: 226

D., F. *The War and the Prophets*. London: Morgan and Scott, 1915.

Dalton, George William. *Who Is to Have Constantinople? A Prophetical Answer to that Political Question*. Dublin: Hodges, Foster & Figgish, 1876.

Dawson, W. Bell. *The Close of the Present Age in the Light of the Periods Predicted by Prophecy*. London: Marshall Brothers, 1917.

Denman, Francis L. "The Capture of Jerusalem." *The Record*. December 20, 1917.

_____. *Turkey — Palestine — and Israel*. London: C. J. Thynne, 1915.

The Destiny of the British Empire as Revealed in the Scriptures. London: William Macintosh, 1865.

Diocesan Reader. *The War: Messiah's Advent: Is It Imminent? Israel's Restoration, 1916–1917*. London: Marshall Brothers, 1915.

Dixon, E. N. *The Divine Plan in the Government of the World*. London: W. Hardwick, 1915.

_____. *The Divine Plan in the Government of the World*, 2nd ed. London: Imperial British-Israel Association, 1919.

E., C. W. *The Identity of the British Nation with The Lost Ten Tribes of the House of Israel: The Clue to the Eastern Question*. London: W. H. Guest, 1880.

"The Editor's Shanty." *The Anglo-American Magazine* 4 (April 1854): 427.

Ellam, John. *Prophetic Studies, or, Some Present Day Facts as Seen in the Light of Prophecy*. London: C. J. Thynne, 1903.

Emmerson, George John. *The End in View*. London: Marshall Brothers, 1920.

"Europe to be Confederated." *The Christian Herald and Signs of Our Times*. September 24, 1914: 280.

"European Partners in Asia." *The Contemporary Review* 67 (May 1895): 609–616.

Frankel, Jonathan. *The Damascus Affair: "Ritual Murder," Politics, and the Jews in 1840*. Cambridge, UK: Cambridge University Press, 1997.

"The Future of Jerusalem." *The Christian Herald and Signs of Our Times*. December 6, 1917: 416

Fyfe, H. Hamilton. "What Russia Will Want." *Daily Mail*. November 30, 1914.

Fysh, Frederich. *The Time of the End, or, The Sultan of Turkey the Wilful King, and Mehemet Ali the King of the South Pushing at Him, as Foretold by Daniel*. London: Simpkin and Marshall, 1839.

Girdlestone, Robert Baker. *The Divine Programme: Suggestions for Its Study*. London: Prophecy Investigation Society, 1915.

Goode, Earnest. "Prophetic Illustrations from Current Events: The Ten-Kingdomed Confederacy." *The Prophetic News and Israel's Watchman*. May, 1915: 115.

Gregg, T. A. "The Drying Up of the Ottoman Power: The Doom of the Gentiles." *The Mail and Empire*. January 13, 1913: 12.

Guinness, H. Grattan. *Light for the Last Days: A Study Historic and Prophetic*. London: Hodder and Stoughton, 1886.

Hawker, John. *Russia's Limits*. London: Elliot Stock, 1878.

Hilbert, Ernie. "Prelude to Armageddon: Apocalyptic Clamour and Complaint in Britain, 1850–1914." *Journal of Millennial Studies* 1 (Winter 1999): 1–22.

Horsefield, Frederick John. *The Return of the King: Its Certainty; Its Meaning; Its Nearness*. London: Marshall Brothers, 1915.

Hurnard, Samuel Fennell. *After Ten Years: A Sequel to "The European War and Prophecy."* London: Morgan and Scott, 1924.

"In the News." *The Jewish Chronicle*. December 31, 1915: 8.

"An Irish Advent Testimony." *The Christian Herald and Signs of Our Times*. January 10, 1918: 28.

Jannaway, Frank George. *Palestine and the Jews, or, The Zionist Movement and the Evidence That the Messiah Will Soon Appear in Jerusalem to Rule the World Therefrom*. Birmingham: C. C. Walker, 1914.

_____. *Palestine and the World*. London: Sampson Low, Marston and Co., 1922.

Kaighin, J. R. *The Bible: The Jew: and The War*. London: Samuel E. Roberts, 1918.

Kelly, M. Harding. *Glory, or, Things to Come*. London: Marshall Brothers, 1916.

Kent, Marian. "Great Britain and the End of the Ottoman Empire, 1900–1923," in *The Great Powers and the End of the Ottoman Empire*. Marian Kent, ed. London: Frank Cass, 1996.

Kerner, Robert. "Russia, the Straits, and Constantinople, 1914–1915." *The Journal of Modern History* 1 (September 1929): 400–415.

"The Kings of the East": An Exposition on the Prophecies. London: Seeley and Burnside, 1842.

Lancaster, George Harold. *Prophecy, the War, and the Near East*. London: Marshall Brothers, 1916.

_____. *Prophecy, the War, and the Near East*, 5th ed. London: Marshall Brothers, 1919.

Landes, Richard. "The Fruitful Error: Reconsidering Millennial Enthusiasm." *Journal of Interdisciplinary History* 32 (Summer 2001): 89–98.

Langston, E. L. *The British Mandate for Palestine and Its Significance*. London: Morgan and Scott, 1920.

_____. *Great Britain, Palestine, Russia, and the Jews: A Third Reprint*. London: C. J. Thynne, 1918.

"Leading Article." *The Record*. November 30, 1916: 936.

"Leading Article: The Russo-Turkish War and Its Issues." *The Stirling Journal*. August 17, 1878: 4.

M. A. of Cambridge. *The Coming Struggle Between England and Russia, Predicted by Ezekiel, Chapters XXXVIII and XXXIX*. London: W. H. Guest, 1879.

McMillan, Charles Duncan Horatio. *The Harvest and the Vintage: An Interpretation of the Times*. London: Robert Scott, 1918.

Mede, Joseph. *The Key of the Revelation Searched and Demonstrated Out of the Naturall and Proper Charecters of the Visions. With a Coment Thereupon, According to the Rule of the Same Key*. Translated by Richard More, with a Preface by Dr. Twisse. London: n.p., 1643.

Middleton, Robert. *The Great War and Its Place in Prophetic History*. London: Jarrold and Sons, 1916.

Millman, Richard. *Britain and the Eastern Question, 1875–1878*. Oxford, UK: Clarendon, 1979.

Moore, Reginald. *The Nearness of Our Lord's Return, as Inferred from Studies in Comparison of Prophecy with History*. London: Robert Scott, 1913.

Moore, William Joseph Bramley. *Ancient Tyre and Modern England, or, The Historical Type of Ancient Tyre in Its Prophetic Application to Modern England*. London: Elliot Stock, 1906.

Moule, Handley C. G. *The Hope and Near Approach of the Lord's Return, and Its Influence on Life*. London: C. J. Thynne, 1919.

Nicklin, James Bernard. *"The Great Shaking."* Halesowen and Blackheath: Parkes, 1918.

"1917: A Fateful Year." *The Christian Herald and Signs of Our Times*. March 22, 1917: 224.

"1917 as a Fateful Year." *The Christian Herald and Signs of Our Times*. January 18, 1917: 52.

Norris, Harold. *When Will Our Lord Return? Prophetic Times and Warning Events*, 2nd ed. London: C. J. Thynne, 1915.

"Notes of the Week." *The Record*. February 14, 1918: 109.

Nurse, Euston John. *Palestine and the War. With Sixteen Illustrations and Maps*. London: Skeffington and Son, 1918.

_____. *Prophecy and the War*, 8th ed., new and revised. London: Skeffington and Son, 1918.

Pae, David. *The Coming Struggle Among the Nations of the Earth, or, The Political Events of the Next Fifteen Years: Described in Accordance with the Prophecies in Ezekiel, Daniel, and the Apocalypse, Showing the Important Position Britain Will Occupy During and at the End of the Awful Conflict*. London: Houlston and Stoneman, 1853.

_____. *The Russo-Turkish War and Its Issues: As Revealed in Scripture Prophecy*. London: William P. Nimmo, 1877.

Patton, D. M. "Russia and Palestine." *Trusting and Toiling on Israel's Behalf: Organ of the Mildmay Mission to the Jews* 21 (February 15, 1915): 9–11.

Pearson, John J. *The Exiles' Return to Their Lost Inheritance*. London: Arthur Stockwell, 1917.

Penson, Lilian M. "The New Course in British Foreign Policy, 1892–1902," *Transactions of the Royal Historical Society*, 4th series, 25 (1943): 121–138.

"Politics and Prophecy." *The Carlisle Patriot*. July 19, 1878: 5.

Pollock, Algernon James. *Things Which Shortly Must Come to Pass*. London: Central Bible Truth Depot, 1918.

Porteous, James Moir. *The Eastern Question. Turkey, Its Mission and Doom; A Prophetical Instruction*. London: n.p., 1876.

Roberts, Lawrence. *Britain's Unveiling, or, Israel in the Book of Revelation*. London: Robert Banks and Son, 1914.

Roberts, Robert. *England and Egypt. Prophecy Fulfilled and Fulfilling*. Birmingham: R. Roberts, 1882.

Rossi, John P. "Catholic Opinion and the Eastern Question," *Church History* 51, no. 1 (1982): 54–70.

Rubinstein, W. D. *A History of the Jews in the English Speaking World: Great Britain.* New York: St. Martin's, 1996.

S., W. [Walter Scott]. *The Eastern Question: and What the Bible Says About Coming Events,* 3rd ed. London: Alfred Holness, 1877.

Saab, Ann Pottinger. "Disraeli, Judaism, and the Eastern Question," *International History Review* 10, no. 4 (1988): 559–578.

Salt, W. F. T. *The Great War in Light of Divine Prophecy. Is it Armageddon?* Bristol: F. Walker, 1915.

Samuel, Elijah Bendor. *Palestine—Turkey—and Egypt.* London: C. J. Thynne, 1915.

Schofield, Alfred Taylor. *The Lord's Coming: Its Near Approach.* London: Prophecy Investigation Society, 1918.

Schor, Samuel. *The Future of Jerusalem.* London: C. J. Thynne, 1917.

Scott, Walter. *The Eastern or Jewish Question Considered: and What the Bible Says About Coming Events.* London: Alfred Holness, 1882.

Semmel, Stuart. *Napoleon and the British.* New Haven, CT: Yale University Press, 2004.

Simpson, A. B. "Britain Fulfilling Prophecy: A Timely and Remarkable Sermon." *The Christian Herald and Signs of Our Times.* April 11, 1918: 257.

_____. "The Midnight Cry." *The Christian Herald and Signs of Our Times.* March 11, 1915: 191–192.

Smith, William, ed. *A Dictionary of the Bible Comprising Its Antiquities, Biography, Geography and Natural History.* London: John Murray, 1863.

Snape, Michael. *God and the British Soldier: Religion and the British Army in the First World War.* Abingdon: Routledge, 2005.

"Striking Prophetic Dates." *The Record.* March 15, 1917: 186.

Sulley, Henry. *Is it Armageddon?* London: Simpkin, 1915.

Tanner, Joseph. *Daniel and the Revelation: The Chart of Prophecy and Our Place in It.* Preface by Hubert Brooke. London: Hodder and Stoughton, 1898.

Thomas, John. *The Coming Struggle Among the Nations of the Earth.* Toronto: Thomas McLear, 1853.

_____. *Destiny of the British Empire as Revealed in the Scriptures. Compiled Chiefly from the Writings of Dr. Thomas.* London: G. J. Stevenson, 1871.

_____. *Elpis Israel: Being an Exposition of the Kingdom of God, with Reference to the Times of the End, and the Age to Come,* 4th ed. West Hoboken, N.J: The Author, 1867.

Tiarks, Hope Charles. *The King's Call for Advent Testimony.* London: C. J. Thynne, 1919.

Titterton, Charles Henry. *Armageddon, or, The Last War, with a Forward by the Rev. E. E. Moore, M.A., Incumbent of Emmanuel Church, Wimbledon.* London: C. J. Thynne, 1916.

"Turkey." *The Morning Star.* February 1, 1915: 25.

"Turkish Bonds and Palestine." *Jewish Chronicle.* April 28, 1876: 52.

Vereté, Mayir. "The Restoration of the Jews in English Protestant Thought, 1790–1840." *Middle Eastern Studies* 8 (January 1972): 3–50.

W., W. M. "The Sequel to the Present War." *The Morning Star.* May 18, 1916: 192–193.

Watts, George. *The Prophecies of Daniel and Their Allusion to the Present War and Defeat of the Kaiser—The Beast, False Prophet and Infidel King—With Copious Notes.* Derby: Mee and Wilson, 1916.

Webster, F. S. "The A.B.C. of Our Manifesto." *The Monthly Bulletin of the Advent Preparation Prayer Union* 1 (June 12, 1919): 2–3.

Wellman, S. A. *The World's Crisis in the Light of Prophecy.* Lucknow: International Tract Society, 1915.

White, Percy F. *Armageddon: The Near Future Great War and the Golden Age of Peace Which Shall Follow.* London: J. F. Belmont and Co., 1918.

Whiteing, Richard. "The Cockpit of the World." *The Daily News.* October 9, 1918: 4.

Wild, Joseph. *The Future of Israel and Judah: Being Discourses on the Lost Tribes, From "How and When the World Will End."* London: Robert Banks, 1880.

_____. *The Lost Ten Tribes and 1882.* London: Robert Banks, 1880.

Wilkinson, Samuel Hinds. *The Future of Jerusalem in Its Successive Phases with Regards to Present Events.* London: Prophecy Investigation Society, 1917.

_____. "Jerusalem!" *Trusting and Toiling on Israel's Behalf: Organ of the Mildmay Mission to the Jews* 24 (January 15, 1918): 1–2.

Wilson, John, *The True Solution to the Eastern Question: England's Duty in Relation to the Christians of Turkey.* London: W. H. Guest, 1877.

Wingate, Andrew. *Mesopotamia, the Gateway to Palestine.* London: n.p., 1911.

_____. *Modern Unrest and the Bible.* London: World's Evangelical Alliance, 1914.

_____. *Palestine, Mesopotamia, and the Jews: The Spiritual Side of History.* Glasgow: Pickering and Inglis, 1919.

Winter, Jay. *Sites of Memory, Sites of Mourning: The Great War in European Cultural History.* Cambridge, UK: Cambridge University Press, 1995.

Wohl, Anthony S. "'Dizzi-Ben-Dizzi': Disraeli as Alien." *Journal of British Studies* 34 (July 1995): 375–411.

Wynn, Walter. *The Bible and the War: Thrilling Addresses.* Letchworth: Garden City, 1915.

_____. *Revelation in the Light of the War and Modern Events.* London: C. J. Thynne, 1916.

Nazi End Times: The Third Reich as Millennial Reich

David Redles

Writing in the wake of a shockingly lost war, with the economy in shambles, and with the specter of a Bolshevik-style revolution looming, Hitler's future mentor Dietrich Eckart saw the unmistakable signs of the End Times in post–World War I Germany. He envisioned however, not the apocalyptic destruction of the Fatherland, but rather its spiritual rebirth in a coming Third Reich:

> Signs and wonders are seen — from the flood a new world will be born. These Pharisees however whine about wretched nest eggs! The liberation of humanity from the curse of gold stands before the door! It's not simply a question of our collapse — it's a question of our Golgotha! Salvation is to befall our Germany, not misery and poverty. No other people on Earth are so thoroughly capable of fulfilling the Third Reich than ours! *Veni Creator spiritus!*[1]

From where did Eckart get this conception of the coming Third Reich as a time of salvation brought on by the descent of the Holy Spirit? One possible source is the idea of the Third *status* as proposed by the medieval apocalyptic writer Joachim of Fiore.[2] That the Italian Giovanni is almost exclusively known by the Germanized name Joachim is a testament to the power of his particular vision of the apocalyptic in German history and scholarship over the centuries, including during the Nazi period. The word *status* is variously translated as stage, age, state, time, and, significantly in Germany, as *Reich*.[3] "Status" signifies not simply duration of time, but also condition of being, a temporal and spiritual state of perfection. Joachim obtained his vision of the End Times through a process he termed *concordia*.[4] This was an analytic technique whereby Joachim discerned correspondences between the Old and New Testaments which, when understood together, gave him clear insight into the coming of "third status," a New Age of spiritual perfection. According to Joachim, humans were evolving toward salvation along a triune series of fixed stages. He associated the three eras with the Trinity. As the Holy Spirit proceeds from the Father and the Son, Joachim believed the third status would proceed from the first and second.[5] According to Joachim the first status (First

173

Reich) began with Adam and continued until the birth of Christ. This was the time of the Father and the order of marriage. The second status (Second Reich) began as a seed during the time of King Josiah and bore fruit with the birth of the Christ. This was the time of the Son and the order of the clerics.[6] Joachim calculated that the third status, that of the Holy Spirit, would proceed forty-two generations later. According to Joachim's calculations this meant the second age of man began with St. Benedict and was the time of the monastic order. The third and final age would bear fruit during the End Times, which Joachim believed was imminent. The beginning of the third age would see the appearance of the Antichrist as well as the "spiritual men," the chosen elite who would defeat the Evil One and usher in this Third and final period of history.[7] This final age would be the time of the "New People of the Third Status," or "the New Order of the People of God," characterized as spiritually perfect humans who would create the millennial third and final Age. The coming of the third status (Third Reich), the time of the Holy Spirit, would be a *renovatio*, a renewal and transformation of the very nature of humanity and existence. Time would be completed and humans perfected.

One possible conduit of Joachim's conception of the Third Reich to Eckart could be the Norwegian playwright Henrik Ibsen, whose *Peer Gynt* provided Eckart with his own greatest literary success.[8] Eckart interpreted Ibsen through the eyes of Otto Weininger, especially as expressed in his *Über die letzten Dinge* (On the Last Things).[9] Written shortly before his suicide, this collection of essays expounds on ideas most famously put forth in Weininger's *Geschlecht und Charakter* (Sex and Character), published the year before. In these works Weininger presented a highly dualistic worldview where the forces of genius and madness, light and dark, good and evil, masculine and feminine, Aryan and Jew, were in constant struggle.[10] In Weininger's reinterpretation of Ibsen, the character Peer represented human genius and the striving for spiritual redemption, while the Boyg, a misshapen figure that impedes Peer's progress, was the "chief salvation negating principle."[11] This latter figure both Weininger and Eckart associated with the Jews. Eckart's version of *Peer Gynt* portrayed the conflict between Peer and the *Grosse Krumme* (the "Great Crooked One" as the Boyg was called in the German translation) as a struggle between eternal opposites.[12] According to Eckart human existence was a perpetual conflict between these opposing forces:

> Truth and lies, Christ and Antichrist, "spirit" and "nature," being and pretense, reason and madness, love and hate, Baldur and Hodur, Siegfried and Alberich, Parsifal and Klingsor.[13]

Ibsen may also have been an important influence in bringing Joachim of Fiore's notion of the Third Reich as the coming kingdom of the Holy Spirit to Eckart. In his 1873 play *Emperor and Galilean*, Ibsen presents a discussion between the Emperor (Kaiser) Julian the Apostate and his intellectual foil Maximus. In this scene Maximus discusses the coming "third Reich, where he who is two in one shall rule." When Julian questions who this figure will be, Maximus responds, the Jewish Messiah. The following dialogue takes place:

> JULIAN: Messiah? Neither Kaiser nor Savior?
> MAXIMUS: Both in one and one in both.
> JULIAN: Kaiser/God — God/Kaiser, Kaiser in the Reich of Spirit and God in Reich of Flesh.
> MAXIMUS: *That* is the Third Reich, Julian!
> JULIAN: Yes, Maximus, *that* is the Third Reich.[14]

Interestingly, although Ibsen first conceived of *Emperor and Galilean* during a visit to Rome in 1864, he completed the play while living in Germany during the Franco-Prussian War (1871), thus witnessing Bismarck's creation of the Second Reich. Ibsen later confided in a friend:

> *Emperor and Galilean* is not the first work I wrote in Germany, but doubtless the first that I wrote under the influence of German spiritual life.... My conception of world history and of human life had hitherto been a national one. It now widened into a racial conception; and then I could write *Emperor and Galilean.*[15]

A potent brew of German nationalism, racialism, and Joachimite millennialism therefore inspired Ibsen's conception of the Third Reich. The belief in the simultaneous arrival of the savior and the Third Reich as the kingdom of spirit as put forth in *Emperor and Galilean* popularized a very different meaning for the term "Reich" than simply a series of geographic empires. It has meaning that is both terrestrial and celestial, especially for those German nationalists who were so disappointed with the Second Reich created by Bismarck and Kaiser Wilhelm.[16] For Dietrich Eckart, the collapse of the Second Reich left a world divided between German nationalists on the right, and Jewish socialists on the left. He desired the coming of a Third Reich that could both bridge the gap between nationalism and socialism and at the same time definitively settle the eternal struggle between good and evil, Aryan and Jew. But exactly how would the millennial Third Reich prophesied by Joachim, and longed for by Eckart, come to pass? And why was Germany envisioned as being so key to its realization? Another German writer believed he had found the answer.

Moeller van den Bruck, the Third Reich, and Germany's "Singular Mission"

That this Third Reich was conceived as something much more profound than simply another in a series of territorial empires was most famously presented in the work of Moeller van den Bruck, whose book, *Das Dritte Reich* (The Third Reich), popularized the term much more than Eckart's obscure musings ever could.[17] Written in 1922 as the new Weimar Republic continued to founder, *Das Dritte Reich* presents a Prussian aristocrat's rejection of the modernized and westernized new Germany. Weimar, with all its overt modernism, could never be the Reich of Moeller's dream. For this writer, and many others, the dream of the new Reich was of a unified, peaceful, prosperous and yet powerful empire that would not only provide the desired regeneration of society, and thus its salvation, but would also enable the purified Germans to finally fulfill the destiny that they ardently believed was their chosen birthright.

The term "Third Reich" for Moeller had a number of interrelated meanings besides its simple historical and chronological implications. In fact he originally considered entitling his book "The Third Way" or the "The Third Party," arguing that a third path which combined the nationalism of the right and the socialism of the left was necessary if Germany was to achieve renewal and salvation. Moeller even flirted with the term "national bolshevism." To achieve this end Moeller, along with Eduard Stadtler and Heinrich von Gleichen, formed the *Juni-Klub*, named for the month in 1919 when the Versailles treaty was signed. The Juni-Klub hoped to attract "Front soldiers," World War I veterans from both sides of the political spectrum, to find this third path to national salvation.[18] According to a contemporary account, the club was founded so that "those who come from the right and those who come from the left shall meet in the fellowship of a third point of view, which we consider to be that of the future."[19] Moeller's book was an extension of the goals of the Juni-Klub, and it is primarily a critique of the much-hated Weimar parliamentary system.

An important influence on Moeller's conceptualization of the Third Reich was Dostoevsky's elaboration of a Russian millennial tradition that conceived of Moscow as the Third Rome.[20] Like the Third Reich, the belief that Moscow would be the Third Rome is part historical and part millennial. The first Rome was the capital of the Roman Empire and the seat of Catholic Christianity. With the fall of Rome in the west, Constantinople, the eastern "Rome" and the seat of Orthodox Christianity, became the second Rome. The conquest of Constantinople by the Turks in 1453 ended the second Rome. Eventually the legend developed that Moscow was seat of the new Caesar (Czar) and the haven of the New Church and its New Patriarch. Consequently, Moscow was the new Constantinople and thus also the Third Rome. Moscow as the Third Rome was subsequently interpreted as the future site of the New Jerusalem, the Heavenly city of the coming millennial kingdom.

According to Dostoevsky's re-interpretation of this myth, Russia had a

divine mission to counter the corrupting influences of western moderniza-
tion and thus inaugurate the millennial New Age, the Third Rome. This
notion most likely came to Moeller through Dmitri Merezhkovski, who along
with Moeller co-edited the first complete German edition of Dostoevsky's
works.[21] Merezhkovski, building upon Dostoevsky, but adding a stronger dose
of Joachimite millennialism, argued that Russian intellectuals, God's new
elect, would overcome the corrupting influences of the West by ushering in
the age of Third Testament Christianity:

> In the first kingdom of the Father, the Old Testament, was revealed the power
> of God, as truth; in the second kingdom of the Son, the New Testament, the
> truth reveals itself as love; in the third and last kingdom of the Spirit, the Com-
> ing Testament, love will be revealed as freedom. And in the last kingdom will be
> pronounced and heard the last name of the Coming Lord, a name as yet unpro-
> nounced and unheard of any: The Liberator.[22]

Merezhkovski further adapted Dostoevsky's millennialism for his German audience. In a preface to the German edition of Dostoevsky's *Political Writings*
(*Politische Schriften*, 1922) entitled "The Religious Revolution," Merezhkovski
argued that Dostoevsky's unfailing promotion of Russian autocracy and the
orthodox faith as a means to world salvation was really a disguise for a hidden desire for the Second Coming:

> Dostoevsky's believed or wanted to believe his religion was Orthodoxy. But his
> true religion was … that which will come after Christianity, after the New Tes-
> tament. It was apocalypse, the coming Third Testament, the revelation of God's
> Trinity, the religion of the Holy Spirit.[23]

Dostoevsky, according to Merezhkovski, longed for the End Times, for with
the apocalypse comes the world cleansing necessary to bring forth the millennial New Age of peace, prosperity, and power.

In Moeller's hands, this Third and Final age became the Third Reich.
In an open "letter" to his Juni-Klub friend Heinrich von Gleichen, which
also serves as the preface for *Das Dritte Reich*, Moeller wrote:

> We put in place of the patronizing treatment of the Party the Third Reich. It
> is an old and great German conception. It arose from the collapse of our first
> Reich. It was fused early on with expectations of a millennial Reich. Yet always
> there lived within it a political conception that aimed to the future, not so
> much upon the end of times, but upon the beginning of a German epoch in
> which the German people will fulfill its destiny on earth.[24]

Moeller worried that such a dream would remain illusory if not pursued
in political reality. He explained that, "the conception of the Third Reich
could be the greatest of all self-deceptions." For the German it could lead to
the end of everything, for "it could ruin him." Moeller understood that mil-

lennial conceptions have an ultimately unattainable character, but it is the attempt to make the imaginary real that generates humanity's greatest achievements:

> It is the essence of all utopias that they never will be realized. It is the essence of all chiliastic hopes that they are never fulfilled. And it is the essence of the millennial Reich that it forever exists only in prophecy, yet men will never partake of it.

However, this does not mean that the millennial dream should be forsaken, only that it should not remain solely a dream, something unrealized. Moeller was fully aware of the dangers of envisioning a Third Reich without enacting its revolutionary nature in practice: "The conception of the Third Reich, of which we cannot let go as our highest and last ideological conception, can only be fruitful as an actualized conception." And, according to Moeller, this Third Reich was not to be actualized in the election booth, but in a bloody eschatological struggle: "The Third Reich, which ends the discord, will not arise in a time of peace...The Third Reich will be a Reich of recapitulation which must succeed politically in a time of European tremors."[25] Towards the end the book, Moeller returns to this theme of the peace to come from the battle for the Third Reich, saying, "the conception of eternal peace is certainly the conception of the Third Reich. However its realization must be fought for, and the Reich must be maintained."[26] If the Third Reich were not achieved, Germany would be annihilated in a glorious final battle of eschatological consequences: "For every people the hour comes in which they die by murder or suicide, and no more magnificent end could be conceived for a great people, than its destruction in a world war in which an entire world gathered arms to conquer a single country."[27] In other words, apocalyptic violence was essentially redemptive, a necessary prerequisite for the coming age of eternal peace. A sword, not a plowshare, would achieve the Third Reich. Moeller's apocalyptic recapitulation of the First World War would find a horrifying realization in the Second World War unleashed by Hitler and the Nazis.

Significantly, Moeller refers to the Third Reich as the *Endreich*, the final empire that would see fulfillment of the Germanic task. As he explained: "German nationalism is a fighter for the Final Reich. It is always promised. And it is never fulfilled. It is the perfection that will only be achieved in imperfection." That the concept of the Reich is something ultimately beyond time and space, a spiritual conception that exists eternally, becomes clear when Moeller states that "there is only one Reich as there is only one Church. Whatever else claims this title may be a state or a community or a sect. There is only *The Reich*."[28]

Moeller envisioned the Third Reich as the time for the fulfillment of the

German mission. It was a task that meant more than simply German unification: it signified a radical transformation of the world and thereby the beginning of the millennial New Age. He explained:

> Nationalism understands the nation through its destiny. It understands it from the antithesis of a people and gives each people its singular mission. German nationalism is in this way an expression of German universalism and thereby looks upon all of Europe...German nationalism thinks of itself in connection with others. It thinks about the shifting focal point of history. It does not want to preserve what is German simply because it is German — how superficial this is, as we have seen, to want to preserve a thing that is past. It wants to preserve much more the German in the Becoming, in the process of creation, in the revolutionary transforming upheavals of the ascending New Age...to give the nation the consciousness that it has, because it is German, a task that no other people can assume.[29]

Joachim's notion of the interlinking of the three stages of humanity, and its completion and perfection in the third, finds its corollary in Moeller's three kingdoms. According to Moeller, the Third Reich is the natural evolution from the Second Reich, and, if it fails to occur, will lead to the final end of all that is German. He wrote: "we believe that the Second Reich was really just the transition to a Third Reich, to a new and final Reich that is promised us, and for which we must live, if we want to live at all."[30] He explained further:

> The conservative thinks of the Third Reich. He knows that it is so that the medieval Reich of our clan-kaiser [*Stammeskaiser*] lived on in the Bismarckian Reich, so also the Second Reich will live on in the Third Reich. The conservative man lives in the consciousness that history is an inheritance: a great transmission and the sum of things, which the people of the past carry forward to the peoples of the future. But this inheritance must be acquired again and again, so that the unity of the great Three completes itself, by which we perceive the past and present, while we at this moment fulfill the future and which we have to fill in with our imagination. The present is but a point in eternity. The past is eternity that survives. The future is eternity which unfolds: but eternity upon which we need not wait, but rather in which we much more live, which invisibly surrounds us and will become visible in the morning — if we today make a resolution to seize it. The Third Reich will exist when we will it. But it can only exist if it is not a copy, rather a new creation.[31]

According to Moeller, Germany, indeed the world, faced an imminent apocalyptic battle: "The reactionary does not know that the war of liberation, which approaches us, can only be led by the entire people. He does not know that each and everyone of us must prepare for it as if it is our last examination, which, if we do not pass it, can only bring the final collapse." He explained further that this eschatological war of liberation should not be a civil war of Right vs. Left; that would only lead the "beloved Fatherland to the abyss." Furthermore, Moeller argued that it was essential to understand that the future war of liberation would be a "war of world views," and that "if we win this final battle, the Reich will be won back for us: one Reich that is not that of the reactionary — but the Reich for us all [*Unser Aller Reich*]."[32]

According to Moeller, as it was for Dietrich Eckart, the German revolution of 1919 was a eschatological turning point. It was a catalyst that had the potential to either usher in the Third Reich and the creation of a new type of man, or lead to the final annihilation of Germany, and ultimately, the world. He explained: "Our revolution was only a beginning; it arose as an insurrection which overthrew the state, but it begins a resurrection which occurs inside men. It is a breakthrough to an altered spiritual frame of mind, and the accompanying self-knowledge — or the revolution is our destruction." Like Joachim of Fiore's coming spiritual men of the Third Age of Spirit, Moeller envisioned a new race or type [*Geschlecte*] of men whose altered consciousness creates the Third Reich. Salvation from the Weimar apocalypse is not possible by following the useless catch phrases of the old type of revolutionary, but "rather in a transformation of humanity which is the only possible thing to save us — from a new and next type which will make good again what we have made so bad." The new revolutionary is a transformed human, a person whose inner spiritual transformation has the power to transform the world. As Moeller described the new type of man: "The revolutionary is he who today already belongs to this new type: in his presentiment, in his spiritual solidarity, in his sense of belonging to destiny — and, what it will ultimately depend on is his political attitude of will and its metapolitical foundation."[33] This revolution is conceived as a transformation of the nature of humanity, and not simply the overthrow of the monarchy, nor even the despised Weimar Republic: "This revolutionary spirit upon which we await and which, as a spiritual process must precede anything political, has nothing to do with the Revolt [of 1919] — that lies behind us. Rather it has everything to do with a revolutionary transformation which occurs in us and against us — and which lies before us."[34]

How was this transformation to occur? And who would lead this new type of man in the creation of the millennial Third Reich? Moeller is silent on this matter. For many Germans, however, only the arrival of a strong personality, the "coming man," could bring salvation from apocalypse. Rudolf Pechel, in an essay for the Juni-Klub's manifesto *Die Neue Front*, wrote: "The West rests silent in spiritual paralysis.... Satan rules under the mask of God. All the great ideas of humanity are distorted and defiled." How to save the world from the apocalyptic rule of Satan? Pechel exclaimed: "We want the Führer as Lagarde once described him, in whom shall be alive the noblest essence of the German nature, who in every fiber of his being possesses the feeling for our true nature, the hatred against everything unnatural, and who breathes the aspiration for a German future."[35]

National Socialism and the Millennial Reich

It was the Nazis who saw themselves as the new type of men capable of creating a Germany that was both national and social, and thus usher in the millennial Third and Final Reich. And of these Nazis it was the Strasser brothers, Gregor and Otto, who most exemplified Moeller's millenarian vision.[36] Gregor Strasser argued that the Nazis were the new type of men endowed with the eternal spirit necessary to achieve the millennium:

> There is, however, only one "correct" spirit, only one spirit with a constructive view; that is the spirit of eternal nature, animated by man, the image of God! It is our strong faith and our profound knowledge that this spirit is in us, in the idea of National Socialism, so that it and no other will build the Millennial Reich![37]

Otto Strasser likewise interpreted the Nazi role as that of an elect whose sacrifice during World War I and after would bring about the millennial New Age:

> The German Revolution recoils from no battle, finds no sacrifice too great, no war too bloody, for Germany must live! Thus we youths feel the heartbeat of the German Revolution pounding, thus we Front soldiers see the face of the future before us and experience, humble-proud, the role of the chosen ones, to fight, to win the battle of the twentieth century satisfied to see the meaning of the war, the Third Reich![38]

Julius Streicher also interpreted the Nazis as an elect minority from whose struggle the coming Reich would be born. In a 1927 speech entitled "With Cross in Hand and the Devil Behind You, You Go Through the People," Streicher told a crowd in Munich that it was not through parliamentary elections that Germany's salvation would come, arguing that "the German people will not be saved by majorities, but rather through a few men who carry in themselves the perception of the new, of the coming Third Reich."[39] In a speech the following year, Streicher returned to the theme of the chosen elect who usher in the New Age through sacrifice and hard work in service of their god-sent savior, Hitler:

> So let us go with new courage and new faith in the struggle! We are indeed few, but we are not alone. A man has arisen who will secure the salvation of our people: Adolf Hitler. He is blessed by God. He will avert the worst for our people. Therefore we believe in him and struggle with him.[40]

For Streicher, like Eckart before him, the Weimar End Times was a sign that the Third Reich was imminent. In the hotly contested elections of 1932 he exclaimed: "The hour is grave, it is admonitory, it shows us however the path that leads to freedom." That path led through Hitler, who will "make free the path to the creation of the new Reich." Reviving the myth of the murder of Jesus by the Jews, as Eckart had earlier, Streicher likened the Nazis to the disciples of the Nazerene:

> We struggle like the apostles after the murder of Golgotha once struggled. These simple insignificant men spoke up and fought. So you go also from here like apostles of the present! It concerns the greatest of things — it is a matter of everything. Germans, perceive the hour! We have a duty to do. If you do not perceive the hour, then you will sink! But do not complain! You will have only yourselves to blame. We National Socialists believe that Adolf Hitler is an emissary for a new Germany. We believe that he has been sent by God to liberate the German people from the blood-sucker Almighty Jewry. It concerns the salvation of the German people, and thereby the world will be saved. March with us! Through struggle to victory![41]

Speeches such as this one, filled with apocalyptic rhetoric and messianic imagery, deeply moved many of those who listened in the audience. These mass gatherings became the most important ritualization of the concept of the millennial Reich. The rallies ritually linked the martyrdom of German soldiers in World War I to those Nazis who died fighting communists after the war, all to be resurrected in the coming Third Reich.[42] The importance of the unity of the German nation in the Third Reich was another key element of these rituals. The observations of Nazi party member Franz Madre demonstrate powerfully the symbolic importance of these so-called Party Days, as well as Hitler's key role as the embodiment of the unity they were meant to visibly express:

> For the first time I saw before my eyes the power of the movement. For the first time I was permitted to see the Führer, and since then I have borne in my heart the strong certainty that we will capture Germany. We all were intoxicated by the powerful experience —100,000 men and all harnessed by one man; 100,000 men and all had one goal and one will, to capture this Germany so that the Führer can build a new Reich, a Reich which should stand after us for a millennium.[43]

The marches were designed to reflect the unity that would be an inherent part of the coming Third Reich. Hugo Döll asked of a Nazi march that he participated in: "Was the goal of the marches reached? Would the German *Volksgenossen* (racial comrades) awaken for the Third Reich?" He answered in the affirmative: "Success was achieved — and so I experienced in exuberant happiness the rebirth of our people."[44]

According to one party member, National Socialism "eradicated class hatred, class spirit and pride of place" and therefore created the conditions necessary for the coming of the Third Reich as a unified community of ethnic Germans. He explained, in thoroughly millenarian fashion:

There is only one German Reich, one German people under one Führer Adolf Hitler, who leads us out of darkness to the light, from misery to happiness. All of Germany strongly supports him and all know that this Third Reich that our Führer created will stand for a millennium, and that after us the Hitler Youth will take this great earth in their loyal hands and build strongly upon it. Thus with a sense of the National Socialist world view as an eternal value and as God sent we will be able to hand over to the loyal hands of the coming Hitler Generation. And still I know one day that through Hitler and his worldview not only Germany, but the entire world will recover. Truth lights the road ahead and so one day the rest of the world will view us as the most harmonious people on earth.[45]

For this man, peace on Earth would come with the racial unity proposed by National Socialism. Erich Jut was likewise moved by the unity expressed in the party rallies and the role of Hitler in creating that sense of community. Describing the crowd's reaction to Hitler, he explained that, "a frenzy of enthusiasm seized the masses. It was a unanimous affirmation for Adolf Hitler." With this sense of community Jut also hoped that religious and class distinctions would vanish and therefore bring forth the millennial Reich: "Possibly, however, all denominational distinctions would fade away and thereby arise a single faith in our Führer and the eternal existence of our Reich."[46]

These rallies also imparted a powerful psychological effect upon both participants and observers, many of who report experiencing something akin to a religious conversion.[47] Emil Sauer described his return home from a party rally in a manner that delineates the process of spiritual transformation that many who converted to Nazism experienced:

This travel home through the dark night, as our headlights ate into the darkness, was symbolic for us. After the torches of the march-by are extinguished, we must again camouflage our brown shirts, as we witness again the seemingly hopeless darkness of the daily struggle against the Terror of the State and the Sub-humans. However, before us shines a light — faith in Germany's future, and the faith that with Adolf Hitler it will be fulfilled. And this light leads us through the darkness till we have reached the goal, the Third Reich.[48]

It was not simply Nazi party members who believed Germans had a special mission to realize the millennial Third Reich. Influential writer Ernst Krieck wrote as early as 1917 in his *Die Deutsche Staatsidee*:

The Third Reich ... knows a new, more deeply grounded human dignity. This is, however, no longer pride in possession of something, but a challenge, a duty: and the spiritual man is always becoming, one whose value and dignity lies before him in the future, in the ideal: the moral Kingdom of God on earth.

Therefore with the coming of the Third Reich would come the Age of the Spirit as foretold by Joachim of Fiore:

> The nation is the protector of a holy fire which is destined to enlighten mankind. When Holy Spirit settles on a people, then it receives a calling, a duty: and the greatness of that people is measured by its fulfillment of its duty.[49]

As Dostoevsky had argued for the Russians, Krieck believed that the Germans had a divine mission to fulfill: realizing the millennial kingdom. It is perhaps not surprising therefore that Krieck asked his readers after the Nazis came into power, "Is not the divine revelation of the original Gospel manifest today in the reality of the Third Reich?"[50]

Professor Julius Petersen succinctly and forcefully expressed the apocalyptic expectations and sentiments of the German populace, building on the notion of the millennial Third Reich as understood by Joachim of Fiore, later revitalized by Moeller van den Bruck, and subsequently realized by Hitler:

> The future has now become today; the sense of the end of the world has changed to an awakening; the final aim appears in the field of vision at the present time and all faith in miracles will be applied to its energetic formation in reality. The mystical number three means no longer termination, but is part of a historical sequence that will find its continuation.

Petersen made it clear at the conclusion of his short book that the realization of the millennial Third Reich was made possible because of the appearance of the prophesied Führer. He concluded by saying: "The new Reich is sown. The Führer, longed for and foretold, has appeared. His words say that the Third Reich is first a becoming, no longer a dream of yearning, but still not a deed yet completed, but a task that has been placed to the renewing German men."[51]

That Hitler was interpreted as key to the coming of the millennial Reich can be seen in the recollections of a Nazi party member. For this man hearing Hitler speak at a mass rally about the coming millennial age was enough to convert him to National Socialism:

> In July the Leader came to Tilsit. I saw him for the first time. About 40,000 people from near and far had gathered to greet him. I heard his voice. His words went straight to the heart. From now on my life and efforts were dedicated to the Leader. I wanted to be a true follower. The Leader spoke of the threatened ruin of the nation and of the resurrection under the Third Reich.[52]

Converted, this man now was committed to help his savior redeem the world, noting: "I was convinced all our work and daily toil was in vain if we did not destroy the prevailing order and erect a new Third Reich on its ruins." The hated Weimar Republic now demolished, the Nazis could then take on the Jewish Bolsheviks in Russia and thereby save the world:

> Another thing the Leader gave us was faith in the German people. If we won, Germany was saved; if we were defeated, a gate would open up in the east and Moscow's Red hordes would swarm in and plunge Europe into night and misery. We had to conquer for the sake of the world, for the sake of Europe.[53]

It is evident in this man's conception, that the coming of the Third Reich would have salvific consequences not simply for Germany, but rather the entire world. But this world salvation, and the eternal peace it would achieve, could only occur if the so-called Jewish-Bolshevik menace was defeated for all time.

Final Reich, Final Battle, Final Solution

For the Third Reich to be the *Endreich* (Final Reich), eternal peace needed to be achieved. According the Nazis this could only be done through an *Endkampf* (Final Battle) against the Jewish-Bolshevik menace, and thus a *Endlösung* (Final Solution) to what was termed the Jewish Question or the Jewish Problem. In other words, the New Age of millennial perfection would come into being if, and only if, the eschatological struggle between Aryans and Jews reached a definitive conclusion. For the Nazis, this was a holy mandate, as Joseph Goebbels explained: "Who cannot hate the devil, cannot love God. Who loves his people therefore must hate his people's destroyer."[54] Nazi anti–Semitism always was conceived, as Saul Friedländer has noted, as an essentially redemptive enterprise.[55]

The successful communist revolution in Russia in 1917 and German loss of World War I the following year, led Dietrich Eckart to the conviction that the Jews were to blame for both. The conflict of opposing forces he so dearly believed in, had now reached an eschatological moment. Writing in 1919, Eckart interpreted World War I as being a component of a larger epic battle that was not over, declaring: "this war was a religious war, that one finally sees clearly! A war between light and darkness, truth and lies, Christ and Antichrist." He concluded therefore: "When light clashes with darkness, there is no coming to terms! Indeed there is only struggle for life and death, till the annihilation of one or the other. Consequently the World War has only apparently come to an end."[56] The final battle that ended this eternal struggle would elicit the Third and Final Reich.

Such a linkage of a coming final battle against so-called Jewish Bolshevism with the subsequent extermination of the Jews also can be seen in Eckart's protégé Hitler. From the early 1920s Hitler conceived of the Nazi movement as one day creating a millennial Reich envisaged as a New World Order led by the Nazis themselves. It was a world that could not be fully realized until a final battle against the demonic force of Jewish Bolshevism had been won, once and for all. The loss of the war and the chaos that followed was seemingly explained in 1919 with the appearance of the German edition of *The Protocols of the Elders of Zion.*[57] This notorious hoax purported that the Jews were using a demonic combination of capitalism, communism, mass media, and world conflict to ultimately take control of the planet. The *Protocols,* and the conspiracy myth it seemingly legitimated, was received by the Nazis as a revelation that the Jews were indeed making a final push for world domination in fulfillment of the covenant. This prophesied Jewish millennial kingdom was interpreted as a counter-millennium to the Third Reich that the Nazis hoped to realize. The Nazis believed that if the Jews were successful, the end result would not be peace on earth, but the extermination of humanity.[58]

The Nazis, however, argued that just as the Jews had fulfillment of their covenant within reach, the end result would not be their victory, but their annihilation. In *The Protocols of the Elders of Zion and Jewish World Policy,* Nazi ideologue Alfred Rosenberg argued that the eschatological moment had indeed arrived, but it would not end as the Jews hoped:

> The Jew stands at the very top of the peak of power which he has so eagerly climbed, and awaits his fall into the abyss. The last fall. After that, there will be no place for the Jew in Europe or America. Today, in the midst of the collapse of a whole world, a new era begins, a fundamental rejection in all fields of many ideas inherited from the past. One of the advance signs of the coming struggle for the new organization of the world is this understanding of the very nature of the demon which has caused our present downfall. Then the way will be open of a New Age.[59]

It was this eschatological perspective that led the Nazis to conclude that humanity had reached a historic turning point that could only lead to salvation, envisioned as the millennial Third and Final Reich, or apocalypse, conceived as the extermination at the hands of the Jews. It is for this reason that Dietrich Eckart argued in 1919, "The hour of decision has come: between existence and non-existence, between Germany and Jewry, between all or nothing, between truth and lies, between inner and outer, between justice and caprice, between sense and madness, between goodness and murder. And humanity once again has the choice!"[60] Hitler certainly agreed that the eschatological moment had arrived between Aryans and Jews. From his earliest political statements to his final political testament, Hitler argued that the final battle between the opposing forces of light and darkness could have but one conclusion. In *Mein Kampf* Hitler wondered whether or not:

> Inscrutable Destiny, perhaps for reasons unknown to us poor mortals, did not with eternal and immutable resolve, desire the final victory of this little nation.

> Was it possible that the earth had been promised as a reward to this people
> which lives only for this earth?

The attainment of world domination, primarily through promulgating Marx-
ism throughout the world, would fulfill the "Jewish prophecy — the Jew would
devour the peoples of the earth, would become their master." The covenant
now achieved, the End Times would follow:

> As a foundation of the universe, this doctrine would bring about the end of any
> order intellectually conceivable to man. And as, in this greatest of all recogniza-
> ble organisms, the result of an application of such a law could only be chaos,
> on earth it could only be destruction for the inhabitants of this planet. If, with
> the help of his Marxist creed, the Jew is victorious over the other peoples of the
> world, his crown will be the funeral wreath of humanity and this planet will, as
> it did millions of years ago, move through the ether devoid of men.[61]

The German people consequently had only two choices — salvation or
apocalypse. In his first important speech after being released from prison in
1925, Hitler returned to the above theme, saying of the Nazi goal:

> Clear and simple: Fight against the satanic power which has collapsed Germany
> into this misery; fight Marxism, as well as the spiritual carrier of this world pest
> and epidemic, the Jews.... As we join ranks in this new movement, we are clear
> to ourselves that in this arena there are two possibilities; either the enemy walks
> over our corpse or we over theirs.[62]

This final battle would have to wait until 1939. That the Second World
War was conceived as an eschatological struggle can be seen in the Nuremberg testimony of Adolf Eichman's deputy, SS Major Dieter Wisliceny. Under
questioning he explained that Nazi anti–Semitism was based on the "mysti-
cal-religious conception that sees the world as governed by good and evil
forces." The Jews were the "evil principle," and therefore:

> Against this world of evil the race-mystics placed the world of good, of light,
> embodied in blond, blue-eyed people, from whom alone all culture-creating
> and state-building forces emanate. Now both of these two worlds were alleged
> to be positioned in a permanent struggle, and the war of 1939, which Hitler had
> begun, represented only the final altercation between these two powers.[63]

On January 30, 1939, the sixth anniversary of the dawning of the Third
Reich with his assumption of the chancellorship, Hitler made a chilling
prophecy. With war plans already underway, Hitler returned to the idea that
the Jews were attempting to use world war and communism to achieve world
domination and fulfill the covenant. He remarked that "quite often in my life
I have been known as a prophet and was mostly laughed at.... I will today
again be a prophet: if international finance Jewry within and without Europe
should succeed in plunging the peoples yet once again in a world war, then

it will result not in the Bolshevization of the earth and thereby the victory of Jewry, but rather the extermination of the Jewish race in Europe."[64] The Second World War was conceived before it even started as the final battle between Aryans and Jews, one that would fully realize the Third Reich as an eternal Reich of peace and prosperity — if, and only if, the Jews were exterminated.

This eschatological interpretation of World War II was especially evident in 1941 as the Nazis prepared to invade the Soviet Union, the home of the supposed satanic threat. A pamphlet entitled "Germany in the Final Battle with the Jewish-Bolshevik Murder-System" was given to education officers as part of the promotional campaign "Führer commands, We Follow." It informed the troops that, "As we at this time enter upon this greatest Front in world history, then it takes place not only on the supposition that it will produce the final settlement of the great war ... but rather to save the entire European civilization and culture." The pamphlet described Bolshevism, characterized as the "demonic invention of our times," in the following way:

> This system of chaos, extermination, and terror was invented by Jews and led by Jews. It is the action of the Jewish race. World Jewry attempts through subversion and propaganda to bring together the uprooted and lesser race elements to accomplish this war of extermination against everything positive, against nationality and nation, against religion and culture, against order and morality. The aim is the production of chaos through world revolution and the establishment of a world state under Jewish leadership.[65]

We have only to look to the letters of German soldiers to see that this millennial worldview of evil Jewish-Bolsheviks and their minions, the Russian sub-humans, locked in apocalyptic battle with Germany, the force of order, was accepted by many of those charged with fighting the final war. These letters often reveal cases of soldiers who, while committing horrible crimes themselves, inverted reality, perceiving the victim to be the true beastly murderer. Indeed, as the war got worse, so did the demonization of the Jew as an Evil Other that had to be annihilated to bring the world eternal peace. In July 1942 one soldier wrote home and explained:

> The great task which is imposed on us in the struggle against Bolshevism lies in the annihilation of eternal Jewry. If one sees what the Jews have produced here in Russia, one can more than ever understand why the Führer began the struggle against Jewry. What sorrows would have come over our Fatherland if these beast men had maintained the upper hand?

This soldier then went on to describe his frustration in not being able to fight the enemy in the open, only to have to deal with partisans, what he termed "furtive rabble," roaming around at night plundering and murdering. After one such night, he reports, a comrade was found murdered. This was not interpreted as being simply a partisan killing, but rather, as this soldier conceptualized it:

> He was cut down from behind. That can only be the Jew who stands behind these crimes. The crack-down that there upon took place indeed yielded an entirely splendid success. The population themselves hate the Jews as never before. They now realize they bare all the blame. This struggle must lead to the most extreme limits and we will fight to the end so that this world will find eternal peace.[66]

The Nazi belief that the coming Third Reich would be a glorious time of eternal peace was always predicated on a final victory over the Aryan's eternal enemy, the Jews. Only one side could realize its millennial dreams. If the Jews achieved their prophesied millennium, the Nazis believed the result would be the extermination of humanity. Aryan victory over the Jewish-Bolshevik menace however would ensure the world's salvation. World War Two would determine which millennium would commence. By this I do not mean to say that the Nazis envisioned death camps and gas chambers from the beginning. The extermination of European Jewry did not result so much from a murderous intention that was decades old, but rather from the apocalyptic expectation that was inherent in Nazi millennialism from the beginning. In other words, belief that the End Times had arrived, that the eschatological final battle between the forces of good and evil had come to pass, led the Nazis to a self-fulfilling prophecy that only one side or the other would be left standing after the final battle. In this way the myth of the Third Reich was transformed from a harmless fantasy into a horrendous reality.[67]

NOTES

1. Dietrich Eckart, "Luther und der Zins," *Auf gut deutsch* (July 5, 1919): 386–387. Unless noted otherwise, this and all translations that follow are my own. Eckart's concluding *Veni Creator spiritus*, literally means "Come, Creator, Spirit," but is usually translated "come Holy Spirit Creator." This is on one level a reference to "the most famous of hymns," a Catholic chant normally sung on special occasions such as the entrance of the Cardinals to the Sistine Chapel during the election of a new pope, the ordination of priests, the consecration of bishops, or the dedication of new churches. However, seen from the perspective of Joachimite millennialism, discussed below, the descent of Holy Spirit upon the Earth takes on a more nuanced meaning. "Golgotha" references the location where the Romans purportedly crucified Jesus. For an anti–Semite like Eckart, however, the linkage of liberation from "the curse of gold" to the crucifixion is a blaming of Jews for both Germany's then economic woes and the death of Jesus.

2. The most complete account of Joachim's life is still Herbert Grundmann, "Zür Biographie Joachims von Fiore und Rainers von Ponza," *Deutsches Archiv für Ersforschung des Mittelalters* 16 (1960): 437–546. In English the standard biographical work is Morton Bloomfield, "Joachim of Flora: A Critical Survey of His Canon, Teachings, Sources, Biography and Influence," *Traditio* 13 (1957): 249–311. Works which stress the influence of Joachim's ideas on later generations include Matthias Riedl, *Joachim von Fiore: Denker der*

vollendeten Menschheit (Würzburg: Königshausen & Neumann, 2004); Bernard McGinn, *The Calabrian Abbot: Joachim of Fiore in the History of Western Thought* (New York: Macmillan, 1985).

3. The word *Reich* can be translated as kingdom, empire, or realm. However, for many German-speaking nationalists, the word had profound and almost mystical connotations. Like the word *Führer* (Leader), Reich became part of the Germanic millennial vocabulary. For a more detailed discussion of Nazi millennialism see David Redles, *Hitler's Millennial Reich: Apocalyptic Belief and the Search for Salvation* (New York: New York University Press, 2005); James M. Rhodes, *The Hitler Movement: a Modern Millenarian Revolution* (Stanford, CA: Hoover Institute Press, 1980); Robert Ellwood, "Nazism as a Millennialist Movement," in *Millennialism, Persecution and Violence*, Catherine Wessinger, ed. (Syracuse, NY: Syracuse University Press, 2000) 241–260.

4. Joachim did not consider himself a passive visionary prophet nor a mystic, but rather a new kind of rational seer, one who used intellectual gifts to perceive the truth. According to Ralph of Coggeshall, Joachim believed that "God who once gave the spirit of prophecy to the prophets has given me the spirit of understanding to grasp with great clarity in His Spirit all the mysteries of sacred scripture, just as the prophets who once produced it in God's Spirit understand these mysteries." Quoted in Bernard McGinn, trans., *Apocalyptic Spirituality: Treatises and Letters of Lactantius, Adso of Montier-en-Der, Joachim of Fiore, the Francisan Spirituals, Savonarola* (New York: Paulist, 1979) 100.

5. This important section of Joachim's *Book of Concordances* is translated by E. Randolph Daniel in McGinn, *Apocalyptic Spirituality*, 120–134.

6. Interestingly, the Spiritual Franciscans, millennialists to the core, interpreted their own order as the fulfillment of this prophecy. See David Burr, *The Spiritual Franciscans: From Protest to Persecution in the Century after Saint Francis* (University Park: Pennsylvania State University Press, 2001).

7. On Joachim's doctrine of the spiritual men see Reeves, *Influence of Prophecy*, 135–144.

8. Eckart composed a free translation of *Peer Gynt* that was first produced in 1914, and it became the second most performed work at the royal playhouse during the war. Dietrich Eckart, *Henrik Ibsens Peer Gynt: in freier Übertragung für die deutsche Bühne eingerichtet* (Munich: Hoheneichen, 1917). See Ralph Max Engelman's discussion in "Dietrich Eckart and the Genesis of Nazism," Ph.D. dissertation, Washington University, 1971, esp., 69–78. That Ibsen's work also may have influenced Hitler as well as been argued by Steven F. Sage, in *Ibsen and Hitler: the Playwright, the Plagiarist, and the Plot for the Third Reich* (New York: Carroll & Graf, 2006).

9. Otto Weininger, *Über die letzten Dinge* (Vienna: W. Braumüller, 1904).

10. Otto Weininger, *Sex and Character: An Investigation of Fundamental Principles*, Ladislaus Löb, trans. (Bloomington: Indiana University Press, 2005). The book failed to achieve critical success, and Weininger, apparently despondent, committed suicide. Eckart, however, believed Weininger killed himself because he was Jewish, and realized, and could not accept, that "he was the devil." Dietrich Eckart, "Das ist der Jude! Laienpredigt über Juden und Christentum." This article is found in undated issues of *Auf gut deutsch* that appeared in the summer of 1920. This quote appears on page 351.

11. Weininger, *Über die letzen Dinge*, 35.

12. Discussed at length in Dietrich Eckart *Ibsen, Peer Gynt, der grosse Krumme und ich* (Berlin-Steglitz: Verlag Herold, 1914).

13. My translation of the German original, as found in Engelman, 70. The latter three associations were inspired by antithetical characters in Richard Wagner's operas, taken from Nordic and Grail legends, which similarly presented a world of opposing forces locked in a struggle for redemption.

14. Quoted in Michael Hesemann, *Hitler's Religion: Die fatale Heilslehre des National-*

sozialismus (Munich: Pattloch, 2004) 174. That Hitler was familiar with the Ibsen/Eckart view of Julian the Apostate can be seen in Hitler's so-called Table Talk during World War II. Here Hitler affirms Julian the Apostate's "clear-sightedness on Christianity and Christians." Hitler saw Julian, and no doubt himself, just like the "Galilean, who later was called the Christ," as "a popular leader who took up his position against Jewry." Found in *Hitler's Table Talk 1941–1944: His Private Conversations*, Norman Cameron and R. H. Stevens, trans. (New York: Enigma, 2000) 75

15. Quoted in Thomas Flanagan, "The Third Reich: Origins of a Millenarian Symbol," *History of European Ideas* 8 (1987): 286.

16. The influence of the myth of the Third Reich in modern German history is discussed in Jean Neurohr, *Der Mythos vom Dritten Reich: zur Geistesgeschichte des Nationalsozialismus* (Stuttgart: Cotta, 1957). How this myth found expression during the chaos of post–world war Germany is best seen in Jost Hermand, *Old Dreams of a New Reich: Volkish Utopias and National Socialism* (Bloomington: Indiana University Press, 1992).

17. Arthur Moeller van den Bruck, *Das Dritte Reich*, 3rd ed., (Hamburg: Hanseatische Verlagsantalt, 1931).

18. Many of the Nazis quoted later in this essay, the so-called Old Guard who joined before 1933, fit this description exactly. Another Front soldier who found his way to Moeller was Adolf Hitler, whose "great idea" of "national socialism" was something along the lines of what Moeller was proposing. When Hitler was asked to address the Juni-Klub in 1922, he attempted to give one of his developing mass audience speeches. Unfortunately for him, the usual crowd of 120 persons was only around thirty. Hitler bombed. Afterward, Hitler met with Moeller, purportedly telling him, "You have everything I lack. You create the spiritual framework for Germany's reconstruction. I am but a drummer and an assembler. Let us work together." Moeller for his part is reported by one attendee as having said afterward, "That fellow will never grasp it." Another recalled Moeller saying "I would rather commit suicide than see such a man in office." Quoted in Fritz Stern, *Politics of Cultural Despair: A Study in the Rise of the Germanic Ideology* (Berkeley: University of California Press, 1974) 237. As both statements were made in 1947, some historical reconstruction and rehabilitation on the part of the authors may have occurred. But it is true that Moeller, despite his talk of bringing the right and left together, was an aristocrat through and through, and he felt Hitler was too common to be the much talked of coming national savior. Despite Moeller's lack of enthusiasm for Hitler, the Nazis would claim Moeller as one of their "prophets."

19. Discussed by Max Hildebert Boehm's in his account of the Juni-Klub, "Die Front der Jungen," *Süddeutsche Monatshefte* 18 (1920): 8, as found in Stern, *Politics of Cultural Despair,* 226.

20. Unlike some conservatives, Moeller was a Russophile. Germany, according to Moeller, naturally belonged to the east and not the west, which he rejected as overly modernized, industrialized and materialistic. For Moeller, Germany's mission lay in the east. On the Dostoevsky/Moeller connection see Christoph Garstka, *Arthur Moeller van den Bruck und die erste deutsche Gesamtausgabe der Werke Dostojewskijs im Piper-Verlag 1906–1919: Eine Bestandsaufnahme sämtlicher Vorbemerkungen und Einführungen von Arthur Moeller van den Bruck und Dmitrij S. Mereschkowskij unter Nutzung unveröffentlichter Briefe der Übersetzerin E.K. Rahsin* (Frankfurt am Main: Peter Lang, 1998). Interestingly, Mereschkowskij (Merezhkovski) was perhaps not only a conduit between Dostoevsky and Moeller, but Ibsen as well. In 1895 Merezhkovski wrote "The Death of the Gods," volume one of his trilogy "Christ and Antichrist." In this work he discussed Julian the Apostate in much the way Ibsen had, and Eckart and Hitler would. See the German edition, *Julian Apostata: Der letzte Hellene auf dem Throne der Cäsaren* (Berlin: Karl Voegels Verlag, 1924).

21. That this belief in Moscow as the Third Rome merged with a growing sense of Russia's special mission is discussed in David G. Rowley "'Redeemer Empire': Russian Millenarianism," *American Historical Review* 104 (1999): 1582–1602. This sense of salvific mission would pass on to Russian bolshevism, connecting the concept of the Third Rome to the third and final stage of Marxist revolutionary theory. See Peter J. S. Duncan, *Russian Messianism: Third Rome, Revolution, Communism and After* (New York: Routledge, 2000).

22. Quoted in Flanagan, "The Third Reich: Origins of a Millenarian Symbol," 290–291.

23. *Ibid.*, 291.

24. Moeller van den Bruck, *Das Dritte Reich*, 6. G. Allen and Unwin published an English translation by E. O. Lorimer, *Germany's Third Empire*, in London in 1934. Unfortunately it is condensed and the translation misleadingly sanitizes and diminishes the millennialism clearly evident in the original German. The quotations that follow are my translations from the third German edition. Moeller uses the term, later employed by the Nazis, "*tausendjährige Reich.*" The Nazi usage of this term is usually translated into English as "thousand-year Reich," but it is more accurately translated as the biblical "millennial kingdom," and therefore, "millennial Reich."

25. *Ibid.*, 7.

26. *Ibid.*, 241.

27. *Ibid.*, 231.

28. *Ibid.*, 244–245.

29. According to Moeller, as it was with Hitler, this special mission of the Germans was to find fulfillment in the East. He wrote: "It is our old and eternal task, in which the Austrian and Prussian and again the Bismarckian pursued. We have yet to definitively understand that we only serve this task toward the East if we are made free in the West. And to make us free is our next and most German task which remains after the error of our western revolution." *Ibid.*, 231.

30. *Ibid.*, 243.

31. *Ibid.*, 185.

32. Here and above, *ibid.*

33. Here and above, *ibid.*, 20–21.

34. *Ibid.*, 21.

35. Quoted in Stern, *Politics of Despair*, 236. Stern notes that this type of statement was typical of the Juni-Klub. Perhaps significantly, it was Pechel who suggested to Moeller that he allow Hitler to address the Juni-Klub, and later, disillusioned, conspired against Hitler. On this see *ibid.*, 237 and 297n. The Lagarde mentioned by Pechel is the anti–Semitic writer Paul de Lagarde, who most famous work is *Deutsche Schriften* (1873). Lagarde called for a Führer who would so represent the will of the people, that they would be united in him and follow his will without hesitation.

36. Otto Strasser was associated with Moeller since the Juni-Klub and has been put forth as the direct link between Moeller's millenarian conception of the Third Reich and the Nazis' similar usage of the term. See Stern, *Politics of Cultural Despair*, 265. However, as we have seen, Hitler's mentor Dietrich Eckart used the term in a millennial context as early as 1919. Otto and Gregor were more to the left politically than Hitler ever was, and their growing independence was never appreciated by the dictatorial leader. Gregor was murdered at Hitler's behest during the infamous Night of Long Knives, and Otto fled into exile. See Karl O. Patel, "Otto Strasser und 'Schwarze Front' des wahren Nationalsozialismus," *Politische Studien* 92 (1957): 269–282.

37. Gregor Strasser, *Kampf um Deutschland: Reden und Aufsätze eines Nationalsozialisten* (Munich: Ehrer, 1932) 139.

38. Quoted in Barbara Miller Lane and Leila J. Rupp, eds. and trans., *Nazi Ideology before 1933: A Documentation* (Austin: University of Texas Press, 1978) 110.

39. Julius Streicher, "Mit dem Kreuz in der Hand und dem Teufel im Rücken geht Ihr durchs Volk," as found in his collection, *Kampf dem Weltfeind: Reden aus der Kampfzeit* (Nuremberg: Verlag der Stürmer, 1938) 78.
40. Julius Streicher, "Ein Mann ist erstanden," as found in *ibid.*, 111.
41. Julius Streicher, "Die Juden sind unser Unglück," as found in *ibid.*, 132.
42. On the Nazi cult of martyrdom see Jay W. Baird, *To Die for Germany: Heroes in the Nazi Pantheon* (Bloomington: Indiana University Press, 1990). The symbolism of the party rallies is explored in Yvonne Karow, *Deutsches Opfer: Kultische Selbstauslöschung auf den Reichsparteitagen der NSDAP* (Berlin: Akademie Verlag, 1997) and Sabine Behrenbeck, *Der Kult um die toten Helden: Nationalsozialistische Mythen, Riten und Symbole* (Vierow: SH-Verlag, 1996). The importance of millennial, messianic, and apocalyptic symbolism is clearly evident in these works.
43. Found in *Die alte Garde sprichts* (The Old Guard Speaks), a four-volume collection of short biographies of early Nazis commission by Rudolf Hess in 1936. Two sets of this collection are housed at the Library of Congress (Washington, D.C.). Hereafter citations to this collection appear as *DAGS*, volume #, author, page #. This quotation is from *DAGS*, vol. 4, Franz Madre, 6.
44. This quotation is found in the Theodore Abel Collection at the Hoover Institute on War, Revolution and Peace (Stanford, CA). The collection contains 580 short autobiographical essays collected by Abel for his sociological study of Nazism, *Why Hitler Came to Power* (New York: Harvard University Press, 1938). I will cite this collection by Abel #, followed by my own pagination. This quotation is from Abel #8, 4. Used together, the autobiographical writings found in *Die alte Garde sprichts* and the Abel collection provide an invaluable glimpse in the motivations and conceptions of those Germans who converted to Nazism.
45. Abel, #60, 26. The phrase *"Ein Reich, Ein Volk, Ein Führer"* (One Empire, One People, One Leader) was a popular expression of Nazi millenarian communalism.
46. *DAGS*, vol. 2, Erich Jut, 3.
47. On the use of religious symbolism and its psychological effects see Klaus Vondung, *Magie und Manipulation: ideologischer Kult und politische Religion des Nationalsozialismus* (Göttingen: Vandenhoeck & Ruprecht, 1971). On the Nazi conversion experience, see Redles, *Hitler's Millennial Reich*, 77–107.
48. *DAGS*, vol. 3, Emil Sauer, 12.
49. As quoted in Flanagan, "The Third Reich: Origins of a Millenarian Symbol," 288.
50. Quoted in Gilmer W. Blackburn, *Education in the Third Reich: A Study of Race and History in Nazi Textbooks* (Albany: State University of New York Press, 1985) 77.
51. Julius Petersen, *Die Sehnsucht nach dem Dritten Reich in deutscher Sage und Dichtung* (Stuttgart: J. M. Metzler, 1934) 1, 61. It is clear in this work that Petersen, like Krieck, interpreted Nazi Germany as the fulfillment of the German mission to bring forth the millennial Reich as first envisioned by Joachim of Fiore.
52. Abel, *Why Hitler Came to Power*, 298.
53. *Ibid.*, 298–299.
54. Quoted in Claus-Ekkehard Bärsch, *Die politische Religion des Nationalsozialismus: Die religiöse Dimension der NS-Ideologie in den Schriften von Dietrich Eckart, Joseph Goebbels, Alfred Rosenberg und Adolf Hitler* (Munich: Wilhelm Fink Verlag, 1998) 126. Goebbels' messianism and millennialism is further explored in Claus-Ekkehard Bärsch, *Der junge Goebbels: Erlösung und Vernichtung* (Munich: Boer, 1995).
55. Saul Friedländer's brilliant discussion of what he termed redemptive anti–Semitism can be found in *Nazi Germany and the Jews: The Years of Persecution, 1933–1939* (New York: HarperCollins, 1997), esp. 73–112.

56. Dietrich Eckart, "Immer lächeln, und doch ein Schurke!" *Auf gut deutsch* (February 7, 1919) 83–84.
57. Gottfried zur Beek, ed., *Die Geheimnesse der Weisen von Zion* (Charlottenberg: Verlag Auf Vorposten, 1919).
58. See David Redles "The Turning Point: *The Protocols of the Elders of Zion* and the Eschatological War Between Aryans and Jews," to appear in the forthcoming volume *Reconsidering the Protocols: 100 Years after the Forgery*, Steven T. Katz and Richard Landes, eds. (New York: New York University Press).
59. Alfred Rosenberg, *Die Protokolle der Weissen von Zion und die jüdische Weltpolitik* (Munich: Deutscher Volksverlag, 1923) 147.
60. Dietrich Eckart, "Die Schlacht auf den Katalaunischen Feldern," *Auf gut deutsch* (February 20, 1920) 86.
61. Adolf Hitler, *Mein Kampf*, trans. Ralph Manheim (Boston: Houghton Mifflin, 1971) 64–65, 452.
62. Adolf Hitler, *Die Rede Adolf Hitlers in der ersten grossen Massenversammlung bei Wiederaufrichtung der Nationalsozialistischen Deutschen Arbeiter Partei* (Munich: Ehrer, 1925) 8.
63. Found in Leon Poliakov and Josef Wulf, eds., *Das Dritte Reich und die Juden: Dokumente und Aufsätze* (Berlin: Arani, 1955), 91–92.
64. Max Domarus, ed., *Hitler: Reden und Proklamationen, 1932–1945* (Neustadt: a.d. Aisch, Schmidt, 1962) 1058.
65. Cited in Redles, *Hitler's Millennial Reich*, 169–170.
66. Letter 351, in Ortwin Buchbender and Reinhold Sterz, eds., *Das andere Gesicht des Krieges: Deutsche Feldpostbriefe, 1939–1945* (Munich: C. H. Beck, 1982) 171. That such apocalyptic interpretations during the Final War were not restricted to this lone soldier is seen in Omer Bartov, *Hitler's Army: Soldiers, Nazis, and War in the Third Reich* (New York: Oxford University Press, 1992) esp. 106–178.
67. I first discussed this Nazi self-fulfilling prophecy in "'The day is not far off...': The Millennial Reich and the Induced Apocalypse," in *War in Heaven, Heaven on Earth: Theories of the Apocalyptic*, Stephen D. O'Leary and Glen S. McGhee, eds. (London: Equinox, 2005) 119–141.

WORKS CITED

Abel, Theodore. *Why Hitler Came to Power.* New York: Harvard University Press, 1938.
_____. Theodore Abel Collection. Hoover Institute Archives, Stanford University.
Baird, Jay W. *To Die for Germany: Heroes in the Nazi Pantheon.* Bloomington: Indiana University Press, 1990.
Bärsch, Claus-Ekkehard. *Die politische Religion des Nationalsozialismus: Die religiöse Dimension der NS-Ideologie in den Schriften von Dietrich Eckart, Joseph Goebbels, Alfred Rosenberg und Adolf Hitler.* Munich: Wilhelm Fink Verlag, 1998.
_____. *Der junge Goebbels: Erlösung und Vernichtung.* Munich: Boer, 1995.
Bartov, Omer. *Hitler's Army: Soldiers, Nazis, and War in the Third Reich.* New York: Oxford University Press, 1992.
Beek, Gottfried zur, ed. *Die Geheimnesse der Weisen von Zion.* Charlottenberg: Verlag Auf Vorposten, 1919.
Behrenbeck, Sabine. *Der Kult um die toten Helden: Nationalsozialistische Mythen, Riten und Symbole.* Vierow: SH-Verlag, 1996.
Blackburn, Gilmer W. *Education in the Third Reich: A Study of Race and History in Nazi Textbooks.* Albany: State University of New York Press, 1985.
Bloomfield, Morton. "Joachim of Flora: A Critical Survey of His Canon, Teachings, Sources, Biography and Influence." *Traditio* 13 (1957): 249–311.

Buchbender, Ortwin and Reinhold Sterz, eds. *Das andere Gesicht des Krieges: Deutsche Feldpostbriefe, 1939–1945.* Munich: C. H. Beck, 1982.

Burr, David. *The Spiritual Franciscans: From Protest to Persecution in the Century after Saint Francis.* University Park: Pennsylvania State University Press, 2001.

Domarus, Max, ed. *Hitler: Reden und Proklamationen, 1932–1945.* Neustadt: a.d. Aisch, Schmidt, 1962.

Duncan, Peter J. S. *Russian Messianism: Third Rome, Revolution, Communism and After.* New York: Routledge, 2000.

Eckart, Dietrich. "Das ist der Jude! Laienpredigt über Juden und Christentum." *Auf gut deutsch* (Summer, 1920): 337–398.

_____. *Henrik Ibsens Peer Gynt: in freier Übertragung für die deutsche Bühne eingerichtet.* Munich: Hoheneichen, 1917.

_____. *Ibsen, Peer Gynt, der grosse Krumme und ich.* Berlin-Steglitz: Verlag Herold, 1914.

_____. "Immer lächeln, und doch ein Schurke!" *Auf gut deutsch* (February 7, 1919): 82–85.

_____. "Luther und der Zins." *Auf gut deutsch* (July 5, 1919): 291–297.

_____. "Die Schlacht auf den Katalaunischen Feldern." *Auf gut deutsch* (February 20, 1920): 81–95.

Ellwood, Robert. "Nazism as a Millennialist Movement" in *Millennialism, Persecution and Violence.* Catherine Wessinger, ed. Syracuse, NY: Syracuse University Press, 2000: 241–260.

Engelman, Ralph Max. "Dietrich Eckart and the Genesis of Nazism." Ph.D. dissertation, Washington University, 1971.

Flanagan, Thomas. "The Third Reich: Origins of a Millenarian Symbol." *History of European Ideas* 8 (1987): 283–295.

Friedlander, Saul. *Nazi Germany and the Jews: The Years of Persecution, 1933–1939.* New York: HarperCollins, 1997.

Garstka, Christoph. *Arthur Moeller van den Bruck und die erste deutsche Gesamtausgabe der Werke Dostojewskijs im Piper-Verlag 1906–1919: Eine Bestandsaufnahme sämtlicher Vorbemerkungen und Einführungen von Arthur Moeller van den Bruck und Dmitrij S. Mereschkowskij unter Nutzung unveröffentlichter Briefe der Übersetzerin E.K. Rahsin.* Frankfurt am Main: Peter Lang, 1998.

Gimbel, Adalbert, ed. *Die alte Garde spricht.* Archival Collection. Library of Congress, Washington, D.C.

Grundmann, Herbert. "Zür Biographie Joachims von Fiore und Rainers von Ponza." *Deutsches Archiv für Ersforschung des Mittelalters* 16 (1960): 437–546.

Hermand, Jost. *Old Dreams of a New Reich: Volkish Utopias and National Socialism.* Bloomington: Indiana University Press, 1992.

Hesemann, Michael. *Hitler's Religion: Die fatale Heilslehre des Nationalsozialismus.* Munich: Pattloch, 2004.

Hitler, Adolf. *Hitler's Table Talk 1941–1944: His Private Conversations.* Norman Cameron and R. H. Stevens, trans. New York: Enigma, 2000.

_____. *Mein Kampf.* Ralph Manheim, trans. Boston: Houghton Mifflin, 1971.

_____. *Die Rede Adolf Hitlers in der ersten grossen Massenversammlung bei Wiederaufrichtung der Nationalsozialistischen Deutschen Arbeiter Partei.* Munich: Ehrer, 1925.

Karow, Yvonne. *Deutsches Opfer: Kultische Selbstauslöschung auf den Reichsparteitagen der NSDAP.* Berlin: Akademie Verlag, 1997.

Lane, Barbara Miller, and Leila J. Rupp, eds. and trans. *Nazi Ideology before 1933: A Documentation.* Austin: University of Texas Press, 1978.

McGinn, Bernard. *The Calabrian Abbot: Joachim of Fiore in the History of Western Thought.* New York: Macmillan, 1985.

_____, trans. *Apocalyptic Spirituality: Treatises and Letters of Lactantius, Adso of Montier-en-Der, Joachim of Fiore, the Francisan Spirituals, Savonarola.* New York: Paulist, 1979.

Mereschkovsky, Dmitry S. *Julian Apostata: Der letzte Hellene auf dem Throne der Cäsaren.* Berlin: Karl Voegels Verlag, 1924.

Moeller van den Bruck, Arthur. *Das Dritte Reich*, 3rd ed. Hamburg: Hanseatische Verlagsantalt, 1931.

Neurohr, Jean. *Der Mythos vom Dritten Reich: zur Geistesgeschichte des Nationalsozialismus.* Stuttgart: Cotta, 1957.

Patel, Karl O. "Otto Strasser und 'Schwarze Front' des wahren Nationalsozialismus." *Politische Studien* 92 (1957): 269–282.

Petersen, Julius. *Die Sehnsucht nach dem Dritten Reich in deutscher Sage und Dichtung.* Stuttgart: J. M. Metzler, 1934.

Poliakov, Leon, and Josef Wulf, eds. *Das Dritte Reich und die Juden: Dokumente und Aufsätze.* Berlin: Arani, 1955.

Redles, David. "'The day is not far off...': The Millennial Reich and the Induced Apocalypse" in *War in Heaven, Heaven on Earth: Theories of the Apocalyptic.* Stephen D. O'Leary and Glen S. McGhee, eds. London: Equinox, 2005: 119–141.

_____. *Hitler's Millennial Reich: Apocalyptic Belief and the Search for Salvation.* New York: New York University Press, 2005.

_____. "The Turning Point: *The Protocols of the Elders of Zion* and the Eschatological War Between Aryans and Jews" in *Reconsidering the Protocols: 100 Years after the Forgery.* Steven T. Katz and Richard Landes, eds. New York: New York University Press (forthcoming 2009).

Rhodes, James M. *The Hitler Movement: A Modern Millenarian Revolution.* Stanford, CA: Hoover Institute Press, 1980.

Riedl, Matthias. *Joachim von Fiore: Denker der vollendeten Menschheit.* Würzburg: Königshausen and Neumann, 2004.

Rosenberg, Alfred. *Die Protokolle der Weissen von Zion und die jüdische Weltpolitik.* Munich: Deutscher Volksverlag, 1923.

Rowley, David G. "'Redeemer Empire': Russian Millenarianism." *American Historical Review* 104 (1999): 1582–1602.

Sage, Steven F. *Ibsen and Hitler: The Playwright, the Plagiarist, and the Plot for the Third Reich.* New York: Carroll and Graf, 2006.

Stern, Fritz. *Politics of Cultural Despair: A Study in the Rise of the Germanic Ideology.* Berkeley: University of California Press, 1974.

Strasser, Gregor. *Kampf um Deutschland: Reden und Aufsätze eines Nationalsozialisten.* Munich: Ehrer, 1932.

Streicher, Julius. *Kampf dem Weltfeind: Reden aus der Kampfzeit.* Nuremberg: Verlag der Stürmer, 1938.

Vondung, Klaus. *Magie und Manipulation: Ideologischer Kult und politische Religion des Nationalsozialismus.* Göttingen: Vandenhoeck and Ruprecht, 1971.

Weininger, Otto. *Sex and Character: An Investigation of Fundamental Principles.* Ladislaus Löb, trans. Bloomington: Indiana University Press, 2005.

_____. *Über die letzten Dinge.* Vienna: W. Braumüller, 1904.

Part II.
Political and Popular

Protestant Evangelicals and U.S. Policy Towards Israel

Husam Mohamad

Introduction

The politicization of the Christian Right movement in the U.S. has caused the group to become a credible force that is able and willing to exert broad influence on U.S. policy towards Israelis and Palestinians. Protestant evangelical leaders, who play a key role in the Christian Right movement, have formulated their own interpretations of their sacred texts in ways that highlight the significance of Israel's interests in their belief system. The success of evangelicals in their capacity to influence U.S. domestic and foreign policymaking has largely derived from their religious appeal that has risen significantly in recent years. Evangelicals generally consider themselves born-again Christians who are assisting in the fulfillment of God's eternal plans, starting with the Rapture that will ascend them into heaven and ending with the Tribulation and Armageddon's battle that would lead to disastrous effects on the world. Their focus on rebuilding the Second Jewish Temple in Jerusalem is intended to facilitate the return of Jesus from heaven onto earth to begin a thousand-year era of peace and harmony, which thus explains the evangelicals' enthusiastic support for Israel. Their backing of Israel has also been influenced by the emergence of radical trends, notably dispensationalism, within the Christian Right movement. Dispensationalist interpreters and their supporters have established a close link between their own theology and the course of human history, which is expected to reach its end in accordance to descriptions found in sacred texts, such as the Books of Genesis, Daniel and Revelations.[1]

From its European origins, the Protestant movement has experienced various theological and ideological transformations and mutations that have enticed its leaders and followers to be more involved in the realms of domestic and foreign policy planning and content. Over the years, the Protestant movement has abandoned the old rigid structure of religious hierarchies, as understood by the Roman Catholic Church, and instead embraced individualism and self-reliance.[2] This situation permits Protestant evangelicals to offer their own independent interpretations of the Old and New Testaments, unlike Catholics who have been restricted by limits imposed by the order of their church. As such, independent interpretations made by dispensationalist theologians about the role of Israel in relation to the end time prophesy, which may have been extreme in comparison to views held by mainstream Christians, enticed their followers to pressure their governments to pursue policies that favor Israel. Dispensationalists have succeeded in translating their rising religious appeal, namely during U.S. elections, into a viable political force that advocates stronger ties between the U.S. and Israel.[3] They have played an increasingly important role in U.S. national elections due to their ability to organize themselves to vote collectively within voting blocs on issues and candidates that matter to their religious beliefs and political agendas.[4]

Initially, the Protestant evangelical movement in the U.S. focused its activism mainly on domestic issues that conflicted with Christian values and beliefs. Some evangelical organizations, such as the Moral Majority and the Christian Coalition, launched locally oriented campaigns targeting women's rights groups, abortion rights advocates and interest groups defending homosexuals. In so doing, their activism has been primarily focused on outlawing abortion laws and suppressing homosexuality.[5] At the same time, they have channeled their efforts towards popularizing traditional values by promoting conservative social and educational agendas such as the teaching of creationism in science classes, promoting abstinence in schools and attempting to secure prayer rights for students in public schools. Although foreign policymaking in the U.S. has not been historically conducted on the basis of religious factors alone, in recent years, however, the theological orientations of evangelicals have gradually and steadily influenced the preparation for, and application of, U.S. policy in the Middle East. Following the September 11th attacks, for instance, along with calling upon the U.S. to boost its clashes with Islamists worldwide, evangelicals focused more on safeguarding Israel's security by linking it with U.S. national interests and with the divine prophesies concerning the end time.[6] In past instances, such as during the Ronald Reagan Administration, evangelicals also played a key role in rallying against the U.S. sale of Airborne Warning and Control Systems to Saudi Arabia. During the George H. Bush Administration, evangelicals participated in pro-Israeli efforts to overturn the United Nations General Assembly's Resolution 3379 that equates Zionism with racism.

Although Christians generally believe in the end time prophesies and in Christ's second coming, dispensationalists focus more on Israel's place in relation to God's final plan for humanity. Dispensationalists also assume that certain preconditions, including those surrounding Israel, its territorial expansion and security concerns, must be met before the end time prophesies are fulfilled.[7] Their views of the Promised Land and of Israel's role during the end time are exclusively based on the groups' interpretation of the texts of Genesis, Exodus, Joshua, Daniel, and Revelation. In Genesis, for instance, evangelicals believe that God had executed a covenant with Abraham promising him and his successors the Promised Land, or *"Eretz Yisrael"* (Land of Israel), which included larger territories than the boundaries of modern-day Israel. God's promise was supposedly then reaffirmed through Abraham's second son, Isaac, and later again by Isaac's son, Jacob. Under the leadership of Moses and Joshua, the Israelites managed to maintain their control of the Holy Land. Evangelicals believe the books of Daniel and Revelation reveal an instance when the Jews will return to the Holy Land and establish their state as a confirmation of God's prophesies. Evangelical leaders and their supporters accept these assumptions as absolute truths. Lobbying efforts on U.S. and British policymakers and advisors have relied heavily on these theological considerations to connect evangelical Christians and the Jews to the Holy Land. For dispensationalist evangelicals, Christ's return, the Apocalypse, and Armageddon cannot occur without enticing Jews to immigrate to the Promised Land and ensuring Israel's lasting existence.[8]

The apocalyptic vision adhered to by dispensationalists in the U.S. is a continuation of contributions found in the writings of John Nelson Darby, who, as an evangelical preacher and a member of the Plymouth Brethren group in nineteenth century England, offered his own interpretations of the end time prophesy. Following earlier writers, Darby divided world history into "seven epochs or dispensations," and concluded that humanity had started its sixth phase, which would lead to "Christ return[ing] to defeat Satan and the Antichrist and establish[ing] the millennium."[9] Based on the end of time theology, dispensationalists believe Christ's second coming and the establishment of his Kingdom may never be reached without the occurrence of the following events and/or conditions:

> The nation of Israel must be re-established..., the Jews must return to the Holy Land and become the sole occupiers of the land.... The Jewish Temple ... must be rebuilt and the temple sacrifices of ancient Israel must be reinstated ... [only then] [Jesus] would hover over the Earth and ... born again Christians would fly up to meet him in the air ... [and] true Christians would leave behind all non-believers.[10]

As a relatively new social movement launched since the early 1970s, Christian Right groups in the U.S. have been engaged in pressuring policymakers, Supreme Court Justices and legislators to pursue policies that serve conservative values with respect to domestic and foreign policy issues. The movement has also managed to institutionalize itself by encouraging its members and activists to run for political positions within major U.S. governmental institutions. Through their use of political pressures on U.S. governmental institutions, along with expanding their own recruitments within the U.S. political system, dispensationalists have become active participants in the process of lobbying and negotiating policies regarding U.S. relations with Israel and the Muslim world. With respect to their influence on British politics, from 1922 until 1947 Protestant evangelical activists have played a crucial role in pressuring politicians, notably Winston Churchill and James Balfour, to aid the Zionist project in Palestine, which eventually resulted in Israel's founding in 1948.[11] The British Labour party, which has strong ties to the Methodist Church, has particularly expressed empathy for Jewish causes. As an eager evangelical member of the British government and the Labour party, James Balfour authorized the Balfour Declaration in 1917, which was incorporated into British Mandate documents in 1922 and thus facilitated the establishment of a Jewish national homeland in Palestine without ever consulting the Arab inhabitants of the country. For its part, the growing influence of dispensationalists on U.S. policy towards Israel is a relatively recent phenomenon that grew significantly in the 1980s, during Ronald Reagan's presidency, and became quite obvious during George W. Bush's Administration. Given their rising role in the realm of domestic and foreign policy conduct, dispensationalists are often viewed by observers and commentators as being more influential than other well-entrenched interest groups, notably the American-Israeli Political Action Committee (AIPAC), in terms of their ability to influence U.S. policy towards Israel. This led some observers to conclude that "America's Christian Zionists," notably dispensationalists, "may be the Jewish State's ultimate strategic asset."[12]

The politicization of the evangelical theology towards Israel has been particularly influenced by key events and transitions that are viewed by evangelicals as deriving from divine prophesies, including Israel's creation in 1948 and its expansion in 1967. The evangelicals' use of theological rationalization to pressure the U.S. government to side with Israel is also viewed by evangelicals and their supporters as an ethical matter concerning the distinction between good versus evil.[13] Following the September 11th terrorist attacks, evangelicals' understanding of the dichotomy between good and evil expanded in ways that has led to the construction of demonizing views of Arabs/Muslims.[14] Furthermore, the use of terms and vocabularies by the G.W. Bush Administration, such as, "the axis of evil" and "crusader" expressions, may have also influenced the mindset of evangelicals who are influenced by religious sentiments.[15]

The dispensationalist trend within the Protestant tradition has particularly become the most influential movement in its ability to pressure the U.S. to continually side with Israel on ideological and theological grounds. For instance, beginning from Reagan's presidency in the 1980s throughout the G.W. Bush Administration, dispensationalists have played a significant role in influencing the White House to refrain from pressuring Israel into making territorial concessions to the Palestinians. Their bond with Israel has more or less been justified as a matter relating to a divine future plan, where modern-day Israel is expected to play an essential role in the fulfillment of upcoming prophesies that would bring the world to a predictive end. Due to the activism of dispensationalists, U.S. backing of Israel has now become an established reality that enjoys wide support among the public, even at times when support for Israel may threaten U.S.'s interests abroad.[16]

This essay argues that U.S. policy towards the Israeli-Palestinian conflict has, mainly during Republican Administrations, been influenced by the theological interpretations and political agendas of evangelicals. It explains how dispensationalists, while awaiting the nearing end of the world, have managed to establish themselves as a new force capable of exerting ample influence on U.S. policy in the Middle East. One of the damaging effects of dispensationalist theologians and activists on Israeli-Palestinian relations is the role they played in the derailing of recent peace efforts, notably the Road Map plan, which consequently led to more deteriorations in Palestinians' living conditions along with hindering Israel's ability to live in peace with its neighbors.

Dispensationalists' Vision of Israel

U.S. policymakers have over the years experienced growing political pressures from dispensationalists, including theologians such as Pat Robertson and policymakers such as Tom DeLay, to pursue policies that favor Israel at all costs. The heightening conflict and chaos in present-day Middle Eastern affairs is, according to dispensationalists, a sign reflective of Christ's second coming.[17] Although Christians believe the timing of Christ's second coming remains obscure, dispensationalists are certain about his arrival in the near future. Being highly influenced by dispensationalists' theology, President Reagan once stated, to a pro-Israeli lobbyist in 1983, that:

> I turn back to your ancient prophets in the Old Testament and the signs foretelling Armageddon, and I find myself wondering if— if we're the generation that's going to see that come about, I do not know if you've noted any of these prophesies lately, but believe me, they certainly describe the times we're going through.[18]

Dispensationalists generally believe that the present time, referred to as a period of dispensation, is approaching an assured end that begins with the Rapture, where the born again Christians join Christ in heaven and achieve eternal salvation. Dispensationalists also assume that the world will then enter into a Tribulation phase which, along with its disastrous effects, will be accompanied by the rise of a charismatic evil figure known as the Antichrist who will establish universal tyranny. Within a seven-year period following the rise of the Antichrist, Jesus will descend back to earth to defeat the Antichrist's evil forces at the battle of Armageddon (*Maggedo*), where the forces of good against evil will collide. With the victory of Christ, a thousand years of peace will resume in the Holy Land, and Jesus will reside at the Second Jewish Temple in Jerusalem.[19]

Dispensationalists' backing for Israel, which contributes in depriving Palestinians of their basic claims, contradicts messages concerning the place of tolerance and compassion in the Christian belief system. For instance, dispensationalists insist on rebuilding the Jewish Temple on the same exact site of the *Al-Aqsa* Mosque, which is revered by Muslims. In response to suggestions concerning the possibility of the Jewish Temple being rebuilt next to the Muslim shrine in Jerusalem and thus avoiding a widening of the Israeli-Palestinian conflict, Tim LaHaye, author of the *Left Behind* series, objected to the idea by explaining: "Some have tried to suggest that perhaps this location [*Al-Aqsa* Mosque] is not the only place in Jerusalem that the [Jewish] temple could be built.... [However, t]here is no substitute on the face of the earth for that particular spot."[20] Consistent with this view, dispensationalists find it necessary to deny the validity of Palestinian claims on theological grounds. Activists such as Pat Robertson, Franklin Graham and Jerry Falwell believe that "the most dramatic evidence for His [Jesus] return is the rebirth of the nation of Israel."[21] Having been viewed as close friends to right-wing Israeli politicians, notably Ariel Sharon and Benjamin Netanyahu, and as spiritual advisors to various Republican Administrations, dispensationalists have focused their efforts on building a strong alliance between the U.S. and Israel to prevent Israel from providing territorial concessions to the Palestinians.

Under the banner of religion, evangelicals are usually socialized to identify themselves with what they consider as the forces of good and express emotionally charged and romanticized views of Israel. They consider those who may object to Israel's policies towards Palestinians as evil doers and enemies of God. Dispensationalists' vision of Israel is deeply rooted in biblical stories about Jesus' life, his miracles, death and resurrection, along with his expected second coming. Their attachment with Israel often begins at their Sunday schools, where stories about Jewish history and Israel's rebirth have resonated in the minds of Christians since childhood. At their congregations, evangelical followers are particularly taught inspirational stories about heroic figures in the history of ancient Israel, such as David and Goliath, and are further coached about the future battle between the forces of good (Christians) and evil (Antichrist) in Armageddon. The socializing effects of Sunday schools on American and British religious and cultural orientations have played an important role in strengthening public ties with Israel. The Sunday schools were initially launched by evangelicals in Britain as an attempt to guide troubled children off the streets and provide them with the proper education. Eventually, this movement began adopting theological interpretations that contributed to indoctrinating children with biblical narratives reflective of the literalist understanding of the Bible. In the U.S., Sunday schools also took a religious shape that addressed Christian values. Schools associated with dispensationalists provided students with vivid messages about the future role of Israel in relation to the end time, which consequently influenced mainstream Christians to express sympathy towards Israel.[22]

In relation to college education and its impact on students, Protestant evangelicals have also established prominent universities and seminaries across the U.S., including, but not limited to, the Dallas Theological Seminary, Wheaton College, Texas Christian University, Oral Roberts University, Bob Jones University and Liberty Baptist. On such campuses, students are generally obligated to obediently internalize the mission of the evangelical tradition, including its unconditional support for Israel. Prominent activists such as Dwight L. Moody, deemed the father of the Protestant evangelical movement in the U.S., have particularly played an influential role in popularizing biblical accounts concerning Israel. Outspoken dispensationalists such as William E. Blackstone have also succeeded in influencing a wide range of audiences among U.S. policymakers and the public at large to become more supportive of Israel.[23] Evangelical groups such as the International Christian Embassy in Jerusalem, the International Fellowships, the Bridges for Peace and the 700 Club have invested ample resources in support of Israel. Not only do evangelical activists, colleges, and groups preach that Jews are the rightful inhabitants of Palestine, but also introduce their own religious interpretations to redirect U.S. policy to serve Israel. Although the balance of power has always been in Israel's favor during the latest Palestinian uprisings against Israel, evangelicals have frequently expressed solidarity with the Jewish people, arranged visits and made donations to Israelis.

To strengthen Christians' ties with Israel, evangelicals have also instilled in the minds of their followers that "the Promised Land belongs to them [Christians] as much as it does to the Israelis."[24] This also explains the increased number of evangelical families residing in various Israeli settlements in the West Bank and Arab East Jerusalem.[25] While overlooking the historical changes that have transpired in the Holy Land over centuries, notably during the rise and expansion of the Islamic empire that maintained its control over Palestine from the 7th century to the early 20th century, evangelicals equate modern-day Israel with the ancient land of David, Solomon and the Hebrew judges. In so doing, evangelicals are legitimizing Israel's right to maintain control over Palestine on religious grounds, along with justifying the U.S.'s official and public backing for Israel as a matter that is also sanctioned by God. For instance, Oklahoma Senator James Inhofe, a born-again Christian, commented, on his understanding of the biblical justifications for the U.S. support for Israel by stating:

> God appeared to Abram [Abraham] and said I am giving you this land.... This is not a political battle at all. It is a contest over whether the word of God is true.[26]

The Antichrist, who is expected to appear in the form of a charismatic leader and may presumably head a world organization, break all treaties and claim that he is saving the world, occupies an important part in dispensationalists rational regarding the need for U.S. continued backing for Israel. Following September 11th 2001, several evangelical leaders in the U.S. implied that the Antichrist was a Muslim figure that aimed at destroying Israel.[27] Indeed, this is consistent with dispensationalists' view of Islam and Islamists, which they see as representing an imminent threat to the U.S. and Israel. In the name of conducting the war on terror, evangelicals were the most enthusiastic supporters of U.S. attacks against Afghanistan and Iraq.[28] Given that Israel's security occupies a central place in their theology, evangelicals have also expressed hostility towards Iran because of its real and/or potential threats to the Jewish State. For dispensationalists, the Messiah's return to destroy the evil doers on earth and the subsequent establishment of peace in the Holy Land has given Israel a special role to play in relation to the end time. While the impact of U.S. backing for Israel may result in high costs and sacrifices for the U.S., evangelicals largely believe that such costs are worth taking.[29]

Ironically, while evangelicals recognize Jews as God's chosen people, it is not the Jews but the born-again Christians whom evangelicals believe would be saved to join Christ in heaven at the end of time. The rest of humanity, including Jews, Muslims, Catholics and all non–born again Christians, will continue to face deadly wars, famines and widespread catastrophes. Dispensationalists further assume that when powerful armies converge at the battle of Armageddon, the forces of the Antichrist will then vanish and Jesus will consequently initiate a new millennial rule. For Jews to be saved and blessed by God, they must convert to Christianity and adhere to Jesus' message, thus inferring that Judaism is not a true, valid religion.[30] Having inferred that, on the verge of the end time, at least two-thirds of the chosen people may also vanish, dispensationalists are often accused of using Israel solely for the fulfillment of their prophesies. For example, John Hagee, a Christian Zionist pastor at the Cornerstone Church in San Antonio, has recently made offensive remarks about Catholics, Jews and the victims of the Holocaust. He stated: "biblical verses made clear that Adolf Hitler and the Holocaust was part of God's plan to chase the Jews from Europe and drive them to Palestine."[31] Consequently, the Republican presidential candidate John McCain rejected Hagee's endorsement, despite Hagee's claim that the remarks were taken out of context.

Indeed, dispensationalists see a strong link between anticipated biblical prophesies on the one hand, and Israel's creation and its continued expansion on the other. They particularly view the founding of Israel, which would not have materialized without crucial U.S. backing, as a fulfillment of God's eternal plan and a product of British and U.S. support for Israel. The presence of Israel on the world's map has also represented a clear precursor from God about the nearing end of the world. On the other hand, dispensationalists express "little or no concern for Palestinian rights — which was ironic since there have always been more Arab Christians in the Middle East than Jewish ones."[32] Dispensationalists are reluctant to express sympathy for Christian Palestinians because a majority of them are of Roman Catholic and Eastern Orthodox background.

Right-wing Israelis and evangelical activists generally believe that the territorial size of the Promised Land is far larger than the boundaries of modern-day Israel. Jordan, for instance, is often assumed by Israelis and evangelicals to be part of the Promised Land as revealed in God's promise to Abraham, the Balfour Declaration and the Palestine Mandate documents. However, disagreements often resurface between evangelicals on the one hand, and Jewish faithful on the other on whether or not prophetic revelations can be fulfilled before Israel controls the entire territories of the Promised Land. There is little disagreement between them on the right of Israel to maintain its control over the West Bank territory, which evangelicals acknowledge as biblical *Judea* and *Samaria*. The far right Jewish settlers' movement, notably *Gush Emmunim*, (Bloc of Faithful), is the strongest ally to evangelicals on the issue of Israel's need to preserve its control over all of historic Palestine.[33] Israel's claim to the entire territory of the Promised Land is also justified by dispensationalists commitment to biblical accounts found in Genesis 15:18:

I am the Lord, who brought you out of Ur of the Chaldeans to give you this land to take position of it ... know for certain that your descendents will be strangers in a country not their own ... your descendents will come back here.... To your descendents I gave this land, from the River of Egypt to the great river, the Euphrates.[34]

Although evangelicals have for the most part been successful in pressuring U.S. policymakers to support Israel on most issues surrounding Israel's conflict with the Palestinians, they continue to protest specific U.S. policies in the region. For instance, many U.S. policymakers, who are motivated by national and strategic considerations regarding U.S. policies in the Middle East, have often pursued plans to meet Israeli and Palestinians' demands for a two-state solution to the conflict. However, evangelicals have continually rejected peace negotiations, including those sponsored by the U.S., because they fear Israel may be pressured into withdrawing from the Palestinian territories, thus hindering Israel's security that might potentially delay the pursuit of God's plans.[35] It is in this context that dispensationalists and right-wing Israelis have effectively voiced their vehement opposition to the U.S. sponsored Road Map formula. The general content of this formula, which was initiated by the G.W. Bush Administration in 2002, expects Israeli and Palestinian negotiators to pursue peace efforts to determine the final fate of the 1967 Palestinian territories, which includes the West Bank, Gaza and Arab East Jerusalem. Indeed, this may entail the expectation of dividing these territories, including East Jerusalem, between Israel and the Palestinians.[36] Evangelical opposition to peace efforts is mainly centered on fears concerning Jerusalem's future status that must, according to them, remain undivided and under Israel's permanent control.

Faced with pressures from evangelicals, the G.W. Bush Administration's commitment to the Road Map was soon transformed into a rhetorical vision that is unable to conclude a peace deal between Israel and the Palestinians. While the Administration has rhetorically continued to this day its pursuit of the two-state plan, in practice, the U.S. has refrained from pressuring Israel into withdrawing from the territories it occupied since the 1967 Arab-Israeli War. Israel's control of the Palestinian territories and its expansion of settlements across Palestinian land have been continually justified by evangelicals, supported by the U.S., mainly on religious grounds.[37] To widen the support of evangelicals for his election campaign, Republican presidential candidate John McCain assured supporters that he would do whatever it took, including the transfer of the U.S. embassy from Tel Aviv to Jerusalem, to ensure Israel's continued control over the unified city of Jerusalem.[38] Obviously, given their political importance in U.S. elections, it is difficult for U.S. politicians, notably Republicans, to ignore evangelical demands, including those relating to their rejection of the peace process. Ultimately, whether for religious or other geopolitical and strategic factors, the U.S.'s unrelenting support for Israel has provoked Arabs and Muslims to question U.S. credibility in the region and to further fuel Arab animosities towards Israel.

Reactions to Dispensationalists' Doctrines

While dispensationalists have invested ample religious and political resources to exert pressures on the U.S. to side with Israel, most Christians limit their view of Israel to the historical ties that usually bond Christians and Jews with the Holy Land. Christian support for Israel has also been motivated by their sense "of spiritual debt to the Jews" given that "the majority of the Bible was written in Hebrew and ordained by God to the ... chosen people."[39] However, dispensationalist theologians, and neo-Conservative politicians affiliated with the G.W. Bush Administration, largely agree that "the key to [God's] plan is the re-founding of Israel as a nation in Palestine." They also assume that "without Israel, the whole plan falls apart."[40] In enticing U.S. backing for Israel, dispensationalists often cite the statement found in Genesis 12:3 stating: "God will bless those who bless the Jewish people"[41] as a guideline for what John Hagee calls "God's foreign policy."[42]

In contrast with dispensationalists, traditional Christian groups who subscribe to replacement theology, for instance, have almost totally eliminated Israel's role from the end-time prophesy. Much of the support for replacement theology derives from non-evangelical Christians, notably Eastern Orthodox, Catholics and liberal Protestants, who assume that the Christian church has supplanted the Jews as God's chosen people. The support for replacement theology particularly comes from Middle Eastern Christians, with an Arab majority, who believe that "the Christian Church is the continuation and heir of biblical historical Israel."[43] Although replacement theology lacks popular appeal among Christians, its doctrine challenges the more dominant belief system of dispensationalism. Replacement theology sees no ties between modern-day Israel and the apocalypse. Thomas McCall summarizes their views as follows:

> [T]he church is the new Israel, a continuation of the concept of Israel which began in the Old Testament ... the Church is the refinement and higher development of the concept of Israel. All of the promises made to Israel ... [in Scriptures] ... find their fulfillment in the [Christian] Church ... the prophesies related to the blessing and restoration of Israel to the Promised Land are spiritualized into promises of blessing to the Church.[44]

Replacement theology does not only conclude that the fulfillment of prophecies is no longer contingent on Israel's possession of the Promised Land, but also dismisses the need for U.S. support of Israel. Although there might be other factors, including geopolitical and strategic considerations, that could explain the strength of U.S. ties with Israel, replacement theology rejects that such a bond should be based on religious grounds. While dispensationalists and most evangelicals hardly question those who support the creation of

Greater Israel in the Holy Land on religious grounds, those affiliated with replacement theology oppose Israel's occupation of the Palestinian territories. Palestinian Christian theologians have also offered interpretations that go beyond replacement theology. Under the influence of Catholic liberation theologians, Palestinian Christian activists "have articulated theologies that see Palestinians, especially Christians, as the lineal successor of the Israelites of the Exodus."[45]

Apparently, both dispensationalist and replacement interpretations of Israel's future role entail an effort to influence the course of U.S. policies in the Middle East. The impact of dispensationalists, given their widespread popular appeal in the U.S., enjoys a more powerful influence in terms of their ability to determine public policies in favor of Israel. Despite its general ineffectiveness in the realm of politics, replacement theology continues to promote an end to Israel's future role in the scriptures. Because replacement theology does not consider the biblical dialogue between God and Abraham, which states: "whoever curses you I will curse; and all people on earth will be blessed through you"[46] as a mandate from God to support modern-day Israel, its supporters find it possible to object to Israel's treatment of the Palestinians in the occupied territories.

The more secular-oriented criticisms of evangelical puritan interpretations generally emphasize that the Christian Bible, like other sacred texts, should not be taken literally. Prominent philosophers, notably Hobbes and Spinoza, for example, were among the first to express skepticism about literalist interpretations of the Bible. Advances in scientific discoveries and critical thinking, mainly at European and U.S. universities, have also encouraged scholars to pursue more critical methods when exploring religious texts, notably Jewish and Christian texts. New findings, particularly in the fields of evolution, archaeology and geology have led to additional critical reviews of interpretations of religious texts across all religions. This situation has ignited backlashes by evangelicals who have played a pivotal role in motivating followers to embrace the dispensationalist view of their sacred texts. In turn, evangelicals have resisted religious and secular criticisms of their beliefs by developing their own interpretations as a counter-balance to the perceived secularization of their society.

For their part, Israelis are largely satisfied with the support they have been receiving from evangelical groups.[47] While welcoming evangelical political, monetary and economic support, Israelis have learned to ignore much of the evangelicals' belief system and theological interpretations that contradict Judaism. Jewish faithful generally discard efforts that aim at converting them to Christianity.[48] Given that evangelicals often make it obvious that their support for Israel is motivated by the need to fulfill certain prophesies, it makes it more possible for their supporters to firmly oppose Jews who might be affiliated with secular and liberal agendas. In this context, one observer concludes that "Christian dispensationalism ... may have simultaneously catalyzed total love for the Jewish State while unwittingly unleashing a wave of anti–Semitism against the Jewish people."[49] Although evangelicals have often caused a certain amount of distress to the diverse Jewish communities in the U.S., most Israelis, however, tend to focus more on the political advantages of evangelism rather than the actual indoctrination of their theology. Along with liberal Jewish and Israeli voices that often expressed resentment to dispensationalists' account of the end time, people within the ultra–Orthodox Jewish community have also voiced their own opposition to evangelical Christians, Zionism and Israel. Based on their own, largely out of the mainstream, theological interpretations of the Old Testament, the ultra–Orthodox Jewish organization, known as Neturei Karta, considers the beliefs and actions of modern-day-Israel, its Zionist ideology and evangelicals backers as contradictory to the Torah.[50]

The apparent theological disagreements between evangelicals and Jews, which are not usually spelled out in public, do not threaten the already existing strong alliance between dispensationalists and right wing-Israelis, especially on the subject of the peace process with the Palestinians. Most dispensationalist evangelicals generally believe that "there's not going to be any real peace in the Middle East until the Lord Jesus sits down upon the throne of David in Jerusalem."[51] While agreeing with the evangelical rejection of the peace process, right-wing Israelis do not view Jesus' possible return as a factor that should ever concern them. Evangelical assumptions concerning what they perceive as an expected Jewish conversion to Christianity is also viewed by Jewish faithful to have no real impact on the Jewish people, their history or religion. Given that the majority of Israelis and Palestinians continue to support the peace process on the basis of a two-state formula, it is questionable whether the alliance between evangelicals and right-wing Israelis will benefit Israel's long-term security status and interests in the Middle East.[52]

Dispensationalist Theology and U.S.-Israeli Relations

While preparing for the return of Christ, evangelicals successfully established themselves as a vital electoral constituency for the Republican Party and therefore flourished significantly during the Reagan and G.W. Bush Administrations. Prominent political leaders and dispensationalist activists, including Pat Robertson, Jerry Falwell, Gary Bauer, John Hagee, Richard Army, John Bolton, Douglas Feith, John Ashcroft, James Inhofe, and Tom

DeLay are among the main players that have exerted significant influence on successive U.S. government policies towards Israel.[53] After the September 11th attacks, evangelical leaders and organizations became more determined to prevent any pressures that may be imposed on Israel to withdraw its forces from the Palestinian occupied territories. Furthermore, in much of their media outlets, evangelicals have described views critical of Israel as acts of anti–Semitism and often against God.[54]

Until his death in 2007, evangelical leader Jerry Falwell was among the main activists who pressured the U.S. government to transfer its embassy from Tel Aviv to Jerusalem. He also called upon U.S. policymakers and advisors to pursue a lenient approach towards Israel's handling of the Palestinians. Falwell has always associated U.S. support for Israel with religious themes. In speeches and rallies supportive of Israel, Falwell reflected on the strength of religious and political connections between Christians and Israel by asking: "Can you love Jesus without loving Israel?" He then went further in explaining his views of the U.S.'s role towards Israel as being part of God's design:

> God has raised up America in these last days for the cause of world evangelism and for the protection of his people, the Jews. I don't think America has any other right or reason for existence than those two purposes.[55]

Believing in Israel's importance in the apocalypse, Pat Robertson has also stated that "Israel has no better friends than American Evangelicals."[56] Reagan's presidency was the turning point for evangelicals whose influence on the administration was quite evident when it addressed Israel's security concerns. The Reagan Administration was the first to be pressured to consider the Palestinian occupied territories, which are recognized as colonized by international law, as a disputed land that is subject to negotiations between Israel and the Palestinians.[57] Furthermore, because the balance of power in the region has always been, and remains, in Israel's favor, along with the presence of continued inequality between Israeli and Palestinian negotiators in the peace talks that began since the early 1990s, it has always been assumed that Israel will maintain some control over the occupied territories. With U.S. support and approval for Israel, evangelicals believe that Israel would continue to assume its right to control the Palestinian territories, regardless of the effects of Israel's policies on the Palestinians' living conditions.

Former Israeli Prime Minister and right-wing hardliner Benjamin Netanyahu, who continues to reject Palestinian national claims, is known in evangelical circles as "the Ronald Reagan of Israel."[58] In recent years, the political ties between right-wing Israeli politicians, U.S. evangelical groups along with neo-Conservatives associated with the Republican Party, have grown significantly.[59] Ilen Prusher's comments on the rising popular appeal of Netan-yahu among U.S. evangelicals shed more lights on the growing alliance between U.S. evangelicals and right-wing Israeli politicians:

> There is perhaps no Israeli Prime Minister who has grasped the passion and political potential of folks like those [evangelicals] ... better than Benyamin Netanyahu.... [H]e has cultivated strong contacts with some of the most senior American figures in the evangelical Christian world.[60]

This alliance between evangelicals and Israeli extremists is best seen in their opposition to the removal of Jewish settlements from the Gaza Strip in August 2005, or what is referred to as illegal outposts, from the Palestinian occupied territories. As an example reflective of their solidarity with Jewish settlers, evangelical congregations in the U.S., have adopted many Jewish settlers in the West Bank to help sustain their settlements. These political links estab-lished between U.S. evangelicals and the Jewish settler movement on the one hand, and political actions and actors associated with mainly neo-Conserva-tive advisors and policymakers in the U.S. on the other, has greatly con-tributed to, the collapse of the Road Map formula for peace between Israel and the Palestinians.

Many members of Congress and the White House continue to lobby for the U.S. backing of Israel's control over the Palestinian territories. For instance, while serving as a majority leader in the House of Representatives in Con-gress, Tom DeLay visited Israel and expressed his support for Israel's control of the entire Palestinian territories, including Arab East Jerusalem, by stat-ing: "I don't see occupied territory, I see Israel."[61] Richard Army, a leading member in the Republican Party in the House of Representatives, expressed similar sentiments in responding to a question concerning Israel's options in dealing with the 1967 occupied Palestinian territories, where he considered these territories as an integral part of Israel and thus called for the transfer of all Palestinians from the West Bank to Jordan.[62] Tim LaHaye along with other evangelicals, namely Jesse Helms, Howard Phillips, Grover Norquist, and Bill Frist, have resisted pressuring Israel into conceding territories that were pre-sumably given by God to the Jewish people.

Above all, in their attempt to preserve the dominance of Israel in the region and establish a Jewish demographic majority in the occupied Palestin-ian territories, evangelicals have continued to funnel millions of dollars into Jewish settlements although international laws have deemed these settlements illegal.[63] As a main contributor to the United Jewish Appeal organization in support of Jewish settlements, John Hagee stood firmly in opposition to U.S. mediations for peace between Israel and the Palestinians. Hagee stated: "I am a Bible scholar and a theologian and from my perspective, the law of God transcends the law of the United States."[64] Evangelical belief in the Biblical mandate given to the Jewish people is the main motivating factor in their unequivocal support for Israel.[65] They believe that "in the Bible, there is not a Green Line ... no occupied territories, and no West Bank ... [there is] only Promised Land [to the Jews]."[66]

Evangelicals in the U.S. have also been particularly successful in utilizing several media outlets across the U.S. that have familiarized Americans with their domestic and foreign policy agendas. Part of the evangelical success derives from an American cultural setting that is usually far more suited, due to religious and historical reasons, to support Israel than they are willing to express sympathy for the Palestinian people.

Conclusions

Obviously, dispensationalists justify their support for Israel on the basis of beliefs found in their sacred texts, namely the Book of Genesis, which often influence other non-dispensationalist Christians to express a degree of sympathy for the Jewish State. Dispensationalist theological interpretations explain their backing for Israel as a matter that is simply sanctioned by God. Dispensationalists also assume that various prophetic signs have already revealed the nearing end of time and the vital role Israel will play in relation to God's plan. Jesus' anticipated return and the events that will surround his arrival are considered by dispensationalists as compelling events to cause Christians worldwide to make it their main duty to support Israel. As such, dispensationalists' support for Israel does not appear to be motivated by what is often explained as Western guilt deriving from the Nazi holocaust or a result of similarities often found between Western and Israeli political systems and cultures. Rather, dispensationalist support for Israel is inspired by a theology concerning the role Israel is expected to play in relation to the end-time.[67]

To further facilitate God's plans, evangelicals generally recognize that they must pressure Western powers, namely the U.S., to unequivocally support Israel regardless of its effects on Palestinians. Through the influence of dispensationalists on U.S. policy in the region, Israeli colonial objectives in the Palestinian territories have largely been achieved. While pursuing their one-sided pro-Israeli approach, dispensationalists, supported by U.S. policymakers, have also endangered Israeli chances to achieve a lasting peace with the Palestinians. Furthermore, dispensationalists, supported by right-wing Israelis, have also contributed in the process of transforming the current Israeli-Palestinian conflict from its historical and political character into more theologically-oriented clashes between religious fanatics on both sides of the conflict.

While not conclusively demonstrating religion as the only underlying factor in U.S. and British historic alliance with Israel, this paper claims that the support for Israel's founding and expansion has generally been at the forefront of U.S. foreign policy agenda. Moreover, the current cultural orientations and ongoing politicization of religious doctrines in both the U.S. and Britain continue to influence policymaking in favor of Israel. Although it should not come as a surprise that British and U.S. public and official support for Israel is largely rooted in religious socialization, education, and training, other factors, notably geopolitical, security and economic issues, have also played a role in their support for Israel, especially during the Cold War era. Meanwhile, at the 60th anniversary of the creation of Israel, President George W. Bush expressed the most vivid, theologically based, and enthusiastic support for Israel. In his speech before the Israeli Knesset, Bush reaffirmed the administration's deeply seeded commitment to Israel on religious grounds. Adopting an evangelical tone and terminology, President Bush was able to express his religious attachments to what he considers as Israel's new rebirth for the fulfillment of God's eternal plans. He pledged the U.S.'s official and public backing of Israel at all costs while confronting the forces of evil,[68] in reference to Hizballah in Lebanon, Hamas in Gaza, and Iran. The dichotomy between good and evil are clearly identified in Bush's speeches and comments concerning Israel's conflict with the Palestinians. While the Bush Administration was quick to condemn Iran's vocal threats to Israel's existence, Democratic Senator Hillary Clinton also vowed, during her primary election campaign in April 2007, to attack Iran if its regime threatened Israel.[69] This statement reveals the lack of real or meaningful differences between Republicans and Democrats in the U.S. when dealing with Israel's security and future. The main difference, however, is that Republican presidents such as Reagan and Bush in general have continually based their support for Israel on evangelical literalist and puritan interpretations of religious texts.

NOTES

1. Jeremy D. Mayer, "Christian Fundamentalists and Public Opinion towards the Middle East: Israel's New Best Friends?" *Social Science Quarterly* 85, no. 3 (2004): 695–712.

2. Marc Schoenit, "The Roots of Christian Zionism," *Theological Review* 26, no. 1 (2005): 3–38.

3. James Kurth, "Religion in World Affairs: The Protestant Deformation and American Foreign Policy," *Orbis: A Journal of World Affairs* 48, no. 2 (1998): 221–239.

4. Miles Pomper, "Religious Right Flexes Muscles on Foreign Policy Matters," *Congressional Quarterly Weekly* 13, no. 3 (2002): 1893–1897.

5. William Martin, *With God on Our Side: The Rise of the Religious Right in America,* (New York: Broadway, 1996) 200–219.

6. Martin Durham, "Evangelical Protestantism and Foreign Policy in the United States after September 11," *Patterns of Prejudice* 38, no. 2 (2004): 145–160.

7. *Chicago Tribune,* "Some Final Words on Armageddon," sec. 1, Feb 1, 1991, pg.7.

8. Marc Schoenit, "The Roots of Christian Zionism," *Theological Review* 26, no.1 (2005): 3–38.

9. *Chicago Tribune,* "As 2000 Nears, End-of-the-World Talk Just Beginning," June 23, 1995, pg. 9.

10. Tony Campolo, "The Ideological Roots of Christian Zionism," *Tikkun* 20, no.1 (2005): 19–20.

11. Irvine Anderson, *Biblical Interpretation and Middle East Policy, the Promised Land, America and Israel, 1917–2002* (Gainesville: University Press of Florida, 2007) 53–74.

12. *Jewish News of Greater Phoenix,* "The Clout of Christian Zionism," July 18, 2003, pg. 8.

13. John Dart, "Bush Religious Rhetoric Riles Critics," *Christian Century* 120, no. 5 (2003): 10–12.

14. *The White House,* "President Bush Addresses Members of the Knesset," May 15, 2008, Office of the President. <http://www.whitehouse.gov/news/releases/2008/05/2008 0515-1.html> (May 16, 2008).

15. Pat Morrison, "The Dangerous Potent Elixir of Christian Zionism," *The Washington Report on the Middle East* 26, no. 3 (2007): 58–60, pg. 58.

16. Abdallah Jaman al-Ghamdi, "The Christian Right and its Influence on American Policy" (Arabic), *Majalat al Ulum al-Ijtimayeh,* (Social Science Journal), 28, no. 3 (2000): 7–41.

17. Tony Campolo, "The Ideological Roots of Christian Zionism," *Tikkun* 20, no. 1 (2005): 19.

18. Anthony Lukas, "The Rapture and the Bomb," *The New York Times,* June 8, 1986. <http://query.nytimes.com/gst/fullpage.html?res=9A0DEFDA153FF93BA35755C0A9609 48260&sec=&spon=> (October 1, 2008).

19. Michael Lienesch, *Redeeming America: Piety and Politics in the New Christian Right* (Chapel Hill, NC: University of North Carolina Press, 1993).

20. Hank Hanegraaff, "Rebuild Temple vs. the Dome of the Rock," August 24, 2007. <http://hankhanegraaff.blogspot.com/2007/08/rebuilt-temple-vs-dome-of-rock.html> (October 1, 2008).

21. Gershom Gorenberg, "Unorthodox Alliance," *Washington Post,* October 11, 2002, A37. <http://www.washingtonpost.com/ac2/wp-dyn/A10067-2002Oct10> (October 1, 2008).

22. Anderson, *Biblical Interpretation and Middle East Policy,* 32–35.

23. Walter Goodman, "Rise of the Religious Right," *The New York Times,* September 28, 1996, pg. 21.

24. Timothy Weber, "How Evangelicals Became Israel's Best Friends," *Christianity Today* 42, no. 11 (1998): 38–50, 38.

25. Donald Wagner, "The Evangelical-Jewish Alliance," *The Christian Century,* June 28, 2003, 20–24. <http://www.religion-online.org/showarticle.asp?title=2717> (October 1, 2008).

26. *Washington Post,* "Unorthodox Alliance," 11, 2002, A37.

27. *J Grant Swank,* "Could Anti-Christ Be Muslim," Magic City Morning Star, October 29, 2007. <http://www.magic-city-news.com/J_Grant_Swank_61/Could_Anti-Christ_ Be_Muslim8896.shtml> (October 17, 2008).

28. Weber. "How Evangelicals Became Israel's Best Friend," *Christianity Today,* 38–50.

29. William Martin, "The Christian Right and American Foreign Policy," *Foreign Policy* 114, no. 3 (1999): 66–80.

30. Grace Halsell, *Prophesy and Politics: Militant Evangelists on the Road to Nuclear War* (Westport, CT: Lawrence Hill, 1986).

31. *The New York Times,* "McCain Rejects Hagee Backing as Nazi Remarks Surface," May 22, 2008.

32. Weber, "How Evangelicals Became Israel's Best Friend," 45.

33. Craig Horowitz, "Israel's Christian Soldiers," *New York Times,* September 22, 2003. <http://nymag.com/nymetro/news/religion/features/n_9255/> (October 1, 2008).

34. Leviticus 26:13, quoted in the New American Standard Bible, 1995. <http://www.bible.cc/leviticus/26-13.htm> (October 1, 2008).

35. Husam Mohamad, "The Peace Process and the Palestinian Political Landscape," *Journal of International and Area Studies* 14, no. 1 (2007): 85–94.

36. "The Road Map," *Palestine-Israel Journal of Politics, Economics & Culture* 10, no. 2 (2003): 115–120.

37. Ted Jelen, "Religion and Foreign Policy Attitudes: Exploring the Effects of Denomination and Doctrine," *American Politics Quarterly* 22, no. 3 (1994): 382–400.

38. *World News,* "McCain Vows U.S. Embassy Move to Jerusalem," July 26, 2007, <http://focusonjerusalem.com/newsroom.html> (October 1, 2008).

39. *The New York Amsterdam News,* "Why Christians Support Israel," April 3-April 9, 2003, pg. 8.

40. Weber, "How Evangelicals Became Israel's Best Friend," 40.

41. Genesis 12:3

42. Christiane Amanpour, "God's Warriors," *CNN Documentary,* Sunday, August 10, 2008.

43. Yaakov Ariel, "An Unexpected Alliance: Christian Zionism and its Historical Significance," *Modern Judaism* 26, no.1 (2006): 74–100, 87.

44. Thomas S. McCall, "Israel and the Church: The Differences," *Levitt Newsletter* 18, no. 5 (1996). <http://www.levitt.com/newsletters/1996-05.html> (October 1, 2008).

45. *Ibid.,* 14.

46. Genesis 12:3.

47. Richard Bernstein, "Evangelicals Strengthening Bonds with Jews," *New York Times,* February 6, 1983, 1.

48. Gustav Niebuhr, "Christian Split: Can Nonbelievers Be Saved?" *New York Times,* August 22, 1996, A1.

49. Colin Shindler, "Likud and the Christian Dispensationalists: A Symbiotic Relationship," *Israel Studies* 5, no.1 (2000): 153–183, 178.

50. *Neturei Karta: Jews United Against Zionism* <http://www.nkusa.org> (October 1, 2008).

51. "A Fitting Farewell to Falwell," *Prospects for Peace,* May 28, 2007. <http://www.prospectsforpeace.com/2007/05> (October 1, 2008).

52. Bill Keller, "Is it Good for the Jews?" *New York Times,* March 8, 2003, A17.

53. Kenneth A. Briggs, "The Influence of Church Leaders in Politics," *New York Times,* September 19, 1980, A13.

54. Husam Mohamad, "The Bush Administration's Vision of the Two-state Solution," in *Where Now for Palestine? The Demise of the Two-State Solution,* (New York: Zed, 2007) 99–102.

55. *La Vista Church of Christ,* "Is the Modern Nation of Israel Important?" <http://www.lavistachurchofchrist.org/LVSermons/IsModernIsraelImportant.htm> (October 1, 2008).

56. Weber, "How Evangelicals Became Israel's Best Friend," 38.

57. Geoffrey R. Watson, *The Oslo Accords: International Law and the Israeli-Palestinian Peace Agreements* (Oxford, UK: Oxford University Press, 2005) 27–34.

58. Donald Wagner, "Reagan and Begin, Bibi and Jerry: The Theopolitical Alliance of the Likud Party with the American Christian Right," *Arab Studies Quarterly* 20, no.4 (1998): 33–52.

59. Nicholas A. Veliotes, "The Bush Vision for Palestine: Realistic or Apocalyptic," *Mediterranean Quarterly* 13, no.4 (2002): 11–19.

60. Ilen Prusher, "Israel's Unlikely Ally: American Evangelicals," *Christian Science Monitor* 90, no. 104 (1998): 1.

61. Daniel Benjamin and Steven Simon, *The Next Attack: the Failure of the War on Terror and a Strategy for Getting it Right* (New York: Times, 2005) 269.

62. *Hardball with Chris Mathews,* "House Republican Leader Calls for the Expulsion of Palestinians," CNBC News, <http://www.awitness.org/journal/palestinians_out.html> (October 1, 2008).

63. W. Thomas Mallison and Sally V. Mallison, *The Palestine Problem in International Law and World Order* (Essex: Longman, 1986) 240–272.

64. *Daily Star,* "The Interregnum: Christian Zionism in the Clinton Years," November 10, 2003. <http://www.informationclearinghouse.info/article4951.htm> (October 1, 2008).

65. John Mearsheimer and Stephen Walt, "The Israel Lobby," *London Review of Books,* March 23, 2006. <http://www.lrb.co.uk/v28/n06/mear01_.html> (October 1, 2008).

66. Ilene R. Prusher, "Israel's Unlikely Ally: American Evangelicals," *Christian Science Monitor* 90, no. 104 (1998): 1.

67. Rammy M. Haija, "The Armageddon Lobby: Dispensationalist Christian Zionism and the Shaping of U.S. Policy towards Israel-Palestine," *Holy Land Studies* 5, no.1 (2006): 75–95 at 81.

68. "Bush: U.S. Stands with Israel, Masada Won't Fall Again," *Haaretz News,* May 16, 2008. <http://www.haaretz.com/hasen/pages/SearchEn.jhtml> (August 3, 2008).

69. *The New York Times,* "Comments: Obliterate Iran" April 28, 2008. <http://thecaucus.blogs.nytimes.com/2008/04/28/rev-wright-defends-church-blasts-media/> (October 1, 2008).

Works Cited

Al-Ghamdi, Abdallah Jaman. "The Christian Right and its Influence on American Policy," (Arabic) *Majalat al Ulum al-Ijtimayeh* (Social Science Journal) 28, no. 3 (2000): 7–41.

Amanpour, Christiane. "God's Warriors." *CNN Documentary.* August 10, 2008.

Anderson, Irvine. *Biblical Interpretation and Middle East Policy, the Promised Land, America and Israel, 1917–2002.* Gainesville: University Press of Florida, 2007.

Ariel, Yaakov. "An Unexpected Alliance: Christian Zionism and its Historical Significance." *Modern Judaism* 26, no. 1 (2006): 74–100.

"As 2000 Nears, End-of-the-World Talk Just Beginning." *Chicago Tribune.* June 23, 1995: 9

Bard, Mitchell. "Israel Lobby Power." *Midstream* 33, no. 1 (1987): 6–8.

Benjamin, Daniel, and Steven Simon. *The Next Attack: The Failure of the War on Terror and a Strategy for Getting it Right.* New York: Times, 2005.

Bernstein, Richard. "Evangelicals Strengthening Bonds with Jews." *New York Times.* February 6, 1983: 1.

Briggs, Kenneth A. "The Influence of Church Leaders in Politics." *New York Times.* September 19, 1980: A13.

"Bush: U.S. Stands with Israel, *Masada* Won't Fall Again." *Haaretz News.* May 16, 2008. <http://www.haaretz.com/hasen/pages/SearchEn.jhtml> (August 3, 2008).

Campolo, Tony. "The Ideological Roots of Christian Zionism." *Tikkun.* 20, no. 1 (2005): 19–23.

"The Clout of Christian Zionism." *Jewish News of Greater Phoenix.* July 18, 2003: 8.

Dart, John. "Bush Religious Rhetoric Riles Critics." *Christian Century* 120, no. 5 (2003): 10–12.

Durham, Martin. "Evangelical Protestantism and Foreign Policy in the United States after September 11." *Patterns of Prejudice* 38, no. 2 (2004): 145–160.

Firestone, David. "Evangelical Christians and Jews United for Israel." *New York Times.* June 9, 2002: 30.

Genesis 12:3. *New American Standard Bible.* 1995. <http://www.biblegateway.com/passage/?search=Genesis%2012:3&version=49> (July 9, 2008)

Goodman, Walter. "Rise of the Religious Right." *The New York Times.* September 28, 1996: 21.

Goodstine, Laurie. "Evangelicals for Israel." *The New York Times.* January 21, 1998: A1.

Gorenberg, Gershom. "Unorthodox Alliance," *Washington Post.* October 11 2002: A37. <http://www.washingtonpost.com/ac2/wp-dyn/A10067-2002Oct10> (October 1, 2008).

Haija, Rammy M. "The Armageddon Lobby: Dispensationalist Christian Zionism and the Shaping of U.S. Policy towards Israel-Palestine." *Holy Land Studies* 5, no. 1 (2006): 75–95.

Halsell, Grace. *Prophesy and Politics: Militant Evangelists on the Road to Nuclear War.* Westport, CT: Lawrence Hill, 1986.

Hanegraaff, Hank. "Rebuild Temple vs. the Dome of the Rock." August 24, 2007. <http://hankhanegraaff.blogspot.com/2007/08/rebuilt-temple-vs-dome-of-rock.html> (October 1, 2008).

Horowitz, Craig. "Israel's Christian Soldiers." *New York Times.* September 22, 2003. http://nymag.com/nymetro/news/religion/features/n_9255/> (October 1, 2008).

"House Republican Leader Calls for the Expulsion of Palestinians." *Hardball with Chris Mathews.* CNBC News. <http://www.awitness.org/journal/palestinians_out.html> (October 1, 2008).

"Is the Modern Nation of Israel Important?" *La Vista Church of Christ.* <http://www.lavistachurchofchrist.org/LVSermons/IsModernIsraelImportant> (October 1, 2008).

Jelen, Ted. "Religion and Foreign Policy Attitudes: Exploring the Effects of Denomination and Doctrine." *American Politics Quarterly* 22, no. 3 (1994): 382–400.

Keller, Bill. "Is It Good for the Jews?" *New York Times.* March 8, 2003: A17.

Kurth, James. "Religion in World Affairs: The Protestant Deformation and American Foreign Policy." *Orbis: A Journal of World Affairs* 48, no.2 (1998): 221–239.

Leviticus 26:13. *New American Standard Bible.* 1995. <http://www.bible.cc/leviticus/26–13.htm> (October 1, 2008).

Levy, Daniel. "A Fitting Farewell to Falwell." *Prospects for Peace.* May 28, 2007. <http://www.prospectsforpeace.com/2007/05/> (October 1, 2008).

Lienesch, Michael. *Redeeming America: Piety and Politics in the New Christian Right.* Chapel Hill, NC: University of North Carolina Press, 1993.

Lukas, Anthony. "The Rapture and the Bomb." *The New York Times.* June 8 1986. <http://query.nytimes.com/gst/fullpage.html?res=9A0DEFDA153FF93BA35755C0A960948260&sec=&spon=> (October 1, 2008).

Luo, Michael. "McCain Rejects Hagee Backing as Nazi Remarks Surface." *New York Times.* May 22, 2008. <http://thecaucus.blogs.nytimes.com/2008/05/22/mccain-rejects-hagee-backing-as-nazi-remarks-surface/?hp> (November 4, 2008).

Mallison, W. Thomas, and Sally V. Mallison. *The Palestine Problem in International Law and World Order.* Essex: Longman, 1986.

Martin, William. "The Christian Right and American Foreign Policy." *Foreign Policy* 114, no. 3 (1999): 66–80.

_____. *With God on Our Side: The Rise of the Religious Right in America.* New York: Broadway Books, 1996.

Marty, Martin. "Bond by Belief." *New York Times.* August 15, 2000: A23.

Mayer, Jeremy D. "Christian Fundamentalists and Public Opinion towards the Middle East: Israel's New Best Friends?" *Social Science Quarterly* 85, no. 3 (2004): 695–712.

"McCain Vows U.S. Embassy Move to Jerusalem." *World News.* July 26, 2007. <http://focus onjerusalem.com/newsroom.html> (October 1, 2008).

McCall, Thomas S. "Israel and the Church: The Differences." *Levitt Newsletter* 18, no. 5 (1996). <http://www.levitt.com/newsletters/1996-05.html> (October 1, 2008).

Mearsheimer, John, and Stephen Walt. "The Israel Lobby." *London Review of Books.* March 23, 2006. <http://www.lrb.co.uk/v28/n06/mear01_.html> (October 1, 2008).

Mohamad, Husam. "The Bush Administration's Vision of the Two-state Solution" in *Where Now for Palestine? The Demise of the Two-State Solution.* New York: Zed, 2007.

_____. "The Peace Process and the Palestinian Political Landscape." *Journal of International and Area Studies* 14, no. 1 (2007): 85–94.

Morrison, Pat. "The Dangerous Potent Elixir of Christian Zionism." *The Washington Report on the Middle East* 26, no. 3 (2007): 58–60.

Neturei Karta: Jews United Against Zionism <http://www.nkusa.org/> (October 1, 2008).

Niebuhr, Gustav. "Christian Split: Can Nonbelievers Be Saved?" *New York Times.* August 22, 1996: A1.

Perko, Michael. "Contemporary American Christian Attitudes to Israel Based on the Scriptures." *Israel Studies* 8, no. 2 (2003): 1–17.

Philips, Kate. "Comments: Obliterate Iran." *New York Times.* April 28, 2008. <http://the-caucus.blogs.nytimes.com/2008/04/28/rev-wright-defends-church> (October 1, 2008).

Pomper, Miles. "Religious Right Flexes Muscles on Foreign Policy Matters." *Congressional Quarterly Weekly* 13, no. 3 (2002): 1893–1897.

"President Bush Addresses Members of the Knesset." *The White House.* May 15, 2008. <http://www.whitehouse.gov/news/releases/2008/05/20080515-1.html> (May 16, 2008).

Prusher, Ilen. "Israel's Unlikely Ally: American Evangelicals." *Christian Science Monitor.* April 24, 1998: 1.

"The Road Map Documents" *Palestine-Israel Journal of Politics, Economics & Culture* 10, no.2 (2003): 115–120. <http://www.pij.org/details.php?id=50> (November 3, 2008).

Schoenit, Marc. "The Roots of Christian Zionism." *Theological Review* 26, no. 1 (2005): 3–38.

Shindler, Colin. "Likud and the Christian Dispensationalists: A Symbiotic Relationship." *Israel Studies* 5, no.1 (2000): 153–183.

"Some Final Words on Armageddon." *Chicago Tribune.* February 1, 1991: 7.

Swank, J. Grant. "Could Anti-Christ Be Muslim?" *Magic City Morning Star.* October 29, 2007. <http://www.magic-city-news.com/J_Grant_Swank_61/Could_Anti-Christ_Be_Muslim8896.shtml> (October 17, 2008).

"3000 Evangelicals Meet in Jerusalem." *New York Times.* October 18, 1981: 17.

Veliotes, Nicholas A. "The Bush Vision for Palestine: Realistic or Apocalyptic?" *Mediterranean Quarterly* 13, no. 4 (2002): 11–19.

Wagner, Donald. "The Evangelical-Jewish Alliance." *The Christian Century.* June 28, 2003: 20–24. <http://www.religion-online.org/showarticle.asp?title=2717> (October 1, 2008).

_____. "The Interregnum: Christian Zionism in the Clinton Years." *Daily Star.* November 10, 2003. <http://www.informationclearinghouse.info/article4951.htm> (October 1, 2008).

_____. "Reagan and Begin, Bibi and Jerry: The Theopolitical Alliance of the Likud Party with the American Christian Right." *Arab Studies Quarterly* 20, no.4 (1998): 33–52.

Watson, Geoffrey R. *The Oslo Accords: International Law and the Israeli-Palestinian Peace Agreements.* Oxford, UK: Oxford University Press, 2005.

Weber, Timothy. "How Evangelicals Became Israel's Best Friends," *Christianity Today* 42, no. 11 (1998): 38–50.

"Why Christians Support Israel." *New York Amsterdam News.* April 3–April 9, 2003: 8.

At the Edge of Tomorrow:
Apocalypticism and Science Fiction

Lorenzo DiTommaso

Apocalypticism is a remarkably persistent and adaptable worldview.[1] Its fertile soil continues to nourish the native beliefs of many Jews, Christians, and Muslims, and has proven equally fecund to new transplants from non–Abrahamic religions. It currently informs foreign and domestic policies of nations across the globe. It is a common feature in nearly every medium of contemporary popular culture, including some of its most *avant garde* forms: anime, graphic novels, and role-playing games. It naturally complements nationalism, enabling it to serve as both the voice of the oppressed and the voice-piece of the oppressors. It freights a teleological orientation which makes it attractive to any group — religious or secular, marginal or mainstream — that considers itself the special object of history. In short, in this post–9/11 era of competing cultural narratives and religious rivalries, the influence of apocalypticism remains undiminished as a mode of explaining the world by way of reference to a transcendent reality, concealed from casual observation, which informs and defines our existence in both time and space.

The many faces of modern apocalypticism, however, have caused two problems for its investigators. The first problem is taxonomical. The ancient Greek word *apokalypsis*, with which the New Testament Revelation of John opens, means "unveiling," and by extension, "revelation." But what does *apokalypsis* mean in the contemporary world? Few modern apocalyptic novels or films, for example, contain revelation in its classic biblical sense. Does a motion picture such as *The Matrix* or an anime such as *Neon Genesis Evangelion* (*Shin seiki Evangelion*), which were designed for mass public consumption in the late twentieth century, convey the same message as the apocalyptic *War Scroll*, which was studied and copied by a small group of Dead Sea sectarians in the early first century? Has "apocalypse" now become a setting, an event, or even a metaphor? If so, has its underlying ideology changed? What is the relationship between the ideology and its many manifestations?

Such questions are all too familiar to scholars of ancient Judaism and

Christianity. For a long time they relied on a single term, "apocalyptic," to describe a distinctive type of literature as well as its worldview, eschatology, and typical motifs, settings, and vocabularies. The result was a state of mind which Florentino García Martínez calls "pan-apocalyptic": a loose set of phenomena whose mutually reinforcing descriptions broadly suggest a concept, rather than define it.[2] The biblical book of Daniel, for example, was considered a prime illustration of early Jewish "apocalyptic" because it had an apocalyptic eschatology, was written in apocalyptic language using apocalyptic motifs, and reflected the eschatological hopes of an apocalyptic movement. The statement embraces everything but defines nothing. It is also unable to distinguish between the elements which are idiosyncratic to Daniel and those which denominate the underlying apocalyptic ideology.

Clearly the scientific study of apocalyptic literature demanded greater taxonomic precision. One response was the Society of Biblical Literature's (SBL) Genres Project, which convened in the mid–1970s under the direction of John J. Collins. It replaced the old, protean designation "apocalyptic" with a new, tripartite taxonomy. Its principal category, *apocalypse*, refers to a "genre of revelatory literature with a narrative framework, in which a revelation is mediated by an otherworldly being to a human recipient, disclosing a transcendent reality which is both temporal, insofar as it envisions eschatological speculation, and spatial as it involves another, supernatural world."[3] There are two types of ancient apocalypse: otherworldly apocalypses, which feature heavenly ascents and the disclosure of cosmological mysteries, and historical apocalypses, which focus on revelations about history and the end of the world. The taxonomy's second category, *apocalypticism*, is the ideology, or worldview, of social movements that share the genre's conceptual framework. The third category is *apocalyptic eschatology*, or the eschatology of apocalypses, "eschatology" being the study of the last things, from the Greek *eschatos*, or "last." Scholars have since debated whether apocalyptic eschatology is distinct from, *e.g.*, prophetic eschatology. Those who argue in its favor pinpoint the expectation of post-mortem corporeal resurrection as a defining characteristic.[4]

It is difficult to overstate the importance of the SBL taxonomy. Since its introduction, it has served as the foundation for most of the advanced research on ancient apocalypses and apocalypticism. Moreover, as with any effective taxonomy, the relationships it proposes also control our conceptions of the subject. Three decades along, however, the foundation has begun to exhibit cracks. This paper is not the venue to identify these cracks or the stresses responsible for them. The point is that the definitions and assumptions of the SBL taxonomy are currently undergoing a re-evaluation in the field of biblical studies. Yet the investigation of modern apocalypticism is largely uninformed by this re-evaluation or, more disturbingly, by the taxonomy and its definitions. With a few notable exceptions, it continues to approach the object of its enquiry firmly indentured to the long-superseded notion of biblical "apocalyptic" that is unable to illuminate the data properly.

The second problem which hinders the investigation of modern apocalypticism is methodological. In attempting to find commonalities among its diverse examples, scholars have focused on observable surface topographies to the virtual exclusion of the ideological bedrock.[5] Science-fiction has proven especially vulnerable to this kind of myopia. Apocalyptic science fiction is nearly always defined, and hence studied, on the basis of easily recognizable motifs and other secondary phenomena. There is no denying that this approach has its advantages and has produced a large amount of fine scholarship. But it is essentially flawed, since motifs and other phenomena devolve from the ideology, not the other way round. Such phenomena, moreover, might rise from multiple ideological sources. The notion of hidden knowledge, for instance, is central to apocalypticism but not unique to it.

Both problems inherent to the investigation of modern apocalypticism, taxonomical and methodological, inhibit the appreciation of its scholarship as a cohesive body of work and obscure its connection with the worldview as a historical phenomenon. One is often unsure as to the grounds on which a study defines "apocalyptic." Consider, for instance, the ubiquitous designation "post-apocalyptic." Among its scores of science-fictional examples are Walter M. Miller Jr.'s *A Canticle for Leibowitz* (1959) and, more recently, Cormac McCarthy's *The Road* (2006). *The Matrix* (1999), written by Andy and Larry Wachowski, is a well-known cinematic example. Strictly speaking, however, "post-apocalyptic" is an oxymoron. In the classic apocalypses, the end of history is a literal event, not a literary setting. Time stops forever with the advent of the eschatological age, at which point the resurrection of the dead occurs (Dan. 12:2–3), the New Jerusalem descends from Heaven (Rev. 21:2), or the Messiah appears for the final judgment (4 Ezra 12:33–34), and the narrative terminates. Different apocalypses, of course, anticipate different events, and are far more complex than indicated here. The bottom line is that none of these narratives can accommodate a sequel. There cannot be "post-apocalyptic" *anything* in these ancient texts, nor in the worldview from which they precipitated. The designation, then, as it applies to science fiction, must originate elsewhere. The obvious suspect is its literary setting. As a result, we seemingly possess two, mutually exclusive conceptions of "apocalyptic," the choice of which depends on the book, film, or other work under review.

A similar problem exists for "apocalyptic eschatology." Although nearly every one of its eschatological motifs derives from the ancient and medieval apocalypses, the eschatology of apocalyptic science fiction is seldom apocalyptic. In science fiction, unlike ancient or medieval apocalypses, apocalyptic eschatology is more often than not identified by the *presence* of eschatological motifs, and not by their function, at least not in the classic sense. Since its narratives do not climax with the end of time, the "last things" of apocalyptic science fiction function purely as background elements of the plot and setting.

Yet we can hardly discard "post-apocalyptic" or "apocalyptic eschatology." The former describes a well-defined category that embraces hundreds of recognizable literary and cinematic examples. The latter is a critical component of the SBL taxonomy, whose attributes distinguish apocalypticism from prophecy and other modes of revelation. For this reason David Ketterer's statement that "the apocalyptic imagination ... finds its purest outlet in science fiction" still rings true.[6] On the other hand, taxonomical imprecision and a focus on surface topographies continues to undermine the investigation of apocalyptic science fiction. In this light it is easy to agree with Andrew Greeley's assessment of the problem: "Science fiction was born from an apocalyptic vision, and currently flourishes on another apocalyptic vision, but does not seem to understand what apocalypse really is."[7]

A potential solution proceeds from the recognition that neither genres nor ideologies are static.[8] The genre apocalypse is typical in this regard, as is the ideology. While no one composes apocalypses like Daniel anymore, apocalypticism thrives today in large part because, a few centuries ago, a secular form gradually evolved alongside the older, biblical form. Apocalyptic science fiction is one of the principal manifestations of secular apocalypticism, preserving, as it does, the central axiom of the worldview: the existence of an ulterior yet ultimate reality.[9] While many philosophies share this view, apocalypticism does not contend that a reliance on our unreliable senses leads to ignorance, as in Hinduism, or that objects in this world are imperfect shadows of their essential forms, as in classic Platonism. Rather, it is distinguished from these and other worldviews by the manner in which the core axiom is articulated along three dimensions that, *mutatis mutandis*, continue to inform its modern secular expressions. These dimensions — temporal, spatial, and existential — define apocalyptic science fiction in novels, films, and other media, even if the underlying ideology is not immediately apparent.

Classic apocalypticism proposes that the singularity of creation, which was disrupted in the distant past, will be reconstituted in the future.[10] This is the ideology's temporal dimension, the teleological orientation of which is retained by all its modern incarnations. The shift to a secular perspective, among other things, eliminated references to a biblical-style new creation and a creator/custodian whose plan regulates human history. In a universe governed by natural law rather than supernatural fiat, history no longer terminates according to a divine timetable, but extends, along with what remains of humanity, into a post-apocalyptic period.

Apocalypticism further proposes that the historical age, which corresponds to the *interregnum disruptus*, is structured by an ontological dualism (good/evil, light/dark, angels/demons) that entirely pervades worldly and otherworldly spaces. This is the ideology's spatial dimension, present also in its secular manifestations, including science fiction. However, because of the historical evolution of the ideology (see below), the spatial dimension of modern secular apocalypticism is frequently unrecognized.

What secular apocalypticism shares in the fullest measure with its ancient antecedents is its existential dimension. It contends that humanity's overriding task is to fathom the hidden patterns that reveal the true temporal and spatial contours of reality. Only when the veil is lifted and reality disclosed can humans discern the proper avenue to follow, the correct course of action to take, the precise frequency of the universe with which to resonate, or whatever else constitutes the author's special path to destiny.

These are the three dimensions of classic apocalypticism, sketched with the broadest of brushstrokes. But the picture is still incomplete without a general sense of the worldview's evolution following the biblical period.

In the late fourth century, the production of historical apocalyptic texts exploded after a hiatus of nearly 300 years, while that of otherworldly apocalypses abruptly declined. The reasons for this change do not concern us here, but are vitally important to the notion of apocalypticism as an organic philosophical system. What is relevant is that, with the change, apocalypticism became associated exclusively with its temporal dimension, *i.e.*, the expectation for the end of the world and a new creation. This type of apocalypticism remained dominant for the next fifteen hundred years, and is known as *millenarianism* (var. *millennialism*). Central motifs such as the Messiah, the Antichrist, Armageddon, Gog and Magog, and the Last Judgment, although germinating in the biblical era, matured and ripened in the millenarian milieu of medieval Christianity, Judaism, and Islam.[11] In fact, today's biblical fundamentalism owes as much to medieval millennialism as it does to Scripture, as it also does to later developments, where in the early modern centuries notions such as the Rapture and the Tribulation fermented from the rich theological must of Anglophone Protestant circles. These circles were different in Judaism and Islam, but the general historical dynamic was similar (*cf.* Islamic Wahabism). The equating of apocalypticism and millenarianism continues to shape the expectations of contemporary authors and audiences alike, and channels the attention of scholars away from motifs and other phenomena not associated with the catastrophic end of the world.

The contours of modernity's contribution to secular apocalypticism, especially its debt to classical humanism and the Enlightenment ethos, are more manifold and consequently less precisely understood.[12] Certain aspects are clear, however. Broadly speaking, the nature of western culture ensures that biblical and medieval motifs, themes, and events remain both typologically important and continually reified to fit new circumstances and fresh perspectives. Jesus is the best example, so much so that he has become the ultimate Rorschach Test — readers tend to project as much into the story of Jesus as they draw out of it. It is in this light that we should appreciate the primary contemporary use of terms such as "apocalyptic," "post-apocalyptic," and "apocalyptic eschatology," and the ongoing relevance of categories such as the Messiah, Armageddon, and Antichrist: old wine in new skins. In its longstanding concern with the approach of the eschaton, Christianity prepared the ground for science fiction.[13]

It is also clear that apocalypticism's temporal dimension found a modern secular analogue in the idea that humanity itself might precipitate or induce Armageddon. Whether by sustaining the politics of racial eugenics or the policies of agricultural monocultures, by designing the trenches of one war or the fallout shelters of another, or by serving totalitarian governments or total-war militaries, twentieth-century science and its attendant horrors steadily eroded the old, nineteenth-century faith in technological progress. By the end of the millennium, the idea of the manufactured apocalypse embraced a grim harvest of engineered calamities on nothing less than a planetary scale, including war, pandemic, and climactic cataclysm.[14] Calamitous devastation, political upheaval, and social collapse, hitherto signs of the fulfillment of God's plan for history, instead became the secularized symbols of humanity's violation of natural law.[15] It goes without saying that one of the chief vehicles by which this sentiment is conveyed is science fiction.

The compass within which apocalyptic science fiction is expressed is wide-ranging; restrictions of space permit a discussion here of a representative sample only. Excluded from this study are novels, films, and other media which describe or envision the end of a present world system but which are devoid of any of the three dimensions of the apocalyptic worldview.

At one end of the spectrum is Cormac McCarthy's *The Road*, a novel which qualifies as a post-apocalyptic novel almost entirely by virtue of its monotonously grey landscape, which provides the setting for the ubiquitous lethality of an earth from which civilization has fled.[16] Whereas in classic apocalypses the seer's dreams and visions divulge information about the true reality toward which the ideology's existential dimension urges its readers to strive, in *The Road* dreams and daydreams serve only to relate the plot's backstory or relay some impossible fantasy. The real world in this novel is the present, not a future world or a heavenly one. The contrast with apocalypticism could not be plainer:

> And the dreams so rich in color. How else would death call you? Waking in the cold dawn it all turned to ash instantly. Like certain ancient frescoes entombed for centuries suddenly exposed to the day.[17]

And again:

> The boy turned away. The man held him. Listen to me, he said.
> What.
> When your dreams are of some world that never was or some world that never will be and you are happy again then you will have given up. Do you understand? And you cant give up. I wont let you.[18]

McCarthy offers no theodicy for the causes of the Apocalypse, no spiritual salves for its effects. Death stalks the land with impunity, pestilence its silent companion. Corpses litter the road. Perhaps, reflects the man, gazing at several impaled bodies, "in the history of the world ... there was more punishment than crime."[19] Such thoughts, though, are alien to apocalypticism, where the account-ledgers of earthly behavior and eschatological recompense must balance to the last soul.

Even so, a faint but persistent note of the existential demand of ancient apocalypticism may be heard in the novel, albeit played entirely in a secular key. True, at one point the man sees himself appointed by God to save his son.[20] But McCarthy consistently frames the transcendental quality of this salvific mission in humanistic terms, not spiritual ones. Its locus is the mysterious "fire," which has been nearly extinguished with the passing of civilization, but whose embers are kept smoldering by the man and his boy. Its obscure description permits multiple interpretations.[21] To my mind, however, the fire represents the indefinable *human* spark which separates civilization from chaos and thus which automatically disallows behaviors such as theft, murder, and cannibalism.

> The boy looked down the road. ...
> We wouldnt ever eat anybody, would we?
> No. Of course not.
> Even if we were starving?
> We're starving now.
> You said we werent.
> I said we werent dying. I didnt say we werent starving.
> But we wouldnt.
> No. We wouldnt.
> No matter what.
> No. No matter what.
> Because we're the good guys.

Yes.
And we're carrying the fire.
And we're carrying the fire. Yes.
Okay.[22]

The fire is inside humans,[23] but it is not supernatural, nor can it be equated
with the soul, since only a few possess it. Yet to know it is to embrace a reality that transcends that of the world in which the other characters of *The Road*
exist. At the end of the novel, it is that which moves the hunter in the grey
and yellow parka to cover the man's dead body with a blanket, because this
is what the hunter had promised the boy, even though blankets were price-
less commodities.

The fire also serves as the yardstick by which good and evil are meas-
ured, framing the ancient apocalyptic dualism which, while never expressed,
is palpably felt throughout the novel. Again, though, the context is entirely
secular. There is no afterlife, no ultimate eschatological courtroom where the
evil of the present age will be redressed.[24] Before the man dies, he assures his
boy that they will still talk.[25] And talk they do, every day.[26] Is it the voice of
God, as the wife of the hunter insists? Or is it the human conscience, which
whispers the code of manners and decency which are to be bequeathed to the
next generation but which must also struggle against the relentless forces of
devolution? In the end perhaps they are the same.

The use of biblical motifs and vocabulary is more overt in Walter M.
Miller's classic triptych, *A Canticle for Leibowitz*, which recapitulates humanity's dark ages, Renaissance, and twentieth century. Its final tale concludes
with a second nuclear Armageddon, articulated with images lifted directly
from Revelation. From this final global catastrophe a small band of humans
escapes by rocket to the stars, unmistakably evoking the theme of salvation:

> The visage of Lucifer[27] mushroomed into hideousness above the cloudbank,
> rising slowly like some titan climbing to its feet after ages of imprisonment in
> the Earth.
> Someone barked an order. The monks began climbing again. Soon they were
> all inside the ship.
> The last monk, upon entering, paused in the lock. His stood in the open
> hatchway and took off his sandals. "*Sic transit mundus*," he murmured, looking
> back at the glow. He slapped the soles of his sandals together, beating the
> dirt out of them. The glow was engulfing a third of the heavens. He scratched
> his beard, took one last look at the ocean, then stepped back and closed the
> hatch.[28]

This salvation is thoroughly secular, despite the overtly spiritual setting. Not
only is this clear in the fact that *Canticle* begins and ends with an Armageddon — surely the antithesis of the "creation → new creation" dynamic of

classic apocalypticism — but in every episode Miller concentrates on the human qualities of his characters, not the spiritual meaning. The five slivers of glass embedded in the body of Mrs. Grales might resemble the stigmata, but, as David Seed perceptively observes, "there is no warrant for reading them as spiritual metaphor rather than metonymy."[29] And if the first and final Armageddons of the novel are articulated in biblical terms, it is only by virtue of the nature of its narrators and in the service of the setting of the novel itself. All three of its parts detail the life and times of members of a religious order, whose stories are told in resonant sympathy to the settings in which they unfold.[30]

Whatever its cinematic merits, *The Matrix* contains one of the more limpid articulations of apocalyptic science fiction.[31] The existential dilemma facing its protagonist, Neo, is precisely that of classic apocalypticism. His task, which also powers the movie's locomotive plot, is to identify the hidden clues which, when considered together, disclose that the world in which Neo lives and operates is actually a synthetically generated "matrix": ignorance masking shadow without substance. The true plane of existence, he soon discovers, is a post-apocalyptic one where artificial intelligences have enslaved humans for use as living batteries. Small groups of humans remain free, fighting a war of resistance. The spatial dualism of good versus evil, formulated in terms of this struggle between humans and the artificial intelligences, thus reveals itself a conflict on multiple planes, exactly as we find in ancient apocalypticism.

Neo achieves awareness of the ultimate reality via an intermediary, Morpheus, the captain of the resistance ship, the *Nebuchadnezzar*,[32] who believes Neo to be the one whom the mysterious "oracle" has foretold. Both Morpheus and the oracle fill the role of the mediating angel in classical apocalypses,[33] while Morpheus also serves as a type of John the Baptist *cum* herald. The rest of the *Matrix* follows that odd amalgam of *Romansbildung* and *Königsrückkehr* that characterizes the narrative arcs of fantastic heroes from *Lord of the Rings'* Aragorn through *Dune's* Paul Atreides to *Star Wars'* Luke Skywalker. Neo discovers himself and the nature of the real world, while simultaneously proceeding towards inheriting his future, which for the movie's characters and audience alike has been prophetically adumbrated.

The apocalypticism of *The Matrix* is largely conveyed christologically. It presents itself not only in the prophetic validation of Neo's mission and his miraculous resurrection through its principal female figure, Trinity, but also in its realized eschatology. In classic apocalypticism, spatial and temporal distinctions operate only in the historical age. As such, they are ultimately unreal, and fade as the singularity of creation is reconstituted in the new age. Accordingly, resurrection prior to the eschaton implies a radical breakdown between boundaries or, from a different perspective, indicates that the new age has been partially realized in the present. This is what Jesus's resurrection represents for Paul, whose letters are preserved in the New Testament. In *The Matrix*, Neo's resurrection completes a metamorphosis that permits him to operate in one plane (the Matrix) with the full awareness of the other. Although each crewmember of the *Nebuchadnezzar* has the ability to access the Matrix, only Neo transcends it. Like Jesus, he is the in-breaking hypostasis of one plane into the other. On one level, this ability allows Neo to perceive the Matrix in its true form, which is graphically represented by lines of marine-green computer code falling against a jet background like electronic rain. The resurrected and transfigured Neo is able to perceive the Matrix not as images produced by the code, but as the code itself, and therein defeats the simulacra which are generated by the artificial intelligences. One might even say that he casts out the electronic demons that invade and inhabit humans who live out their lives within the artificial reality of the Matrix. On another level, the culmination of Neo's metamorphosis signals the beginning of what the audience perceives as the abrogation of the *interregnum disruptus* and the reconstitution of an original state, which in this case involves the beginning of the end of the machines (so we must presume, without foreknowledge of the movie's sequels) and the renaissance of humankind. The fact that all these variables are expressed in science-fiction terminology is unimportant to the issue of their apocalyptic qualities. What is significant is that, despite the overtly apocalyptic tenor of *The Matrix* and the quasi-spiritual nature of the "oracle," they are entirely secular.

No doubt other literary and cinematic examples of apocalyptic science fiction would illustrate the full spectrum of its manifestations.[34] For the purpose of this paper, however, it is necessary to revisit the SBL definition of apocalypse, specifically regarding the issues of pseudonymity and fiction. From the modern standpoint, unless one clings to the conservative view that Daniel actually lived during the Babylonian Exile, or that Adam, Enoch, Moses, Baruch, and Ezra wrote the apocalyptic literature ascribed to them, ancient apocalypses attributed to Daniel and other biblical figures are pseudonymous and therefore spurious.[35] Yet this ancient literature was never intended as fiction, nor, for most of the past two millennia, was it received as fiction. The book of Daniel was assembled for a community who believed that the terrible events it described would come to pass. Most of its subsequent interpreters, commentators, and readers believed this as well. For this reason, issues of pseudonymity and authenticity, while certainly not overlooked by the SBL group, simply did not inform its definition of either genre or worldview.

But if we extend our investigation into the modern period, where secular apocalypticism exists alongside biblical apocalypticism, then we must acknowledge this unstated assumption in the definition: ancient apocalyptic literature is *non-fiction*.[36] Apocalyptic science fiction, on the other hand, is *fiction*. It exhibits the qualities of all three constituents of its title: *apocalyptic*, *science*, and *fiction*, with *secular* understood. Moreover, its forms bear the hallmarks of mercantile consumerism and authorial professionalism, motivations that do not precisely overlap their pre-modern counterparts. For example, most impending- and post-apocalyptic motion pictures and anime are created principally for financial purposes. Put plainly, the setting sells. Accordingly, both *The Matrix* and *Neon Genesis Evangelion* contain endless combat scenes that appear designed chiefly to attract the adolescent dollar. Moreover, whereas the prime motivation of both biblical and secular apocalypticism is to transmit information about a transcendent reality,[37] only in the former does the audience actually believe this reality to exist. The literary or cinematic examples of secular apocalypticism are regarded as fictional or, in their more sublime illustrations, allegorical or metaphorical.[38] The distinction is between expectation and extrapolation.[39]

There are two special types of literature which are related to apocalyptic science fiction but which are neither fictional nor secular. As with exceptions in general, each helps define the category by delineating its boundaries.

The first exceptional type is science-fictional apocalypticism, or modern-day biblical apocalyptic literature whose ancient variables (but not the axioms) have been recalibrated in terms of pseudo-science, and whose overall tenor is science-fictional. A textbook example is the theology of the Heaven's Gate, the new religious movement that became infamous for its March 1997 mass suicide at Rancho Santa Fe, California.[40] The movement's leaders, Bonnie Lu Nettles and Marshall Herff Applewhite (a.k.a. "Peep" and "Bo"; also "Ti" and "Do"), saw themselves as intermediaries of the revelation of a hidden transcendent reality. Like Jesus, who 2000 years ago had been dispatched to earth at God's behest in order to reveal the truth about the impending advent of the Kingdom of Heaven, Nettles and Applewhite preached the imminent end of the world, the result of divine dissatisfaction with, as they saw it, the weeds that were choking Garden Earth.

Unlike Jesus's message, though, their revelation had an extra, science-fictional stratum. Heaven's Gate theology held that terms like "God" and "Heaven" were merely labels that had been imposed on the evidence, principally by the ancient Gospel writers, who could not help but tell the story of Jesus in scriptural terms. The reality was that God and Jesus were highly evolved aliens, and that the "Kingdom of Heaven" was their plane of existence, properly known as the Evolutionary Level above Human. So whereas, for example, the evangelists recorded Jesus' baptism, whereupon he was filled by the descending Holy Spirit (Mark 1:10–11 par.), what had actually occurred was that an alien, functioning as the leader of a *Star Trek*-like "away mission" to Earth, arrived on the planet to inhabit the body of the adult Jesus, which had been specially prepared for it. The alien's revelation — the "good news"— was that Earth's inhabitants must evolve beyond their mammalian limitations in order to progress to the next Evolutionary Level. The mission's success was thwarted by evil space aliens known as Luciferians.

Two millennia later, the message still unheeded, the members of Heaven's Gate received their special revelation. This set the stage for the 1997 suicide, precipitated by the discovery of the comet Hale-Bopp. The group members believed that their souls, liberated from their bodily prisons at the proper moment, would embark on a spacecraft that was traveling behind the comet. The craft, piloted by Nettles (who had predeceased the mass suicide) would then transport their incorporeal selves to the next Evolutionary Level, leaving behind the weed-filled Garden Earth to be ploughed under.

To paraphrase Xenophanes, one horse's god might be one person's horse. From one vantage, the label "science-fictional apocalypticism" applies to many religions. But we are assaying Heaven's Gate theology in its modern, secular contexts, wherein the vast majority of persons in the West, religious or otherwise, would regard it as science fiction. Heaven's Gate is not special in its theological blending of biblical apocalypticism and modern scientific terminology and paradigms.[41] More nebulous still is what Tom Doyle designates "Christian apocalyptic fiction,"[42] which includes Christian millenarian novels such as *Left Behind* (1995) and its multiple sequels. Even if they read such works as fiction, many Christians, I suspect, are in general agreement that signs and portents will precede the return of Jesus, as the New Testament proclaims.

The second exceptional type of literature is represented by Philip K. Dick's novel, *VALIS* (1981). Dick was obsessed with issues surrounding human identity, authenticity, and artificiality. Since he normally framed these issues in religious terms, his writing is often considered to be apocalyptic.[43] Yet, other than a few post-apocalyptic novels like *The Penultimate Truth* (1964) and *Dr. Bloodmoney* (1965), and of course *VALIS*, his science fiction is better classified as "dualistic," despite the recurrent presence of typically apocalyptic motifs and, at times, their ideological axioms.

Dick's early fiction is colored by his experimentation with various models of dualistic thought. An extreme illustration is *The Cosmic Puppets* (1957), which, perhaps unique in the annals of science fiction, employs the full-blown dualism and overt terminology of Zoroastrianism. More moderate in tenor is *The Man in the High Castle* (1962), whose dualistic inclinations are, strangely enough, filtered through the Chinese oracular compendium, the *I Ching*.[44] In contrast, the novels of Dick's middle period, including those for which he is best known, are typified by an internalization of his thoughts and the gradual development of a personal philosophy. In *Martian Time-Slip* (1964), *The Three Stigmata of Palmer Eldritch* (1964), *Do Androids Dream of Electric Sheep?* (1968), and *Ubik* (1969), Dick is more confident in his own reflections concerning the paradoxically dualistic nature of existence, rather than awkwardly framing his ideas through external models like Zoroastrianism. Although he never ceased experimenting with new ways of appreciating the problem, his own views came to dominate his writing, the examples of which are increasingly underpinned by an extensive (if superficial) knowledge of the world's religions and philosophies, both mainstream and esoteric.

By his later novels, Dick had settled on classical gnosticism[45] to explain what by now was a complicated personal theology.[46] The culmination of this process was the so-called *VALIS* trilogy, which includes *The Divine Invasion* (1981) and *The Transmigration of Timothy Archer* (1982). *VALIS*, though, is by far the best of the three novels, and in my opinion stands as Dick's masterpiece. It relates the psychological breakdown of its protagonist, Horselover Fat, and his subsequent attempt to understand its causes. A narcotics user, Fat suffers from mental illness (or at least thinks he does, having been institutionalized after a suicide attempt), and claims to have repeatedly received otherworldly information transmitted directly into his brain from an extraterrestrial entity named "Zebra." In his quest to understand these phenomena, which are interrelated, Fat touches on nearly every meaningful question of human existence. He also begins composing a long "Exegesis," whose synopsis appears as an appendix to the novel.

At a critical point in the novel, Fat and a few friends, one of whom is Philip K. Dick, watch a motion picture called *VALIS*. The title is an acronym for Vast Active Living Intelligence System, an orbital satellite that transmits information to persons on Earth. VALIS also plays a role in the struggle to overthrow the U.S. President, Ferris Fremount, a thinly disguised Richard M. Nixon. Fat and the others soon realize that Zebra and VALIS are identical. They contact the filmmakers, who are either cognizant of VALIS' true nature or barking mad, and meet their young daughter, Sophia (Greek for "wisdom"), the living oracle of VALIS. The meeting with Sophia represents the climax of Fat's intellectual quest. The novel ends with a report of her death, prompting Fat to leave his friends to travel the world, seeking the next incarnation of the oracle.

As with apocalypticism, gnosticism exhibits modern manifestations which, while having their antecedents in the ancient forms, are distinctively secular.[47] Dick, however, was interested in its ancient Christian variety, which he knew principally through English translations of the Nag Hammadi texts. The systematic theology of *VALIS*—highly personalized and culturally updated — contains key elements of both classic gnosticism and apocalypticism. The plot of *VALIS* involves the protagonist's first recognition of and then attempt to understand a higher-order and hidden reality which both influences his life and structures his phenomenological world. This is the existential dimension of apocalypticism as it appears in all its forms. In most of his other novels, Dick focuses on the recognition of *gnosis*, or knowledge, and less on a millenarian emphasis on the end of the world and its attendant eschatological demands. This in turn indicated a more mystical destination to his protagonists' journeys.

In *VALIS*, though, the mysticism is less evident, even if it is clear, through its manifold references to Gnostic Christian terminology of late antiquity, that classical gnosticism remained Dick's principle theological lens. In its place is an ontological dualism that is closer to the spatial dimension of classic apocalypticism, more so than that which appears in any other of his novels. Like Neo in *The Matrix*, Horselover Fat is able to perceive both worlds, although unlike Neo, he is neither hero nor savior; this role is accorded to Sophia. Furthermore, in its startling claim that time ceased in the year 70 and resumed only in 1974, *VALIS* demonstrates the temporal dimension of the apocalyptic worldview, which posits the existence of the *interregnum disruptus* and the expectation of its impending abrogation.

Dick tells the story of *VALIS* in the first person. Its narrative transpires over several years, during which Horselover Fat's ideas on reality and existence coalesce. What emerges from this process is *VALIS* itself: a theologically substantive, fully modernized, internally consistent, and thoroughly insane version of early Christian Gnosticism. It is also autobiographical. Philip K. Dick *is* Horselover Fat: not only is he a character in his own novel, he is *two* characters, "horselover" being a translation of the Greek *philhippos*, and *Dick* the German for "fat." This existential dualism also has a parallel in time and space: Dick/Fat believed that he was simultaneously a Gnostic Christian during the Roman Empire and a science-fiction writer in 1970s California. Like Fat, Dick suffered a mental breakdown, attempted suicide, and believed that an extraterrestrial entity was beaming coherent information into his brain. Dick, too, was obsessed about the nature of reality, particularly its binary aspects, and in his attempts to understand the tension between his inner life and the outside world wrote a million-word "Exegesis," out of which precipitated the systematic theology of the novel. *VALIS* therefore falls outside the pale of apocalyptic science fiction because, like the theology of groups like Heaven's Gate or that of the *Left Behind* novels, it is not fiction, at least in the normal sense of the word. Instead, it, too, is science fictional apocalypticism, but *deliberately* disguised as science fiction, in contrast to these other theologies.

In conclusion, the multi-form nature of contemporary apocalypticism, which in part reflects the secularization of the ideology in modern times, has given rise to methodological problems that have hindered its scientific investigation. Apocalyptic science fiction is no exception. This paper has attempted to study the literature from a proper taxonomical basis, and has proceeded from the ideological foundations of the worldview rather than typical secondary elements such as settings, motifs, or vocabulary. The paper's observations, necessarily abbreviated in places, are intended as a prolegomenon to a series of future studies, including one on apocalyptic anime[48] and another on Philip K. Dick's post–1974 novels.[49]

NOTES

1. Research for this paper was supported by 2005–2008 and 2008–2011 Research Grants from the Social Sciences and Humanities Research Council of Canada, and by a 2007–2008 FAS Grant from Concordia University. I am indebted to Andrea Lobel, doctoral candidate in Religion, for her assistance in identifying and obtaining secondary sources.

2. Florentino García Martínez, "Is Jewish Apocalyptic the Mother of Christian Theology?" W.G.E. Watson, trans. from the Spanish original (1991), in *Qumranica minora I: Qumran Origins and Apocalypticism* (Leiden: Brill, 2007) 129–151 at 146.

3. John J. Collins, *The Apocalyptic Imagination: An Introduction to Jewish Apocalyptic Literature* (Grand Rapids, MI: Eerdmans, 1998) 1–42 (for a history of research), and 4–5 (for the definition of the genre).

4. See, among others, John J. Collins, "Apocalyptic Eschatology in the Ancient World," in *The Oxford Handbook of Eschatology*, Jerry L. Walls, ed. (Oxford, UK: Oxford University Press, 2008) 40–55 at 47, and Lorenzo DiTommaso, "Apocalypses and Apocalypticism. III. Judaism," forthcoming in the *Encyclopedia of the Bible and Its Reception*, 30 vols., H.-J. Klauck, Bernard McGinn, et al., eds. (Berlin, New York: W. de Gruyter).

5. A welcome exception is Robert M. Geraci, "Apocalyptic AI: Religion and the Promise of Artificial Intelligence," *Journal of the American Academy of Religion* 76 (2008): 138–166, which traces the ancient antecedents of modern thinking about AIs. However, his view that "the victory of good over evil is not necessary in apocalypticism" (160) finds little support in the ancient and medieval apocalyptic texts (see also n. 4, above, and n. 24, below).

6. David Ketterer, *New Worlds for Old: The Apocalyptic Imagination, Science Fiction, and American Literature* (Bloomington and London: Indiana University Press, 1974).

7. Andrew Greeley, "Varieties of Apocalypse in Science Fiction," *Journal of American Culture* 2 (1979): 279–287.

8. See Alistair Fowler, "The Life and Death of Literary Forms," *New Literary History* 2 (1971): 199–216, and, more recently, Wai Chee Dimock, "Introduction: Genres as Fields of Knowledge," and Stephen Owen, "Genres in Motion," *Publications of the Modern Language Association* 122 (2007): 1377–1388 and 1389–1393.

9. Apocalypticism also assumes several consequential propositions; see Lorenzo DiTommaso, *From Antiquity to Armageddon. The Architecture of Apocalypticism*, forthcoming from Oxford University Press.

10. One of the finest essays on time in modern apocalyptic literature is Stephen R.L. Clark, "The End of the Ages," in *Imagining Apocalypse: Studies in Cultural Crisis*, David Seed, ed. (New York: St. Martin's, 2000) 27–44.

11. See Bernard McGinn, *Visions of the End: Apocalyptic Traditions in the Middle Ages* (New York: Columbia University Press, 1998 [orig. 1979]).

12. I will address this issue in *From Antiquity to Armageddon*. Valuable early studies include Eric Hobsbawm's *Primitive Rebels* (Manchester, 1959), and Frank Kermode's classic *The Sense of an Ending* (Oxford, UK: Oxford University Press, 2000 [orig. 1967]). Many post–9/11 works attempt to trace the trajectories from ancient apocalypticism to modern political thought. A more successful example is John Gray's *Black Mass: Apocalyptic Religion and the Death of Utopia* (New York: Random House, 2007), particularly in his synopsis of the forces and figures that have shaped contemporary neo-conservativism in the United States. Cf. Catherine Keller, *God and Power: Counter-Apocalyptic Journeys* (Minneapolis, MN: Fortress, 2005); her examination of the apocalyptic basis of neo-conservativism is less nuanced than Gray's, however.

13. Cseslaw Milosz, "Science Fiction and the Coming of the Antichrist," in *Emperor of the Earth. Modes of Eccentric Vision* (Berkeley: University of California Press, 1977) 15–31 at 19–20.

14. On the ecological dimension of apocalyptic science fiction, see Ernest J. Yanarella, "Critical Political Theory and Apocalyptic Science Fiction," in *The Cross, the Plow and the Skyline* (Parkland, FL: Brown Walker, 2001) 43–76, and Martin Griffiths, "Apocalypse: Its Influence on Society and British SF," *Foundation* 31 (2002): 35–45.

15. Lewis Fried, "A Canticle for Leibowitz: A Song for Benjamin," *Extrapolation* 42 (2001): 362–374. Interestingly, even though it is not apocalyptic per se, a closely related modern analogue of the sharp dualism of the ideology's spatial dimension is the conspiracy theory, especially in its political forms. On conspiracy theories and modern millenarianism, see Michael Barkun's insightful study, *A Culture of Conspiracy: Apocalyptic Visions in Contemporary America* (Berkeley: University of California Press, 2003).

16. In such cases "post-holocaust" or an equivalent term is as appropriate as "post-apocalyptic." See Peter Nicholls, "Holocaust and After," in *The Encyclopedia of Science Fiction* J. Klute and P. Nicholls (New York: St. Martin's, 1993) 581–584.

17. Cormac McCarthy, *The Road* (New York: Vintage, 2006) 21.

18. *Ibid.*, 189.

19. *Ibid.*, 33.

20. *Ibid.*, 77.

21. Michael Chabon, review of *The Road* in *New York Review of Books* 54.2, February 15, 2007.

22. McCarthy, 128–9.

23. *Ibid.*, 279.

24. For this reason post-mortem resurrection is an essential quality of classical apocalypticism.

25. McCarthy, 279.

26. *Ibid.*, 286.

27. Not the Devil, but a Device.

28. Walter M. Miller, Jr., *A Canticle for Leibowitz* (New York: Bantam, 1988) §30, 310.

29. David Seed, "Recycling the Texts of Culture: Walter M. Miller's *A Canticle for Leibowitz*," *Extrapolation* 37 (1996): 257–270 at 264. This lucid essay contains other examples of Miller's inversion of spiritual categories.

30. As Thomas J. Morrissey notes, "the servants of truth in Miller's novel speak the truth insofar as they apprehend it." See "Armageddon from Huxley to Hoban," *Extrapolation* 25 (1984): 197–213 at 207–208.

31. In an insightful study, Elizabeth K. Rosen argues that *The Matrix*, along with its two cinematic sequels and an anime derivative, *The Animatrix*, represents the culmination of two apocalyptic traditions. The first tradition is one where robots or computers

bring on the end of the world. This is an important insight, although it approaches apocalypticism via motif rather than at the axiomatic level. The second tradition "relocates the apocalyptic scenario to an internal landscape" (98), a penetrating observation that also sheds light on the function of the visionary and the vision's effect on his/her intended audience in classic apocalyptic literature. See *Apocalyptic Transformation: Apocalypse and the Modern Imagination* (Lanham: Lexington, 2008).

32. The name's symbolism is obvious upon reading Daniel 4 and recalling Morpheus' retrospective account of human history, especially the point in his story immediately preceding the genesis of the artificial intelligences.

33. The oracle is an information vector passing data about one plane to another, dynamically equivalent to the seer's visions in classical apocalypses.

34. See especially James, "Rewriting the Christian Apocalypse," for many examples, although like many other authorities he approaches the issue principally on the level of theme and motif.

35. The Revelation of John is not pseudonymous, and there are other examples from medieval literature. The issue, while not complicated, falls outside the scope of the present study. On whether the authors of apocalypses actually experienced the visions they describe, see Michael E. Stone, "A Reconsideration of Apocalyptic Visions," *Harvard Theological Review* 96 (2003): 167–180.

36. I have proceeded from "apocalypse" to "apocalyptic literature" without comment. In other studies I describe how the scholarly distinction between these categories detracts from their proper appreciation of the ideology outside the ancient period.

37. The adjective "spiritual" is the key difference: secular apocalypticism also envisions a transcendent reality. But see the following note.

38. Stephen King's novel, *The Stand* (1978, rev. 1990) represents a type of science-fiction apocalypticism located closest to its ancient roots. Set in a world devastated by a biological agent, this long novel, arguably his best, climaxes in a final battle that involves overt supernatural forces, individuals who make a "stand" on good or evil, and a "holy fire" of a final conflagration. King recycles biblical types such as Moses and motifs such as Armageddon in a manner extending beyond the merely secular. See James Egan, "Apocalypticism in the Fiction of Stephen King," *Extrapolation* 25 (1984): 214–227. The supernatural backdrop permits this effect by providing the novel with an underlying philosophical basis, which in turn substitutes for the theology of classical apocalypticism. On the one hand, many persons still believe in supernatural phenomena *per se*. As such, the temporal and spatial dimensions of *The Stand*, which are expressed in the progression towards the final battle and in the novel's radical dualism, find a reception with the audience on a level beyond that of works like *The Road* or *The Matrix*. On the other hand, despite this innate reception, I suspect that neither the author nor the majority of the intended audience believes that *The Stand* describes reality, unlike the Revelation of John.

39. Frederick A. Kreuziger, *Apocalypse and Science Fiction: A Dialectic of Religious and Secular Soteriologies,* AAR Academy Series 40 (Chico, CA: Scholars, 1982) 191–192.

40. The group's theology evolved over the decades. I am greatly synthesizing and harmonizing elements from its mature form, which at one time could be accessed freely on the internet. The literature on Heaven's Gate is extensive. Fine starting-points are John R. Hall, *Apocalypse Observed: Religious Movements and Violence in North America, Europe and Japan* (London, New York: Routledge, 2000) 149–182, and Catherine Wessinger, *How the Millennium Comes Violently: From Jonestown to Heaven's Gate* (New York: Seven Bridges Press, 2000) 229–246. See also the essay in this volume by Benjamin Zeller, "Apocalyptic Thought in UFO Religions."

41. In 1999 I interviewed several post–Waco Branch Davidians, who informed me (and

presented me with literature) that the New Jerusalem that would descend from Heaven at the end of time, as in Revelation 21, was actually a spacecraft on which the chosen would escape the impending doom of the planet.

42. Tom Doyle, "Christian Apocalyptic Fiction, Science Fiction and Technology," in *The End That Does: Art, Science and Millennial Accomplishment,* Cathy Gutierrez and Hillel Schwartz, eds. (London, Oakville: Equinox, 2006) 195–209. See also Edward James, "Rewriting the Christian Apocalypse as a Science-Fictional Event," in *Imagining Apocalypses: Studies in Cultural Crisis,* David Seed, ed. (London: Macmillan, 2000) 45–61.

43. See, most recently, Steven Best and Douglas Kellner, "The Apocalyptic Vision of Philip K. Dick," *Cultural Studies/Critical Methodologies* 3 (2003): 186–202. Their paper does not discuss *VALIS* and has little to do with apocalypticism, being more an examination of Dick as an example of postmodernism.

44. "A *logós* or Two Concerning the *logoz* of Umberto Rossi and Philip K. Dick's *Time Out Of Joint,*" *Extrapolation* 39 (1998): 287–298; "Redemption in Philip K. Dick's *Man in the High Castle,*" *Science Fiction Studies* 26 (1999): 91–119; and "Gnosticism and Dualism in the Early Fiction of Philip K. Dick," *Science Fiction Studies* 28 (2001): 49–65, which is reprinted in *Short Story Criticism. Volume 57: John Cheever, Philip K. Dick, Steven Millhauser, Elizabeth Spenser, Ivan Turgenev,* Janet Witalec, ed. (Detroit: Gale, 2003) 126–136.

45. Like apocalypticism, gnosticism is currently experiencing a re-evaluation of its definition and taxonomy. See M.A. Williams, *Rethinking "Gnosticism": An Argument for Dismantling a Dubious Category* (Princeton: Princeton University Press, 1996), and Karen King, *What Is Gnosticism?* (Cambridge, MA: Belknap, 2003). According to Kreuziger (*Apocalypse and Science Fiction,* 187), both science fiction and apocalyptic literature "are built upon a body of (secret) knowledge and tend toward gnosticism." But the motif of hidden knowledge is by no means present in all science fiction, nor is it limited to the genre.

46. See Michel Desjardins, "Retrofitting Gnosticism: Philip K. Dick and Christian Origins," *Violence, Utopia and the Kingdom of God: Fantasy and Ideology in the Bible,* George Aichele and Tina Pippin, eds. (London, New York: Routledge, 1998) 122–133. The usefulness of the study, however, is hampered by its author's decision to work from feature films such as *Blade Runner,* which have few points of contact with their literary antecedents (in this case *Do Androids Dream of Electric Sheep?*).

47. On gnosticism in the modern world, see Kirsten J. Grimstad, "On Gnostic Modernity and Modern Gnosticisms," *The Modern Revival of Gnosticism and Thomas Mann's Doktor Faustus* (Rochester, NY: Camden House, 2002) 35–91, and the sources she cites.

48. The term "superflat," introduced by the artist Takashi Murakami, signifies the manner in which art, design, and culture in Japan are curiously flattened or compressed. See *Sûpaafuratto/Superflat* (Tokyo: Madra, 2000). It also refers, self-referentially, to the emptiness of contemporary Japanese life, particularly its consumer aspects. It seems to me that "superflat" does very well in explaining the nature and study of modern apocalypticism, and all the more so since the notion developed from and remains intimately associated with anime, especially in its liaison with history and apocalypse. See Noi Sawaragi, "On the Battlefield of 'Superflat': Subculture and Art in Postwar Japan," in *Little Boy: The Arts of Japan's Exploding Subculture,* Takashi Murakami, ed. (New York/New Haven: Japan Society/Yale University Press, 2005) 187–207, and Thomas Looser, "Superflat and the Layers of History in 1990s Japan," in *Mechademia 1: Emerging Worlds of Anime,* Frenchy Lunning, ed. (Minneapolis/London: University of Minnesota Press, 2006) 92–109. Nothing is privileged: super flatness assigns equal value to all elements, which appear in two dimensions rather than three. Modern apocalypticism seems strangely hyper-present, over-

lapping multiple, ultra-fine layers of motifs, themes, and imagery to create the *illusion* of depth. One cannot help but recall Erich Auerbach's view of the peculiar flatness of the Homeric tales, as compared with the biblical stories.

49. Academics have largely neglected the deeper theological aspects of these novels. But see now the fine study by Gabriel Mckee, *Pink Beams of Light from the God in the Gutter: The Science Fictional Religion of Philip K. Dick* (Dallas, TX: University Press of America, 2004).

Works Cited

Barkun, Michael. *A Culture of Conspiracy: Apocalyptic Visions in Contemporary America.* Berkeley: University of California Press, 2003.

Best, Steven, and Douglas Kellner. "The Apocalyptic Vision of Philip K. Dick." *Cultural Studies/Critical Methodologies* 3 (2003): 186–202.

Chabon, Michael. Review of Cormac McCarthy, *The Road. New York Review of Books* 54, no. 2 (February 15, 2007). <http://www.nybooks.com/articles/19856> (November 15, 2008).

Collins, John J. "Apocalyptic Eschatology in the Ancient World" in *The Oxford Handbook of Eschatology.* Jerry L. Walls, ed. Oxford, UK: Oxford University Press, 2008: 40–55.

_____. *The Apocalyptic Imagination: An Introduction to Jewish Apocalyptic Literature.* Grand Rapids, MI: Eerdmans, 1998.

Clark, Stephen R.L. "The End of the Ages" in *Imagining Apocalypse: Studies in Cultural Crisis.* David Seed, ed. New York: St. Martin's, 2000: 27–44.

Desjardins, Michel. "Retrofitting Gnosticism: Philip K. Dick and Christian Origins" in *Violence, Utopia and the Kingdom of God: Fantasy and Ideology in the Bible.* George Aichele and Tina Pippin, eds. London and New York: Routledge, 1998: 122–133.

Dimock, Wai Chee. "Introduction: Genres as Fields of Knowledge." *Publications of the Modern Language Association* 122 (2007): 1377–1388.

DiTommaso, Lorenzo. "Apocalypses and Apocalypticism. III. Judaism" in *The Encyclopedia of the Bible and Its Reception.* H.-J. Klauck, Bernard McGinn et al., eds. Berlin and New York: W. de Gruyter. Forthcoming.

_____. *From Antiquity to Armageddon. The Architecture of Apocalypticism.* New York: Oxford University Press. Forthcoming.

_____. "Gnosticism and Dualism in the Early Fiction of Philip K. Dick." *Science Fiction Studies* 28 (2001): 49–65. Reprinted in *Short Story Criticism. Volume 57: John Cheever, Philip K. Dick, Steven Millhauser, Elizabeth Spenser, Ivan Turgenev.* Janet Witalec, ed. Detroit: Gale Research Corporation, 2003: 126–136.

_____. "A *logós* or Two Concerning the *logoz* of Umberto Rossi and Philip K. Dick's *Time Out Of Joint.*" *Extrapolation* 39 (1998): 287–298.

_____. "Redemption in Philip K. Dick's *Man in the High Castle.*" *Science Fiction Studies* 26 (1999): 91–119.

Doyle, Tom. "Christian Apocalyptic Fiction, Science Fiction and Technology" in *The End That Does: Art, Science and Millennial Accomplishment.* Cathy Gutierrez and Hillel Schwartz, eds. London and Oakville: Equinox, 2006: 195–209.

Egan, James. "Apocalypticism in the Fiction of Stephen King." *Extrapolation* 25 (1984): 214–227.

Fowler, Alistair. "The Life and Death of Literary Forms." *New Literary History* 2 (1971): 199–216.

Fried, Lewis. "A Canticle for Leibowitz: A Song for Benjamin." *Extrapolation* 42 (2001): 362–374.

García Martínez, Florentino. "Is Jewish Apocalyptic the Mother of Christian Theology?"

W.G.E. Watson, trans. *Qumranica minora I: Qumran Origins and Apocalypticism.* Leiden: Brill, 2007: 129–151.

Geraci, Robert M. "Apocalyptic AI: Religion and the Promise of Artificial Intelligence." *Journal of the American Academy of Religion* 76 (2008): 138–166.

Gray, John. *Black Mass: Apocalyptic Religion and the Death of Utopia.* New York: Random House, 2007.

Greeley, Andrew. "Varieties of Apocalypse in Science Fiction." *Journal of American Culture* 2 (1979): 279–287.

Griffiths, Martin. "Apocalypse: Its Influence on Society and British SF." *Foundation* 31 (2002): 35–45.

Grimstad, Kirsten J. *The Modern Revival of Gnosticism and Thomas Mann's* Doktor Faustus. Rochester, NY: Camden House, 2002.

Hall, John R. *Apocalypse Observed: Religious Movements and Violence in North America, Europe and Japan.* London and New York: Routledge, 2000.

Hobsbawm, Eric. *Primitive Rebels.* Manchester, 1959.

James, Edward. "Rewriting the Christian Apocalypse as a Science-Fictional Event" in *Imagining Apocalypses: Studies in Cultural Crisis.* David Seed, ed. London: Macmillan, 2000: 45–61.

Keller, Catherine. *God and Power: Counter-Apocalyptic Journeys.* Minneapolis, MN: Fortress, 2005.

Kermode, Frank. *The Sense of an Ending.* Oxford: Oxford University Press, 2000.

Ketterer, David. *New Worlds for Old: The Apocalyptic Imagination, Science Fiction, and American Literature.* Bloomington and London: Indiana University Press, 1974.

King, Karen. *What Is Gnosticism?* Cambridge, MA: Belknap, 2003.

Kreuziger, Frederick A. *Apocalypse and Science Fiction: A Dialectic of Religious and Secular Soteriologies.* AAR Academy Series 40. Chico, CA: Scholars, 1982.

Looser, Thomas. "Superflat and the Layers of History in 1990s Japan." *Mechademia 1: Emerging Worlds of Anime.* Frenchy Lunning, ed. Minneapolis and London: University of Minnesota Press, 2006: 92–109.

McCarthy, Cormac. *The Road.* New York: Vintage, 2006.

McGinn, Bernard. *Visions of the End: Apocalyptic Traditions in the Middle Ages.* New York: Columbia University Press, 1998.

Mckee, Gabriel. *Pink Beams of Light from the God in the Gutter: The Science Fictional Religion of Philip K. Dick.* Dallas, TX: University Press of America, 2004.

Miller, Walter M., Jr. *A Canticle for Leibowitz.* New York: Bantam, 1988.

Milosz, Cseslaw. *Emperor of the Earth. Modes of Eccentric Vision.* Berkeley: University of California Press, 1977.

Morrissey, Thomas J. "Armageddon from Huxley to Hoban." *Extrapolation* 25 (1984): 197–213.

Murakami, Takashi. *Sûpaafuratto/Superflat.* Tokyo: Madra, 2000.

Nicholls, Peter. "Holocaust and After" in *The Encyclopedia of Science Fiction.* J. Klute and P. Nicholls, eds. New York: St. Martin's, 1993: 581–584.

Owen, Stephen. "Genres in Motion." *Publications of the Modern Language Association* 122 (2007): 1389–1393.

Rosen, Elizabeth K. *Apocalyptic Transformation: Apocalypse and the Modern Imagination.* Lanham: Lexington, 2008.

Sawaragi, Noi. "On the Battlefield of 'Superflat': Subculture and Art in Postwar Japan" in *Little Boy: The Arts of Japan's Exploding Subculture.* Takashi Murakami, ed. New York and New Haven, CT: Japan Society and Yale University Press, 2005: 187–207.

Seed, David. "Recycling the Texts of Culture: Walter M. Miller's *A Canticle for Leibowitz.*" *Extrapolation* 37 (1996): 257–270.

Stone, Michael E. "A Reconsideration of Apocalyptic Visions." *Harvard Theological Review* 96 (2003): 167–180.
Wessinger, Catherine. *How the Millennium Comes Violently: From Jonestown to Heaven's Gate.* New York: Seven Bridges Press, 2000.
Williams, M.A. *Rethinking "Gnosticism": An Argument for Dismantling a Dubious Category.* Princeton, NJ: Princeton University Press, 1996.
Yanarella, Ernest J. *The Cross, the Plow and the Skyline.* Parkland, FL: Brown Walker, 2001.

"A Human Incarnate":
Puritans and Parody in *Good Omens*
Therese-Marie Meyer

Introduction

In 1990, Neil Gaiman, author of *The Sandman*, a serialized graphic novel published under the Vertigo line from DC Comics and which ran from 1988 to 1996, wrote the novel *Good Omens* with Terry Pratchett, of serial humour and *Discworld* fame.[1] *Good Omens* tells of a failed apocalypse. In a bungled-up baby-swapping, the Antichrist, Adam, is placed into the English Young family. He grows up in Lower Tadfield as the head of "Them," a small gang of two boys, Brian and Wensleydale, and a girl, Pepper. After eleven years of competition over the wrong boy, Aziraphale, an angel, and Crowley, a demon, cooperate in a quest for Adam. Their attempt to intercept the apocalypse is foiled by their supernatural superiors. Two human couples also try to uncover the Antichrist while apocalyptic portents are sweeping Britain. Eventually, all participants gather at the Tadfield Airbase for a showdown in which Adam prevents the apocalypse and restores order. This action is framed by a prologue set at the Eastern Gate of Paradise after the Fall, and an epilogue which relates the closures of the various plotlines and ends with a second Fall.

Despite its circulation in paperback for eighteen years and a consequent level of dissemination, as well as the fact that co-authored contemporary novels are rare (which in itself should have alerted critics), *GO* has been passed by as trivial in criticism. If at all, it is only briefly mentioned in studies on apocalyptic writing or the Antichrist. Interestingly, even these few comments disagree. Bernard McGinn considers *GO* an "apocalyptic novel" because of its "comic inversions of Fundamentalist views."[2] T.M. Doyle contradicts McGinn due to "the anti-apocalyptic view" of the novel which is "a much more radical retelling."[3] Johannes Rüster comments on the prologue, and concludes that the novel de-mythologizes its metaphysical agents.[4] As such, it would be a parody though Rüster does not employ the term.[5] Lastly, Brian Murdoch, claims the novel as a "double parody" of Richard Donner's movie

The Omen (1976) and of Salman Rushdie's *The Satanic Verses* (1988).[6] While the parody of *The Omen* is apparent already from the title, the connection with Rushdie's *Satanic Verses* is flimsy.[7] *The Satanic Verses* are based in Islamic traditions; *GO* addresses Christian apocalyptic concepts. Strikingly, the appearance of a Kabbalistic angel (Metatron) and the Islamic Archangel of Death (Azrael) towards the end of *GO* attempts to extend this Christian focus briefly into a more universal reading of apocalyptic narratives of Abrahamic religions. Nonetheless, the novel remains grounded in Christianity.

Such brief treatment fails to do justice to what is a surprisingly complex text (an important *caveat* for anyone who tends to class bestsellers automatically as trivia). *Good Omens* appears to be a palimpsest of Christian apocalyptic traditions, an homage in Gérard Genette's sense of the term, overwriting texts inscribed into the Christian history of Western civilization, and oscillating between admiration, parody, and social satire.[8] Palimpsests by their very nature create an impression of ambiguity when coterminous textual elements unite disparate concepts.[9]

The novel's form combines features of romance and thriller. The plots show various protagonists engaging in quests for salvation and/or love. Conventional paratexts frame the main body of the text.[10] As genre, an apocalypse would call for a "narrative framework, in which a revelation is mediated by an otherworldly being to a human recipient."[11] *Good Omens*, however, is no visionary epiphany. There is a heterodiegetic narrator, omniscient and overt, and variable focalization coupled with ample free indirect discourse. Stylistically, the novel is marked by abrupt changes between plotlines and by jumps in time. Adding narrative technique, plot and some characterization to this stylistic consideration, there is little doubt of the genre. *Good Omens* presents a thriller: fast-paced reading, suspense, and repeated *in medias res* experiences.

Nonetheless, the events *GO* describes — three-and-a-half days' run-up[12] to an apocalypse — largely confirm some apocalyptic expectations while ridiculing others. An apocalypse as text also entails a "transcendental reality which is both temporal, insofar as it envisages eschatological salvation, and spatial, insofar as it involves another, supernatural world."[13] There are metaphysical agents which interact with humans in *GO*, though all events take place on earth.[14] Eschatological salvation, conversely, is postponed and could be questionable, enhancing the playful aspect of the novel. The final twist of the outcome, however, strongly confirms metaphysical agency and represents a transcendental understanding of contemporary reality, which affirms traditional apocalyptic expectations. Thus, the novel combines the formal features of a fantasy thriller with an homage to the apocalypse in its structure and content, re-writing traditions not uncritically, yet in itself featuring a transcendental reality and an apocalyptic ending. Parodic elements are embedded into this background.

The next focus of analysis proceeds along comparatist lines. Having established the apocalyptic structure of the novel, it is necessary to analyze the agents that people the action and whose features mingle early Christian, medieval, Puritan, New Age and Evangelical concepts. Adam Young, the Antichrist protagonist, will be briefly exempted from this analysis. He takes centre stage towards the end of the novel, and functions as a *deus-ex-machina* figure, providing closure and restoring order.

Adam will be examined in the third part of this paper, at which point it is argued that the critical "anti-apocalypse" or "parody" verdicts clearly fail to describe *GO*. The Antichrist tradition, which the novel uses extensively in the character of Adam, seems to collide with his restorative function in the plot. The ambiguity here resembles that of the novel's structure. A medieval concept (the Antichrist), interacting with the theology of Fall and Redemption, is overlaid with post–Darwinist concerns of the current nature vs. nurture debate. Superficially, the result seems to validate the modern (nurture: human) and dismiss the medieval (nature: demonic), as the Antichrist refuses to fulfil his predetermined role in the apocalyptic scenario. Yet the method and result of his refusal and the epilogue of the novel clarifies a striking return of medieval concepts of the Antichrist as the central metaphysical agent and divine antagonist of an apocalyptic scenario.

The engagement of the readers' sympathy with Adam is of consequence, and the results are deliberately disturbing. The readers are gradually made party to a child Antichrist, whose immanence and power is eventually affirmed, and whose actions will determine the future. In consequence, the epilogue leaves readers to question to what extent their own hypocrisy and nostalgic need for (narrative) order and closure would entail their complicity with an Antichrist in a traditional apocalyptic scenario, which the last sentences of the novel briefly anticipate.

Apocalypse and Allegory in *Good Omens*

Unfashionable as it may seem, it is helpful to contemplate the structure of *GO* with a character chart (fig. 1), as apocalyptical writing "has no room for moral ambiguity, for any shades of grey."[15] In consequence, the binary opposition of divine vs. demonic creates a doubling of figures and the formulaic simplicity of a character chart carries this point very well.

In part, binary oppositions in *GO* function as a splitting between good and bad, and metaphysical characters are accordingly clear-cut apocalyptic

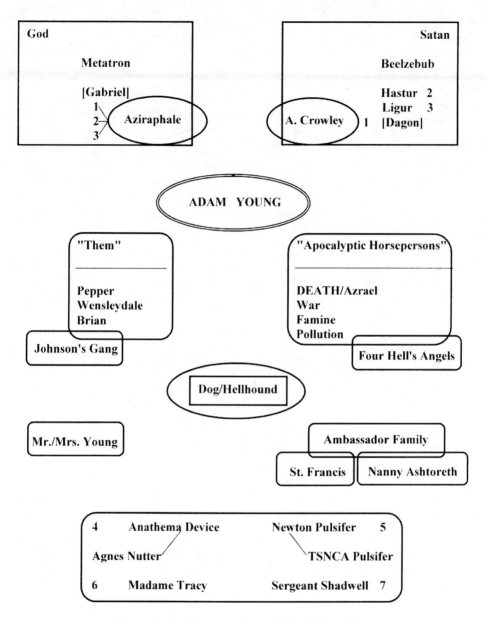

Figure One. Character chart of *Good Omens.*

antagonists. In part however, due to the novel's romance features, binary oppositions provide compatibility, analogy and correspondence (often satirical, and depending on the nature of the figures in question). Human or humanized characters are accordingly more complicated. They show, however, less the shades of grey modern readers would call the co-existence of good and evil within a rounded character. The narrator only once endorses such a shade-of-grey morality:

> It may help to understand human affairs to be clear that most of the great triumphs and tragedies of history are caused, not by people being fundamentally good or fundamentally bad, but by people being fundamentally people.[16]

For instance, Sergeant Shadwell accepts payment for a fictional witchfinder army from either side (demonic and heavenly) and cheats on both.[17] Similarly, Satanists are ridiculed as leading lives of "mild unassuming mediocrity," in which Satanism provides suburban titillation.[18] On a more complex plane, the witch Agnes Nutter, who is harmlessly eccentric throughout, kills her entire village when burnt to death, suicide bomber style:

> There was much subsequent debate as to whether this [explosion] had been sent by God or by Satan, but a note later found in Agnes Nutter's cottage indicated that any divine or devilish intervention had been materially helped by the contents of Agnes's petticoats, wherein she had with some foresight concealed eighty pounds of gunpowder and forty pounds of roofing nails.[19]

There is no immediate evaluation of this otherwise sympathetic character; readers are left to draw their own conclusions. Yet much later, in a dialogue, there is an ironic reply which qualifies Agnes' eulogy as well as her possible idealization by readers: "'What a nice person,' said Newt. 'You could almost overlook her blowing up an entire village.'"[20] Thus, in contrast to *GO*'s otherwise stated need of human characters to assign clear sides, human actions in the novel emerge as having sometimes a share in both. The extremes that humans are also capable of are due to their free will.[21]

Ultimately though, an action's strategic value to the cause of either side (divine, demonic or human) depends not on its agent's intent but on its outcome. This key concept extends from human characters to the two main metaphysical figures, the angel Aziraphale and the demon Crowley, demonstrating their contagion with human features which they acquired by having been involved in human affairs for too long. Aziraphale with best intent gives his flaming sword to Adam and Eve as a defensive weapon — it re-emerges as the attribute of War, and hence allegorically embodies the moral dilemma of defensive aggression.[22] Crowley with worst intent attempts to twist many events into evil, most of which, however, fail to achieve his purpose. Evil intent contributing to divine planning explicitly culminates in theology's *felix culpa*, when original sin leads to the redemption of the world.[23]

As intricate as the moral interaction between agents, intent, action and outcome is, the apocalyptic placing of characters into *pro* and *contra* camps remains to shape the action; the litmus test of a character's moral value is the existence of the Antichrist. Generally, choice of action and its impact are crucial issues to apocalyptic texts:

Apocalyptic symbols are not merely images to be pondered; they are also stimuli to action. Even the earliest apocalypses combined a literal sense of a divinely predetermined plan for history with an insistence on the necessity for choice within history.[24]

Humans thus may embody both good *and* evil while their actions are assignable to good *or* evil (with some bungling up for good comic measure). In the case of the gardener St Francis and Nanny Ashtoreth, this co-existence dwindles to extremes that caricature "Saint" and "Satanist" respectively.[25] In the case of all other human characters, the co-existence is more pronounced, placing the main three human couples into the middle between the opposing forces of good vs. evil ... which is where they belong in an apocalyptic scenario, "civilian casualties either way."[26]

Humanity's moral ambiguity in *GO* confirms the traditional identification of apocalyptic opponents to Christianity as external as well as internal. Dating back to Augustine, the Antichrist is also within any Christians' actions or thoughts against God.[27] This ambiguity extends via "the radical wing of the Reformation"[28] into contemporary Evangelical Millenarianism, where "the Antichrist is conceived of both as an external force that will threaten or attack the 'righteous,' and as something that will come from the righteous themselves, even from the believer's own heart."[29]

As *GO* subscribes to the traditional concept of metaphysical figures' lack of free will, such figures are determined in their antagonism. Aziraphale and Crowley certainly attempt to exert opposing influences upon their own side, infected by long-term contact with humanity.[30] Their intent remains angelic or demonic, however. Despite some shared interest, they remain antagonists.

Looking at the character chart then, there is little left to comment on in the opposition of God vs. Satan. Satan in *GO* is medieval and not biblical. His demons occupy the murky air assigned to them by Peter Lombard's *Sentences* (ca. 1150),[31] as the "hosts of Heaven and Hell, wingtip to wingtip" fill the "crystallized" air above the final showdown: "If you looked really closely, and had been specially trained, you could tell the difference."[32] Satan is also "a Fallen Angel" and, consequently, placed underground in Hell, where demons punish humans in quite the medieval, physical way, for instance by ice-skating over the bodies of their victims.[33] God makes no appearance. Though Providence (or the "ineffable plan,"[34]) is discussed at length, and though Satan once threatens to emerge personally from underground,[35] God remains absent. Even more strikingly, there is no mention of Jesus in the entire text. Adam Young, in keeping with the theology of the Fall and his telling name, yet in clear contrast to his function as Antichrist, faces Death as antagonist.[36]

Instead, God is represented through the Kabbalistic angel Metatron,[37] who opposes Beelzebub as the other metaphysical Second-in-Command.[38] Gabriel is mentioned, and Milton's Dagon has a minor part, but Hastur and Ligur are detailed demonic figures.[39] There are thus more demons than angels at work. The most elaborated opposition is that of the angel Aziraphale and the demon Crowl(e)y, who engage in a quest of the whereabouts of Adam.[40] The quest plot sets Adam firmly at the center of the action. His human foster family remains in the background.

As Death is flanked by the riders of Revelation 6, Adam is flanked by his gang. In the final showdown between these two groups, Adam pits the children in symbolic duels against the apocalyptic Riders. Pepper, a red-head girl, opposes War, a red-head woman, Wensleydale faces down Famine and Brian fights against Pollution, who has replaced Pestilence, who "muttering about penicillin, had retired in 1936."[41] These two groups have a shadowy doubling in Greasy Johnson's Gang in the case of "Them," and a group of four human Hell's Angels in the case of the apocalyptic Riders. Adam, in turn, is flanked by Dog, a hellhound sent for his eleventh birthday by Satan (in reference to *The Omen*). Dog embodies a scholastic conflict echoing Adam's Darwinist own between nature and nurture: his essence (demonic hellhound) struggles against his form (small mutt).

Finally, the most important three human pairs are the modern witch Anathema Device, who is paired with Newton Pulsifer, a weak and unconvinced modern witchfinder. This couple repeats and redeems their respective ancestors: The witch Agnes Nutter, whose "prophecies" feature as embedded parodies of Renaissance prophecies *and* of contemporary attempts at assigning meaning to them,[42] and her murderer, the Witchfinder General Thou-shalt-not-commit-adultery Pulsifer, obviously a blend of the Puritan Nicholas Barebone (in name) and Matthew Hopkins (in profession).[43] Madam Tracy, a.k.a. Marjorie Potts, a middle-aged part-time medium and part-time prostitute, is paired with old Sergeant Shadwell, Newton's superior. In these two contemporary couples (not in Agnes Nutter and her murderer), former hostility in humans towards each other resolves into love, exposing the figures as compatible. Still, even within its human protagonist couples *GO* retains a binary structure essential to an apocalyptic text.

Numbers are significant. Sets of three in *GO* are owed to romance rather than to apocalypse, though, and are connected with the plots, such as the quest for the Antichrist conducted by three pairs of searchers (angel/demon; witch/witchfinder; "painted Jezebel"[44]/witchfinder); or the detailed quest of Aziraphale and Crowley in three steps. Also, the romance's *topos* of the baby exchange involves here three instead of two babies. The Cultural Attaché's child emerges in the course of the novel to have ended up in Lower Tadfield as well: it is Greasy Johnson. His gang shadowing "Them" in the character

chart is as meaningful to the apocalyptic structure of *GO* as Johnson's existence in Tadfield and will be examined below, in the analysis of Adam Young.

In *GO* Adam is additionally surrounded by the seven vices (Pride, Wrath,
Envy, Lust, Sloth, Greed, and Gluttony) countered by the cardinal virtues
(Humility, Patience, Kindness, Chastity, Diligence, Temperance and Abstinence); this is also part of many medieval Antichrist plays.[45] In the character
chart, relevant characters are numbered from one to seven. This explains the
higher number of demons. Aziraphale embodies Humility, Patience and Kindness (virtues one to three).[46] Crowley, on the other hand, embodies Pride.[47]
Hastur's foremost feature is blind Wrath[48] and Ligur is driven by Envy.[49]

In keeping with the more complex characterization of humans, the two
contemporary human pairs searching for Adam embody both their assigned
vice and to a certain extent its corresponding virtue. Anathema Device
("church-banned vice") is connected to Lust as well as Chastity. She certainly
arouses lust in virginal Newton and her sexual behaviour is casual, while she
leads a celibate existence prior to their meeting.[50] Newton Pulsifer in turn
embodies Sloth as well as an obsessive, dysfunctional Diligence.[51] His telling
name connects Isaac Newton and his apocalyptic computations with Lucifer.
This is not merely indicative of the sense of "Lucifer" as "the brightest of all
stars"[52] but also of Newton (the character)'s lack of belief[53] and the corresponding connection between unbelief and a scientific world-view still considered
demonic by fundamentalist Christians.[54] In opposition, Anathema's further
distinguishing feature is her intensity of belief.[55]

Madam Tracy's occultism and prostitution originate in grubby materialism,[56] an indication of Greed. Her lower middle-class, restricted imagination provides Temperance: thrift is the result.[57] Her telling name (Marjorie
Potts) indicates this homely side to her character. Sergeant Shadwell's chain-
smoking and drinking of sweet condensed milk, which has rotted his teeth
to stumps,[58] make him an example of Gluttony, while his austere surroundings, reduced needs and sexual ignorance[59] pronounce his Abstinence. Telling
names and allegorical constellations thus provide further layers of meaning
to *GO*. Some of them are clearly parodic yet they nonetheless function as struc-
turing elements. This, too, is traditional:

> Though some critics have dismissed the apocalypse as replete with puerile
> allegories (and there are certainly many of these), apocalyptic texts are actually
> filled with images that call into question any simplified modern distinction
> between "bad" allegory and "good" symbolism.[60]

The action of *GO* takes place partly in London, where Crowley and Aziraphale live, partly in Lower Tadfield, a fictional rural English community, in
which the Antichrist (the demonic tadpole) is raised. Such a rural English setting for the Antichrist is an enacting of Puritan apocalyptic concepts. Vari-

ous medieval texts already assigned to the Britons a crucial function in apocalyptic events.[61] The English as providentially chosen apocalyptic protagonists
is a subject that echoes through medieval Lollard publications. It was later
extended to an explicit equation of the English with the Israelites by, for
example, the Digger Gerrard Winstanley.[62] British Israelism enjoyed a measure of popularity with the Puritans and well into the Victorian Age.[63] In *GO*,
the narrator comments on the automatic identification of Aziraphale as English
by casual observers,[64] which resonates of Bede's famous anecdote of the
angli/angeli pun by Pope Gregory.[65] While the English-as-Israelites is not
made a topic in *GO*, there is no doubt that the setting affirms Puritan notions
of England's providential centrality to apocalyptic events. Even the Antichrist's
originally intended American foster family stays in London, so the setting
choice the novel suggests is one between London or Tadfield — a division of
urban vs. rural English space. The planned setting for Armaggedon, however,
remains biblical.[66]

The parody of apocalyptic features, by comparison, is social satire directed
at ignorance and narrow-mindedness. *GO* ridicules people's lack of religious
knowledge, for instance in their inability to recognize apocalyptic portents,[67]
or conversely their narrow-minded fundamentalism.[68] Human mediocrity
and banality again and again provide comic deflation. Materialism is also sat-
irized in attempts at making money from apocalyptic fears by publishers,[69]
Christian fundamentalists,[70] or New Age and ecological conspiracy theorists.[71]
In turn, these apocalyptic fears emerge as ubiquitous. The contemporary
occupations of the four apocalyptic Riders justify these fears. War,[72] Famine
(orchestrating the dieting craze, anorexia and junk food) and Pollution (the
ecological equivalent of Pestilence) are as omnipresent as Death, and though
their personas ride motorbikes, their attributes are biblical. Contemporary
reality in *GO* is of itself apocalyptic.

The placement of the four Riders on the side of the demonic is an interesting point. In Revelation 6:2–8, they embody heaven-sent tribulations. Revelation 6:8 stresses, however, that Death is followed by Hell in his destructive
ride, and *GO's* War, Famine and Pestilence hyperbolically declare themselves
the original Hell's Angels.[73] Yet Death's riders, though clearly evil-minded,
are embodiments of man-made misery.[74] *GO* departs much further than the
satirical from traditional apocalypse in its categorical distinction of these
figures from Death. Death is actually an angel (Azrael), while the other riders are part of "the minds of men."[75] Azrael and Metatron declare the world
a divine creation, a Christian prerequisite to any apocalyptic scenario. However, Azrael also declares his own creation as "creation's shadow," thus not as
the result of a first Fall but as part of "normal entropy"[76] and inherent to existence. As the allegory of Adam Young's name and his function as antagonist

to Death relies on the theology of the Fall, *GO* here presents an incongruity in its world-view. A conflict between a largely affirmative depiction of Christian apocalyptic and theological concepts and what is, at bottom, a scientific world-view (in which death is indeed the expression of entropy) can be traced in the figure of Death/Azrael.

Angels, Demons, Humans

Good Omens is even closer to Christian theology in its depiction of categorical differences. As has been mentioned in the context of Satan, angels and demons in *GO* share an immortal nature. While their rebellion, which features briefly in *GO*,[77] is traditional and not in the Bible,[78] their grouping into hierarchies, with an inclination to the bureaucratic,[79] is biblical. Crowley's inferiority in status may be the reason for his grumbling compliance with Aziraphale's demands[80]; then again, in a passage echoed once by the narrator, Aziraphale lectures Crowley in theology:

> "You see, evil always contains the seeds of its own destruction," said the angel. "It is ultimately negative, and therefore encompasses its downfall even at its moments of apparent triumph. No matter how grandiose, how well-planned, how apparently foolproof an evil plan, the inherent sinfulness will by definition rebound upon its instigators. No matter how apparently successful it may seem upon the way, at the end it will wreck itself. It will founder upon the rocks of iniquity and sink headfirst to vanish without a trace into the seas of oblivion."[81]

Naturally, as a demon, Crowley does not agree; yet he remains subject to Aziraphale's wishes. It may appear part of a satire on (angelic/demonic) bureaucracy that both Aziraphale and Crowley shift within their respective hierarchies. Aziraphale is a Cherubim in the prologue[82]; next, he is a demoted Principality.[83] Crowley starts out as serpent in the prologue in keeping with Genesis,[84] but receives commendations for his involvement in human affairs (such as his invention of Welsh-language television).[85] This involvement as well as the application of career paths to metaphysical entities seems hyperbolic and in consequence satirical. Yet it is firmly part of Christian traditions and connects very disparate groups, from early apocryphal Christianity and medieval legends[86] to (scholastic) theology[87] and including contemporary Evangelicalism.[88]

A blend of a specifically Miltonian understanding of angels/demons with wider Puritan concepts can be found in *GO*'s depiction of angelic bodies. In opposition to Catholic theology's claim for the spiritual nature of angelic beings some reformed and Puritan definitions stressed their corporeal nature, making them capable of sensual actions.[89] *GO* depicts angelic beings eating or drinking.[90] Milton especially insisted on a difference between an angelic body's appearance as human and its genuine shape, a concept *GO* applies extensively to both demons and angels.[91]

According to Thomas Aquinas, the intellect of angels and thus also of demons is superior to humans,[92] a point that narrative commentary in *GO* as well as plot developmentonly conditionally assert.[93] Technology, namely, is problematic and the resulting limitations in knowledge evinced by demons and angels alike confirm Milton over Aquinas.

> In this, Milton departed from the common seventeenth-century notion that angels were endowed with "an intuitive knowledge that transcends man's bondage to 'discoursive reason.'" In *De Doctrina*, Milton was to observe that even the "good angels do not see into all God's thoughts," and further, that there "are many things of which they are ignorant."[94]

Thus, Metatron himself does not know God's ultimate plan.[95] Satan's fall results in restrictions in demonic power as well as nature. Demons are destroyed by holy water, and they hate, distrust and despise each other to the point of paranoia.[96] Though Satan is God's adversary, he is not his equal — *GO* is not a Manichaean apocalypse. Every demonic action, including temptations,[97] is "part of the ineffable divine plan."[98]

The foremost human feature, as stated above, is free will, but humans struggle with determining forces. Genetics determines Anathema's mental similarity to Agnes Nutter as well as Newton's similarity to T. Pulsifer, and the closure to their plotline adds Newton's assertion of individuality against descent to the happy ending of romance.[99] He means their love to prove their individuality in *not* repeating their ancestors' actions. However, as humans in *GO* are pathetically deluded in the importance of their actions,[100] Newton's assertion has to be taken with a grain of salt: In general, events are providential (and not simply fated[101]) and this includes Newton and Anathema's meeting and coupling.

The human propensity for belief, another important feature of human characters in *GO*, is restricted by their limited understanding. People cling to prophecy, astrology,[102] New Age beliefs[103] and occultism,[104] all of which *GO* mercilessly ridicules: "Offer people a new creed with a costume and their hearts and minds will follow."[105] On the battleground of Armaggedon, humans are pawns in a cosmic game. Though choice and action are important for humans in *GO*, and despite their defining characteristic of free will, only Adam can claim full freedom of choice and only his actions avert the apocalypse.

> "Of course I have to take sides," said Pepper. "Everyone has to take sides in *something*." Adam appeared to reach a decision. "Yes. But I reckon you can make your own side."[106]

Then again, the Antichrist is not just human.

Adam, Old and New

In the context of the Fall, Adam Young's name, nature and function are of cosmic importance. In a tell-tale comment by a Tadfield old lady: "That young Adam's full of the Old Adam."[107] *GO* dramatizes here concepts that, though not biblical, are at the very heart of Christian apocalypse and redemption theology:

> If the origin of evil is to be explained on the basis of the Fall of the First Adam, and salvation is made available through the New Adam who is Jesus Christ, then final victory (that is, ultimate salvation) will not be achieved until the defeat of that last and most evil Adam, Antichrist. Given the anthropological nature of the central Christian myth of evil, Antichrist is as necessary to it as Adam and Christ.[108]

Naming the Antichrist "Adam" connects Adam's demonic (Anti-Christ) function with his representative function towards humanity.[109] As a child he has no Eve nor does he need one yet.[110] Growing up incognito, he may embody the hidden "mystery of iniquity" of 2 Thess. 2:7. Until his coming into his powers, he cannot be recognized by metaphysical figures or human reason.[111] He is revealed at the age of eleven, the number of iniquity (twelve minus one), at three o'clock in the afternoon (the hour of Jesus' death) by the manifestation of the hellhound. In reference to Revelation 13:8's "number of a man," his (phone) number, which identifies him to Aziraphale, is Tadfield 666.[112]

Adam's nature is kept deliberately ambiguous[113] yet the text provides clues. He is delivered to Crowley at midnight, apparently newly-born, but his origins are left obscure.[114] As "the Devil's child"[115] he has uncanny faculties; his screaming, for example, is

> a sound that a mere mortal should not have been able to utter. [...] It resounded around the universe, which is a good deal smaller than physicists would believe. It rattled the celestial spheres.[116]

All of this indicates a demonic incarnation, as does Adam's appearance. As a baby Adam looks "ominously normal." And, as an eleven-year old, he is "like a prepubescent Greek god. Or maybe a Biblical illustration, one which showed muscular angels doing some righteous smiting. It was a face that didn't belong in the twentieth century. It was thatched with golden curls that glowed. Michelangelo should have sculpted it."[117] Further attesting to his demonic identity, Adam performs miracles unconsciously, while sleeping or simply by imagining reality: he "warp[s] the world around him to his own desires, shaping it in his own image."[118]

His demonic nature is positioned against a human upbringing. This conflict of nature versus nurture is probably his most human feature. His two other human faculties, aura and belief, are so intensified they are superhuman.[119] His characterization (verbal style, implied situational understanding) is that of a child while his maturity of action in the showdown is again superhuman. Some features thus point towards Adam's other function as "a *human incarnate*,"[120] as the representative embodiment of humanity's strengths and dilemmas, while others focus on his superhuman nature. Discussing Adam's specific nature versus nurture situation, Crowley mixes scientific and theological argument:

> "Hey, if you're going to go on about genetics, you might as well say the kid will grow up to be an angel. After all, his father was really big in Heaven in the old days. Saying he'll grow up to be a demon just because his father *became* one is like saying a mouse with its tail cut off will give birth to tail-less mice. No. Upbringing is everything."[121]

This is Crowley, of course, at his most demonic, tempting Aziraphale into action — are we as readers to trust the "old serpent" and assume, as all witnesses to the showdown do, that Adam's human upbringing has successfully fought his demonic nature?[122] There'd be no need then for the epilogue; *GO* would break with its former theological consistency, and be an anti-apocalypse indeed.

Not so. Three clues point towards the epilogue's surprising conclusion of this question. The first clue is Warlock, the Young's baby mistaken for the Antichrist. Hyperbolically close monitoring by Heaven and Hell[123] cannot change his being at bottom "too bloody *normal*," to quote again Crowley.[124] No matter how intense the nurture, it cannot transform a categorically different nature.

The second clue is the list of actions of the Antichrist. Adam's effect on Tadfield, apprehended by both Aziraphale and Anathema, is love — crucially.[125] How could love be suspicious? The results of this superhuman love are Tadfield's "superb" rural landscape, its climate of picture-book perfection, and its "rural changelessness"[126]: Adam's childhood closely reproduces Richmal Crompton's *Just William* (1922–70) series.[127] At heart, *GO*'s Antichrist is conservative, even nostalgic.

Yet Adam's miraculous actions (conscious or unconscious) correspond to traditional Antichrist expectations. He has a natural affinity to occultism, though his understanding of it is limited by his age.[128] He produces warped miracles.[129] He consciously draws the four apocalyptic Riders towards Tadfield, and is the node connecting all plots.[130] In fact, even his attractiveness is traditional. In Wynkyn de Worde's Humanist Antichrist pamphlet, for instance,

[...] the Antichrist appears a most charming fellow. He is the ideal student, a model young man, so selfless he gives away all his possessions to the poor; everyone adores him, especially the religious. [...] Upon reaching adulthood, unexpectedly, the Antichrist reveals his true colours.[131]

De Worde's Antichrist is written to suit Renaissance readers; *GO*'s Antichrist must charm modern readers, who nostalgically sigh for Crompton's boyhood of milk-crate meetings, gangs whose offences consist in stealing fruit or ringing at doorbells, and a rural idyll. Yes, Adam divides the earth amongst his friends,[132] yet for himself, he only wants Tadfield and the continuation of his childhood. This is his moment of crisis: the realization that he cannot have both, his childhood and the apocalypse.[133]

The apocalypse is averted not for higher reasons but for selfish ones — because Adam changes reality to maintain Tadfield and his friends.[134] In contrast to the narrator's final call for reader empathy with an imagined "summer that never ends,"[135] Adam does *not* imagine his childhood summer to be perpetual but is willing to seize the day regardless. This is his chosen third side in the conflict: "calculated innocence."[136] At no point does it fully change his nature, on the contrary, "possibly more of Adam Young than there had ever been before" results from his crisis.[137] By putting his resolution into action, Adam comes into his own. In the epilogue Adam steals apples from a primordial tree, "with the speed of a striking cobra."[138] Only the readers (and perhaps God?) witness this second fall closing the novel's frame. The apples are green. The real Fall, the harvest, and Adam's adulthood are still in the future. In his hands, however, they transform into "tart and perfect" fruit.

In the final pages, the closures provided suggest Adam's childish influence in restoring cosmic order; Adam has become "the power that [is] controlling the fate of all mankind."[139] He also changes reality at whim (as an alibi, displaying a charmingly simple hypocrisy, 381). *GO* thus ends with Adam installed as World Ruler,[140] and as he wipes the minds of the human witnesses to the events in Tadfield he is, indeed, now the fully-fledged "mystery of iniquity" at work (2 Thess. 2:7).[141]

At this point we touch upon the possible explanation of God's and Jesus' absence in the apocalypse of *GO*. Should this Antichrist be just the first one of the two envisaged by Joachim of Fiore, or should this failed apocalypse be just one of the many typological apocalypses then neither God's nor Jesus' personal involvement would be necessary yet.[142] The *Dramatis Personae* actually lists Adam as "an Antichrist," not as "the Antichrist."[143] As the reference to Yeats' "Second Coming" in the last lines of *GO* indicates, the future that Adam slouches towards is his twenty-first birthday in the year 2000 — another apocalypse becomes suddenly possible in the last paragraphs of the novel.[144]

Conclusion: Readers and the Antichrist Within

Yet what is there to dread from an endearingly nostalgic child? Undoubtedly, Adam has the full sympathies of his readers in his preference of apple stealing over Armaggedon. At the end of *GO*, we are prepared to smile benignly at his selfish changes of reality. He just cannot resist improving things to what he believes the better, despite his former avowal not to do so.[145] Putting it less nicely, Adam does not keep his word and is a very endearing, thoroughly selfish hypocrite.[146] He is, in short, an Antichrist, yet the *Dramatis Personae* did not specify whether readers will witness a *ludus de Antichristo* or a *ludus Antichristi*.

This brings us to the last clue of the three. There is one other moment apart from the epilogue in which the narrator calls for emphatic imagination.[147] This address concerns the third baby, Baby B, and it begs readers to imagine an ordinary, happy future for this baby as well (currently at the mercy of Satanists). The ending is significant:

> Possibly, you would like to imagine some children, and a hobby — restoring vintage motorcycles, perhaps, or breeding tropical fish. / You don't want to know what *could* happen to Baby B. / We like your version better anyway. / He probably wins prizes for his tropical fish.[148]

The style suggests that what readers imagine is simply a result of their own wishful thinking. Later, an annotation on Greasy Johnson links to this metafictional paragraph.

> [Greasy Johnson] was instead secretly devoted to his collection of tropical fish, which won him prizes. Greasy Johnson was the same age as Adam Young, to within a few hours, and his parents had never told him he was adopted. See? You were *right* about the babies.[149]

Johnson's identification with Baby B thus depends on the repetition of a motif (breeding tropical fish), his age, the fact that he is adopted — and his structural function. In a providential, apocalyptical reality, Johnson's leading of the "Johnsonites" vs. "Them" must be significant, as the few flimsy items listed must be indicative of his identity with Baby B. The readers' need for narrative significance and closure supplies the rest. Only by the readers' token is Adam's world rule cutesy, and by the same token, at the end of *GO*, the future to be imagined not that of another apocalypse approaching but of an everlasting summer.

> If you want to imagine the future, imagine a boy and his dog and his friends. And a summer that never ends. / And if you want to imagine the future, imagine a boot ... no, imagine a sneaker, laces trailing, kicking a pebble; [...] imagine a figure, half angel, half devil, all human....[150]

The syntax quotes Orwell's *1984*, yet the readers are asked to dismiss Orwell's "boot stamping on a human face forever"[151] for a much more complacent vision of the future and for a full identification with humanity's new representative, Adam ... an Antichrist. Within a witty and hilarious apocalyptic text, *GO* therefore contains thought-provoking insights into human nature quite in line with the Christian fiction of Chesterton, to whom the novel is dedicated. It needs indeed Baudelaire's and Eliot's "*hypocrite lecteur*" to fully identify with Adam, "*mon semblable, mon frère.*"

NOTES

1. Neil Gaiman and Terry Pratchett, *Good Omens* (London: Corgi, 1991). Referred to in this paper as *GO*.
2. Bernard McGinn, *Antichrist: Two Thousand Years of the Human Fascination with Evil* (New York: Columbia University Press, 2000) 271.
3. T. M. Doyle, "Competing Fictions: The Uses of Christian Apocalyptic Imagery in Contemporary Popular Fictional Works, vol. II: Anti-Apocalyptic Fictions," <http://www.mille.org/publications/ winter2001/Newtwo.pdf> (March 22, 2008) 21.
4. Johannes Rüster, *All-Macht und Raum-Zeit: Gottesbilder in der englischsprachigen Fantasy und Science Fiction*, Erlanger Studien zur Anglistik und Amerikanistik vol. 8 (Berlin: Lit Verlag, 2007) 92.
5. On parody see Beate Müller, *Komische Intertextualität: Die Literarische Parodie* (Trier: Wissenschaftlicher Verlag, 1994); Margaret Rose, *Parody: Ancient, Modern, Postmodern* (Cambridge, UK: Cambridge University Press, 1993).
6. Brian Murdoch, *Adam's Grace: Fall and Redemption in Medieval Literature* (Cambridge, UK: D. S. Brewer, 2000) 9–10.
7. Two characters in *GO* are a demon and an angel. The main protagonists in *The Satanic Verses* are two humans, transformed into metaphysical entities: one Shaitan (a jinn and *not* the Christian Lucifer/Satan), the other Gibreel (an archangel, corresponding to the Christian Gabriel, yet additionally medium of the prophet Muhammad's divine inspiration). Here the similarity ends.
8. Gérard Genette, *Palimpsestes: La littérature au second degré* (Paris: Éditions du Seuil, 1982), esp. chapter xviii.
9. *GO* does not conform to Rose's definition of a post-modern "general parody" (Rose, *Parody*, 47–53). Though the novel partly provides "comic refunctioning" (*ibid.*, 52) and ambivalently implicates structures of its parodied texts, the epilogue reasserts metaphysical reality and apocalyptic expectations.
10. There are a prologue, an epilogue, a parodic title leaf with a list of *Dramatis Personae*, dedications and annotations.
11. Quoted in McGinn, *Antichrist*, 11.
12. For half-of-seven as "an obvious marker of failure and imperfection" in apocalyptic texts, see McGinn, *Antichrist*, 21. The main text is structured into "Wednesday" (3 A.M.) to "Saturday" (night) chapters.
13. Quoted in Doyle, "Competing Fictions," 20.
14. Paradise, the setting of the prologue, is terrestrial (*GO*, 11) as the Middle Ages and the Renaissance believed.
15. McGinn, *Antichrist*, 16.
16. *GO*, 32.
17. *Ibid.*, 181–2.

18. *Ibid.*, 84.

19. *Ibid.*, 195.

20. *Ibid.*, 211.

21. *Ibid.*, 41.

22. *GO*, 10, 51; 357.

23. *Ibid.*, 11.

24. McGinn, *Antichrist*, 278. See also Christopher Rowland, "'Upon Whom the Ends of the Ages Have Come': Apocalyptic Writing and the Interpretation of the New Testament," Malcolm Bull, ed., *Apocalypse Theory and the Ends of the World* (Oxford, UK: Blackwell, 1995) 38–57; esp. 43.

25. *GO*, 67–9. For Ashtoreth as demonic see John Milton, *Paradise Lost*, Christopher Ricks, ed. (London: Penguin Classics, 1968), I.422. The satire of nanny Ashtoreth additionally targets *Mary Poppins* (1964).

26. *GO*, 270.

27. Richard K. Emmerson, *Antichrist in the Middle Ages: A Study of Medieval Apocalypticism, Art, and Literature* (Seattle: University of Washington Press, 1981) 65; L. J. Litaert Peerbolte, *The Antecedents of Antichrist: A Traditio-Historical Study of the Earliest Christian Views on Eschatological Opponents* (Leiden: Brill, 1996) 88, 102–3; McGinn, *Antichrist*, xv–xvi.

28. McGinn, *Antichrist*, xv.

29. Orestis Lindermayer, "Europe as Antichrist: North American Pre-Millenarianism," Stephen Hunt, ed. *Christian Millenarianism: From the Early Church to Waco* (Bloomington: Indiana University Press, 2001) 48.

30. *GO*, 41, 46.

31. Henry Ansgar Kelly, *Satan: A Biography* (Cambridge, UK: Cambridge University Press, 2006) 238.

32. *GO*, 340–1.

33. *Ibid.*, 138, 289.

34. *Ibid.*, 352.

35. *Ibid.*, 356.

36. *Ibid.*, 344.

37. *GO*, 348. *GO* is exact in its depiction of Metatron's functions, cf. Andrei A. Orlov, *The Enoch-Metatron Tradition* (Tübingen: Mohr Siebeck, 2005), but for one detail: his limited knowledge.

38. *GO*, 233, 349. Beelzebub traditionally is Hell's vice-regent. See Milton, *Paradise Lost*, I.79; Christopher Marlowe, "Doctor Faustus," 5.263, M. H. Abrams, Stephen Greenblatt et al., eds. *The Norton Anthology of English Literature: Volume One* (London: Norton, 2000), 1007.

39. *GO*, 78, 107; Milton, *Paradise Lost*, I.462.

40. "Crawley" (*GO*, 9) is a pun on the serpent. The changed spelling targets Aleister Crowley, the self-styled black magus. Crowley's first name "Anthony" anticipates his fight with Hastur and Ligur (*GO*, 244–7), referring to legends of St Anthony the Hermit. Significantly, Aziraphale's is not a telling name nor does he use an alias. Crowley's demonic name is a "complex wiggly sigil" (*GO*, 24).

41. *GO*, 263.

42. See Agnes Nutter's telling surname. "The English edition of Nostradamus' *Centuries* had just gone into its third printing, and five Nostradamuses, all claiming to be the only genuine one, were on triumphant signing tours. [...] 'It is a licence to printe money!' said Master Bilton to Master Scraggs. 'The public are crying out for such rubbishe! We must straightway printe a booke of prophecie by some hagge!'" (*GO*, 52) The satire targets the publication business as well as (Renaissance) credulity and spelling. The histori-

cal *and* contemporary satire is evident also pp. 220 and 300, where dramatic irony over the meaning of Agnes' prophecies is employed to comic effect.

43. *GO*, 167.

44. *GO*, 14. A reference to 1 Kings 16–31 as well as to Rev. 2:20: "that woman Jezebel, which calleth herself a prophetess" (AV).

45. The Beast of Rev. 13, traditionally seen as representing the Antichrist (see McGinn, 51), has seven horns, which were connected by medieval exegesis to the seven vices. See also the essay in this volume by Lisa LeBlanc, "Social Upheaval and the English Doomsday Plays."

46. Aziraphale never takes credit for his good actions, is very patient (e.g. *GO*, 309) and always helpful (e.g. *GO*, 90–2). He is also notoriously optimistic about the possibility of good in others, including within Crowley (*GO*, 105, 347, 357).

47. Crowley's pride is the display of luxury possessions (*GO*, 20, 23, 77, 239–40), which indicate his mastery of technologies other demons are said to be ignorant of (*GO*, 21, 25, 243, 249). He is also very arrogant. The result is vainglory, an egocentric variety of Aziraphale's optimism (*GO*, 295).

48. See his mass murder *GO*, 297.

49. *GO*, 23, 245.

50. *GO*, 221, 283.

51. *GO*, 43–4.

52. Kelly, *Satan*, 167.

53. "Newton Pulsifer had never had a cause in his life. Nor had he, as far as he knew, ever believed in anything. It had been embarrassing, because he quite *wanted* to believe in something, since he recognised that belief was the lifebelt that got most people through the choppy waters of Life" (*GO*, 175).

54. Lindermayer, "Europe as Antichrist," 46.

55. "[Anathema] didn't compartmentalize her beliefs. They were welded into one enormous, seamless belief, compared with which that held by Joan of Arc seemed a mere idle notion" (*GO*, 144).

56. *GO*, 253, 278. Her matter-of-fact occultism echoes of T. S. Eliot's Madam Sosostris in "The Waste Land."

57. *Ibid.*, 290, 376.

58. *Ibid.*, 174–75, 286.

59. *Ibid.*, 252, 282.

60. McGinn, *Antichrist*, 20.

61. For instance Brut's *Register Trefnant*, qtd. in Curtis V. Bostick, *The Antichrist and the Lollards: Apocalypticism in late Medieval and Reformation England* (Leiden: Brill, 1998) 150.

62. Christopher Hill, "Till the Conversion of the Jews," in *Millenarianism and Messianism in English Literature and Thought, 1650–1800,* Richard H. Popkin, ed. (Leiden: Brill, 1988), 12–36; 21.

63. See *ibid.*; also Richard H. Popkin, "Christian Interest and Concerns about Sabbatai Zevi," in *Millenarianism and Messianism in Early Modern European Culture, vol. 1: Jewish Messianism in the Early Modern World*, Matt D. Goldish and Richard H. Popkin, eds. (Dordrecht: Kluwer Academic, 2001) 91–106; 92.

64. *GO*, 160.

65. Bede, *The Ecclesiastical History of the English People,* Judith McClure and Roger Collins, eds. (Oxford, UK: Oxford University Press, 1969) 70.

66. *GO*, 243, 377–8; see Rev. 16:16.

67. *Ibid.*, 271, 310–11, *passim*.

68. Such episodes provide the few explicit parodies of Fundamentalist Christianity in

GO. The disembodied Aziraphale, for example, possesses three humans, all of whom try to fit him (to no avail) into their religious framework: a voodoo healer (*GO,* 265–6), an Australian Aborigine (*GO,* 264), and a television preacher (*GO,* 266–70). In the last case, Aziraphale at length refutes the Rapture, and is promptly considered demonic. Similarly, Shadwell considers Aziraphale demonic for employing kabbalistic conjuring methods and possessing Madam Tracy (*GO,* 287): "He'd seen it all. He'd heard it all. He hadn't understood any of it, but he knew what people did with circles and candlesticks and incense" (*GO,* 236).

69. *GO,* 52.

70. *Ibid.,* 266–7.

71. *Ibid.,* 145, 160, passim.

72. Female War parodies political correctness. She changes in the final showdown, like the other Riders, to "humanoid shapes made up of all the things they were or represented" (*ibid.,* 341).

73. *Ibid.,* 263.

74. *Ibid.,* 62, 64, 186.

75. *Ibid.,* 344.

76. *Ibid.,* 344, 350.

77. *Ibid.,* 373.

78. Kelly, *Satan,* 13.

79. See Harold Bloom, *Omens of Millenium: The Gnosis of Angels, Dreams, and Resurrection* (London: Fourth Estate, 1996) 45. Ephesians 6:12 applies hierarchies to demons as well. Narrative comments stress the contemporary human ignorance of these metaphysical hierarchies in *GO,* 13, 45, *passim.*

80. *Ibid.,* 246.

81. *Ibid.,* 95.

82. *Ibid.,* 9, wielding the flaming sword of Gen 3:24.

83. *Ibid.,* 45, 51.

84. *Ibid.,* 9. On the biblical serpent as a snake and not a demon cf. Kelly, *Satan,* 13, 74–75, 152, 176.

85. *GO,* 19, 41, 23.

86. In the *Vita Adae,* angels function as hands-on helpers. Michael e.g. shows Adam how to till the soil (Murdoch, 24) and advises Eve on breastfeeding (ibid, 36). In the *Golden Legend* of Jacobus de Voragine, the most important medieval anthology and a blockbuster (Kelly mentions forty editions in French alone from 1483 to 1557; see *Satan,* 221), devils are whipped by their superiors if they have been bested by humans (Kelly, *Satan,* 226).

87. Kelly, *Satan,* 239, 243.

88. Martyn Percy, "Whose Time is It Anyway? Evangelicals, the Millennium, and Millenarianism," in *Christian Millenarianism: From the Early Church to Waco,* Stephen Hunt, ed. (Bloomington: Indiana University Press, 2001) 26–38; 35.

89. Kelly, *Satan,* 244 and Leland Ryken, *The Apocalyptic Vision in Paradise Lost* (Ithaca, NY: Cornell University Press, 1970) 134.

90. *GO,* 47, 53, *passim.*

91. Ryken, *The Apocalyptic Vision,* 160 and *GO,* 18, 20, 100, *passim.*

92. Kelly, *Satan,* 244.

93. *GO,* 160, 170–1, 270–1.

94. William Kolbrenner, *Milton's Warring Angels: A Study of Critical Engagements* (Cambridge, UK: Cambridge University Press, 1997) 159–60.

95. *GO,* 353.

96. The fate of Ligur, *ibid.,* 245. "Hastur was paranoid, which was simply a sensible

and well-adjusted reaction to living in Hell, where they really were all out to get you" (*ibid.*, 247).

97. Crowley's temptations consist of asking questions, such as the traditional *unde malum* applied to the Fruit of Knowledge (9–10, 11, 373), which "Tertullian claimed was the kind of thing that made people heretics" (Murdoch, *Adam's Grace*, 23). Adam echoes these demonic arguments (350–1).

98. *GO*, 57.

99. *Ibid.*, 93, 160, 195, 371.

100. The apocalyptic Riders start a world-wide chemical, nuclear and computer disaster that the Antichrist stops with a word (*ibid.*, 344). Newton assumes *he* has fixed it, by placing his hand on top of one of the computer cabinets (*ibid.*, 346–7).

101. "Could be Fate," [Newton] said hopefully. [Anathema] shook her head. "'No,' she said. 'No such thing.'" (*ibid.*, 207)

102. *Ibid.*, 18.

103. UFOs, Atlanteans, hollow Earth, rainforest preservation, health food, modern witches, and theosophy since Helen Blavatsky (*ibid.*, 166) are ridiculed by clashing with the common sense of "Them." When Adam wills some of these beliefs into being (Atlanteans, 162–4; UFOs, 198; Tibetan monks emerging from hollow earth, 201, 203, 211, 214; Brazilian rainforests replacing cities 224–6) they turn out to be either dangerous or pathetic. Only two fragments of New Age spirituality are affirmed: ley-lines (which twist to indicate the presence of the Antichrist, *ibid.*, 162), and auras (which Anathema can see and all humans have, *ibid.*, 145). The apocalyptic Riders, embodiments of man-made suffering, have "negative ones," "like black holes" (*ibid.*, 339).

104. *Ibid.*, 278–80.

105. *Ibid.*, 32.

106. *Ibid.*, 308, original italics.

107. *Ibid.*, 139.

108. McGinn, *Antichrist*, 45.

109. The name is significant rather than merely amusing (cf. Doyle, 20), nor is it in opposition to the character's Antichrist function (cf. Murdoch, *Adam's Grace,* 9).

110. Pepper is Adam's potential future mate, *GO*, 307.

111. *Ibid.*, 108, 141.

112. *Ibid.*, 70, 171.

113. Though Polycarp addresses the Antichrist as "the firstborn of Satan" (Peerbolte, *The Antecedents of Antichrist,* 110), early Christianity generally imagined the Antichrist as human. The Middle Ages favoured a demonic incarnation either coupled to human nature (again in imitation of Christ, Bostick, *The Antichrist and the Lollards*, 27; Emmerson, *Antichrist in the Middle Ages*, 75) or as fully demonic ("the visible devil," Emmerson, *Antichrist in the Middle Ages*, 82; Bostick, *The Antichrist and the Lollards*, 43).

114. *GO* evades thus the anti–Semitic tradition that made the Antichrist Jewish (Bostick, *The Antichrist and the Lollards*, 25; Emmerson, *Antichrist in the Middle Ages*, 46, 79; McGinn, *Antichrist*, 59), as well as it evades detailing the perversions supposed to be his origin (rape, incest, bestiality). It follows instead Joachim of Fiore's "false Christian from the West" (McGinn, *Antichrist*, 141).

115. *GO*, 30, 58, 350, 353 and 356.

116. *Ibid.*, 302.

117. *GO*, 30, 33; 139.

118. *Ibid.*, 70.

119. He has an aura the size of England (*ibid.*, 146); his faith literally moves mountains (*ibid.*, 144).

120. *Ibid.*, 353, original italics.

121. *Ibid.*, 59, original italics.
122. *Ibid.*, 56, 353.
123. *Ibid.*, 66–9.
124. *Ibid.*, 69, original italics.
125. *Ibid.*, 89, 222.
126. *Ibid.*, 141, 180, 219.
127. Breebaart and Kew, annotation to pp. 79/46.
128. *GO*, 144.
129. Antichrist's miracles traditionally are illusions or otherwise inferior (cf. 2 Thess. 2:9; McGinn, Antichrist, 71); as demonic *simia dei* he could not but produce simulacra.
130. *GO*, 300. Bringing together people scattered abroad, sealing his followers, and appearing in the form of a man are all features of the Antichrist in Hippolytus (McGinn, Antichrist, 61).
131. Bostick, *The Antichrist and the Lollards*, 43.
132. *GO*, 217; see for this feature of the Antichrist Orlov, *The Enoch-Metatron Tradition*, 216.
133. *GO*, 301, 302.
134. *Ibid.*, 351.
135. *Ibid.*, 383.
136. *Ibid.*, 359.
137. *Ibid.*, 302.
138. *Ibid.*, 382.
139. *Ibid.*, 378.
140. On Jewish apocryphal Adam as king, see Orlov, *The Enoch-Metatron Tradition*, 216; on a medieval (benevolent) World Ruler preceding the manifestation of the Antichrist, see Emmerson, *Antichrist in the Middle Ages*, 58; McGinn, *Antichrist*, 89; on a demonic World Ruler and Y2K in Evangelical writings, see Nancy E. Shaefer, "Apocalypse Now: Evangelical Visions of Dystopia at the End of the Last Millenium," Jaap Verheul, ed. *Dreams of Paradise, Visions of Apocalypse: Utopia and Dystopia in American Culture* (Amsterdam: VU University Press, 2004) 183–197.
141. *GO*, 354.
142. McGinn, *Antichrist*, 140. A widely popular medieval exegesis of Mark 13:5–8, see Bostick, *The Antichrist and the Lollards*, 72, 122; McGinn, *Antichrist*, 39.
143. *GO*, 14.
144. Murdoch, *Adam's Grace*, 10.
145. *GO*, 354.
146. Hypocrisy and corruption is an essential feature of late-medieval/Renaissance concepts of the Antichrist, see McGinn, *Antichrist*, 198.
147. *GO*, 42–3.
148. *Ibid.*, 43, original italics.
149. *Ibid.*, 129, original italics.
150. *Ibid.*, 382.
151. See Breebart and Kew, annotation to p. 383/267.

WORKS CITED

Bede. *The Ecclesiastical History of the English People*. Judith McClure and Roger Collins, eds. Oxford, UK: Oxford University Press, 1969.
Bloom, Harold. *Omens of Millenium: The Gnosis of Angels, Dreams, and Resurrection*. London: Fourth Estate, 1996.

Bostick, Curtis V. *The Anti-Christ and the Lollards: Apocalypticism in Late Medieval and Reformation England.* Leiden: Brill, 1998.

Breebaart, Leo and Mike Kew. "The Annotated Pratchett File v.9.0: Good Omens." *The L-Space Web.* <http://www.lspace.org/books/apf/good-omens.html> (November 1, 2008).

The Bible: Authorized King James Version with Apocrypha. Robert Carroll and Stephen Prickett, eds. Oxford, UK: Oxford University Press, 1997.

Doyle, T. M. *Competing Fictions: The Uses of Christian Apocalyptic Imagery in Contemporary Popular Fictional Works: Vol. II: Anti-Apocalyptic Fictions.* <http:www.mille.org/publications/winter2001/Newto.pdf> (March 20, 2008).

Emmerson, Richard K. *Antichrist in the Middle Ages: A Study of Medieval Apocalypticism, Art, and Literature.* Seattle: University of Washington Press, 1981.

Gaiman, Neil, and Terry Pratchett. *Good Omens.* London: Corgi, 1991.

Genette, Gérard. *Palimpsestes: La Littérature au Second Degré.* Paris : Éditions du Seuil, 1982.

Hill, Christopher. "Till the Conversion of the Jews" in *Millenarianism and Messianism in English Literature and Thought, 1650—1800.* Richard H. Popkin, ed. Leiden: Brill, 1988: 12–36.

Kelly, Henry Ansgar. *Satan: A Biography.* Cambridge, UK: Cambridge University Press, 2006.

Kolbrenner, William. *Milton's Warring Angels: A Study of Critical Engagements.* Cambridge, UK: Cambridge University Press, 1997.

Lindermayer, Orestis. "Europe as Anti-Christ: North American Pre-Millenarianism" in *Christian Millenarianism: From the Early Church to Waco.* Stephen Hunt, ed. Bloomington: Indiana University Press, 2001.

Litaert Peerbolte, L. J. *The Antecedents of Antichrist: A Traditio-Historical Study of the Earliest Christian Views on Eschatological Opponents.* Leiden: Brill, 1996.

Marlowe, Christopher, "Doctor Faustus" in *The Norton Anthology of English Literature: Volume One.* M. H. Abrams, Stephen Greenblatt, et al., eds. London: Norton, 2000: 990–1025.

McGinn, Bernard. *Antichrist: Two Thousand Years of the Human Fascination with Evil.* New York: Columbia University Press. 2000.

Milton, John. *Paradise Lost.* Christopher Ricks. London: Penguin Classics, 1968.

Müller, Beate. *Komische Intertextualität: Die Literarische Parodie.* Trier: Wissenschaftlicher Verlag, 1994.

Murdoch, Brian. *Adam's Grace: Fall and Redemption in Medieval Literature.* Cambridge, UK: DS Brewer, 2000.

Orlov, Andrei A. *The Enoch-Metatron Tradition.* Tübingen: Mohr Siebeck, 2005.

Percy, Martyn. "Whose Time is It Anyway? Evangelicals, the Millenium, and Millenarianism" in *Christian Millenarianism: From the Early Church to Waco.* Stephen Hunt, ed. Bloomington: Indiana University Press, 2001: 26–38.

Popkin, Richard H. "Christian Interest and Concerns about Sabbatai Zevi" in *Millenarianism and Messianism in Early Modern European Culture, vol. I: Jewish Messianism in the Early Modern World.* Matt D. Goldish and Richard H. Popkin, eds. Dordrecht: Kluwer Academic Publishers, 2001: 91–106.

Rose, Margaret. *Parody: Ancient, Modern, Postmodern.* Cambridge, UK: Cambridge University Press, 1993.

Rowland, Christopher. "'Upon Whom the Ends of the Ages Have Come': Apocalyptic Writing and the Interpretation of the New Testament" in *Apocalypse Theory and the Ends of the World.* Malcolm Bull, ed. Oxford, UK: Blackwell, 1995: 38–57.

Rüster, Johannes. *All-Macht und Raum-Zeit: Gottesbilder in der englischsprachigen Fantasy und Science-Fiction*. Erlanger Studien zur Anglistik und Amerikanistik vol. 8. Berlin: Lit Verlag, 2007.

Ryken, Leland. *The Apocalyptic Vision in Paradise Lost*. Ithaca, NY: Cornell University Press: 1970.

Shaefer, Nancy E. "Apocalypse Now: Evangelical Visions of Dystopia at the End of the Last Millenium" in *Dreams of Paradise, Visions of Apocalypse: Utopia and Dystopia in American Culture*. Jaap Verheul, ed. Amsterdam: VU University Press, 2004: 183–197.

The End-Times Narratives of the American Far-Right

Johann Pautz

> The apocalyptic cannot rest easy. He feels always under pressure to impose his world view — antagonistic to much contemporary rationality — on others, in part to stifle his own doubts and affirm the values of his convictions. He is a restless missionary who can become a righteous killer.
> — Robert Jay Lifton, *Destroying the World to Save It.*[1]

Apocalyptic and millennialist texts describe the fears and wishes of their authors and targeted audiences, characterizing the enemies and circumstances which antagonize the "chosen group," and juxtaposing these trials with remembrance of the world "as it should be." Social and cultural stresses, often described as amounting to inversions of the natural order, provide the background for apocalyptic and millennialist narratives. Frequently, these situations are described as so dire that only divine intervention, whether in the form of a deity or by a force of nature or history, can right these wrongs. Once the millennial triumphs are realized, the chosen survivors experience their utopia, portrayed as a time in which the prevailing group experiences the conversion or annihilation of its foes to enjoy an "end of history."

The apocalyptic fiction of the American far-right — here exemplified by the *John Franklin Letters*[2] (1959), *The Turner Diaries*[3] (1978), *The Left Behind series*[4] (1995–2007), and *Survivors*[5] (2006), not only provide insight into the fears of various American far right factions, but likewise the world that such groups hope for following their respective millenarian scenarios. Whether accomplished through a victorious guerrilla war against the United Nations or the establishment Christian dominion, these novels each end with the realization of their community of readers' earthly utopia. Each of these texts can be viewed as a foundational novel — a text through which the post–Apocalyptic society is expressed as a longed-for imagined community. Because the protagonists largely derive their identities from their opposition to the Other, these texts can be characterized as extremist.

265

In a cultural phenomenon similar to a sort of socio-political *agnosia*, the proponents of such mythologies do not recognize the United States as such. Instead, these groups understand contemporary America as a counterfeit substituted for the imagined nation. This America is variously imagined as white, Christian, patriarchal, invincible, privileged, and features minimal taxation or government interference. Contradictions to these conceptions are detrimental to such groups' integration into an ever-evolving body politic. The resulting dissonance between the *nation as it is imagined* and the *nation as it is* prompts nefarious explicatory conspiracies. In these myths, the United States, once favored by God, has invited elements of tolerance and subversion which remove this divine mantle. Apocalyptic and millennialist texts allow those sub-cultures alienated by the cultural evolution of the United States to experience the narrative destruction of their opponents and the achievement of their inevitable victories and dominion.[6]

For the extremist proponents of these utopias, it is only after the apocalypse takes its course and the other is eliminated that, in Benedict Anderson's words, [the community can be imagined]

> regardless of the actual inequality and exploitation that may prevail in each, the nation is always conceived as a deep, horizontal comradeship. Ultimately it is this fraternity that makes it possible, for so many millions of people, not so much to kill as willingly to die for such limited imaginings.[7]

American extremist groups have long recognized their lack of an organized front. Mirroring the actual strategy of militia movements, the protagonists of these novels form "leaderless" resistance cells[8] which carry out guerrilla attacks. During the fictional process of fighting those elements considered antithetical to their ideal America (or world), various leaderless cells of the disorganized resistance come together for the final push against their enemy. Thus, in constructing the ideals and values of the imagined community, slight differences in doctrine are minimized in the agenda of destroying common enemies, whether the United Nations, non-whites, non–Christians, communists, or a combination thereof. Anderson states that,

> No nation imagines itself coterminous with mankind. The most messianic nationalists do not dream of a day when all members of the human race will join their nation in the way that it was possible, in certain epochs, for, say, Christians to dream of a wholly Christian planet.[9]

This claim rings true in the narratives of the anti-globalist and anti-communist right wing due to the rabid nationalism of these texts. However, William Pierce's novel of mass genocide ends with the eventual promise of a white world and in the case of Tim LaHaye's *Left Behind*, the "Christian dream of a wholly Christian planet" mentioned by Anderson indeed exists in our epoch.

While these novels express the desires implicit in the millennial agendas of the fringes of the American right, the common spirit of these texts can be traced to their authors' associations with the John Birch Society. Though the appeal of these millennial narratives is largely limited to the radical right, their fantasies of armed resistance to globalism, multiculturalism and "collectivism" have transcended their customary bounds. Indeed, these themes have demonstrated not only their continual adaptability, but in the form of LaHaye's *Left Behind* franchise, they have achieved an unquestionable mainstream circulation. Though all of these texts share aspects of the Birchist tradition which fears subversion of the nation-state at hands of global elites and complicit insiders, *Left Behind* is exceptional, not only due to its mass distribution but the high-level political involvement of its author, LaHaye. Given these factors, as well as the prominent influence of John Birch alumni within the political apparatuses of the United States, these apocalyptic themes and their potential impacts are worthy of closer attention.

In contrast to these mid to late 20th century end times narratives, American millennial movements have generally sought to actualize the promises of the new nation's mythical exceptionalism and destiny. For much of American history, post-millennial thought informed the periodic religious and civic campaigns which were intended to cleanse American culture and elevate the nation as a beacon of morality. Movements in favor of evangelism, abolitionism and temperance aspired to perfect American society in preparation for the millennium. Following World War II, hopes of the United States' trajectory as a shining "City on the Hill" and a "New Jerusalem," were increasingly exchanged for a fear of a fall of from glory and impending enslavement or destruction. As the nuclear age emerged, apocalyptic discourse was no longer restricted to the religious sphere. However, a constant theme remains in the belief that internal corruptions and moral declines within the United States might open the door for apocalyptic scenarios. In examples of the American far right's post World War II apocalyptic narratives, the protagonists' anxieties describe a world in which traditional cultural values are undermined, national sovereignty is threatened, and social hierarchies are upset.

Despite the Soviet Union's collapse in the last decade of the 20th century, fears of communism survived alongside end times scenarios ranging from the religious to the economic and technological. During this *fin de siècle*, both American popular culture and mass-mobilization of politicized religious revivalism reflected paranoia of a New World Order.[10] The entertainment industry capitalized conspiracy theories involving secret government collaboration with the Other — whether in the form of extra-terrestrials or international elites.

Many cultural and economic trends were understood as signifying the collapse of the United States as it had existed. "Buy American" campaigns rose in prominence as deindustrialization prompted consumer xenophobia. Cultural traditionalists were shocked by radical changes in race and gender status, the likes of which had not been seen since the counter-cultural revolution of the 1960s and 70s. For many, particularly on the right, a menacing tapestry was woven between the massacres at Ruby Ridge and Waco, gun control legislation, federal control of land, multi-national military exercises on U.S. soil, and an increasingly complex global economy in which distant events had drastic impacts.

In impoverished rural areas and the Pacific Northwest in particular, tax protests and conspiracy theories denouncing the Federal Reserve as an agency of a One World Government became increasingly common.[11] "Patriot" and "Citizen Militias" sprang up, claiming to exist in order to defend the United States from a takeover by a global supergovernment. Historically, membership in militant extremist groups had generally been fairly limited, though they also fluctuated with the times, as seen in the revival of the Ku Klux Klan in the 1920s.[12] Frequently, such quasi-terrorist organizations consist of small nebulous cells which are often loosely associated and whose notable personalities drift to and from various extremist groups.[13] Several prominent leaders of the 1990s militia movement have had ties to such notorious organizations as Posse Comitatus, Christian Identity and Aryan Nations.[14] Cultural and economic malaise provided ample opportunities for recruitment into militias tangentially associated with extremist groups. While many of the participants may have been unaware of many militia leaders' extremist ties, their repackaged anti–Semitic conspiracies resonated with the anxieties of those who feared the Federal Reserve, United Nations, and gun control.

Though the above-mentioned groups represent the extremes of the far-right, during the Reagan-era, religious conservatives became a significant constituency of the American right, both politically and culturally. Conservative evangelicals may be brought to the polls to confront political wedge-issues ranging from same-sex marriage and abortion to Middle East policy. However these issues are not "ends in themselves." Whether reacting to the "intrusion" of the Federal government into education (banning school prayer, teaching evolution, providing sex education), or campaigning against abortion and equal rights for women and homosexuals, many members of the religious right seek to purify the United States in preparation for its millennial destiny — an agenda that can be traced back to the "new lights" of the Great Awakening. While the mainstream evangelical movement is undeniably distinct from the militia movement, there nonetheless exists an area of overlap in which an impending apocalypse is evidenced by a conspiratorial understanding of a "culture war" through which secular humanists threaten traditional moral boundaries. Basing their understanding of the United States on a myth of religious purity sullied by encroaching secularization and loosening morals, many notable Evangelists have described any opposition to a theocratic agenda as religious persecution, and in some instances, the implicit need for armed defense.

The fears of American cultural traditionalists are illustrated by the initial pages of Donald McAlvany's book, *Toward a New World Order*.[15] The first chapter, "The Decline of America," begins:

Remember back when:
Teenagers answered "Yes, Sir and "No, Sir" to their elders?
When helping the enemy was treason and punishable by death?
When a farmer could plant what he wanted to? ...
When the *New York Times* was pro–American?
When our Government was the servant of the people, instead of the master?
When the poor were too proud to take charity? ...
When it was preposterous to believe that America could lose a war?
When you went to church and heard a preacher who believed in the divinity of
   Christ and preached from the Bible?
When a white wedding gown meant something?
When the courts protected society, rather than the criminal? ...
When people used the phrase, "Sound as a Dollar"?
When pornography in the classroom was illegal, but prayers weren't?[16]

According to McAlvany, these are signs not only of America's decline but of the associated rise of the tyrannical New World Order (NWO). These "memories" of an idealized past portray the present as an inversion of the proper order and a certain sign that the end times are near. The author cautions "traditionalists" against complacency, urging them to arm themselves, invest in gold and silver, and make survivalist preparations. Warning of opposition by the forces of evil, McAlvany comforts his readers, claiming "God is still in control of nations, of history, and of individual's lives, and He is the winning side!"[17]

While McAlvany's writing may be dismissed as appealing only to fringe elements of the American religious right, the same themes make up the core of the fictional *Left Behind* series of novels based on the concept of a pre-tribulation rapture. According to this belief, Christ will spirit the faithful to paradise before the tribulation — a period of plagues, wars, and famine which anticipate Armageddon. This rapture is to be followed by the dawning of the millennium during which Christ will rule on earth for one thousand years.

The story uses several stock elements of older apocalyptic narratives, continuing the tradition of keeping their prophecies relevant to a changing world.[18] The attack on Israel by a coalition Middle Eastern states and Russia, ending in the antagonists' miraculous defeat as a trigger of the end times is a popular convention in such literature.[19] While particularly due to the influence of the *Scofield Reference Bible* on pre-millennialist narratives, such a scenario was understandably applicable to the Cold War (as well as to those who think of the Soviet Union's demise as a ploy against the West). To describe the rise of the Antichrist, *Left Behind* combines a standard — the resurrected Roman Empire, often associated with the European Union in contemporary prophecy — with contemporary concerns of the American right, the United Nations.[20] As in many of the earlier versions of rapture narratives, the novels include the break-up of the nuclear family as rebellious teenagers are separated from their pious parents and unfaithful husbands from their wives.[21] Accompanying the rapture is large scale chaos, particularly in urban areas, as the hard-working "everyman" or woman is revealed to be a saved Christian, their identity as a believer evidenced their disappearances.[22]

Anguishing over his wife's disappearance, protagonist Rayford Steele tracks down her former assistant pastor, Bruce Barnes, who convinces him that the disappearances are the Rapture of which his wife had warned him. Rayford begins proselytizing to his daughter, Chloe, and new associates, joining the remainder of the church's congregation. In the ensuing chaos of the Rapture, Nicolai Carpathia, a Romanian diplomat is propelled to the leadership of the United Nations. Through his inexplicable charisma, rhetoric of world peace and disarmament, and shadowy dealings with international financiers, he forms a world government named the Global Community (GC). This "One World" government results loss of national sovereignty. Carpathia uses the climate of fear surrounding a failed Russian attack on Israel and the mass disappearances to rally support for an era of peace and disarmament. Chief among his plans are the destruction of 90 percent of the world's weaponry, with the remaining 10 percent put into GC control. Observing these events, Bruce Barnes tells his followers that according to Biblical prophecy, Carpathia is the likely Antichrist.

Though many previous works of this genre have identified the papacy with the Antichrist (particularly during periods of religious strife), LaHaye instead casts the Roman Catholic Pope as the founder of a laissez-faire, New Age, "One World Religion."[23] The new religion's advocacy of tolerance and inclusion at the cost of morality and doctrine drives true, post–Rapture Christians underground and results in their persecution by the GC.

Once the GC's consolidation of power is set in motion, resistance begins to build. The American president regrets agreeing to give up the United States' weapons while anti–United Nations forces mount a guerrilla war. The resulting counter-attack by the GC levels most major cities in the United States.

Meanwhile Rayford Steel and his son-in-law, Buck Cameron, are chosen to work in high-level positions for the GC, affording them opportunities to spy on their enemies.

Barnes warns his followers of the harsh times to come and suggests that they form a resistance, named the "Tribulation Force." Bruce Barnes tells Rayford and Chloe that he intends to establish a group which would carry out a resistance effort against the GC, both spiritually and militarily. During the uncertain times being experienced, Barnes explains to Chloe and Rayford that,

> "It's great to pray for the witnesses springing up out of Israel.... But doesn't part of you want to jump into the battle? ...
> "So your little group inside the group, a sort of Green Berets, would be your Tribulation Force."[24]

As this resistance force is formed, the subsequent novels describe the group traveling around the globe, using high-tech means to proselytize and spy on Carpathia and the GC. Sequentially, the prophecies of the Tribulation are fulfilled with non-believers punished and the Tribulation Force skirmishing with GC forces. The standards of survivalist planning are covered: food is stockpiled, bunkers are equipped, and the extraordinary circumstances are used to justify the protagonists' new moral flexibility.

The various socio-political concerns of the religious right are echoed throughout the series. Independent women and homosexuals are portrayed as allied with the GC and Antichrist, betraying members of the Tribulation Force and aiding in the persecution of Christians. One character who works in an abortion clinic laments the disappearances of fetuses in the rapture because it will have a negative effect on business. Similarly, there is a shootout in a GC abortion clinic while the Tribulation Force members rescue Carpathia's mistress from a forced abortion. Actions against the GC (or at the expense of non-believers) are represented as actions on behalf of bringing about the millennium. Thus, the apocalyptic paradox is illustrated as the Christian protagonists are permitted to abandon traditional morality in order to survive in a world in which they are persecuted. The result is that the members of the Tribulation Force steal, murder, and rationalize these normally universal transgressions as actions towards the greater good.

The novels' pre-tribulation doctrine encourages an especially hard sentiment against the unconverted for two reasons. Primarily, from the Rapture through the Tribulation, the unconverted are looked down upon for their apparent refusal to acknowledge the prophetic signs. Secondly, this Manichaeism is further exacerbated by the appearance of two marks. The first appears on all believers as a valid testimony of their salvation. The second is issued by the GC as an official means of identification and is refused under penalty of death. As this is the "Mark of the Beast," willing submission to the GC is an allegiance to the Antichrist, removing any ambiguity and identifying believers and non-believers as mortal enemies by default.

The *Left Behind* novels draw parallels between prophecies and many of the anxieties of the far right in the era of globalization. These include concerns over a one-world currency, the erosion of national boundaries in favor of a global governing body, and changes in the historical social standings of traditionally subaltern groups both domestically and abroad. The series clearly capitalizes on anti–United Nations hysteria, merging the concerns of the militant right with those of Christian Evangelicals. Of particular concern is the melding of foreign policy and religious prophecy as the traditional myth of America's divine mission has adapted readings of the *Left Behind* franchise to the post–9/11 world and its ensuing conflicts. Thus, aspects of the books' contents, such as the GC's Iraqi headquarters and the undeniable religious framing of global conflict, have been melded in ways that present these wars as "prophecy manifest" to significant portions of the population.[25] As a result, such wars seem inevitable (due to their having been prophesied) and seem to serve a divine purpose.[26] Such contextualization of current United States involvement in Middle Eastern wars is evidenced in the distribution of "freedom packages" containing the *Left Behind: Eternal Forces* video game to American soldiers by the evangelical Operation Straight Up.[27]

While Tim LaHaye's best-selling books have made him a household name, his political accomplishments may not be as widely known. Like many architects of the New Right, LaHaye was a member of the John Birch Society, an organization which has spawned its share of right wing leaders as well as several extremists.[28]

In his article titled, "Reverend Doomsday," Robert Dreyfus describes the late 1950's and early 1960's San Diego political environment in which Tim and Beverly LaHaye participated:

> At that time, southern California was a hotbed of former McCarthyites, neo–Nazis and the John Birch Society.... They all muttered darkly about secret societies, the evil United Nations and one-world-government conspiracies, views that LaHaye would soon make his own. For years, LaHaye spoke at Birch Society training sessions, getting to know many of its leaders and building his ministry in the part of California that, twenty years later, would be the launching pad for Ronald Reagan's 1980 presidential bid.[29]

The "New Right" as such was the creation of a faltering Republican party seeking to supplement its base of anti–New Deal conservatives by creating ties to the growing Evangelical movement and campaigning on a platform of "traditional values." Goldberg states,

The Christian nationalist movement has its roots in the John Birch Society. Rushdoony[30] was a sympathizer; in *Institutes of Biblical Law*, he compared the group's cellular structure to the early Christian church. Summit Ministries president and Christian worldview author David Noebel was a member, as was Tim LaHaye who ran John Birch Society training seminars in California in the 1960s and 1970s.[31]

Conventional wisdom holds that the John Birch Society lost influence with the decline of the McCarthy era's witch hunts and that by the late 1970s it was simply a minor embarrassment to the American political right. However, Birch membership reportedly doubled following George H. W. Bush's description of a New World Order and the role of the United Nations in the course to the 1991 Persian Gulf War.[32]

Founded in 1958 by candy baron Robert Welch, the John Birch Society (JBS) is fearful of the economic and foreign affairs changes which have been associated with the United States' rise to superpower status. Known for its ardently anti-communist rhetoric, the JBS was named for a Baptist missionary and World War II Army intelligence officer who was killed in China during that country's communist revolution. By virtue of their careers in religion, politics and the military, many prominent members were influential in organizations outside of the JBS. The JBS's most important means of political activism were its letter writing campaigns, its grass root recruitment, and its "reading rooms" where its propaganda materials were distributed.

Welch was influenced by Oswald Spengler's concept of the cyclical decline of civilizations which, according to Daniel Levitas, was used by fascists and anti–Semites "to justify their own ideas about how Judaism, communism, and other 'unclean elements' threatened the integrity of Western culture." Levitas states that in Welch's appropriation of this theory, the culprit is the "disease of collectivism."[33] Just as religious millennialists are wary of current events which may portend the actualization of scriptural prophecy, so the JBS looks for clues to the "international communist conspiracy." According to the JBS, the current mechanisms of this conspiracy are the United Nations and the Council on Foreign Relations. With their paleo-conservative and nationalist business agendas, Birchers fear the United Nations and Federal Reserve, advocating for a return to the gold standard. Birchers fear both taxes and social programs and particularly detest labor unions. The origin of the "U.S. out of the UN" movement lies in the JBS as does the oft-resurrected "War on Christmas." Michelle Goldberg cites this war as first appearing in a 1959 Birch pamphlet titled, "There Goes Christmas" which described department store holiday displays in which Christmas decorations were marked with the United Nations logo.[34]

Birch doctrine claims that communism is simply a present instance of a much older conspiracy. The core of this historical conspiracy consists of elite international bankers manipulating world events in order to bring about a one world government.[35] According to these conspiracies, the inventions of this elite group include fascism, Nazism, and communism. Though Welch denied that Jews were the "insiders,"[36] these claims bear a close resemblance to the centuries old anti–Semitic conspiracies. Forever concerned with the "insiders" or "enemies within," the JBS reached the height of its infamy when it denounced President Eisenhower as an "agent of the communist conspiracy."

The JBS hinged many of its beliefs on its claim that the United States was founded as a republic, not a democracy,[37] and that the widening political influence of the masses was a creeping form of communist subversion.[38] As an organization, the JBS advocated neither racism nor anti–Semitism and it did not endorse violence. However, the same cannot be said for many of its members. Levitas states that, "although Welch avoided overt anti–Semitic ranting, he had a bad habit of gathering anti–Semites around him and recommending anti–Semitic publications." When individual members, sometimes high ranking, were exposed as racists or neo-Nazis, the JBS was frequently slow to distance itself from them.[39]

Claims of the JBS' decline are belied by the influence of many prominent Birchers in the political apparatuses of the New Right. JBS member Tim LaHaye was influential in uniting business interests with the early religious right to form this new political front. For example, the Moral Majority was formed by the Reverends Tim LaHaye and Jerry Falwell while funding was provided by figures such as Amway founder Richard Devos and oil tycoon Nelson Bunker Hunt.[40] Similarly, LaHaye founded the Council for National Policy, an elite conservative organization through which candidates lobbied for by conservative and Republican policy makers are given the seal of approval for "values voters."[41] Later, he worked on behalf of his wife's organization, Concerned Women for America, and championed the Nicaraguan Contras and school prayer.[42]

The Council on National Policy was conceived as an answer to the Council on Foreign Relations, an organization which figured heavily in JBS conspiracies. In her description of the origins of the Council on National Policy, Michelle Goldberg writes that,

> Nelson Bunker Hunt, a member of the John Birch Society's national council, was influential in helping LaHaye form the Council on National Policy, which has counted a number of Birch veterans as members.[43]

Thus, the apparent decline of the traditional John Birch Society in the 1980's may instead be viewed as a transition to a new (and more powerful) institutional infrastructure.

Among the Council's religious right activists, the signifiers of "communist" and "socialist" were replaced by "secular humanist." Tim LaHaye coordinated the mobilization of Christian conservative voters on behalf of the Reagan campaign and formed the American Coalition on Traditional Values.[44] The leadership of these groups is gripped by the same paranoia as the Birchers and their discourse retains the themes of small groups infiltrating, corrupting, and eventually enslaving the nation, which is here represented as Christian Americans. Sara Diamond states, "The theme of 'religious persecution' was a staple in the Christian Right's 1984 organizing." She cites LaHaye and Noebel's statements in their book *Mind Siege*,

> We are being ruled by a small but very influential cadre of committed humanists. These politicians are determined to turn America into an immoral, humanist country, ripe for merger into a one world state.[45]

This creeping persecution is described at length in the various far-right apocalypses, whose authors have been John Birch members. As Donald McAlvany advises in his book, *Storm Warning*,

> the levers of power in America today are dominated by activists from these groups who operate in the government, the judiciary, the media, the educational system.... And they have dictated an agenda ... that has taken prayer and any mention of God out of the public schools ... denigrated Christians and traditionalists on television, ... and which is now beginning to portray Christians and traditionalists as a dangerous threat to the nation.[46]

Citing the precedent of Waco, McAlvany claims that there is an agenda at work which seeks to characterize Christians and traditionalists as "cults" in the public consciousness. Similarly he states that the Clinton Administration, aided by the Reagan administration's rapprochement of the Soviets and George H. W. Bush's proclamation of a New World Order, furthers this scheme.

Though some of the John Birch membership has become part of the political establishment and power elite, the evolution of its conspiratorial and apocalyptic rhetoric is evidenced in the end times narratives written by past and present members. While the views expressed in these novels vary in extremity, the similarities among their themes and plots demonstrate common ideological roots, adapted to the concerns of the Birch Society's numerous offshoots. In demonstrating this paranoid lineage, the *John Franklin Letters* provides what is likely the original example of JBS ideology in fictional form.

The Birch Society is credited with promoting a 1959 epistolary novel titled the *John Franklin Letters*. Though the novel is anonymous, its association with the JBS is so close that it is generally considered to be a piece of JBS propaganda.[47] The novel is based upon the character John Franklin's letters to his uncle Jake. Made up of correspondence from 1959 to 1976, these letters are sent by the World War II and Korean War veteran to his uncle's Illinois farm (using the rural Midwest as the iconic representation of the untainted "true America").[48] Organized by year, *The John Franklin Letters* combines didactic style with elements of the conspiracy and adventure genres in a propagandistic monologue. Through the necessary limitations of its format, the reader has access only to John Franklin's opinions — without shred of his Uncle Jake's responses (except as quoted within John Franklin's replies).

The first portion of the book describes social trends which Franklin finds disturbing including increasing multiculturalism, New Deal and Keynesian economics, and workers unions, all of which he associates with rising urban crime rates. As he sends alarming news from the East Coast, John Franklin states to his Midwestern relative, "you still live in America."[49] Franklin critiques the "educated blind" and laments the growing socialism in American universities.

The apocalyptic portion of Franklin's story begins in 1963 as Franklin describes rampant, United Nations-sanctioned injustices perpetrated by minority groups and foreigners against professionals and patriots. He begins by describing the arrest of the "Dayton Defenders." These are a group of anti-labor business men who are accused of "'obstructing international justice in regard to man's right to organize to protect the rights of workers'" and are arrested by "Marshals of the World Court," made up of United Nations headquarters' security guards.[50] Franklin describes the "International Labor Organization" and World Court as communist fronts whose treaties override American law and are "rather distasteful for those who cling to the traditions of American Nationalism."[51] With the realization of Franklin's predictions, Americans become the first victims of international communism as American exceptionalism functions as an anti-communist parallel to the religious "city on the hill."

When protests outside of the U.N. building are dispersed by a police crackdown on orders of the mayor, "Alejandro Jesus de la Flores," Franklin uses this to connect the rise of Puerto Rican and minority power within government to the supposed rise of communist internationalism in the United States government. While citizens write to their congressmen to complain, not only do the congressmen respond that the procedures are legal, but these petitions are subject to searches by the postal service, "'looking for possible violation of the Javits 'hate literature' law.'"[52]

In response to anti-communist resistance, a nationwide "disciplinary strike" is carried out by the Teamsters Union. This strike, the brainchild of a Mr. Schwartzfelder, seeks to discipline those Americans "who want to conduct business without buying Mr. Schwartzfelder's permission." This correspondence is concluded by Franklin asking his uncle if Franklin's rifle is still being stored at the uncle's farm — a clear foreshadowing of impending armed conflict.

In Franklin's second letter of 1963, he relates an incident that represents the true magnitude of internationalism trumping any sort of United States civil code.[53] In this incident an American businessman is the victim of the United Nations' World Health Organization due to a 1959 law allowing "health inspectors" to access private residences. According to the anecdote, a stereotypic "drunken Eastern European" named Kuprasck overhears Martinson describing a file of anti-communist journals. The drunken health inspector uses his clout to not only have Martinson thrown out of the bar but the next day, attempts to force his way into Martinson's home with the predictable consequences: Martinson kills him and is tried by an international tribunal. The resounding themes are the dismantling of traditional privacy and civil rights by a transnational bureaucracy, the inversion of social status with the drunken foreigner having authority over the ostensibly hard-working and, according to Franklin, exemplary American. However, it is the violation of the sanctity of the home and the transfer of the justice process to a foreign court which brings the anecdote to its climax. By 1964 Franklin describes a vastly devalued currency and expresses envy towards his uncle's fully-stocked larder and other survivalist provisions. He believes that he might be able to acquire gold — a stable form of universally-accepted currency. Franklin criticizes the removal of the gold standard, international loans and U.S. overseas debt, Keynesian economics, and social security. He claims that currency devaluation, foreclosure on farms, etc, are a conspiracy by communists and social-engineering bankers to cheaply buy-off debt-ridden Americans.

Beginning in 1967, John Franklin initiates coded correspondence with his uncle through an underground network. Franklin claims that the loss of civil liberties in America has "gone so far that it cannot be reversed" and describes such a condition as "living in exile in our own land."[54] With such unbearable circumstances Franklin states that,

> We are now setting up the underground organization of American patriots which will be the resistance movement to the alien government — miscalled a "World Government" — which almost certainly will take over the United States within a few years. If we can't throw it off we will die fighting it.

Franklin continues by stating that such a resistance must begin organizing immediately due to the "capture of Americans within ... the United States by ... international foreign courts and bureaus." Franklin predicts that the United States has been rendered "ripe for the picking" by the Soviet Union due to fantasies of universal brotherhood.

Franklin proposes to fight this with an "American Underground" that will be "first and foremost ... a military organization"[55] which Franklin states will be known as the Rangers.[56] Predicting that the formal military will be disbanded, Franklin anticipates many veterans will join the ranks of his organization which he describes as

> Thousands of trained men and many caches of weapons. Sportsmen, athletes ... will be in Ranger ranks, not to mention women and even children. Sporting weapons and home-made weapons will be used. There will be large areas of sparse population which never will be completely under international control.[57]

Franklin suggests that his uncle and associates begin being cautious in their social appearances and in expressing their opinions.

The remainder of the novel describes the exploits of Franklin's militia and the excesses of the Soviet-style bureaucracy which it battles. Franklin's communist opposition is conveniently incompetent (explained by the laziness and mediocrity engendered by socialism) and eventually the system, bringing its governmental bulk to the extreme of completely duplicating itself to the point of redundancy, accommodates the resistance by beginning to crumble under its own weight. In an early literary example of the militant right's "leaderless resistance" strategy, the protagonists of the *John Franklin Letters* work in small guerrilla groups independent of any central authority. In descriptions of tactics duplicated in the later *Turner Diaries* and *Survivors*, these small, independent militias are described as operating independently in detailed anecdotes of sabotage, bombings, and assassinations, but then come together in large alliances for the final push against globalist forces. The ensuing victories are described nebulously at best.

On the bicentennial of the American Revolution, John Franklin proclaims the final defeat of communism and the United States' rebirth. Foreign aid is ended as "Africans and Indians have now finally realized that they can run their own show."[58] South African apartheid has been resolved as blacks and whites have come together to throw off the communist yoke. The new government of the United States has been installed and apparently John Franklin is a part of it as he mentions he is writing the letter from the "new State Department building." Symbolic of the new government's stance on economics and trade, the new president was formerly under-secretary of Commerce. John Franklin states that there is no hurry to reinstall Congress. Though the process is in the works he states,

> We don't need legislation right now. Nobody in the world needs more laws. We need to work, nation by nation, town by town, family by family to rebuild what was torn apart by international bureaucracy.[59]

In an aside, Franklin mentions that the new president is a "Negro" and had served as a Ranger in the anti–WPA resistance. This hollow attempt at negating earlier racist aspects of the narrative glares in the face of the characterizations of nearly every instance of non-white ethnicity to that point.

As noted, various groups founded or championed by former Birch members have had agendas of fascism, anti-communism, nativism and racial or religious supremacy. Following the 1995 Oklahoma City bombing, media accounts of the American militia movement brought attention to the neo-Nazi novel, *The Turner Diaries*. Due to similarities between the book and the bombing of the Murrah Federal Building, as well as Timothy McVeigh's well-documented interest in the novel, this book is thought to have inspired the terrorist attack. According to Richard Mitchell,

> Pierce admits the idea for his diaries was not original. Many years earlier Robert Welch, founder of the John Birch Society, had recommended another book to him, *The John Franklin Letters* (1959).[60]

Incorporating many elements of the *John Franklin Letters*, the infamous *Turner Diaries* retains the militant struggle against a foreign element which has gradually subverted the government of the United States. *The Turner Diaries* is a short novel presented in the form of a personal journal which chronicles Earl Turner's role in the Great Revolution, a race war which ushers in the New Era. Turner is an engineer living in the Washington D.C. area and a low-level member of a white supremacist rebel group. In a style similar to the *John Franklin Letters*, the novel is characterized as archival material in a post–Great Revolution America, recording the events leading up to the revolution as well as Turner and his group's actions within it. Thus, the text, sharing the monologue of its diary format with the *John Franklin Letters* is intended to function as a foundational text for the post–"Great Revolution" America.

The novel begins in 1989 with the enforcement of the "Cohen Act" which is intended to confiscate firearms from white citizens. As the name implies, this law is attributed to Jews within the U.S. government. Turner watches as African-American police, under the supervision of a "Caucasian of unusually dark complexion" search the homes of whites for weapons, raping white women, and threatening whites in general. Having attempted to hide a weapon, Turner is arrested. According to the story, the government has been secretively taken over by Jews and their collaborators who use African-Americans and other minorities as a means of suppressing whites while orchestrating their enslavement and "racial defilement."[61] Turner claims that this is accomplished through control of the media and use of social issues such as integration and affirmative action. Among the sensationalist atrocities mentioned, white women are forced into prostitution and racial miscegenation, the black police forces exist to intimidate whites, blacks are frequently described as "lapsing into cannibalism," and anyone who claims any victimhood by non-whites is charged with racism and is sent to prison for reeducation.

Upon his release, Turner joins a terrorist cell, bombing federal offices and communications complexes, and in a scene borrowed from *The John Franklin Letters*, setting up a printing press as a front company for guerrilla activities. As an engineer, Turner is given the tasks of maintaining communications equipment and weapons as well as devising alarms and bombs, including reverse-engineering a nuclear bomb. Such tasks make Turner an intellectual warrior, demonstrating his ingenuity and skill, while fetishizing the technical means by which the race war is carried out, the high-tech methods of the genocide intended as a demonstration of white supremacy.[62] In addition to attacking strategic targets, Turner's rebels carry out a cultural war, lynching interracial couples and liberal university professors and leaving placards on their corpses stating, "I Betrayed My Race."[63]

Whites are increasingly marginalized by The System and resistance begins, resulting in social and economic collapse. Like the preceding narratives, Pierce uses the inevitable incompetence of the oppressive regime and its henchmen (here attributed to racial inferiority) as a means of explaining the protagonist's victory against overwhelming odds. Nevertheless, this produces a paradoxical turn of events in which Turner is captured and tortured, giving up information before being rescued by his peers. After his release, he is chastised for his failure to commit suicide when captured but is offered a deal: should he undertake a suicide mission, he will be given posthumous membership in the elite core of The Organization — a group known as The Order.[64] Eventually The Organization takes over Vandenberg Air Force base, acquiring its nuclear weapons and eventually bombing the east coast of the United States. In a suicide mission, Turner drops a nuclear bomb on the Pentagon from a commandeered crop duster, thus ending the "diary."

The archival notes serving as an epilogue describe the subsequent events as a global genocide and nuclear war culminating in December of 1999. This history states that The Organization "[achieved] its world-wide political and military goals, and that the Order would spread its wise and benevolent rule over the earth for all time to come."[65] Just as the Christian millennium entails the elimination of non–Christians, so the utopia imagined by William Pierce is an all-white world. Short of scapegoating and genocide, the adolescent plot of *The Turner Diaries* presents little in the way of proposing solutions to the social ills which it claims plague the country. There is only faith in the proposition that the elimination of obstacles to white dominion will in itself usher in an "end of history." While *The Turner Diaries* is riddled with logical inconsistencies and plot problems (the general premise included) contemporary end times fiction of the far right has become more sophisticated, as exemplified by the economic apocalypse scenario proposed in the novel *Patriots*.

James Wesley Rawles' survivalist novel, *Patriots: Surviving the Coming Collapse*, is set in the early 21st century and is, for all intents and purposes, a narrated survival manual.[66] The book extensively details the canning of food, the preparation of ordnance, and various medical procedures. Similarly, the equipments specified, from firearms to hiking and communications gear, are brand and model specific, with descriptions amounting to "product place-ment" advertisements.

The novel begins with Todd Gray, an economist, discussing an impend-ing global financial crisis with representatives of several major international banks. Realizing the critical nature of the situation, Todd rallies the mem-bers of his Christian survivalist group. From disparate locations across the country and various walks of life, they converge on their "hardened" home in rural Idaho, a self-sufficient bunker prepared for such eventualities. As the "Crunch" hits hard, the unprepared are victims of starvation, roving bands of looters and rapists, and deadly epidemics. Meanwhile at their "Valley Forge" retreat, the members of the survivalist group (who begin to refer to them-selves as the Northwest Militia) are used to illustrate how such a survivalist group should deal with the various stereotyped groups who drift by their "observation post." These range from a family who, because of their skills are taken in to contribute to the effort, to a pair of looters who are revealed to be communists and cannibals who are shot on sight after Maoist literature and human flesh are found in their provisions.

Various armed encounters with bands of looters and vandals are described with the protagonists invariably winning and scavenging weapons and pro-visions. Loose alliances with other militias in the region lead to an atmos-phere of purity, self-righteousness and an idealization of the "new frontier" lifestyle. Four to five years into the "post–Crunch" period, order begins to return, barn dances are held, farmers markets and swap meets are organized, and church services resume.

However, hot on the heels of this rebirth, a new conflict emerges in the form of a newly formed and non-elected federal government which, along with United Nations troops (primarily German), claims to have "pacified" some of the Eastern States. A representative of this interim government arrives and lists several demands, including replacing the worthless American cur-rency with a new currency which is similarly not backed by precious metals, confiscating firearms, and instituting a national identification card. The rep-resentative is sent packing by the various militia leaders who have congregated to listen and ask questions. Anticipating a response, the militias store provi-sions and manufacture munitions in preparation for war with the United

Nations. Fighting as individual groups, the independent militias form a coordinated resistance, albeit while each maintaining their independence.[67] The novel ends with a future anecdote exemplifying cultural acceptance of firearms and eternal vigilance as a result of the "Second Civil War."[68]

Many of the preceding texts have not achieved more than underground circulation or "cult" status. The *John Franklin Letters* was advertised in JBS publications. *The Turner Diaries* was sold almost exclusively at gun shows, receiving little notoriety outside of neo-Nazi and white supremacist circle until its association with the Oklahoma City bombing was noticed in late 1995. Unlike these preceding examples, the thematically similar *Left Behind* novels have been phenomenally popular, even outside of Evangelical circles.[69]

Robert Jay Lifton describes the memberships of apocalyptic cults as an extensions of their gurus and claims that as a leader's needs to extend control increases, so does the likelihood that the cult will either engage in mass suicide (as the guru's omnipotence is threatened) or an exercise of "forcing the end" (in an attempt to make apocalyptic prophecies manifest). To initiate a millennial cataclysm, the guru inverts traditional morality and rationalizes anti-social behavior.

Citing *The Turner Diaries'* influence on American extremists, Lifton proposes that in the absence of a guru, a text may influence an individual to take actions intended to bring about the millennium. As he observes, the novel inspired not only the far right's "leaderless resistance" strategy, but key aspects of the terrorist acts carried out by Timothy McVeigh and Robert Matthews. While Lifton acknowledges various thought-leaders of the movement, he maintains that the text of *The Turner Diaries* is perhaps among the most significant mobilizing factors in an otherwise fragmented extremist milieu. In this sense, an apocalyptic text of the American far right has already inspired terrorist acts, the intents of which were to initiate chain reactions of racial violence which would bring about the millennium.

As many of the architects of the contemporary American political right have passed through the John Birch Society, the organization's influence can hardly be considered marginal. Despite the differences in their specific agendas, the apocalypse narratives of the John Birch Society and its extremist offshoots have substantial common ground. Though many of these texts may be dismissed as having only fringe appeal, their shared themes have mobilized armed groups and informed the popular culture's apocalyptic imaginings. Just as the militia movement might be considered a mainstreamed version of smaller and more virulent extremist groups, *Left Behind* has been referred to as "*Turner Diaries* Lite"[70] for its thinly-veiled Christian Dominionist and anti–Semitic agenda.

Due to its wide circulation, and the cultural agenda which it promotes, *Left Behind* should be examined as an artifact of a much broader social movement which has gained considerable influence in American politics. Domestically, the consequences of the religious right's climb to power range from limit-setting on civil rights to the use of the American government as an instrument of proselitization. In foreign policy, the United States' participation in the United Nations is undermined while policies in the Middle East are influenced in ways that could potentially ignite region-wide conflicts. Such a situation, taken at face value, offers two frightening possibilities. The first is that circumstances perceived as prophetic and contributing to the millennium's realization may be dismissed as part of a cosmic plan. Even more disturbing is the possibility that catastrophic situations resembling prophesied events may be actively encouraged in an effort to force the end.

NOTES

1. Robert Jay Lifton, *Destroying the World to Save It: Aum Shinrikyo, Apocalyptic Violence, and the New Global Terrorism* (New York: Metropolitan, 1999).

2. Anonymous, *The John Franklin Letters* (New York: Bookmailer, 1959).

3. William Pierce (as Andrew Macdonald), *The Turner Diaries 2nd Ed.* (New Jersey: Barricade, 1996).

4. Tim LaHaye and Jerry Jenkins, *Left Behind* (Wheaton, IL: Tyndale House, 1995).

5. James Wesley Rawles, *Patriots: Surviving the Coming Collapse* (Philadelphia: Xlibris, 2006).

6. The means of victory are often vague and divine favor in some form is frequently as important as tactics and strategy.

7. Benedict Anderson, *Imagined Communities: Reflections on the Origin and Spread of Nationalism* (New York: Verso, 2003).

8. Morris Dees, *Gathering Storm: America's Militia Threat* (New York: HarperCollins, 1996).

9. Anderson, *Imagined Communities*, 7.

10. A phrase made famous by George H.W. Bush in a speech to Congress on September 11, 1990. It has since become synonymous with a conspiracy to undermine American sovereignty in favor of a one world government.

11. Conspiracy theories concerning the Federal Reserve (including many openly anti–Semitic theories) are as old as the organization though they became increasingly mainstream as the militia and tax-protest movements grew.

12. Posse Comitatus, Ed DePugh's Minutemen and the various Klan-affiliated groups are examples. While they may have significant moral support, their estimated membership is in the low tens of thousands. Such organizations frequently overstate their actual numbers, making accurate counts difficult.

13. The lines between criminal opportunism and "political violence" are often blurred. Groups such as The Order have engaged in armored car heists and firearms thefts intended to finance anti-government plots as well as carrying out assassinations and intimidating government officials.

14. These are extensively detailed in the following: David A. Neiwert, *In God's Country: The Patriot Movement and the Pacific Northwest* (Pullman, WA: Washington State

University Press, 1999); Richard Abanes, *American Militias: Rebellion, Racism, and Religion* (Downers Grove, IL: InterVarsity Press, 1996); Daniel Levitas, *The Terrorist Next Door: The Militia Movement and the Radical Right* (New York: St. Martin's Press, 2002).

15. McAlvany, a John Birch Society and Council on National Policy member is a major gold investor and publishes an "intelligence report" which warns of turbulent times and the need to invest in precious metals.

16. Douglas McAlvany, *Towards a New World Order: A Countdown to Armageddon* (Oklahoma City: Heartstone, 1990).

17. *Ibid.*, 244.

18. Paul Boyer, *When Time Shall Be No More: Prophecy Belief in Modern American Culture* (Cambridge, MA: Harvard University Press, 1992).

19. *Ibid.*, 155.

20. The prophecy of Jack Van Impe is an example of this.

21. Paul Boyer, *When Time Shall Be No More*, 256.

22. In particular, Boyer discusses the writings of Leon Bates' *Projection for Survival*, 1979, and Charles Taylor's *Destiny of America*, 1972. Left Behind's rapture scenarios share many similarities with those of the preceding works.

23. Paul Boyer, *When Time Shall Be No More*, 274–275.

24. LaHaye, *Left Behind*, 419–420.

25. Robert Dreyfuss, "Reverend Doomsday: According to Tim LaHaye, the Apocalypse is Now," *Rolling Stone*, January 28, 2004.

26. Dreyfuss states that LaHaye has speculated on Iraq's role in the apocalypse since the 1970s with the reconstruction of ancient Babylon. More recently he has claimed that Hussein was a forerunner to the Antichrist and that the end times would be ushered in by a war between Iraq and Israel.

27. Max Blumenthal, "Kill or Convert, Brought to You by the Pentagon." The Nation Blog, entry posted August 7, 2007 <http://www.thenation.com/blogs/notion?bid=15&pid=220960> (October 2, 2008).

28. The John Birch Society can claim among its past and current members such figures as Tim LaHaye, oilman Nelson Bunker Hunt, neo–Nazis William Pierce and Tom Metzger, Christian Identity advocate and Posse Comitatus organizer William Potter Gale, neofascist Willis Carto, far-right activist Phyllis Schaffley, Christian survivalist author James Wesley Rawles, Christian intelligence advisor and precious metals broker Don McAlvany, militia movement notable Robert Depugh, Major General Edwin Walker and far right evangelist Billy James Hargis.

29. Dreyfuss, "Reverend Doomsday."

30. Rousas J. Rushdoony was the founder of the Christian Reconstructionist movement which advocated a return to biblical law and the gold and silver currency. He also was John Birch member, and an early and influential advocate of home schooling. His son-in-law, Gary North, has been a member of the Council on National Policy.

31. Michelle Goldberg, *Kingdom Coming: The Rise of Christian Nationalism* (New York: W.W. Norton, 2006) 162.

32. Political Research Associates, "John Birch Society" Political Research Associates, 2007 <http://www.publiceye.org/tooclose/jbs.html> (October 2, 2008).

33. Levitas, *The Terrorist Next Door*, 69.

34. Goldberg, *Kingdom Coming*.

35. Neiwert, *In God's Country*, 49.

36. Political Research Associates, "John Birch Society," 2.

37. Neiwert, In God's Country, 41.

38. The JBS viewed the 1960's civil rights movement as "communist" for this reason.

39. Levitas, *The Terrorist Next Door*, 70–71.

40. Stephenie Hendricks, *Divine Destruction: Wise Use, Dominion Theology, and the Making of American Environmental Policy* (Hoboken, NJ: Melville House, 2005).

41. *Ibid.*, 73–4.

42. Sara Diamond, *Roads to Dominion: Right-Wing Movements and Political Power in the United States* (New York: Guilford, 1995).

43. Goldberg, *Kingdom Coming*, 161.

44. Diamond, *Roads to Dominion*, 243.

45. *Ibid.*, p. 242.

46. Donald S. McAlvany, *Storm Warning: The Coming Persecution of Christians and Traditionalists in America* (Oklahoma City: Heartstone, 1999).

47. The publisher, "Bookmailer, Inc." and its president, Lyle H. Munson, who editorializes in the introduction, appear to have been primarily a vendor of "red-scare" novels and non-fiction.

48. According to the fictional forward, this collection of letters would have been archived in the University of Illinois library in 1989, thirty years after the novel's publication.

49. Anonymous, *The John Franklin Letters*, 39.

50. *Ibid.*, 66.

51. *Ibid.*, 66.

52. *Ibid.*, 67.

53. Here, Franklin also laments the decline of Anglo-Saxon common law, which is frequently cited as legal precedent by tax protestors and sovereign citizenship activists.

54. *Ibid.*, 85.

55. *Ibid.*, 86.

56. Incidentally this is the name given to the California militia organized by Posse Comitatus founder and John Birch alumnus William Potter Gale.

57. *Ibid.*, 86.

58. *Ibid.*, 176.

59. *Ibid.*, 178.

60. Richard G. Mitchell, *Dancing at Armageddon: Survivalism and Chaos in Modern Times* (Chicago: University of Chicago Press, 2002).

61. In neo–Nazi and white supremacist discourse, this conspiracy is referred to as ZOG or Zionist Occupational Government.

62. Lifton, *Destroying the World to Save It*, 334.

63. Pierce, *The Turner Diaries*, 160–1.

64. This name was the inspiration for a neo–Nazi group founded by Robert Matthews which robbed pawn shops and armored cars and carried out assassinations including the killing of radio host Alan Berg.

65. Pierce, *The Turner Diaries*, 211.

66. Rawles is a former Army intelligence officer (who tendered his resignation upon Bill Clinton's presidential inauguration), John Birch member, and publisher of SurvivalBlog, an internet survivalist resource site.

67. The leaders of the Northwest Militia specifically refer to the concept of "leaderless resistance" and "phantom cells." The groups include many named after notable personalities on the right wing fringe including "Gordon Kahl Company," "Samuel Weaver Company," referring to the sovereign citizenship activist and tax-protestor, killed during a series of shootouts with Federal officers and the murdered son of far-right martyr Randy Weaver.

68. Rawles, *Patriots*, 384.

69. Dreyfuss, "Reverend Doomsday."

70. Edmund Cohen, "Turner Diaries Lite," *Free Inquiry* 21 (2001): 58–76.

WORKS CITED

Abanes, Richard. *American Militias: Rebellion, Racism, and Religion*. Downers Grove, IL: InterVarsity Press, 1996.

Anderson, Benedict. *Imagined Communities: Reflections on the Origin and Spread of Nationalism*. New York: Verso, 2003.

Blumenthal, Max. "Kill or Convert, Brought to You by the Pentagon." *The Nation Blog*. August 7, 2007. <http://www.thenation.com/blogs/notion?bid=15&pid=220960> (October 2, 2008).

Boyer, Paul. *When Time Shall Be No More: Prophecy Belief in Modern American Culture*. Cambridge, MA: Harvard University Press, 1992.

Cohen, Edmund. "Turner Diaries Lite." *Free Inquiry* 21 (2001): 58–76.

Dees, Morris. *Gathering Storm: America's Militia Threat*. New York: HarperCollins, 1996.

Diamond, Sara. *Roads to Dominion: Right-Wing Movements and Political Power in the United States*. New York: Guilford, 1995.

Dreyfuss, Robert. "Reverend Doomsday: According to Tim LaHaye, the Apocalypse is Now." *Rolling Stone*. January 28, 2004. <http://www.rollingstone.com/politics/story/5939999/reverend_doomsday/> (November 1, 2008).

Goldberg, Michelle. *Kingdom Coming: The Rise of Christian Nationalism*. New York: W.W. Norton, 2006.

Hendricks, Stephenie. *Divine Destruction: Wise Use, Dominion Theology, and the Making of American Environmental Policy*. Hoboken, NJ: Melville House, 2005.

The John Franklin Letters. New York: Bookmailer, 1959.

LaHaye, Tim, and Jerry Jenkins. *Left Behind*. Wheaton, IL: Tyndale House, 1995.

Levitas, Daniel. *The Terrorist Next Door: The Militia Movement and the Radical Right*. New York: St. Martin's, 2002.

Lifton, Robert Jay. *Destroying the World to Save It: Aum Shinrikyo, Apocalyptic Violence, and the New Global Terrorism*. New York: Metropolitan Books, 1999.

McAlvany, Donald S. *Storm Warning: The Coming Persecution of Christians and Traditionalists in America*. Oklahoma City: Heartstone Publishing, 1999.

McAlvany, Douglas. *Towards a New World Order: A Countdown to Armageddon*. Oklahoma City: Heartstone, 1990.

Mitchell, Richard G. *Dancing at Armageddon: Survivalism and Chaos in Modern Times*. Chicago: University of Chicago Press, 2002.

Neiwert, David A. *In God's Country: The Patriot Movement and the Pacific Northwest*. Pullman, WA: Washington State University Press, 1999.

Pierce, William (as Andrew Macdonald). *The Turner Diaries* 2nd ed. Fort Lee, NJ: Barricade, 1996.

Political Research Associates. "John Birch Society." *Political Research Associates*. 2007. <http://www.publiceye.org/tooclose/jbs.html> (October 2, 2008).

Rawles, James Wesley. *Patriots: Surviving the Coming Collapse*. Philadelphia: Xlibris, 2006.

The *Left Behind* Series and Its Place Within the American Evangelical Subculture

Nancy A. Schaefer

Combines Tom Clancy–like suspense with touches of romance, high-tech flash and biblical references.

—The New York Times

Visions of euphoria and despair — held in uneasy embrace — are deeply embedded in the American religious landscape. Early on, utopian dreams of the New Jerusalem, a "city upon a hill" were married to apocalyptic nightmares about the end of the world. Four centuries later, "endism"[1] arguably constitutes a major component of the national zeitgeist, evident in the dystopian images and narratives that permeate U.S. popular culture: TV shows, films, music, novels, comic books, computer games, and the Internet. Secular and religious variants — ranging from nuclearism to New Ageism — exist side-by-side. Among American evangelicals, pop eschatology has reached faddist proportions if the sales figures of the *Left Behind* series (*LBS*) of books are a reliable gauge. Part of an apocalyptic literary genre, *LBS* has topped the best-seller lists of the *New York Times, Publishers Weekly* and Amazon.com, rivaling the sales of the most popular fictional writers in the U.S. today. In this essay, I examine the *LBS* phenomenon and locate it within the historical context of American evangelicalism.[2] I also attempt to explain the persistence of prophecy beliefs in American society and the current fascination with end-time speculation.

Historical background — The End of Days

"Apocalypse" stems from the Greek verb *apokalypsis* meaning "to uncover or disclose."[3] Originally an apocalypse was a text in which the events leading up to the world's denouement were hidden, decipherable only by true believers.[4] Gradually the term came to connote "disaster" and became a core tenet of eschatology, the doctrine concerning the end of the world.[5] Biblical apocalypticism, derived from ancient Hebraic thought, is found primarily in the books of Daniel, Ezekiel, and Revelation. Over time, "apocalypse" increasingly became associated with "millennium," the thousand year period of peace and justice when Christ would return (*parousia* or "Second Coming") to reign over His earthly Kingdom. Then the dead would be resurrected and the Last Judgment unleashed.[6]

While the Roman Catholic Church adopted St. Augustine's position that the Book of Revelation was allegorical, biblical literalism survived in the folkways of popular belief. And millenarism,[7] the view of salvation as collective, terrestrial, impending, total, and miraculous[8] — coupled with eschatological visions of calamitous destruction — persisted, sparking hundreds of movements from the Middle Ages onwards.[9]

Popular belief in apocalypticism not only survived but thrived outside the sanction of clerical authority, becoming part of America's founding myth. Christopher Columbus, an avid student of biblical prophecy, interpreted his "discovery" of the New World as part of a divine script. He wrote: "God made me the messenger of the new heaven and the new earth of which He spoke in the Apocalypse of St. John ... and He showed me where to find it."[10] Likewise the Puritans — convinced that they had been chosen by God to carve out a New Jerusalem in the wilderness — held apocalyptic beliefs while anticipating Christ's return.[11] These beliefs were hardly aberrant either but were widely held and transmitted across generations. As historian Paul Boyer explains:

> From the early seventeenth century through to the late eighteenth century,
> the entire span of American colonial history was marked by speculation about
> America's role in God's plan. That the colonizing century began at a time of
> intense apocalyptic awareness in England meant that it, like everything else in
> these years, took on an aura of eschatological meaning.[12]

By the nineteenth century apocalyptic fervency was on the wane, yet prophecy-beliefs about the world's end continued to mobilize new separatist religious movements, including the Millerites (Seventh-day Adventists) in the 1830s and 1840s, the Jehovah's Witnesses, and the Church of Latter Day Saints (Mormons). Apocalyptic anticipation likewise leavened the revivalism of Methodist and Baptists churches during this period, persisting in these traditions today. As religion scholar Lorne Dawson notes, "One need only listen to a Billy Graham crusade to hear the familiar apocalyptic refrains and the admonitions repeated over and over again."[13]

After the Second World War, a new wave of religious conservatism (sometimes called neo-evangelicalism) dawned on the national horizon, taking many observers by surprise.[14] During the Cold War period, a reconstituted Christian movement emerged and gathered momentum, led by urban revivalist-cum-presidential adviser Billy Graham. Largely absent from public view after the fundamentalist debacles of the 1920s, these born-again believers had *not* capitulated (as many thought at the time) but actually had been busily constructing the institutional scaffolding necessary to sustain a burgeoning subculture which would further develop into a full-blown sociopolitical movement to "take back America": The Religious Right. Now known as "evangelicals," their key organizations included the National Association of Evangelicals (1942), Evangelical Foreign Missions Association (1945), National Religious Broadcasters (1944), and Graham's flagship publication *Christianity Today* (1956). Leading expert Mark Juergensmeyer aptly summarizes the period:

> At the end of the Cold War the talk of a "new world order" alarmed many evangelical Christians, who took this to mean the global domination of secular government. Some conservative Christians interpreted it as opening up American society to a variety of religions, races, and sexual orientations, all of which they regarded as contrary to their desire for a Christian nation that would fulfill the messianic expectations of the coming of Christ. As a result, many evangelical Christians turned to electoral politics to increase their power, and in the late twentieth century, their efforts bore fruit.[15]

During the 1960s, evangelicals were most assuredly feeling beleaguered and aggrieved. The country had elected its first Roman Catholic president, a liberal Democrat, and the winds of social and civic reform blew stronger than at any time since the Civil War. Reeling from the onslaught of liberalism (in all its attendant forms) and the loosening of traditional social norms, Bible believers saw themselves as the defenders of old-time religion. They were especially outraged by the *Roe v. Wade* Supreme Court ruling (1973) — emblematic, in their view, of the country's slide into degeneracy and secularism. As a result, evangelicals mounted a fight back, entering a new phase of political and social activism marked by Jimmy Carter's successful presidential bid (1976) and the creation of Jerry Falwell's Moral Majority organization (1979).[16] Thanks to a stronger post-war economy in the Sun Belt (a traditional fundamentalist stronghold), many evangelicals benefited from rising prosperity and upward social mobility, growing political acumen and media acuity.[17] Flexing their political muscles, the Religious Right was instrumental in sending Ronald Reagan to the White House (and Carter packing).[18] The ongoing cultural skirmishes (culture wars) have been well documented.

By the mid–1980s, evangelicalism had become "the dominant religious force" in America.[19] A 1986 Gallup poll found 32 percent of those surveyed identified themselves as "born-again" or "evangelical."[20] Conservative Christians have erected an impressive infrastructure to sustain a thriving subculture. Besides a widespread network of churches, these include numerous schools, colleges and universities, missionary agencies, alongside other parachurch organizations, such as the National Religious Broadcasters mentioned earlier, as well an extensive (alternative) media network.[21] By the early 1990s evangelicals commanded three TV networks, 200 TV stations, and nearly 1,300 radio stations; a billion dollar book industry with 80 publishers and over 6,000 book stores; and a thriving multi-million dollar music industry catering to a range of tastes — from rock 'n' roll, folk, and country to rap and heavy metal.[22] Evangelicals too were quick to seize the opportunities afforded by the Internet to propagate their gospel message. By 2002, the Christian entertainment industry (publishing, music and other producers of Christian-themed consumer goods) was generating yearly revenue of $4.2 billion.[23]

An important consequence of the evangelical movement's growing media sophistication has been the diffusion of apocalyptic themes (traditionally on the cultural margins) into the popular mainstream.[24] Political scientist Steve Barkun believes that, "[n]ot since the days of the 'Second Great Awakening' before the Civil War have so many Americans been so relentlessly exposed to chiliastic arguments and imagery."[25] Closely associated with apocalyptic thinking is premillennial dispensationalism. Attributed to John Nelson Darby (1800–82) and the Plymouth Brethren in Britain, this doctrine was popularized in the U.S. by Cyrus Scofield's (1843–1921) Reference Bible (1909), and is still used by dispensationalists today.[26] Anticipating Christ's return *before* the millennium,[27] history is conceived as a pattern of seven "dispensations" or periods when humanity is repeatedly tested — and punished — for failure: the expulsion from Eden (1st era); the Flood (2nd), the Tower of Babel (3rd) and so on. The present Church Age (6th), too is doomed, destined to terminate with the (looming) Tribulation — a seven year period of discord, destruction, and disaster — culminating in the Lord's return, triumph over Antichrist and his hordes at Armageddon, and millennial reign.[28] Though most devotees are pre–Tribulationists who expect to be divinely rescued or raptured[29] (physically transported from earth) *before* the tumult, there are also mid– and post–Tribulationists.[30] The latter (fringe minority) assume that they must suffer through the turbulence along with the unsaved. Adopting survivalist tactics, they create their own communities to wait out the seven-year storm.[31] Tribulationists — whether pre-, mid-, or post-leaning — anticipate a "literal fulfillment of Scripture prophecy"[32] whereby historical and current events are filtered through the particular lens of biblical prophecy they adopt. According to this worldview — counter to modernity's optimism — society spirals downward into degeneracy, apostasy, and violence, destined (soon!) for annihilation.[33] It is little wonder, then, that believers remain alert for end-time signs, described in Matthew 24:3–14, as wars, and rumors of wars, pestilence, and disaster.

This also explains why the signs of the times — even the possibility of worst-case scenarios such as the outbreak of World War III or a nuclear holocaust, along with activities that could conceivably work to bring these disasters about (e.g. stockpiling nuclear weapons) — may be seen by some enthusiasts as *positive* developments within the framework of dispensationalist thinking. Conversely, attempts to avoid such calamities — United Nations peace initiatives, for example — are rejected as impediments to God's doomsday plan.[34] Thus fervent believers may even welcome (albeit anxiously) wars, natural or man-made disasters, global warming, AIDS, crime, terrorism, Ebola, and so forth, as signs of Christ's imminent return and their own much-anticipated escape from physical death and suffering. These are recurrent themes in apocalyptic literature more generally and in the books examined more closely below.

Importantly for this discussion, "[p]remillennial dispensationalism ... is the predominant form of popular apocalypticism in the United States today," according to folklorist Daniel Wojcik.[35] A handful of individuals were instrumental in spreading premillennial dispensationalism early on: Jerry Falwell and Tim LaHaye (via their political activism and media ministries), and Hal Lindsey, author (with Carole C. Colson) of *Late Great Planet Earth* (1970). Lindsey's book dealt with the rapture, the Tribulation, and the Second Coming from the perspective of nuclear war; it was *the* best-selling "nonfiction" book in the U.S. during the 1970s, with nine million copies in print by 1978 (28 million by 1990).[36] Endism became a dominant mood in American society; *Time* magazine profiled "The Deluge of Disastermania" (March 5, 1979) and identified "Armageddon" a growth industry.[37] Controversy swirled around the issue of prophecy belief again in the 1980s when journalists reported that the sitting president, Ronald Reagan, and several top members of his administration, expressed interest in eschatology. At the time, serious concerns were raised about how these beliefs could adversely affect U.S. foreign policy — especially troubling in light of the collapse of détente with the Soviets and America's major build-up of conventional and nuclear weapons. (Recall that President Reagan delivered his Evil Empire speech at a National Religious Broadcaster conference.)[38] In 1981, the testimony of then Secretary of the Interior James Watt also raised alarm bells when he told a congressional committee "I don't know how many future generations we can count on until the Lord returns."[39]

Further evidence that apocalyptic and millennial motifs migrated from the fringes into the mainstream may be found in a steady stream of films[40] such as *The Omen* (1976), *Damien Omen II* (1978), *The Final Conflict* (1981),

The Rapture (1991), *Independence Day* (1996), *Armageddon* (1998), and *The Day After Tomorrow* (2004), and TV shows like *The X-Files, Millennium,* and *Revelations* (2005), NBC's six-part TV miniseries purportedly created to cash in on the interest generated by *LBS* and Mel Gibson's *The Passion of the Christ* (2004) . As Barkun observed: "What were once regarded as exotic sectarian manifestations have become part of popular culture...."[41] To this list we should add the growing list of paperbacks crowding bookstore shelves penned by prophecy populizers, both religionists and secularists alike. Top sellers (both fiction and non-fiction) include Michael Drosnin's *Bible Code* (1998) and *Bible Code II* (2003), Pat Robertson's novel *The End of the Age* (1996) and Joel Rosenberg's *Dead Heat* (2008), the fifth in the *Left Behind* political series spin-off (carrying an endorsement by right-wing radio personality Rush Limbaugh on its cover). Arguably *the* major purveyor of apocalyptic speculation is LaHayes's and Jenkins's tour de force *Left Behind* series as we will see next.

The *Left Behind* Series (*LBS*) — a Quintessential American Phenomenon

Nowhere is endism more apparent than in the runaway best-selling *Left Behind* series (*LBS*) of books which continue to popularize and spread apocalyptic speculation; as *Time* magazine enthused, co-authors "Tim LaHaye and Jerry B. Jenkins ... are doing for Christian fiction what John Grisham did for courtroom thrillers."[42] Part of an American apocalyptic literary tradition,[43] *LBS* is a serialization of events leading up to TEOTWAKI (the end of the world as we know it),[44] when the faithful (theologically conservative born-again Christians) will be divinely snatched (raptured) and the unsaved will be left behind when the Tribulation hits and the world slides into apostasy and turmoil. The first book, *Left Behind* (1995), kicks off with the rapture and its immediate aftermath. The story opens with the following passage:

> Rayford Steele's mind was on a woman he had never touched. With his fully loaded 747 on autopilot above the Atlantic en route to a 6 A.M. landing at Heathrow, Rayford had pushed from his mind thoughts of his family.

Moments later, millions of people suddenly disappear, leaving behind personal effects (e.g., clothing, belts, contact lenses, hearing aids, jewelry etc.) as well as loved ones. Chaos ensues: planes crash, cars careen out of control, ships sink, and fires rage, leaving survivors stunned and grieving by the magnitude of the global disaster. Amid the confusion (people suspect UFOs or radiation fallout are to blame for the disappearances), law and order breaks down and suicides are rampant. Readers are introduced here to the main recurring characters, including: Cameron "Buck" Williams, senior staff writer for a prestigious newsmagazine; Captain Rayford Steele, the (pseudo-philandering) airplane pilot; Chloe Steele, Rayford's college-aged daughter and Buck's love interest; Pastor Bruce Barnes, the (African American) pastor of New Hope Village Church; Nicolae Carpathia (aka Antichrist), the Romanian secretary-general of the UN; and Hattie Durham (aka Whore of Babylon), the airline stewardess who becomes Nicolae's personal assistant.

The central premise is laid in this first book and then subsequently worked out over the next eleven novels in the core series[45]: In order to survive, the heroes band together as the Tribulation Force, pledging to fight evil and expose Carpathia as Antichrist whilst converting as many unbelievers as possible (hence the books are laced with sermonettes and biblical passages explaining the finer points of dispensationalism and born-again beliefs, steeped in the political ideology of the Religious Right). In a nutshell, *LBS*— set in the present time — chronicles what happens to a small band of post-rapture penitents who must battle Satan's proxy, Antichrist (and his evil minions) to survive until the Second Coming. Then, in a final cataclysmic showdown between good and evil at Armageddon, Christ triumphs over his nemesis, casts the wicked into an eternal fiery furnace, and sets up a heavenly kingdom on earth for a thousand years.[46]

LBS was the brainchild of the Southern Baptist minister-cum-author Tim LaHaye. Now in his late 70s, he was recently described by one polemicist as "a small, elderly, gnome-like man with ... dyed coal black hair, a battery-powered earpiece and a pedantic, cold demeanor."[47] Diminutive physique notwithstanding, LaHaye is a titan in evangelical circles, known for his political activism. It turns out that this frail-looking minister is in fact a tough evangelical politico (culture warrior), who, next to his direct involvement in the cut and thrust of American politics, coauthored the blockbuster *Left Behind* series using Christian literary fiction as yet another delivery device to disseminate his particular brand of conservative evangelical ideology (about which more later).

LaHaye says he hatched his original book idea based on a real-life incident he experienced at 30,000 feet: aboard a routine flight he observed a (married) male pilot (with wedding band) flirting with an attractive stewardess (not his wife —*sans* ring). He started to fantasize about what would happen if the rapture struck that instant.[48] Afterwards LaHaye recruited middle-aged sportswriter Jerry Jenkins as his coauthor. Apparently Jenkins fleshes out the stories while LaHaye supplies the conservative[49] (theological and political) Christian framework that, among other things, features premillennial dispensationalism writ large.[50] In interviews both men assert that their main motivation is "soul saving" not profit, though neither denies that their books have proven a financial bonanza for themselves as well as their publisher, Tyndale House. Thanks to *LBS*, Tyndale's operations nearly doubled and its earnings trebled — registering $122 million in net revenue — propelling Tyndale House to first place as the nation's largest Christian publisher.[51]

A top-shelf brand in the crowded cultural marketplace, the series' success is due in no small measure to Tyndale's savvy marketing strategies. Moving beyond traditional Christian stores, the series is sold by general booksellers and retailers such as Barnes & Noble, Wal-Mart and Target, as well as airport bookstores across the country. The marketing budget for *The Mark* (book 8) alone was a purported $3.5 million, which paid for ads in *USA Today*, ABC Radio Network, and The Rush Limbaugh Show, among others.[52] The *LBS* literary franchise has also generated two new book series — one with a military theme, the other, political — by freshly recruited authors, alongside a Web site and virtual "Prophecy club" with weekly email newsletters. Further merchandizing spin-offs range from audio books and graphic novels, to children's books (targeting 9–12 year olds) and study guides designed for church groups. The *LBS* logo adorns a growing array of merchandized products: calendars, bible covers, key rings, magnets, mugs, teddy bears, greeting cards, T-shirts, a computer game, worship CD and interactive CR-ROM.[53] Three films have been made so far (available on DVD and video), although they have been much less profitable.

LaHaye and Jenkins' premillenialist end-time thrillers are among the best-selling fiction in the U.S. today, topping the best-seller lists of the *New York Times*, *Publishers Weekly*, *USA Today* and the *Wall Street Journal* as well as the Christian Booksellers Association. *LBS* had reached a staggering 60 million items by 2006 and is still climbing, achieving first print run sales exceeding two million copies — in the same league as John Grisham, Stephen King, Tom Clancy and J.K. Rowling.[54] Given these phenomenal sales, it is little wonder that *LBS* attracted the attention of the mainstream media. In 2002, for example, the authors were interviewed on CNN, ABC, NPR, CBS, and CNBC,[55] whereas *Time* magazine (U.S. edition) in July 2002 featured a burning cross emblazoned on the cover with the caption "The Bible and the apocalypse: why more Americans are reading and talking about the End of the World."[56] (*Newsweek* followed suit with its May 24, 2004 cover). *Entertainment Weekly* gushed, "Christian thriller. Prophecy-based fiction. Juiced-up morality tale. Call it what you like, the *Left Behind* series ... now has a label its creators could never have predicted: blockbuster success."[57] No doubt such media exposure boosted sales, but it does not explain the books' continuing popularity after the spotlight faded.

Reception among Audiences — Fans and Critics

An obvious question arises about consumers — just who is buying these products? In 2001, Tyndale hired Barna Research Group to find out.[58] According to this study carried out in October that year, almost one in ten American adults (9 percent of the general population), had read at least one of the *Left Behind* books. The overwhelming majority, 71 percent of readers, lived in the South and West, while only 6 percent resided in the Northeast (hence the Red State label used by journalists.) The typical customer was a Southern born-again (evangelical) white woman who was middle-aged, married with children, attended church regularly, and probably lacked a university degree.[59] As one journalist quipped, this "isn't the 'Sex and the City' crowd."[60] (This demographic may also help to explain Tyndale's sponsorship of a NASCAR racing car, replete with *Left Behind* logo — irony notwithstanding — probably aimed at *LBS'* core readers' husbands).

The evidence suggests that *LBS'* conservative evangelical fan-base correlates (albeit roughly) with specific church membership. Those denominations that embrace dispensationalism naturally are more favorably predisposed to the *Left Behind* series. For instance, the Assemblies of God (AOG), the largest white Pentecostal denomination in America, continues to promote the series. At the time of this writing (July 2008), affable interviews with both LaHaye (2000) and Jenkins (2007) are featured on the official website. Moreover, AOG posted its own doctrinal position on the rapture to demonstrate its accord with the views expressed in the books for the convenience of its members.

Not everyone is so enthralled by the series, of course. Some critics have disparaged the novels' prosaic style, grisly violence, and political conservatism. Others have objected primarily on theological grounds. These responses were predictable given the authors' insistence, aptly summed up by one *USA Today* reporter, that

> the end is imminent. And only those who accept Jesus as their personal savior and the Scripture as the sole source of God's word will know eternal life. Horrors await those who don't, including faithful Catholics and most mainline Protestants, Mormons, Muslims, Hindus, Buddhists and Jews.[61]

Thus LaHaye and Jenkins continue to draw sharp criticism from various quarters, including Jews and Catholics, as well as other Protestants at various points along the ideological spectrum.

Jewish scholars and journalists have repeatedly expressed unease and alarm regarding the depiction of Jews in the books. The centrality of Israel and the Jewish people during the Last Days is a prominent feature of *Left Behind* and reflects, to some extent, prevailing evangelical attitudes towards both today.[62] Taking a pro-Zionist stance, Jewish characters such as Rabbi Tsion Ben-Judah, scientist Chaim Rosenzweig, and the Wailing Wall prophets are rendered in a more sympathetic light, according to religion scholar Yaakov Ariel.[63] Though a case can be made that 144,000 evangelical Jews are actually saved during the Tribulation, there is a major catch — they must convert to Christianity or be destroyed along with the rest of the world's unbelievers (that is, everyone who is not a born-again conservative Protestant evangelical). In Ariel's estimation, *LBS* reflects, at best, "the mixed and ambivalent feelings toward Jews" that many conservative evangelicals harbor.[64] Israeli-based journalist Gershom Gorenberg's condemnation is less equivocal when he writes that the books' "anti–Jewishness is exceeded [only] by their anti–Catholicism."[65]

Many Catholics undoubtedly agree — at least the few familiar with the series. The Barna survey found that Catholics — the largest Christian church is the U.S. today — were among the *least likely* to have read any of the books, making up only 3 percent of all *LBS* readers.[66] Like their Jewish counterparts, Catholic writers and officials were highly critical of the series: at least two books by freelancers[67] have appeared to controvert what they call "rapture doctrine," while an online publisher charged that *Left Behind* "is prejudiced against Catholics and seeks to undermine their faith."[68] Official renunciation by the Catholic Church appeared in *The Living Light,* published by the U.S. bishops' Department of Education, which devoted half of its winter 2003 issue to *Left Behind.* Declaring the series "both subtly and overtly anti–Catholic,"[69] the articles detailed how *LBS* contradicted central Catholic teachings. Next to erroneous doctrine, Catholic critics also complained about the negative portrayal of the pope. Although he actually gets raptured (as readers discover in book two, *Tribulation Force),* it was only after embracing Protestant beliefs at the last moment. His successor in the series, American Peter Mathews, is a corpulent toady whose sham election is choreographed by Antichrist. In the ultimate betrayal, "Pontifex Maximus Peter II" sells out the Church of Rome to head up the new one-world religion which worships Antichrist as God.[70]

Among Protestants, broadly speaking, the reaction has been three-fold. Some churches enthusiastically embraced the series, such as the Assemblies of God, mentioned earlier. In contrast, liberal mainstream Protestants have given *LBS* the cold shoulder, choosing to ignore the books altogether.[71] However, there is at least one notable exception: the Presbyterian Church (U.S.). At its 2001 General Assembly, the denomination's elected representatives passed a strongly-worded resolution stating that the theology espoused in *LBS* is "not in accord with our Reformed understanding" and encouraged ministers to hold study sessions about the novels if they were becoming a source of "confusion and dissension" among congregants.[72]

Next to Catholics and Jews, some of the strongest indictments have been lobbed by other conservative Christians who found fault with the series even as they shared some theological valences with the authors. The dean of the Southern Baptist Theological Seminary in Louisville, Danny Aiken, conceded his agreement with LaHaye's general theology but expressed grave concerns about the authors' handling of Scripture in the storyline. Another evangelical theologian, Ben Witherington III of Asbury Theological Seminary, ridiculed the dispensational theology expressed in the novels as "'Beam me up, Scotty' belief."[73] In a similar vein, A.L. Barry, (the late) president of the Lutheran Church — Missouri Synod (second-largest Lutheran denomination in the U.S.) ridiculed the books. In his December 2000 statement titled "The 'Left Behind' View is out of Left Field," he argued, among other things, that the Book of Revelation is "written in highly symbolic language" and "is not meant to be read as a literal account."[74] Dismissing the authors' claim that *LBS* is "true to prophecy," Barry rejoined "The entire 'Left Behind' series ... is an unbiblical flight of fancy (known by the term 'dispensational premillennialism') receiving far more press than it deserves."[75]

Regardless of the criticisms offered by evangelical elites however, it is clear that many conservative Christians share the basic tenets of prophecy belief reflected in the *Left Behind* series, even if they dispute the fine print. As indicated above, the Barna Research Group found that evangelicals were *LBS*' core readership. This is not accidental, since the prevalence of prophecy belief has been closely linked to the relatively high rates of evangelical belief and practice in contemporary American society.[76]

A Tentative Explanation of *LBS*' Sustained Popularity

As noted earlier, the preoccupation with eschatological signs is nothing new, nor is setting dates for the world's end; history contains many examples, along with corresponding disconfirmations.[77] Yet it seems paradoxical that in the United States — a highly modern society in many other respects — ancient ideas of apocalypticism and millennialism are "commonplace,"[78] albeit with a more recent dispensational twist. Endism accelerated at the *fin-de-millennium*[79]; the Y2K computer glitch, followed by the 9/11 attacks on the U.S. by foreign extremists, triggered fresh waves of apocalyptic anxieties among evangelicals, confirming Boyer's claim about the prevalence of these beliefs. According to a Time/CNN poll taken in 2002, a staggering 59 percent of Americans asked said that they expected the events portrayed in the Book of Revelation to come true in a literal sense. Over *one-third* indicated that they were watching news reports more closely to determine how current events related to TEOTWAKI. Those polled likewise admitted that they had discussed relevant Bible passages on the subject with others and almost *one-fourth* were convinced that the 9/11 attacks were predicted in the Bible. (This enhanced apocalypticism was also manifest in *LBS* sales which skyrocketed 60 percent).[80] Such surveys must be used judiciously of course, yet the figures are nevertheless striking. They continue to point to a longstanding trend concerning the relatively higher levels of religious belief that distinguish the U.S. from other advanced Western economies in the world today.[81]

When trying to explain the popularity of the *Left Behind* series, a number of relevant factors come into play. The stories are multi-layered and function at a variety of levels. Scholars remain divided about *LBS'* principle purpose. Literature professor Amy Frykholm asserts that the authors' primary purpose is to entertain: "They want to tell a fast-paced, action-packed story with adventure and drama that will capture and hold readers' attention."[82] Brian Wilson of Western Michigan University suggests that *LBS* fills a particular niche in the evangelical marketplace, arguing that the *Left Behind* series "provide a horror story with doctrinal sanction" among a constituency "that still denies itself Stephen King, fearing his books' occult overtones."[83] Several observers have noted that *LBS* undoubtedly provides a form of escapism, as popular culture does more generally; the novels' formulaic storylines enable readers to know the outcome in advance: the good guys (Tribulation Force) win and the bad guys (Carpathia and his henchmen) lose. Randall Balmer and Lauren Winner, in their book *Protestantism in America* suggest that, however improbable to non-evangelicals, prophecy speculation itself—'Could those UPC codes in the supermarket [be] the Mark of the Beast?'—is actually a lot of fun.[84]

At the same time, the books are clearly didactic, as evidenced for example by myriad exhortations and Bible passages running throughout the novels. Catholic critic Jimmy Akin insists that there are actually two conflicting motives in the series: prophet vs. profit. The first involves "a sincere desire to advance people's knowledge of God's prophetic words — what we may call a prophet motive. The second is the simple desire to make a buck — a plain, old, ordinary profit motive."[85] Many critics openly accused the authors of being driven purely for personal financial gain; independent Catholic writer Carl Olson warned his readers that "millions of people have left behind their cash at their local book store in exchange for LaHaye's and Jenkin's vision of the future — will you be next?"[86]

Supporters and fans who were initially more favorably inclined to the novels lauded the novels as evangelistic tools to reach the unsaved. George Barna, head of the Research Group bearing his name, discovered in his survey that, while the core readership of *Left Behind* were indeed "born again" adults, as many as three million "non–born again" individuals had read one or more books in the series. Welcoming *LBS* as an effective evangelistic or teaching tool, he pointed out that *Left Behind* actually reached a wider unchurched audience than had most religious TV or radio ministries.[87] Others largely agreed with Barna about the proselytizing potential of the novels and objected to them on those very grounds. These critics implied that *LBS* was simply unadulterated propaganda intended to "sheep steal" (that is, "convert" Christians from other faith traditions). Catholic writer Carl Olson, for instance, declared that

> the real point of the series is to present a theological system, as evidenced by the nearly endless number of pages filled with sermons, lectures and explanations about the Rapture, impending doom and ... well, the Rapture. In essence, the books were simply "tract-novels," stories wrapped around huge chunks of blatant proselytizing.[88]

Although downplayed in much of the scholarly analysis, there are commentators who concur that the novels are indeed propagandistic but not for the purpose of soul-saving. Instead, these critics insist, the real motivation behind the series entails an old-fashioned ploy for political power. Michael Standaert, in his book *Skipping Towards Armageddon*, calls the series "conscious propaganda" and maintains that the series is ultimately intended to further LaHaye's and the Religious Right's political agenda. He claims that the books "have little to do with spiritual faith and a great deal to do with power over how millions of Americans view the intersection of faith and politics."[89]

LaHaye remains an outspoken doyen of the Religious Right, involved in key organizations and institutions whose reach has moved well beyond the evangelical subculture. He helped found the Moral Majority (with Falwell), the Institute for Creation Research, and Concerned Women for America (with his wife Beverly). LaHaye also served briefly as co-chair of Jack Kemp's 1988 presidential bid (until he was forced to resign after allegedly making anti–Catholic remarks). Most important of all, LaHaye has played a strategic role in organizing the Council for National Policy in 1981. The Council has been hailed by CBS News as "the most influential organization you've never heard of."[90] In 2004 the *New York Times* likewise described the CNP as "a little known club of a few hundred of the most powerful conservatives in the country [who for 23 years] have met behind closed doors at undisclosed locations ... to strategize about how to turn the country to the right."[91] CNP membership reportedly includes such right-wing Illuminati as William F. Buckley, Grover Norquist, John Ashcroft, Oliver North, Tommy Thompson, Holland Coors (of beer fame), James Dobson (Focus on the Family radio host), Wayne LaPierre (National Rifle Association), and Phyllis Schlafly (anti–ERA campaigner). The Council has played host to Vice President Dick Cheney, former Defense Secretary Donald Rumsfeld, and former Senate majority leader Bill Frist. In fact, President George W. Bush (then governor of Texas) addressed the group in 1999 but has steadfastly refused to make his speech available to the public. For his part, LaHaye has been recognized by those in the know as the most influential American evangelical of the 20th century,[92] a tribute that is not merely hyperbole. In a 2004 interview with the *Los Angeles Times*, Jerry Falwell described LaHaye's political clout: "His impact subliminally is probably greater than it ever has been, such that if you were to ask him he would tell you that he's no longer crusading, he's evangelizing.... Once his converts get in our churches, we pastors have a tendency to tell them how to vote."[93] Thus the allegation leveled by critics like Standaert about LaHaye's scheme to push the nation further to the right is credible and consequently *LBS* may be seen as simply another tool in the Religious Right's arsenal to disseminate its ideological message.

The melding of religious and spiritual concerns is not new in American history of course. As Juergensmeyer points out, what *had* changed by the turn of the 21st century was "the way that religion became infused into a radical critique of the secular political order."

> Though Christianity has always contained the idea of a kingdom of God that contrasts with the worldly human order, the notion of a catastrophic moment history in which this godly kingdom intersects with the human order is peculiar to Evangelical Protestant Christianity. It began to take shape in the modern era with the theology of John Nelson Darby, a nineteenth-century British theologian, who believed that the time of the kingdom would be at hand when pious Christians experienced the "rapture" of being united with heavenly existence. This vision reemerged with remarkable popularity in the United States after the end of the Cold War. It has provided the framework for the *Left Behind* novels of Tim LaHaye and Jerry Jenkins, which have sold tens of millions of copies. Many of the sixteen volumes ... made the *New York Times* best-seller list.[94]

Juergensmeyer further suggests that the American evangelical movement, the acknowledged *LBS* audience, "has had *a profound impact on American politics*. It required American political society to take on a Christian character in order to fulfill society's role in the coming of Christ."[95] Indeed, while there exists broad diversity among evangelicals today, their numbers remain formidable, as is their collective political clout. In 2004, CBS news reported that an estimated 70 million Americans call themselves evangelical, and in the 2000 presidential election, 40 percent of the ballots cast for George W. Bush came from this constituency.[96] This does not mean however, that every evangelical reads the series, or subscribes to the views expressed in the novels, political or otherwise. As cultural studies theorists have long pointed out, audiences may decode texts in a variety of ways that are ultimately outside the control of the producers. In our case, we ought to take a closer look at the other functions that the novels may fulfill.

From an external perspective, prophecy belief appears to be a major component in the construction of individual and collective evangelical identity. For devotees, products such as *LBS* are edifying and may even be used for ritual purposes, elevated to the status of religious relics[97] — that is, when profane cultural artifacts become imbued with sacred meaning. These goods, in aggregate, help to reinforce existing beliefs and worldviews, which in turn, provide support in promoting and sustaining the evangelical subculture, forging shared identities among constituents and serving as boundary markers for outsiders. As Andre Corten and Ruth Marshall-Fratani make clear, although a spiritual rebirth (born-again) conversion experience involves the individual breaking with his or her past life, actually *being* born again is a lifelong existential undertaking, not a static state achieved once and for all.[98]

Thus cultural products such as *LBS* reinforce existing beliefs, helping to sustain a belief system constantly under pressure from outside forces. Although some scholars have seen "fundamentalism" in broad strokes as a kind of collective illness,[99] prophecy belief may play a significant social-psychological role as a therapeutic tool to relieve emotional stress. Religion scholar George Marsden for example, contends that dispensationalism, based on a teleological view of history, envisions "divine intervention [as] the direct solution to the modern problem of change."[100] Glenn Shuck agrees: In his book *Marks of the Beast: The Left Behind Novels and the Struggle for Evangelical Identity*, he convincingly argues that LaHaye and Jenkins, like other conservative evangelicals more generally, feel besieged and "threatened by pervasive yet elusive economic, political, and cultural forces ... [and thus] articulate their anxieties in the familiar language of apocalypse, creating protagonists who give voice to their deepest concerns."[101] Shuck suggests that these born-again believers require a certain amount of tension for boundary maintenance to distinguish themselves from mainstream American society. So in effect, prophecy belief strengthens evangelical identity by serving as a sort of' "cultural thermostat" that can be adjusted up or down, giving these believers "just the right amount of tension vis-à-vis the contemporary world."[102]

Dispensationalists may receive emotional benefits associated with belonging to a network of like-minded believers, along with the satisfaction of possessing a "privileged source of knowledge"[103] that eschews formal training or elaborate study. Even more importantly, the apparent fulfillment of specific predictions, or even disconfirmations that may be adequately explained from their perspective of faith, provide empirical proof substantiating the dispensational system and evangelical faith as well. Devotees may derive comfort in deciphering order and meaning from seemingly chaotic historical events, and perceive their own importance as actors in God's end time plan.[104]

Lastly, one should not discount that for many fans, the *Left Behind* series are a rip-roaring read, as some critics begrudgingly admit. In reality, the appeal value of the entertainment element of these sorts of products appears beyond dispute — after all, as the argument goes, they would quickly disappear if consumers stopped buying them. As long as evangelicals continue to feel threatened by the cultural mainstream and can use their belief system to adequately explain current events — and have fun doing so — there seems little evidence that these believers will abandon the activity anytime soon. Meanwhile, at the time of this writing (July 2008), another series generated by the *Left Behind* culture-religion industry will be out shortly, insuring the demand for these goods will continue to be met, at least for the foreseeable future.

NOTES

1. Coined by Charles B. Strozier, *Apocalypse* (Boston: Beacon, 1994 [reprint WIPF and Stock publishers] 2002).

2. Following Randall Balmer, I use evangelicalism here as an umbrella term for conservative Protestants who include Pentecostals, charismatics, fundamentalists, and of course, evangelicals. In general these believers hold that an individual born-again experience is necessary for salvation, emphasize the importance of having a personal relationship with Jesus, and underscore the Great Commission to spread the Gospel. They adopt various degrees of biblical literalism, underline the inerrancy of Scripture and insist upon certain behavioral standards or moral codes within their ranks. Many object to the fundamentalist label, preferring to be called evangelical instead. For further discussion, see Randall Balmer, *Mine Eyes Have Seen the Glory* (New York and Oxford: Oxford University Press, 2000) xv–xviii.

3. Stozier, *Apocalypse*, 1.

4. Paul Boyer, *When Time Shall Be No More* (Cambridge, MA, and London: Belknap, 1992) 23.

5. Eugen Weber, *Apocalypses* (Cambridge, MA: Harvard University Press, 1999) 29.

6. Norman Cohn, *The Pursuit of the Millennium* (London: Paladin, 1970) 24–25.

7. Here millenarism, millennialism or chiliasm are used interchangeably for the belief in the future millennium.

8. Cohn, *The Pursuit of the Millennium*, 13.

9. Millenarians are found in movements outside Christianity, both religious and secular; see Catherine Wessinger, ed. *Millennialism, Persecution, & Violence* (Syracuse, NY: Syracuse University Press, 2000).

10. Quoted in Jeanne Halgren Kilde, "How Did Left Behind's Particular Vision of the End Times Develop?" in *Rapture, Revelation, and The End Times,* Bruce David Forbes and Jeanne Halgren Kilde, eds. (New York: Palgrave, 2004) 46.

11. *Ibid.*, Daniel Wojcik *The End of the World As We Know It* (New York and London: New York University Press, 1997) 21.

12. Boyer, *When Time Shall Be No More,* 68. See also Carmen Gomez-Galisteo's "Flight from the Apocalypse" in this volume.

13. Lorne L. Dawson, *Comprehending Cults,* (Oxford, UK: Oxford University Press, 2006) 147.

14. Edwin Gaustad and Leigh Schmidt, *The Religious History of America* (New York: Harper San Francisco, 2002) 336.

15. Mark Juergensmeyer, *Global Rebellion* (Berkeley: University of California Press, 2008) 182–3.

16. George Marsden, *Understanding Fundamentalism and Evangelicalism* (Grand Rapids, MI: Wm. B. Eerdmans, 1991) 105–109. See also Evelyn Stiller's essay "Gaming Armageddon," in this volume.

17. Michael Barkun, "Afterward: Millennial Violence in Contemporary America," in *Millennialism, Persecution, & Violence*, Catherine Wessinger, ed. (Syracuse, NY: Syracuse University Press, 2000) 353; also E. Weber, *Apocalypses,* 234.

18. Ironically, many conservative evangelicals did not support fellow evangelical Carter because he was "too liberal."

19. George Marsden, ed. *Evangelicalism and Modern America* (Grand Rapids, MI: Wm. B. Eerdmans, 1984) 43.

20. Boyer, *When Time Shall Be No More*, 3.

21. Christian Smith, *American Evangelicalism* (Chicago: University of Chicago Press, 1998) 12–13.

22. James Davison Hunter, *Culture Wars* (New York: Basic, 1991) 229–230.

23. Michael Standaert, *Skipping Towards Armageddon* (Brooklyn, NY: Soft Skull Press, 2006) 60.

24. Michael Barkun, *Disaster and the Millennium* (New Haven, CT: Yale University Press, 1974 [reprint Syracuse University Press, 1986]) 160.

25. *Ibid.*

26. See Mark Noll, *A History of Christianity in the United States and Canada* (London: SPCK, 1992) 376–378; Grace Halsell, *Prophecy and Politics* (Westport, CT: Lawrence Hill, 1986).

27. There are also *postmillennialists* who expect the Lord to return after the Church has built a worthy society, and *amillennialists* who believe that the millennium is figurative, occurring in the hearts of believers; Timothy Weber, *Living in the Shadow of the Second Coming* (Grand Rapids, MI: Academie, 1983) 9.

28. Marsden, *Understanding*, 40; Boyer, *When Time Shall Be No More*, 87–88; Noll, *A History of Christianity in the United States and Canada*, 376–378.

29. The term does not appear in the Bible but is inferred from I Thessalonians 4:16–17.

30. Robert Clouse, "Rapture of the Church" in *The Concise Evangelical Dictionary of Theology*, Walter Elwell, ed. (London: Marshall Pickering, 1993) 415–417.

31. Michael Barkun, "Language of Apocalypse: Premillennialists and Nuclear War" in *The God Pumpers: Religion in the Electronic Age,* Marshall Fishwick and Ray Browne, eds. (Bowling Green, OH: Bowling Green State University Popular Press, 1987) 172, fn. 3.

32. E. Weber, *Apocalypses*, 172.

33. Marsden, *Understanding*, 41.

34. Halsell *Prophecy and Politics*; Wojcik, *The End of the World As We Know It.*

35. Wojcik, *The End of the World As We Know It*, 37.

36. Boyer, *When Time Shall Be No More*, 5; Marsden, *Understanding*, 159.

37. E. Weber, *Apocalypses*, 207–208.

38. Boyer, *When Time Shall Be No More*, 162.

39. E. Weber, *Apocalypses*, 202; Boyer, *When Time Shall Be No More*, 141; other administrative officials included Secretary of Defense Casper Weinberger and the Surgeon General C. Everett Koop.

40. E. Weber, *Apocalypses*, 207; Barkun, "Aftermath," 362.

41. Barkun, *Disaster*, viii.

42. Tim LaHaye and Jerry B. Jenkins, *Indwelling* (Carol Stream, IL: Tyndale House, 2000), back flap.

43. "The Left Behind Books," discussion between Randall Balmer and Michael Maudlin, *Slate* June 20, 2000, <http://www.slate.com/id/2000179/entry/1005543/> and <http://www.slate.com/id/2000179/> (October 15, 2008).

44. TEOTWAKI "was used a lot prior to the year 2000 in anticipation of the Y2K date change" *The Free Dictionary.* <http://www.theFreeDictionary.com> (July 21, 2008).

45. The core *LBS* is: *Left Behind* (1995), *Tribulation Force* (1996), *Nicolae* (1997), *Soul Harvest* (1998), *Apollyon* (1999), *Assassins* (1999), *The Indwelling* (2000), *The Mark* (2000), *Desecration* (2001), *The Remnant* (2002), *Armageddon* (2003) and *Glorious Appearing* (2004). The series has ballooned to 16 titles: three prequels: *The Rising* (2005); *The Regime* (2005), and *The Rapture* (2006); and one sequel, *Kingdom Come* (2007). All are published by Tyndale House.

46. Bruce David Forbes, "How Popular Are the Left Behind Books ... and Why?" in *Rapture, Revelation, and the End Times*, Bruce David Forbes and Jeanne Halgren Kilde, eds., 7.

47. Chris Hedges, *American Fascists* (Glencoe, IL: Free Press, 2007) 183.

48. David Gates, "The New Prophets of Revelation" *Newsweek*, May 24, 2004. <http://www.prnewsire.com/cgi-bin/micro_stories.pl?ACCT=6178> (January 8, 2008).

49. For good discussions about LaHaye's conservative political and theological agenda, see Standaert, *Skipping Towards Armageddon*; also Melani McAlister, "Prophecy, Politics, and the Popular: The *Left Behind* Series and Christian Fundamentalism's New World Order" *The South Atlantic Quarterly* 102, no. 4 (2003): 773–798.

50. Jenkins said, "We each play a different role in the creation of the books. Dr. LaHaye develops a detailed biblical outline for each book. I do all the writing." Quoted in Jimmy Akin, "False Profit: Money, Prejudice, and Bad Theology in Tim LaHaye's *Left Behind Series*" *Catholic Answers Special Report*, undated: last modified March 1, 2004 <http://www.catholic.com/library/false_profit.asp> (June 13, 2008).

51. Corrie Cutrer "Publishing: *Left Behind* Series Puts Tyndale Ahead" *Christianity Today*, November 13, 2000 <http://christianitytoday.com/ct/2000/november13/20.26.html> (October 28, 2007).

52. *Ibid.*

53. Malcolm Gold, "The *Left Behind* Series as Sacred Text?" In *Reading Religion in Text and Context.* Elisabeth Arweck and Peter Collins, eds. (Aldershot, UK: Ashgate, 2006) 35–36; Cutrer, "Publishing: *Left Behind* Series Puts Tyndale Ahead."

54. Forbes, "How Popular Are the Left Behind Books ... and Why?" 7–8; Gold, "The *Left Behind* Series as Sacred Text?" 36; Nancy Gibbs, "Is It Good for the Jews?" *Time,* July 1, 2002 <http://www.time.com/time/magazine/article/0,9171,1002761,00.html> (January 11, 2008).

55. McAlister, "Prophecy, Politics, and the Popular: The *Left Behind* Series and Christian Fundamentalism's New World Order," 774.

56. Gibbs, "Is It Good for the Jews?"

57. LaHaye and Jenkins, *Indwelling*, back flap.

58. Despite its evangelical Christian leaning, Barna is considered a reliable pollster by scholars (Forbes, "How Popular Are the Left Behind Books ... and Why?" 8–9).

59. Gold, "The *Left Behind* Series as Sacred Text?" 36–7.

60. Gates, "The New Prophets of Revelation."

61. Cathy Lynn Grossman, "Prophecy feeds fires of debate: End-of-the-world books have an eternal appeal" *USA Today,* April 22, 2004, D.07 <http://pqasb.pqarchiver.com/TSAToday/622180421.html> (July 23, 2004).

62. Gibbs, "Is It Good for the Jews?"

63. Yaakov Ariel, "How are Jews and Israel Portrayed in the Left Behind Series?" in *Rapture, Revelation, and The End Times*, 131–166.

64. Ariel, "How are Jews and Israel Portrayed in the Left Behind Series?" 146.

65. Quoted in Forbes, "How Popular Are the Left Behind Books ... and Why?" 27.

66. "Different Groups follow Harry Potter, Left Behind and Jabez" *The Barna Update*, October 22, 2001 <http://www.barna.org/FlexPage.aspx?Page=BarnaUpdateNarrow&B> (January 16, 2008).

67. Paul Thigpen, *The Rapture Trap: A Catholic Response to "End Times" Fever* (West Chester, PA: Ascension Press, 2001) and Carl E. Olson, *Will Catholics Be Left Behind?: A Critique of the Rapture and Today's Prophecy Preachers* (Ft. Collins, CO: Ignatius, 2003).

68. Akin, "False Profit: Money, Prejudice, and Bad Theology in Tim LaHaye's *Left Behind Series.*"

69. Quoted in Jerry Fiteau, "Left Behind series called 'overtly anti–Catholic'" *Catholic News Service*, April 12, 2004 <http://www.catholicnews.com/data/stories/cns/20040412a.html> (June 13, 2008).

70. LaHaye firmly rejects the anti–Catholic charge, although he is an alumni of Bob Jones University, a fundamentalist stronghold known for its virulent anti–Catholicism. More telling is the fact that LaHaye was dropped during the Kemp campaign when it was reported that he had called Catholicism a "false religion." See Standaert, *Skipping Towards Armageddon*, 43, 51.

71. Forbes, "How Popular Are the Left Behind Books ... and Why?" 16.

72. Quoted in John Dart, "Beam Me Up Theology" *The Christian Century*, September 25-October 8 (2002): 8–9.

73. *Ibid.*

74. A.L. Barry, "The 'Left Behind' View is out of Left Field" Lutheran Church — Missouri Synod, December 11, 2000 <http://www.lifeoftheword.com/believe/statements/left behind.php> (June 14, 2008).

75. *Ibid.*

76. Boyer, *When Time Shall Be No More*, 293; Marsden, *Understanding*, 158.

77. Normally divorced from a temporal millennium, famous disconfirmations include the Anabaptists' prediction of 1533 and the Millerite prophecies of 1843–4; see Cohn *The Pursuit of the Millennium*; also Leon Festinger et al., *When Prophecy Fails* (New York: Harper Torchbooks, 1956) 3–32.

78. Boyer, *When Time Shall Be No More*, 337

79. E. Weber, *Apocalypses*, 221–222; also Boyer, *When Time Shall Be No More*, 337; Barkun, "Afterward," 352.

80. Gibbs, "Is It Good for the Jews?"

81. Pippa Norris and Ronald Inglehart, *Sacred and Secular: Religion and Politics Worldwide* (Cambridge, UK: Cambridge University Press, 2004) 83–110.

82. Amy Johnson Frykholm, "What Social and Political Messages Appear in the Left Behind Books?" in *Rapture, Revelation, and The End Times*, 193.

83. David Van Biema, "The End: How It Got That Way" *Time*, July 1, 2002 <http://www.time.com/time/magazine/artcle/0,9171,1002760,00.html> (January 1, 2008).

84. Quoted *ibid.*

85. Akin, "False Profit: Money, Prejudice, and Bad Theology in Tim LaHaye's *Left Behind Series.*"

86. Carl E. Olson, "No Rapture for Rome: The anti–Catholics Behind the Best-selling *Left Behind* Books" *This Rock* magazine, November, 2000 <http://www.catholic.com/thisrock/2000/0011fea2.asp> (October 18, 2008).

87. "Different Groups follow Harry Potter, Left Behind and Jabez" *The Barna Update*,

October 22, 2001 <http://www.barna.org/FlexPage.aspx?=BarnaUpdateNarrow&B> (January 1, 2008).

88. Olson, "No Rapture for Rome: The anti–Catholics Behind the Best-selling *Left Behind* Books."

89. Standaert, *Skipping Towards Armageddon*, 4–5. See also Johann Pautz's essay in this volume, "The End-Times Narratives of the American Far-Right."

90. Michelle Goldberg, "Fundamentally Unsound" *Salon* July 29, 2002. <http://www.salon.com/story/books/feature/2002/07/29/left_behind> (January 1, 2008).

91. David D. Kirkpatrick, "The 2004 Campaign: The Conservatives; Club of the Most Powerful Gathers in Strictest Privacy" *New York Times*, August 28, 2004, <http://query.nytimes.com/gst/fullpage.html?res=9C0CE3DA1E3EF93BA1575BC0A9629C8B63> (October 18, 2008).

92. See Forbes, "How Popular Are the Left Behind Books ... and Why?" 14–15.

93. Nancy Shepherdson, "Writing for Godot," *Los Angeles Times*, April 25, 2004, <http://articles.latimes.com/2004/apr/25/magazine/tm-lahaye17> (October 18, 2008).

94. Juergensmeyer, *Global Rebellion*, 182.

95. *Ibid.*, my emphasis.

96. CBS News, "Rise of the Righteous Army," February 8, 2004, <http://www.cbsnews.com/stories/2004/02/05/60minutes> (January 8, 2008).

97. See Gold, "The *Left Behind* Series as Sacred Text?" for further discussion.

98. Andre Corten and Ruth Marshall-Fratani, eds. *From Babel to Pentecost* (Bloomington and Indianapolis: Indiana University Press, 2002) 7.

99. Strozier, *Apocalypse*, 3.

100. Marsden, *Understanding*, 41.

101. Glenn Shuck, *Marks of the Beast: The Left Behind Novels and the Struggle for Evangelical Identity* (New York: New York University Press, 2004) 2.

102. *Ibid.*, 4.

103. Boyer, *When Time Shall Be No More*, 309.

104. *Ibid.*, xi, 315.

WORKS CITED

Akin, Jimmy. "False Profit: Money, Prejudice, and Bad Theology in Tim LaHaye's *Left Behind Series*" *Catholic Answers Special Report*. March 1, 2004. <http://www.catholic.com/library/false_profit.asp> (June 13, 2008).

Ariel, Yaakov. "How are Jews and Israel Portrayed in the Left Behind Series?" in *Rapture, Revelation, and The End Times*. Bruce David Forbes and Jeanne Halgren Kilde, eds. New York: Palgrave, 2004: 131–166.

Balmer, Randall. *Mine Eyes Have Seen the Glory*. New York and Oxford: Oxford University Press, 2000.

Barkun, Michael. "Afterward: Millennial Violence in Contemporary America" in *Millennialism, Persecution, and Violence*. Catherine Wessinger, ed. Syracuse, NY: Syracuse University Press, 2000: 352–366.

_____. *Disaster and the Millennium*. New Haven: Yale University Press, 1974. Reprint Syracuse University Press, 1986.

_____. "Language of Apocalypse: Premillennialists and Nuclear War" in *The God Pumpers: Religion in the Electronic Age*. Marshall Fishwick and Ray Browne, eds. Bowling Green, OH: Bowling Green State University Popular Press, 1987: 159–173.

The Barna Update. "Different Groups follow Harry Potter, Left Behind and Jabez." October 22, 2001. <http://www.barna.org/FlexPage.aspx?Page=BarnaUpdateNarrow&B> (January 16, 2008).

Barry, A.L. "The 'Left Behind' View is out of Left Field." Lutheran Church — Missouri Synod. December 11, 2000. <http://www.lifeoftheword.com/believe/statements/left behind.php> (June 14, 2008).

Boyer, Paul. *When Time Shall Be No More.* Cambridge, MA, and London: Belknap, 1992.

Clouse, Robert. "Rapture of the Church" in *The Concise Evangelical Dictionary of Theology.* Walter Elwell, ed. London: Marshall Pickering, 1993: 415–417.

Cohn, Norman. *The Pursuit of the Millennium.* London: Paladin, 1970.

Corten, Andre, and Ruth Marshall-Fratani, eds. *From Babel to Pentecost.* Bloomington and Indianapolis: Indiana University Press, 2002.

Cutrer, Corrie. "Publishing: *Left Behind* Series Puts Tyndale Ahead." *Christianity Today.* November 13, 2000. <http://christianitytoday.com/ct/2000/november13/20.26.html> (October 28, 2007).

Dart, John. "Beam Me Up Theology." *The Christian Century.* September 25-October 8 (2002): 8–9.

Dawson, Lorne L. *Comprehending Cults.* Oxford: Oxford University Press, 2006.

Festinger, Leon, et al. *When Prophecy Fails.* New York: Harper Torchbooks, 1956.

Fiteau, Jerry. "Left Behind Series Called 'Overtly Anti-Catholic.'" *Catholic News Service.* April 12, 2004. <http://www.catholicnews.com/data/stories/cns/20040412a.html> (June 13, 2008).

Forbes, Bruce David. "How Popular Are the Left Behind Books ... and Why?" in *Rapture, Revelation, and the End Times.* Bruce David Forbes and Jeanne Halgren Kilde, eds. New York: Palgrave, 2004: 5–32.

Frykholm, Amy Johnson. "What Social and Political Messages Appear in the Left Behind Books?" in *Rapture, Revelation, and The End Times.* Bruce David Forbes and Jeanne Halgren Kilde, eds. New York: Palgrave, 2004: 167–195.

Gates, David. "The New Prophets of Revelation." *Newsweek.* May 24, 2004. <http://www.prnewswire.com/cgi-bin/micro_stories.pl?ACCT=6178> (January 8, 2008).

Gaustad, Edwin, and Leigh Schmidt. *The Religious History of America.* New York: Harper San Francisco, 2002.

Gibbs, Nancy. "Is It Good for the Jews?" *Time.* July 1, 2002. <http://www.time.com/time/magazine/article/0,9171,1002761,00.html> (January 11, 2008).

Gold, Malcolm. "The *Left Behind* Series as Sacred Text?" in *Reading Religion in Text and Context.* Elisabeth Arweck and Peter Collins, eds. Aldershot, UK: Ashgate, 2006: 34–49.

Goldberg, Michelle. "Fundamentally Unsound." *Salon.* July 29, 2002. <http://www.salon.com/story/books/feature/2002/07/29/left_behind> (January 1, 2008).

Grossman, Cathy Lynn. "Prophecy Feeds Fires of Debate: End-of-the-World Books Have an Eternal Appeal." *USA Today.* April 22, 2004, D07. <http://pqasb.pqarchiver.com/TSAToday/622180421.html> (July 23, 2004).

Halsell, Grace. *Prophecy and Politics.* Westport, CT: Lawrence Hill, 1986.

Hedges, Chris. *American Fascists.* Glencoe, IL: Free Press, 2007.

Hunter, James Davison. *Culture Wars.* New York: Basic, 1991.

Jeurgensmeyer, Mark. *Global Rebellion.* Berkeley: University of California Press, 2008.

Kilde, Jeanne Halgren. "How Did Left Behind's Particular Vision of the End Times Develop?" in *Rapture, Revelation, and The End Times.* Bruce David Forbes and Jeanne Halgren Kilde, eds. New York: Palgrave, 2004: 33–70.

Kirkpatrick, David D. "The 2004 Campaign: The Conservatives; Club of the Most Powerful Gathers in Strictest Privacy." *New York Times.* August 28, 2004. <http://query.nytimes.com/gst/fullpage.html?res=9C0CE3DA1E3EF93BA1575BC0A9629C8B63> (January 1, 2008).

"The Left Behind Books," discussion between Randall Balmer and Michael Maudlin. *Slate.*

June 20, 2000. <http://www.slate.com/id/2000179/entry/1005543/> and <http://www.slate.com/id/2000179/> (October 15, 2008).

LaHaye, Tim, and Jerry B. Jenkins. *Indwelling*. Carol Stream, IL: Tyndale House, 2000.

Marsden, George. *Understanding Fundamentalism and Evangelicalism*. Grand Rapids, MI: Wm B. Eerdmans, 1991.

_____, ed. *Evangelicalism and Modern America*. Grand Rapids, MI: Wm B. Eerdmans, 1984.

McAlister, Melani. "Prophecy, Politics, and the Popular: The *Left Behind* Series and Christian Fundamentalism's New World Order." *The South Atlantic Quarterly* 102, no. 4 (2003): 773–798.

Noll, Mark. *A History of Christianity in the United States and Canada*. London: SPCK, 1992.

Norris, Pippa, and Ronald Inglehart. *Sacred and Secular: Religion and Politics Worldwide*. Cambridge, UK: Cambridge University Press, 2004.

Olson, Carl E. "No Rapture for Rome: The Anti-Catholics Behind the Bestselling Left Behind Books." *This Rock*. November 2000. <http://www.catholic.com/thisrock/2000/0011fea2.asp> (October 18, 2008).

_____. *Will Catholics Be Left Behind?: A Critique of the Rapture and Today's Prophecy Preachers*. Ft. Collins, CO: Ignatius, 2003.

"Rise of the Righteous Army." *CBS News*. February 8, 2004. <http://www.cbsnews.com/stories/2004/02/05/60minutes> (January 8, 2008).

Shepherdson, Nancy. "Writing for Godot." *Los Angeles Times*. April 25, 2004. <http://www.pqasb.pqarchives.co./latimes/ access/623523641.html?> (January 10, 2008).

Smith, Christian. *American Evangelicalism*. Chicago: University of Chicago Press, 1998.

Standaert, Michael. *Skipping Towards Armageddon*. Brooklyn, NY: Soft Skull Press, 2006.

Strozier, Charles B. *Apocalypse*. Boston: Beacon, 1994. Reprint WIPF and Stock Publishers 2002.

"TEOTWAKI." *The Free Dictionary*. <http:www.theFreeDictionary.com> (July 21, 2008).

Thigpen, Paul. *The Rapture Trap: A Catholic Response to "End Times" Fever*. West Chester, PA: Ascension, 2001.

Van Biema, David. "The End: How It Got That Way." *Time*. July 1, 2002. <http://www.time.com/time/magazine/artcle/0,9171,1002760,00.html> (January 1, 2008).

Weber, Eugen. *Apocalypses*. Cambridge, MA: Harvard University Press, 1999.

Weber, Timothy. *Living in the Shadow of the Second Coming*. Grand Rapids, MI: Academie, 1983.

Wessinger, Catherine, ed. *Millennialism, Persecution, & Violence*. Syracuse, NY: Syracuse University Press, 2000.

Wojcik, Daniel. *The End of the World As We Know It*. New York and London: New York University Press, 1997.

Gaming Armageddon: Leaving Behind Race, Class and Gender

Evelyn Stiller

Introduction

Left Behind Eternal Forces is a real-time strategy videogame which is a spin-off from the popular *Left Behind* fiction series. As a cultural artifact of the evangelical movement, *Left Behind Eternal Forces* embodies many of the cultural contradictions faced by the modern evangelical movement, which must grapple with such opposing forces as its historic rejection of modern culture as it seemed to appeal to people who participate in many aspects of modern culture. The evangelical engagement in secular aspects of society rose under Jerry Falwell's influence, resulting in a distinct change in the manner that gender, race, and homosexuality are addressed in evangelical rapture fiction created before and after this time, as will be discussed later. As a product of the computing industry that is geared to appeal to the stereotypical game-player, expected to be a white, middle-class male between the age of 13 and 50, the world of this videogame is fraught with contradictions that mirror evangelical tensions such as the simultaneous needs to reject modern technology and yet to embrace technology as an effective means to communicate a message. For example, game characters and evangelical Christians need to be both culturally separate and politically engaged; Christian teachings prompt people to love one another, yet this game marginalizes groups of people.

As a post-apocalyptic real-time strategy game, *Left Behind Eternal Forces* allows players to control characters to acquire resources and convert people to join a Christian army (the Tribulation Force), and thus "save as many people as possible from the clutches of the Antichrist (Global Community Peacekeepers) as possible," as is stated in the game's how-to manual.[1] A more detailed sequence of events is introduced through a group of *storyline missions,* as they are called in the game, which a player must successfully complete in order to advance through the game. Each mission corresponds to a level of difficulty that one encounters in conventional video games, so players advance their skill and knowledge of the game as the story unfolds. The videogame is itself a form of rapture fiction as a result of the narrative that is embodied in its sequence of storyline missions.

The videogame is a spin-off of the *Left Behind* series (*LBS*), which consists of sixteen novels by Tim LaHaye and Jerry B. Jenkins. This series started in 1995 with *Left Behind: A Novel of the Earth's Last Days* and ended in 2007 with the final novel, *Kingdom Come: The Final Victory*. The novel series as well as the video game embody a dispensational premillennialist eschatology. Premillennialism is the Christian belief that we are living in a period prior to a 1,000 year reign of Christ that will occur upon his second coming.[2] Premillennialists also stress a "secret rapture" in which no one knows the day or the time of the rapture in which all faithful Christians and young children disappear from Earth and are taken to heaven. Dispensational premillennialism involves the belief that the rapture and Christ's return will occur prior to the seven year period of tribulation.[3] In fact, the primary narrative of rapture fiction focuses on the chaotic tribulation period in which the forces of good and evil struggle against each other. A particularly controversial aspect of rapture fiction is that individuals may be saved after the rapture, which introduces an important dimension of hope to the storyline. However, not all evangelicals agree with this perspective.[4] Another distinguishing element of an evangelical religious perspective is that in order to be saved (raptured), one must establish a personal relationship with Christ.[5] In rapture fiction, the distinction between those who have established this personal relationship and those who consider themselves Christian but do not have this relationship, establishes the dividing line between the raptured and those who must suffer through the horrors of the tribulation period but may redeem themselves. The primary narrative of *Left Behind* revolves around the adventures of these believers as they struggle against the Antichrist and nonbelievers during this period.

Retelling/Telling Anew: The Game and the Novel Series

Left Behind Eternal Forces embodies the narrative from the *Left Behind* novel series in a number of ways. First, the videogame starts with an introductory video that summarizes the fundamental narrative context for the *Left Behind* novel series and sets up the premise for the game. The video takes place moments before the Rapture as people are engaged in their everyday lives. Suddenly, in a flash of light, certain individuals disappear, leaving only their clothes. Chaos ensues as driverless cars crash, and people are shocked to find that people have suddenly disappeared. The next scene opens eighteen months later, showing a TV reporter preparing to give a report for *Wolfe News* on the ascent of Nicolae Carpathia to leader of the world. The reporter makes no pretence of objectivity as he describes Carpathia's mission as "freeing us from the bondage of religion.... The Global Community Peacekeepers," he states, "are protecting us from the rebels and their treasonous beliefs." Here, the media is portrayed as a tool of the Antichrist, a common element of rapture fiction.[6] The next scene shows us the Global Community Peacekeepers aggressively rounding up a group of individuals quietly praying in a basement by candlelight. The video ends with the Antichrist/Carpathia gazing out of a window in the former UN building and declaring "This is *my* time." Just as with the introductory video, the game play establishes a stark contrast between good and evil. Descriptive text and narration often remind the players of the allegiance of a particular character in the game. For example, players are cautioned to avoid the rock musicians as they may influence you with their "screaming guitars."

Game players are instructed to recruit as many characters as possible for the Tribulation Force and to avoid members of the Global Community Peacekeepers. As players advance through the storyline missions of the game, various characters from the novel series appear: players guide Rayford Steele, his daughter Chloe, and her husband Buck Williams through the streets of New York as they carry out mission objectives. Similar to the novels, the game unfolds as a series of either storyline missions (or books) culminating in the final battle, Armageddon.

There are aspects of the game *Left Behind Eternal Forces* that create a unique experience from other forms of rapture fiction. In some ways the video game is a more intense evangelical experience than reading a novel, primarily because praying and evangelizing (recruiting) are prominent strategic aspects of the game, and players are actively involved in both of these crucial activities; players must decide which characters must pray and when, and they must select who to recruit to their side. Players are rewarded when they engage in these behaviors by succeeding in the storyline missions. As a player, one finds oneself directing characters in the game to pray and recruit often. To the extent that the characters we guide through the environment serve as our avatars, we feel that we are taking a moment to pray or recruit, as these activities cause the character to block other functions while the prayer or recruitment take place.

In other ways the videogame departs quite distinctly from its prose counterpart. Although players are concerned with the spiritual wellbeing of their characters, material matters are also important. As players build the Tribulation Force, they must acquire more real estate and provisions for their forces, and thus bank-building, the only means to earn money available in the game, becomes increasingly important. The emphasis on bank-building seems rather odd and in contradiction to the usual need for Christian characters to opt out of the mainstream economy in order to avoid the mark of the devil, as will be discussed later. Banks, whether owned by the Tribulation Forces or not, are an element of the game's formal economic structure. Thus, building banks draws the evangelicals into the mainstream economy, and this need for bank ownership never changes throughout the game. Another odd aspect of bank-building is that eighteen months after the rapture (the time frame established in the introductory video), there is insufficient social fabric left to clear away smoldering cars (they are strewn about in the game environment), but rather than squatting in empty real estate, evangelicals politely build banks to justify the acquisition and transformation of property. I will take up this contradiction later in the paper, as I explore the historical suspicion evangelicals have toward modern and secular aspects of society.

Retelling: The Novel Series and Previous Rapture Fiction

Just as the video game borrows narrative elements from the book series inspiring it, LaHaye and Jenkins' *Left Behind* book series reflects a similar storyline to Salem Kirban's novel *666*.[7] From a religious perspective, *Left Behind* embodies dispensational premilleniallist eschatology as does *666*, producing many similarities in the storylines. However LaHaye and Jenkins have borrowed many more narrative elements beyond what is dictated by the common eschatology.[8] The father figures in both storylines are imperfect in their pre-rapture incarnations, but become deeply religious and committed to defeating the Antichrist. George, the father figure in *666* and journalist in the antichrist's inner circle, is split into two characters in the *LBS*. LeHaye and Jenkins' father-figure Rayford Steele becomes the Antichrist's airplane pilot and Buck Williams takes on the reporter role, covering the Antichrist. Rayford is sought after by Carpathia (the Antichrist) to serve as his pilot, much like Kirban's George was recruited by the Antichrist in *666*. Other parallel narrative elements exist, such as the initial depiction of the rapture unfolding on an airplane and the pregnancy and subsequent persecution by the Antichrist of the daughter-figures. Many other similarities between the *666* and the *Left Behind* series exist.[9] While both *666* and the *Left Behind* series are published by Tyndale House, LaHaye and Jenkins do not acknowledge *666* as their inspiration, claiming to have created an original work of fiction.[10]

These works of fiction emanating from evangelical culture create characters that express popular beliefs and take part in relationships that model norms found in evangelical communities. However, from Kirban's publication of *666* in the 1970s to the first decade of the new millennium, pressures of modern society have exerted influence on evangelical communities that conflict with their cultural roots. These conflicting influences will be examined next.

Culturally Separate Yet Politically Engaged

When one looks at the origins of the modern evangelical movement, some common evangelical perspectives can be traced. Ernest Sandeen credits James Nelson Darby with bringing this religious perspective to Britain and North America between 1862 and 1877.[11] According to Betty DeBerg, the rise of the fundamentalist movement in the U.S. was primarily the mobilization of white, middle class Protestants in response to major social and economic restructuring resulting from the industrial revolution. This social upheaval resulted in liberalizing moral standards, the rise of the labor movement, a new consumer culture, secular public education, a more international perspective after World War I, and more women in the workforce, causing a shift in gender roles.[12] Louis Gasper points to additional social phenomenon that fundamentalists reacted to such as science education, especially evolutionary theory, and biblical criticism.[13] The resulting attitudes developed by the evangelical community include conservative moral codes, anti-globalization, an intellectual insecurity, and a suspicion of technology, science, and industrialization.[14] While evangelicals have historically had an anti-consumerist bent, the success of religious book stores and book series like *Left Behind,* complicate this perspective.[15] Religious web sites have also provided positive examples of technology use.[16]

Although evangelicals are primarily white, they view their doomsday-focused belief system and criticism by biblical scholars as creating for them the status of a persecuted minority.[17] This attitude provides a sense of cohesion and purpose to evangelicals and gives them a reason to close themselves off from non-evangelicals who might question their eschatology. The sense of isolation expressed by the characters in all examples of rapture fiction investigated here is clear. In the *LBS*, *666*, and *Left Behind: Eternal Forces* a small band of newly saved Christians combats the larger forces of evil controlled by the Antichrist. In the videogame the sense of isolation is reinforced by the lack of lighting throughout the virtual world. The lighting is limited to a small area around the immediate location of the character that the player controls.

As the character moves through the game environment, the light follows the character. In the early stages of the game, players have a single character to guide through the dark and lonely game. Every other character encountered is either hostile or neutral, so the game starts with the main character not having a single ally.

Although the cultural roots of evangelical isolation can be seen in both recent forms of rapture fiction, the 1970s and 1980s brought additional influences on evangelical culture through the activities of a new generation of ministers, typified by the actions of Jerry Falwell. By 1976 Falwell attributed the idea that "religion and politics don't mix" to the devil, stating that this idea was meant to keep "Christians from running their own country."[18] With the advent of the Moral Majority, Falwell was encouraging evangelicals to work publicly in opposition of "existing evils" such as homosexuality, the Equal Rights Amendment, pornography, and women's liberation.[19] Thus, we see a new emerging force directing evangelicals to engage in the world of politics when evangelical leaders had previously directed followers to reject all things secular, including politics.

Issues mentioned by Falwell such as homosexuality find expression in the *Left Behind* series, whereas homosexuals are simply omitted from Kirban's novel. LaHaye and Jenkins' Nicolae Carpathia (*Left Behind's* Antichrist) is the product of genetic engineering which combines the genetic code of a male homosexual couple to form a hybrid sperm. This sperm is then used to impregnate a Romanian woman. Carpathia then becomes a successful business man and politician who ascends to lead the United Nations in the wake of the chaos that results from the rapture. Carpathia renames the UN the Global Community Peacekeepers (GCP), associating "global" with evil and making another argument for isolation. On the other hand, in Kirban's *666*, Brother Bartholomew (the Antichrist) is the product of a virgin birth from an Iraqi woman. The characterization of the Antichrist in *LBS* illustrates a shift in rapture fiction from omission of homosexuality to aggressive hostility towards it, as well as a call for isolationism, asking the U.S. to stay out of world affairs.

None of the Kirban characters in *666* are described as homosexual (such omission is a common homophobic tactic). Instead, the cultural depravity ushering in the end time in *666* is represented by sexual liberty and drug use. In the *LBS* homosexuality is one prong of the "downfall of man." In addition to giving rise to the Antichrist, homosexuality is portrayed in an unflattering light through both a lesbian and a gay male character. Verna, the lesbian, is contrasted with the feminine and domesticated Chloe and gives Buck "the willies," while Guy Blod introduces comic relief as he prances and giggles in various scenes.[20] Further, Guy Blod creates a statue of the Antichrist, which he then worships. The gay and lesbian characters are portrayed as inauthentic males and females, representing those who will not be saved.[21]

The videogame simply does not include homosexuals. Instead it features expressions of sexual modesty. The videogame, *Left Behind Eternal Forces (LB Eternal Forces)* starts with an introductory animation which shows a stylized version of the *Creation of Adam* from the Sistine Chapel fresco by Michelangelo. This version drapes a cloth over Adam to conceal his penis and transforms Eve from a naked, dark haired woman with a look of concern to a tranquil blond haired woman wearing what appears to be a strapless dress. This covering of nakedness is suggestive of the sexually conservative nature of fundamentalists, while the look of tranquility expresses women's more submissive role in society and the family.

To summarize briefly, the shift we see in rapture fiction from Kirban's *666* to LaHaye and Jenkins' *Left Behind* series is one from strict isolation in which the characters simply avoid "cultural depravity" and issues such as homosexuality simply do not exist, to one in which homosexuality is clearly represented and mocked or shown as evil. As we shift to the *LB Eternal Forces* videogame, we see a return to sexual modesty and omission of homosexuality, but the theme of isolation appears to remain strong in all three forms of rapture fiction, giving a sense of purpose and brotherhood to evangelicalism.

Gender: To Embrace and to Marginalize

The personal relationships presented in rapture fiction often model conventional evangelical family structures. Much research suggests that strict gender roles are cornerstones of evangelical life with men serving as authority figures and women behaving submissively toward men.[22] Thus, evangelical families tend to be patriarchal, having the father act as head of household as well chief money earner and women taking charge of domestic life. According to Brenda Brasher, "one of the more significant fruits a believer can show is a life aligned with biblically based order ... the cornerstone of this order is heterosexual marriage headed by an adult male: a family." While women are expected to defer to their husbands, they are viewed as being spiritually equal and are in charge of the spiritual upbringing of the children.[23] Women who do not fit this mold of deference to men are criticized in the evangelical movement as feminists, or according to T. DeWitt Talmage, reeking lepresses who need to be soaked in carbolic acid for three weeks.[24] These women are portrayed in an unflattering light in rapture fiction as the Whore of Babylon, who is the ultimate embodiment of evil. She is described in the Book of Revelation:

The great whore that sitteth upon many waters: with whom the kings of the earth have committed fornication, and the inhabitants of the earth have been made drunk with the wine of her fornication.[25]

Jerry Falwell's influence on the evangelical movement has been to eliminate the prohibition on evangelical involvement in the secular world by encouraging active involvement in politics. Other modernizations include encouraging spreading the evangelical truth through means other than the ministry. Falwell encouraged evangelicals to spread their moral vision through all professions, as creationist teachers, antiabortion doctors and nurses, and as lawyers who defend the right to pray in the classroom.[26] Further, since Falwell's Liberty University prepares both male and female students to enter a variety of fields, the prohibition of women's participation in the secular realm is not maintained by Falwell's organization.[27] While these developments took place during the 1970s and 1980s, they are not reflected in the portrayal of women from *666* to the *LBS* and to the videogame.

In *666* the archetypical authoritative father figure is represented in the main character George, and the misguided but good-intentioned female role is expressed through his daughter Gaye, who is redeemed in the end by obeying her father. George's wife and younger children are raptured, reflecting a conventional family structure in line with evangelical norms in which the wife is expected to be in charge of the spiritual well-being of the family, so she and the small children are ready at the time of the rapture to ascend to heaven. George, as the head of the household, engages in worldly activities that support the family financially. He is recruited to work closely with the Antichrist as an advisor, so he travels around the world in nuclear powered helicopters, carrying out projects for the Antichrist. George reunites with his older daughter, Gaye, who was willful and skeptical about religious matters prior to the rapture, but is later filled with deep regret that she did not listen to her mother. When George refuses the mark of the beast by not participating in economic life, he and Gaye must go into hiding from the Antichrist. Much like Kirban's *666*, LaHaye and Jenkins' *LBS* features a worldly, money earning, father figure, Rayford Steele whose wife and small child have mysteriously disappeared with the rapture. He shares many experiences with his oldest, strong-willed daughter, Chloe. Rayford Steel, like Kirban's George, is imperfect in his pre-rapture incarnation, but becomes deeply religious and committed to defeating the Antichrist as the novels proceed.

Gaye's role in Kirban's *666* is to play the misguided woman who sees the error in her willful ways and is finally redeemed because she aligns her behavior with evangelical norms. When George reunites with Gaye, she is pregnant, but does not have a birth coupon, which is required due to overpopulation of the planet. So, she is required to take the drug, 666, which causes the pregnancy to terminate and her to, according to the narrator, "lose every reason to live." Unlike her father, Gaye takes the mark of the beast, but regrets her decision soon thereafter. Shortly before the final battle, in which George and Gaye see all of their loved ones return from heaven, the mark disappears, and she and George ascend into heaven, as a result of her decision to obey her father. In this text, women tag along with men, are a source for male concern, and are in need of rescue. They otherwise have few active roles to play in the narrative. This changes in the *Left Behind* series where women are more actively involved in the storyline. The initially willful Chloe redeems herself when she marries Buck, and becomes the obedient wife. In addition to the lesbian Verna, *LBS* has a Whore of Babylon figure, Hattie Durham, who portrays what becomes of the misguided, independent woman. Hattie initially acts as a temptress for Rayford, but later becomes involved with the Antichrist, becomes pregnant, and aborts his child.

We see the role of women is to conform to strict evangelical gender norms in the rapture fiction. However, the role of women becomes somewhat more important to the narrative as we move from *666* to the *Left Behind* series. And yet, in the videogame women take a severe setback. Women are initially omitted from the early stages of game play. For example, in the first mission the player is instructed to guide Leonard to find Brad and then meet Taylor at the Church. Leonard, Brad, and Taylor are portrayed as white men. In this mission the only character that one can control is Leonard, so Leonard serves as the player's avatar. This mission requires the player to navigate Leonard through a subset of New York City, trying to avoid the Global Community Peacekeepers' (GCP) musicians, who are also all male.

The next mission, called "New Beginnings," has the player guide Taylor to recruit eight friends and bring them to the abandoned church. One friend must be a builder so that the Tribulation Force can reclaim the church. Only Taylor has the power to recruit friends, so Taylor is the player's avatar for this storyline mission. Although a player can control other characters once they have been recruited, in order to succeed in the mission, Taylor must be the central character. Having all nine characters in the second mission represented as white men is clearly a choice made by the game developers which models the authoritative centrality of men in evangelical culture.

For the first three missions women have no role in the game. Chloe, does not appear until the twenty-fifth mission (out of thirty-seven missions), where she enters the storyline as the newlywed wife of Buck Williams. Her importance to the storyline is as the marital partner of a central male character. Her purpose in the mission is to heal injured characters, a stereotypical care-giving role. Even Chloe-based missions are still populated predominantly by white men.

As the game advances, players encounter additional types of characters that are affiliated with either the Tribulation Force or the Global Community Peacekeepers. The Tribulation Force has a series of character types, each with special capabilities that are suited to the character's function in the game. The character types are *friend*, three levels of *recruiters*, three levels of *builders*, four levels of *influencer*, three levels of *healers*, and five different types of *soldiers*. When a character type has multiple levels, it simply means that a sequence of character types exist, with each successive level suggesting a more advanced or powerful role for character of that type. For example, the three levels of healers are medic, nurse and doctor, and the ability to heal increases from medic to doctor.

There are only three types of characters on the Tribulation Force that have one or more level that can be portrayed by a female character according to the game manual. One of these types is friend, which can be either a white male or white female. Friends either appear in certain storyline missions or they are neutral men or women who are recruited by the player to become friends. Friends who appear without recruitment are invariably men. So, despite having two friend genders, men are most heavily, if not exclusively, represented in the missions. A second category of character that has female portrayal is influencer. Although three of the four levels of influencers are depicted by white female characters in the game manual, they also are often actually male in the game. For example, the first level of influencer is musician, and the game manual shows a white female character. In missions where musicians are present, they are male. However, a player may decide to train a female friend to become a musician; thus there are potentially white female musicians in the game. The third category of character that has female representation is healer, which includes medics, nurses, and doctors. Here, the game makers perpetuate the stereotype that women are innately drawn to care-giving professions and state that by having women serve as healers, they are "tapping into their exceptional, unconditional care for people."

The element of the game that epitomizes its gender stereotyping is found in the male and female friend definitions on the Tribulation Force. When one clicks on a woman friend, the description says, "Untrained woman friend can start a medical or musician career." When one clicks on a male friend, the description says, "Untrained male unit can start any career." This opens up the male-only options of builder, advanced builder, foreman, soldier, spy, Special Forces, sniper, disciple, evangelist, and missionary.

The treatment of women develops slightly in the transition from *666* to the *LBS* and is marked by a more aggressive critique of feminism in the more recent fiction. The dutiful and subservient women in both novels are raptured at the beginning of each story because they have successfully fulfilled their spiritual roles in the family. It is the role of the initially willful daughters and the father-figures to keep the memory of the mothers alive throughout the story by expressing their regret for not having followed the guidance of the mother. The *LBS* takes a lesson from Jerry Falwell and actively criticizes women who do not conform to the evangelical norms. Hattie Durham simultaneously represents the Whore of Babylon and the self-determining feminist. Thus, the authors connect the two aspects of female non-conformity as a critique of feminism.

The role of women in the videogame represents an abrupt change, though it still conforms to evangelical norms. The videogame presents a virtual world that is initially empty of women that participate in any strategic elements of the game. They are clearly marginalized and only later in the game do women have even a small role in meaningful game play. The game makers claim that they wish to market their game to game players and Christian mega churches.[28] While game players are indeed stereotypically teenaged to middle aged males, the makers appear to have no interest in marketing to girls or women. Perhaps the extreme degree to which women are omitted from this game is a result of combining computer culture with evangelical culture. Sexism is pervasive throughout many aspects of the computing industry including computer mediated communication, gaming, and technology education. Numerous authors such as Sherry Turkle, Susan Herring, Joel Cooper, and Whitney Butts have addressed the phenomenon.[29] The game is clearly the product of two highly sexist cultures, evangelical and computer.

The development of rapture fiction from the 1970s until today has illustrated increasingly aggressive homophobia and sexism. Racism will be looked at in the next section.

From Racism by Omission to Overt Racism

Race is not explicitly mentioned in either the *666* or *Left Behind* series storyline. Because the eschatology espoused in both appeals to a primarily white audience, most readers assume that the characters are white by default, setting up a situation of racism by omission. However, the *LBS* has three spin-off movies in which one prominent character is portrayed by an African-American actor, Clarence Gilyard.[30] The character he plays is Pastor Barnes, an inauthentic religious leader who fails to be taken in the rapture, but sees the error of his ways like the other Tribulation Force members.

The videogame is comprised of three distinct elements: an introductory animation, a video which sets context for the game, and the interactive game itself. Each of these elements treats race differently. The characters of the contextual video are somewhat racially diverse. One of the raptured characters is an African American waitress, as are the reporter for Wolfe news and some members of the prayer circle, for example.

However, the introductory animation seems curiously racist on two counts. The opening scene of the introductory animation offers the player a god-like view from space, looking at a spinning planet Earth. Suddenly, beams of light emanate from Earth into space. The beams of light are presumably souls ascending into heaven during the rapture. Most beams come from the United States of America, with a few coming from Central and South America. There is another cluster of beams that come from the other side of the Earth, which appear to be coming from Europe. No beams come from the continent of Africa at all. If these localized sources of souls represent Christian areas, a viewer might ask, have the centuries of missionary work in Africa resulted in nothing? The remainder of the animation features a single African American character who happens to be a thug-like character and who also appears in the game play. When consulting the game manual, the *thug* character is clearly depicted as African-American. The web version of this character's description shows the thug as being a bit lighter skinned, and therefore more racially ambiguous.

In the interactive portion of the game racism is explicit. In addition to the African American thug, the game features a single Asian character, who is the "cult leader," perhaps suggesting that eastern religions are cult-like or exotic. As one plays the game, the race of the characters in the game environment is visually obvious, but additional racial and cultural clues exist as well. Each character in the videogame has a profile which is displayed when one clicks the mouse on that character. Sometimes non–Euro-American names are given to the characters, but mostly the names are common Anglo-American names such as Taylor Malone, Cindy Potter, or Joel Webber. Based on an unscientific survey of character profiles, the majority of Tribulation Force members have common Anglo-Saxon names. On occasion one will encounter a Hispanic name such as Chico Perez or Cruz Torres. Many members of the Global Peacekeeper Force (the force of evil) also often have Euro-American names. However they also have Hebrew (Al Rossberg) or Muslim (Ahmir Mohammad) names. These names suggest anti–Semitism and an anti–Arabic sentiment as there are neither Jewish nor Arabic names on the Tribulation Force side.

The *Left Behind* movies seem to present a liberalizing of racial perspective with an African-American playing the role of a key character. However, with the advent of the videogame we see an abrupt turn towards extreme racial stereotypes, including anti–Semitism as well as anti–Asian and anti–Arabic sentiments. While the preceding issues of sexism and homophobia that stem from a call to action from evangelical leaders such as Jerry Falwell or James Dobson, we do not see evangelicals publicly calling for more racial exclusion.[31] So, how does one explain the almost childish representations of race in the videogame's animation and interactive portion, which contradict the more balanced racial representations in the game's introductory video? One explanation is derived from recognizing that different industries, the film and the computing industries, produced each element. It appears the film industry created a video that is racially diverse, while the computing industry was willing to create a videogame that contains almost exclusively white characters, and any racial diversity is seen only on the side supporting the Antichrist.

Heeding Falwell's call for societal engagement, we have seen evangelical fiction aggressively move into the fray of political dialogues, characterizing marginalized groups such as women, homosexuals, and racial and ethnic minorities in unflattering ways and associating them with the side of evil. Next, we will see another dimension of social involvement.

Culturally Separate yet Technologically Savvy

Kirban presents the traditional evangelical attitude concerning modern society and technology by showing technology use in a negative light. The story of *666* unfolds in the year 2000 with the United States portrayed as a futuristic dystopia. People eat protein cakes made from a mixture of crude oil and bacteria or from reprocessed human remains in a manner similar to the 1973 film *Soylent Green*. Industrial advances have lead to a highly polluted world, and only government officials may drive cars due to the excessive pollution. Only people who have been given birth coupons may have children because of overpopulation due to "sex without marriage." Nuclear weapons are used by the Antichrist to achieve his domination of the world. The prominent scientist in the narrative, Dr. Curtier, is in the service of the Antichrist, who uses Curtier's advances to conduct extensive surveillance to control people and dominate the world. Kirban portrays technology as a surveillance and control tool of the Antichrist and government as a privileged organization that he leads.

Attitudes concerning media and technology shift between Kirban's *666* and Lahaye and Jenkins' *Left Behind*. The Antichrist in *666* charms the news media and thus produces a positive message without technical interference. However, in *Left Behind* the Antichrist uses technology to interfere with media broadcasts by inserting his own message to replace any negative news about the Global Community. Because the media in *Left Behind* attempts to report objectively on matters and must be "hacked" by the Antichrist, the series presents a more positive portrait of the media as an organization than *666*. Both Antichrists use technology to spy on and control individuals; however, the *LBS*'s Tribulation Force (the "good" side) also uses technology extensively to communicate with each other, tamper with information belonging to the Antichrist, as well as spy on him. Rather than simply controlling them, technology also assists the righteous side in *LBS*. In this later work of rapture fiction, technology is harnessed for both good and evil.

Ironically, the characters in the videogame use little technology, with the exception of conventional military weaponry such as machine guns, Humvees, and helicopters. Although the characters have little exposure to non-military technology, they participate in modern economic culture at a level that goes beyond the other forms of rapture fiction discussed here. As one recruits people into the Tribulation Force, one must acquire more real estate and provisions for the forces, and thus bank-building, the only means to earn money available in the game, becomes increasingly important. The emphasis on bank-building runs against the grain of traditional rapture fiction, which requires believers to step out of the mainstream economy when they refuse the mark of the devil. Given the historical suspicion evangelicals have toward large corporations, making banking central to Tribulation Force progress seems odd, unless one views this bank-building as a nod to capitalism.

Given that the Tribulation Force members are equipped with more and more weaponry as one advances through the game, they are armed and dangerous and must kill members of the opposition in order to be successful. In conventional rapture fiction the Christian side cleverly evades the armed attackers or relies on supernatural help, but are not themselves armed and aggressive. The videogame's display of aggressive violence from the Christian side has generated quite a bit of controversy in the evangelical community, as one might expect.[32]

Another aspect of social involvement is engaged through the videogame's dual perspectives on rock music. Especially in the early missions, the forces of the Antichrist are embodied by rock musicians, so we see the old evangelical warning that rock music will cause one's soul to turn towards the devil. However, just as the modern evangelical movement has a more complex relationship with technology and capitalism, the videogame vilifies rock music, while promoting Christian rock bands and their albums. In an element outside the storyline called *clues*, players may choose to read clues at the conclusion of tutorial lessons and after completing a mission. Clues are opportunities for the game makers to proselytize about issues ranging from evolution to the proper interpretation of the Book of Revelation. While players read each clue, a different Christian rock album plays in the background with information appearing in the clue window explaining how to purchase this music.

In rapture fiction we see evangelicals being portrayed as an isolated and persecuted minority, yet their membership is portrayed as white and middle class. Additionally, evangelicals have taken an active role in transforming society through promoting Christian rock music and adapting technology to promote evangelical perspectives over the Internet.

Conclusion

There is a noticeable change in perspective from Kirban's 1970 rapture fiction novel *666* to the *Left Behind* novel series by LaHaye and Jenkins. This new perspective is driven by the change in attitude concerning evangelical involvement in modern culture. During the 1970s and 1980s Jerry Falwell encouraged evangelicals to take an active role in modern society to help transform it to meet evangelical norms. This participation in society can take an apparently liberal form of shifting from criticizing rock music to creating Christian rock, or it can take an aggressively conservative form of openly criticizing women who do not conform to evangelical standards of behavior. These simultaneously developing phenomena taking on both liberal and conservative expression create apparent contradictions.

As one examines the *Left Behind Eternal Forces* videogame, additional factors enter into this evangelical transformation. The primary factor is the influence of the culture of the computing industry which appears to intensify the expression of racism and sexism. The sexism and racism of evangelical culture are expressed more explicitly through the videogame. In rapture fiction one can be racist by omission (by simply not addressing race), and allowing the predominantly white audience to fill in their preference. In a videogame one cannot omit race. To explicitly portray all good characters as white and to have the only African-American character be a thug constitutes an outrageous level of racism. The gender-stereotyping is similarly extreme. It is clear that this game not meant for women, girls, or racial minorities to play.

In surveying reviews of *Left Behind Eternal Forces*, I became alarmed at the absence of concern for the racism and sexism embodied in the game. In his GameSpy review Allen Rausch critiques *Left Behind Eternal Forces* as an uninteresting, poorly designed real-time strategy game.[33] He finds the elements of fundamentalism innocuous and inoffensive, not noting the absence of women or people of color. During his review Rausch says, "that unit (friend) can then be trained in purchased buildings as soldiers, medical technicians, builders or spiritual influencers," when only male friends can be trained in this manner.[34] Other game reviews are similar to the Rausch review, although

Ben Kuchera raised concern about the anti-evolution "clue" presented to players of the game.[35] Reviews that regard *Left Behind Eternal Forces* as an intolerant game are referring to the religious intolerance of converting or killing non-believers, rather than the sexism or racism embodied in the game.[36]

This insensitivity to matters of race and gender in *Left Behind Eternal Forces* seems to be a product of two cultures, evangelical and computer cultures. It is shocking to see recently developed computer games embody such a sexist and racist perspective with little challenge by those who review computer applications.

NOTES

1. *Left Behind Games*, 2006 <http://www.leftbehindgames.com/> (May 7, 2007).

2. Amy Johnson Frykholm, *Rapture Culture: Left Behind in Evangelical America* (New York: Oxford University Press, 2004) 15.

3. *Ibid.*

4. See for example Frykholm, *Rapture Culture*, 176. See also Biblical Discernment Ministries. *Book Review: The Left Behind Series.* January 2005 <http://www.rapidnet.com/~j beard/bdm/BookReviews/left.htm> (October 10, 2007).

5. Hal Lindsey, *The Late Great Planet Earth* (Grand Rapids, MI: Zondervan, 1970) 144.

6. A similar portrayal of the media also occurs in Salem Kirban's *666* (Chattanooga, TN: Future Events, 1970).

7. Carl E. Olsen, "Recycled Rapture," *This Rock*, September 2001, <http://www.catholic.com/thisrock/2001/0109fea3.asp> (August 12, 2007).

8. Ernest Sandeen, *The Roots of Fundamentalism: British and American Millenarianism 1800–1930* (Chicago: University of Chicago Press, 1970) 62.

9. Olsen, *Recycled Rapture.*

10. Pentecostal Evangel, *Conversation with Tim LaHaye, Prophecy-based fiction*, 2002, <http://www.ag.org/pentecostal-evangel/articles/conversations/4490_LaHaye.cfm> (August 20, 2007).

11. Sandeen, *The Roots of Fundamentalism*, 15.

12. Betty DeBerg, *Ungodly Women: Gender and the First Wave of American Fundamentalism* (Minneapolis, MN: Mercer University Press, 2000) 5.

13. Louis Gasper, *The Fundamentalist Movement, 1930–1965* (Grand Rapids, MI: Baker Bookhouse, 1981) v.

14. DeBerg, *Ungodly Women*, 4; Frykholm, *Rapture Culture*, 124. R. Laurence Moore, *Religious Outsiders and the Making of Americans* (New York: Oxford University Press, 1986) 163.

15. Frykholm, *Rapture Culture*, 126.

16. Frykholm, *Rapture Culture*, 126. Stephen Pfohl, *Left Behind: Religion, Technology, and Flight from the Flesh. Ctheory.net.* Arthur and Marilouise Kroker, eds. November 1 2006, <www.ctheory.net/articles.aspx?id=554> (October 19, 2008).

17. Moore *Religious Outsiders*, 163.

18. Susan Harding, *The Book of Jerry Falwell: Fundamentalist Language and Politics* (Princeton, NJ: Princeton University Press, 2000) 23.

19. *Ibid.*

20. Tim LaHaye and Jerry B. Jenkins, *Nicolae: The Rise of The Antichrist* (Wheaton, IL: Tyndale House, 1997) 281. Tim LaHaye and Jerry B. Jenkins, *The Indwelling: The Beast Takes Possession* (Wheaton, IL: Tyndale House, 1997) 60.

21. Frykholm, *Rapture Culture*, 78.

22. Betty DeBerg, *Ungodly Women*, 13. Brenda Brasher, *Godly Women: Fundamentalism and Female Power* (New Brunswick, NJ: Rutgers University Press, 1998) 131. Margaret Bendroth, *Fundamentalism and Gender: 1875 to the Present* (New Haven, CT: Yale University Press, 1993) 11.

23. Brasher, *Godly Women*, 140.

24. DeBerg, *Ungodly Women*, 1.

25. Rev 17:1–2 (King James).

26. Harding, *The Book of Jerry Falwell*, 13.

27. *Liberty University*, 2008, <http://www.liberty.edu> (March 2, 2008).

28. *Left Behind Eternal Forces*, FAQ, 2008, <http://www.eternalforces.com/faq.aspx> (February 20, 2008).

29. Sherry Turkle, *Life on the Screen : Identity in the Age of the Internet* (New York: Touchstone, 1995). Susan Herring, et al. "Women and Children Last: The Discursive Construction of Weblogs" in *Into the Blogospher: Rhetoric, Community, and Culture of Weblogs,* Laura Gurak et al., eds. 2004, <http://blog.lib.umn.edu/blogosphere/women_and_children. html> (August 23, 2007). Joel Cooper and Kimberlee D. Weaver, *Gender and Computers: Understanding the Digital Divide* (Mahwah, NJ: Lawrence Erlbaum, 2003). Whitney Butts, "OMG Girlz Don't Exist on teh Intarweb!!!!1" *The Escapist,* November 1, 2005 <http:// www.escapistmagazine.com/articles/view/issues/issue_17/109-OMG-Girlz-Dont-Exist-on-teh-Intarweb-1> (September 12, 2007).

30. Vic Sarin, *Left Behind, The Movie* (Los Angeles, CA: Columbia TriStar Picture, 2000), videorecording.

31. Sara Diamond, *Not By Politics Alone: The enduring influence of the Christian Right* (New York: Guilford, 1998).

32. Ilene Lelchuk, "'Convert or die' game divides Christians," *San Francisco Chronicle*, December 12, 2006, <http://www.sfgate.com/cgi-bin/article.cgi?file=/c/a/2006/12/12/ MNG8TMU1KQ1.DTL> (June10, 2008). "Liberal Christians Want Wal-Mart to Drop 'Left Behind' Video Game," Fox News, December 13, 2006, <http://www.foxnews.com/ story/0,2933,236209,00.html> (June 15, 2008).

33. Allen Rausch, "What Would Jesus Play? Not this." *PC Game Spy,* Dec. 7, 2006, <http://pc.gamespy.com/pc/left-behind-eternal-forces/749748p1.html> (October 18, 2008).

34. *Ibid.*

35. Ben Kuchera, "Left Behind: Eternal Forces: In the Future, All Restaurants Are Taco Bell," *ARS Technica.* December 13, 2006, <http://arstechnica.com/reviews/games/leftbehind.ars/2> (September 12, 2007). Mike Musgrove, "Fire and Brimstone, Guns and Ammo," *The Washington Post.* August 17, 2006, D01. Brett Todd, "Another Good Thing About the Rapture Is That It Will Take You Away from Disastrous, Buggy Games Like Left Behind: Eternal Forces," *GameSpot,* November 28, 2006, <http://www.gamespot.com/ pc/strategy/leftbehindeternalforces/review.html?mode=gsreview> (August 13, 2007).

36. Musgrove, "Fire and Brimstone."

WORKS CITED

Biblical Discernment Ministries. *Book Review: The Left Behind Series.* January 2005. <http://www.rapidnet.com/~jbeard/bdm/BookReviews/left.htm> (October 10, 2007)

Brasher, Brenda. *Godly Women: Fundamentalism and Female Power.* New Brunswick, NJ: Rutgers University Press, 1998.

Bendroth, Margaret. *Fundamentalism and Gender: 1875 to the Present.* New Haven, CT: Yale University Press, 1993.

Butts, Whitney. "OMG Girlz Don't Exist on teh Intarweb!!!!1." *The Escapist*. Julianne Greer, ed. November 2005. <http://www.escapistmagazine.com/articles/view/issues/ issue_17/109-OMG-Girlz-Don-t-Exist-on-teh-Intarweb-1> (September 12, 2007).

Cooper, Joel, and Kimberlee D. Weaver. *Gender and Computers: Understanding the Digital Divide*. Mahwah, NJ: Lawrence Erlbaum, 2003.

DeBerg, Betty. *Ungodly Women: Gender and the First Wave of American Fundamentalism*. Minneapolis, MN: Mercer University Press, 2000.

Diamond, Sara. *Not by Politics Alone: The Enduring Influence of the Christian Right*. New York: Guilford, 1998.

Frykholm, Amy Johnson. *Rapture Culture: Left Behind in Evangelical America*. New York: Oxford University Press, 2004.

Gasper, Louis. *The Fundamentalist Movement, 1930–1965*. Grand Rapids, MI: Baker Bookhouse, 1981.

Halliday, Fred. "Cold War" in *The Oxford Companion to the Politics of the World*, 2nd edition. Joel Krieger, ed. Oxford: Oxford University Press, 2001.

Harding, Susan. *The Book of Jerry Falwell: Fundamentalist Language and Politics*. Princeton, NJ: Princeton University Press, 2000.

Herring, Susan, et al. "Women and Children Last: The Discursive Construction of Weblogs" in *Into the Blogospher: Rhetoric, Community, and Culture of Weblogs*. Laura Gurak et al., ed. 2004. <http://blog.lib.umn.edu/blogosphere/women_and_children.html> (August 23, 2007).

Kirban, Salem. *666*. Chattanooga, TN: Future Events, 1970.

Kuchera, Ben. "Left Behind: Eternal Forces: In the Future, All Restaurants Are Taco Bell." *ARS Technica*. December 13, 2006. <http://arstechnica.com/reviews/games/leftbehind. ars/2> (September 12, 2007).

LaHaye, Tim, and Jerry B. Jenkins. *The Indwelling: The Beast Takes Possession*. Wheaton, IL:Tyndale House, 1997.

_____. *Left Behind: A Novel of the Earth's Last Days*. Wheaton, IL.: Tyndale House, 1995.

_____. *Nicolae: The Rise of the Antichrist*. Wheaton, IL: Tyndale House, 1997.

Left Behind Games. 2006. <http://www.leftbehindgames.com/> (May 7, 2007).

Lelchuk, Ilene. "'Convert or Die' Game Divides Christians." *San Francisco Chronicle*. December 12, 2006. <http://www.sfgate.com/cgi-bin/article.cgi?file=/c/a/2006/12/12/MN G8TMU1KQ1.DTL> (June10, 2008).

"Liberal Christians Want Wal-Mart to Drop 'Left Behind' Video Game." *Fox News*. December 13, 2006. <http://www.foxnews.com/story/0,2933,236209,00.html> (June 15, 2008).

Liberty University. 2008. <http://www.liberty.edu/> (March 2, 2008).

Lindsey, Hal. *The Late Great Planet Earth*. Grand Rapidsm, MI: Zondervan, 1970.

Manker, Dayton A. *They That Remain: A Story of the End Times*. Grand Rapids, MI: Zondervan, 1941.

Marsden, George. *Fundamentalism and American Culture: The Shaping of Twentieth-Century Evangelicalism: 1870–1925*. Oxford, UK: Oxford University Press, 1982.

Molpus, David. *Televangelist, Christian Leader Jerry Falwell Dies*. May 15, 2007. <http:// www.npr.org/templates/story/story.php?storyId=10188427> (May 15, 2007).

Moore, R. Laurence. *Religious Outsiders and the Making of Americans*. New York: Oxford University Press, 1986.

_____. *Selling God: American Religion in the Marketplace of Culture*. New York: Oxford University Press, 1994.

Musgrove, Mike. "Fire and Brimstone, Guns and Ammo." *The Washington Post*. August 17, 2006: D01.

Oilar, Forrest Loman . *Be Thou Prepared for Jesus Is Coming*. Boston: Meador Publishing, 1937.

Olson, Carl E. "Recycled Rapture." *This Rock*. September 2001. <http://www.catholic.com/thisrock/2001/0109fea3.asp> (August 12, 2007).

Pfohl, Stephen. "Left Behind: Religion, Technology, and Flight from the Flesh." *Ctheory. net*. Arthur and Marilouise Kroker, eds. November 1, 2006. www.ctheory.net/articles.aspx?id=554> (October 19, 2008).

Rausch, Allen. "What Would Jesus Play? Not This." *PC Game Spy*. December 7, 2006. <http://pc.gamespy.com/pc/left-behind-eternal-forces/749748p1.html> (July 12, 2007).

Sandeen, Ernest. *The Roots of Fundamentalism: British and American Millenarianism 1800–1930*. Chicago: University of Chicago Press, 1970.

Sarin, Vic. *Left Behind, The Book*. Los Angeles, CA: Columbia TriStar Pictures, 2000. Videorecording.

Todd, Brett. "Another Good Thing About the Rapture Is That It Will Take You Away from Disastrous, Buggy Games Like Left Behind: Eternal Forces." *GameSpot*. November 28, 2006. <http://www.gamespot.com/pc/strategy/leftbehindeternalforces/review.html?mode=gsreview> (August 13, 2007).

Turkle, Sherry. *Life on the Screen: Identity in the Age of the Internet*. New York: Touchstone, 1995.

Watson, Sydney. *In the Twinkling of an Eye*. New York: Fleming H. Revell, 1933.

Apocalyptic Thought in UFO-Based Religions[1]

Benjamin E. Zeller

Americans woke up on March 27, 1997, to a grisly news item: in a suburban California mansion, police had discovered thirty-nine decomposing bodies, all neatly dressed in a black uniform and covered by a purple shroud. In the coming days, journalists would come to call this group Heaven's Gate, though the movement had used a different name for most of its twenty-year existence. Soon, scholars discovered the reason for the mass suicide: the members of Heaven's Gate left behind their physical bodies because they believed it represented the only way to escape an immanent apocalypse destined to consume human civilization.

In combining apocalyptic thought and belief in unidentified flying objects (UFOs), Heaven's Gate was unusual but not unique. The movement followed in a long line of UFO religions that similarly looked to the physical heavens for signs of the End Times. Throughout the twentieth century and into the twenty-first, UFO religions have mixed belief in flying saucers and space aliens with apocalypticism, messianism, and eschatological fervor. This essay considers apocalyptic thought within the four largest and most influential UFO religions in the Western world, the Aetherius Society, the Unarius Academy of Science, the International Raëlian Movement, and Heaven's Gate.

Though the UFO religions varied in the specifics of their apocalyptic thought, each used what I term an "extraterrestrial hermeneutic" to read apocalyptic materials inherited from their shared Christian tradition. Like all hermeneutical methods, extraterrestrial hermeneutics is an ordered method of reading a set of texts, where "text" includes not only the Bible, but also channeled messages from deceased spirits or space aliens, culturally inherited stories or motifs, and the lived experiences of members of the movement. Though those outside the communities may find it difficult to understand (or take seriously) extraterrestrial hermeneutics, the hermeneutical method itself is internally coherent, if not always consistent. Members of these groups interpret their texts and experiences vis-à-vis belief in extraterrestrial existence. Since these four religious groups deploy their extraterrestrial hermeneutics to interpret the same Biblical texts and traditions, certain commonalities emerge: the God of the Bible is actually a space alien, apocalyptic texts such as Daniel and Revelation describe technological events associated with the coming of space aliens, and the millennium itself represents a new era in the relationship between humankind and extraterrestrial life. Beyond those shared understandings, the religions differ in their millennial and wider theological ideologies.[2]

The Aetherius Society, for example, adopts the Manichean dualism closely identified with many strands of Christian apocalypticism. Rather than look to Christ to defeat the Antichrist, however, Aetherius envisions a race of benevolent extraterrestrials fighting on Earth's behalf against another group of hostile space aliens. The Unarius Academy of Science, by contrast, uses an extraterrestrial hermeneutic to reread Christian millennialism and utopianism. Employing the classic language of postmillennialism, Unarius hoped to create a utopian new age that will usher in the arrival of the cosmic "Space Brothers." The Raëlians and Heaven's Gate likewise read apocalyptic conceptions through the interpretive lens of extraterrestrial visitations. The International Raëlian Movement assumes a utopian millennialism similar to Unarius, but adds to it a salvific image of the resurrection of the flesh, albeit in the form of genetic cloning mediated by space aliens. Heaven's Gate represents the apex of UFO millennialism: before imploding in self-directed violent apocalypticism, the movement produced a theological anthology rereading the Christian Bible, especially the Apocalypse of John, through an extraterrestrial hermeneutic. They read Satan as a space alien, Christ as an extraterrestrial visitor, and the millennial tribulations most often associated with the popular concept of apocalypse as a UFO-induced planetary disaster.

Each of the UFO religions considered here has its roots in the post-war explosion of interest in flying saucers, extraterrestrials, the new world of science engendered by the discovery of nuclear physics, and the new world of potential Armageddon born of atomic weaponry. Each is part of a "UFO subculture" that employs an extraterrestrial hermeneutic in order to make sense of this new world. This subculture has several origins: Kenneth Arnold's June 1947 sighting of a "flying saucer" in the Pacific Northwest; an unexplained explosion and crash a month later in Roswell, New Mexico; a Department of Defense investigation the following year (and an accused cover-up); and the foundation of several ufology groups in the decade thereafter, most notably the Mutual UFO Network (MUFON). Soon, a group calling themselves "contactees" began to claim direct communication with the crews of the flying saucers. George Adamski, who in 1953 published an account of his close encounter with Venusian extraterrestrials, was representative of the contactees when he declared that the space aliens came to Earth in order to bring new moral guidelines, scientific information, and truths about the nature of the universe. Referring to a strange set of symbols that the Venusians left him, Adamski declared:

> From a very practical standpoint, these markings may be giving to Earth men [*sic*] celestial positions already known by us, which those who are now traveling the vastness of space are using as navigational points along the way. From a philosophical viewpoint, these markings may be divulging great secrets of life which we on Earth today have either forgotten or have never known.... Our own Bible tells us that we must work for that which we have. And this includes intangible as well as tangible possessions. "Seek and you shall find." ... A belief there is a great deal of wisdom being handed down to us in these symbolic markings.[3]

Observers have noted the implicitly religious nature of such messages and the UFO subculture more widely, but it would take until 1954, when the Aetherius and Unarius societies were founded, for explicit UFO religions to emerge.[4]

Millennial Mysticism: The Case of Aetherius Society

In 1954, the English spiritual seeker George King (1919–1997) founded the Aetherius Society, dedicated to promulgating the messages he claimed to receive from the Cosmic Masters, extraterrestrial beings hailing primarily from the planets Venus and Mars. What little biographical information on King that exists has been heavily influenced by the Aetherius Society's hagiographic reading, though it is clear that he was a spiritual seeker who had tried forms of yoga, psychic projection, metaphysical study, and self-healing, as well as the Anglican Christianity of his childhood.[5] Unlike many other contactees, most notably George Adamski, King did not claim direct physical contact with space aliens. Rather, King rested his religious claims on the practices of channeling and psychic projection, making Aetherius a distinct form of religion, a *channeled* UFO religion. Channeling, as Suzanne Riordan defines it, is "a process in which information is accessed and expressed by someone who is convinced that the source is not their own consciousness."[6] Or, as Michael F. Brown elucidates, "[channeling's] practitioners believe that they can use altered states of consciousness to connect to wisdom emanating from the collective unconscious or even from other planets, dimensions, or historical eras."[7] Methods of channeling vary, but generally channelers use some form of trance. Aetherius's founder George King employed several varieties of Hindu yoga, particularly "Raja, Gnani [jñana], and Kundalini Yoga," as members of his movement later explained, each methods of meditation popular in the New Age subculture.[8] In order to gain knowledge, channelers access beings ranging from deceased historical figures to religious leaders to angels to space aliens. In the case of King, he mentally contacted a group of Venusians and Martians, most notably those using the pseudonyms "Aetherius" and "Mars Sector 6." According to King's explanations, these extraterrestrials reached out to him with an urgent message.

The message that these two extraterrestrials — and eventually many others, called the Devas, Great White Brotherhood, Cosmic Masters, Cosmic Adepts, and Solar Hierarchy[9]— brought King combined an optimistic view of human potential and a warning of the possibility of dire ramification if Earthlings failed to live up to their potential. The space aliens used explicitly millennial language, but also invoked a soteriological individualism prevalent in both New Age religion and the Protestant Christianity of King's childhood.

> The Lords have declared that the great Millenium [*sic*] of Peace and Enlightenment must come, but only those who have expended the necessary efforts to learn the Divine Law and have fashioned their lives within the framework of its lasting Truth, will be left upon the Earth. For only such as these will deserve to enjoy this new, wonderful age.[10]

The message encapsulated the foundational position of Christian millennialism as well: human beings who cleaved to Truth and Divine Law could experience the peaceful tranquil millennium. In the case of Aetherius, however, one found Divine Law not in the Bible or other ancient text, but the channeled knowledge given to King.

King's extraterrestrial sources revealed to him a salvific drama quite similar to that undergirding Christian theology, beginning with a fall from grace and culminating in the coming millennium. In the case of Aetherius, the fall actually happened thrice, though in the second and third cases, benevolent space aliens acted to mitigate its disastrous effects. King describes the first Fall in a strikingly Edenic tone:

> Hundreds and thousands of years ago there was another Planet in this Solar System [named Maldek]. This planet made an orbit between Mars and Jupiter. It was a small mass about the size of Earth. A green prosperous world inhabited by a people who where, for the most part, reasonably satisfied with their progression.... The Planet was so highly mechanized that robots took care of all menial tasks.... They could control their weather so that drought and famine became long forgotten.[11]

However, Maldek's people became lazy, and eventually became infected with the "mental disease" of "lust for great power." In a clear parallel to the

Genesis account of the forbidden fruit, the inhabitants of the planet discovered the secret of the atom. "They completely destroyed the Planet Maldek and murdered the whole populace in one blinding flash of searing flame."[12] Though only a few of the Maldek scientists were actually involved, the whole paid the price: their planet was destroyed, and their souls had to journey to a new planet, Earth, and create a new society from the ground-up. The second and third falls resulted when the transplanted Maldekians reverted to their warlike ways, annihilating their settlements on the mythic lost continents of Lemuria and Atlantis through nuclear war. In each of these latter cases, members of the Solar Hierarchy from Mars and Venus acted to protect the other inhabitants of Earth. This narration of the Fall employs an extraterrestrial biblical hermeneutic to interpret the Biblical text of Genesis and relate its meaning to Aetherius's belief in extraterrestrial life.

This prehistory provides the frame for the millennialism of the Aetherius Society. Like other millennialists, King taught that the present moment was pivotal, with the decisions of contemporary humans shaping their eventual fate. Specifically, Aetherius and Mars Section 6 informed King that the recent discovery of atomic energy and nuclear weapons forced humankind to either repeat the errors of Maldek (and to a lesser extent, Lemuria and Atlantis), or ascend to a higher level of consciousness. Like the biblical account in the Book of Revelation, the certainty of the dawning millennium has been already predetermined, but individual humans faced the decision of whether they would join the millennial kingdom, in which case the benevolent space aliens would protect them from the horrors of war, or face the hellish flames of nuclear annihilation. King affirmed, "this Declaration is irrevocable and cannot in any way be changed by any Power in the Solar System."[13] Just as in the closing chapter of Revelation, however, individuals could choose their fate by siding with the Truth.

In keeping with the Christian concept of the millennium, the future "Millennium of Peace on Earth," as King called it, would be entirely physical and earthy. Much like the tribulations described in Revelation, the nuclear war would purge the Earth of its sinful inhabitants. He specifically explained that "under no account will the Planet itself be destroyed. If man chooses to debase his energy by engaging in war he will leave the Earth, through death, to be born again upon another Planet." The upright remainder would then enjoy the "great Cosmic Initiation of Earth," in King's terminology, a functional equivalent to the "new heaven and new earth," in the words of Revelation (Rev. 21:1).[14] King summarized the teachings of Aetherius and Mars Sector 6 in his introduction to his book of channeled liturgical blessings: "Humanity needs this Power, this Teaching, this Cosmic Love, in order to survive the ordeal of coming painful experiences."[15]

In this context of apocalyptic urgency, King experienced the prototypical experience of the prophetic revelator, the mystical vision of the heavens. He included details of this experience in the sacred text that he produced, *The Nine Freedoms,* and members of the Aetherius Society continue to reference his experiences.[16] Like the protagonists of the books of Daniel, Ezekiel, 1 and 2 Enoch and Revelation, King personally encounters a heavenly realm, one that can be read as a functional parallel to both the vision of the throne of God (in Ezekiel) and the New Jerusalem (in Revelation).

King ascended, in psychic form, to what he called "Third Satellite," an invisible orbiting space station hovering one thousand five hundred fifty miles above Earth. Like heavenly voyagers before him, he paid particular attention to the shapes, colors, and materials of the world that greeted him.

> In the middle of the ceiling, covering about a quarter of its huge domed surface, there was a large circular window. This was made of pure crystal, very finely ground and completely free from all flaws such as those which might be found in terrestrial glass.... Beneath the huge window stood three large crystal prisms which broke up the Solar spectrum into its primary colours. Each spectromatic colour was then split into seven further shades by another large crystal which held my fascinated gaze.[17]

This description, reminiscent of Ezekiel's new temple (Ezek. 40) and John's New Jerusalem (Rev. 21), accomplishes the same effect: it represents the promise of a better future. On Third Satellite, King witnesses the ascension of an unnamed human girl from India, a young woman who has completely accomplished her spiritual growth and has joined the Cosmic Hierarchy as a fully evolved and transcendent human being. This is the future that the Aetherius Society holds out as the possibility for everyone in the millennial age.[18]

It is clear that the Aetherius movement possessed a millennial worldview. They looked to a dawning "Millennium of Peace," and read from a text describing their founder's miraculous vision of the heavens. Yet the group possessed another additional element that typically marks millennial groups: dualism. In the case of the Aetherius Society, this dualism manifested itself in the form of the "white and black magicians." The black magicians represented a chronic force of evil focused on the accumulation of destructive power. King's channeled extraterrestrial sources indicate that these forces were responsible for the destruction of Lemuria and Atlantis, and currently threaten all of human society. In each case, these "dark ones" and "evil factions" probed the atom and developed atomic weaponry. The Aetherius Society invokes this Manichean dualism in its appraisal of its current global situation, "[a]gain the forces of the atom have been unleashed. Again the world is divided against itself. Again we stand in a similar position to the one we occupied before the destruction of Maldek, before the destruction of Lemuria. We stand in a similar position now, as you read this, to the one we stood in before the atomic destruction of Atlantis."[19] Elsewhere, Aetherius warned of nefarious robotic and insectoid aliens in league with the black magicians, and bent on destruction of the Earth.[20]

Aetherius explicitly contrasted the black magicians with the white magicians of Venus and Mars, elsewhere called the Cosmic Adepts or Masters. Contrasting with the black magicians, the white magicians seek only to help humanity:

> These Beings, realizing Their interrelationship with all other lifestreams, have forged ahead through unimaginably hard work and suffering, have Evolved to such a point that Their existence within this Solar System helps to rise all other life forms within it.[21]

Like other millennialists, members of the Aetherius Society seek to align themselves and emulate the positive forces of the white magicians, rejecting their Manichean opposites. Adherents of Aetherius engage in ritual prayer intended to charge the earth with positive energy, reinforce the planet's protection atmosphere, and heal damage to the ecosystem.[22] In this regard, the Aetherius Society hopes to usher in the new millennium of peace.

Unarius

Like the Aetherius Society, the Unarius Academy of Science also adopted a millennialist outlook emphasizing the possibility of global peace and tranquility. As two ethnographers of Unarius, Diana Tumminia and R. George Kirkpatrick, wrote, Unarius possesses a "totalistic utopian vision of millenarian transformation."[23] Except for a brief period during the 1970s and 1980s (as detailed below), Unarius has emphasized a millenarian transformation predicated upon individual development and growth. Like Aetherius, Unarius envisions a individualistic millennium, wherein each individual has achieved a higher evolution. Distinctly different from Aetherius, Unarius lacks any semblance of Manichean dualism. However like all millenarian groups, Unarius recognized that a new era was fast approaching. Writing in 1989 and looking forward to a day when extraterrestrials would one day land and guide humankind, Unarius co-founder Ruth Norman wrote, "[t]his is man's 21st century development, the new age of reason, the new age of logic, the *new age of spiritual renaissance.*"[24]

Ernest L. Norman (1904–1971) and Ruth E. Norman (1900–1993) founded Unarius in 1954. Both were spiritual seekers and had previously encountered spiritualism, channeling, psychic visions, and past-life regressions.[25] After meeting at a California psychic convention and subsequently marrying, the two founded the movement in order to promulgate Ernest's channeled messages. After his death, Ruth began channeling as well. Both of the co-founders generally channeled the spirits of famous scientists and historical figures, among them Michael Faraday (1791–1867), Nikola Tesla (1856–1943), and the recently deceased Albert Einstein (1879–1955). These spirits brought knowledge of the extraterrestrial cosmos, including details of the inhabitants of the planets Venus, Eros, Hermes, Orion, Muse, Elysium, the Pleiades, and Unarius, the headquarters of an interplanetary confederacy and source of the group's name.

The content of the channeled message changed over time, but always retained a millennial core. At first, Ernest received a message that encapsulated a classically escapist millennialism. Like the premillennial dispensationalism that swept through American Evangelical Christianity during the twentieth-century, Ernest's channeled wisdom prophesied a coming rapture during which the elect few would advance to a greater existence. Norman explained,

> Planned and masterminded by millions of Super-Intelligent Beings from a higher world, this mission had been formulated to accomplish two important purposes: first, to rescue, as it were, a limited number of earth people who had certain preconditioning and life experiences which would enable them to be, in the future, suitably acclimated to a higher world existence. The second purpose was to achieve through projection a certain preparatory phase to millions of other Earth inhabitants ... which would enable the Unariun Brothers to come to their assistance and lead them to the halls of the Unariun Universities where they would be suitably trained for future incarnation, life in higher worlds, etc.[26]

Although not precisely a rapture in the technical sense of bodily removal from Earth, Norman's vision of the evolution of individual human souls into a higher level of being certainly repeats a central millennial tenet: the salvation of the elect few.

Ernest Norman explicitly invoked the millennium in explaining that a crisis moment had arrived when human beings had to choose salvation. "We have heard in our circles and in our own way of life various interpretations, such as the Aquarian Age and we might even say in the terms of the more fundamentalist [Christian], such things as the approaching millennium, the second coming, etc. There is also at this time, considerable confusion which is naturally evident in times of a great change or a metamorphosis which is taking place among the races of peoples of the world."[27] Citing the "grave dangers" of atomic warfare, Norman declared an immanent world transformation. Unlike dispensationalists, however, he characterized the millennium as one of opportunity rather than destruction. During this new era, individuals could seek "development in our personal progression which would lead us to our pathway to the stars."[28] Those who did not progress would merely remain on Earth. Unarius offered rapture without apocalypse.

Over time, Unarius adopted a more utopian view of the world, expanding its millennial outlook from rapture to world-transforming extraterrestrial advent. Following Ernest Norman's death in 1971, Ruth Norman became the main Unarius channeler. Before her death more than two decades later, she promulgated a vision of Unarius as building a utopian millennial world. Like Christian postmillennialists, Ruth taught that Unarius would usher in world-transforming salvation. But whereas Christian postmillennialists envision themselves laying the groundwork for Christ's second Advent, Unarius understood itself to be — quite literally — paving a landing strip for extraterrestrial saviors.

"This then, is a time of great change," Ruth Norman declared in her text, *Interdimensional Physics*. "It is the Spiritual Renaissance of Man. [It is a time of] a greater humanity who, as Brothers on higher frequency worlds, is [sic] working to balance the negative polarity of earth by inputting greater positive powers."[29] Norman taught that these "Brothers," elsewhere called the "Space Brothers," would soon land on Earth and establish a millennial utopia. All that humans had to do was welcome them, something that Unarius sought to accomplish through building a landing strip in the mountains outside San Diego, California.[30] After landing, the Space Brothers promised to inaugurate a golden age by restoring the lost libraries of the sunken Atlantis and Lemuria, civilizations which Unarius identified as ancient super-advanced human societies. The Space Brothers would also create a central hospital wherein a technological device called a "psychic anatomy viewer" would heal people of mental, physical, and emotional disorders. As a result, the Space Brothers would cure humanity of disease, crime, and emotional upheaval. Finally, they would establish a university where humans could learn cosmic secrets and advance towards their eventual place in the stars.[31]

Clearly, Ruth Norman's utopian vision represented a form of millennialism, specifically the postmillennial outlook of a dawning golden age. Unfortunately for Unarius, the Space Brothers failed to land during each of the predicted moments.[32] Responding to the cognitive dissonance engendered by such failed prophecies, following the death of Ruth Norman, the movement reverted to a more privatized rapture-oriented millennialism. The Unarius webpage indicates this transition. The site's frequently asked questions section declares that "the objective of Unarius"

> is to help the individual progress in his evolution.... The Unarius curriculum is a "Science of Life," which when applied by the student, places the individual on a higher frequncy [sic] position in his spiritual evolution.[33]

This more individualized approach reiterates the quasi-rapture orientation of Ernest Norman and shifts away from the postmillennial view of Ruth Norman. Nevertheless, a millennial outlook still characterizes the group. The Unarius webpage maintains, "a New Age beckons, [and] the energy fiber that procreates our physical anatomy and generates our spiritual being is regenerating a new and higher potential!"[34] Though Unarius now views the New Age as one of individual transformation, the utopian millennial outlook of their message remains throughout their worldview.

Raëlians

The International Raëlian Movement, sometimes called the Raëlian Church, assumes the same utopian postmillennialism that characterized Unarius during the Ruth Norman years, but adds to it a salvific image of the resurrection of the flesh (albeit in the form of genetic cloning mediated by space aliens) as well a messianic faith in the movement's founder, Claude Raël, né Claude Vorilhon (1946-). Founded in 1974, the Raëlian movement predicates its worldview on Raël's claims of encountering the extraterrestrial operator of a flying saucer in December 1973, followed by his visitation of an extraterrestrial world three years later.[35] This extraterrestrial, later revealed to be named Yahweh, the biblical name of God sometimes incorrectly transliterated as Jehovah, revealed to Raël that humankind had entered the age of Apocalypse, and that the inhabitants of Earth were now ready to inaugurate a glorious new age. In other words, Raël offered a postmillennial utopian vision.

The crux of the Raëlian millennial outlook is a prophesied landing of extraterrestrials that will inaugurate the Apocalypse. Deploying an extraterrestrial biblical hermeneutic, the Raëlian movement has interpreted the biblical text as the scientific log of an alien race called the Elohim (another name for God used in the Bible, but one that is grammatically plural) who created life on Earth, interacted with terrestrial life as its Creators, and have slowly allowed humanity to mentally evolve and socially develop. Like all hermeneutics, the Raëlian method specifies particular Biblical sections to highlight, dismissing what is considers less relevant as "merely poetic babblings." In the Raëlian reading, different factions of the Elohim disagreed over how to treat their new human creations. Eventually the more liberal faction ("the serpent") attempted to teach genetic science to humanity, and was subsequently punished. Since then ("the Fall"), the Elohim have sent occasional messengers ("prophets") to guide humankind, as well as a skeptical scientist ("Satan") who tests the value of humanity. Eventually, human history will culminate in the discovery of genetic science and the ability of Earth scientists to understand the methods the Elohim used to create the first humans. At this point, humans will face the choice of establishing a new utopian society and welcoming the Elohim, or destroying themselves through war and ignorance.[36]

Employing New Age terminology in an explicitly millennial turn of phrase, the Raëlian movement assesses human history as having reached its most pivotal moment.

> The time of the end of the world has arrived. Not the end of the world as in a catastrophe destroying the Earth, but the end of the Church, which has completed its work.... People of Earth: ... the time has come for you to know the truth. As it has been foretold, everything is happening now that the Earth has entered the Age of Aquarius.[37]

Glossing Revelation, the Raëlians look to the millennium as the end of the age of the church and the beginning of a new epoch. For this reason, they recognize the present age as "the Apocalypse — literally the 'age of revelation,'" when human society must transform itself in response to that revelation.[38] Notably, the movement has titled its internal newsletter "Apocalypse."

The Raëlian movement adopted as the heart of its millennialism a postmillennial ambition of creating a utopian human society and thereby demonstrating to the Elohim that their creations have reached the pinnacle of their social and mental development. Like the early twentieth-century postmillennial American Christian Social Gospel movement, which looked to improve sanitation, labor laws, and taxation, the Raëlians offer particular proposals meant to create the millennium. First, humans must create a new governmental system of "geniocracy" wherein the most intelligent members of society — the geniuses — rule. "To vote," Raël explained, "individuals would need an intellectual coefficient of at least ten per cent above average." The Raëlians argue that by disenfranchising the lower sixty percent of the populace, the upper echelons would eliminate graft and empower Earth's geniuses to solve humanity's greatest problems. Like Plato's republic of enlightened philosopher kings, the Raëlians envision their utopia as one where the most intelligent rule.[39]

The Raëlian movement offers several additional methods of establishing a utopian millennial society, including the abolition of most forms of private property and the institution of a world government. However the most important way in which people can contribute towards the dawning Apocalyptic age, they argue, is the creation of a embassy to welcome the Elohim and their flying saucers. Similar to the biblical Yahweh's instructions to Moses on how to build the Tabernacle (Ex. 25–26), what most scholars consider the basis for the Jerusalem Temple as well, Raël proclaims that the extraterrestrial Yahweh has furnished him with the details of the embassy. Like the temple, the embassy is to be built in Israel, and the instructions include the precise dimensions and materials to be used. In essence a third temple, the Raëlian embassy will demonstrate to the Elohim that humankind is now ready to inaugurate the new millennium.[40]

The International Raëlian Movement adds another piece to their millennial view, one in keeping with the classic Christian understanding of millennialism: the resurrection of the flesh. The apocalyptic books of Daniel and Revelation famously describe this resurrection: "many of those who sleep in the dust of the earth shall awake, some to everlasting life, and some to shame and everlasting contempt."[41] In the Raëlian understanding, the Elohim will accomplish this resurrection through scientific cloning. A Raëlian text explains that Yahweh demonstrated this to Raël during his second close encounter: "from a sample cell like the one we took from between your eyes we can create a total replication of the individual whose cell we took, complete with the memory, personality and character."[42] Reread in their extraterrestrial hermeneutic, for the Raëlians, the resurrection is a scientific process offered by the Elohim space aliens. The context is still millennial, however. Like Daniel and Revelation, the Raëlians envision this resurrection as reserved only for those judged worthy, those with "an unambiguously positive assessment at the end of one's life," as Raël explains.[43] Like Revelation's vision of the post-apocalyptic utopia of the New Jerusalem, the Raëlians envision an eternal life of joy awaiting the elect. Perhaps reflecting the desires of contemporary culture, Raël singled out that the new life will include limitless food and robotic servants designed to provide endless sexual pleasure.

Though the Raëlians generally adopted a postmillennial utopian vision of the apocalypse, their material does provide hints that the movement recognizes the possibility of a more catastrophic or premillennial apocalypse as well. "When the cataclysm takes place — and there is a good chance it will happen quite soon, given the way human beings are presently behaving — there will be two sorts of people: those who have not recognized their creators ... and those who have opened their eyes and ears."[44] Such destructive apocalyptic material is muted in the actual Raëlian texts, but ethnographer Susan J. Palmer noted it in her participant observation of the group. She summarized the Raëlian position: "If we spread the message, unite the world in peace, and build an embassy to greet them, they will return on or before [the year 2035] and award us the gift of their advanced technology. If we fail, they will turn their backs on us in disgust as we blow ourselves to smithereens in a final holocaust."[45] Thus, while the International Raëlian Movement overall demonstrates a postmillennial vision, a premillennial concern with Armageddon still exists within their worldview.

Heaven's Gate: Armageddon Arrived

The new religious group known as Heaven's Gate best demonstrates the premillennial fervor and apocalyptic expectation one most often associates with millennialism. Founded in 1972 by Marshall Herff Applewhite (1932–1997) and Bonnie Lu Nettles (1928–1985), Heaven's Gate's extraterrestrial hermeneutic eventually drove the group to ritual suicide, an act the group intended in order to escape from an immanent global destruction that they saw predicted in biblical apocalyptic literature. Before the movement ended through its members' suicides, the group upheld a worldview strongly millennial in orientation. Its founders, Applewhite and Nettles, saw themselves as prophetic figures foretold in Revelation, and the group looked to heavenly rapture as the only means of escape from the apocalyptic tribulations soon to engulf the earth. Heaven's Gate represents the apex of a premillennial UFO religion.

Like King, the Normans, and Vorilhon-cum-Raël, Applewhite and Nettles were both spiritual seekers before cofounding their movement. Nettles had been a member of a Theosophical group, a religious tradition that fuses Asian religious influences with Western occultism. Both Nettles and Applewhite had been involved in astrology and channeling, and Applewhite was a dropout from a Presbyterian seminary.[46] The two had also become active in ufological circles and reached out to fellow ufologists in forming their religion. Despite their interest in flying saucers, it was actually a Christian millennialism that drove them to create Heaven's Gate. They saw their work together as part of "a task that had something to do with the Bible, an update in understanding, and prophesy fulfillment."[47] For Nettles and Applewhite, extraterrestrials and UFOs were the interpretive lens (hermeneutic), but the core of their ideology emerged from the Christian Bible, particularly the apocalyptic books. Applewhite and Nettles, or "the Two" as they called themselves, eventually taught that they were the two witnesses foretold in Revelation 11, destined to preach of the dawning millennial era, be mocked by a disbelieving public, martyred, and resurrected from the dead. This reading is a relatively straightforward gloss of Revelation 11. Reading the text in light of their particular hermeneutic, however, the Two explained that they would use extraterrestrial technology so as to biologically and chemically transform themselves into new alien creatures, making the resurrection of Revelation more akin to a metamorphosis. They would then depart in UFOs. In their interpretation, Revelation's mention of the two witnesses ascending "in a cloud" (Rev 11:12) was a coded message for their ascension aboard a flying saucer.[48] Having completed their mission, a new era or millennium would commence in which human beings could evolve to a new level, a "level beyond human" as the group called it, and migrate to outer space. Neither premillennial nor postmillennial, the Two offered an individualized millennium focusing on the possibility of personal rapture.

The failure of Applewhite and Nettles to be martyred led the Two, and later the entire Heaven's Gate movement, to eventually reinterpret their understanding of Revelation 11 as well as millennialism more broadly. Heaven's Gate continued to look to a rapture during which the faithful few would ascend to the heavens, similar to the Unarius position. Unlike the other UFO groups however, Heaven's Gate adopted a specifically dispensationalist premillennial understanding of the Bible, declaring that an immanent set of tribulations and eventual destruction awaited those who stayed behind on Earth.[49] Using their extraterrestrial hermeneutic, Heaven's Gate interpreted contemporary culture and historical developments as evidence of the dawning Armageddon. Applewhite wrote two years before the mass suicides, "[s]ince this is the close of the Age, the battle in the Heavens with their servants on Earth will be the means of the closing and the spading under of the plants (including humans) of this civilization. 'Weeds' are now getting rid of weeds — from gang wars to nations involved in ethnic cleansing."[50] Much like Christian dispensationalists, most notably best-selling author Hal Lindsey, Heaven's Gate envisioned itself as surrounded by cultural decline that evidenced the arrival of the End Times.

The millennium that Heaven's Gate envisioned, however, was far greater than even that promulgated by Christian dispensationalists, which describes wide-scale destruction but also some hope for those left alive on Earth. In Heaven's Gate's understanding, after the few true believers evacuate earth in a technologically-induced rapture, all those remaining will die. "Last Chance to Advance Beyond Human!" declared a headline the group used in newspaper advertisements and posters for their talks. Those who stayed behind, not advancing beyond human, faced the "spading under."[51] Applewhite elucidated, "between now [1992] and the end of the decade — and I'm afraid I feel like we're off a number of years, that it's going to be significantly before the end of this decade — will be the end of this Age. So, it's spade time. And the big, big, surprise will come."[52] This big surprise, or spading under, was the complete annihilation of every human being on Earth, and the creation of a new terrestrial species less conducive to violence, chaos, and sin. Employing language alluding to Eden, Heaven's Gate declared that humankind — and perhaps all life on Earth — would find itself on the receiving end of an extraterrestrial shovel, "spaded under" so that a new garden could begin on Earth.

The millennium, Heaven's Gate indicated, would actually occur in space, where the few persons who "advanced beyond human" would receive new extraterrestrial bodies and achieve their final reward as new members of the heavenly society. Unlike the Raëlian vision of an Edenic heaven filled with infinite supplies of food and sex, Heaven's Gate looked to their millennial future as one devoid of all troublesome human relationships, one that will "rise above ... all forms of sexuality, human family ties, addictions, and self-serving ways." It is also "'outside of time'—from whence all Creation originates, both terrestrial and extraterrestrial."[53] Like some Christian visions of heavenly bliss, Heaven's Gate looked to the millennial future as a completely non-human state defined by its difference from the troubles and corporality of Earth. The Heaven's Gate millennium, one member declared, is "a genderless, crew-minded, service-oriented world that finds greed, lust, and self-serving pursuits abhorrent."[54] Abandoning the Earthly New Jerusalem-style millennialism of most utopian millenarian movements, Heaven's Gate looked to heavenly rapture as the only escape from earthly hellish tribulation.

Like many other millennially oriented movements, for example Aetherius, Heaven's Gate adopted a dualistic view of the cosmos. The group's negative assessment of the human condition and belief in cultural declension were certainly part of this, but on a broader level Heaven's Gate employed its extraterrestrial hermeneutic to understand the battle described in Revelation, normally read as one between Christ and Antichrist, or Satan and God, as actually between the heavenly extraterrestrials of the "next level" and a group of disobedient hellish space aliens. "There are space aliens (humanoid remnants from other civilizations) who travel in the nearby heavens. They are dependent upon Earth's atmosphere for harvesting hybrid bodies to 'wear.' ... We call them Luciferians because of their lineage," Applewhite explained.[55] Combining images from science fiction classics such as *Invasion of the Body Snatchers* or *The X-Files* with that of 1 Enoch and Revelation, Heaven's Gate explained that the Luciferian space aliens stole human bodies, performed grotesque experiments, instigated wars and oppression, and infiltrated human government.

> These "Luciferian" space aliens are the humans' *greatest enemy*. They hold humans in unknown slavery only to fulfill their own needs. They cannot "create," though they develop races and biological containers through genetic manipulation and hybridization. They even try to "make deals" with human governments to permit them (the Luciferians) to engage in biological experiments (through abductions) in exchange for technologically advanced modes of travel.[56]

Combining tropes from the UFO subculture, conspiracy theory, science fiction, and millennialism, Heaven's Gate saw evidence of Luciferians everywhere, in a constant Manichean struggle with the benevolent next level extraterrestrials.

Heaven's Gate's millennialism erupted in self-directed violence when this Manichean dualism combined with a fervent premillennial belief that the time of tribulations had arrived. Looking to the heavens, as several millenarian groups had done before, Heaven's Gate identified the Hale-Bopp comet as a sign of the advent of the End Times. Deciding that their souls stood a better chance of admission into the next level if they immediately left the doomed planet earth, the thirty-nine active members of Heaven's Gate (and two semi-active members over the following year) committed ritual suicide. Their final act stands as a testament to the power of millennial belief in UFO oriented religious movements.

Concluding Thoughts

Though the four UFO religions considered here vary in their specific apocalyptic perspectives, they shared a worldview shaped by the UFO subculture that envisioned the stars populated with positive and negative intelligences. Because the Aetherius Society, Unarius Academy of Science, International Raëlian Movement, and Heaven's Gate are religious movements, each of them transformed the assumptions and worldview of the UFO subculture into a hermeneutic useful in analyzing religious texts. This hermeneutic called for analyzing texts in light of belief in the existence of extraterrestrial life and the involvement of alien beings in Earth's spiritual life. Since each of the groups emerged in the modern West, they deployed this extraterrestrial hermeneutic to interpret the Bible and the biblical tradition. Each of the groups also looked to an immanent and transformative new age, and hence they focused their extraterrestrial hermeneutic on millennial material. The four UFO religions came to different conclusions regarding how to understand the millennium, ranging from Aetherius's Manicheanism, Unarius's postmillennialism, Raëlian technological resurrection of the flesh, and Heaven's Gate's escapist apocalypticism. Though outsiders scoff at the beliefs of the UFO religions, and even many ufologists consider these religions unbelievable, the groups each possessed an internally coherent religious worldview constructed through their application of an extraterrestrial hermeneutic to Biblical texts. The millennialisms of UFO religions may be unusual, but within their own interpretive frameworks, they make sense.

NOTES

1. The author wishes to thank several readers who offered helpful suggestions and criticisms on earlier drafts of this essay: Emily R. Mace and Kathryn E. Lofton. Of course, none are responsible for any remaining mistakes or oversights. I also wish to thank Brenda G. Spillman, interlibrary loan librarian at Brevard College, who provided crucial help in locating numerous primary sources.

2. For more on hermeneutics, see Van A. Harvey, "Hermeneutics," in *Encyclopedia of*

Religion, vol. 6, Lindsay Jones, ed. (Detroit: Macmillan Reference USA, 2005) 3930–3936. For the background and history of various approaches of biblical hermeneutics, see Steven L. McKenzie and Stephen R. Haynes, eds., *To Each Its Own Meaning: An Introduction to Biblical Criticisms and Their Application* (Louisville, KY: Westminster John Knox, 1993).

3. Adamski's account is the second part of a book that he coauthored with another ufologist, Desmond Leslie. In the omitted portions of this quotation, Adamski muses on the possibility of ancient Earth civilizations having lost this knowledge and destroyed themselves. The possibility of atomic self-destruction and the extraterrestrial warnings against nuclear warfare reappear as a motif in Adamski's account. Desmond Leslie and George Adamski, *Flying Saucers Have Landed* (New York: British Book Centre, 1953) 223–224.

4. There are several excellent sources on the UFO subculture and the contactee movement. See especially Brenda Denzler, *The Lure of the Edge: Scientific Passions, Religious Beliefs, and the Pursuit of UFOs* (Berkeley: University of California Press, 2001). Depending on how one defines "UFO," one might also consider the pre-history of UFO religious movements such as eighteenth century Swedenborgianism and nineteenth century Theosophy.

5. For examples of the hagiographic literature, see Charles E. Abrahamson, "Introduction to the Author," in George King, *The Nine Freedoms* (Hollywood, CA: Aetherius Society, 1963) 8–10; The Aetherius Society, "Biography of Dr. George King, Our Founder," The Aetherius Society, <http://www.aetherius.org/index.cfm?app=content&SectionID=29> (March 17, 2008). For a consideration of this literature, see Mikael Rothstein, "Hagiography and Text in the Aetherius Society: Aspects of the Social Construction of a Religious Leader," in *Alien Worlds: Social and Religious Dimensions of Extraterrestrial Contact*, Diana G. Tumminia, ed. (Syracuse, NY: Syracuse University Press, 2007) 3–24.

6. Suzanne Riordan, "Channeling: A New Revelation?" in *Perspectives on the New Age*, James R. Lewis and Gordon Melton, eds. (Albany: State University of New York Press, 1992) 105.

7. Michael F. Brown, *The Channeling Zone: American Spirituality in an Anxious Age* (Cambridge: Harvard University Press, 1997) 6.

8. Abrahamson, "Introduction to the Author," 8. Raja yoga is the yoga of breath and body control most often associated with the term "yoga" in the west. Jñana yoga is a yoga of mental development. Kundalini yoga involves awakening the energy centers (chakras) of the body and enlivening the mind.

9. Many of these corporate names for the space aliens have origins in Western occult and Theosophical movements, which used the term to refer to spiritual masters beyond normal earthly existence, e.g. Great White Brother, Masters, Adepts, Brothers.

10. George King, *The Nine Freedoms* (Hollywood, CA: Aetherius Society, 1963) 19.

11. *Ibid.*, 13.

12. *Ibid.*, 13–14. Though it is perhaps coincidental, I am struck by the name of the planet, Maldek, which is a contraction of a biblical name for a high priest of Jerusalem described in Genesis, Malchizedek.

13. *Ibid.*, 18–19.

14. *Ibid.*, 19.

15. *Ibid.*, 10.

16. The Aetherius Society, "Biography of Dr. George King, Our Founder," The Aetherius Society, "Magnetization Periods," Aetherius Society, <http://www.aetherius.org/index.cfm?app=content&SectionID=45&PageID=74> (March 17, 2008).

17. King, *The Nine Freedoms*, 123.

18. There are numerous other parallels to the Biblical apocalyptic literature, most notably King's "angelic" (as he calls them) Martian and Venusian guides and his vision of the great crystal throne at the heart of Third Satellite, a classically Ezekielian image.

19. *Ibid.*, 17. For more on the Black Magicians see J. Gordon Melton, *The Encyclopedia of American Religions* (Detroit: Gale Research, 2003) 798. Compare also the description of the "dark forces" in George King, *The Twelve Blessings* (Hollywood, CA: Aetherius Society, 1958) 59.

20. Details on these threats are available only in the esoteric materials reserved for members of the Aetherius Society. I rely on the secondary scholarship in this regard. See John A. Saliba, "The Earth is a Dangerous Place — The World View of the Aetherius Society," *Marburg Journal of Religion* 4 no. 2 (December 1999): 7.

21. King, *The Nine Freedoms*, 170.

22. Details of the Aetherius Society's efforts are available both in print and on their website. Abrahamson, "Introduction to the Author," 8–10; The Aetherius Society, "Global Healing," The Aetherius Society, <http://www.aetherius.org/index.cfm?app=content&SectionID=36> (March 17, 2008). See also secondary material: Simon G. Smith, "Opening a Channel to the Stars: the Origins and Development of the Aetherius Society," in *UFO Religions*, Christopher Partridge, ed. (London: Routledge, 2003) 89–92; Saliba, "The Earth is a Dangerous Place," 8–9.

23. Diana Tumminia and R. George Kirkpatrick, "Unarius: Emergent Aspects of an American Flying Saucer Group," in *The Gods Have Landed: New Religions From Other Worlds*, James R. Lewis, ed. (Albany: State University of New York Press, 1995) 85.

24. Emphasis in the original. Ruth Norman, *Interdimensional Physics: The Mind and the Universe* (El Cajon, CA: Unarius, 1989) 41.

25. For a brief hagiographic biography of Ernest Norman, see the introductory material in Ernest L. Norman, *The Voice of Venus* (El Cajon, CA: Unarius, 1956) 1–10. Ruth Norman has written her own spiritual autobiography, Ruth Norman, *Bridge to Heaven: Revelations of Ruth Norman*, 2nd ed. (El Cajon, CA: Unarius, 1969). For both, see also the Unarius webpage, The Unarius Academy of Science, "Founders of Unarius, Cosmic Visionaries," The Unarius Academy of Science, <http://www.unarius.org/bio.html> (March 17, 2008).

26. Ernest L. Norman, *The Infinite Concept of Cosmic Creation* (1956; reprint, El Cajon, CA: Unarius, 1970) xiii–xiv.

27. *Ibid.*, 1.

28. *Ibid.*, 381.

29. Ruth Norman, *Interdimensional Physics*, 330.

30. Because the Space Brothers failed to land, Unarius has purged its webpage and new editions of its books of details on the landing strip. Interested parties can still visit it on the web at "Unarius Landing Site," The Center for Land Use Interpretation, <http://ludb.clui.org/ex/i/CA3234/> (October 13, 2008).

31. Ruth Norman, *Tesla Speaks*, 13 volumes (El Cajon, CA: Unarius, 1973–1977). See also Tumminia and Kirkpatrick, "Unarius," 90–93.

32. For more on the failed prophecies and how Unarius responded, see Diana G. Tumminia, *When Prophecy Never Fails: Myth and Reality in a Flying Saucer Group* (New York: Oxford University Press, 2005).

33. The Unarius Academy of Science, "Introduction to Unarius," <http://www.unarius.org/resume.html> (March 17, 2008).

34. The Unarius Academy of Science, "You are not Alone in the Universe," <http://www.unarius.org/resume.html> (March 17, 2008).

35. Raël recounts both events in his self-published books, *Le Livre Qui Dit la Vérité* (1974) and *Les Extra-Terrestres M'Ont Emmené sur Leur Planète* (1975). These books have

been published in English under various titles, notably *The Message Given to Me by Extraterrestrials* (1986), *The Final Message* (1998), and *The True Face of God* (1998). With the exception of pagination and illustrations, these translations are identical. I cite *The Final Message* here.

36. See Raël, *The Final Message* (London: Tagman, 1998) 25–73. While I have cited only the main primary source material here, an excellent scholarly treatment of the Raëlian movement is Susan J. Palmer, *Aliens Adored: Raël's UFO Religion* (New Brunswick, NJ: Rutgers University Press, 2004).

37. Raël, *The Final Message*, 73–74.
38. *Ibid.*, 182.
39. *Ibid.*, 88–89.
40. *Ibid.*, 90–92. Illustrations are also printed *ibid.*, 106–107.
41. Daniel 12:2, cf. Revelation 20:11–15
42. *Ibid.*, 150. Interestingly, the Elohim sampled Raël very close to the location of the "third eye," a concept drawn from Hinduism and quite popular in the New Age subculture.
43. *Ibid.*, 188.
44. *Ibid.*, 190.
45. Palmer, *Aliens Adored*, 80.
46. Benjamin E. Zeller, "Storming the Gates of the Temple of Science: Religion and Science in Three New Religious Movements," Ph.D. Dissertation (Chapel Hill: University of North Carolina, 2007) 259–263. See also Robert W. Balch, "Waiting for the Ships: Disillusionment and the Revitalization of Faith in Bo and Peep's UFO Cult," in *The Gods Have Landed*, 141–42.
47. When citing Heaven's Gate materials, I reference their self-produced anthology. This anthology repaginates every section, hence a page number such as "1.5" refers to section 1, page 5. Heaven's Gate, *How and When "Heaven's Gate" (The Door to the Physical Kingdom Level Above Human) May Be Entered* (Mill Spring, NC: Telah Foundation, 1997) 3.3.
48. *Ibid.*, 3.6.
49. See Zeller, *Storming the Gates*, 285–289.
50. Heaven's Gate, *How and When Heaven's Gate May Be Entered*, 1.11.
51. *Ibid.*, 6.4.
52. *Ibid.*, 4.45.
53. *Ibid.*, 6.10.
54. *Ibid.*, A.22.
55. *Ibid.*, 1.5.
56. *Ibid.*, 5.3. Emphasis in the original. Note that many of these accusations against the Luciferian space aliens mimic the views of other conspiracy theorists who posit government collusion with extraterrestrials. For details of the conspiracy theory subculture from which Heaven's Gate drew, see Michael Barkun, *A Culture of Conspiracy: Apocalyptic Visions in Contemporary Culture* (Berkeley: University of California Press, 2003).

WORKS CITED

Abrahamson, Charles E. "Introduction to the Author" in *The Nine Freedoms*. George King, ed. Hollywood, CA: Aetherius Society, 1963.
Aetherius Society. "Biography of Dr. George King, Our Founder." Aetherius Society. <http://www.aetherius.org/index.cfm?app=content&SectionID=29> (March 17, 2008).
_____. "Global Healing." Aetherius Society. <http://www.aetherius.org/index.cfm?app=content&SectionID=36> (March 17, 2008).

_____. "Magnetization Periods." Aetherius Society. <http://www.aetherius.org/index. cfm?app=content&SectionID=45&PageID=74> (March 17, 2008).

Balch, Robert W. "Waiting for the Ships: Disillusionment and the Revitalization of Faith in Bo and Peep's UFO Cult" in *The Gods Have Landed: New Religions From Other Worlds.* James R. Lewis, ed. Albany: State University of New York Press, 1995.

Barkun, Michael. *A Culture of Conspiracy: Apocalyptic Visions in Contemporary Culture.* Berkeley: University of California Press, 2003.

Brown, Michael F. *The Channeling Zone: American Spirituality in an Anxious Age.* Cambridge, MA: Harvard University Press, 1997.

The Center for Land Use Interpretation. "Unarius Landing Site." The Center for Land Use Interpretation. <http://ludb.clui.org/ex/i/CA3234/> (March 17, 2008).

Denzler, Brenda. *The Lure of the Edge: Scientific Passions, Religious Beliefs, and the Pursuit of UFOs.* Berkeley: University of California Press, 2001.

Heaven's Gate. *How and When "Heaven's Gate" (The Door to the Physical Kingdom Level Above Human) May Be Entered.* Mill Spring, NC: Telah Foundation, 1997.

King, George. *The Nine Freedoms.* Hollywood, CA: Aetherius Society, 1963.

_____. *The Twelve Blessings.* Hollywood, CA: Aetherius Society, 1958.

Leslie, Desmond, and George Adamski. *Flying Saucers Have Landed.* New York: British Book Centre, 1953.

McKenzie, Steven L., and Stephen R. Haynes, eds. *To Each Its Own Meaning: An Introduction to Biblical Criticisms and Their Application.* Louisville, KY: Westminster John Knox, 1993.

Melton, J. Gordon. *The Encyclopedia of American Religions.* Detroit: Gale Research, 2003.

Norman, Ernest L. *The Infinite Concept of Cosmic Creation.* El Cajon, CA: Unarius, 1956. Reprint 1970.

_____. *The Voice of Venus.* El Cajon, CA: Unarius, 1956.

Norman, Ruth. *Bridge to Heaven: Revelations of Ruth Norman,* 2nd edition. El Cajon, CA: Unarius, 1969.

_____. *Interdimensional Physics: The Mind and the Universe.* El Cajon, CA: Unarius, 1989.

_____. *Tesla Speaks.* Thirteen volumes. El Cajon, CA: Unarius, 1973–1977.

Palmer, Susan J. *Aliens Adored: Raël's UFO Religion.* New Brunswick, NJ: Rutgers University Press, 2004.

Raël. *The Final Message.* London: Tagman, 1998.

Riordan, Suzanne. "Channeling: A New Revelation?" in *Perspectives on the New Age.* James R. Lewis and Gordon Melton, eds. Albany: State University of New York Press, 1992.

Rothstein, Mikael. "Hagiography and Text in the Aetherius Society: Aspects of the Social Construction of a Religious Leader" in *Alien Worlds: Social and Religious Dimensions of Extraterrestrial Contact.* Diana G. Tumminia, ed. Syracuse, NY: Syracuse University Press, 2007.

Saliba, John A. "The Earth is a Dangerous Place — The World View of the Aetherius Society." *Marburg Journal of Religion* 4, no. 2 (December 1999): n.p. <http://web.uni-marburg.de/religionswissenschaft/journal/mjr/pdf/1999/saliba1999.pdf> (November 11, 2008).

Smith, Simon G. "Opening a Channel to the Stars: the Origins and Development of the Aetherius Society" in *UFO Religions.* Christopher Partridge, ed. London: Routledge, 2003.

Tumminia, Diana, and R. George Kirkpatrick. "Unarius: Emergent Aspects of an American Flying Saucer Group" in *The Gods Have Landed: New Religions From Other Worlds.* James R. Lewis, ed. Albany: State University of New York Press, 1995.

Tumminia, Diana G. *When Prophecy Never Fails: Myth and Reality in a Flying Saucer Group.* New York: Oxford University Press, 2005.

Unarius Academy of Science. "Founders of Unarius, Cosmic Visionaries." Unarius Academy of Science. <http://www.unarius.org/bio.html> (March 17, 2008).

_____. "Introduction to Unarius." Unarius Academy of Science. <http://www.unarius.org/resume.html> (March 17, 2008).

_____. "You are not Alone in the Universe." Unarius Academy of Science. <http://www.unarius.org/resume.html> (March 17, 2008).

Zeller, Benjamin E. "Storming the Gates of the Temple of Science: Religion and Science in Three New Religious Movements." Ph.D. Dissertation. Chapel Hill: University of North Carolina, 2007.

Zombie Apocalypse:
Plague and the End of the
World in Popular Culture

Rikk Mulligan

Something black and of the night had come crawling out of the
middle ages. Something with no framework, or credulity, something that had been consigned, fact and figure, to the pages of
imaginative literature.
— Richard Matheson, *I Am Legend*

Many prophets, seers, and writers have presented the final chapter of
human civilization in apocalyptic terms. Contemporary western representations of the end of the world often draw from medieval iconography, particularly Albrecht Dürer's woodcut of the Four Horsemen of the Apocalypse, as
convincingly offered by Andrew Cunningham and Ole Peter Grell.[1] While
scholars and theologians debate what each horsemen represents, most interpretations include death, war, and pestilence or plague. Speculative fiction
and media, including science fiction, fantasy, and horror, envision the apocalypse from a number of perspectives. Science fiction frequently focuses on
post-apocalyptic civilization or the use of technology in attempts to prevent
disaster; only rarely does it depict the end of all human life.[2] Horror, on the
other hand, typically portrays humanity's annihilation, often by supernatural forces; it echoes earlier fears, including plague and the hungry dead, both
of which define the zombie apocalypse sub-genre. The ur-text of this genre
is Richard Matheson's novella *I Am Legend* that tells the story of mankind's
destruction by germ-born vampirism. Matheson's end-of-the-world story
rationalizes older supernatural tropes by using science to demythologize the
vampire and to cast doubts on contemporary medicine and its control over
disease. Matheson's plague of vampires inspired George Romero's flesh-eating zombies in the *Living Dead* movies; they became the template for most
subsequent zombies. These films internalize the fears of disease and war, and
shift their manifestations to both zombies and vampires, while also using

medieval and millennialist motifs to contrast with science and technology. Narratives of the zombie apocalypse secularize the eschatological and replace supernatural agencies by offering scientifically plausible explanations for the end of the world that draw on recurring fears of contagion, infection, and the dead themselves.

The modern zombie can be traced backwards through the B-movie monsters of the twentieth century, the Gothic romances of the nineteenth, to the anxieties of the Middle Ages popularized by scenes themselves drawn from Revelations and the Book of Daniel. Medieval images of the Hell Mouth fade after the mid-seventeenth century, but the Dürer-inspired Horsemen are secularized and propagated to this day, as described by Frances Carey and other scholars.[3] The Romantic response to industrialization includes a reworking of the medieval revenant that transformed it into the decadent, aristocratic Victorian vampire. The figures of Lord Ruthven, Carmilla, and Count Dracula drifted from literature into the films of popular culture that emphasize their foreign and seductive aspects while maintaining the underlying fear of corruption and disease. Matheson uses science to explain the modern vampire, but draws heavily from Gothic and medieval imagery to create a story of contagion, apocalyptic transformation, and the rise of a new society. Stories of the zombie apocalypse correspond to historical nodes of social anxiety: nuclear weapon tests, race conflict during the fight for Civil Rights, the riots and assassinations of the 1960s, the mid–1980s and the AIDS epidemic, and the events of September 11, 2001. The vampire is first romanticized from medieval fears, then rationalized, and finally zombified; in the computer games of the late 1990s, and on screen after 9/11, the monster is faster, stronger, and unstoppable. These zombies are not the slow, easily subjugated automatons of black-and-white films; rather their current incarnations charge from the grave to devour the living and spread contagion.

Medieval Roots: Disease and the Hungry Dead

First millennial fears of the early Middle Ages included invasion, war, death, and disease. At the turn of the millennium, 999 CE, after conversions and military campaigns against Vikings, Magyars, and Moors, "Christian Europe had [largely] become a reality."[4] Fears faded and transformed into millennialist sects as new doctrine rendered many end-of-days beliefs unorthodox; but as Norman Cohn argues, they "persisted in the obscure underworld of popular religion," especially for many who felt marginalized and dispossessed.[5] However, beginning in the fourteenth century, successive waves of plague — the Black Death — devastated Europe and reignited apocalyptic memories of death and social collapse. Norman Cantor elaborates that "the level of mortality in the Black Death was so high and so sudden that ... Western Europe [was shaken] to its foundations."[6] Contemporary Western society remains haunted by the Black Death; "to find a modern parallel we must look more toward a nuclear war than a pandemic."[7] As with the plague in Matheson, the Black Death spread from East to West, from port and river inland, following previous invasion routes. Mary Shelley describes a plague ravaging westward from China in *The Last Man*, and Matheson's contagion surfaces in Europe before spreading to America. The role of disease is now emphasized in regional depopulation and the fall of civilizations, particularly in the devastation visited by accident and design on indigenous peoples by Europeans, an argument elaborated first by William H. McNeill, later by Alfred W. Crosby, and most recently by Jared Diamond.[8] In the nineteenth century John Snow and Louis Pasteur helped expose the formerly "invisible" threat of disease and germs; in the twentieth century the supposed eradication of smallpox and new vaccines for polio, rubella, and measles suggested man's control over disease. This confidence in modern medicine is troubled, however, by memories of the 1918 Spanish Flu epidemic and its parallels to the bubonic plague.[9] The more recent HIV and AIDS crisis, and outbreaks of SARS, the West Nile Virus, and Bird Flu, keep the contemporary threat of plague and disease very active in the public consciousness. Modern medicine offers rational, scientific reasons for the spread of disease, but the media project lurid images provoking the public's worst anxieties.

The unquiet dead, who were believed to prey on the living as revenants or vampires, stalked the folklore of medieval Europe long before they inspired the Gothic romances of John Polidori, Sheridan Le Fanu, and Bram Stoker. In *Vampires, Burial, and Death*, Paul Barber provides evidence of the vampire as a global phenomenon, as "dead people who, having died before their time, not only refused to remain dead but returned to bring death to their friends and neighbors."[10] Barber ties the fear of vampires directly to disease, and stresses that preliterate societies lacked "a proper grounding in physiology, pathology, and immunology ... [so] blame[d] death on the dead."[11] The revenant is a persistent medieval fear "often manifested in decapitation motifs or the images of plague-ridden corpses that roam the night. From Icelandic narratives like *Grettis saga* to continental folk tales, the fear of human transformation was pervasive and often linked to images of the apocalypse and fears of the walking dead."[12] Harte ties fears of physical transformation, disease, and the risen dead together in his discussion of an incident from 1090 A.D., where corpses were disinterred and then decapitated to end a plague epidemic.[13] Medieval sermons that invoked Cain, Abel, and Jezebel, created another vampiric image by connecting sinners, murderers, and sometimes

Jews, often describing them as blood-drinkers, according to Bettina Bild-hauer.[14] The outsiders — whether outlaw, foreigner, or Jew — are portrayed as unclean predators, and thus as valid targets for violence and retribution from the (Christian) community at large.

Cold War Vampire: Science Displaces Superstition

I Am Legend is the story of Robert Neville, the only person immune to a plague that has transformed the rest of humanity into vampires. Set twenty years into Matheson's future, in the Los Angeles of 1976, flashbacks reveal the onset of a post-war plague caused by global dust storms that carry the contagion around the world, infecting every human and transforming them into vampires. Neville remains barricaded in his fortified suburban home by night, and systematically hunts the lairs of vampires by day. For three years he struggles to understand the illness, but the cure remains beyond his abilities. Neville is finally hunted down not by the vampires, but by humans whose transformation has been halted halfway, and who have formed a new society. To these half-vampires Neville is the day-walker who indiscriminately slays everyone in their sleep. He has become the outsider, the monster, and the legend of their post-apocalyptic society.

Matheson incorporates a number of tropes drawn from Gothic romances: the story centers on Neville within his fortified suburban home, and includes his struggles with despair, depression, alcoholism, and sexual temptation. Neville ultimately fails to master the science needed to craft a cure, although he does offer an innovative explanation of vampirism and discovers a germ he thinks is responsible for the infection. An atmosphere of death and decay pervades the novella: the city, home, suburbs, and experiments are suffused with darkness and forebodings of an inevitable defeat. Vampire biology and delusion on the one hand, and bombs and mutations on the other, offer a blend of science fiction and horror that ends with a new species, humans "living" with the vampire germ. These hybrids rise from the ashes of Los Angeles and the world to build a new society, after bug and bomb render the "last judgment."

When Matheson wrote *I Am Legend*, the American public had had little time to cope with the memories of World War II and the Holocaust, or the atomic bombings of Hiroshima and Nagasaki, before Russia developed its own atomic weapons. By 1954, when the book was published, China had staged its own communist revolution, the Iron Curtain had fallen across Eastern Europe, and both the U.S. and USSR had successfully tested a new generation of hydrogen bombs; fears of global annihilation had become disturbingly plausible. As Paul Boyer notes in *When Time Shall Be No More*, nuclear weapons forced some mainstream theologians to reconsider scriptural interpretations while the more radical pre-millennialists connected tanks, bombs, and even radiation poisoning to specific verses of The Book of Revelation.[15] Fear and paranoia ran rampant through American society, fueled by the House Un-American Activities Committee hearings and McCarthyism, and were given a voice by a new generation of science fiction and horror writers. The science fiction magazine market began to diversify in the 1950s and writers began exploring new themes, many of which dealt with the new nuclear fear: man could now destroy not merely a city, or a country, but the entire planet. Horror writers such as Shirley Jackson and Robert Bloch looked to psychology and parapsychology, delving into the monster within. Matheson combines the tropes of science fiction and horror, melding modern and medieval fears of apocalypse and plague, coupling them with the terror of the undead to bring a monster from the Middle Ages into the modern, suburban living room.

Based on a foundation drawn from apocalyptic iconography, Matheson creates the model for the modern vampire in *I Am Legend* and many of its elements form basis of the flesh-eating Romero zombie and more recent milieus of the zombie apocalypse. Matheson's use of biology and psychology becomes a core component of the modern apocalypse, but the collapse of society, civil authority, and community are also integral to these cataclysmic narratives. Neville's inability to create a cure prefigures the failures of science, and warns of the misuse of science that forces some global annihilations to occur. Matheson demythologizes the vampire of folklore through Neville's fevered experiments that prove many of the superstitions false. Neville analyzes the weapons of legend — garlic, the stake, and running water — under a microscope and applies psychoanalysis to explain the "undead" in terms of their lack of abilities and dread of mirrors and holy symbols. In one respect John Cawelti regards this rationalization as part of a shift from Gothic to modern horror when "vampire-film makers ... resort to a variety of devices to regenerate the sense of horror ... [by] inventing quasi-scientific rationales to replace the traditional symbolism of the vampire story."[16] By subjecting the vampire to scientific observation, analysis, and experimentation, the figure is separated from its medieval roots of the all-devouring maw and the risen dead. Matheson's vampires are killers who can be kept at bay by garlic or killed with a stake, but they cannot change form, entrance victims, or turn to mist. They are unhinged and demented after their return from deathbed or burial, but they are not the revenants of Norse saga or vampires of Slavic folklore; faith in psychoanalysis and empirical science replaces superstition.

Neville's attempts to discover and understand the vampire germ are based on observable phenomena and reproducible data. However, Neville's hypotheses are pulled from legends and myth, *a priori* knowledge that was the basis of formal sciences, such as mathematics, and the natural philosophy of the Middle Ages. Neville reads Stoker's *Dracula* for clues, but finds it "a hodgepodge of superstitions and soap opera clichés ... no one believed in them and how could they fight something they didn't believe in?"[17] Medieval fears and superstitions are displaced by experimentation, but the effort to approach a cure systematically also fails, offering an indictment of the mid-twentieth century faith in science. Matheson's rationalization of the vampires is predicated on the details Neville is able to derive his work with book, slide, and microscope. The discovery of the vampire germ and its ability to form a body glue that protects vampires from bullets comes from his experiments, but idea that the germ spread through sporulation on the winds of global dust storms remains but a theory. Understanding the germ helps him dispatch the infected but provides no cure, in the same way that medieval legend attempted to contextualize the plague as a sign of the apocalypse, or as divine punishment. Neville can only speculate about his personal immunity, but he can neither test it nor reproduce it. Those who have not died, but are only infected can be "saved" by being transformed into transhuman hybrids dependent on their technology—a pill—to keep them alive, but they are no longer human. Science, or medicine, only partially defines the new society of hybrids; the pills that control the vampire germ as allow them to maintain a half-life but are not a cure, therefore failing them as tools to control their world. The human race succumbs to its newest manifestation, the vampire, embodying the primal apocalyptic fear of medieval societies in this transformation.

When the microscope fails him, Neville turns to the latest pseudo- or soft science, psychoanalysis, to understand and combat his vampires. Psychoanalysis became especially popular for urban and suburban encounter groups after World War II, and Matheson deployed it as one of Neville's barely understood armchair weapons. To understand their fear of the crucifix, Neville captures a vampire and questions her; he eventually tortures her to death with no answer, an act reflecting modern misconceptions of the Middle Ages. Later, during a fight with his former friend and nemesis, Cortland, who is Jewish, he discovers that while the crucifix does nothing a Torah drives him away.[18] He hypothesizes that the dread of holy symbols and mirrors is psychologically based and that their death activates a "self-hatred," creating hysterical blindness in the case of the mirror and fear of damnation in reaction to holy symbols.[19] Neville explains, "...neither a Jew nor a Hindu nor a Mohammedan nor an atheist ... would fear the cross," though symbols that invoked their particular moral beliefs would serve the same function.[20] Their violent reactions and the attempts by some to fly even though they cannot shift forms, are all behaviors that Neville considers from a psychological perspective, but he can never confirm those theories. Before Neville considered psychology, he had almost turned back to superstition when "phenomena did not fit in with the bacilli," as in the case of mirrors.[21] But psychology and psychoanalysis are tools of a secular faith; they imply causation without meeting the criteria of empirical methodology and further destabilize science. When science and reason fail a society, its members often retreat into religion and grasp at superstition as alternatives, much as a return to prophecy to explain plague, famine, or war.

Neville is frustrated in his attempts to master science and by his failure to produce a cure, which David A. Oakes argues is an example of the "doubt and suspicions surrounding science and technology in American society."[22] In his discussion Oakes ties Freud's "uncanny" and other definitions of horror to the analysis of contemporary anxieties; as he points out, "science and technology ... have become integral parts of human life ... [but] so complex that the vast majority of people are no longer able to understand them."[23] Neville is a layman who attempts to reconcile these new concepts; he continually acknowledges his lack of an analytical mind and only gradually develops a systematic approach in his research and extermination efforts. His education is haphazard as he selects book at random from the public library. Neville wonders why stakes and garlic work, and knows that he "should collect all the questions before I try to answer them. Things should be done the right way, the scientific way."[24] Unfortunately his methods resemble those of medieval European "doctors" and their rudimentary grasp of biology and anatomy. Neville uses stakes — the weapons described by Stoker — only after bullets fail to injure the undead; *Dracula* becomes his pop culture manual for dealing with vampires, a text that itself reflected Western fears of "Oriental" contagion. It is chance that leads him to discover that he can kill the vampires by exsanguinations; modern weapons are impotent but the crossbow, pike, and sword are surprisingly effective. Limited studies and a sparse knowledge of science inhibit Neville's work: "I won't believe anything unless I see it in a microscope."[25] He sums up his doubts as a product of superstition blocking out scientific inquiry, "...before science had caught up with the legend, the legend had swallowed science and everything."[26] As a child of the modern and rational world, Neville is unable to completely let go of the "laws" he knows and understands to explore a greater range of possibilities in his quest for a cure.

As few as they may seem, Neville's successes are far greater than the combined efforts of the pre-vampire society to understand their impending annihilation. As John May argues, "apocalypse is a response to cultural crisis...[and grows from] the passing of an old worldview."[27] Written in 1953, Matheson's novella is on the cusp of the post-atomic shift towards a postmodern society; by bending atomic bombs and disease he creates a post-modern world, where as Isabel Cristina Pinedo explains, traditional "categories break down, boundaries blur...Enlightenment narratives collapse, [and] the inevitability of progress crumbles."[28] War and the failures of civil and government authorities are the basis for the vampire apocalypse in *I Am Legend*, incorporating first millennial anxieties with those of the Cold War. In a flashback, atomic explosions are revealed as the cause of the global dust storms as well as the appearance of "a strain of giant grasshoppers found in Colorado."[29] Matheson may have drawn from contemporary Hollywood projects when he wrote the novella, as the mutated insect or animal became a popular theme for films like *Them* (1954), *Gojira* (1954), and its American release as *Godzilla* (1957), and *Tarantula* (1955). Mutations became a staple of Hollywood's vision of nuclear fear but insects also resonate with the plagues of grasshoppers and locusts drawn directly from biblical books including Daniel, Exodus, and Revelation. In the flashback, authorities cannot determine the source of contagion, a failure that leads the Nevilles to inadvertently expose their daughter, Kathy, to the germ, because authorities did not order a quarantine early enough. After her death, Neville asks himself "Why had he followed so blindly, listening to those fools who set up their stupid regulations during the plague?"[30] Neville is complicit in the social collapse when he chooses to disobey the civil directives and bury his wife Virginia's body in a field rather than bring her to the central fire pit outside the city. He pays for his "crime" by being forced to stake her when she returns from the dead; neither love nor law can forestall the hunger of vampirism or its spread across the world.

Arguably, the most memorable vampire in popular culture is Bela Lugosi's portrayal of Count Dracula in Tod Browning's 1931 film adaptation of Stoker's novel *Dracula*. Ray B. Browne defines popular culture as "the system of attitudes, behavioral patterns, beliefs, customs, and tastes that define the people of any society."[31] In popular culture, formulas develop as "cultural products ... [and] become conventional ways of representing and relating certain images, symbols, themes, and myths."[32] These conventions provide the audience with a familiar and comfortable experience that allows them to relax into an escapist fantasy and "the construction of an ideal world without the disorder, the ambiguity, the uncertainty, and the limitations of the world of our experience."[33] Unfortunately, by the end of the 1940s the Count had become such a comfortable icon, that he inspired laughter rather than terror, as in the 1948 film *Abbott and Costello meet the Wolfman*. By the 1950s, the vampire seemed an obsolete superstition as science fiction turned to invasions from space as an analog for anti-communist paranoia. But it was after viewing Browning's *Dracula* after World War II that Richard Matheson considered the persistent fear of the undead; "if one vampire was frightening, then a whole world of vampires would be really frightening."[34] Matheson inverts the vampire formula by using his anti-hero protagonist to subject the vampire to scientific and psychological analysis rather than a supernatural explanation; this rationalizes the creature into a threat that the new faith — science — is unable to oppose, and wraps a modern horror story with the mythic.

The vampires of *I Am Legend* are no stronger nor faster than the average human, and their derangement keeps them from communicating and cooperating on anything other than the most basic level; individually these vampires are weak and their threat relies on the strength of the mob. The themes Matheson introduces: the failure of reason and science, of community and state become the basic elements for the future zombie apocalypse stories, but were first adapted in three separate films derived "directly" from the text and share apocalyptic themes. *The Last Man on Earth* (1964), with Vincent Price as scientist Robert Morgan (not Neville), follows the plot of the novella the most closely.[35] Price manages to convey Neville's desperation and utter loneliness, but not his social devolution that so resonates with medieval imagery. The 1971 version, *The Omega Man*, with Charleton Heston as Colonel Robert Neville, departs the most from the novella with a script was specifically written to highlight the race and class conflicts of the 1960s, and to make a veiled anti-war statement about the conflict in Vietnam.[36] In Will Smith's recent portrayal of Neville in *I Am Legend* (2007) the protagonist is now updated as a military virologist, reflecting more recent anxieties spawned by AIDS, Ebola, and Russian anthrax factories.[37] By making Neville a trained scientist, rather than a floundering autodidact, these scripts twist Matheson's theme by offering the potential of a cure and the chance for the victims of the plague to regain their humanity. By allowing the possibility that human civilization can be rebuilt, rather than the new society of the hybrids, Matheson's exploit of a "Renaissance" to leave the old, "Dark Ages" of the Cold War world behind is elided from the story.

While the producers and scriptwriters of *The Omega Man* felt that vampires were no longer relevant, they did incorporate even more medieval tropes including cloaked and torch wielding mobs, catapults, conflagrations of the vanities (in the form of bookburnings), and an attempted burning at the stake. As with Matheson's novella there is nothing supernatural in this story, but it uses the "Dark Age" motif to emphasize a response to and attack on the military-industrial complex. The "family" is a cult of diseased maniacs who seek to kill Neville and destroy all aspects of modern technology as they blame it (and Neville) for their diseased, mutated condition. Neville refers to the family as mutants, their condition caused by germ warfare between Russia and China. Neville is a military biowar specialist who creates an experimental vaccine that gives him immunity to the virus. Everyone other than Neville is infected: those in the tertiary stages become albino, are light-sensitive and also burn in sunlight, and become irrational and highly suggestible, especially under the guidance of Mathias, the leader of the family. Rather than hunt Neville for blood as in the novella and earlier film, the family try to destroy him as a symbol of the military-industrial complex that unleashed the nuclear weapons and germ warfare that destroyed the world. Mathias ultimately kills Neville, but only after he had developed a serum from his blood to treat a small group of racially mixed children and teens that were not yet fully mutated. The final scene of the film offers Neville as Christ, lying in a pool stained red with his blood, arms to spread to each side, legs crossed, exsanguinated and crucified on a statue in a fountain. Although this script implies a "second coming" there will be no new world, but a return to the old.

From Thirst to Hunger: The Vampire Becomes the Zombie

The contemporary zombie rises from the Apocalypse and medieval images of torment and Hell. The Book of Revelation describes the dead rising from their graves for final judgment; those who fail will be cast into Hell, an image popularized through the Hell Mouth. Aleks Pluskowski describes the Hell Mouth in the Winchester Psalter (mid-twelfth century) as "typical of medieval conceptions of the apocalypse and the infernal, with its principal focus on the devouring mouth of a monstrous predator."[38] Pluskowski emphasizes the fear of a rapid and unnatural death, especially that of being devoured by a predator. The natural decay and consumption of the corpse was barely understood, and anything considered "unnatural" was given "monstrous depiction typically focus[ed] on the violent consumption of living beings."[39] This concept reappears in contemporary popular culture through the hell mouths, demons, and vampires of Joss Whedon's *Buffy the Vampire Slayer*. These images speak of a pervasive dread of transformation and existence after death that has only altered in medium and expression.

The actual zombie apocalypse begins with the work of George Romero in the 1968 film, *The Night of the Living Dead*, with an enemy comprised of reanimated corpses who eat the flesh of the living.[40] Romero realized that the vampire had too many weaknesses, and once the novelty of science wore off, it was little worse than the old supernatural haunt and medieval revenant. In *The Night of the Living Dead*, the zombies are corpses who may be reanimated by a mysterious radiation; science is never given the chance to understand the cause for the dead rising because the world collapses too quickly. Radiation factors into the array of a more general fear of contagion that persists from the Cold War through recent events, as Jacqueline Foertsch offers in her analysis of mid to late twentieth century literature and films, *Enemies Within*. Foertsch finds these fears of contagion interconnected and redolent with a "postmodern plague" of fear that begins in the paranoia, panic, and the social rejection of the McCarthy years, runs through the 1960s, the Reagan-era, and continues during the post–Cold War 1990s; these fears actually have medieval roots. She incorporates B-movie science fiction, such as *The Thing* and *The Blob*, into her sources but avoids horror films for the most part, as she argues the interrelation among themes of infection, contamination, and invasion.[41] Her argument complements Paul Boyer's observations of the fears of nuclear proliferation and contamination in *By the Bomb's Early Light*, as well as his insight into the influence of premillenialist apocalyptic beliefs on the policies of President Reagan, and his approach to the USSR as servant of the forces of the Anti-Christ. But neither traces these fears back to the embedded imagery of Revelation or the medieval plagues, nor do they associate these new zombies with undead and contagion as transformation.[42] Romero's films are not within Foertsch's analysis, but the *Living Dead* reflect the paranoia of the Red Scare, the racial tensions of the 1960s, and the homophobia of the 1980s, binding all three eras together with a homicidal, cannibalistic, and contagious other that links back to Matheson.

Romero's *Night of the Living Dead* introduces flesh-eating zombies in a story about a small group of people who attempt to live out a night barricaded in a farmhouse in rural Pennsylvania surrounded by a horde of the risen dead who crave their flesh. These zombies are even less dangerous than Matheson's vampires: they shy away from fire, cannot speak, and only move slowly and haltingly. Still, they are able to use simple tools — sticks and stones — and their numbers grow over the course of the night, slowly surrounding the house with a shambling, infected mob. Some critics view *Night* "as much like a documentary on the loss of social stability as an exploitation film. Battle lines are drawn: black versus white, children versus parents, the un-silent minority versus the silent majority."[43] Romero's microcosm is an analog for "America devouring itself"[44] during the paranoia and tensions of the Red Scare, the FBI response to the Reverend King during the civil rights movement, and even the social and class tensions between urban, suburban, and rural lifestyles. A multi-racial, socially mixed group replaces Neville even as the farmhouse replaces his suburban ranch house. There is no clear explanation for the reanimation of corpses in *Night*, although the leaking radiation from a Venus probe is strongly implied, and the death of the girl, Karen Cooper, confirms infection; both vectors offer a vague explanation for the reanimation, but not their homicidal actions.

Romero's zombies are the new apocalypse. However, unlike Matheson's vampires, or the cult from *The Omega Man*, the zombies do not deliver taunts, threats, or sermons; they only groan. The moans of the zombie are as constant as their hunger and desire for living humans. Unlike the vampires, who must hide from the sun and daylight, zombies are inexhaustible and implacable both day and night. The zombies do not appear intelligent initially, yet they do have an awareness and fear of fire. Bullets and other weapons do little to stop them, unless they are burned or have their brain destroyed. Once a victim has been bitten, there is no way to halt the infection and transformation other than amputation and cauterization of a limb, an option almost as likely to cause death as not. The infection moves quickly, and beyond a certain point is impossible to stop, echoing medieval fears of miasma and contagion. In every story of the zombie apocalypse, infection by bacteria, virus, or body fluid is tantamount to death, calling on those old atavistic fears of the devouring maw earlier depicted in the Hellmouth and monsters on the margins of early maps. This is not an "unveiling" of a new society but the annihilation of all society, all community, and almost all humans.

Over the course of the sequels, *Dawn of the Dead* (1978),[45] *Day of the Dead* (1985),[46] and *Land of the Dead* (2005),[47] Romero fleshes out his world, but this is no post-apocalypse paradise, but a grim, decaying future with the hungry dead at the community gate. The farmhouse becomes a shopping mall, an underground military bunker, and finally, a fortified project within Pittsburgh; the racial tensions of *Night* and *Dawn* are replaced by those between the military and civilian scientists in *Day*, and appear alongside those of class in *Land*. In *Dawn*, the survivors theorize that the zombies gather at the mall because of latent memories of its importance to them, Romero's way of critiquing rampant 70s American commercialism. In *Day*, Dr. Logan brings science back into sharp focus by giving a detailed analysis of the zombie's physiology, and his attempts to train and domesticate the creature, Bub, show that they can remember bits of their past and even learn, that their human minds have not been entirely destroyed. Bub later "remembers" how to use gun and shoots the commander of the base during the climactic invasion by the zombies that destroys the bunker and most of its personnel. *Land*, set several years after the zombie apocalypse, depicts Dennis Hopper's character, Kaufman, as the "lord" of this modern manor. He controls the condominiums and slums of walled and defended river-side sector of Pittsburgh; he uses mercenaries drawn from the underprivileged in his ghettos to raid outlying towns for food, supplies, and remaining luxury goods. These most recent Romero zombies resemble the new society sketched by Matheson; a group of town-zombies are led by "Big Daddy," invading and annihilating the city after being raided, reflecting the typical Romero view of "live and let live," that pervades the movies. These zombies have learned: they use machetes, rifles, and jackhammers to invade the city, and Big Daddy shows empathy, anger, and command when he leads the rest of his people. After four films the zombies have formed a self-supporting community; humans, however, have failed to adapt and continue to prey on their own, or ignore the consequences of their actions, in effect abdicating their position on the evolutionary ladder.

Postmodern Dead: Fast Zombies and Rage-Zombies

In the 1990s, after the collapse of the Soviet Union and most Cold War fears and the discovery of sustainable treatments for the HIV virus, audience appetite for apocalyptic horrors faded from the screen for a time. However, the end of the 1990s brought the technological panic of the Y2K Bug, the collapse of the Internet bubble and economic recession of 2000, and the cascade of apocalyptic imagery and discussion in the media after the attacks of September 11, 2001. In the wake of these foreign attacks on American soil, pundits and politicians scrambled to explain these actions as religious fanaticism born in medieval Islamic extremism rather than class-based anger or as a response to globalization and American cultural imperialism. The contamination of the United States Postal Service with anthrax-laced envelopes and other mysterious powders made the authorities accidentally complicit in the "infection" of its own citizens while fear of disease and contagion became the staple of the 24-hour new cycle. The application of the term "crusader," and the religious rhetoric of President George W. Bush calling for a holy war, leading to the invasions of Afghanistan and Iraq in 2001 and 2003, drew from medieval precedent. Deliberate poisoning and infection by fanatics still falls into the domain of man-made disaster, but the media has tracked a new possibility since the 1980s, often adding an irrational twist to spike the fear: animals. Investigations into the causes of HIV and AIDS stretched back to monkeys and Africa, but in the 1990s "mad cow" disease provoked fears of food and the more recent West Nile Virus and Bird Flu extended new anxieties to backyards and local pools. Disease, once something cured in the industrialized, modern first world and the subject of pity in the third world, has returned to the industrialized world as a seasonal, if not daily, concern. The blend of medieval and postmodern terrors inform the barrage of zombie movies produced in the early twenty-first century, among them the *Resident Evil* franchise, inspired by a series of computer games, Danny Boyle's British variants in *28 Days Later* and *28 Weeks Later*, and the 2004 remake of Romero's *Dawn of the Dead* with its "upgraded" faster and stronger zombie.[48]

The *Resident Evil* (*RE*) films are derived from a popular series of computer games created in Japan as *Biohazard*, and released in the United States for the Sony Playstation in 1996. The games emphasize puzzle solving over plot-driven elements, a feature incorporated into the 2002 *Resident Evil*, but dropped from the later sequels, *Resident Evil: Apocalypse* (2004) and *Resident Evil: Extinction* (2007).[49] While the games are part of a sub-genre called survivor horror, the movies take much of their inspiration from Romero's *Living Dead* films. The *RE* zombies combine elements taken from Matheson, the movies based on his novella, and various aspects of Romero's *Dead*. The *RE* zombies are corpses reanimated by the T-virus, an experiment created by a researcher for the Umbrella Corporation, later weaponized by senior management. These films pull a page from the film variants of Matheson's story by offering a vaccine for the T-virus; rather than a single hero, the embattled teams of the first two movies spend a great deal of effort to retrieve and apply the cure. Matheson's vampires are immune to bullets but not other weapons, while the *RE* reanimates only "die" the same way as Romero's, by having their brains blown out. The settings for the film resemble both Romero and Matheson in that *RE* occurs in an underground bunker where a small team of mercenaries struggle to survive and escape; they have no outside help and do not recognize their full danger until late in the movie — similar in some respects to Romero's *Day*. In *RE: Apocalypse*, the heroine of the first film, Alice, now mutated by her own exposure to the virus and possessed of superhero-like powers, attempts to bring a team out of the devastated city above the research complex but she dies during the escape. As a twist on the zombie reanimation, Alice is resurrected with more powers in the third film, by cloning rather than zombification. The end of the film leaves the audience with the impression that there will soon be an army of Alices to wage war on the Umbrella Corporation, now two "undead" hosts with which to contend. *RE: Extinction* aligns itself fully with the end of the world as a small convoy of survivors search for fuel, food, and supplies in a blasted, virus-devastated landscape. *RE* incorporates mutated Dobermans as zombie dogs, a nod to Matheson's vampire-dogs, but this third film extends the animal threat and parallels fears of both the West Nile Virus and Bird Flu by assaulting the survivors with zombie-crows, infected after eating the flesh of zombies.

Romero's *Dead* films inspired Danny Boyle's *28 Days Later* in 2002. The so-called "rage zombies" are not undead, but humans infected with an extremely fast acting viral agent that sends them into a permanent homicidal rage. Rage, a virus accidentally released from an animal testing lab by animal rights extremists, can be passed through any bodily fluids, echoing the initial panic surrounding the AIDS crisis. As with Romero's films, a small group of survivors barricade themselves, this time a fortified manor house. Also in keeping with Romero, the survivors turn on themselves, as soldiers turn on the civilians they should be protecting. The sequel, *28 Weeks Later* (2007), opens with the United States Army escorting British survivors into a "green zone" to begin repopulating England. The discovery of a survivor who is actually a carrier of Rage leads to rapid infection throughout the green zone, to the U.S. Army personnel, and eventually, once again beyond London. The final scene has a brief radio signal from Paris suggesting the contagion has spread to the Continent. In keeping with the *RE* movies incautious science leads to the world's end; corporate scientists cause the initial contagion, and the later outbreak is caused by an attempt to find a cure and poor security, echoing Neville's failure and fate and reinscribing fears of disease, contagion, and the failure to control science and technology.

The sub-genre is cannibalistic, as is most horror and science fiction, and new ideas are taken from recent projects and reused in new films, matching Cawelti's thesis of innovation and convention in formula narratives.[50] The "fast zombie," quickly spread through the canon after Boyle's "rage-zombies" pushed the envelope and Zack Snyder's evolution of faster, more dangerous zombies in the 2004 remake of *Dawn of the Dead*. In *Night* and the opening scene of the original *Dawn*, a television studio relays the little information known about the attacks and reanimated dead. In the 2004 remake of *Dawn* the opening credits insert a news-media montage showing the explosion of rioting, disorder, and mayhem as the infection spreads; one scene captures zombies attacking a CNN film crew in Istanbul, a possible oblique reference to the Crusades. This montage is accompanied by Johnny Cash's apocalyptic song, "When the Man Comes Around," with its references to Armageddon and quotes from *Revelation* 6:8. The slow moving zombie had become a known quantity that it was comically lampooned by Saturday Night Live, Kids in the Hall, and even Mad TV; both the "fast zombie" and "rage-zombie" made audiences jump. News snippets fill in the backstory of the films, but also extend a critique of news agencies that have become little more than opinionated talking-heads or slices of reality TV, leaving the audience ill-informed and effectively in the dark (ages).

The most recent film to expand the zombie apocalypse is more a mutant apocalypse, but the reuse of signature themes is crucial to the story of the 2007 version of *I Am Legend* as it incorporates many of the elements from Matheson and those of the zombie apocalypse. In this most recent story, the agent of transformation is the K-Virus, an initially successful, genetically altered strain of measles that cured cancer. Then ninety percent of humanity died. The "dark-seekers" who hunt Will Smith are not undead; they are the nine percent of humanity who survived mutation and hunt the one percent who have a natural immunity to the virus. These mutants are stronger, faster, and more agile than humans — they can tear open steel shutters and break armor-glass, but sunlight burns them and bright lights blind them, combining both the vampiric aspects of Matheson's undead with the zombie apocalypse motif of the later films. While Neville thinks they have completely devolved socially, their pack leader does learn how to set a trap after Neville takes a female for testing; they learn, they organize, and they overwhelm Neville's fortified brownstone in Manhattan. In the theater-release version of the film, Neville kills himself and many of the dark-seekers to preserve the vaccine he has created and passed to an uninfected woman and boy. The alternate ending is much closer to the novella in that Neville realizes all too late that the mutated were intelligent and reactive and that his efforts to hunt them cast him outside their new society as a genocidal murderer. The scenes of an empty New York City, with deer running through the streets choked with abandoned vehicles, and the tangled remnants of the Brooklyn Bridge are apocalyptic reminders of the 9/11 attacks. While Neville, by way of Bob Marley's biography and lyrics, preaches love and peace, and the final scene of a small, walled Vermont town with a prominent steepled church reinforces the impression of a society under attack from outsiders.

The death of the last uninfected man on Earth, an idea first projected by Richard Matheson and later modified through the stories of zombie apocalypse that he inspired, suggests that man will change, that he must change, in order to adapt to the realities of modern science and society. However, that change often draws on secularized religious fears and superstitions deeply embedded in the collective consciousness. The vampire and zombie are personifications of ancient fears that survived the industrial revolution in Gothic romances and grew stronger through the postmodern crises of the Cold War, the AIDS epidemic, and now, during the renewed fears of intolerance and religious fanaticism. Plague, radiation, germ, virus, genetic manipulation — these monsters have incorporated every post-bomb scientific advancement and remain atavistic myths that incorporate critiques of institutions, governments, the military, and religion as each fails to support, protect, or renew the societies for which they exist. Speculative fiction reconfigures the anxiety of disease and death into the zombie and the vampire because such avatars can be fought, evaded, and possibly defeated; they fulfill a need for escapist fantasy when unremitting media coverage of war, terrorist bombs, and natural disaster threaten to reduce daily life to a monotonous, painful existence. Romero has said in interviews that his movies are about revolution, about change and even hope; Will Smith's Neville presented the hope for love and life in the face of anger, fear, and death. The worlds of the zombie apocalypse are those of the evening news and cable television, but the potential for both life and love exist through the symbol of hope these stories convey. The real contagion is fear and hopelessness, in doing nothing and hiding or merely praying for the daylight to come.

NOTES

1. Andrew Cunningham and Ole Peter Grell, *The Four Horsemen of the Apocalypse: Religion, War, Famine and Death in Reformation Europe* (Cambridge, UK: Cambridge University Press, 2000).

2. For the term "post-apocalyptic" as problematic, see the essay by Lorenzo DiTommaso "At the Edge of Tomorrow: Apocalypticism and Science Fiction" in this volume.

3. Frances Carey, "The Apocalyptic Imagination: Between Tradition and Modernity" in *The Apocalypse and the Shape of Things to Come*. Frances Carey, ed. (Toronto: University of Toronto Press, 1999) 270–297.

4. James Reston Jr., *The Last Apocalypse: Europe at the year 1000 A.D.* (New York: Anchor, 1988) 276.

5. Norman Cohn, *The Pursuit of the Millenium* (New York: Oxford University Press, rev. 1970; rpt 1974 [1957]]) 30.

6. Norman F. Cantor, *In the Wake of the Plague: The Black Death & The World it Made* (New York: Free Press, 2001) 25.

7. *Ibid.*, 25.

8. McNeill was one of the earliest to argue the devastating impact of diseases brought by Europeans and African slaves to Amerindian populations. William H. McNeill, *Plagues and Peoples* (New York: Anchor Books, rpt 1998 [1976]). Crosby extends this discussion to New Zealand and the South Pacific; both works predate Diamond's analysis, although he also incorporates the impact of technology in concert with disease as weapons of depopulation and empire. Alfred W. Crosby, *Ecological Imperialism: The Biological Expansion of Europe, 900–1900* (Cambridge, UK: Cambridge University Press, rpt 2000 [1986]). Jared Diamond, *Guns, Germs, and Steel: The Fate of Human Societies* (New York: W.W. Norton, 1997).

9. John M. Barry, *The Great Influenza: The Epic Story of the Deadliest Plague in History* (New York: Penguin, 2004) 240.

10. Paul Barber, *Vampires, Burial, and Death: Folklore and Reality* (New Haven, CT: Yale University Press, 1988) 2.

11. *Ibid.*, 3.

12. Larissa Tracy, "So he smote of hir hede by myssefortune": *The Real Price of the Beheading Game in SGGK and Malory* delivered at the International Medieval Congress at Western Michigan University, Kalamazoo, May 2008.

13. Two walking corpses "took to wandering the streets of the village at night ... shouting 'Come along!' Everyone who heard this died of the plague, until the walking corpses were dug up. Their heads were cut off, the hearts pulled out and burnt and Drakelow was at peace." Jeremy Harte, "Hell on Earth: Encountering the Devils in the Medieval Landscape" in *The Monstrous Middle Ages*. Bettina Bildhauer and Robert Mills, eds. (Toronto: University of Toronto Press, 2003) 177–195 at 180.

14. Bettina Bildhauer, "Blood, Jews and Monsters in Medieval Culture," in *The Monstrous Middle Ages*, 75–96 at 88.

15. Paul Boyer, *When Time Shall Be No More: Prophecy Belief in Modern American Culture* (Cambridge, MA: Belknap, 1992) 115–125.

16. John G. Cawelti, *Adventure, Mystery, and Romance: Formula Stories as Art and Popular Culture* (Chicago and London: University of Chicago Press, 1976) 49.

17. Richard Matheson, *I Am Legend*. (New York: Tom Doherty Associates, rpt 1995) 28.

18. *Ibid.*, 140.

19. *Ibid.*, 115.

20. *Ibid.*, 135.

21. *Ibid.*, 114.

22. David A. Oakes, *Science and Destabilization in the Modern American Gothic: Lovecraft, Matheson, and King* (Westport, CT: Greenwood, 2000) 9–12.

23. *Ibid.*, 8.

24. Matheson, *I Am Legend*, 27.

25. *Ibid.*, 135.

26. *Ibid.*, 29. Neville's insight reflects concerns that the shift from a Newtonian to an Einsteinian scientific paradigm marks an intellectual dislocation for even the college educated; by the 1950s only a handful of experts understood the redefinitions of reality described by relativity and quantum mechanics.

27. John R. May, "The Judaeo-Christian Apocalypse" in *The Revelation of Saint John the Divine.* Harold Bloom, ed. (New York: Chelsea House, 1988) 35–44 at 40.

28. Isabel Cristina Pinedo, "Postmodern Elements of the Contemporary Horror Film" in *The Horror Film.* Stephen Prince, ed. (New Brunswick, NJ: Rutgers University Press, 2004) 85–117 at 86.

29. Matheson, *I Am Legend*, 56.

30. *Ibid.*, 36.

31. Ray B. Browne and Pat Browne, "The Generalities of Cultures" in *Profiles of Popular Culture: A Reader.* Ray B. Browne, ed. (Madison: The University of Wisconsin Press, 2005) 3–12 at 3.

32. Cawelti, *Adventure, Mystery, and Romance*, 20.

33. *Ibid.*, 13.

34. Paul M. Riordan, "He is Legend: Richard Matheson," in *Sci-Fi Masters Series*, Sci-Fi Station <http://www.scifistation.com/matheson/matheson_index.html> (October 8, 2008).

35. *The Last Man on Earth.* Dir. Ubaldo Ragona. API. 1964

36. *The Omega Man.* Dir. Boris Sagal. Warner Bros. 1971.

37. *I Am Legend.* Dir. Francis Lawrence. Warner Bros. 2007.

38. Aleks Pluskowski, "Apocalyptic Monsters: Animal Inspirations for the Iconography of Medieval North European Devourers," in *The Monstrous Middle Ages*, 155–176, 155.

39. *Ibid.*, 161. See also Michael Camille, "Visionary Perception and Images of the Apocalypse in the Later Middle Ages" in *The Apocalypse in the Middle Ages.* Richard K. Emmerson, Bernard McGinn, eds. (Ithaca, NY, and London: Cornell University Press, 1992) 276–292, esp. 282–283. The relationship between death, decay, change, and consumption persists through late-medieval images of the Hell Mouth in manuscript illuminations, and is later used in the paintings of Hieronymus Bosch, and the 1498 woodcut series of Albrecht Dürer.

40. *Night of the Living Dead.* Dir. George Romero. Image Ten. 1968.

41. Jacqueline Foertsch, *Enemies Within: The Cold War and the AIDS Crisis in Literature, Film, and Culture* (Urbana and Chicago: University of Illinois Press, 2001).

42. Paul Boyer, *By the Bomb's Early Light: American Thought and Culture at the Dawn of the Atomic Age* (Chapel Hill: University of North Carolina Press, 1985).

43. Joseph Maddrey, *Nightmares in Red, White and Blue: The Evolution of the American Horror Film* (Jefferson, NC: McFarland, 2004) 51.

44. *Ibid.*, 51.

45. *Dawn of the Dead.* Dir. George Romero. Laurel Group. 1978.

46. *Day of the Dead.* Dir. George Romero. Dead Films. 1985.

47. *Land of the Dead.* Dir. George Romero. Atmosphere Entertainment. 2005.

48. *28 Days Later.* Dir. Danny Boyle. British Film Council. 2002 (UK), 2003 (U.S.). *28 Weeks Later.* Danny Boyle. Fox Atomic and DNA Films. 2007. *Dawn of the Dead.* Dir. Zack Snyder. Strike Entertainment. 2004.

49. *Resident Evil.* Dir. Paul W.S. Anderson. Constantin Film Produktion. 2002. *Resident Evil: Apocalypse.* Dir. Alexander Witt. Constantin Film Produktion. 2004. *Resident Evil: Extinction.* Dir. Russell Mulcahy. Constantin Film Produktion. 2007.

50. Cawelti, *Adventure, Mystery, and Romance,* 49.

WORKS CITED

Barber, Paul. *Vampires, Burial, and Death: Folklore and Reality.* New Haven, CT: Yale University Press, 1988.

Barry, John M. *The Great Influenza: The Epic Story of the Deadliest Plague in History.* New York: Penguin, 2004.

Bildhauer, Bettina. "Blood, Jews and Monsters in Medieval Culture" in *The Monstrous Middle Ages.* Bettina Bildhauer and Robert Mills, eds. Toronto and Buffalom, NY: University of Toronto Press, 2003: 75–96.

Boyer, Paul Boyer. *By the Bomb's Early Light: American Thought and Culture at the Dawn of the Atomic Age.* Chapel Hill: University of North Carolina Press, 1985.

Browne, Ray B. and Pat Browne. "The Generalities of Cultures" in *Profiles of Popular Culture: A Reader.* Ray B. Browne, ed. Madison: University of Wisconsin Press, 2005: 3–12.

Camille, Michael. "Visionary Perception and Images of the Apocalypse in the Later Middle Ages" in *The Apocalypse in the Middle Ages.* Richard K. Emmerson and Bernard McGinn, eds. Ithaca, NY, and London: Cornell University Press, 1992: 276–292.

Cantor, Norman F. *In the Wake of the Plague: The Black Death & The World it Made.* New York: Free Press, 2001.

Carey, Frances. "The Apocalyptic Imagination: Between Tradition and Modernity" in *The Apocalypse and the Shape of Things to Come.* Frances Carey, ed. Toronto: University of Toronto Press, 1999: 270–297.

Cawelti, John G. *Adventure, Mystery, and Romance: Formula Stories as Art and Popular Culture.* Chicago and London: University of Chicago Press, 1976.

Cohn, Norman. *The Pursuit of the Millenium.* New York: Oxford University Press, 1957. Revised 1970; reprint 1974.

Crosby, Alfred W. *Ecological Imperialism: The Biological Expansion of Europe, 900–1900.* Cambridge, UK: Cambridge University Press, 1986. Reprint 2000.

Cunningham, Andrew, and Ole Peter Grell. *The Four Horsemen of the Apocalypse: Religion, War, Famine and Death in Reformation Europe.* Cambridge, UK: Cambridge University Press, 2000.

Dawn of the Dead. Dir. George Romero. Laurel Group. 1978.

Dawn of the Dead. Dir. Zack Snyder. Strike Entertainment. 2004.

Day of the Dead. Dir. George Romero. Dead Films. 1985.

Diamond, Jared. *Guns, Germs, and Steel: The Fate of Human Societies.* New York: W.W. Norton, 1997.

Foertsch, Jacqueline. *Enemies Within: The Cold War and the AIDS Crisis in Literature, Film, and Culture.* Urbana, IL, and Chicago: University of Illinois Press, 2001.

Harte, Jeremy, "Hell on Earth: Encountering the Devils in the Medieval Landscape" in *The Monstrous Middle Ages.* Bettina Bildhauer and Robert Mills, ed. Toronto: University of Toronto Press, 2003: 177–195.

I Am Legend. Dir. Francis Lawrence. Warner Bros. 2007.

Land of the Dead. Dir. George Romero. Atmosphere Entertainment. 2005.

Maddrey, Joseph. *Nightmares in Red, White and Blue: The Evolution of the American Horror Film*. Jefferson, NC: McFarland, 2004.

Matheson, Richard. *I Am Legend*. New York: Tom Doherty Associates, 1954. Reprint 1995.

May, John R. "The Judaeo-Christian Apocalypse" in *The Revelation of Saint John the Divine*. Harold Bloom, ed. New York: Chelsea House, 1988: 35–44.

McNeill, William H. *Plagues and Peoples*. New York: Anchor, 1976. Reprint 1998.

Night of the Living Dead. Dir. George Romero. Image Ten. 1968.

Oakes, David A. *Science and Destabilization in the Modern American Gothic: Lovecraft, Matheson, and King*. Westport, CT: Greenwood, 2000.

Pinedo, Isabel Cristina. "Postmodern Elements of the Contemporary Horror Film" in *The Horror Film*. Stephen Prince, ed. New Brunswick, NJ: Rutgers University Press, 2004: 85–117.

Pluskowski, Aleks. "Apocalyptic Monsters: Animal Inspirations for the Iconography of Medieval North European Devourers" in *The Monstrous Middle Ages*. Bettina Bildhauer and Robert Mills, eds. Toronto and Buffalo, NY: University of Toronto Press, 2003: 155–176.

Resident Evil. Dir. Paul W.S. Anderson. Constantin Film Produktion. 2002.

Resident Evil: Apocalypse. Dir. Alexander Witt. Constantin Film Produktion. 2004.

Resident Evil: Extinction. Dir. Russell Mulcahy. Constantin Film Produktion. 2007.

Reston, James Jr. *The Last Apocalypse: Europe at the Year 1000 A.D.* (New York: Anchor, 1988).

Riordan, Paul M. "He is Legend: Richard Matheson" in Sci-Fi Masters Series. *Sci-Fi Station*. <http://www.scifistation.com/matheson/matheson_index.html> (October 8, 2008).

The Last Man on Earth. Dir. Ubaldo Ragona. API. 1964.

The Omega Man. Dir. Boris Sagal. Warner Bros. 1971.

Tracy, Larissa. "'So He Smote of Hir Hede by Myssefortune': The Real Price of the Beheading Game in SGGK and Malory" delivered at the International Medieval Congress at Western Michigan University, Kalamazoo, May 2008.

28 Days Later. Dir. Danny Boyle. British Film Council. 2002 (UK), 2003 (U.S.).

28 Weeks Later. Danny Boyle. Fox Atomic and DNA Films. 2007.

About the Contributors

Lorenzo DiTommaso is assistant professor of theology at Concordia University, Montréal. He is writing *From Antiquity to Armageddon: The Architecture of Apocalypticism*, to be published by Oxford University Press.

Carmen Gómez-Galisteo is a Ph.D. candidate in American studies at the Universidad de Alcalá, Madrid, Spain. She was assistant editor of *Interpreting the New Milenio* (Cambridge Scholars, 2008). Her work has appeared in international journals such as *Clepsydra* and *AdAmerican*. She is a contributor to *The Literary Encyclopedia*.

Karolyn Kinane holds a Ph.D. from the University of Minnesota and is assistant professor of English at Plymouth State University, New Hampshire, where she directs the annual Medieval and Renaissance Forum. She researches, presents and publishes on medieval saints' lives, pedagogy, and Arthuriana. She is the contributing editor of the online journal *The Once and Future Classroom*.

Lisa LeBlanc is an associate professor of English literature and chair of the Division of Humanities at Anna Maria College in Paxton, Massachusetts, where she has taught for over ten years. She earned her doctorate in English literature from the Catholic University of America in Washington, D.C., where she focused on the influence of apocalypticism on secular medieval literature.

Therese-Marie Meyer holds an M.A. in English, German, and comparative literary studies and a doctorate in English literature. She is the author of *Where Fiction Ends* (2006), an analysis of literary scandals. Her research interests include contemporary international literatures in English, and (post-)colonial literatures especially from the Caribbean, Australia, New Zealand and Canada.

Husam Mohamad is an associate professor of political science and Middle Eastern studies at the University of Central Oklahoma in Edmond. He has served as a Fulbright scholar at the University of Qatar and has published a number of journal articles, book chapters and book reviews in several refereed publications.

Tessa Morrison is an Australian Research Council fellow in the School of Architecture and Built Environment at the University of Newcastle, Australia. At the present she is translating Book five of Villalpando's *De Postrema Ezechielis*

Prophetae Visione and Newton's work on the Temple of Solomon from Latin into English.

Rikk Mulligan, doctoral candidate in American studies at Michigan State University, is working on a dissertation involving post-apocalyptic societies in speculative media. His research focuses on intersections between popular culture and political criticism in science fiction and horror. He has published on *Battlestar Galactica* and presented on the zombie apocalypse at the International Conference for the Fantastic in the Arts.

Johann Pautz holds an M.A. in literature from the University of Louisiana–Lafayette. He is completing his Ph.D. in humanities at Florida State University, focusing on the apocalyptic narratives of American far-right groups. His research and teaching interests include cultural imperialism as well as globalization and culture.

Kevin R. Poole has degrees in Spanish literature, linguistics, and cultural studies from the University of Kentucky and the Ohio State University. He teaches at Clemson University in South Carolina. His areas of specialization are medieval Spanish visual culture and medieval theology.

David Redles is associate professor of history at Cuyahoga Community College in Cleveland, Ohio, and is an associate scholar of the Center for Millennial Studies at Boston University. He is the author of *Hitler's Millennial Reich: Apocalyptic Belief and the Search for Salvation* (New York University Press, 2005), which appeared in paperback in 2008.

Eric Michael Reisenauer earned his Ph.D. in history from Loyola University–Chicago in 1997. He is the Williams-Brice-Edwards Professor of Humanities at the University of South Carolina, Sumter. His articles have appeared in such journals as *British Scholar*, *The Historian*, and *The Journal of the Georgia Association of Historians*.

Michael A. Ryan, assistant professor of history at Purdue University, holds an M.A. in history from Western Michigan University and a Ph.D. from the University of Minnesota. He has completed a scholarly monograph on the intersection of magic, astrology, apocalyptic ideas, and political authority in the late medieval Crown of Aragon and is the author of several book reviews, book chapters, and articles.

Nancy A. Schaefer, Ph.D., University of Aberdeen, United Kingdom, is assistant professor of sociology at Western Illinois University–Quad Cities. She formerly taught American studies at the University of Groningen, Netherlands, and has written about Pentecostal-charismatic movements, professional revivalism, gospel music and globalization/Americanization.

Richard Smith works in the Department of Media and Communications, Goldsmiths University of London. His first book, *Jamaican Volunteers in the First World*

War, was published in 2004. He researches the imperial dimensions of race and masculinity and the work of black Caribbean intellectuals during the early twentieth century.

Casey Starnes, doctoral candidate in classics at the University of Missouri, is writing a dissertation on the Culex as parodic epyllion. His research projects include "Constructing Greek Masculinity: Cretan and Spartan Drinking Rituals" and "Giants, Fratricide, and Exile in the Narrative Technique of *Beowulf.*"

Evelyn Stiller worked in the computing industry for a decade prior to teaching in the Computer Science and then Communications and Media Studies Departments at Plymouth State University, New Hampshire. She has been interested in making the use and study of technology appealing to women and underrepresented minorities and her current work considers how computer mediated communication differs between genders and races.

Brett Edward Whalen, assistant professor of history at the University of North Carolina, Chapel Hill, works on Christian intellectual and cultural history from late antiquity to the high middle ages. His forthcoming book, *The Pursuit of Christendom: The Medieval Church and the Conversion of the World*, explores how the Roman papacy, its supporters, and its critics invoked prophecy and apocalyptic thought to theorize the proper ordering of the world during the European expansion of the eleventh to the fourteenth centuries.

Benjamin E. Zeller holds a Ph.D. from the University of North Carolina and a M.T.S. from Harvard University. He serves as assistant professor of religion at Brevard College. Dr. Zeller researches new and alternative religions in America, focusing on religious engagements with science, both in new religions and more broadly.

Index